MEDIEVAL JEWISH PHILOSOPHY AND ITS LITERARY FORMS

NEW JEWISH PHILOSOPHY AND THOUGHT

Zachary J. Braiterman

MEDIEVAL JEWISH PHILOSOPHY AND ITS LITERARY FORMS

Edited by Aaron W. Hughes and
James T. Robinson

INDIANA UNIVERSITY PRESS

This book is a publication of

Indiana University Press
Office of Scholarly Publishing
Herman B Wells Library 350
1320 East 10th Street
Bloomington, Indiana 47405 USA

iupress.indiana.edu

Manufactured in the United States of America

Names: Hughes, Aaron W., [date] editor.
Title: Medieval Jewish philosophy and its literary forms /
edited by Aaron W. Hughes and James T. Robinson.
Description: Bloomington : Indiana University Press, 2019. |
Series: New Jewish philosophy and thought | Includes bibliographical references and index.
Identifiers: LCCN 2018049717 (print) | LCCN 2019014651 (ebook) | ISBN 9780253042552 (e-book) | ISBN 9780253042514
(cl : alk. paper) | ISBN 9780253042521 (pb : alk. paper)
Subjects: LCSH: Jewish philosophy—History. | Philosophy, Medieval.
Classification: LCC B755 (ebook) | LCC B755 .M435 2019 (print) |
DDC 181/.06—dc23
LC record available at https://lccn.loc.gov/2018049717

1 2 3 4 5 24 23 22 21 20 19

To the memory of our beloved colleague,
Kalman P. Bland (1942–2017)

CONTENTS

Introduction / Aaron W. Hughes and James T. Robinson *1*

1 Animal Fables and Medieval Jewish Philosophy / Kalman P. Bland, z'l *8*

2 Biblical Commentaries as a Genre of Jewish Philosophical Writing / Raphael Dascalu *40*

3 Commentaries on *The Guide of the Perplexed*: A Brief Literary History / Igor H. de Souza *79*

4 Philosophical Commentary and Supercommentary: The Hebrew Aristotelian Commentaries of the Fourteenth through Sixteenth Centuries / Yehuda Halper *104*

5 The Author's *Haqdamah* as a Literary Form in Jewish Thought / Steven Harvey *133*

6 Does Judaism Make Sense? Early Medieval Kalam as Literature / Gyongyi Hegedus *161*

7 Dialogues / Aaron W. Hughes *185*

8 Poetry / Aaron W. Hughes *213*

9 Poetic Summaries of Scientific and Philosophical Works / Maud Kozodoy *238*

10 The Philosophical Epistle as a Genre of Medieval Jewish Philosophy / Charles H. Manekin *264*

11 The Sermon in Late Medieval Jewish Thought as Method for Popularizing Philosophy / Chaim Meir Neria *288*

12 Lexicons and Lexicography in Medieval Jewish Philosophy / James T. Robinson *313*

13 Theological Summas in Late Medieval Jewish Philosophy / Shira Weiss *337*

Index *359*

MEDIEVAL JEWISH PHILOSOPHY AND ITS LITERARY FORMS

INTRODUCTION

Aaron W. Hughes and James T. Robinson

> To raise the issue of the nature of narrative is to invite reflection on the very nature of culture and, possibly, even on the nature of humanity itself. . . . Far from being a problem, then, narrative might well be considered a solution to a problem of general human concern, namely, the problem of how to translate knowing into telling, the problem of fashioning human experience into a form assimilable to structures of meaning that are generally human rather than culture-specific.[1]

With this statement, Hayden White suggests that the only meaning that history can have is the one that narrative imagination assigns to it. In this volume, we wish to suggest, in a similar vein, that the only meaning that philosophy can have is through the various literary genres that provide it form. There is not one abstract notion of philosophy, in other words, to which we assent but only various narratives of philosophy that organize, build an argument, and, in the process, ultimately seek to influence a readership. This is as true for Jewish philosophy, as White suggests, as it is for all types of philosophy.

The academic study of medieval Jewish philosophy began in Central Europe in the middle of the nineteenth century. In their desire to make Jews rational and to show how Jewish philosophy coincided with the various species of non-Jewish rationalism, towering figures such as Moritz Steinschneider (1816–1907), Hermann Cohen (1842–1918), and Jakob Guttmann (1845–1919) created the parameters of a field of study that is still largely in place to this day.[2] Such individuals wrote during a period of inner turmoil within Judaism to be sure, one wherein all of the major denominations of Judaism were created, all of which revolved around the perceived relationship between Jews and non-Jewish ideas and culture.[3] While none of this was unique to the nineteenth century—Jews after all had been intimately involved in other cultures since at least the first century CE—what was new was the creation of a distinct field devoted to the academic study of Judaism in general and medieval Jewish philosophy in particular. Methods supplied by larger disciplinary frameworks such as history and philology formed the context for this new endeavor.[4] Wissenschaft des Judentums, the predecessor to the modern field of Jewish studies, also established many of the categories and subdisciplines—medieval Jewish philosophy, Kabbalah, rabbinics, *parshanut* (i.e., biblical exegesis), and so on—that continue to structure how premodern Jewish texts are categorized and studied both in North America and Israel. In addition to these rubrics, the non-Jewish temporal periodizations of medieval Jewish philosophy, which continue to be employed, were also developed to subdivide medieval Jewish philosophy: Platonic, Aristotelian, Neoplatonic, Averroistic, humanist, and so on.

While recent years have witnessed many new trends and developments in the more general study of the Middle Ages, many of these trends and developments have made few or no inroads into the field of medieval Jewish philosophy.[5] The field continues to develop largely along the technical and insular lines laid out by Wissenschaft des Judentums over a century and a half ago. Despite the increased intersection between medieval studies and the larger humanities in which they are located, the study of medieval Jewish philosophy remains a fairly technical and unwelcoming field. The present volume seeks to redress this oversight by providing what we believe to be a set of new and critical investigations into the study of medieval Jewish philosophical texts by focusing on the important role of genre.

This overwhelming evidence on a generically constructed "medieval Jewish philosophy" too often overlooks the ways in which ideas contained within the texts associated with them are presented, articulated, and developed. While this may be forgiven in the modern period, in which philosophy tends to be written in technical monographs and disseminated through university presses, this has not always been the case. The medieval period, for example, witnessed a host of different genres and forms to express, to communicate, and to teach the more technical aspects of Platonic and Aristotelian philosophy. Because of this diversity of genres, proper attention must be paid to the various literary forms of these texts and not just their contents. It is not insignificant, for example, that some philosophers chose to express their ideas using the genre of dialogues, that some did so using poetic meter, or that others chose to present their ideas through commentaries of either earlier philosophers or sacred scripture.

Such literary genres, of course, need not mean that the contents are not philosophical. However, too often within Jewish studies that deal with the medieval period, "nontraditional" genres are written off as unoriginal and then subsequently lumped into another subfield created by Wissenschaft des Judentums, such as *parshanut* or poetry. It is frequently assumed, for example, that a philosophical commentary is an unoriginal genre because it simply restates, albeit in different language, that which is found in an earlier composition (be it Plato, Aristotle, Maimonides, or Averroes). Such an assumption, however, overlooks the often extremely original and creative ideas embedded in the genre. Indeed, one could even go so far as to claim that the genre provides a certain conservative cover under which innovative or even dangerous ideas could be expressed. A similar case could be made for poetry. Today there is a tendency to think, and this may well be part of our Platonic inheritance bequeathed to us by our Wissenschaft forebears, that poetry is the antithesis of philosophy. Yet we all know that Plato was an expert in mythopoesis, and that some of the great Islamic philosophers, such as Al-Farabi and Avicenna, argued for the philosophic importance of the genre. Such a conceit also ignores the fact that many medieval Jewish philosophers—especially the Neoplatonists associated with the Andalusi tradition—were highly accomplished poets and made a conscious effort to write their philosophy in poetic style. This does not mean they were inept philosophers, as Hermann Cohen implied,[6] but, as Aaron Hughes argues in his chapter devoted to poetry, these philosophers felt that the poetic medium offered a particular way of thinking about the cosmos and metaphysics that the standard philosophical treatise fundamentally lacked.

A renewed attention to genre shows us to what extent medieval thinkers made connections between the literary, the exegetical, the philosophical, and the mystical—three spheres that Wissenschaft des Judentums tore asunder and made into separate subdisciplines. However, this artificial and retroactive distinction betrays both the creativity and what we today call the "interdisciplinarity" of medieval philosophical thought. In order to correct some of these wrongs, we have commissioned chapters from some of the leading voices currently engaged in the study of medieval Jewish philosophy. The result, *Medieval Jewish Philosophy and Its Literary Forms*, is meant to challenge many of the conventions that have grown up around the field and to simultaneously set an outline for new and future research into the material.

In so doing, we also hope to widen the scope of what gets to count as medieval Jewish philosophy. Rather than perpetuate tradition and confine analysis to the usual suspects—such as Solomon ibn Gabirol, Judah Halevi, Maimonides, and Gersonides—we hope that a renewed attentiveness to genre might open up the traditional canon. Unfortunately, it is the types of assumptions documented above that were responsible for constituting that canon in the first place. Maimonides's *Guide* is the perfect example. Although Leo Strauss famously defined it as a book of biblical exegesis,[7] it has nevertheless been held up by generations of scholars as the most original work of medieval Jewish philosophy. While there can be no denial of this treatise's importance, its elevation may come at the expense of other works and other thinkers, most of whom are imagined either as leading up to Maimonides or as his subsequent epigones.[8] This can be seen in the overwhelming volume of secondary works published on Maimonides to the detriment of other medieval Jewish thinkers.

This is certainly not to deny that there exist several important introductory books, edited collections, and monographs devoted to some of the more technical features of medieval Jewish philosophy. Very few of them, however, focus specifically on genre.[9] We would further not be so bold as to imply that no work has been done on the role of several literary forms employed by medieval Jewish philosophers. Much important work has been done, for example, on the genres of commentary on the Bible,[10] commentary on rabbinic Aggadah,[11] dialogue,[12] encyclopedias,[13] sermons,[14] and poetry,[15] to name a few. What is unique about the present volume is the sustained theoretical focus on all of these forms, an abiding interest in the various ways that genres produce content, and an attentiveness to the various contexts in which this occurs. When taken as a whole, as opposed to considering individual parts, we are able to see some of the lines that connect these diverse genres, thereby appreciating how these literary forms develop and disseminate philosophical ideas and, in the process, what features they have in common.

Within this context, our goal as editors has been to assemble a leading team of internationally recognized scholars and to charge them with the task of writing a chapter on a particular genre or literary form. While chapters are rooted in medieval sources, they are also forward-looking, and authors are not afraid to engage with more modern issues in both literary studies and contemporary philosophy. The end result is a unified collection that seeks to reframe some of the questions traditionally asked of both medieval and modern Jewish philosophy and to begin the process of breathing new life into a field of study that has unfortunately remained isolated from some of the larger frames of analysis supplied by the humanities.

Medieval Jewish Philosophy and Its Literary Forms has several aims. Our primary goal is to create a new path into the field of medieval Jewish philosophy by developing a set of questions about form as well as content and by focusing on how an argument is presented in addition to the actual argument. Whereas we possess many studies that focus on the latter, our claim is that we also need to spend time contextualizing and assessing the former. How a philosophical (or indeed any) text generates an argument is intimately connected to the argument itself. The frame and what is framed cannot be neatly extracted from each other. Instead, an appreciation of the complex entanglements between genre and content shows us the ways texts are imagined and constructed and the purposes for which they are written. In this way we see something of the larger contexts of medieval Jewish philosophy. Do Jewish philosophers, for example, employ genres that are similar to or different from those of non-Jewish philosophers? If similar, do they deviate in important ways from the others and, if so, for what purposes? Likewise, if Jewish thinkers compose philosophical treatises using genres that differ from the majority, why do they do so and again for what purposes?

Second, a sustained analysis of genre and literary form illumines the social construction of meaning. Rather than imagine philosophical treatises as existing in hermetically sealed and timeless bubbles, the chapters that follow demonstrate clearly that philosophy takes place in specific communities and often in response to distinct concerns within them. Despite the claims of many philosophers, philosophy is not an unembodied and timeless activity. Instead, individuals who write philosophy are connected to and embedded in real communities. Within these contexts, philosophical texts are written with specific audiences in mind and as a way to persuade them of a particular position. It is thus important to understand the connections between philosophers and their social and intellectual environments. Our goal in the present volume is to understand how various literary forms relate to the social production and dissemination of philosophy.

Third, we hope to create a new understanding of medieval Jewish philosophy by opening it up to questions supplied by other fields, such as literary studies, religious studies, and medieval studies. Within this context, we seek to develop an analytical framework that will focus not just on a text's content, as mentioned, but also upon the form wherein that content is expressed. An understanding of genre, the way in which an argument is framed and constructed, is just as important as the argument. With so many genres to choose from, why did certain philosophers choose one over another? Why, for example, are some arguments framed as dialogues as opposed to poems, and vice versa? What does the literary and technical structure of a dialogue provide an argument that a poem cannot?

Fourth, most the chapters focus on some of the minor or at least lesser known thinkers of medieval Jewish philosophy. Many of these thinkers were often seen as unoriginal or epigonic precisely on account of the genres in which they expressed themselves. By examining them and their treatises, we hope to widen the canon of medieval Jewish philosophy. In this sense, we sincerely hope that our volume will function as an accessible and nontechnical introduction to the breadth of medieval Jewish philosophy by focusing on one aspect of its production—that of genre.

Notes

1. Hayden White, *The Content of the Form: Narrative Discourse and Historical Representation* (Baltimore, MD: Johns Hopkins University Press, 1987), 1.

2. For general historical context of this period, see Christian Wiese, *Challenging Colonial Discourse: Jewish Studies and Protestant Theology in Wilhelmine Germany*, trans. Barbara Harshav and Christian Wiese (Leiden: Brill, 2005); Michael Brenner, *Prophets of the Past: Interpreters of Jewish History*, trans. Steven Rendall (Princeton, NJ: Princeton University Press, 2010).

3. See the important collection of essays in Ismar Schorsch, *From Text to Context: The Turn to History in Modern Judaism* (Hanover, NH: University Press of New England, 1994).

4. See, for example, Aaron W. Hughes, "'Medieval' and the Politics of Nostalgia: Ideology, Scholarship, and the Creation of the Rational Jew," in *Encountering the Medieval in Modern Jewish Thought*, ed. James A. Diamond and Aaron W. Hughes (Leiden: Brill, 2012), 17–39.

5. There are, of course, some exceptions. See, in particular, the essays devoted to the medieval period in *Women and Gender in Jewish Philosophy*, ed. Hava Tirosh-Samuelson (Bloomington: Indiana University Press, 2004).

6. Cohen equates bad philosophy with pantheism, something that he maintained was one of the hallmarks of the Neoplatonic philosopher-poets of Al-Andalus. Such individuals, for him, became intoxicated by pantheism and "the other seductive charms of Neoplatonic fantasy [noch von den anderen Reizen Neuplatonischer Phantasie]." See his "Charakteristik der Ethik Maimunis," in *Werke*, vol. 15, ed. Hartwig Wiedebach (Hildesheim: Georg Olms Verlag, 2009), 186. English translation in *Ethics of Maimonides*, trans. with commentary by Almut Sh. Bruckstein (Madison: University of Wisconsin Press, 2004), 41.

7. Leo Strauss, "How to Begin to Study the *Guide of the Perplexed*," in Maimonides, *The Guide of the Perplexed*, 2 vols., trans. Shlomo Pines (Chicago: University of Chicago Press, 1963), xiv.

8. See, for example, James T. Robinson, "We Drink Only from the Master's Water: Maimonides and Maimonideanism in Southern France, 1200–1306," in *Epigonism in Jewish Culture*, ed. Shlomo Berger and Irene Zwiep, *Studia Rosenthaliana* 40 (2007–2008), 27–60.

9. Important works include Isaac Husik, *A History of Mediaeval Jewish Philosophy* (Philadelphia, PA: Jewish Publication Society of America, 1916); Julius Guttmann, *Philosophies of Judaism: A History of Jewish Philosophy from Biblical Times to Franz Rosenzweig*, trans. David W. Silverman (New York: Schocken, 1964); Colette Sirat, *A History of Jewish Philosophy in the Middle* Ages (Cambridge and Paris: Cambridge University Press and Editions de la Maison des Sciences de l'Homme, 1985); Raphael Jospe, *Jewish Philosophy: Foundations and Extensions. Vol. 1: General Questions and Considerations* (Lanham, MD: University Press of America, 2008). Important edited works include *History of Jewish Philosophy*, ed. Daniel Frank and Oliver Leaman (London: Routledge, 1997); and the more recent *The Cambridge History of Medieval Philosophy: From Antiquity to the Seventeenth Century*, ed. Tamar Rudavsky and Steven Nadler (Cambridge: Cambridge University Press, 2009). Again, both provide excellent overviews of the subject matter, but, for the most part, literature and literary forms are marginal to the presentation. As for specialized studies on either individual philosophers or topics, the number is too great to mention in the present context.

10. E.g., James A. Diamond, *Maimonides and the Hermeneutics of Concealment: Deciphering Scripture and Midrash in the "Guide of the Perplexed"* (Albany: State University of New York Press, 2002); Robert Eisen, *The Book of Job in Medieval Jewish Philosophy* (New York: Oxford University Press, 2002); James T. Robinson, *Samuel ibn Tibbon's Commentary on Ecclesiastes: The Book of the Soul of Man* (Tübingen: Mohr Siebeck, 2007).

11. See, e.g., *Marc Saperstein, Decoding the Rabbis: A Thirteenth-Century Commentary on the Aggadah* (Cambridge, MA: Harvard University Press, 1980).

12. See, e.g., Aaron W. Hughes, *The Art of Dialogue in Jewish Philosophy* (Bloomington: Indiana University Press, 2008).

13. See *The Medieval Hebrew Encyclopedias of Science and Philosophy*, ed. Steven Harvey (Dordrecht: Kluwer Academic Publishers, 2000).

14. See, e.g., Marc Saperstein, *Jewish Preaching 1200–1800: An Anthology* (New Haven, CT: Yale University Press, 1989).

15. See, e.g., Adena Tanenbaum, *The Contemplative Soul: Hebrew Poetry and Philosophical Theory in Medieval Spain* (Leiden: Brill, 2002); Aaron W. Hughes, *The Texture of the Divine: Imagination in Medieval Islamic and Jewish Thought* (Bloomington: Indiana University Press, 2004).

AARON W. HUGHES is the Philip S. Bernstein Professor of Jewish Studies at the University of Rochester. He is the author of many books, including *Rethinking Jewish Philosophy: Beyond Particularism and Universalism.*

JAMES T. ROBINSON is the Caroline E. Haskell Professor of the History of Judaism, Islamic Studies, and the History of Religions at the University of Chicago Divinity School. He is the author of several books and articles on medieval Jewish philosophy, literature, and biblical exegesis.

1

ANIMAL FABLES AND MEDIEVAL JEWISH PHILOSOPHY

Kalman P. Bland, z'l

"Wolf at Grammar School" is a medieval Hebrew tale, a fiction, a captivating sample of a storyteller's art. Yet philosophy often prefers the medium of the theoretical or scientific treatise; allergic to "counterfactuals," philosophy tends to distance itself from the telling of mere fictions.[1] This preference illuminates why "Wolf at Grammar School" and its kindred tales have been ignored by prospectors who have assayed the terrain of medieval Hebrew literature and discovered rich veins of philosophy in unexpected places, including law codes, poetry, and biblical commentaries.[2] This chapter argues that the neglect of Aesopian fables diminishes readers' understanding of medieval Jewish philosophy.

The argument addresses three questions: (1) Taking "Wolf at Grammar School" as the point of departure, which features typify the genre of Aesopian fable? (2) What is it about the genre that elicits philosophy's multiplex reactions? and (3) Using the terms *right*, *center*, and *left* in their political sense, where do Aesopian fables stand in relation to philosophy? My argument presupposes that in medieval Jewish culture Aesopian fables and philosophy converged: they were products of similar historical circumstances; their authors were uniformly accustomed to absorbing and interpreting biblical and rabbinic narratives; and both fabulists and philosophers earnestly probed or modeled life conduct. "Wolf at Grammar School" is therefore a congenial gateway leading to a more inclusive vista of currents and crosscurrents in medieval Jewish philosophy.

Typology of Aesopian Fables

"Wolf at Grammar School" belongs to *Mishle Shuʿalim* (Fox fables), a collection of stories written in northwestern Europe in the late twelfth or early thirteenth century by Berakhiah ha-Naqdan.[3] The tale, composed in elegant rhyming prose and suffused with biblical idioms, reflects a society that prizes literacy. Readers encounter a teacher and a student during a beginner language lesson. The teacher, not unexpectedly, is human. The student, to the readers' dismay and delight, is not. He is a wolf, a carnivore, a ferocious, feral predator. The lessons nevertheless proceed smoothly. The teacher pronounces "aleph" and asks the student to repeat it. The wolf, rather than blasting a lupine howl, articulates an "aleph." After introducing the entire alphabet, the teacher demonstrates how the letters combine to form words. To encourage mastery, the teacher offers an incentive: the forging of "one family" or a single peoplehood (*ʿam eḥad*) between the two of them, or perhaps between all humans and wolves. The teacher prompts the wolf to imitate the way he combines letters, "Aleph, beth." The wolf replies, "Hinneh ha-seh" (behold, the sheep). The tale ends abruptly, without revealing whether the teacher was pleased or scandalized by the wolf's statement; without explaining who initiated the lessons; without describing the time, place, and setting of the lessons; and without clarifying the wolf's true identity.

In true rabbinic fashion, Berakhiah reveals part of the puzzle in the *epimythium*, or didactic commentary, he appends to the narrative. He explains that the wolf is a metaphor, a "figure" (*mashal*) representing wicked people whose appearances deceive but whose speech betrays the evil lurking within their hearts. Explicating the tale's phrase, "one family" (*ʿam ʾeḥad*)—an allusion to Genesis 34:16, which describes the ruse perpetrated by Jacob's sons on behalf of their violated sister Dinah against the wrongdoing of the uncircumcised, gentile inhabitants of Shechem—Berakhiah identifies the wolf with Esau, the typological brother who "despises Jacob." Berakhiah was living in medieval England or northwest France, perhaps Rouen, when he composed the tale.[4] By that time and in those places, Esau had become standard code in Jewish parlance for Rome and Christianity.[5] Berakhiah's identification of the wolf with Esau, the paradigmatic Other, the archetype of wickedness and physical violence, signals a barely disguised polemic against his contemporaries.

Perhaps Berakhiah meant to disparage the utopian thought that socioeconomic, ethnic, and religious differences conducive to hostility can be neutralized and replaced with a social order made peaceful by a common language, presumably Hebrew. Perhaps his targets were naive Jews who thought some good might come of teaching Hebrew to Christian scholars. Perhaps his narrative was meant to warn the Jewish community against the danger of Christians who dissimulate in order to proselytize, who only pretend affirmative friendliness with Jews and Jewish culture.

On the other hand, Berakhiah's tale may have been a strictly intramural polemic, a parodic critique or caricature of his society's idealistic faith in the civilizing power of education. Berakhiah was likely acquainted with any number of Jewish students who resisted bookish paideia, whose native temperaments rendered them incorrigibly more like alien Esau than nonthreatening Jacob. Perhaps the didactic commentary, which is noticeably skewed in dilating on the wolf while scarcely mentioning the teacher, conveys esoteric, subtle assurance that there is no harm in studying extramural sciences or mastering a foreign language, including ecclesiastical Latin.

Regarding all of these interpretive possibilities, there is no certainty. Muddles and vagaries prevail. A fanciful figment of imagination, the tale is nevertheless wrapped in a thin veneer of philosophic dignity, a composite of respect for naturalism, ontological realism, and epistemological moderation. The tale strains credulity but stops short of bursting it. Perched precariously on the border between verisimilitude and falsification, the tale reasonably ascribes to the wolf desire, appetite, imagination, potential for being trained, and an oral-aural capacity for communication, but it avoids the outrageous suggestion that the wolf is capable of learning to read and write a human language.[6] The tale also blurs the distinction between individuals and universals; it takes no precautions against stereotypical thinking. Its characters are dull abstractions: they lack personal names, and nothing differentiates them from other humans and wolves, from other teachers and students. As for the combination of tale and didactic commentary, its descriptions and judgments presuppose that the reader will recognize the distinction between virtue and vice, but its messages seem indistinct, irreverent, and indeterminate. The tale indulges in hyperbole, implying that carnivores are moral agents and necessarily wicked. If a wolf is faulted because it naturally thinks of sheep, what is a reader to think of the patriarch Isaac, who naturally asks his father Abraham in Genesis 22:7, "Here [*hinneh*] is the fire and the wood, but where is the sheep [*ha-seh*]?"

"Wolf at Grammar School" exudes a distinctive aura, the consequence of skewed commentary and the byproduct of narrative fiction interacting with the complexity latent in all metaphors.[7] The aura of dubious logic and uncertainty may typify the strain of Aesopian literature exemplified by "Wolf at Grammar School."

A more complete sketch of that Aesopian strain can be drawn by juxtaposing Berakhiah's tale with kindred stories from different times and circumstances in medieval Jewish history.[8] Traveling eastward in space and backward in time, we encounter *The Tales* (*or Alphabet*) *of Ben Sira*, a late ninth- or early tenth-century Hebrew text composed in Arabophone, Islamicate, Geonic Babylonia, most likely Baghdad. It contains several fantastic narratives, including "Raven with Wobbly Gait" and "Fox without Heart."[9]

In "Raven with Wobbly Gait," the anonymous fabulist explains that one day, under unspecified circumstances, a raven admires the graceful walk of a dove. Attempts to emulate the dove are unsuccessful. All the other birds ridicule the ungainly raven, who consequently decides to revert to its natural walk. These attempts, too, are unsuccessful. The raven is hobbled, doubly incapacitated, unable either to imitate the dove or recover its former locomotion.

"Fox without Heart" is an episode in an elaborate tale about folklore's paradigmatic trickster, "the most clever [*piqeaḥ*] of any creature." The fox first outsmarts the angel of death, subsequently arouses the envy of the mythological Leviathan, and eventually outsmarts both the Leviathan and his minions, the fish. Lured by the fish into the ocean with false promises of replacing the Leviathan as king, the fox realizes his mortal danger when the fish inform him that they are carrying him to the Leviathan, who plans to eat his heart. The fox, feigning regret, persuades the gullible fish that one customarily leaves his heart at home when traveling. He proclaims his readiness to surrender his life and to guarantee their reward. Convinced by his compelling rhetoric, the fish return the fox to dry land in order to retrieve his heart from home. Safely on shore, the sophistic fox gloats, ridiculing the foolish (*shotim*) fish.

The patterns exhibited in the tales are dissimilar. "Wolf at Grammar School" features dialogue between a feral beast and a human being; "Fox without Heart" lacks human characters but features dialogue between animals, between the fox and the angel of death and between the fish and the mythological Leviathan; "Raven with Wobbly Gait" lacks both human characters and verbal dialogue. "Wolf at Grammar School," couched in biblical Hebrew, is inseparable from its skewed and didactic commentary; the other two tales, composed in the idiom of Talmud and Midrash, speak ambiguously for themselves. Two of the three tales are etiological[10] or cosmological: one explains how ravens acquired their awkward gait, the other accounts for why the seas lack a foxlike creature.

Complementing these differences are the "family resemblances" that demarcate the contours of Aesopian fable. The narratives conform to a pattern recognized by Walter Benjamin: they are meant to entertain, to be memorable, and to be practical or "useful"; their style is "chastely compact," unconcerned with conveying information.[11] The fabulists are unburdened with the task of describing the times and places of the action; they neither detail the biographical background of their characters nor do they provide explicit theoretical explanation for their characters' behavior. Another critic has noticed that a fable's characters tend to "act on the basis of desire" and are "thwarted in that desire because another character . . . opposes and defeats it, also by desire. Desire is thus vanquished by desire."[12] Other critics have remarked that, unlike fairy tales, fables "have no element of magic" and "no happy ending, except for the villains";[13] unlike fairy tales, fables do not allow for supernatural intervention or deus ex machina either to advance the aims of their characters or to save them from catastrophe.[14] Aesopian fables simulate the writing of history; they describe the singularity of a past event. The import of their moral message is often questionable, ambiguous, or elusive.[15] More allusive and provocative than dogmatic, the fables invite contemplation and stimulate thought rather than supply definitive answers. The fables tend to depict the implications of fixed identity, illustrating the futility of efforts to escape destiny. Typically, their preferred dramatis personae are nonhuman animals. Aesopian fables are therefore easily distinguished from the popular genre of exempla, in which the heroes to be emulated are not fictitious animals with questionable morality but actual or legendary human saints and scholars whose piety and righteousness are exemplary.[16]

Philosophy's Polar Reaction: Discord and Compatibility

Aesopian fables blend more comfortably with other genres of medieval Jewish literature. Whimsically, innocently, ironically, subversively, or sarcastically, the fables ascribe to animals behaviors conventionally restricted to human beings. Among those behaviors are practices and virtues considered supreme in the medieval Jewish philosophic tradition: wisdom; rational deliberation; recognition of fixed laws in nature; and rhetorical prowess.

Similar to philosophy, Aesopian fables stimulate critical thought and favor the formation of abstract universals and generalizations. As Maimonides declares, "The Law does not pay attention to the isolated . . . [and] was not given to things that are rare."[17] Aesopian fables and philosophy are both preoccupied with the management of desire; both genres engage the pragmatic question of how best to conduct life.[18] The parallels and analogies between philosophy and fables are noteworthy but not conclusive. The resemblances may be superficial or coincidental. Even if the resemblances indicate substantive overlap, they do not necessarily imply concordance or homogeneity in timbre, form, content, and social purpose. Philosophers commanded a rich array of genres at their disposal. They nevertheless preferred expository prose in formulating their arguments; they spared the use of parables in constructing their treatises and commentaries. Fabulists were restricted to storytelling. Medieval Jewish philosophy was constrained by several needs: justifying itself before the bar of religious law,[19] interpreting sacred texts,[20] mastering the natural sciences,[21] and wrestling with the vexatious problems of faith and reason. Medieval Hebrew fables were unfettered by these constraints. Regardless of precise measurement, the overlap between medieval Jewish philosophy and fables evoked an array of reactions—ranging from the pleasure of piquant harmonies to the irritation of jangling cacophony.

Discord, the more familiar relationship, will be considered first. The clash between fables and philosophy is not mysterious. Fables belong to the family of stories, myths, far-fetched fictions, and narratives. They evoke a philosopher's discomfort. Motivated by moral concerns and epistemological scruples and inclined toward science and naturalistic explanation, philosophers flex the muscles of rationality, analytic criticism, logical rigor, and empirical investigation. The effort is directed at liberating truth from fantasy or protecting truth from the vagaries of metaphor.[22] As Plato famously observes in the *Republic* (607b), "There's been a long-standing dispute [*diaphora*] between philosophy and poetic [fictions]."[23] Fables invite nonbelievers in transmigration to suspend disbelief; philosophers decline the invitation, adamantly. Aesopian fables "are readily understandable, not esoteric or couched in obscure or technical terms . . . [having] in mind an audience of ordinary readers, rather than one of a relatively few"[24] experts and scholars. The same cannot be said of premodern, elitist, highbrow philosophy, which made no secret of its devotion to specialized terminology and its disdain for the kind of storytelling that egregiously misrepresents reality.

The disdain was calibrated. It ranged from polite, amicable pique to brusque dismissal. Aristotle was altogether resolute but respectful when he chided Hesiod and the other "theologians" for speaking about the gods and the natural order in a mythological language that was "beyond our comprehension."[25] Aristotle was less patient with Democritus for believing "that the sea was decreasing in volume and that it will in the end disappear." Such a belief resembled "something out of Aesop's fables [*muthōn*]. For Aesop has a fable about Charybdis in which he says that she took one gulp of the sea and brought the mountains to view, a second one and the islands appeared, and that her last gulp will dry up the sea altogether. A fable like this was a suitable retort for Aesop to make when the ferryman annoyed him, but is hardly suitable for those who are seeking the truth."[26] In the early thirteenth century, when this passage made its way from Arabic to Hebrew via Samuel ibn Tibbon's translation, the philosophers' reaction to the fable had shifted from mild demurral to derisive erasure. Aesop's very name became unmentionable: "Whosoever claims that the sea had a beginning and [eventually] will perish, while the world will remain forever, is in error. Similarly he [Aristotle] explains the error of Democritus, who thought that the sea is always decreasing until it will have wholly disappeared because it is dried up by the sun and because the great amount of vapor that rises from it. He [Aristotle] also brings forward the theory of another twaddler [*mahbīl*], whose [irrational, falsifying, delirious, raving, and sophistic] words need not be mentioned."[27]

Aristotle's remarks concerning Hesiod and Democritus, together with Samuel ibn Tibbon's use of the pejorative Hebrew term *mahbīl*—meaning twaddler of sophistic or fanciful nonsense—suggest a provisional, working hypothesis: within the Aristotelian tradition, resistance to fables has little to do with blanket repugnance for storytelling and everything to do with intolerance for misrepresentations of the natural. The working hypothesis can be corroborated with the help of a passage in Maimonides's Arabic commentary on the Mishnah, in which the translator, perhaps Samuel ibn Tibbon himself, uses the same Hebrew term, *mahbīl*, to castigate proponents of the pseudoscience astrology.[28]

According to Maimonides, people interpret rabbinic literature diversely. They interpret inappropriately when they attend to the literal, superficial, exclusively exoteric, or manifest meaning; they interpret appropriately when they attend to the metaphorical, symbolic, esoteric, or latent meaning. The misguided literalists subdivide into two large groups: those who honor and those who ridicule the rabbinic sages. Those who ridicule are "so pretentiously stupid that they can never attain genuine wisdom. Most of those who fall into this belief are affiliated with medicine or twaddle the sophistic nonsense [*al-hādhīn*; *ha-mahbīlīm*] of astrology." The members of this "cursed group" also fail to understand how to communicate metaphysical and related truths to both the masses and the elite sages. Nor do they properly understand the contours and practices of "practical philosophy" (*al-juz' al-'amalī, ha-heleq ha-ma'asī*). In contrast to the small number of people who properly grasp rabbinic discourse, the far more numerous members of the "cursed group" fail to understand that when the rabbinic sages "spoke of things that seem impossible, they were employing the style of riddle and parable which is the method of truly great thinkers."[29]

The same terminology and conceptual framework surface in Maimonides's pungent critique of ancient pagan idolatry. Displaying their utter disregard for the scientific understanding of reality, the credulous pagans harbored such "absurdities," "fanciful nonsense" (*khurāfa*), and "crazy notions" as the beliefs "that in India there is a tree whose branches, if taken and thrown on the earth, move, crawling as snakes do; and also that there is another tree there whose root has a human form; this root may be heard to growl and emit isolated words." Maimonides takes the trouble of recounting this nonsense for the benefit of people who had yet to "acquire such sciences as will prevent [one's] mind from becoming attached to the superstitious, foolish fables [*khurāfāt*] of the Sabians and the ravings [*hadhayān, shig'onoth*] of the Chasdeans and Chaldeans who are devoid of all science that is truly a science."[30]

Maimonides's strictures against astrology and ancient paganism reveal that philosophy, in the Aristotelian tradition, found no fault with storytelling,[31] as long as the narratives did not interfere with the aims of "theoretical philosophy," as long they avoided confounding the distinction between true and false, and as long as they refused to compromise the truths of physics, mathematics, and metaphysics. Conversely, narratives were deemed compatible with philosophy if they advanced the cause of "practical philosophy" and offered guidance on action to be taken, restricting themselves to the distinction between good and evil in the domains of ethics and politics.[32] Illustrating the alliance between practical philosophy and storytelling, Aristotle's dissatisfaction with cosmology according to Hesiod and Democritus differs from Aristotle's approval of the rhetorically effective Aesopian fable of a loquacious fox and hedgehog. Their conversation conveys a salutary, practical lesson in political behavior.[33] Similar considerations account for Plato's moving portrayal of Socrates's preoccupation with Aesopian fables while awaiting execution.[34] Speaking more generally for philosophy's nuanced approval of storytelling, Plato, in the *Republic*, distinguishes between "two kinds of stories: true ones and fictional [*pseudos*] . . . in which there can be [moral] truth."[35] Plato's distinctions made their way into Hebrew literature in the early fourteenth century when Ibn Rushd's commentary on the *Republic* was translated by Samuel ben Yehudah of Marseilles, the same translator of another classic in political philosophy, Aristotle's *Nicomachean Ethics*:[36] "Among the tales by which the citizens are educated, as we have said, are tales about theoretical [*madda'iyim*] and practical [*ma'asiyim*] matters. These tales are of two kinds, demonstrative statements, and dialectical, rhetorical and poetical ones . . . As for practical matters, they have also been examined in this science. A representation [of reality], as [Plato] says, is either close or distant, false *(kozvim)* or true *(ṣodqim)*."[37] Recognition of the nexus between Aesopian storytelling and practical philosophy, the domain of ethics and politics, brings harmony to the discussion and the doing of philosophy in medieval Jewish culture.

Political Themes: Degrees of Disrupting the Social Order

Recognition of the nexus between Aesopian fables and practical philosophy also reveals the political dimension of "Wolf at Grammar School" and its kindred tales. Politics is the arena in which asymmetries in power and status are examined and negotiated. "Wolf at Grammar School" investigates the asymmetry of authority and knowledge between teachers and students. "Wolf and Lamb at Riverbank," another of the tales told by Berakhiah ha-Naqdan, depicts different asymmetries: king versus subject, predator versus prey, corrupt judges and magistrates versus the common folk, and rich versus poor.

In the tale, a wolf known as Thirsty goes to a river where he encounters a lamb. Finding the lamb agitates the wolf, who growls menacingly, "Why have you upset me, the river is mine, I made it?" Deferential and abjectly pleasant, the lamb replies, "My royal majesty, the King, I did not upset you. . . . I left my dwelling to drink the river's water, but if this displeases you, I will return, silence being the way to respond to your words." The wolf replies angrily, "Who are you that you have no fear of me? Do a wolf and a lamb graze as one? Who has ever seen them together, slaking their thirst, at the riverbank?" Changing tack from a breach in decorum to guilt by hereditary descent, the wolf excoriates the lamb for being the offspring of an "ancestor who, for the past four years, has rebelliously defied" the wolf. The lamb insists on his innocence, appealing to historical facts and invoking principles of justice: "I'm a newly arrived little lamb, not yet even one year old, and offspring are not put to death on account of ancestors." The arguments prove irrelevant and futile. "Because of you, I am thirsty and disgraced, so you will never see me again," the wolf declares. He thereupon "struck the sheep, flayed its skin, ripped it apart, and consumed its flesh." In the *epimythium*, Berakhiah explains that the story is a "parable, a metaphor [*mashal*]," representing the relations between rich and poor, designating the "mighty [*gadol*] of society, the judges and magistrates, who swallow their [impoverished] fellows by perverting justice, emptying their purses, and stripping them of their shirts."[38]

Berakhiah's preoccupation with injustice in human society, especially his loathing for wealthy people and corrupt officials who oppress the poor and powerless, is as evident in the commentary to "Wolf and Lamb at Riverbank" as it is in many of his other stories, as well as in the introduction to his *Fox Fables*. His preoccupation exerts an orthodox, centripetal force on the fable, deflecting attention both from its full array of asymmetries and from its more centrifugal, radical, and tantalizing implications. Deflection, however, is not permanent erasure. The discrepancy between tale and didactic commentary at work in "Wolf at Grammar School" is recurrent. Berakhiah first has the meek lamb abjectly declare the wolf a king. Berakhiah then sublimates the lamb's declaration of loyalty into the less politically dangerous figuration of submission to wealth. Doing so, Berakhiah has removed the evidence of lèse-majesté. In hiding his rejection of monarchy, he shows himself to be writing artfully in an age of "persecution."[39] Along similar lines, when the wolf holds the lamb responsible for an ancestor's treason, which goes unmentioned in the commentary, Berakhiah may well be exploiting rhetorical stealth to make his critique of monarchy, a rare stance in medieval Jewish political thought.[40]

Unlike the clever protagonist in "Fox without Heart" who outwits the angel of death and Leviathan's fish, the lamb does not get the better of his adversary. The lamb's meticulously reasoned arguments fail to dissuade the wolf from committing characteristic violence. This failure dramatizes the belief that facts, language, truth, and logic cannot overcome the elemental forces of appetite and desire. As if it were a "good play," as described by Paul Feyerabend, "Wolf and Lamb at Riverbank"

> uses the *physical manifestations of reason* to irritate our senses and disturb our feelings so that they get in the way of a smooth and "objective" appraisal. It tempts us to judge an event by the interplay of *all* the agencies that cause its occurrence. Even better, a good play does not merely tempt us; it deflects us from our intention to use rational criteria only; it gives the material manifestations of the idea business a chance of making an impression, and it thus forces us to *judge reason* rather than use it as a basis for judging everything else.[41]

Berakhiah entrusts his message to a story featuring nonhuman animals. The story conveys resignation; it formulates a quietistic counsel of despair. By allowing the wolf to mock and mangle Isaiah 11:6–9—"the wolf and lamb grazing together," a phrase not appearing in scripture—Berakhiah appears to have found a way to express, perhaps defend, the heterodox rejection of utopian or messianic hope. Intentionally or not, he plants the idea in his readers' minds that corrupt officials and wealthy people can no more cease oppressing the powerless than wolves can stop feasting on sheep. The lesson is already implicit in "Raven with Wobbly Gait": identity and behavior are fixed. It is as impossible for a raven to imitate a dove as it is for a wealthy person to treat the poor kindly, for a government official to deal with the powerless justly, and for a poor person to escape poverty and injustice. So too in "Wolf at Grammar School": no matter how adept in Hebrew a wolf might be, it is as impossible for that wolf to forgo its feral desire and appetite for sheep. Another of Berakhiah's fictitious wolves more humorously displays the same subordination of ego to id and the same ineradicable, irrepressible appetite for sheep and goats.[42] In "Wolf and Lamb at Riverbank," the natural order and human society are irremediably dystopic. They are isomorphs, identically "red in tooth and claw."[43] Speaking for the multitudes of powerless and impoverished humans he represents, Berakhiah's lamb would fault Thomas Hobbes for claiming that "nature hath made men so equal in the faculties of body . . . for as to the strength of body, the weakest has the strength to kill the strongest." Without quibbling, however, the lamb would readily concede that Hobbes was right about the "time of war, where every man is enemy to every man . . . and worst of all, [where there are] continual fear and danger of violent death, and life of man, [is] solitary, poor, nasty, brutish and short."[44] It is also unlikely that

Berakhiah's lamb would rejoice in Hobbes's remedy to war: the absolutely sovereign king.

In composing a story featuring wolves and sheep who play universal roles, Berakhiah produces an artist's vision of human collectivity. As if adapting philosophic abstractions for performance on a theatre's stage, Berakhiah dramatizes a law of human behavior. He seems to have decided that the best way to accomplish his goal of encouraging the poor and powerless, of "strengthening hands that are weak,"[45] is to dispense with empty promises and wish-fulfilling illusions and instead to describe things as they naturally *are* rather than to dwell on how they *ought to be.*

The decision to describe rather than prescribe resonates partially with methodological procedures adopted in the seventeenth century by Bento/Barukh/Benedict Spinoza, who faulted his predecessors in philosophy who "conceive men not as they are, but as they would like them to be."[46] Spinoza investigated politics and human nature "with the same unfettered spirit as is habitually shown in mathematical studies, [taking] great care not to deride, bewail, or execrate human actions, but to understand them";[47] he concludes, as did Maimonides,[48] that "man is necessarily always subject to passive emotions, and that he follows the common order of Nature, and obeys it, and accommodates himself to it as far as the nature of things demands."[49] Spinoza's axiom might fairly be understood as addressing the lamb's predicament, if not soothing its existential grief: "There is in Nature no individual thing that is not surpassed in strength and power by some other thing. Whatsoever thing there is, there is another more powerful by which the said thing can be destroyed."[50] The resonance with Spinoza is only partial, because Berakhiah is not inspired by "mathematical studies," nor does he forgo "deriding, bewailing, or execrating" the oppressive behavior of wealthy and powerful people. Unlike Spinoza, Berakhiah does not aim at the dispassionate understanding of human behavior. A product of the twelfth century, not the seventeenth, Berakhiah was nevertheless more intellectually adventurous than most of his medieval peers.

Not all of Berakhiah's medieval fables are as radical as "Wolf and Lamb at Riverbank." Not all of them resonate so audibly with the early modern, "radical enlightenment"; not all of them so profoundly challenge androcentric and ethnocentric prejudices; not all of them so powerfully question the efficacy of reason and intellect; not all of them defy so much of the cultural logic that makes ideas robust and persuasive; not all of them are so dismissive of theological traditions.[51] Even the most politically innocuous and philosophically moderate of Berakhiah's fables are nevertheless capable of disrupting ideological complacency and rousing people from dogmatic slumber.[52] The disruption, as described by Pierre Hadot, is integral to the practice of philosophy; it induces a change in outlook, it acclimates a person "to a new way of being-in-the-world, which consists in becoming aware of oneself as a part of nature . . . at this point one no longer lives in the usual, conventional human world, but in the world of nature . . . this implies a radical transformation of perspective, and contains a universalist, cosmic dimension."[53] To varying degrees of intensity, the same disruptive capacity is latent within all the other medieval Hebrew animal fables, including the two twelfth/thirteenth-century translations of the immensely popular Arabic collection of *Kalilah wa-Dimnah*;[54] the cluster of fables in Joseph ibn Zabara's twelfth-century *Book of Delight*;[55] the unforgettable tale of the hypocritical, sacrilegious Chanticleer in Judah al-Ḥarizi's *Book of Taḥkemoni*;[56] and the eight fables artfully deployed in Abraham ibn Ḥasdai's early thirteenth-century reworking of the Buddha's biography, *Ben ha-Melekh ve-ha-Nazir* (The prince and the ascetic).[57] Also to be included are the thirteenth-century tales composed by Isaac ibn Sahula in *Meshal ha-Qadmoni* (Fables from the distant past),[58] which are notably conservative in their display of cultural chauvinism and advocacy of promonarchic politics. In all of these medieval Hebrew texts, originating in Christian Spain, nonhuman animals are envisioned as persons, acting as ethical agents, moved by passions and desires, capable of reasoning, and proficient in speech.[59] Endowed with these attributes, they manifest a commonality with human beings. The disruptive, medieval affirmations of that commonality reverberate with themes and motifs that are Montaignesque, anti-Cartesian, and proto-Darwinian.[60]

The medieval affirmations of commonality were articulated directly and obliquely. The affirmations were oblique, as the fables show, when the commonalities were mined by the Aesopian fabulists for double-hinged symbols, metaphors, allegories, and parables. The affirmations were direct and explicit when Islamic and Jewish poets and thinkers had their human characters overcome conventional, androcentric points of view, exercise a modicum of empathy in their perception of nonhuman animals, translate theoretical insight into practical behavior, and recommend to one another that they "lighten their load and show them some kindness, sympathy, and pity. For they are flesh and blood like us. They feel and suffer. We have no special merit in God's eyes that He was rewarding when he subjected them to us."[61] The direct affirmation of commonality was articulated less begrudgingly when poets and thinkers proclaimed that there is no "difference" (*hevdel*) between human and nonhuman animals, that exactly like humans, beasts "die and are born / They sleep and wake at morn / They sit /They stand . . . / They have a soul like you; also heart, like you, to make them wander the earth / Never's a time when mortals do not die, never a time when begetters do not beget."[62] The poetically exuberant denial of categorical difference between human and nonhuman animals clashes with a principle cherished by medieval Jewish thinkers. Originating with Aristotle, the principle asserted that the "lower animals cannot partake of happiness [*eudaimonia, haṣlaḥah*], because they are completely devoid of the contemplative activity [*po'al ha-sekhel*] . . . Human beings, by contrast, do partake of happiness to the extent of this [contemplative] activity within them, whereas the other animals . . . have nothing within them conducive of happiness and related to reasoning [*sevara*], neither in theoretical science [*yedi'ah*] nor in applied practice [*ma'aseh*]."[63] The principle of categorical human superiority is endorsed, ironically, by a nonhuman animal in one of Isaac ibn Sahula's Aesopian fables, "Courtiers of King Lion: Fox and Hart," in which the hart (*ṣevi*), a barely disguised Jewish sage, lauds humanity's "noble soul" (*nefesh nikhbedeth*). The praise unfolds in the course of a learned exposition of Aristotelian physics, during which the hart identifies the human soul as the uppermost stratum in the tripartite hierarchy of living things: plant (*ha-ṣomeaḥ*), animal (*ha-ḥayyoth*), and intellect. Human intellect, the hart explains, is the exclusive guarantor of immortality; it is also the source of additional superiorities over nonhuman animals, including "imagination, laughter," and the capacity for inventing rhetorical figures of speech.[64] The hart's lecture recapitulates doctrines enunciated by Ibn Sahula in the introduction to his fables: God emanates into each human being "a noble and supernal form, which constitutes superiority over earthbound creations, for 'man's superiority over the beast' [*motar ha-'adam min ha-behemah*] is the rational soul [*nefesh medabbereth*] . . . the ultimate perfection [*takhlith, telos*] in the world of lower beings, for it persists eternally but they come to an end."[65] Human intellect, according to Ibn Sahula, offers more immediate advantages, as well: "To those whom fortune's slings / Make victims, intellect redemption brings." To prove the point, Ibn Sahula might have invoked "Fox without Heart," were he familiar with it. To disprove the point, he might have invoked the futile efforts of the hapless lamb described in "Wolf and Lamb at Riverbank," were he familiar with that story. In actuality, Ibn Sahula refers to his own Aesopian tale in which the hart uses his prudential intelligence to outwit his foe, the scheming and ambitious fox. "Consider the beasts," Ibn Sahula counsels. If they, with their inferior grade of mind, can outwit their enemies, "How much more so can human beings succeed, [*kol she-khen ha-'adam*], given their superior grade of intellect."[66]

Conservative fables like "Courtiers of King Lion: Hart and Fox" propagate conventional wisdom: they advocate the inferiority of nonhuman animals vis-à-vis human beings. Such fables nevertheless concede that all living creatures are linked in a continuum of commonalities. Their concession induces or maintains minimal awareness of "our entwinement with the nonhuman world of animals."[67] Fables like "Wolf and Lamb at Riverbank" are more radical. They urge the denial of difference between human and nonhuman animals. Their fabulous denial induces or maintains not only "our entwinement with . . . animals" but more fully promotes the state of consciousness described by Hadot: the "radical transformation of human perspective, containing a universalist, cosmic dimension."[68]

To the Left of Radical

Medieval Aesopian fables that posit the superiority of animals over humans complete the picture. Such fables engage the politics of asymmetrical power. They broadcast on the same wavelength that carries Michel de Montaigne, Spinoza, and radical enlightenment. They resonate with themes and motifs associated with Plutarch, who credits "the soul of beasts" with having "a greater natural capacity and perfection [than human beings] for the generation of virtue."[69] They side with the ancient and scandalous Cynics, who believed that "civilisation is bunk."[70] They foreshadow George Orwell's *Animal Farm* and its wise character, Old Major, the pig who declared that "there, comrades, is the answer to all our problems. It is summed up in a single word—Man. Man is the only enemy we really have."[71]

In 1316 Qalonymus ben Qalonymus translated an extended Aesopian fable from Arabic into Hebrew.[72] It is an exercise in political philosophy, lamentably ignored by historians of the field.[73] The fable recounts a dispute between humans and animals. Humans claim that they are superior to animals in every respect. Humans further claim that this superiority justifies their ownership of animals. Humans assert that they are the masters and animals their slaves. The animals deny the principle of human superiority and reject its practical correlate, hierarchy. They protest the socioeconomic subjugation of animals. Nonviolently, they rebel, seeking justice from the court of an impartial third party, Birasaf the Wise. In the original Arabic, his title was king of the Jinn; in Hebrew, it became king of the Shedim, the demons.

Addressing the question of provenance, Qalonymus explains in the introduction to his translation that the fable derives from "'Iggereth Ba'ale Ḥayyim," (Epistle on animals), one of fifty-one epistles comprising an encyclopedia composed by the Ikhwān al-Ṣafā', the Brethren of Purity, a group of "extraordinarily learned, anonymous Islamic sages and philosophers."[74] Qalonymus describes their encyclopedia as a unified work of literature. He notes that it combines diverse genres, "narrative, storytelling, proofs, and demonstrative proofs" (*haggadah ve-sippur ve-re'ayoth u-moftim*). He adds that "the demonstrative proofs, however, are not many." He also observes that "many of the propositions follow the paths of religion, while other propositions follow the footsteps of philosophy, with the result that in every Epistle both an assertion and its contrary appear, except for statements involving the mathematical sciences."

Qalonymus explains that his Hebrew version inexactly transposes the Arabic. He acknowledges deleting numerous passages, many of them poetic, difficult to fathom, or repetitious, in which he finds no "deep meanings" (*'amuqoth*). He also excludes "the sections preceding the story [*sippur*]." They contain "what Aristotle and his successors had said" regarding the natural history, anatomy, and physiology of the various species of animals.

Despite these deletions and other embellishments tailoring the text for a Jewish audience, Qalonymus preserves the drama, ethical fervor, and philosophic intensity of the original fable. Whether speaking Arabic or Hebrew, the protagonists form the same, equally loquacious parties: humans, animals, and demons. The staging is "debate" (*vikkuaḥ*), the term used by Qalonymus, or courtroom drama, since most of the action occurs in tribunals presided over by the king of demons. The narrative unfolds in a sequence of three phases. The first phase depicts a preliminary hearing initiated by the animals. The plaintiffs are creatures who endure the most intense interaction with humans: mule, ox, ram, camel, elephant, horse, pig, and rabbit. Poignantly, they describe the physical abuse and emotional suffering inflicted upon them by human cruelty; they condemn humanity's indecent exploitation of animal labor; they ridicule allegations of human superiority. Humans mount a weak defense. The animals prevail. They persuade Birasaf to convene a formal tribunal.

In the second phase of the fable, the three parties prepare for the judicial hearing. Birasaf consults with his demon scholars and viziers. They speculate on possible outcomes of the tribunal; they review the history of antagonism between demons and humans. Meanwhile, the humans also caucus. Their group of seventy is cosmopolitan. It includes a Hindu from Ceylon, a Syrian Jew, a Syrian Christian, a Byzantine Greek philosopher, a Bedouin, an Arabian Muslim, and a Persian Muslim. They too speculate on possible outcomes of the trial. They briefly consider ameliorating their treatment of animals. They ponder methods for swaying King Birasaf and his advisers in humankind's favor. One corrupt speaker suggests bribes; another mendacious one proposes fabricating the claim that documents proving ownership of the animals were lost during the flood. While humans and demons caucus, the animals convene to consider their plight and organize their forces. They dispatch messengers to all the animal domains, requesting that litigators be sent. Six are chosen. Land-based carnivores settle upon Kalilah the jackal; birds choose Nightingale; flying insects choose Bee; birds of prey, predators marked by hooked beaks and curved talons, choose Parrot; aquatic creatures, including the amphibians, choose Frog; and crawling creatures, including the snakes, chose Cricket.

Their choices are not arbitrary. Descriptions of the selection process are opportunities for invidious comparisons that shame human behavior. We learn, for example, that after considerable deliberation the flying insects decide that only their monarch, Bee, possesses traits that work effectively at the court of the demons: "lawful rectitude, justice, keen thinking, clear reasoning, and lucid arguments."[75] As for the aquatic creatures, they too understand that they cannot prevail in court by exerting "brute force and aggressiveness but only by moderation and tolerance, tranquility of mind and discernment, justice and rectitude." Crocodile therefore excuses himself because he acknowledges being "irascible, mercurial, destructive, and treacherously harmful." Crocodile then recommends that Frog be sent, because "he's wise, mild, patient, and abundantly devout, for he copiously sings praises to his God by night and day, with hymns in afternoon and psalms at night."[76]

The six animal litigators dominate the third, longest, and final phase of the fable. Their displays of rhetorical prowess are brilliant. The delegate from the rulers of Byzantium boasts that mankind's "marvelous capacity for managing our lives and collaborating in the arts, industries . . . and commerce . . . confirms our claim that we are their masters and they are our slaves."[77] Bee replies by calling attention to the way his own subjects "cooperate to secure our interests . . . having knowledge, understanding, awareness, discernment, thought, and judgment [that are] more subtle and finer than [humans]." Maintaining the hive requires discipline, effective social organization, and a sagacious division of labor. Similar ethological traits are to be found among ants, locusts, silkworms, and wasps, Bee argues. And if the Byzantines were to consider the life of insects, they "would find that [insects] have knowledge, discernment, awareness, and ingenuity . . . and [Byzantines] would not boast of being our masters and us their slaves."[78] Parrot advances a complementary argument. He punctures human pride with a barrage of facts illustrating the productivity achieved by bees who build without tools and nevertheless outmatch human architects; spiders who outdo human tailors and weavers; termites who perform prodigies, first manufacturing clay and then building complex structures with it; and all the other birds and beasts who build homes and raise their offspring intuitively and with more success than humans.[79]

A Jew from the land of Israel argues that religion signifies human superiority and provides the credentials for human dominion. He itemizes divine revelation of law, prophecy, promises of reward and punishment, regulations for observing "prayers, fasts, charity and alms, festivals, holidays, gatherings, and attendance at houses of worship and synagogues." His inventory elicits a feisty rejoinder from Nightingale: "All this counts against you, not in your favor, because all these are penalties, chastisements to expiate sin and atone for wrong-doing, or to restrain you from foul, shameful doings." Furthermore, Nightingale proclaims, humans only obey these laws because they fear punishment. "But we [animals] are free of sin and evil, indecency and disgrace. We don't need the rituals you boast of. Besides, you must know, O human, that God sent His prophets and messengers only to miscreant people and the ignorant masses . . . but we are clear of all these things . . . You must know, O human, that prophets are physicians of the soul. No one but the sick needs a doctor . . . You [humans] need teachers and admonishers, because of the paucity of your knowledge of beneficial and harmful things, but we [animals] are instructed directly with all we need to know from the very beginning of our existence."[80] Parrot joins the chorus, insisting that

> were it not for the ignoble nature of humans, their base characters, vicious mores, depraved customs, and uprooting of goodness, God would not have commanded them to show gratitude to God and parents. God gave us no such commands, for we have no betrayers and rebels. Command and prohibition are addressed only to you because you are bad slaves who always fall into the trap of rebellion. You are therefore more fit for slavery and we for freedom. How then can you so arrogantly claim to be our masters and we your slaves, were it not for your being swept away by sheer effrontery and unmitigated gall.[81]

Animals such as these are not realistic; they do not exist outside the fable in the way that humans depicted in the fable exist outside it. What then does Qalonymus make of these nonmimetic, fabulous, and argumentative crocodiles, bees, parrots, and nightingales? Comparison with his handling of the demons provides an oblique answer. In the introduction to his translation, he reports that the authors of the Arabic fable did not "believe in them." Qalonymus therefore concludes that the demons were meant as literary devices, entertainments, products of playful imagination, fictions exemplifying the need for impartial judges in settling disputes. Alluding to the analysis of parables provided by Maimonides,[82] Qalonymus explicitly classifies the demons as "ornaments [*maskiyyot*] which do not belong to the overall intended meaning [of the text] but are needed to complete the dramatic give and take and to flesh out the aesthetic beauty of the story's narrative [*noy ḥiqqui ha-sippur*]."

Qalonymus deals differently with the fable's animals. He does not explain them away by reducing them to mere literary ornament. He says nothing to obscure their verisimilitude to biological counterparts in the world outside the fable. Despite his understanding that the fable is primarily *haggadah ve-sippur*, narrative and fictional, and despite his awareness that its authors, the Ikhwān al-Ṣafā', the Brethren of Purity, intentionally contradict themselves at every turn, Qalonymus concludes that the fable is univocal and apodictic. Despite its aura of vagaries, he understands it to proclaim unassailable scientific truths: truths about the forces of nature, truths about the capacities of practical intellect, and unsettling truths about behavioral parity between humans and animals. He does not believe that living animals can speak Arabic, Hebrew, or any other human language, but he does believe that what they cannot tell in words they show in activity. Qalonymus's fable is a dual translation: it transposes Arabic into Hebrew, and it transmutes the nonverbal idiom of animal behavior into eloquent human speech.

"What became clear to me after reading the book numerous times," Qalonymus writes in the introduction,

> was that with respect to matters political [*mediniyim*] and practical, or productive [*ma'asiyim*], man has no superiority over the animals. Nor is the rank of [man] over the [beast] higher in any matter subject to the practical intellect [*sekhel ma'asi*], for whatever man does by rational choice [*proairesis, ba-veḥirah*] exists in animals naturally [*ba-teva'*], with the consequence that [animal] work is more estimable [*ḥashuvah*], as explained in the book, *De anima*. It is nevertheless made clear at the end of the fable that [man] does enjoy superiority over the beast: it resides in the human intellect, but if and only if it is actual and in its state of final perfection. With this truth, only a fool [*sakhal*] or sophist [*mit'aqesh*] would disagree.

This passage forcefully overturns the judgment that Qalonymus "wrote no philosophical works, except for the letter addressed to Joseph Kaspi."[83]

The passage also makes clear that Qalonymus neither understands the fable's animals to be literary fictions, distinguishing them from the nonexistent demons, nor does he dodge quotidian reality by construing the animals as metaphors or symbols signifying deeper, perhaps more spiritual, esoteric meanings. Two allegorical readings of literary texts were possible: psychological and sociological. In the psychological hermeneutics favored by medieval thinkers, animals represent the bestial, nonrational, or irrational strata of the human soul: desires, passions, and appetites.[84] Their drama is subjugated to intellect and reason, the process by which humans achieve liberation from enslavement to corporeality, thereby setting the stage for achieving intellectual enlightenment.[85]

In the medieval sociological reading, animals are thinly veiled metaphors for types of human beings. For the conservative and parochial Isaac ibn Sahula, the humans are Jews. For Berakhiah ha-Naqdan and the other fabulists, the humans are unspecified and generic. In our own time, a third kind of sociological reading was argued by the eminent historian of philosophy, Shlomo Pines, who explicitly rejects Qalonymus's interpretation of the fable for being tendentiously "Averroistic." Pines insists that the fable's animals transmit a "hidden meaning." They are symbols representing the mass of commoners who are obliged to subordinate themselves to the hierarchical regimen of belief and practice imposed upon them by elite leaders and ontological superiors, the prophets or imams.[86]

Qalonymus refuses to allegorize the fable. His philosophic tradition privileged deductive logic and theoretical science but credited practical intellect with responsibility for ethics, political life, arts, crafts, and technologies of all sorts. Qalonymus applies that tradition to the fable and concludes that it affirms parity between humans and other animals in practical realms. Reminiscent of Berakhiah's didactic commentaries to "Wolf at Grammar School" that ignored the teacher and to "Wolf and Lamb at Riverbank" that bypassed the antimonarchic politics in favor of castigating the wealthy classes, Qalonymus's introduction is noticeably silent on the scathing critiques of human culture and the claims of animal superiority. Animals might prefer his more radical conclusions: not parity, but the superiority of animal life over the systemic depravity of human life and the abolition of animal slavery. Animals might then be reminded of his numerous deletions from the Arabic original and sigh in relief, knowing that he refused to bowdlerize, that he preserved in Hebrew all the passages voicing both profound admiration for animal life and utter discontent with human civilization.

From the animals' point of view, Qalonymus may have been too subtle, too reticent, or too moderate on the topics of human degeneracy and animal superiority. From the point of view of other Jewish thinkers, however, Qalonymus's conclusions were far too radical. In fifteenth-century Spain, in a rare medieval reference to Qalonymus's version of the fable, Joseph Albo readily concedes that, in the practical domains of arts and crafts, nonhuman animals are superior to humans. Albo nevertheless defends androcentrism. He subordinates the practical, or mundane, "welfare of the body" to the transcendental "welfare of the soul."[87] He understands the soul's transcendence to consist of metaphysical enlightenment and theological rectitude. He declares that

> we cannot say that the purpose of the human intellect is exclusively practical, to enable man to invent arts and trades. For it is made clear in the *Treatise on Animals*, composed by the Brethren of Purity, that as a general rule the lower animals are more adept in the arts and trades than man. Moreover, were it the case [that the purpose of human intellect is exclusively practical], then since the purpose is more important than that which comes before the purpose, the practical arts would be more noble than the speculative, and those speculative arts which lead to no practical result at all would be vain and of no value whatsoever.[88]

Albo's concession that "the lower animals are more adept in the arts and trades than man" is not idiosyncratic. Roughly two centuries earlier, Shem-Tov Falaquera (ca. 1225–1295) invokes the *Sefer Ba'ale Ḥayyim*, the corpus of Aristotle's zoological treatises, to corroborate the assertion that "the most skilled human artisans" cannot match the "astonishing" productivity and behavior of nonhuman animals, especially the "ants, spiders, silk-worms, and bees."[89] Similar claims of animal superiority in bodily capacities and technology are articulated earlier in the thirteenth century by Abraham ibn Ḥasdai.[90] Conspicuously absent from these statements by Ibn Ḥasdai, Falaquera, and Albo is the stunning assertion made by Qalonymus regarding the parity in matters political, ethical, or social (*mediniyim*) between human and nonhuman animals.

The divergent interpretations of the fable given by Albo and Qalonymus, together with the gap between the fable itself and the meaning imposed upon it by Qalonymus, are compelling reminders that Aesopian fables constitute a capacious genre. In medieval Jewish literature, they gave voice to the parochial orthodoxies of an Isaac ibn Sahula; the mythological, pseudoscience of *The Tales (or Alphabet) of Ben Sira*; the disruptive heterodoxies of a Berakhiah ha-Naqdan; and the ultraradical critiques of human civilization in Qalonymus's version of the fable. Regardless of their place on the spectrum of ideological affiliation, the fables and their fabulists were inescapably engaged with the political. They shared this orientation with the medieval philosophers. Unlike the philosophers, however, the fabulists were primarily storytellers. They tended to see the world through the lens of storytelling. Paradoxically, the imaginative fabulists often beheld a this-worldly, Machiavellian, somber realism that eluded their more idealistic and optimistic counterparts, the practitioners of medieval Jewish philosophy.

Notes

1. See Elaine Scarry, "A Defense of Poesy (The Treatise of Julia)," in *On Nineteen Eighty-Four: Orwell and Our Future*, ed. Abbot Gleason, Jack Goldsmith, and Martha C. Nussbaum (Princeton, NJ: Princeton University Press, 2005), 13–28, see Joseph Dan, *The Hebrew Story in the Middle Ages* (Jerusalem: Keter Publishing House, 1974), 7–11, 27–30 [Hebrew].

2. To sample the evidence of neglect, see Daniel H. Frank and Oliver Leaman, eds., *The Cambridge Companion to Medieval Jewish Philosophy* (New York: Cambridge University Press, 2003); Steven Nadler and T. M. Rudavsky, eds., *The Cambridge History of Jewish Philosophy: From Antiquity to the Seventeenth Century* (New York: Cambridge University Press, 2009); and Colette Sirat, *A History of Jewish Philosophy in the Middle Ages* (New York: Cambridge University Press, 1985). For a sampling of philosophy discovered in law codes, see Isadore Twersky, *Introduction to the Code of Maimonides (Mishneh Torah)* (New Haven, CT: Yale University Press, 1980), 356–514; in poetry, see Aaron W. Hughes, *The Texture of*

the Divine: Imagination in Medieval Islamic and Jewish Thought (Bloomington: Indiana University Press, 2004), and Adena Tanebaum, *The Contemplative Soul: Hebrew Poetry and Philosophical Theory in Medieval Spain* (Leiden: Brill, 2002); and in biblical commentary, see Isadore Twersky, "Aspects of the Social and Cultural History of Provençal Jewry," in *Jewish Society through the Ages*, ed. H. H. Ben-Sasson and S. Ettinger (New York: Schocken Books, 1971), 187n9; Barry Mesch, *Studies in Joseph ibn Kaspi: Fourteenth-Century Philosopher and Exegete* (Leiden: Brill, 1975); James T. Robinson, "Philosophy and Science in Medieval Jewish Commentaries on the Bible," in *Sciences in Medieval Jewish Cultures*, ed. Gad Freudenthal (New York: Cambridge University Press, 2011), 454–75.

3. For the Hebrew text, see *Mishle Shu'alim le-Rabbi Berakhiah ha-Naqdan*, ed. A. M. Haberman (Jerusalem: Schocken, 1946), 125. For a complete English translation, see *Fables of a Jewish Aesop, Translated from the Fox Fables by Berechiah ha-Nakdan*, trans. Moses Hadas (Boston: Nonpareil Books, 2001), 213–14. For indispensable monographic discussion informed by folklore studies that delight in assembling cross-cultural parallels, see Haim Schwarzbaum, *The "Mishle Shu'alim" (Fox Tales) of Rabbi Berechiah ha-Nakdan: A Study in Comparative Folklore and Fable Lore* (Kiron: Institute for Jewish and Arab Folklore Research, 1979), 533–36.

4. For the historical context and scant biographical data, see Norman Golb, *The Jews in Medieval Normandy: A Social and Intellectual History* (New York: Cambridge University Press, 1998), 318, 324–47.

5. See Gerson D. Cohen, "Esau as Symbol in Early Medieval Thought," in *Jewish Medieval and Renaissance Studies*, ed. Alexander Altmann (Cambridge, MA: Harvard University Press, 1967), 19–48, and Israel Jacob Yuval, *Two Nations in Your Womb: Perceptions of Jews and Christians in Late Antiquity and the Middle Ages*, trans. Barbara Harshav and Jonathan Chipman (Berkeley: University of California Press, 2006).

6. For an indispensable overview of the ancient and late ancient philosophic debates over animal capacities, see the compendium of arguments assembled by Abraham Terian in *Philonis Alexandrini De Animalibus: The Armenian Text with an Introduction, Translation, and Commentary* (Chico, CA: Scholars Press, 1981), and the critical scholarship of Richard Sorabji in *Animal Minds and Human Morals: The Origins of the Western Debate* (Ithaca, NY: Cornell University Press, 1993), 78–96. To complement Sorabji's philosophic focus, see Ingvild Saelid Gilhus, *Animals, Gods, and Humans: Changing Attitudes to Animals in Greek, Roman, and Early Christian Ideas* (New York: Routledge, 2006), 1–137, 205–26. For a handy collection of primary texts, see Stephen T. Newmyer, *Animals in Greek and Roman Thought: A Sourcebook* (New York: Routledge, 2011).

7. For additional comments on the disparity between moral lessons "inside . . . and outside the story," see Laura Gibbs, *Aesop's Fables* (New York: Oxford University Press, 2002), xvi–xviii.

8. For comparative perspectives and a sense of the Aesopian in classical Greek culture, see Leslie Kurke, *Aesopic Conversations: Popular Tradition, Cultural Dialogue, and the Invention of Greek Prose* (Princeton, NJ: Princeton University Press, 2011); in medieval European culture, see Jan M. Ziolkowski, *Talking Animals: Medieval Latin Beast Poetry, 750–1150* (Philadelphia: University of Pennsylvania Press, 1993); in early modern and modern Europe, see Annabel Patterson, *Fables of Power: Aesopian Writing and Political History* (Durham, NC: Duke University Press, 1991); in postcolonial, postmodern, multimedia, and global cultures, see Gert Reifart and Phillip Morrisey, eds., *Aesopic Voices: Re-framing Truth*

through Concealed Ways of Presentation in the 20th and 21st Centuries (Newcastle upon Tyne: Cambridge Scholars Press, 2011).

9. For monographic treatment, including two distinct recensions of the Hebrew original, see Eli Yassif, *The Tales of Ben Sira in the Middle-Ages: A Critical Text and Literary Study* (Jerusalem: Magnes Press, 1984) [Hebrew]. "Raven with Wobbly Gait" appears on p. 246 and is subject to folkloristic analysis on pp. 86–88; "Fox without Heart," pp. 250–52, 100–4. An English translation of the entire *Alphabet of Ben Sira*, based on yet a third distinctive Hebrew recension originally published by Moritz Steinschneider and reprinted in *Otzar Midrashim*, ed. J. D. Eisenstein (New York: Hotsa'at Reznik, Menshel ve-Shutafim, 1928), 1:43–50, is accessible in David Stern and Mark J. Mirsky, eds., *Rabbinic Fantasies: Imaginative Narratives from Classical Hebrew Literature* (New Haven, CT: Yale University Press, 1990), 190 ["Raven with Wobbly Gait"], 191–94 ["Fox without Heart"].

10. See Yassif, *Tales of Ben Sira in the Middle Ages*, 87, 91.

11. See Walter Benjamin, "The Storyteller: Reflections on the Works of Nikolai Leskov," in *Illuminations: Essays and Reflections*, ed. and intr. Hannah Arendt, trans. Harry Zohn (New York: Schocken Books, 1968), 83–109.

12. See Berel Lang, "The Animal-in-the-Text: Fables and Literary Origins," in *The Anatomy of Philosophical Style* (Cambridge: Basil Blackwell, 1990), 200. Like Benjamin, Lang stresses the concision of narrative style; unlike Benjamin, Lang's insight regarding desire introduces a psychological explanation.

13. See C. M. Woodhouse, introduction to George Orwell, *Animal Farm: A Fairy Story*, preface by Russell Baker (New York: Signet Classic, 1956), xvii–xxi.

14. Similar conclusions have also been reached by Galit Hasan-Rockem in the entry "Fable," *Encyclopedia Judaica*, 2nd ed. (Detroit, MI: Macmillan Reference with Keter Publishing, 2007), 6:666–70.

15. See Lang, "The-Animal-in-the-Text," 204–7.

16. For medieval and early modern samples of the genre accessible in English translation, see Nissim ben Jacob ibn Shahin, *An Elegant Composition concerning Relief after Adversity*, trans. William M. Brinner (New Haven, CT: Yale University Press, 1977) and *Ma'aseh Book: Book of Jewish Tales and Legends Translated from the Judeo-German*, ed. and trans. Moses Gaster (Philadelphia, PA: Jewish Publication Society of America, 1934). For an analytic overview of the genre, see Eli Yassif, *The Hebrew Folktale: History, Genre, Meaning*, trans. Jaqueline S. Teitelbaum (Bloomington: Indiana University Press, 1999), 283–96, 321–42. For additional comments distinguishing the genre of Aesopian fables from closely related forms of literature, see Dov Noy, *The Jewish Animal Tale of Oral Tradition* (Haifa: Ethnological Museum and Folklore Archives, 1976), 138–46 [Hebrew].

17. See Moses Maimonides, *The Guide of the Perplexed*, trans. Shlomo Pines (Chicago: University of Chicago Press, 1963), 534 [3:34] (hereafter Pines trans.)

18. For justification of the claim that premodern philosophy was preoccupied with the management of desire and the pragmatic search for peace of mind, see Martha C. Nussbaum, *The Therapy of Desire: Theory and Practice in Hellenistic Ethics* (Princeton, NJ: Princeton University Press, 1994); Pierre Hadot, *What Is Ancient Philosophy?* trans. Michael Chase (Cambridge, MA: Belknap Press of Harvard University Press, 2002), 55–233, and *Philosophy as a Way of Life*, ed. Arnold I. Davidson and trans. Michael Chase (Cambridge, MA: Blackwell Publishers, 1995), 47–125, 147–276; and A. A. Long and D. N. Sedley, *The Hellenistic Philosophers*, vols. 1–2 (New York: Cambridge University Press, 1987).

19. See Herbert A. Davidson, "The Study of Philosophy as a Religious Obligation," in *Religion in a Religious Age*, ed. S. D. Goitein (Cambridge, MA: Association for Jewish Studies, 1974), 53–68; and Steven Harvey, *Falaquera's "Epistle of the Debate": An Introduction to Jewish Philosophy* (Cambridge, MA: Harvard University Press, 1987).

20. For an overview of the hermeneutical, apologetic, and polemical issues, see "Socioreligious Controversies" in Salo Baron, *A Social and Religious History of the Jews* (New York / Philadelphia: Columbia University Press and Jewish Publication Society of America, 1957), 5:82–137, 326–52; and Marc Saperstein, *Decoding the Rabbis: A Thirteenth-Century Commentary on the Aggadah* (Cambridge, MA: Harvard University Press, 1980), 1–20.

21. See, for example, Y. Tzvi Langermann, *The Jews and the Sciences in the Middle Ages* (Brookfield, VT: Ashgate Variorum, 1999); Gad Freudenthal, *Science in the Medieval Hebrew and Arabic Traditions* (Burlington, VT: Ashgate Variorum, 2005); and Gad Freudenthal, ed., *Science in Medieval Jewish Cultures* (New York: Cambridge University Press, 2011).

22. For a prime example of how a medieval Jewish philosopher systematically dismantled a charming metaphor, "The world is a single animal," see Maimonides, *Guide of the Perplexed*, 1:72 ("Man is a small world . . . but you never hear that one of the ancients has said that an ass or a horse is a small world," [Pines trans., 190–4]). *Locus classicus* for philosophy's discomfort with myths and storytelling is Plato's *Republic* 2. For discussion, see the still-pertinent comments in Werner Jaeger, *Paideia: The Ideals of Greek Culture*, vol. 2, *In Search of the Divine Center*, trans. Gilbert Highet (New York: Oxford University Press, 1943), 211–24. Typical of post-Platonic, premodern philosophy's moral concerns and epistemological scruples is John Locke's polemic against the "abuse of words" formulated in his *Essay Concerning Human Understanding*, 3:10. Typical of major trends in modern Anglo-American philosophy antagonistic to "stories" is Alex Rosenberg, *The Atheist's Guide to Reality: Enjoying Life Without Illusions* (New York: W. W. Norton & Company, Inc., 2011), 8–19, 310–15. For an altogether useful discussion of Locke and philosophy's perennial quarrel with stories, see Martha Nussbaum, *Love's Knowledge: Essays on Philosophy and Literature* (New York: Oxford University Press, 1990), 3–53, 251, 261–85. For the sometimes ragged seams between *logos* and *muthos*, when naturalistic science began its emancipation from irrationality in ancient Greece, see G. E. R. Lloyd, *The Revolutions of Wisdom: Studies in the Claims and Practice of Ancient Greek Science* (Berkeley: University of California Press, 1987).

23. See Plato, *Republic* 6–10, ed. and trans. Christopher Emlyn-Jones and William Preddy (Cambridge, MA: Harvard University Press, 2013), 437.

24. See Norman Golb, *The Jews in Medieval Normandy: A Social and Intellectual History* (New York: Cambridge University Press, 1998), 341.

25. See Aristotle, *Metaphysics*, 3:4 (1000a9–21), trans. Hugh Tredennick (Cambridge, MA: Harvard University Press, 1933), 127–28.

26. See Aristotle, *Meteorologica*, 2:3 (356b9–18), trans. H. D. P. Lee (Cambridge, MA: Harvard University Press, 1951), 143–44.

27. See *Otot Ha-Shamayim: Samuel ibn Tibbon's Hebrew Version of Aristotle's* Meteorology, ed. and trans. Resianne Fontaine (New York: E. J. Brill, 1995), 91. *Mahbīl* is perfectly translated as "twaddler"; one who bloviates or drivels might also convey the underlying biblical Hebrew, *hevel*. Jacob Klatzkin's *Philosophicus Thesaurus* (s.v. *mahbīl*) calls attention to the possibility of translating the term "deceiving, errant sophist," based on Ahituv's version of *Treatise on Logic*, ch. 8, in which the author, presumably Maimonides, distinguishes the various hierarchic grades of syllogism, from the most to the least scientific: demonstrative,

dialectic, rhetorical, sophistic, and poetic. For the original texts, see Israel Efros, "Maimonides' Treatise on Logic," *Proceedings of the American Academy for Jewish Research* 7 (1937–1938): 41, 81, 114 [Hebrew] and 48–49 [English], [ch. 8].

28. For a summary of scholarly consensus regarding Samuel ibn Tibbon's biography and works, see James T. Robinson, *Samuel ibn Tibbon's Commentary on Ecclesiastes: The Book of the Soul of Man* (Tübingen: Mohr Siebeck, 2007), 3–17. For an inventory of sources indicating the controversial status of astrology in medieval Jewish philosophy, see Herbert A. Davidson, *Moses Maimonides: The Man and His Works* (New York: Oxford University Press, 2005), 494–501; and Shlomo Sela, "Astrology in Medieval Jewish Thought (Twelfth–Fourteenth Centuries)" in *Science in Medieval Jewish Cultures*, 292–300. For an unforgettable portrayal of the imbrication of astrology in medieval Islamicate Jewish life, see Judah Alḥarizi, *The Book of Taḥkemoni: Jewish Tales from Medieval Spain*, trans. David Simha Segal (Portland, OR: Littman Library of Jewish Civilization, 2003), 205–9, 526–28. For a critical and annotated edition of the Hebrew original, see *Taḥkemoni; or The Tales of Heman the Ezraḥite by Judah Alḥarizi*, ed. Joseph Yahalom and Naoya Katsumata (Jerusalem: Ben Zvi Institute for the Study of Jewish Communities in the East, 2010), 327–32. To enrich critical understanding, see "The Silence of the Jews: Judah al-Ḥarizi's Picaresque Tale of the Muslim Astrologer," in Ross Brann, *Power in the Betrayal: Representations of Jews and Muslims in Eleventh- and Twelfth-Century Islamic Spain* (Princeton, NJ: Princeton University Press, 2002), 140–59.

29. A (slightly unreliable) English translation of the passage is readily available in Isadore Twersky, *A Maimonides Reader* (New York: Behrman House, 1972), 407–9. For the Hebrew translation, see Moshe ben Maimon, *Haqdamot le-Ferush ha-Mishnah (Pereq Heleq)*, ed. M. R. Rabinowitz (Jerusalem: Mossad Harav Kook, 1961), 116–23. For the Arabic original, see *Selections from the Arabic Writings of Maimonides*, ed. Israel Friedlander (Leiden: E. J. Brill, 1909), 12.

30. See Maimonides, *Guide of the Perplexed*, 3:29 (Pines trans., 516–20) in which the terms for *raving, absurdity, foolish nonsense*, and *twaddle* (*hevel*) recur some fifteen times.

31. Scholarly consensus affirms that, in these matters, Maimonides followed the lead of Al-Farabi. Literature on the topic is immense. Initial foothold and stabilizing orientation are available in Muhsin S. Mahdi, *Alfarabi and the Formation of Islamic Political Philosophy* (Chicago: University of Chicago Press, 2001); *Al-Fārābī on the Perfect State*, ed. and trans. Richard Walzer (New York: Clarendon Press, 1985), 209, 219, 390; Miriam Galston, "The Theoretical and Practical Dimensions of Happiness as Portrayed in the Political Treatises of al-Fārābī," in *The Political Aspects of Islamic Philosophy*, ed. Charles E. Butterworth (Cambridge, MA: Harvard University Press, 1992), 95–151; Joel L. Kraemer, *Maimonides: The Life and World of One of Civilization's Greatest Minds* (New York: Doubleday, 2008); and Herbert A. Davidson, *Moses Maimonides* (New York: Oxford University Press, 2005).

32. For the distinctions between good/bad and true/false, see Averroës, *Middle Commentary on Aristotle's "De Anima,"* ed. and trans. Alfred L. Ivry (Provo, UT: Brigham Young University Press, 2002), 121. ["True and false are to theoretical science as good and bad are to practical science."] See also the illuminating discussion by Shlomo Pines, "Truth and Falsehood versus Good and Evil: A Study in Jewish and General Philosophy in Connection with the *Guide of the Perplexed*, 1:2" in *Studies in Maimonides*, ed. Isadore Twersky (Cambridge, MA: Harvard University Press, 1990), 95–157. For an overview of the Aristotelian taxonomy of knowledge—distinguishing the practical, productive, and theoretical—see W. K. C. Guthrie, *A History of Greek of Greek Philosophy*, vol. 6, *Aristotle: An Encounter* (New York: Cambridge

University Press, 1981), 132–34. For a medieval Arabic statement of the taxonomy, focused on practical philosophy, traditionally ascribed to Maimonides, and subsequently translated into a widely read Hebrew version, see Muhsin Mahdi, "Maimonides: Logic," in *Medieval Political Philosophy*, ed. Ralph Lerner and Muhsin Mahdi (Ithaca, NY: Cornell University Press, 1972), 188–90. For the entire text, all of chapter 14 dealing with the divisions of philosophy, see Efros, "Maimonides' Treatise on Logic," 61–65. For a critique of the ascription to Maimonides, see Herbert A. Davidson, *Moses Maimonides: The Man and His Works*, 313–22. For monographic treatment of the medieval taxonomies of science, see Harry A. Wolfson, "The Classification of Sciences in Medieval Jewish Philosophy" and "Note on Maimonides' Classification of the Sciences" in *Studies in the History of Philosophy and Religion*, vol. 1, ed. Isadore Twersky and George H. Williams (Cambridge, MA: Harvard University Press, 1973), 493–560.

33. See Aristotle, *Art of Rhetoric*, trans. J. H. Frese (Cambridge, MA: Harvard University Press, 2006), 273–77 (2:20, 1393a30–1394a8). See also the following note.

34. See Plato, *Phaedo*, trans. Harold N. Fowler (Cambridge, MA: Harvard University Press, 2001), 207–13 (59d–61b). I have discussed both this text and the passage in Aristotle's *Rhetoric* cited in the prior note in "Liberating Imagination and Other Ends of Medieval Jewish Philosophy" in *Journal of Jewish Thought and Philosophy* 20 (2012): 35–53.

35. See Plato, *Republic Books 1–5*, ed. and trans. Chris Emlyn-Jones and William Preddy (Cambridge, MA: Harvard University Press, 2013), 193 (bk. 2, 377a).

36. See *Averroes' Middle Commentary on Aristotle's Nicomachean Ethics in the Hebrew Version of Samuel ben Judah*, ed. Lawrence V. Berman (Jerusalem: Israel Academy of Sciences and Humanities, 1999); and Lawrence V. Berman, "Greek into Hebrew: Samuel ben Judah of Marseilles, Fourteenth-Century Philosopher and Translator," in *Jewish Medieval and Renaissance Studies*, ed. Alexander Altmann (Cambridge, MA: Harvard University Press, 1967), 289–320.

37. See *Averroes' Commentary on Plato's Republic*, ed. and trans. E. I. J. Rosenthal (New York: Cambridge University Press, 1966), 29–30 [Hebrew], 124–25 [English].

38. For the Hebrew original, *see Mishle Shu'alim le-Rabbi Berakhiah ha-Naqdan*, 10–11; for a parallel English translation, see *Fables of a Jewish Aesop*, 12–13. For the comparative folklore, see Haim Schwarzbaum, *The "Mishle Shu'alim" (Fox Tales) of Rabbi Berechiah ha-Nakdan*, 9–14.

39. See the title essay in Leo Strauss, *Persecution and the Art of Writing* (Glencoe, IL: Free Press, 1952), 22–37; and more generally, Arthur M. Melzer, *Philosophy between the Lines: The Lost History of Esoteric Writing* (Chicago: University of Chicago Press, 2014). Strauss and his disciples enjoy no monopoly on the recognition of need for skill in outsmarting censorship, political and otherwise; see, for example, Sigmund Freud, *The Interpretation of Dreams*, ed. and trans. James Strachey (New York: Basic Books, 2010), 166–68 [chapter 4, Distortion in Dreams].

40. To date, scholarship has identified only one medieval Jewish antimonarchist, Don Isaac Abravanel (1437–1508). For general orientation, see Eric Lawee, *Isaac Abarbanel's Stance toward Tradition: Defense, Dissent, and Dialogue* (Albany: State University of New York Press, 2001). For the details on monarchy, see Robert Sacks, "Abravanel: Commentary on the Bible," in *Medieval Political Philosophy*, ed. Ralph Lerner and Muhsin Mahdi, 254–70; and *The Jewish Political Tradition*, vol. 1, *Authority*, ed. Michael Walzer, Menachem Lorberbaum, Noam J. Zohar, and Yair Lorberbaum (New Haven, CT: Yale University Press, 2000), 108–65

[ch. 3, Kings]. See also Abraham Melamed, *The Philosopher-King in Medieval and Renaissance Jewish Political Thought*, ed. Lenn E. Goodman (Albany: State University of New York University Press, 2003).

41. See Paul Feyerabend, "Let's Make More Movies," in *The Owl of Minerva: Philosophers on Philosophy*, ed. Charles J. Bontempo and S. Jack Odell (New York: McGraw-Hill Paperbacks, 1975), 201–2. A similar claim, that "poetry and art, rather than science and argument . . . can change our sense of which features of the world demand our attention and our love," is made in Catherine Osborne, *Dumb Beasts and Dead Philosophers: Humanity and the Humane in Ancient Philosophy and Literature* (New York: Oxford University Press, 2007), 11.

42. For the Hebrew, see *"Mishle Shu'alim" le-Rabbi Berakhiah ha-Naqdan*, 45; for an English translation, see *Fables of a Jewish Aesop*, 69–70. For the comparative folklore, see Haim Schwarzbaum, *The "Mishle Shu'alim" (Fox Tales) of Rabbi Berechiah ha-Nakdan*, 218–23. The motif of irrepressible lupine appetite for sheep and goats also surfaces in *Sefer Meshalim*, the early thirteenth-century collection of picaresque stories composed in rhymed prose by Jacob ben Elazar. For the annotated Hebrew text, see Yonah David, ed., *The Love Stories of Jacob ben Eleazar (1170–1233)* (Tel Aviv: Ramot Publishing, 1992–1993), 107–14. For critical discussion of Jacob ben Elazar's career and poetic vision, including evidence that the motif of wolves remaining irrepressibly wolves had "clear parallels in [medieval] Arabic and European sources" (143), see Jonathan P. Decter, *Iberian Jewish Literature: Between al-Andalus and Christian Europe* (Bloomington: Indiana University Press, 2007), 136–45.

43. See Alfred Lord Tennyson, *In Memoriam A. H. H.* [canto 56], which reads, "Who trusted God was love indeed / And love Creation's final law / Tho' Nature, red in tooth and claw / With ravine, shriek'd against his creed," as reproduced in *Tennyson's Poetry*, ed. Robert W. Hill Jr. (New York: W. W. Norton, 1999), 238.

44. See Thomas Hobbes, *Leviathan*, ed. Edwin Curley (Indianapolis, IN: Hackett, 1994), 74-76 [part 1: 13 (1, 9)].

45. See *Mishle Shu'alim*, 5 [Hebrew]; *Fables of a Jewish Aesop*, 5 [English].

46. See *Spinoza: Complete Works*, trans. Samuel Shirley (Indianapolis, IN: Hackett, 2002), 680 [*Political Treatise*, chapter 1].

47. Ibid., 681. For fuller description of the mathematical spirit in Spinoza's discussion of emotion, see Baruch Spinoza, *The Ethics*, trans. Samuel Shirley (Indianapolis, IN: Hackett, 1992), 58, 102–3 [part 1, appendix; part 3, preface].

48. See Maimonides, *Guide of the Perplexed*, 2:36 ("He should rather regard all people according to their various states with respect to which they are indubitably either like domestic animals or like beasts of prey" [Pines trans. 372].)

49. See Baruch Spinoza, *The Ethics*, 157 [part 4: prop. 4, corollary].

50. Ibid., 155 [part 4, axiom].

51. See Jonathan Israel, *Radical Enlightenment: Philosophy and the Making of Modernity, 1650–1750* (New York: Oxford University Press, 2001) and *A Revolution of the Mind: Radical Enlightenment and the Intellectual Origins of Modern Democracy* (Princeton, NJ: Princeton University Press, 2010).

52. I have discussed fables of this sort in "Liberating Imagination and Other Ends of Medieval Jewish Philosophy" and "Construction of Animals in Medieval Jewish Philosophy" in *New Directions in Jewish Philosophy*, ed. Aaron W. Hughes and Elliot R. Wolfson (Bloomington: Indiana University Press, 2010), 181–86.

53. See Hadot, *Philosophy as a Way of Life*, 211.

54. See *Deux Versions Hébräiques du Livre Kalîlâh et Dimnâh*, ed. Joseph Derenbourg (Paris: F. Vieweg, 1881). For additional critical analysis, see Ángeles Navarro Peiro, "La Versión Hebrea de *Calila y Dimna de Ya'ăqob ben El'azar*" in *Jewish Studies at the Turn of the Twentieth Century*, ed. Judith Targarona Borrás and Angel Sáenz-Badillos (Leiden: Brill, 1999), 468–75. For an English translation of the underlying Arabic, see Thomas B. Irving, *Kalilah and Dimnah: An English Version of Bidpai's Fables Based on Ancient Arabic and Spanish Manuscripts* (Newark, DE: Juan de la Cuesta, 1980). For the Arabic original, I consulted Ibn al-Muqaff'a, *Kalīlah wa-Dimnah* (Beirut: Dar Sadr, 1984).

55. For the Hebrew text, see *Sepher Shaashuim: A Book of Medieval Lore by Joseph ben Meir ibn Zabara*, ed. Israel Davidson (New York: Jewish Theological Seminary of America, 1914), 20–35, 98–99, 127–28. For an English translation, see *The Book of Delight by Joseph ben Meir Zabara*, trans. Moses Hadas (New York: Columbia University Press, 1932), 55–70, 124–25, 146–47. For indispensable critical analysis, see Judith Dishon, *The Book of Delight Composed by Joseph ben Meir Zabara* (Jerusalem: Reuven Mas, 1985), esp. 119–122 [Hebrew].

56. See *Taḥkemoni* 186–92 [Hebrew] and *The Book of Taḥkemoni*, 105–110, 479–81 [English].

57. See Abraham ben Shmu'el ha-Levi ibn Ḥasdai, *Ben ha-Melekh ve-ha-Nazir*, ed. Ayelet Oettinger (Tel Aviv: Tel Aviv University / Hayyim Rubin, 2011); 82 (ch. 9); 127 (ch. 17); 142 (ch. 19); 150 (ch. 21); 161 (ch. 23); 166 (ch. 24); 197 (ch. 30); 203 (ch. 31); and for critical commentary, 36–38.

58. See the two-volume edition of Isaac ibn Sahula, *Meshal Haqadmoni: Fables from the Distant Past, a Parallel Hebrew-English Text*, ed. and trans. Raphael Loewe (Portland, OR: Littman Library of Jewish Civilization, 2004).

59. For insight into the particularities of this temporal and cultural setting, see Decter, *Iberian Jewish Literature*.

60. For the Montaignesque, see "Apology for Raymond Sebond" in *The Complete Essays of Montaigne*, ed. Donald M. Frame (Stanford, CA: Stanford University Press, 1965), 318–58; for a sample of the Cartesian, see *The Philosophical Writings of Descartes*, trans. John Cottingham, Robert Stoothoff, and Dugald Murdoch (New York: Cambridge University Press, 1985), vol. 1: 134, 139–41 [*Discourse on Method*, part 5]. For a delightful sketch of the contrast between Montaigne and Descartes, see Stephen Toulmin, *Cosmopolis: The Hidden Agenda of Modernity* (New York: Free Press, 1990), 36–44.

61. For the Arabophone, Islamic original, see *Epistles of the Brethren of Purity: The Case of the Animals versus Man Before the King of the Jinn*, ed. and trans. Lenn E. Goodman and Richard McGregor (New York: Oxford University Press, 2009), 148. For the fourteenth-century Hebrew translation, to be discussed below, see *Sefer Ba'ale ḥayyim*, Bibliothèque Nationale (Paris) Hebrew MSS 899, 22r. For a printed edition, the more readily available version of the Hebrew, see *Sefer Igereth Ba'ale ḥayyim* (Warsaw, 1877), 22 [2:3].

62. For the Hebrew text of this poem by Samuel ha-Nagid (993–1056), critical interpretation, and a far more elegant English translation, see Raymond P. Scheindlin, *Wine, Women, and Death: Medieval Hebrew Poems on the Good Life* (New York: Oxford University Press, 1999), 159–61. See also my comments in "Construction of Animals in Medieval Jewish Philosophy," 190–95.

63. See Aristotle, *Nicomachean Ethics*, trans. H. Rackham (Cambridge, MA: Harvard University Press, 1926), 623–25 [10:8, 1178b24-32]. For the fourteenth-century Hebrew translation, see *Aristotle's Middle Commentary on Aristotle's "Nicomachean Ethics" in the Hebrew Version of Samuel ben Judah*, 343 [63]. For overall guidance to the topic, see Hava Tirosh-Samuelson,

Happiness in Premodern Judaism: Virtue, Knowledge, and Well-Being (Cincinnati, OH: Hebrew Union College Press, 2003). I discuss the medieval Jewish philosophic emphasis on human superiority in two essays: "Human-Animal Dualism in Modernity and Premodern Jewish Thought" in *Light against Darkness: Dualism in Ancient Mediterranean Religion and the Contemporary World*, ed. Armin Lange, Eric M. Meyers, Bennie H. Reynolds, and Randall Styers (Oakville, CT: Vandenhoeck and Ruprecht, 2010), 277–82; and "Cain, Abel, and Brutism" in *Scriptural Exegesis: The Shapes of Culture and the Religious Imagination—Essays in Honor of Michael Fishbane*, ed. Deborah A. Green and Laura S. Leiber (New York: Oxford University Press, 2009), 165–85.

64. See Isaac ibn Sahula, *Meshal Haqadmoni*, I, 93–98.

65. Ibid., 22. The biblical reference to "man's superiority over the beast" is Eccles. 3:19.

66. Ibid., 54.

67. See Stanley Cavell, "Companionable Thinking" in Stanley Cavell, Cora Diamond, Cary Wolfe, et al., *Philosophy and Animal Life* (New York: Columbia University Press, 2008), 92.

68. See supra, note 56.

69. See Plutarch, "Whether Land or Sea Animals Are Cleverer," "Beasts Are Rational," and "On the Eating of Flesh" in *Moralia 12*, trans. Harold Cherniss and William C. Helbold (Cambridge, MA: Harvard University Press, 1957), 311–579. For critical discussion, see Stephen T. Newmyer, "Animals in Plutarch" in *A Companion to Plutarch*, ed. Mark Beck (Malden, MA: Wiley Blackwell, 2014), 223–34; and Phillip S. Horky, "The Spectrum of Animal Rationality in Plutarch" in *Apeiron* 49 (2016):1–3; see Plutarch, "Beasts Are Rational," 501.

70. See Sorabji, *Animal Minds and Human Morals*, 160. See also Hadot, *Philosophy as a Way of Life*, 247.

71. See Orwell, *Animal Farm*, 28–29.

72. For a biographical sketch, see Ḥayyim Schirmann, *Hebrew Poetry in Spain and Provence* (Jerusalem: Mosad Bialik, 1960), 2:2, 499–502 [Hebrew]. For additional data and a list of his translations, roughly thirty, see Ernest Renan, *Les Écrivains Juifs Français du XIV Siècle* (Paris: Imprimerie Nationale, 1893), 71–114. For a critical edition of the premodern Arabic text underlying the translation, see *The Case of the Animals versus Man before the King of Jinn*, ed. and trans. Lenn E. Goodman and Richard McGregor. For background on the Brethren of Purity and their *Epistles*, see Nader el-Bizri, ed., *The Ikhwān al-Ṣafā' and Their Rasā' il: An Introduction* (New York: Oxford University Press, 2008) and Godefroid de Callatay, *Ikhwan al-Safa': A Brotherhood of Idealists on the Fringe of Orthodox Islam* (Oxford: One World, 2005).

73. For details of the deficit in Jewish studies, see Abraham Melamed, *Wisdom's Little Sister: Studies in Medieval and Renaissance Political Thought* (Brighton, MA: Academic Studies Press, 2012), 16–76. [chapter 1: "Is There a Jewish Political Philosophy?: The Medieval Case Reconsidered" and chapter 2: "Medieval and Renaissance Jewish Political Philosophy: An Overview."] For additional evidence of the absence, see supra, note 4. The fable fared slightly better in Islamic studies: see Patricia Crone, *God's Rule: Government and Islam, Six Centuries of Medieval Islamic Political Thought* (New York: Columbia University Press, 2004), 209, 327, 355–56. For notice that the fable's authors were attentive to political philosophy, see E. I. J. Rosenthal, *Political Thought in Medieval Islam* (New York: Cambridge University Press, 1962), 143; and J. L. Kraemer, "The Jihād of the Falāsifa" in *Jerusalem Studies in Arabic and Islam* 10 (1987): 305n46.

74. Unless otherwise noted, all the following citations translate Qalonymus's introduction as recorded in *Sefer Ba'ale ḥayyim*, Bibliothèque Nationale (Paris) Hebrew MSS 899, 5r–6r. For comparison, see the Hebrew edition printed in Warsaw (1887), 3. For a modern edition, collating the handful of printed versions, see *Iggeret Ba'ale ha-ḥayyim*, ed. I. Toporovski (Jerusalem: Mossad Harav Kook, 1949). For an annotated German translation of the entirety of Qalonymus's text, see Julius Landsberger, *Iggereth Baale Chajjim* (Darmstadt: G. Jonghaus'sche Hofbuchhandlung Verlag), 1–6, 214–19. All of the printed editions, including that of Toporovski, should be used with extreme caution, because they show unmistakable signs of censorship and other editorial interventions that deviate from Hebrew MSS 899 and the underlying Arabic in Qalonymus's translation.

75. See *The Case of the Animals versus Man*, 174–75 [English, Arabic]; Paris MS 899, 29v [Hebrew]; Warsaw, 1877, 30 [2:8].

76. See *The Case of the Animals versus Man*, 185–86 [English, Arabic]; Paris MS 899, 29v–32r [Hebrew]; Warsaw, 1877, 30–2 [2:8].

77. See *The Case of the Animals versus Man*, 242 [English, Arabic]; Paris MS 899, 46r [Hebrew]; Warsaw, 1877, 51 [4:1].

78. See *The Case of the Animals versus Man*, 242–7 [English, Arabic]; Paris MS 899, 46r–47v [Hebrew]; Warsaw, 1877, 51–4 [4:1–2].

79. See *The Case of the Animals versus Man*, 275–8 [English, Arabic]; Paris MS 899, 55v–56v [Hebrew]; Warsaw, 1877, 65–6 [5:3–4].

80. See *The Case of the Animals versus Man*, 254–8 [English, Arabic]; Paris MS 899, 50r–51r [Hebrew]; Warsaw, 1877, 58 [4:5].

81. See *The Case of the Animals versus Man*, 269–71 [English, Arabic]; Paris MS 899, 54r [Hebrew]; Warsaw, 1877, 64 [5:2].

82. See Maimonides, *Guide of the Perplexed*, introduction to part 1 (Pines trans., 10–14).

83. See Colette Sirat, *A History of Jewish Philosophy in the Middle Ages* (New York: Cambridge University Press, 1985), 330.

84. For examples of this intrapsychic understanding of the animal imagery, see the full-scale medieval Jewish commentaries to the Song of Songs: Joseph ben Judah ben Jacob ibn 'Aḳnīn, *Divulgatio Mysteriorum Luminumque Apparentia*, ed. and trans. Abraham S. Halkin (Jerusalem: Meqize Nirdamim, 1964) [Arabic, Hebrew]; Moses ibn Tibbon, *Moses ibn Tibbons Kommentar zum Hohelied und sein poetologisch-philosophisches Programm*, trans. and ed. Otfried Fraisse (New York: Walter de Gruyter, 2004) [Hebrew, German]; and Levi ben Gershom, *Perush le-Shir ha-Shirim*, ed. Menahem Kellner (Ramat-Gan: Bar-Ilan University, 2001) [Hebrew]; and *Commentary on Song of Songs of Levi ben Gershom (Gersonides)*, trans. Menachem Kellner (New Haven, CT: Yale University Press, 1998). For a sample of the philosophic perspective as articulated in technical treatises, see Abraham ibn Da'ud, *Sepher ha-Emunah ha-Ramah*, ed. S. L. Weil (Frankfurt-am-Main: np, 1853), 20–33 [book 1:6]; and for an English translation, Abraham ibn Daud, *The Exalted Faith*, trans. Norbert M. Samuelson (Cranbury, NJ: Associated University Presses, 1986), 83–107; Maimonides, *Guide of the Perplexed*, 2:36 ["By then, he will have detached his thought from, and abolished his desire for bestial things." (Pines trans., 371)]; and Shem-Tov ibn Falaquera, *Sepher ha-Nephesh* in Raphael Jospe, *Torah and Sophia: The Life and Thought of Shem Tov ibn Falaquera* (Cincinnati, OH: Hebrew Union College Press, 1988), 296–304, 307–17, 335–40, 342–47 [e.g., "When the [rational soul] turns toward the bestial faculties in order to subdue them and guide them in the way of justice, its function is called governance, and it is called practical intellect

(p. 335).”] As Jospe points out, Falaquera's intellectual debts are owed to Ibn Sina (Avicenna). In addition to Falaquera, there was a second, parallel channel in which Ibn Sina's psychology entered medieval Hebrew literature; for a critical edition of the text and erudite analysis, see Gabriella Elgrably-Berzin, *Avicenna in Medieval Hebrew Translation: Todros Todrosi's Translation of "Kitāb al-Najāt," on Psychology and Metaphysics* (Leiden: Brill, 2015), 40–43, 137, 143–44.

85. For guidance on conducting comparative analysis, tracking parallels, and discovering possible influence, see Peter Garnsey, *Ideas of Slavery from Aristotle to Augustine* (Cambridge: Cambridge University Press, 1996), especially chapter 14, "Slavery as Metaphor." See also Franz Rosenthal, *The Muslim Conception of Freedom Prior to the Nineteenth Century* (Leiden: Brill, 1960); Patricia Crone, *God's Rule: Government and Islam, Six Centuries of Medieval Islamic Political Thought*, 350–54; and, with caution, Bernard Lewis, *Race and Slavery in the Middle East* (New York: Oxford University Press, 1990), 3–15.

86. See "Shīʿite Terms and Conceptions in Judah Halevi's *Kuzari*" in Shlomo Pines, *Studies in the History of Jewish Thought*, ed. Warren Zev Harvey and Moshe Idel (Jerusalem: Magnes Press, 1997), 185–88, esp. 187n166.

87. For the distinction in categories, see Maimonides, *Guide of the Perplexed*, 3:27 (Pines, trans. 510–12): "Welfare of the soul (*iṣlāḥ al-nafs, tiqqun ha-nephesh*) . . . consists in the multitude's acquiring correct opinions . . . as for the welfare of the body (*iṣlāḥ al-badn, tiqqun ha-guf*), it comes about by the improvement of their way of living one with the other . . . the latter consists in the governance of the city and the well-being of the people." For a glance at the existential stakes in betting on the mundane instead of the metaphysically transcendent, see the chapter "Transcending Humanity" in Martha C. Nussbaum, *Love's Knowledge: Essays on Philosophy and Literature*, 365–91.

88. See Joseph Albo, *Sefer Ha-ʿIkkarim: Book of Principles*, ed. and trans. Isaac Husik (Philadelphia, PA: Jewish Publication Society, 1946), vol. 3, 15 [3:2].

89. See *Schemtob ben Joseph ibn Falaqueras Propädeutik der Wissenschaften Reschith Chokmah*, ed. Moritz David (Berlin: M. Poppelauer, 1902), 7. For an English translation of the parallel passage, see *Falaquera's Book of the Seeker* (Sefer Ha-Mabaqqesh), ed. M. Herschel Levine (New York: Yeshiva University Press, 1976), 36–37. For the Hebrew, see *Sefer Ha-Mevaqqesh*, ed. Mordecai Tama (Hague: 1779), 29. For monographic treatment of Falaquera's polymathic output, see Raphael Jospe, *Torah and Sophia: The Life and Thought of Shem Tov ibn Falaquera* (Cincinnati, OH: Hebrew Union College Press, 1988).

90. See *Ben ha-Melekh ve-ha-Nazir*, ch. 15.

KALMAN P. BLAND (1942–2017) was Professor Emeritus in the Department of Religious Studies at Duke University. His publications include *The Epistle on the Possibility of Conjunction with the Active Intellect by Ibn Rushd with the Commentary by Moses Narboni* and *The Artless Jew: Medieval and Modern Affirmations and Denials of the Visual.*

2

BIBLICAL COMMENTARIES AS A GENRE OF JEWISH PHILOSOPHICAL WRITING

Raphael Dascalu

FROM THIS POINT IN HISTORY, LOOKING BACK AT over a millennium of Jewish commentaries on scripture, it is difficult to appreciate what a profound transformation the adoption of this genre marked for Jewish literature. To be sure, scriptural interpretation is a classical vehicle for Jewish thought and literary activity and has remained so from antiquity until the present.[1] However, prior to the Islamic conquests, coherent commentaries written by a single author were not the dominant genre of Jewish scriptural exegesis.[2] Nor do rabbinic Jews seem to have engaged directly with Greek philosophy.[3] The production of systematic and running commentaries by a single author within the rabbinic tradition would have to wait until the Islamic period, when Jewish intellectual life would undergo some of its most profound transformations.[4] The openness of the dominant culture enabled Jews to join with Muslims, Christians, and members of other minorities in the pursuit of knowledge, drawing on a vast corpus of literature in Arabic, including a great deal of material that had been translated from Greek.[5] Engagement with the philosophical tradition led in turn to radical reinterpretations of the meaning of the Torah and the commandments, while exposure to Christian and Islamic exegetical traditions encouraged the production of the first coherent Jewish biblical commentaries. It is thus no coincidence that Jewish philosophy and commentaries as we now know them first developed in tandem in the early centuries of the Islamic era.

In what follows, I will explore the use of biblical commentaries as a genre of philosophical writing among medieval Jews.[6] By *commentaries*, I mean coherent running interpretations of the Torah by a single author. Defining the term *philosophy* is more difficult, because many authors who did not self-identify as philosophers drew on material from the Greek, Arabic, and Latin philosophical traditions. I shall thus adopt a broad interpretation of the term and discuss any works that draw on philosophical sources, generally as transmitted in the Arabic and Latin traditions. This will necessarily include authors who were hostile toward the "philosophers," particularly the Peripatetics, but who read and employed philosophical sources and methodology. It is also worth recalling that philosophy itself encompassed a much broader range of disciplines than is generally understood today, including arithmetic, geometry, astronomy, physics, and metaphysics.

In order to present a broad treatment of the subject, I shall present an overview of the major philosophical traditions as they are represented in Jewish biblical commentaries, providing illustrative examples. Although I draw examples from commentaries across the Hebrew Bible, the reader may notice that the opening chapters of Genesis feature prominently among them. Indeed, in the medieval period those passages became a major locus for the exploration of philosophical themes—most notably physics, cosmology, and psychology.[7] I shall then present a (necessarily incomplete) discussion of a single biblical theme that would become the focus of a great deal of philosophical reflection and debate: the creation of human beings in *imago Dei* (the image of God) in Genesis 1:26. This will provide an instructive example of the ways in which philosophical material was not only transmitted in commentaries but also informed, constrained, and enriched scriptural exegesis. From this overview, supported by concrete examples, it is my hope that the reader will be afforded a glimpse into the breadth of philosophical material that was integrated into medieval Jewish commentaries and the degree to which the engagement with philosophy shaped the Jewish encounter with scripture.

Philosophical Traditions in Jewish Biblical Commentaries

Kalam and Philosophy in the Islamic East

Kalām (lit., "speech" or "discourse") is the general term for a number of streams of systematic theology that emerged in the early centuries of the Islamic era. The proponents of kalam (Arabic: *mutakallimūn*) developed distinctive approaches to physics and metaphysics, ethics and theodicy. They often drew on Hellenistic philosophical material that had become marginal to the Peripatetic and Neoplatonic traditions.[8] In addition, kalam left its mark on philosophical discourse outside the confines of its own circles.[9] Thus, despite the fact that they were distinguished from the philosophers (*al-falāsifa*), it would be misleading to deny the mutakallimūn a place in our discussion of philosophy in Jewish commentaries. Furthermore, it was through engagement with kalam that Jewish authors first seriously adopted philosophical discourse in the production of biblical exegesis.[10]

Jewish engagement with kalam emerges in history in the ninth century with the figure of Dāwūd al-Muqammiṣ (fl. ninth century), who likely functioned as a bridge between the Syriac Christian and Jewish traditions.[11] Al-Muqammiṣ apparently converted to Christianity, became thoroughly acquainted with the Syriac literary and intellectual tradition, and produced theological works and commentaries in Arabic after reverting to Judaism. Although his commentaries to Genesis and Ecclesiastes (which are the only ones that he is known to have composed) are no longer extant apart from a single brief fragment, James T. Robinson has speculated concerning their likely character based on the Syriac cultural and literary context in which Al-Muqammiṣ was educated after his conversion to Christianity and which colored his literary output after his reversion to Judaism.[12] Following in the tradition of the patristic school of Antioch,[13] it is likely that Al-Muqammiṣ's commentaries would have included systematic introductions, verse-by-verse commentaries, and linguistic, stylistic, and rhetorical discussions pertaining to the text in question. From the period of Al-Muqammiṣ's activity onward, such features would become characteristic of much of the Jewish biblical exegesis produced within the Islamic world.[14] Although his role in shaping these norms is impossible to appraise with any certainty, his activity allows us to trace some of the central elements of Judeo-Arabic exegesis as far back as the ninth century. Al-Muqammiṣ's own affiliation as a Rabbanite or Karaite remains unclear, and he was a notable early literary figure for both traditions.[15] Following in the Syriac tradition, shaped as it is by Hellenistic thought and culture, it is most likely that Al-Muqammiṣ would have adopted a systematic mode of theological argumentation informed by philosophical discourse and kalam, as is evident from his extant writings.[16] Jewish philosophical and theological discourse in the kalam tradition was further developed both in the Rabbanite and Karaite traditions.[17]

Elements of Muʿtazilite kalam were widely adopted by Karaite thinkers, along with elements from other philosophical sources, and these often shaped their attitudes toward exegesis.[18] One of the most notable examples is Jacob al-Qirqisānī (fl. tenth century), whose extant works include a commentary on the narrative portions of the Pentateuch entitled *Kitāb al-riyāḍ wa'l-ḥadā'iq* (The book of gardens and parks), and a separate commentary on Genesis (*Tafsīr bereshit*, Commentary on Genesis).[19] In his interpretation of Genesis 1, he identifies elements of physics and Aristotelian-Ptolemaic cosmology, such as the four elements and the celestial spheres.[20] In the same commentary, he appears to reject an atomistic theory of time that was adopted by many mutakallimūn in favor of the Aristotelian theory.[21] In a later period, Aristotelian philosophy would gain greater sway among Karaite thinkers in Byzantium, often as a result of contact with Rabbanite intellectuals.[22]

The most prominent Rabbanite figure to engage seriously with kalam was Saadia Gaon (d. 942), and he was followed in this orientation by Samuel b. Ḥofni Gaon (d. 1013).[23] Departing from earlier Geonic practice, both authored major exegetical, theological, and legal works in Arabic.[24] Both also adopted many of the literary conventions and concepts of kalam literature. Saadia Gaon is of central significance in the Judeo-Arabic literary canon. Much of his importance lies in the extent to which he engaged with contemporary Arabic thought across a number of fields, his adoption of Arabic literary conventions, and his attempt to formulate systematic and fundamentally rationalistic accounts of Jewish thought and practice.

For our purposes, his incorporation of a broad range of philosophical material into his biblical commentaries is of particular significance.[25] Illustrative examples may be found in his long commentary to Genesis.[26] Saadia not only interprets the biblical narrative as reflecting a philosophical cosmology, with a spherical Earth surrounded by concentric spheres in which are set the heavenly luminaries, but he goes to great lengths to find the basic principles of Greco-Arabic physics in scripture. Like his Karaite contemporary Al-Qirqisānī, with whom he was apparently unacquainted, Saadia maintains that the Torah is familiar with and communicates the concept of the four elements.[27] The identification of the elements in the creation narrative would be reformulated and refined over the centuries, and it is possible that Saadia contributed to Maimonides's understanding of the esoteric science of *ma'aseh bereshit* (the work of the creation) as corresponding with Aristotelian physics. Interestingly, aspects of Saadia's physics have been shown to reflect Stoic sources, most notably his theory that a subtle air-like element pervades all existence, and that the Earth is held in place by a vortex of wind. However, how exactly he encountered such theories remains unknown.[28] Another curious example of Saadia's integration of philosophical sources into his commentary on Genesis is his discussion of the vitality of plants, based on Theophrastus's work *On Plants*.[29]

Neither Al-Qirqisānī, nor Saadia, nor Samuel b. Ḥofni fit neatly into a single school of philosophy or kalam.[30] Still, it might be said that their stance toward reason and revelation in general and toward the interpretation of scripture in particular, most clearly reflect the Muʿtazilite school of kalam.[31] Kalam is thus the earliest stream of philosophically informed thought in medieval Jewish commentaries on the Hebrew Bible, although it helped to open the door to a broader range of philosophical material as well. Through the commentaries of Saadia Gaon in particular, elements of kalam would continue to resurface in Jewish literature throughout its subsequent history.

Neoplatonism in the Islamic West

It may be said that, whereas kalam-inflected discourse dominated in the Islamic East (*al-mashriq*), Neoplatonism was the dominant intellectual current in the West (*al-maghrib*).[32] Particularly notable Neoplatonists include Isaac Israeli (d. c. 955), a resident of North Africa and contemporary of Saadia, and the Spanish Hebrew poet Solomon ibn Gabirol (d. c. 1058).[33] The great medieval Iberian Hebrew poets generally inclined primarily toward Neoplatonism, and some of them—such as Ibn Gabirol and Moses ibn Ezra (d. after 1138)—authored philosophical works.[34] However, most of the extant Judeo-Arabic commentaries from the Islamic West focus on linguistic analysis, integrating philosophical material only to a minimal degree. Indeed, one of the crowning achievements of Iberian and North African Jewish scholarship would be the development of a rigorous philological approach to scriptural interpretation, usually referred to as the *peshaṭ* tradition.[35]

Arguably the first exegete to integrate elements of the Spanish *peshaṭ* methodology with a significant amount of philosophical material was Isaac ibn Ghiyāth of Lucena (d. 1089) in his commentary to Ecclesiastes.[36] Ibn Ghiyāth called Ecclesiastes *Kitāb al-zuhd* (The book of renunciation), echoing the asceticizing interpretations of Ecclesiastes that had been advanced by Karaite exegetes (and Saadia to a degree).[37] However, in contradistinction to the Karaite approach, Ibn Ghiyāth advocated a scholastic mode of asceticism that was inextricably bound to the pursuit of knowledge of the sciences and intellectual discipline, through which one might purify the body and mind and ultimately attain felicity in the hereafter.[38] Indeed, he maintained that Ecclesiastes refers in some way to each of the philosophical sciences.[39]

Despite his critique of the Geonim for their lengthy scientific digressions, Abraham ibn Ezra (d. 1164) did not shy away from integrating philosophical material into his commentaries. He was particularly focused on astronomical and astrological themes, and this interest informed a significant portion of his biblical interpretations.[40] Although he demonstrates an affinity with some of the more Neoplatonizing aspects of medieval Greco-Arabic philosophy, he evades neat categorization.[41] His commentaries generally focus on philological (*peshaṭ*) exegesis, but he occasionally alludes to esoteric meanings in the text, and these references inspired the production of numerous supercommentaries that sought to unlock the secrets of scripture.[42] Not infrequently, Ibn Ezra integrates clearly philosophical material, whether in the course of direct exegesis or in excurses.[43] Indeed, he draws on elements of philosophical cosmology, astronomy, and psychology to elucidate verses from all over scripture.[44]

Possibly inspired by Ibn Ghiyāth, Ibn Ezra appears to have associated Ecclesiastes broadly with the philosophical sciences.[45] This identification shaped his interpretation of specific verses. For example, Ibn Ezra interprets Ecclesiastes 3:15 through a scientific prism. The verse reads: "What is occurring occurred long since [*mah she-hayah kebar hu*], and what is to occur occurred long since; and God seeks the pursued [*ve-ha-elohim yebaqqesh et nirdaf*]."[46] According to Ibn Ezra, the pronoun *hu* refers to the present, as opposed to what occurred in the past and what is to occur in the future. Ibn Ezra understands the "pursued" (*nirdaf*) to refer to the present moment in time, and he states that the verse refers to the divine will for time to remain continuous.[47] He then moves on to the topic of celestial motion, which has its own midpoint or *nirdaf*, the center of the terrestrial sphere.[48] In the Aristotelian tradition, time was generally understood to be a measure of motion. Implicit in Ibn Ezra's commentary is that there exists some relationship (beyond mere homology) between time and cosmic motion and that this scientific concept is alluded to in the Hebrew Bible.[49]

Ibn Ezra's tendency to incorporate philosophical material into his commentaries would help to secure his place as the biblical exegete favored by philosophically inclined Jews in the post-Maimonidean period.[50] Furthermore, his wanderings helped to expose the Jewish communities of Italy,

France, and England to the rich exegetical and scientific traditions of Islamic Spain.

The Beginnings of Jewish Peripateticism (Aristotelianism)

Although Jews had engaged with Aristotelian thought for centuries prior, the first writers who exhibit an interest in engaging in distinctly Jewish literary activity through a Peripatetic prism emerged only in the twelfth century.[51] The pioneering Jewish Peripatetic philosopher Abraham ibn Daud (d. c. 1180) appears to have left his mark on the thought and literary oeuvre of Moses Maimonides.[52] However, he is not known to have authored any biblical commentaries. Not so Abū al-Barakāt al-Baghdādī (d. after 1164), who composed a commentary on Ecclesiastes.[53] Al-Baghdādī, author of a philosophical work entitled *Kitāb al-muʿtabar* (The book of that which has been derived from contemplation), was a convert to Islam late in life.[54] He occupies a peculiar position, at once identifying with the Peripatetic tradition and reading it critically. In the segments of the commentary that have been edited, translated into Hebrew, and studied by Shlomo Pines, Al-Baghdādī discusses questions of theodicy and psychology.[55] He also touches upon cosmology, insofar as it is relevant to questions of theodicy and psychology.[56] Based on Pines's selection and study, Al-Baghdādī may have viewed Ecclesiastes as a kind of compendium on various topics.[57] The question of coherence aside, Al-Baghdādī's treatment of Ecclesiastes reflects his integration of a wide array of sources, including philosophical ones.[58]

Another Jewish exegete of the twelfth and thirteenth centuries who engaged with the Peripatetic tradition was Joseph b. Judah ibn ʿAqnīn (d. c. 1220).[59] Ibn ʿAqnīn is the earliest known medieval exegete to write a systematic commentary to the Song of Songs that interprets the book as an allegory for the human rational soul's desire to attain union with the Active Intellect.[60] He thus assumes and promotes central elements of Peripatetic cosmology, psychology, and soteriology. Although Maimonides argued for a similar reading of the Song of Songs, it appears that Ibn ʿAqnīn was not dependent on him in this regard.[61] Indeed, in a certain sense, Ibn ʿAqnīn's interpretation is at odds with that of Maimonides: Ibn ʿAqnīn does not understand the Song of Songs as Maimonides puts it, as an allegory for the soul's intense love of God; rather, he understands it as a dialogue between the rational soul and the active intellect. That is to say that (a) the Song of Songs not only expresses the desire of the individual for the Beloved, but also the active intellect's guidance of the substance that bears an affinity with it toward itself; and (b) the soul's desire is not for God—whose emanation of sublunar forms and governance of the world takes place via the active intellect—but for the active intellect.[62] This interpretation would facilitate much discussion of philosophical conceptions of psychology and soteriology in his commentary, in addition to cosmological discussions. Ibn ʿAqnīn also cites explicitly from philosophical sources, perhaps most notably from the works of Abū Naṣr al-Fārābī (d. mid-tenth century).[63]

Maimonides and Beyond

Moses Maimonides exerted a powerful influence on the commentators of subsequent generations, despite not having authored a biblical commentary himself. His impact upon future exegetes would be ensured in particular by three factors: (1) His articulation of a hermeneutical method according to which certain biblical passages are to be viewed as allegories for philosophical matters;[64] (2) his provision of what amounts to a lexicon of philosophical exegesis in the first section of the *Guide of the Perplexed*;[65] and (3) his identification of the classical esoteric sciences of rabbinic literature, *ma'aseh bereshit* (the work of creation) and *ma'aseh merkabah* (the work of the chariot), with physics and metaphysics respectively.[66] Together, these factors would provide later exegetes with the tools to neutralize theologically and philosophically problematic passages and to develop philosophical allegoresis of scripture to an extent not seen among Jews since first-century Alexandria. Insofar as *ma'aseh bereshit* and *ma'aseh merkabah* are classically conceived of as exegetical disciplines, focused on the creation narrative and Ezekiel's visions of the divine chariot respectively, Maimonides provided a theoretical basis for the scientific interpretation of key passages in scripture. In addition, he furnished his readers with many examples of his own philosophical exegesis, particularly throughout the *Guide*, providing them with models to which they could aspire in their own writing.[67]

In the period following Maimonides's activity, a range of "Maimonideanisms" would emerge, with considerable variation based on local intellectual trends and the inclinations of individual authors. In Egypt and the Levant, Jews—including Maimonides's own descendants—continued the project of interpreting the Torah and commandments through a philosophical prism and read Maimonides in conjunction with Ibn Sīnā (Avicenna) and Sufi thought.[68] In the Yemen, a philosophical mode of Jewish religious thought would emerge that integrated Maimonidean Peripateticism with elements appropriated from Neoplatonic, Hermetic, and Ismaili (Shiite) sources.[69] Both of these trends stretched roughly from Maimonides's lifetime until the Spanish expulsion in the late fifteenth century and often emphasized non-Aristotelian elements in Maimonides's thought. In contrast, in Western Christendom Maimonides's philosophy was primarily read in a more exclusively Aristotelian fashion, with Ibn Rushd (Averroes) occupying the place as the central (but by no means exclusive) mediator of the Aristotelian tradition.[70] This was particularly the case in medieval Languedoc and would also inform Jewish philosophy in Italy.

Maimonideanism in Egypt and the Levant

Maimonides's son Abraham wrote biblical commentaries, and those on Genesis and Exodus are largely extant.[71] Perhaps best known for his engagement with Sufism, his commentaries draw most closely on earlier Geonic exegesis and the Spanish *peshaṭ* school.[72] However, he does find occasion to comment on philosophical and theological matters, albeit sparingly.[73] In his interpretation of the creation and Eden narratives, Abraham finds opportunities to articulate a basically Peripatetic psychology.[74] He also describes (and implicitly prescribes) a program of intellectual discipline and meditation that is directly based on passages in his father's *Guide*, which may have ultimately been inspired by Ibn Sīnā.[75]

The biblical commentaries of Tanḥum b. Joseph ha-Yerushalmi (d. 1291), a former resident of Jerusalem who relocated to Egypt, reflect the author's tremendous erudition and his broad commitment to philology and philosophy.[76] He is prone to both linguistic and philosophical excurses. In Tanḥum's commentaries, one finds explicit discussions of ethics, physics, cosmology, psychology, and soteriology. He appears to be the first Jewish author to identify the Solomonic corpus—namely, Proverbs, Ecclesiastes, and the Song of Songs—as a philosophical curriculum, corresponding with ethics, physics, and metaphysics. This bears a striking resemblance to Origen's classification of the same works.[77] The identification is further reflected in Tanḥum's exploration of scientific and philosophical themes at length in his commentaries to Ecclesiastes and the Song of Songs (only a small fragment survives of his commentary to Proverbs, which also appears to have had a distinctly philosophical focus).[78] In the introduction to his commentary on Ecclesiastes, he presents a full classification of the philosophical sciences,[79] while in his introduction to the Song of Songs he includes an original psychological bird allegory in the Avicennan tradition.[80] Indeed, he cites a passage from Ibn Sīnā's *Epistle of the Bird* verbatim.[81] In his commentaries, he also finds opportunity to discuss ethics, theories of time, and matters of cosmology and psychology.[82]

Similar philosophical orientations may be seen in a number of post-Maimonidean works from Egypt and the Levant, including a commentary to the Song of Songs in the hand of David b. Joshua Maimonides (d. c. 1415).[83] In general, it may be said that the Peripatetic element in the Levantine and Egyptian context tends to be Avicennan and is often informed by a deep engagement with Sufi thought and praxis.[84]

Philosophy in Yemeni Biblical Commentaries

In Yemen in the thirteenth to fifteenth centuries, there flourished an intellectual climate in which Jewish scholars advanced a philosophical understanding of rabbinic Judaism in a Maimonidean mode. Yemenite Jewish thinkers of this period tended to emphasize non-Peripatetic elements in Maimonidean thought and to draw on more distinctly Neoplatonic and Ismaili sources, sometimes exhibiting a self-conscious eclecticism.[85] Authors penned anthological commentaries (called midrashim) that compiled classical midrashic material with medieval philosophical citations and glosses and excurses that reveal their own distinctive philosophical worldview.[86]

An informative example of the Yemeni context may be furnished by *Nūr al-ẓalām* (Light of the darkness), a commentary on the Torah by Nathaniel b. Isaiah (fourteenth century).[87] In his commentary, the author follows standard Yemeni practice by citing rabbinic interpretations in Hebrew and Aramaic and interspersing that material with discussions in Arabic that reveal a much more distinctly philosophical orientation. In his commentary on Genesis 1:1, the author casually points out that the verse employs the divine name Elohim (a plural form) because it is an equivocal term, referring to the emanation of the sublunary world from the separate intellects.[88] This quite startling interpretation sets the author off on an excursus in which he presents a detailed philosophical cosmology.[89] In his interpretation of Genesis, Nathaniel b. Isaiah insists on the remoteness of God from the act of creation: All existence depends upon God as its remote cause and is ontologically anchored in the divine; however, the world that we observe is the product of a chain of causation that more directly involves the celestial spheres and separate intelligences.[90]

Perhaps the most famous of the Yemenite midrashim is David ʿAdanī's *Midrash ha-gadol*, authored in the mid-fourteenth century.[91] Unlike other Yemenite midrashim, this work is written entirely in Hebrew and Aramaic. However, it betrays a distinctly Maimonidean orientation and lacks the philosophical eclecticism of the other Yemenite commentaries.

Finally, we must mention Zekhariah ha-Rofe (fifteenth century). In his commentary on the Pentateuch, entitled *Midrash ha-ḥefets*, he adopts astrological positions and ascribes them to "the philosophers."[92] This is in harmony with several other contemporaneous philosophically inclined works from the Yemen.[93] He includes a considerable amount of cosmological and psychological discussion in his commentary on Genesis. Elements of his emanationist psychology echo Neoplatonic sources, likely mediated through Ismaili works.[94] In his commentary to the Song of Songs, he interprets the work as an allegory for the emanation, tribulations, and ultimate salvation of the human rational soul. In so doing, he promotes a basically Avicennan psychology and repeatedly returns to the theme of autognosis (self-knowledge), three times citing the Delphic maxim in its Arabic version.[95] In all, the Yemenite midrashim are a rich source of philosophical material that provide a window into Jewish engagement with a broad spectrum of intellectual currents.

Maimonideanism in the Jewish Commentaries of Western Christendom

Peripatetic activity and an engagement with Maimonides's works began among Jews in Western Christendom within Maimonides's own lifetime, at the initiative of Samuel ibn Tibbon (c. 1165–1232).[96] Rather than inclining toward Ibn Sīnā and Sufi discourse, as was the case in the Islamic East, Maimonidean writers in the Christian West would be more informed by the teachings of Ibn Rushd (Averroes, d. 1198). This reflects a general trend in Latin scholasticism and is particularly evident in the return to the study of Aristotle's own works, rather than engaging primarily with the later Arabic Peripatetics and in the translation of those works into Hebrew.[97]

The Ibn Tibbon family played a central role in the emerging Maimonidean movement in Languedoc.[98] The patriarch of the family, Judah ibn

Tibbon, was an important translator of Judeo-Arabic works into Hebrew. Subsequent generations of the family continued to translate from Arabic and to author their own exegetical works. Samuel ibn Tibbon, Judah's son and translator of Maimonides's *Guide of the Perplexed* into Hebrew, wrote a commentary on Ecclesiastes, as well as a sustained interpretation of the creation narrative from Genesis entitled *Ma'amar yiqqavu ha-mayim* (Discourse [on] "Let the waters be gathered" [Gen. 1:9]).[99] He self-consciously and explicitly modeled his exegesis on Maimonidean hermeneutics and expressed his disappointment in earlier exegetes whose works focus on philological analysis to the detriment of philosophical interpretation. Indeed, he critiques even those exegetes whose approach to the text is most deeply informed by philosophy, notably Ibn Ghiyāth and Ibn Ezra.[100] In his view, Ecclesiastes is fundamentally intended as an argument for belief in the immortality of the soul.[101] However the author finds opportunity to explore other themes along the way, such as the limitations of human knowledge, theodicy, ethics, and the dangers of philosophy for the unprepared.[102]

Another family of interpreters that migrated from Islamic Spain to Languedoc was the Qimḥi clan of Narbonne.[103] Joseph Qimḥi (d. c. 1170), the first of his family to settle in Narbonne, composed several biblical commentaries, of which few survive.[104] Little is known of Joseph's son Moses Qimḥi, but we note that he alludes to elements of philosophy in his commentary on Proverbs.[105] David Qimḥi (d. 1235) in particular earned his place as one of the foremost Hebrew grammarians and as an heir both of the *peshaṭ* tradition and of Maimonidean philosophy.[106] His philosophical tendencies are clearly evident in his commentaries.[107] In his commentary to the first verse of the Torah alone, he provides an Aristotelian account of the nature of time, affirms an emanationist cosmogony, and discusses principles of philosophical cosmology such as the celestial spheres and the four sublunary elements. David Qimḥi would not hesitate to employ philosophical conceptions in explaining verses throughout scripture, drawing on elements of the various sciences to illuminate and enrich his reading of the text.[108]

Another major philosophical exegete in the Western tradition is Levi b. Gershom (Gersonides, d. 1344), who authored commentaries on the Torah and certain parts of the Prophets and Hagiographa.[109] He divides his commentary on the Torah into lexical and paraphrastic sections, both of which employ distinctly philosophical terminology. A striking example of philosophical discourse in his commentaries may be found in the opening lines of his commentary to Genesis, in which he provides a summary account of pre-Socratic materialism, referring explicitly to Aristotle's *Metaphysics*. He states that philosophy (*ha-pilosofiya*) in Moses's time was severely deficient, and that in response to a lack of understanding of the distinction between matter and form, the Torah provides an account of the formal and efficient causes.[110] In essence, Gersonides argues that the Torah does precisely the same thing as Aristotle in the *Metaphysics*: It provides a corrective to the opinion of ancient materialists and introduces the concept of a remote cause of all things. His presentation of Aristotelian physics and cosmology is framed in soteriological terms: A correct understanding of these sciences (in addition to the doctrine of creation ex nihilo) provides a demonstration of the Creator's existence, and this knowledge is necessary for the soul to attain the requisite degree of intellectual development to survive the death of the body.[111]

Gersonides goes on to identify the central elements of Peripatetic (Aristotelian-Ptolemaic) cosmology in the creation narrative, including the four elements,[112] the separate intellects (identified with angels),[113] and the celestial spheres.[114] Gersonides's commentary explores these themes in particular detail and with great clarity. Indeed, his commentary appears not only to represent an attempt to interpret scripture through the prism of Aristotelian philosophy but also to employ the genre of biblical commentary as a vehicle for philosophical instruction. Interestingly, he rarely cites Maimonides in his commentaries, preferring instead to appeal directly to Aristotle when presenting philosophical ideas.[115]

The above discussion presents but a glimpse into the rich world of Jewish philosophical exegesis in Languedoc in the post-Maimonidean era. Moses ibn Tibbon (fl. 1244–1283), Samuel Ibn Tibbon's son and the translator of a great number of philosophical and scientific works into Hebrew, authored a philosophical commentary on the Song of Songs, interpreting the work through the prism of Peripatetic psychology and cosmology.[116] Apart from a number of nonexegetical works, Joseph ibn Kaspi (d. c. 1345) penned several commentaries on the Bible that promote a radical Maimonidean philosophy.[117] Nissim b. Moses of Marseille (fl. early fourteenth century) composed a Maimonidean-oriented commentary on the Pentateuch, prefaced by a philosophical treatise and suffused with philosophical material entitled *Ma'aseh Nissim* (a wordplay: Nissim's work, or Account of miracles).[118]

Peripatetic thought and exegesis also made inroads into Italy.[119] Owing to its unique geographic situation and political fragmentation, the Italian

Peninsula sat at the crossroads between diverse currents of Jewish culture. Italian communities initially came into contact with Peripatetic thought when Occitanian and Spanish scholars sojourned or settled in Italy. For example, Jacob Anatoli spent time at the royal court in Naples; Judah ha-Kohen of Toledo (d. after 1247), author of the philosophical encyclopedia *Midrash ḥokhmah* and an avid Aristotelian, relocated to Lombardy and Tuscany as a young adult; and Zeraḥyah b. Isaac b. She'alti'el Ḥen of Barcelona (fl. late thirteenth century), a translator of philosophical works into Hebrew and a biblical commentator, was primarily active in Rome.[120] Thereafter, Italian Jewry would produce its own Peripatetically inclined philosophers and exegetes, who often engaged directly with the broader Latin intellectual culture around them.[121]

Immanuel of Rome (d. before 1336) authored biblical commentaries that synthesized a range of earlier philosophical interpretations, drawing on Ibn Ezra, Maimonides, the Tibbonids, and others. His relative Judah Romano (d. after 1330) held the belief that at the moment of conjunction with the active intellect, scripture may convey different insights to *an individual reading the same text on different occasions*, each time according to the intellectual development of the reader.[122] In proposing this model, he expanded Maimonidean hermeneutical dualism, now conceiving of scripture as a vast body of polysemic potential, containing all philosophical insights. For example, in his commentary to Song of Songs 1:3, he presents nine interpretations that together constitute a broad summary of metaphysics (with a distinctly Plotinian orientation).[123] In his commentary on the creation narrative in Genesis, Judah Romano not only presents a detailed account of physics, metaphysics, psychology, and cosmology but also documents some of the raging debates among his contemporary Latin scholastics. Beyond this, his work provides important evidence of the reception and influence in the Latin West of Ibn Sīnā's more Neoplatonizing interpretations of Aristotle (via the works of Albertus Magnus), alongside those of Ibn Rushd.[124]

Philosophy in Kabbalistic Commentaries from Christian Spain

In the Iberian Peninsula, the continuing Reconquista brought larger numbers of Jews under Christian rule and opened up new channels of cultural communication between Franco-German Jewish communities and those of Iberia.[125] Kabbalistic literature first emerged in Occitania in the twelfth century, and in the thirteenth century Spain became the center of kabbalistic activity. Circles of masters and disciples soon sprang up in several different regions, each with its own particular approach to Jewish esoteric and mystical thought and praxis.[126] By this time, the philosophical sciences had become largely naturalized into Iberian Jewish culture, and many kabbalists continued to exhibit an interest in philosophy or integrate elements of it into their works.[127]

From its beginnings, kabbalistic literature exhibits an engagement with philosophy, in particular Neoplatonism.[128] However, Isaac ibn Laṭīf (d. late thirteenth century) remains unusual in the extent to which he straddled both worlds. By formulating a synthesis of Neoplatonic philosophy and Spanish Kabbalah, he ensured that later Jewish writers would relate to him as an outsider, whether they belonged to the former or latter school of thought.[129] In some ways, Ibn Laṭīf appears to be consciously resisting the post-Averroesian return to a purer Aristotelianism.[130] Indeed, Ibn Laṭīf has been identified as a pioneer of the anti-Aristotelian trend that would reach its apogee in the works of Ḥasdai Crescas (d. 1410/1411).[131] In addition to his major work *Sha'ar ha-shamayim* (The gate of heaven), Ibn Laṭīf penned a commentary to Ecclesiastes.[132] He explicitly states that the work contains references to physics, metaphysics, ethics, and political science, all based upon sound logical reasoning.[133]

Although he is popularly characterized as the great mystical opponent of philosophy, Naḥmanides (Moses b. Naḥman, d. 1270) also exhibited a complex attitude toward philosophy and integrated elements of it into his commentaries, albeit to a lesser extent than Ibn Laṭīf.[134] A native of Catalonia, his commentaries on the Torah mediate between the Andalusian exegetical tradition as represented by Abraham ibn Ezra and the classical midrashic tradition as applied to systematic commentary by Rashi (Solomon b. Isaac of Troyes, d. 1105).[135] Into this discussion Naḥmanides incorporated elements of Kabbalah and frequently displayed his own fine literary sensibilities.[136] Despite his deemphasis of the role of philosophy in his exegesis, Naḥmanides found ample opportunity to discuss philosophical and scientific concepts in his commentaries.[137] For example, in his commentary to Genesis 1:8, he makes casual reference to elements of philosophical cosmology, such as the existence of the separate intellects;[138] in his commentary to Genesis 1:20, he discusses philosophical psychological theories, focusing on the tripartite division of the human soul; and in his commentary to Genesis 9:12, he refers to and accepts the opinion of "the Greeks" concerning the natural cause of a rainbow.[139]

We would be remiss if we did not mention the *Zohar* (Book of radiance), parts of which began to circulate in the 1280s.[140] The text is modeled on ancient midrashim, written predominantly in a peculiar style of Aramaic, and largely structured as a commentary but broken up in dialogic fashion. Despite some scholarly debate on this matter, the main body of the text appears to be the product of a single author, most likely Moses de León (d. 1305). The author is profoundly influenced by Neoplatonic thought; indeed, the earliest stratum of the *Zohar, Midrash ha-ne'elam* (The hidden midrash), reads scripture straightforwardly as Neoplatonic allegory.[141] The bulk of later material in the *Zohar* emphasizes more mythical themes, often inspired by classical rabbinic exegesis. However, in the background emanationist cosmology and the impact of Plotinian apophasis remain.[142] In addition, the *Zohar* directly and indirectly draws from philosophical and scientific sources, such as the doctrine of the tripartite human soul.[143]

Later Spanish exegesis would continue to bring philosophy and Kabbalah into dialogue as two distinct traditions that complemented or conflicted with one another. Baḥya b. Asher ibn Ḥalawa (d. mid-fourteenth century) consciously employs four modes of exegesis in his commentary: literal-contextual (*peshaṭ*), midrashic, philosophical, and kabbalistic.[144] His initial presentation of the philosophical stratum of interpretation exhibits a degree of ambivalence. He calls the method "the way of the intellect" (*derekh ha-sekhel*) and states that his aim is to demonstrate that "our Torah is inclusive of all of the sciences [*she-toratenu kelulah mi-kol ha-ḥokhmot*]." However, he somewhat derisively refers to philosophers not with the standard term *pilosofim* but as *mitpalsefim*—those who posture as philosophers, or would-be philosophers.[145] His discomfort notwithstanding, Baḥya does indeed integrate a considerable amount of philosophical material into his commentaries. Like many exegetes before him, including a number of those discussed above, he explored the basics of physics and cosmology in his commentary to Genesis.[146] A particularly unique aspect of Baḥya's cosmological discussions is his comparative approach: Rather than presenting a single model as authoritative or offering a harmonized account, he treats rabbinic, philosophical, and kabbalistic cosmologies separately, summarizing the central elements of each.[147] Similarly, he expands upon Naḥmanides's discussion of philosophical theories of the human soul, adding a defense of the immortality of the intellectual soul (*ha-nefesh ha-ḥakhamah*).[148]

Although he sits at the edge of our period, Isaac Abarbanel (d. 1508) provides a striking illustration of the integration of diverse sources into his commentaries. If the Iberian Judeo-Arabic commentaries were lacunose and Abraham ibn Ezra's commentaries filled out many of the gaps, the style in late medieval Spain tended toward the expansive. The sheer breadth of sources to which Abarbanel referred in his commentaries is worth noting:[149] Alongside a wide array of Jewish sources, he refers to "Pythagoras, Empedocles, Anaxagoras, Aristotle and Plato, Seneca, Ptolemy, Sallust and Virgil, Pliny, Plotinus, Porphyry, Galen and Hermes Trismegistus, Valerius Maximus, ancient Spanish historians, 'the books of the Latins,' the New Testament, Jerome, Augustus, the Venerable Bede, Sextus Julius Africanus, Isidore of Seville, Thomas Aquinas, Albertus Magnus, Nicholas de Lyra and others."[150] Perhaps more than any other medieval exegete, Abarbanel stood at the margins of philosophy and Kabbalah, never entirely committing to any party and yet drawing deeply from the entire spectrum of literature available to him.[151] The Christian Spanish context is a thoroughly eclectic one, as writers engage and struggle with kabbalistic and philosophical traditions, both pushing against philosophical discourse and never entirely letting go of it.

Implicit Philosophical Concerns: The Creation of Human Beings in the Image of God

Medieval Jewish interpretations of Genesis 1:26 provide an illuminating example of the ways in which the Jewish encounter with philosophy enabled new and innovative scriptural exegesis. The verse reads: "Let us make man in our image [*be-tsalmenu*], after our likeness [*ki-demutenu*]." For philosophically inclined Jews, the verse was problematic both in its use of the first-person plural and in its implicit anthropomorphism. Indeed, the rhetorical and ethical power of the biblical account lies precisely in its imagistic quality, situated within the aniconic Israelite culture. The transposition of the representation of the divine from the temple sanctum to the individual human being is nothing short of startling and carries profound ethical and legal implications.[152] Both imagistic and nonimagistic conceptions of the human being as *imago Dei* are attested in rabbinic thought.[153] By the medieval period, philosophically inclined Jewish writers had to reinterpret texts that carried anthropomorphic and anthropopathic overtones in new and innovative ways.[154] In this case, that meant arguing for an understanding of Genesis 1:26 in a way that would explain the plural formulation while affirming a strict monotheism and explain the concept of *imago Dei* in as nonimagistic a fashion as possible. The tension between the mythical theology of Genesis and the abstractly conceptual discourse of the philosophical tradition opened up a space to explore some of the central themes of psychology, cosmology, and other fields of philosophical inquiry.

In tracing the interpretation of this verse, it would do us well to make a distinction between essentialist and functional approaches. By "essentialist," I refer to those interpretations that emphasize some intrinsic property of the human being that constitutes an affinity with the divine. By "functionalist," I refer to interpretations that identify some mode of behavior or role that human beings enact in the world that might be analogous to the role or actions of God in the cosmos.[155]

Essentialist

In his commentary to Genesis 1:26, Abraham ibn Ezra states that human beings may only be considered to be "in the Divine Image" insofar as "the supernal soul of the human being [*nishmat ha-adam ha-'elyonah*]" shares something of the divine nature—namely, immortality and incorporeality. The verse affords him the opportunity to articulate a dualistic anthropology, apparently informed by Neoplatonic sources, which constitutes the basis for human distinctness from the other creatures of the sublunary realm. That the biblical conception of *imago Dei* is expressive of some intrinsic property of the human soul or intellect appears to first have been stated by Philo, who identified the mind (*nous*) as that particular quality of the human being that represents the divine.[156] This conception echoes the Platonic conception of the human soul as sharing a kinship (*sungeneia*) with the gods, a notion that was enthusiastically embraced by the Stoics.[157] Furthermore, Philo emphasizes that the human mind's relation to the body is analogical to that of the deity to the cosmos.[158] Although Philo had little or no impact on rabbinic Jewish thought, it is notable that this understanding resurfaces among Jewish thinkers in the medieval period.

Functionalist

Saadia Gaon's reading of the verse is particularly rich in polemical material and ultimately settles on a political reading of the creation of human beings in *imago Dei*.[159] After presenting and critiquing Christian, Karaite, and alternative Rabbanite views, Saadia offers his own interpretation: The expression *in our image, after our likeness* employs the majestic plural; in substance it emphasizes the cherished status of human beings in the world and expresses the particular role of the human being as a ruler (*sulṭān*) over all other creatures.[160] The latter interpretation is reflected succinctly in his Arabic translation of the verse: "Let us make a human being in our form [and] in our likeness [*bi-ṣūratinā bi-shabahinā*], *appointed as a ruler* [*mus-allaṭan*]; they shall rule over the fish of the sea and the birds of the sky."[161] Saadia's political interpretation of *imago Dei* is thus more functionalist, insofar as the formulation reflects the particular role that human beings play in the world. This echoes the Qur'ān's account of the creation of Adam as the appointment of a representative of God to rule the world.[162] It also resembles an idea articulated by Saadia's contemporary and fellow resident of Baghdad, Al-Fārābī: The latter identified the concept of *imitatio Dei* (Arabic *al-tashabbuh bi-allāh*) with political activity. Later, Maimonides would follow Al-Fārābī in describing ethically and intellectually grounded political governance as *imitatio/tashabbuh* but would make a clear distinction between that concept and *imago Dei*.[163] But as we see, according to Saadia, the ability to rule over creation is precisely the sense in which humans are created in the image of God.

Post-Maimonidean Thinkers

The terms *tselem* (image) and *demut* (likeness) are the subjects of the first chapter of Maimonides's *Guide*, emphasizing both the centrality of psychology in Maimonides's thought and the magnitude of the problem posed by the verse's strongly implicit anthropomorphism. According to Maimonides, human beings share some likeness with the divine insofar as they have the potential for intellectual perfection.[164] Thus, like Ibn Ezra and Saadia, Maimonides adopts a nonimagistic interpretation of Genesis 1:26–27, tending more toward Ibn Ezra's essentialist approach. However, he formulates his understanding in distinctly Aristotelian terms: Since the human intellect is an entelechy of the organism rather than an emanated entity, the divine image and likeness (*tselem* and *demut*) consist of the human ability to attain true intellectual insight.[165] Thus, according to Maimonides, all human beings are *said* to be created in the divine image, but not all are able to attain its fullest expression.

Maimonides's interpretation of Genesis 1:26 had a significant impact upon exegetes that followed him. In his commentary on Genesis 1:26, Maimonides's son Abraham bases elements of his discussion directly on *Guide* 1:1, in particular his emphatic rejection of the notion that the terms *tselem* and *demut* might refer here to a physical form or configuration (*shakl, takhṭīṭ*).[166] However, he also articulates a highly dualistic anthropology according to which the human intellectual soul emanates from the angelic realm, that is, that of the separate intellects.[167] Whereas Moses Maimonides's view of the human soul as an entelechy of the organism most closely echoes Al-Fārābī, his son's view is more distinctly Avicennan (and therefore, on this point, Neoplatonic).[168]

The Yemenite midrashim also reflect the functionalist and essentialist interpretations of *imago Dei* in the Judeo-Arabic tradition. Nathaniel b. Isaiah's discussion of Genesis 1:26–27 in *Nūr al-ẓalām* is rich in philosophical concepts and language.[169] Not only does he propose an emanationist theory of the origin of the human soul, but also he employs a distinctly Avicennan expression to refer to the active intellect: *Wāhib al-ṣuwar* (the giver of forms).[170] After locating *imago Dei* specifically in the human rational faculty (*al-quwwa al-nāṭiqa*), Nathaniel proposes a microcosmic interpretation: There is a structural homology between the cosmos as a whole, governed by God, and the human body, governed by the intellect.[171] David ʿAdanī's *Midrash ha-gadol* walks a line between these approaches, ascribing the formulation to (1) the existence of the rational soul (*nefesh ḥakhamah*) that knows and apprehends (*yodaʿat u-masseget*) the rest of creation, (2) a human being's service of the Creator in imitation of the ministering angels, and (3) the additional consciousness (*ha-deʿah ha-yeterah*) that a human possesses, in distinction from other sublunary beings. In *Midrash ha-ḥefets*, Zekhariah ha-Rofe follows Nathaniel b. Isaiah in understanding *imago Dei* through the prism of a microcosmic anthropology. However, he develops considerably on this idea, stating that each major aspect of the cosmos is represented in the human being: The body is composed of the sublunary elements, the soul of the subtle substance of the celestial spheres, and the intellect emanates directly from the active intellect (*wāhib al-ṣuwar*). According to Zekhariah, human beings are considered to be in the image and likeness of the Creator and the entire cosmos that it governs.[172]

Like many other commentators, David Qimḥi suggests that the plural form of *let us make* alludes to the angels (i.e., the separate intellects). However, he also offers an alternative interpretation that he attributes to his father: That the plural form refers to the elements, and therefore to the human body. However, it is the former interpretation that he develops most fully in his commentary to the verse, and it leads him into a discussion of the dual nature of human beings.[173] In his reading, the prepositional prefix in the expression *after our likeness* (*ki-demutenu*, literally "like our likeness") alludes to the fundamental difference between humans and other rational beings, such as the heavenly bodies and the separate intellects, insofar as the former are composed of corruptible sublunary matter. However, the expression also offers a hope of attaining a degree of likeness: "If he wishes, he can become a little like us [*lehiddamot elenu qetsat*] for the choice is his." *How* exactly one attains a degree of likeness with the angels may only be surmised, but his formulation is suggestive of a classical rabbinic interpretation according to which one becomes godly by embodying the divine impulses of compassion and graciousness.[174] In Maimonidean thought, this concept becomes deeply enmeshed with the cultivation of moderate ethical dispositions, very much in the Aristotelian tradition.[175]

In his interpretation of the verses, Baḥya b. Asher cites explicitly from *Guide* 1:1, offering Maimonides's interpretation that *imago Dei* consists in intellectual apprehension (*hassagah sikhlit*). He offers an alternative interpretation, according to which human beings contain the three parts (*ḥalaqim*) of the cosmos: the intellectual, the celestial, and the terrestrial-elemental. Humans are thus created in the divine image insofar as they are a microcosm. This leads Baḥya into an excursus on the topic of cosmic emanation and the sense in which God remains the cause of all things, while actually generating sublunary beings via a chain of intermediaries.[176] His reading of these verses echoes *Midrash ha-ne'elam* and also bears a striking resemblance to the interpretations of Abraham Maimonides and many of the Yemenite midrashim, with which Baḥya was apparently unacquainted.[177]

From this very brief and incomplete survey, we may see a few of the ways in which medieval exegetes interpret Genesis 1:26 through the prisms of philosophical cosmology, psychology, and politics. In their reading of scripture, they draw deeply from ancient and medieval Jewish exegesis on the one hand and the Greco-Arabic and Latin philosophical traditions on the other. Here, philosophy informs and enriches exegesis, enabling new and innovative interpretations, while scripture lends its bold mythical language to Jewish philosophical discourse.

Conclusion

In the above study, I hope to have provided a glimpse into the richness of scriptural commentaries as a locus of medieval Jewish philosophical writing. Commentaries constituted a worthy and versatile vehicle for philosophical discourse and facilitated the inclusion of the sciences in a Jewish educational curriculum. Philosophical concerns also shaped exegesis in profound ways, informing, enriching, and constraining the interpreter's encounter with scripture. Any full account of Jewish philosophy must take commentaries into consideration, just as any full account of Jewish scriptural exegesis must confront its engagement with the philosophical tradition.

Virtually every tendency in Jewish thought finds expression in commentaries, including a broad range of philosophical trends adopted by Jews in diverse cultural and historical settings. From the earliest medieval Jewish engagement with philosophy in connection with kalam to the post-Maimonidean syntheses of Peripateticism with Sufi, Neoplatonic, and Ismaili thought, each development in Jewish intellectual culture has left its mark upon scriptural exegesis. Indeed, if reading and interpreting scripture is considered to be a sacred obligation, it is inevitable that generations of Jews would bring their full hearts and minds to such a task, seeking to bring philosophical truth into conversation with revealed truth.

Notes

1. Biblical exegesis begins within the Hebrew Bible itself. For inner-biblical exegesis, see Michael Fishbane, "Inner-Biblical Exegesis," in *Hebrew Bible/Old Testament*, vol. 1/1, ed. Magne Sæbø (Göttingen; Vandenhoeck and Ruprecht, 1996), 33–48; ibid., *Biblical Interpretation in Ancient Israel* (New York: Oxford University Press, 1985). For narrative expansion as a classic mode of biblical exegesis, exhibited in Second Temple literature and midrashic works among others, see James Kugel, *In Potiphar's House: The Interpretive Life of Biblical Texts* (San Francisco, CA: Harper, 1990).

2. Rabbinic midrash was not composed in the form of running commentary, although it was sometimes redacted into something resembling such a genre. The literature on *midrash*, which in part seeks to define the term, is vast. A good introductory study to midrashic exegesis is James Kugel's "Two Introductions to Midrash," *Prooftexts* 3 (1983), 131–55. For works and genres of classical rabbinic literature, see H. L. Strack and G. Stemberger, *Introduction to the Talmud and Midrash*, trans. Markus Bockmuehl (Minneapolis, MN: Fortress Press, 1992). Two informative studies of the *Mekhilta de-rabbi yishma'el*, an early rabbinic midrash, are Daniel Boyarin, *Intertextuality and the Reading of Midrash* (Bloomington: Indiana University Press, 1990) [on non-legal material], and Azzan Yadin, *Scripture as Logos: Rabbi Ishmael and the Origins of Midrash* (Philadelphia: University of Pennsylvania Press, 2004) [on legal hermeneutics].

3. Hellenized Alexandrian Jews composed allegorical commentaries that were deeply informed by Platonic thought but had little or no influence upon rabbinic tradition. Most

notable were Philo (d. mid-first century CE), and Aristobulus (second century BCE). See Folker Siegert, "Early Jewish Interpretation in a Jewish Style," in *Hebrew Bible/Old Testament*, vol. 1/1, 130–98. For general introductions to Philo, see Erwin R. Goodenough, *An Introduction to Philo Judaeus* (Oxford: Oxford University Press, 1962); Ronald Williamson, *Jews in the Hellenistic World: Philo* (Cambridge: Cambridge University Press, 1989). For a more extensive study, see Harry Austryn Wolfson, *Philo: Foundations of Religious Philosophy in Judaism, Christianity, and Islam*, 2 vols. (Cambridge, MA: Harvard University Press, 1948). For the genres of his commentaries, some of which are running and some of which are thematic and for his general attitude toward scripture and its relationship to philosophy, see Wolfson, *Philo*, vol. 1, 87–199; James R. Royse, "The Works of Philo," in *The Cambridge Companion to Philo*, ed. Adam Kamesar (Cambridge: Cambridge University Press, 2009), 32–64; Adam Kamesar, "Biblical Interpretation in Philo," in ibid., 65–91. For the absence of Philo in rabbinic tradition (until the works of Azariah dei Rossi, d. c. 1578), see David T. Runia, *Philo in Early Christian Literature: A Survey* (Minneapolis, MN: Fortress Press, 1993), 12–16; David Winston, "Philo's *Nachleben* in Judaism," *Studia Philonica Annual* 6 (1994), 103–10; David Winston, "Philo and Rabbinic Literature," in Kamesar (ed.), *The Cambridge Companion to Philo*, 231–53.

4. For the emergence and development of the biblical commentary among medieval Jews, see Daniel Frank, *Search Scripture Well: Karaite Exegetes and the Origins of the Jewish Bible Commentary in the Islamic East* (Leiden: Brill, 2004), 249–57.

5. For the Arabic translation movement, see Dimitri Gutas, *Greek Thought, Arabic Culture: The Graeco-Arabic Translation Movement in Baghdad and Early 'Abbāsid Society (2nd–4th/8th–10th centuries)* (London: Routledge, 1998). See also Joel L. Kraemer, *Humanism in the Renaissance of Islam: The Cultural Revival during the Buyid Age* (Leiden: Brill, 1986).

6. For earlier studies on this theme, see James T. Robinson, "Philosophy and Science in Medieval Jewish Commentaries on the Bible," in *Science in Medieval Jewish Cultures*, ed. Gad Freudenthal (Cambridge: Cambridge University Press, 2011), 454–75; Howard Kreisel, "Philosophical Interpretations of the Bible," in *The Cambridge History of Jewish Philosophy: From Antiquity through the Seventeenth Century*, ed. Steven Nadler and T. M. Rudavsky (Cambridge University Press: 2009), 88–120. See also James T. Robinson, "Secondary Forms of Philosophy: On the Teaching and Transmission of Philosophy in Non-Philosophical Literary Genres," in *Vehicles of Transmission, Translation, and Transformation in Medieval Textual Culture*, ed. Carlos Fraenkel, Jamie Fumo, Faith Wallis, and Robert Wisnovsky (Turnhout: Brepols, 2011), 254–57.

7. Cf. Giuseppe Sermoneta, "Ha-Perush le-'parashat bereshit' le-r' yehudah ben mosheh ben daniyyel romano u-meqorotav," in *Proceedings of the World Congress of Jewish Studies* vol. 2 (1965), 341.

8. For kalam in general, see Harry Austryn Wolfson, *The Philosophy of Kalam* (Cambridge, MA: Harvard University Press, 1976); M. Abdel Haleem, "Early *kalām*," in *History of Islamic Philosophy*, ed. Seyyed Hossein Nasr and Oliver Leaman (London: Routledge, 1996), 71–88; James Pavlin, "Sunni *Kalām* and Theological Controversies," in ibid.., 105–18. For the reception of and engagement with Greek philosophical sources among the mutakallimūn, see Wolfson, *Philosophy of Kalam*, 64–66; Dimitri Gutas, *Greek Thought, Arabic Culture*, 69–74; and cf. Harry Austryn Wolfson, *Repercussions of the Kalam in Jewish Philosophy* (Cambridge, MA: Harvard University Press, 1979), 124–62. For the importance of John Philoponus (fl. sixth century CE), a Christian commentator on Aristotle and an innovative and

independent philosopher in his own right, in the Arabic philosophical and in particular kalam traditions, see Herbert Davidson, "John Philoponus as a Source of Medieval Islamic and Jewish Proofs of Creation," *Journal of the American Oriental Society* 89 (1969), 357–91.

9. For example, on the connections between the early Islamic Neoplatonist philosopher Al-Kindī (d. after 870) and the *Mu'tazilī* school of kalam, see Peter Adamson, "Al-Kindī and the Mu'tazila," in *Arabic Sciences and Philosophy* 13 (2003), 45–77.

10. For the impact of kalam on Jewish thinkers, including a number of pioneering commentators in the Judeo-Arabic tradition such as Al-Muqammiṣ and Saadia, see Wolfson, *Repercussions of the Kalam in Jewish Philosophy*. Cf. Al-Kindī's role in the development of philosophical exegesis of the Qur'ān; Jules Janssens, "Al-Kindī: The Founder of Philosophical Exegesis of the Qur'an," *Journal of Qur'anic Studies* 9 (2007), 1–21.

11. For Al-Muqammiṣ in general, see Sarah Stroumsa, *Dawūd ibn Marwān al-Muqammiṣ's Twenty Chapters ('Ishrūn Maqāla)* (Leiden: Brill, 1989).

12. James T. Robinson, *Asceticism, Eschatology, Opposition to Philosophy: The Arabic Translation and Commentary of Salmon ben Yeroham on Qohelet (Ecclesiastes)* (Leiden: Brill, 2012), 11–12; Stroumsa, *Twenty Chapters*, 19–20, 23–26, 29, 32.

13. For the extended period that Al-Muqammiṣ spent in Nisibis, see Stroumsa, *Twenty Chapters*, 15–16. For a study of the School of Nisibis, its establishment, history, and place at the intellectual and cultural crossroads of the Hellenistic and Near Eastern worlds, see Adam Becker, *Fear of God and the Beginning of Wisdom: The School of Nisibis and Christian Scholastic Culture in Late Antique Mesopotamia* (Philadelphia: University of Pennsylvania Press, 2006).

14. Cf. James T. Robinson, *Samuel ibn Tibbon's Commentary on Ecclesiastes: The Book of the Soul of Man* (Tubingen: Mohr Siebeck, 2007), 19.

15. For the lack of clarity surrounding Al-Muqammiṣ's Karaite or Rabbanite affiliation—indeed, for the possibility that such distinctions were not so clear at the time—see Stroumsa, *Twenty Chapters*, 16–19.

16. Robinson, *Asceticism, Eschatology, Opposition to Philosophy*, 12; cf. Stroumsa, *Twenty Chapters*, 19–33. For Al-Muqammiṣ's relationship with kalam, see Stroumsa, "Saadya and Jewish *kalam*," 78–79; Haggai Ben-Shammai, "Jewish Thought in Iraq in the 10th Century," in *Judaeo-Arabic Studies*, ed. Norman Golb (Reading: Harwood Academic Publishers, 1997), 25.

17. For Judah al-Baṣīr and Yeshu'ah b. Judah, both devoted mutakallimūn of the Mu'tazilite school, see Isaac Husik, *A History of Mediaeval Jewish Philosophy* (New York: Macmillan, 1916), 48–58; and the discussions of these thinkers in Wolfson, *Repercussions of the Kalam in Jewish Philosophy*.

18. See Daniel Lasker, *From Judah Hadassi to Elijah Bashyatchi: Studies in Late Medieval Karaite Philosophy* (Leiden: Brill, 2008); ibid., "Medieval Karaism and Science," in Freudenthal, *Science in Medieval Jewish Cultures*, 427–37; Frank, *Search Scripture Well*.

19. Daniel Frank, "Karaite Exegesis," in *Hebrew Bible/Old Testament*, 1/2, 116–19. For Al-Qirqisānī in general, see Leon Nemoy, *Karaite Anthology: Excerpts from the Early Literature* (New Haven, CT: Yale University, 1952), 42–68; Hartwig Hirschfeld, *Qirqisāni Studies* (London, 1918).

20. Frank, "Karaite Exegesis," 118–19.

21. See Hirschfeld, *Qirqisāni Studies*, 14. It is hard to read this passage as anything other than a reference to Aristotle's definition of time in *Physics* 4.11.219b, 4.12.221b (*pace* Hirschfeld). For the difference between medieval Islamic atomism and ancient Greek

atomism and for the affinity between the former and Indian conceptions, see Shlomo Pines, "The Middle Ages. Introduction to Mediaeval Science," in *The Collected Works of Shlomo Pines*, vol. 2 (Jerusalem: Magnes Press, 1986), 355. For an alternative argument, which identifies the emergence of an atomistic theory of time with Diodorus Cronus, its adoption by Epicurus, and the possibility of its revival in Islamic thought by Abū al-Hudhayl al-ʿAllāf (d. c. 841) based ultimately on Greek sources, see Richard Sorabji, "Atoms and Time Atoms," in *Infinity and Continuity in Ancient and Medieval Thought*, ed. Norman Kretzmann (Ithaca, NY: Cornell University Press, 1982), 37–86. For two mutakallimūn who adopted alternative positions on the nature of time—Muʿammar and Al-Naẓẓam (ninth century)—see L. E. Goodman, "Time in Islam," in *Religion and Time*, ed. Anindita Niyogi Balslev and J. N. Mohanty (Leiden: Brill, 1993), 142–47.

22. For example, Elijah Bashyatchi (d. c. 1490) would prescribe a complete Aristotelian curriculum of study, after a student had gained a sufficient grasp of biblical and legal subjects. See Lasker, "Medieval Karaism and Science," 431, 435–37.

23. Both stood at the head of the academy of Sura in Baghdad, Samuel b. Ḥofni after it was reestablished following a period of inactivity. See Robert Brody, *The Geonim of Babylonia and the Shaping of Medieval Jewish Culture* (New Haven, CT: Yale University Press, 1998), 235–39; David E. Sklare, *Samuel ben Ḥofni Gaon and His Cultural World: Texts and Studies* (Leiden: Brill, 1996), 6–10. For Saadia, his thought, and his works in general, see Henry Malter, *Saadia Gaon: His Life and Works* (Philadelphia, PA: Jewish Publication Society of America, 1921); Brody, *The Geonim of Babylonia*, 235–332. For Samuel b. Ḥofni in general, including central elements of his exegesis, see Sklare, *Samuel ben Ḥofni*.

24. For Saadia's engagement with kalam, see Sarah Stroumsa, "Saadya and Jewish *Kalam*," in *The Cambridge Companion to Medieval Jewish Philosophy*, ed. Daniel H. Frank and Oliver Leaman (Cambridge: Cambridge University Press, 2003), 71–90.

25. For Saadia's broad interest in the sciences, see Y. Tzvi Langermann, "Saʿadya and the Sciences," in *The Jews and the Sciences in the Middle Ages* (Burlington, VT: Variorum/Ashgate, 1999), 2:1–21.

26. Saadia's commentary to Genesis has been edited and translated into Hebrew by Moshe Zucker, *Saadya's Commentary on Genesis* (New York: Jewish Theological Seminary of America, 1984). For the passages discussed here, see ibid., 27–50 [Arabic], 209–51. [Hebrew].

27. For Saadia's unfamiliarity with Al-Qirqisānī, see Nemoy, *Karaite Anthology*, 44. Cf., however, Malter, 230, n. 511, in which the author suggests that Al-Qirqisānī may have been familiar with Saadia. Saadia and Al-Qirqisānī also shared a rationalist approach to scripture that was colored by kalam; see Robinson, "Philosophy and Science," 456–57.

28. See Gad Freudenthal, "Stoic Physics in the Writings of R. Saadia Ga'on al-Fayyumi and Its Aftermath in Medieval Jewish Mysticism," in *Arabic Sciences and Philosophy* 6 (1996), 113–36. For the ways in which these theories are reflected in Saadia's commentary on Genesis, see ibid., 124–25, 129.

29. See his commentary to Gen. 1:20, 24; and Gen. 2:7. Translated into English and discussed in Langermann, "Saʿadya and the Sciences," 18–21.

30. Stroumsa, "Saadya and Jewish *Kalam*," 76, 84–86. In his production of commentaries accompanied by Arabic translations of scripture, he mirrored the literary project of the Jerusalem Karaite school. For the argument that Saadia's literary project was effectively enabled by Karaite authors, see Rina Drory, *Models and Contacts: Arabic Literature and Its Impact on Medieval Jewish Culture* (Leiden: Brill, 2000), 126–57. For a counterargument that the

parallels between Rabbanite and Karaite thought and literary production were the product of common engagement in contemporaneous Islamic and Christian discourse, see Stroumsa, "Saadya and Jewish *Kalam*," 87–88.

31. Cf. Robinson, "Philosophy and Science," 456–57.

32. Cf. Sarah Pessin, "Jewish Neoplatonism: Being above Being and Divine Emanation in Solomon ibn Gabirol and Isaac Israeli," in *The Cambridge Companion to Medieval Jewish Philosophy*, ed. Daniel H. Frank and Oliver Leaman (Cambridge: Cambridge University Press, 2003), 92–93. For a survey of scientific discourse in the works of Iberian Jews, see Y. Tzvi Langermann, "Science in the Jewish Communities of the Iberian Peninsula," in *The Jews and the Sciences in the Middle Ages*, 1:1–54.

33. For Isaac Israeli, see Alexander Altman and Samuel M. Stern, *Isaac Israeli: A Neoplatonic Philosopher of the Early Tenth Century* (Chicago: University of Chicago Press, 1958). For Solomon ibn Gabirol, see Jacques Schlanger, *La Philosophie de Salomon ibn Gabirol: Étude d'un néoplatonisme* (Leiden: Brill, 1968); Jochanan Wijnhoven, "The Mysticism of Solomon ibn Gabirol," in *The Journal of Religion* 45 (1965), 137–52.

34. See Adena Tanenbaum, *The Contemplative Soul: Hebrew Poetry and Philosophical Theory in Medieval Spain* (Leiden: Brill, 2002); Paul Fenton, *Philosophie et exégèse dans le Jardin de la métaphore de Moïse ibn 'Ezra* (Leiden: Brill, 1997).

35. The term *peshaṭ* is usually understood to refer to the plain meaning of the biblical text. For the rabbinic expression *en miqra yoṣe mi-yde peshuṭo* (a biblical verse does not leave the realm of its *peshaṭ*) and its transmission and interpretation in medieval sources, see Mordechai Z. Cohen, *Opening the Gates of Interpretation* (Leiden: Brill, 2011), 347–81. My translation of the principle is taken from ibid., xvii. For Cohen's discussion of his translation, see ibid., 495–99. The understanding of *peshaṭ* that this school promoted entailed "an empirical, contextual reading of Scripture that adheres to the rules of language, biblical literary conventions and historical context." (For this formulation, see Mordechai Z. Cohen, *Three Approaches to Biblical Metaphor: From Abraham ibn Ezra and Maimonides to David Kimhi* (Leiden: Brill: 2003), 3.

36. For a broad study of Ibn Ghiyāth, see Sarah Katz, *Rabbi Yitzḥaq ibn Giyat: Monografiyah* (Reuven Mas, 1994). For his commentary on Ecclesiastes, see George Vajda, "Quelques Observations en Marge du Commentaire d'Isaac ibn Ghiyāth sur l'Ecclésiaste," *Jewish Quarterly Review* 57 (seventy-fifth anniversary volume, 1967), 518–27; Hagit Mittelman (Kiel), "A Description of *Perishut* (*Al-Zuhd*, 'Abstinence') in a Commentary on Ecclesiastes Ascribed to Isaac ibn Ghiyath and Its Comparison to Islamic Mysticism," *Da'at* 48 (2002): 57–81. The commentary and Arabic translation, accompanied by a Hebrew translation, was published by Yosef Qafiḥ in *Ḥamesh megillot*, 161–296. For Qafih's mistaken attribution of the commentary to Saadia Gaon, see Shlomo Pines, "Four Extracts from Abu'l-Barakat al-Baghdadi's Commentary on Ecclesiastes," *Tarbiz* 33 (1963): 198, 212–13; Katz, *Rabbi Yitzḥaq ibn Giyat*, 122.

37. Robinson, *Samuel ibn Tibbon's Commentary*, 21, 26.

38. Robinson, *Samuel ibn Tibbon's Commentary*, 21–22.

39. Qafiḥ, *Ḥamesh megillot*, 168.

40. Y. Tzvi Langermann, "Some Astrological Themes in the Thought of Abraham ibn Ezra," in *Rabbi Abraham ibn Ezra: Studies in the Writings of a Twelfth-Century Polymath*, ed. Isadore Twersky and Jay M. Harris (Cambridge, MA: Harvard University Press, 1993), 28–85; Shlomo Sela, *Astrology and Exegesis in Abraham ibn Ezra's Thought* (Givat Ram: Bar-Ilan University Press, 1999) [Hebrew].

41. For discussions of Ibn Ezra that locate him within the Neoplatonic tradition, see Husik, *History of Mediaeval Jewish Philosophy*, 187–96; Colette Sirat, *A History of Jewish Philosophy in the Middle Ages* (Cambridge and Paris: Cambridge University Press/Editions de la Maison des Sciences de l'Homme, 1985), 104–12; Aaron W. Hughes, "The Three Worlds of Ibn Ezra's *Ḥay ben Meqitz*," *Journal of Jewish Thought and Philosophy* 11 (2002): 1–24. For a study that argues for his closer alignment with the Peripatetic tradition, see Joseph Cohen, *The Philosophy of R. Abraham ibn Ezra* (Ramle: Shai, 1996) [Hebrew].

42. Kreisel, "Philosophical Interpretations of the Bible," 95–96; Uriel Simon, "Interpreting the Interpreter: Supercommentaries on Ibn Ezra's Commentaries," in *Rabbi Abraham ibn Ezra: Studies in the Writings of a Twelfth-Century Polymath*, 86–128.

43. The excursus is a literary unit embedded in the commentary, which may provide necessary background but is fundamentally independent; see Sela, *Ibn Ezra and the Rise of Medieval Hebrew Science*, 288–89, 326; cf. L. Rabinowitz, "Lecture IV: Abravanel as Exegete," in *Isaac Abravanel: Six Lectures*, ed. J. B. Trend and H. Loewe (Cambridge: Cambridge University Press, 1937), 83–84. For an example of Ibn Ezra's use of philosophical material, see his long commentary on Exod. 33:20–21, which includes an extensive excursus on cosmological themes, concluding with a parable that appears to be borrowed from the Brethren of Purity. See Robinson, "Philosophy and Science," 459–60.

44. See, for example, Ibn Ezra's commentary to Eccles. 1:3, his commentary to Ps. 8:5–6, and his elaborate astronomical interpretation of Ps. 19.

45. See Mariano Gómez Aranda, "The Meaning of Qohelet According to Ibn Ezra's Scientific Explanations," *Aleph* 6 (2006): 339–70.

46. Translation from the Jewish Publication Society Tanakh (2003).

47. For an English translation of this passage in Ibn Ezra and a discussion of its contents, see Aranda, "The Meaning of Qohelet," 351–52. Here, the sentence "ve-ha-'inyan she-ha-elohim biqqesh me-ha-zeman she-yihyeh nirdaf" is translated: "The meaning of the verse is that God wanted time to be continuous" (Ibid., 351). For discussions of this passage, see also Sela, *Astrology and Biblical Exegesis*, 215–16, 228.

48. Aranda, "The Meaning of Qohelet," 351.

49. Aranda, "The Meaning of Qohelet," 351–52.

50. See Tamás Visi, "Ibn Ezra a Maimonidean Authority: The Evidence of the Early Ibn Ezra Supercommentaries," in *The Cultures of Maimonideanism: New Approaches to the History of Jewish Thought*, ed. James T. Robinson (Leiden: Brill, 2009), 89–131.

51. For the involvement of Jews in philosophical correspondence on matters of Aristotelian teaching in the mid-tenth century with the great Christian Aristotelian Yaḥyā ibn 'Adī (d. 974), see Shlomo Pines, "A Tenth Century Philosophical Correspondence," *Proceedings of the American Academy for Jewish Research* 24 (1955): 103–36.

52. For a broad biographical sketch of Ibn Daud and an overview of his works, see Katja Vehlow, *Abraham ibn Daud's Dorot 'Olam (Generations of the Ages)* (Leiden: Brill, 2013), 14–24. See also Husik, *A History of Medieval Jewish Philosophy*, 197–235. For Maimonides as following in Ibn Daud's footsteps in a number of important ways, despite never actually citing him directly or mentioning him by name, see Resianne Fontaine, "Was Maimonides an Epigone?" *Studia Rosenthaliana* 40 (2007–2008), 9–26; and cf. Husik, *A History of Medieval Jewish Philosophy*, 235.

53. See Shlomo Pines, "Toward the Study of Abū al-Barakāt al-Baghdādī's Commentary on Qohelet: Four Texts," *Tarbiz* 33 (1964), 198–213 [Hebrew]; Samuel Poznanski, "Aus

Abū-l-Barakāt Hibat-Allah's arabischem Kommentar zu Qohelet," *Zeitschrift für Hebraeische Bibliographie* 16 (1913), 32–36. Following the precedent of Saadia, Karaite exegetes, and Ibn Ghiyāth, Al-Baghdādī's commentary is accompanied by an Arabic translation of the biblical text. See Pines, "Toward the Study of Abū al-Barakāt al-Baghdādī's Commentary," 198.

54. For Abū al-Barakāt al-Baghdādī in general, see the articles collected in Shlomo Pines, *Studies in Abu'l-Barakāt al-Baghdādī: Physics and Metaphysics* (Jerusalem and Leiden: Magnes Press / E. J. Brill: 1979); and Sirat, *History of Jewish Philosophy*, 131–40.

55. Pines, "Toward the Study of Abū al-Barakāt al-Baghdādī's Commentary," 199.

56. See the text presented, translated into Hebrew, and discussed in Pines, "Toward the Study of Abū al-Barakāt al-Baghdādī's Commentary," 200–6. Here, Al-Baghdādī also discusses questions connected to human intuition.

57. Al-Baghdādī may be influenced here by rabbinic attitudes to Ecclesiastes. For the possibility of Ecclesiastes Rabbah as reflecting a curriculum of study across topics, structured as a commentary, see H. L. Strack and G. Stemberger, *Introduction to the Talmud and Midrash*, trans. Markus Bockmuehl (Minneapolis, MN: Fortress Press, 1992), 317–18.

58. For his use of Euclid, see Pines, "Toward the Study of Abū al-Barakāt al-Baghdādī's Commentary," 204–6. For an affinity with the Brethren of Purity, see ibid., 210. He also cites and critiques verses from Abū 'Alī al-Muḥassin ibn 'Alī al-Tanūkhī (d. 994), for which see ibid., 207.

59. For a general treatment of the work, see A. S. Halkin, "Ibn 'Aknin's Commentary on the Song of Songs," in *Alexander Marx Jubilee Volume* (New York: Jewish Theological Seminary of America, 1950), 389–424. For an edition of the Arabic with a Hebrew translation, see *Inkishāf al-asrār wa-ẓuhūr al-anwār/hitgallut ha-sodot ve-hofa'at ha-me'orot/Divulgatio Mysteriorum Luminumque Apparentia*, ed. and trans. A. S. Halkin (Jerusalem: Mekize Nirdamim, 1964).

60. For the background to this interpretation, see Shalom Rosenberg, "Philosophical Hermeneutics on the Song of Songs, Introductory Remarks," *Tarbiz* 59 (1990), 133–41 [Hebrew].

61. Ibn 'Aqnīn was aware of Maimonides and appears to have known him personally in Fez. (See Halkin, "Ibn 'Aknin's commentary on the Song of Songs," 405.) However, his interpretation of Song of Songs does not seem to be dependent on Maimonides's treatment of the work. (See ibid., 399–401; Rosenberg, "Philosophical Hermeneutics," 135.) For Maimonides's understanding of Song of Songs, see *Mishneh Torah*, "Book of Knowledge, Laws of Repentance," 10:3.

62. In shifting the object of human desire from God to the active intellect, Ibn 'Aqnīn's commentary prefigures certain trends in post-Maimonidean exegesis of the Song of Songs as attested in the interpretations of Joseph ibn Kaspi (d. 1340), Moses ibn Tibbon (fl. 13th century), and Levi b. Gershom (Gersonides; d. 1344). Cf. Yosef Marciano, "Ha-rambam u-farshanut shir ha-shirim," in *Teshurah le-'Amos: Collected Studies in Biblical Exegesis - Presented to 'Amos Hakham*, eds. Moshe Bar-Asher, Noaḥ Ḥakham, and Yosef 'Ofer (Tevunot: 2007), 106–8; Wolfson, "Asceticism and Eroticism," 94–95.

63. See the references listed in Halkin, *Inkishāf al-asrār*, 513. Halkin lists seven references to Al-Fārābī—more than any other source, Jewish or non-Jewish.

64. See Maimonides's introduction to the *Guide*, in Shlomo Pines, *The Guide of the Perplexed* (Chicago: University of Chicago Press, 1963), 11–12.

65. *Guide* 1:1–70.

66. See *Mishneh torah*, "Laws of the Foundations of the Torah," 2:11–12, 4:10–13; Maimonides's commentary to Mishnah *Ḥagigah* 2:1.

67. For Maimonides as an exegete, see Alfred Ivry, "Strategies of Interpretation in Maimonides's *Guide of the Perplexed*," *Jewish History* 6 (1992), 113–30; Sara Klein-Braslavy, *Maimonides as Biblical Interpreter* (Boston, MA: Academic Studies Press: 2011); Mordechai Z. Cohen, *Three Approaches to Biblical Metaphor*; ibid., *Opening the Gates of Interpretation*.

68. See David R. Blumenthal, "Was There an Eastern Tradition of Maimonidean Scholarship?" *Revue des études juives* 138 (1979): 57–68; Elisha Russ-Fishbane, *Judaism, Sufism, and the Pietists of Medieval Egypt: A Study of Abraham Maimonides and His Times* (New York: Oxford University Press, 2015).

69. See Y. Tzvi Langermann, "Yemenite Philosophical Midrash as a Source for the Intellectual History of the Jews of Yemen," in *The Jews of Medieval Islam: Community, Society, and Identity*, ed. Daniel Frank (Leiden: Brill, 1995), 335–47.

70. For the place of Ibn Rushd in the philosophical Jewish culture of Languedoc, see Gregg Stern, "Philosophy in Southern France: Controversy over Philosophical Study and the Influence of Averroes upon Jewish Thought," in *Cambridge Companion to Medieval Jewish Philosophy*, ed. Oliver Leaman and Daniel Frank (Cambridge: Cambridge University Press, 2003), 281–303.

71. See *Perush rabbenu abraham ben ha rambam za"l 'al bereshit u-shmot*, trans. Ernest Wiesenberg, ed. S. D. Sassoon (London, 1959) [Hebrew].

72. For Abraham Maimonides's engagement with Sufism, see Paul Fenton, "Abraham Maimonides (1186–1237): Founding a Mystical Dynasty," in *Jewish Mystical Leaders and Leadership in the 13th Century*, ed. Moshe Idel and Mortimer Ostow (New York: Jason Aronson, 1998), 127–54; Russ-Fishbane, *Judaism, Sufism, and the Pietists of Medieval Egypt*.

73. See Nahem Ilan, "Theological Assumptions and Hermeneutical Principles in Abraham Maimuni's Commentary on the Pentateuch," in *A Word Fitly Spoken: Studies in Mediaeval Exegesis of the Hebrew Bible and the Qur'ān, Presented to Haggai Ben-Shammai*, ed. Meir M. Bar-Asher, Simon Hopkins, Sarah Stroumsa, and Bruno Chiesa (Jerusalem: Ben-Zvi Institute, 2007), 31–70 [Hebrew].

74. See his commentary to Gen. 1:24, which presents an emanationist theory of the origins of the souls of animals, in Wiesenberg, *Perush rabbenu abraham*, 2–3. Cf. Ibn Sīnā's formulation in *Ibn Sina's Remarks and Admonitions: Physics and Metaphysics*, trans. Shams C. Inati (New York: Columbia University Press, 2014), 165. See also Abraham's commentary on Gen. 2:15, which assumes a process of intellectual actualization drawing on Peripatetic sources and prescribes the acquisition of some additional perfection that a person is born without (although humans are believed to have a capacity for such perfection), in Wiesenberg, *Perush rabbenu abraham*, 38–41.

75. Abraham Maimonides explains the perception of the divine described in Exod. 24:11 as the product of a regimen of self-isolation (*khalwa*), during which the participants were "exclusively devoted to Him [*munqaṭi'īn lahu*]" to the point that they attained their respective levels of perfection, nearness (*qurb*), and worship (*'ibāda*)—here certainly referring to intellectual contemplation. See Wiesenberg, *Perush rabbenu avraham ben ha-rambam*, 379; the passage is cited in an English translation in Russ-Fishbane, *Judaism, Sufism, and the Pietists of Medieval Egypt*, 121. For intellectual worship (*al-'ibāda al-aqliyya*) as nearness to God (*al-qurb min allāh*) in *Guide* 3:51, see Pines, 623 (English); Salomon Munk, *Dalālat al-ḥā'irīn (sefer moreh nevukhim) le-rabbenu mosheh ben maimon* (Yunovits, 1930), 459 lines 1–2 [Arabic]. Cf. Ibn Sīnā chapter on the stations of the knowers/Gnostics in *Al-ishārāt wa'l-tanbīhāt li-abī*

ʿalī bin sīnā, ed. Sulayman Dunya (Dār al-maʿārif: 1958), part 4, 789–852 [Arabic]; cf. English translation in *Ibn Sīnā and Mysticism: Remarks and Admonitions: Part Four*, trans. Shams C. Inati (London: Kegan Paul International, 1996).

76. For editions of Tanḥum's commentaries, most of them accompanied by studies, see Hadassa Shy, *Tanḥum Ha-Yerushalmi's Commentary on the Minor Prophets* (Jerusalem: Magnes Press, 1991) [Hebrew]; Michael Wechsler, *Strangers in the Land: The Judaeo-Arabic Exegesis of Tanhum ha-Yerushalmi on the Books of Ruth and Esther* (Jerusalem: Magnes Press, 2010); Arye Zoref, "Tanchum Ha-Yerushalmi's Commentary on Canticles: Studies in its Tendencies and Its Jewish, Sufi-Islamic and Christian Sources, with a Critical Edition," 2 vols. (PhD diss., Hebrew University, 2012) [Hebrew]; ibid., *Tanchum Yerushalmi's Commentary on Ecclesiastes: Edited and Translated from Arabic to Hebrew* (self-published, Jerusalem, 2013) [Hebrew]. See also Joseph Alobaidi's edition of Tanḥum's commentary on Song of Songs, which is unfortunately riddled with errors in transcription and translations and inexplicably incomplete at the beginning: *Old Jewish Commentaries on the Song of Songs II: The Two Commentaries of Tanchum Yerushalmi—Text and Translation*, ed. Joseph Alobaidi (New York: Peter Lang, 2014). For studies of Tanḥum, see Samuel Poznanski, "Tanhoum Yerouschalmi et son commentaire sur le livre de Jonas," *Revue des études juives* 40 (1900): 129–53; ibid., "Tanhoum Yerouschalmi et son commentaire sur le livre de Jonas (suite et fin) [Appendice: Tanhoum Yerouschalmi et Moïse ibn Chiquitilla]," *Revue des études juives* 41 (1900): 45–61; Avi Tal, "Parshanuto ha-maddaʿit ve-ha-re'alistit shel rabbi tanḥum ha-yerushalmi mi-tokh be'urav le-sifre melakhim b, yeshaʿyahu, yirmiyahu vi-yehezqel," in *Mi-tuv Yosef*, ed. Eilat Ettinger and Dani Bar-Maʿoz (Haifa: Haifa University Press, 2011), vol. 3, 120–44; Avi Tal, "Rabbi Tanḥūm Ha-yerūšalmī's Exegetic Methods in His Commentary on the Books of II Kings, Isaiah, Jeremiah and Ezekiel According to Manuscripts from the Bodleian Library and St. Petersburg Library" (PhD diss., Bar-Ilan University, 2007) [Hebrew]; Raphael Dascalu, "Between Intellect and Intoxication: An Exploration of Tanḥum ha-Yerushalmi's Commentary to the Book of Jonah," *Jewish Quarterly Review* 105 (2015): 42–71; ibid., "Philology, Philosophy, and Sufism: Towards an Understanding of Tanḥum Ha-Yerushalmi's Exegesis and Thought, with a Focus on His Commentaries on Jonah, the Song of Songs, and Qohelet" (PhD diss., University of Chicago, 2016).

77. See Dascalu, "Philology, Philosophy, and Sufism," 180–84.

78. See Zoref, *Tanchum Ha-Yerushalmi's Commentary on Canticles*, vol. 1; Dascalu, "Philology, Philosophy, and Sufism," 180–281, 310–97. The fragment of his commentary to Proverbs survives as an interpolation into a Muslim commentary on Maimonides's *Mishneh Torah*. See G. Margoliouth, "A Muhammadan Commentary on Maimonides' Mishneh Torah. Chs. I-IV," in *Jewish Quarterly Review* 13, no. 3 (April 1901), 501, 505–6.

79. See Dascalu, "Philology, Philosophy, and Sufism," 190–230.

80. See Dascalu, "Philology, Philosophy, and Sufism," 324–42.

81. Zoref, *Tanchum Ha-Yerushalmi's Commentary on Canticles*, 1:102–3; Dascalu, "Philology, Philosophy, and Sufism," 436–37 and n. 11.

82. Dascalu, "Philology, Philosophy, and Sufism," 230–61, 372–96.

83. For which, see Paul Fenton, "A Mystical Commentary on the Song of Songs in the Hand of David Maimonides II," in *Esoteric and Exoteric Aspects in Judaeo-Arabic Culture*, ed. Benjamin Hary and Haggai Ben-Shammai (Leiden: Brill, 2006), 19–53.

84. For Jewish engagement with Sufism in this context, see Paul Fenton, *The Treatise of the Pool: Al-Maqāla al-Ḥawḍiyya* (London: Octagon Press, 1981), 4–20. There were exceptions to this orientation—for an example of an antiphilosophical position, see Paul Fenton "Daniel

ibn Māshiṭa's *Taqwīm al-Adyān*: New Light on the Oriental Phase of the Maimonidean Controversy," in *Genizah Research after Ninety Years: The Case of Judaeo-Arabic*, ed. Joshua Blau and Stefan Reif (Cambridge: Cambridge University Press, 1992), 74–81. There is also at least one commentary to the Song of Songs from this milieu that presents a Jewish Sufi spiritual path, mostly free of Peripatetic material, for which see Paul Fenton, "Some Judaeo-Arabic Fragments of Rabbi Abraham He-Ḥasid, the Jewish Sufi," *Journal of Jewish Studies* 26 (1981): 47–72; ibid., "Mystical Commentary on the Song of Songs in the Hand of David Maimonides II," 43–53.

85. Langermann, "Yemenite Philosophical Midrash"; Y. Tzvi Langermann, *Yemenite Midrash: Philosophical Commentaries on the Torah* (San Francisco, CA: Harper, 1996), xvii–xxx. Particularly striking is Ḥoṭer ben Shelomo's rephrasing of a maxim in Mishnah Tractate Avot 4:1 in defense of his eclectic approach: "Who is wise? One who collects from every place" (for which, see Langermann, "Yemenite Philosophical Midrash," 345.)

86. See Y. Tzvi Langerman, "The Debate between the Philosopher and the Mutakallim," *Proceedings of the American Academy for Jewish Research* 60 (1994): 190–91.

87. For a discussion of the work and its author, see Langermann, *Yemenite Midrash*, 265–66. For an edition and translation into Hebrew, see *Nūr al-ẓalām/Me'or ha-'afelah*, edited and translated into Hebrew by Joseph Qafiḥ (Ha-Agudah le-Hatsalat Ginze Teman, 1957).

88. This interpretation is based on Maimonides's understanding of the semantic range of the term *Elohim*, for which see *Guide* 1:2 (Pines, 23). Cf. also Ibn Ezra to Gen. 1:1, s.v. *Elohim*.

89. See Qafiḥ, *Nūr al-ẓalām*, 5-6.

90. Cf. Qafiḥ, *Nūr al-ẓalām*, 24.

91. See Langermann, *Yemenite Midrash*, 267–68. For an edition, see *Midrash ha-gadol*, ed. Mordekhai Margaliot (Jerusalem: Mossad Harav Kook, 1947).

92. For the work, published with Hebrew translations of the Arabic sections, see *Midrash ha-ḥefets*, 3 vols., ed. and trans. Meir Havazelet (Jerusalem: Mossad Harav Kook, 1990–1992).

93. Langermann, "Yemenite Philosophical Midrash," 338.

94. See Havazelet, *Midrash ha-ḥefets*, 1:25–26 (Hebrew pagination). For the theme of the "traces" or "effects" (*āthār*) left by causes (in this case intellects), in Muḥammad al-Nasafī, drawn from *Pseudo-Ammonius*, see Paul E. Walker, "The Ismaīlīs," in *The Cambridge Companion to Arabic Philosophy*, ed. Peter Adamson and Richard C. Taylor (Cambridge: Cambridge University Press, 2005), 78–79. Cf. David R. Blumenthal, *The Commentary of Ḥōṭer ben Shelōmō to the Thirteen Principles of Maimonides* (Leiden: Brill, 1974), 17–19. Cf. also Zekhariah's reference to the universal soul in Havazelet, *Midrash ha-ḥefets*, 1:22 [Arabic], 23 [Hebrew, Hebrew pagination]. Ḥoṭer and Zekhariah share a synthesis of Aristotelian and Neoplatonic elements; see Blumenthal, ibid.

95. In *Ḥamesh megillot: shir ha-shirim, rut, qohelet, ester, ekhah*, ed. Josef Qafiḥ (Jerusalem: Ha-Agudah le-Hatsalat Ginze Teman, 1962). For a study of the commentary, see Y. Tzvi Langermann, "Saving the Soul by Knowing the Soul: A Medieval Yemeni Interpretation of Song of Songs," *Journal of Jewish Thought and Philosophy* 12 (2003), 147–66.

96. See James T. Robinson, "We Drink Only from the Master's Water: Maimonides and Maimonideanism in Southern France, 1200–1306," *Studia Rosenthaliana* 40 (2007–2008), 27–60.

97. For the primacy of Aristotle in Ibn Rushd's thought, see Richard C. Taylor, "Averroes: Religious Dialectic and Aristotelian Philosophical Thought," in *The Cambridge Companion to Arabic Philosophy*, ed. Peter Adamson and Richard C. Taylor (Cambridge: Cambridge University Press, 2005), particularly 189–96; Craig Martin, *Subverting Aristotle: Religion, History,*

and Philosophy in Early Modern Science (Baltimore, MD: Johns Hopkins University Press, 2014), 13. It must be noted that other Islamicate thinkers played a role in the development of Christian Aristotelianism, notably Ibn Sīnā and Maimonides. See Étienne Gilson, "Avicenne en Occident au moyen âge," *Archives d'histoire doctrinale et littéraire du moyen âge* 44 (1969): 89–121; Georges C. Anawati, "Saint Thomas d'Aquin et la métaphysique d'Avicenne," in *St. Thomas Aquinas, 1274–1974: Commemorative Studies*, ed. Armand A. Maurer et al. (Toronto: Pontifical Institute of Mediaeval Studies, 1974), 449–65. For the participation of members of the Tibbonid family in an extensive project of translating philosophical works, see Robinson, *Samuel ibn Tibbon's Commentary*, 3–4. For a table of Hebrew translations of philosophical texts (mainly from Arabic and Latin), see Mauro Zonta, "Medieval Hebrew Translations of Philosophical and Scientific Texts: A Chronological Table," in Freudenthal, *Science in Medieval Jewish Cultures*, 17–73.

98. Robinson, "Philosophy and Science," 461–64; Robinson, "We Drink Only from the Master's Water." For Spain as a major route through which philosophical discourse entered southern France, see Gad Freudenthal, "Science in the Medieval Jewish Culture of Southern France," *History of Science* 33 (1995): 23–58.

99. For a translation and study of his commentary to Qohelet, see Robinson, *Samuel ibn Tibbon's Commentary*. For a critical edition of the Hebrew text, see James T. Robinson, *Perush Qohelet li-Shemuel ibn Tibbon* (Jerusalem: World Union of Jewish Studies, 2016). *Ma'amar yiqqavu ha-mayim* was edited by M. L. Bisliches (Pressburg, 1837).

100. For Ibn Tibbon's fraught relationship with the Andalusian *peshaṭ* tradition and his critique of Ibn Ghiyāth's approach to Qohelet, see Robinson, *Samuel ibn Tibbon's Commentary*, 34–35, 68–73. For his critique of Ibn Ezra's astrological interpretation of verses from Qohelet, see ibid., 73–75.

101. Robinson, *Samuel ibn Tibbon's Commentary*, 35–36.

102. Robinson, *Samuel ibn Tibbon's Commentary*, 36–40.

103. For a study of David Qimḥi, which also explores his background and family, see Frank Ephraim Talmage, *David Kimhi: The Man and the Commentaries* (Cambridge, MA: Harvard University Press, 1975).

104. See *The Book of the Covenant*, trans. Frank Ephraim Talmage (Toronto: Pontifical Institute of Mediaeval Studies, 1972). For his commentary to Proverbs, along with that of his son Moses, see *Perushim le-sefer mishle le-bet Qimḥi*, ed. Frank Ephraim Talmage (Jerusalem: Magnes Press, 1990). His commentary to the Song of Songs has been published in *Mikra'ot Gedolot 'Haketer'*, ed. Menachem Cohen (Jerusalem: Bar-Ilan University Press, 2012).

105. See for example, his reference to the philosophical sciences in his commentary to Prov. 9:1. For a discussion of this passage, accepting the mistaken attribution of the commentary to Ibn Ezra, see Harry Austryn Wolfson, "The Classification of Sciences in Mediaeval Jewish Philosophy," in *Studies in the History of Philosophy and Religion*, ed. Isadore Twersky and George H. Williams (Cambridge, MA: Harvard University Press, 1973), 507–9. For the misattribution of Moses Qimḥi's commentary on Proverbs to Abraham ibn Ezra in rabbinic Bibles and the discovery of this error by Jacob Reifmann, see *A Commentary on the Book of Proverbs Attributed to Abraham ibn Ezra*, ed. Samuel Rolles Driver (Oxford: Clarendon, 1880), v–vi. For Moses Qimḥi in general, see Talmage, *David Kimhi*, 7–8.

106. Indeed, he participated directly in the Maimonidean controversies. See Talmage, *David Kimhi*, 27–39. His commentary to the Torah is included in *Torat ḥayyim: ḥamishah ḥumshe torah*, 7 vols. (Jerusalem: Mossad Harav Kook, 1993).

107. For philosophy in David Qimḥi's commentaries, see Talmage, *David Kimhi*, 70–72; Frank Ephraim Talmage, "David Kimhi and the Rationalist Tradition," *Hebrew Union College Annual* 39 (1968): 177–218. In the present chapter, I refer primarily to David Qimḥi's commentary to the Torah, published as *Perushe rabbi David Qimḥi (radaq) 'al ha-torah*, ed. M. Kamelhar (Jerusalem: Mossad Harav Kook, 1970); and his commentary to Psalms, *Ha-Perush ha-shalem 'al tehillim*, ed. Abraham Darom (Jerusalem: Mossad Harav Kook, 1971).

108. See for example his reference to philosophical anthropology in his commentary to Ps. 103:14; his references to philosophical cosmology in ibid., vs. 20 and to the Aristotelian classification of sublunary beings in ibid., vs. 22; and his extensive use of philosophical cosmology and physics in his commentary to Ps. 104.

109. On Gersonides in general, see Seymour Feldman, *Gersonides: Judaism within the Limits of Reason* (Oxford/Portland: Littman Library of Jewish Civilization, 2010); For an annotated bibliography of studies on Gersonides's relationship to Maimonides, see Israel Jacob Dienstag, "The Relationship of Gersonides to the Philosophy of Maimonides: An Annotated Bibliography," *Da'at* 23 (1989): 5–13 [Hebrew]. See also the studies included in Menachem Kellner, *Torah in the Observatory: Gersonides, Maimonides, Song of Songs* (Boston, MA: Academic Studies Press, 2010).

110. For the passages discussed below, see *Perushe ha-Torah le-rabbenu Levi ben Gershom (ralbag)*, ed. Jacob Leyb Levi (Jerusalem: Mossad Harav Kook, 1992), 1:20 30. (in Hebrew pagination).

111. Levi, *Perushe ha-Torah*, 20.

112. Levi, *Perushe ha-Torah*, 22–25.

113. Levi, *Perushe ha-Torah*, 26.

114. Levi, *Perushe ha-Torah*, 28–29.

115. Kellner, *Torah in the Observatory*, 19–20.

116. For Moses ibn Tibbon's extensive literary activity, see Robinson, *Samuel ibn Tibbon's Commentary*, 4. For the commentary, see *Perush 'al shir ha-shirim me-r' Mosheh ibn Tibbon* (Mekize Nirdamim, 1874); and the more recent synoptic edition by Otfried Fraisse, *Moses ibn Tibbons Kommentar zum Hohelied und sein poetologisch-philosophisches Programm* (Berlin: Walter de Gruyter, 2004).

117. For a broad and detailed study of Ibn Kaspi, see Isadore Twersky, "Joseph ibn Kaspi: Portrait of a Medieval Jewish Intellectual," in *Studies in Medieval Jewish History and Literature* (Cambridge, MA: Harvard University Press, 1979), 231–57; Adrian Sackson, *Joseph ibn Kaspi: Portrait of a Hebrew Philosopher in Medieval Provence* (Leiden: Brill, 2017). For a list of his biblical commentaries, see ibid., 68–69. See also Robert Eisen, "Joseph ibn Kaspi on the Book of Job," *Jewish Studies Quarterly* 13, no. 1 (2006): 50–86; ibid., "Joseph ibn Kaspi on the Secret Meaning of the Scroll of Esther," *Revue des études juives* 160, no. 3 (2001): 379–408; Hannah Kasher, "On the Book of Esther as an Allegory in the Works of Joseph ibn Kaspi: A Response to R. Eisen," *Revue des études juives* 161 (2002): 459–64; ibid., "Joseph ibn Kaspi's Aristotelian Interpretation and Fundamentalist Interpretation of the Book of Job," *Da'at* 20 (1988): 117–26.

118. See Howard Kreisel, "Some Observations on Ma'aseh Nissim by R. Nissim of Marseilles," in *Perspectives on Jewish Thought and Mysticism*, ed. Alfred L. Ivry, Elliot R. Wolfson, and Allan Arkush (Harwood Academic Publishers, 1998), 201–22; Ḥayyim (Howard) Kreisel, "Ha-Parshanut ha-filosofit-allegorit la-torah bi-yme ha-benayim: sefer ma'aseh nissim le-r' nissim mi-marsey," in *Me'ah she'arim: Studies in Medieval Jewish Spiritual Life in Memory of*

Isadore Twersky, ed. Ezra Fleischer, Yaakov Blidstein, Carmi Horowitz, and Bernard Septimus (Jerusalem: Magnes Press, 2001), 297–316. For an edition of the work, see *Ma'aseh nissim: perush la-torah*, ed. Howard Kreisel (Mekize Nirdamim, 2000).

119. For an overview, see Robinson, "Philosophy and Science," 466–67.

120. See Robinson, "Philosophy and Science," 466. On Judah ha-Kohen, see Resianne Fontaine, "Judah ben Solomon ha-Cohen's *Midrash ha-Ḥokhmah*: Its Sources and Use of Sources," in *The Medieval Hebrew Encyclopedias of Science and Philosophy*, ed. Steven Harvey (Dordrecht, Kluwer Academic Publishers, 2000), 191–210; Tony Lévy, "Mathematics in the *Midrash ha-Ḥokhmah* of Judah ben Solomon ha-Cohen," in ibid., 300–312.

121. See Mauro Zonta, *Hebrew Scholasticism in the Fifteenth Century: A History and Source Book* (Dordrecht: Springer, 2006), 3.

122. For Judah Romano in general, see Caterina Rigo, "Yehudah ben Mosheh Romano: Traduttore degli Scholastici latini," *Henoch* 17 (1995): 141–70; ibid., "Human Substance and Eternal Life in the Philosophy of Rabbi Judah Romano," *Jerusalem Studies in Jewish Thought: Joseph Baruch Sermoneta Memorial Volume* (1998): 181–222 [Hebrew]; Giuseppe Sermoneta, "'Thine Ointments Have a Goodly Fragrance': Rabbi Judah Romano and the Open Text," in *Jerusalem Studies in Jewish Thought: Shlomo Pines Jubilee Volume on the Occasion of His Eightieth Birthday: Part II* (1990), 77–113 [Hebrew]; ibid., "Jehudah ben Mošeh ben Dani'el Romano, traducteur de Saint Thomas," in *Hommage à G. Vajda, études d'histoire et de pensée juives*, ed. G. Nahon and C. Touati (Leuven: Peeters, 1980), 235–62. For his particular approach to biblical exegesis, see Sermoneta, "Ha-Perush le-'parashat bereshit' le-r' yehudah ben mosheh ben daniyyel romano u-meqorotav"; Caterina Rigo, "Judah Romano's Commentaries on the Bible: His Philosophical System as Contained in Them and His Sources in Jewish Thought and Christian Scholasticism" (PhD diss., Hebrew University, 1996) [Hebrew].

123. Sermoneta, "Rabbi Judah Romano and the Open Text." For the nine positions that he articulates and a detailed discussion, see ibid., 92–100.

124. Sermoneta, "Ha-Perush le-'parashat bereshit' le-r' yehudah ben mosheh ben daniyyel romano u-meqorotav."

125. Bernard Septimus, *Hispano-Jewish Culture in Transition* (Cambridge, MA: Harvard University Press, 1982), 1–2; Robert Chazan, *Fashioning Jewish Identity in Medieval Western Christendom* (Cambridge: Cambridge University Press, 2004), 9, 93. For a discussion of the significance of the opening up of new channels of cultural exchange between Spanish Jewry and the Jewries of Provence, northern France, and Ashkenaz in the twelfth and thirteenth centuries, see Yom Tov Assis, "The Judeo-Arabic Tradition in Christian Spain," in *Jews of Medieval Islam: Community, Society, and Identity*, ed. Daniel Frank (Leiden: Brill, 1995), 117–22.

126. For the emergence of kabbalah, see Gershom Scholem, *Origins of the Kabbalah*, trans. Allan Arkush, ed. R. J. Zwi Werblowsky (Philadelphia, PA and Princeton, NJ: Jewish Publication Society/Princeton University Press, 1987). For a brief history of the Kabbalah and its development until the emergence of the *Zohar*, see Arthur Green, *A Guide to the Zohar* (Palo Alto, CA: Stanford University Press, 2004), 9–27.

127. For the place of the sciences in the Jewish cultures of the Iberian Peninsula, both under Islamic and Christian rule, see Y. Tzvi Langermann, "Science in the Jewish Communities of the Iberian Peninsula," in *The Jews and the Sciences in the Middle Ages*, 1:1–54.

128. Green, *A Guide to the Zohar*, 22–23, 26, 37, 42, 58. See also Hava Tirosh-Samuelson, "Kabbalah and Science in the Middle Ages," in Freudenthal, *Science in Medieval Jewish Cultures*, 476–510.

129. See Sara O. Heller Wilensky, "Isaac ibn Laṭif—Philosopher or Kabbalist?" in *Jewish Medieval and Renaissance Studies*, ed. Alexander Altmann (Cambridge, MA: Harvard University Press, 1967), 185–223; Sara O. Heller Wilensky, "The 'First Created Being' in Early Kabbalah: Philosophical and Isma'ilian Sources," in *Binah: Jewish Intellectual History in the Middle Ages* 3, ed. Joseph Dan (Praeger, 1994), 65–77. For Ibn Laṭīf's general identification with the Jewish Neoplatonists and with Ibn Gabirol in particular, see Wilensky, "Isaac ibn Laṭif—Philosopher or Kabbalist?" 200–210. For his relationship with Spanish kabbalah, see ibid., 210–21.

130. For his Platonic sympathies, despite knowing Plato only indirectly, and his criticism of the tendency to accept Aristotle's views as authoritative, see Wilensky, "Isaac ibn Laṭif—Philosopher or Kabbalist?" 188–95.

131. Wilensky, "Isaac ibn Laṭif—Philosopher or Kabbalist?" 192. However, it should be noted that Ibn Laṭīf did often align himself with Al-Fārābī. See ibid., 195–200. For the anti-Aristotelian trend and Ḥasdai Crescas, see James T. Robinson, "Hasdai Crescas and Anti-Aristotelianism," in *The Cambridge Companion to Medieval Jewish Philosophy*, 391–413.

132. Published as *Perush megillat qohelet* (Constantinople, ca. 1585). For a partial list of Ibn Laṭīf's works, see Wilensky, "Isaac ibn Laṭif—Philosopher or Kabbalist?" 186 and n. 11.

133. Ibn Laṭīf states that the work contains elements of "the natural sciences and some metaphysics, based upon demonstrative analogy, weighed upon the scales of the science of logic, accompanied and contained by the principles of the Torah and faith. [. . .] Further, included in it are matters that provide instruction concerning the rectification of human dispositions, and the arrangement of the association of some people with others."

134. For an introduction to Naḥmanides, see Yaakov Elman, "Moses ben Nahman/Nahmanides (Ramban)," in *Hebrew Bible/Old Testament*, 1/2, 416–32. See also Nina Caputo, *Nahmanides in Medieval Catalonia: History, Community, and Messianism* (Notre Dame, IN: University of Notre Dame Press, 2007). His commentary to the Pentateuch has been published as *Perushe ha-torah le-rabbenu mosheh ben naḥman (ramban)*, 2 vols., ed. Ḥayyim Dov (Charles Ber) Chavel (Jerusalem: Mossad Harav Kook, 1959); for an English translation, see *Ramban/Nahmanides: Commentary on the Torah*, 5 vols., trans. Charles B. Chavel (New York: Shilo, 1971–1976). For his attitude to philosophy, see Warren Zev Harvey, "Aspects of Jewish Philosophy in Medieval Catalonia," in *Mossé ben Nahman i el seu Temps: Simposi commemoratiu del vuitè centenari del seu naixement 1194–1994 / The Life and Times of Moses ben Nahman: A Symposium to Commemorate the 800th Anniversary of His Birth 1194–1994* (Girona: Ajuntament de Girona, 1994), 145–47.

135. For a study of Naḥmanides's relationship with the Andalusian tradition, in which the author also discusses his relationship with Rashi, see Bernard Septimus, "'Open Rebuke and Concealed Love': Nahmanides and the Andalusian Tradition," in *Rabbi Moses Nahmanides: Essays in His Religious and Literary Virtuosity*, ed. Isadore Twersky (Cambridge, MA: Harvard University Press, 1983), 11–34.

136. For a study of Naḥmanides's literary approach, see Michelle Levine, *Nahmanides on Genesis: The Art of Biblical Portraiture* (Providence, RI: Brown University Press, 2009).

137. He attempted to restrict the study of philosophy to a limited elite, and he opposed central elements of Peripatetic philosophy, but he also adopted a moderate position in the Maimonidean controversies and employed philosophical discourse in a number of contexts. See Benjamin R. Gampel, "A Letter to a Wayward Teacher: The Transformations of Sephardic Culture in Christian Iberia," in *Cultures of the Jews: A New History*, ed. David Biale

(New York: Schocken, 2002), 406. For Naḥmanides's rejection of Aristotelian philosophy as severely limited in comparison with astral magic and Kabbalah, see Dov Schwartz, "From Theurgy to Magic: The Evolution of the Magical-Talismanic Justification of Sacrifice in the Circle of Nahmanides and His Interpreters," *Aleph* 1 (2001): 174–76. In some ways, Naḥmanides's commentary on the Pentateuch mediates between the exegetical methods of Rashi and Ibn Ezra, who typified classic midrashic methodology and Spanish *peshaṭ* respectively.

138. For his adoption of such elements, and the ways in which he synthesizes them with more mythical cosmological and theological elements, see Elliot Wolfson, "The Secret of the Garment in Naḥmanides," *Da'at* 24 (1990–91): xxv–xlix.

139. For Aristotle's theory, to which Naḥmanides's brief formulation may allude, see *Meteorology* 3:4. Cf. Saadia's opinion that the rainbow was produced during creation but here became meaningful as a symbol, referred to and rejected by Ibn Ezra in his commentary to Gen. 1:13.

140. For an edition, see *Sefer ha-Zohar*, 3 vols., ed. Reuben Margaliot (Jerusalem: Mossad Harav Kook, 1999). A recent annotated English translation may be found in *The Zohar (Pritzker Edition)*, 12 vols., trans. and commentary by Daniel Matt [vols. 1–9], Nathan Wolski [vol. 10], Joel Hecker [vol. 11], Wolski and Hecker [vol. 12] (Palo Alto, CA: Stanford University Press, 2004–2017). For early evidence of the Zoharic texts and their earliest circulation in the 1280s and 1290s, see Gershom Scholem, "The Earliest Citation from *Midrash ne'elam*," *Tarbiz* 3 (1932): 181–83 [Hebrew]; Boaz Huss, "The Early Dissemination of 'Sefer ha-Zohar,'" *Tarbiz* 70 (2002): 507–42 [Hebrew].

141. Nathan Wolski, "Radical Allegoresis and Neoplatonic Myth in *Midrash ha-Ne'elam*," *Kabbalah* 34 (2015): 133–75. For the *Zohar*'s complex attitude toward the Hellenistic heritage in general and philosophy in particular—see Elliot R. Wolfson, "Light through Darkness: The Ideal of Human Perfection in the Zohar," *Harvard Theological Review* 81 (1988): 82n32. For Moses de León's admiring citation of the *Theology of Aristotle*, referring to the author (whom he apparently believed to be Aristotle) by the messianic title of *moreh tsedeq*, see *Sefer Mishkan ha-Edut*, ed. Avishai Bar-Asher (Los Angeles: Cherub Press, 2013), 81, lines 1327–29 and notes.

142. See the opening passages of the work, translated into English in *The Zohar*, trans. Daniel Matt (Palo Alto, CA: Stanford University Press, 2004), vol. 1, beginning at page 107. Here, as throughout the *Zohar*, the Plotinian motif of a cosmic flow is prominently employed. For this motif in Plotinus, see Dominic J. O'Meara, *Plotinus: An Introduction to the Enneads* (Oxford: Oxford University Press, 1993), 60.

143. This had already been adopted by others, notably Saadia. See Isaiah Tishby, *The Wisdom of the Zohar: An Anthology of Texts*, trans. David Goldstein (Portland, OR: Littman Library of Jewish Civilization, 2008), 684–92. It seems that Galen was the first to identify the Platonic tripartite soul with the Aristotelian division of living beings into vegetable, animal, and human; see Majid Fakhry, *Ethical Theories in Islam* (Leiden: Brill, 1994), 95 and n. 9. For Plato's threefold division of the human soul, including the localization of its parts, see *Timaeus* 69d–73a. For Aristotle's division of beings in a psychological context, see *De Anima* 2:3 (414a–415a). For Galen's reception of elements of Platonic and Aristotelian psychology, see Christopher Gill, *Naturalistic Psychology in Galen and Stoicism* (Oxford: Oxford University Press, 2010).

144. For an edition of Baḥya's commentary, see *Rabbenu baḥya: be'ur 'al ha-torah*, 3 vols., ed. Ḥayyim Dov (Charles Ber) Chavel (Jerusalem: Mossad Harav Kook, 2006).

145. The passage appears in Baḥya's introduction to his commentary, Chavel, *Rabbenu baḥya*, 1:4–5 (Hebrew pagination). Cf. the Arabic form *mutafalsif.*

146. See Chavel, *Rabbenu baḥya*, 1:16, 18, 19, 25 (Hebrew pagination).

147. See Chavel, *Rabbenu baḥya*, 1:18–19, 21–23 (Hebrew pagination; for a kabbalistic reception of the neo-Pythagorean account in *Sefer yetsirah*).

148. Chavel, *Rabbenu baḥya*, 1:62–65 (Hebrew pagination).

149. On Abarbanel, see Eric Lawee, "Divine Perfection and Methodological Inconsistency: Towards an Understanding of Isaac Abarbanel's Exegetical Frame of Mind," *Jewish Studies Quarterly* 17 (2010): 302–57; Moshe Idel, "Kabbalah and Ancient Philosophy According to R. Isaac and R. Judah Abravanel," in *Filosofiyat ha-ahabah shel Yehudah Abarbanel*, ed. Menahem Dorman and Zeev Levy (Jerusalem: Ha-Kibbutz Ha-Meuhad, 1985), 73–112. See also Robinson, "Philosophy and Science," 473–74.

150. L. Rabinowitz, "Lecture IV: Abravanel as Exegete," in *Isaac Abravanel: Six Lectures*, ed. J. B. Trend and H. Loewe (Cambridge: Cambridge University Press, 1937), 79.

151. See Lawee, *Abarbanel's Stance toward Tradition.*

152. For which, see Gen. 1:26–27, 5:1–2, 9:6. For imagistic understandings of these passages, see Benjamin D. Sommer, *The Bodies of God and the World of Ancient Israel* (Cambridge: Cambridge University Press, 2009), 69–70. See also Esther J. Hamori, *"When Gods Were Men": The Embodied God in Biblical and Near Eastern Literature* (Berlin: De Gruyter, 2008).

153. For a comprehensive study of the concept in classical rabbinic Judaism, see Yair Lorberbaum, *In God's Image: Myth, Theology, and Law in Classical Judaism* (Cambridge: Cambridge University Press, 2015). For a distinctly imagistic understanding of *imago Dei* in rabbinic thought, see *Avoth de-Rabbi Nathan: Solomon Schechter Edition*, ed. Menahem Kister, version B, chapter 30, p. 66 [Hebrew].

154. See Marc Saperstein, *Decoding the Rabbis: A Thirteenth-Century Commentary on the Aggadah* (Cambridge, MA: Harvard University Press), 1–20.

155. Both approaches are represented in classical rabbinic sources. For a strikingly imagistic understanding of *imago Dei* in a classical rabbinic text, see *Avoth de-Rabbi Nathan*, ed. Solomon Schechter (New York: Jewish Theological Seminary of America, 1997), version B, # 30, 66. See also Yair Lorberbaum, *In God's Image: Myth, Theology, and Law in Classical Judaism* (Cambridge: Cambridge University Press, 2015). For an implicitly functionalist interpretation, see the following interpretation of the unusual Hebrew lexeme *ve-anvehu* (Exod. 15:2) ascribed to Abba Shaul: "Become alike unto Him. Just as He is gracious, you be gracious; just as He is compassionate, you be compassionate." For text and translation, see *Mekhilta de-Rabbi Yishma'el*, ed. Jacob Z. Lauterbach (Philadelphia, PA: Jewish Publication Society, 2004), Tractate Shirata 3, 185, lines 43–44, and variants; cf. the parallel in Babylonian Talmud, Tractate Shabbat 133b, in which the standard (Vilna) text reads "heve domeh lo" (be like him). These sources evoke Gen. 1:26–27 in their use of the root *d-m-h*, the basis of the form *demut*.

156. See "On the Creation," in *Philo*, vol. 1, *Loeb Classical Library*, trans. F. H. Colson and G. H. Whitaker (William Heinemann Ltd., 1929), 50–57 (sections 66–71).

157. See John R. Lenz, "Deification of the Philosopher in Classical Greece," in *Partakers of the Divine Nature: The History and Development of Deification in the Christian Traditions*, ed. Michael J. Christensen and Jeffery A. Wittung (Madison, NJ: Fairleigh Dickinson University Press, 2007), 59; Guy G. Stroumsa, *The End of Sacrifice: Religious Transformations in Late Antiquity* (Chicago: University of Chicago Press, 2009), 12.

158. "It is in a fashion a god to him who carries and enshrines it as an object of reverence; for the human mind (*ho anthrōpinos nous*) evidently occupies a position in men precisely

answering to that which the great Ruler (*ho megas hēgemōn*) occupies in all the world. It is invisible while itself seeing all things, and while comprehending the substance of others, it is as to its own substance unperceived." (Text and translation from Colson and Whitaker, "On the Creation," 54–55.) Philo goes on to emphasize the visionary power of the human mind.

159. See *Saadya's Commentary on Genesis*, ed. and trans. M. Zucker, 50–53 [Judeo-Arabic], 252–258 [Hebrew].

160. Cf. Al-Qirqisānī's similar discussion of Gen. 1:26–27 in *Kitāb al-Anwār wal-Marāqib: Code of Karaite Law by Ya'qūb al-Qirqisānī (Second Quarter of the Tenth Century)*, 5 vols., ed. Leon Nemoy (New York: Alexander Kohut Memorial Foundation, 1939), vol. 1, 2.28.12–2.28.13 (176–77); and cf. Wolfson, *Philosophy of the Kalam*, 103.

161. Emphasis mine. For the Judeo-Arabic text, see *Oeuvres Complétes de R. Saadia ben Iosef al-Fayyoûmî*, vol. 1, ed. J. Derenbourg (E. Leroux, 1893), 6.

162. The Arabic term is *khalīfa* (ruler, representative, successor, viceregent); see Qur'ān, *Sūrat al-Baqara* [2], v. 31.

163. Lawrence V. Berman, "The Political Interpretation of the Maxim: The Purpose of Philosophy Is the Imitation of God," *Studia Islamica* 15 (1961): 53–61.

164. *Guide*, 1:1 (Pines, 21–23). On intellectual perfection as the *telos* of human existence, see *Guide*, 3:27 (Pines, 511), and *Guide*, 3:54 (ibid., 635).

165. *Guide*, 1:1 (Pines, 21–23).

166. See Wiesenberg, *Perush rabbenu avraham ben ha-rambam*, 5. Cf. Pines, 21–22; *Dalālat al-ḥā'irīn (sefer moreh nevukhim) le-rabbenu mosheh ben maimon*, ed. Salomon Munk (Yunovits, 1930), 14.

167. "Just as he brought Adam's physical matter into being from the world of elements that was created before him—as He made clear with the statement *and the Lord God formed the human being from the dust of the earth* (Gen. 2:7) —in like manner He brought his form into being from the supernal world [*al-'ālam al-malakūtī*]. [The] only [difference is] that the world of the elements from which his physical matter was brought into being by the decree and will of his Creator is non-rational inanimate being, whereas the angelic world [*'ālam al-malā'ika*] from which his form emanated is rational living being" (Wiesenberg, *Perush rabbenu avraham ben ha-rambam*, 6–7.)

168. For Ibn Sīnā's emphasis of Neoplatonic elements in Peripatetic psychology as a response to internal problems, see Herbert Davidson, *Alfarabi, Avicenna, and Averroes, on Intellect* (Oxford: Oxford University Press, 1992), 47, 80–82. For a broad discussion of Ibn Sīnā's psychology as expressed in distinct literary contexts, see Peter Heath, *Allegory and Philosophy in Avicenna (Ibn Sînâ): With a Translation of the Book of Muḥammad's Ascent to Heaven* (Philadelphia: University of Pennsylvania Press, 1992), 53–79. For Ibn Sīnā's conception of the soul as a simple substance that governs the physical body, see Shams C. Inati, *Ibn Sina's Remarks and Admonitions*, 96–97, 101–2. For his conception of the active intellect as the emanating cause of the soul, see Davidson, *On Intellect*, 76, 94. For a discussion of the possible influence of Al-Ghazālī's *Iḥyā' 'ulūm al-dīn* on Maimonides's *Mishneh torah*, see Steven Harvey, "Alghazali and Maimonides and their Books of Knowledge," in *Be'erot Yitzhak: Studies in Memory of Isadore Twersky*, ed. Jay M. Harris (Cambridge, MA: Harvard University Press, 2005), 99–117.

169. Note in particular his use of Maimonides's terminology (*shakl wa-takhṭīṭ*), as discussed above, in Qafiḥ, *Nūr al-ẓalām*, 25 (Hebrew pagination).

170. See Qafiḥ, *Nūr al-ẓalām*, 24 (Hebrew pagination). For *wāhib al-ṣuwar* as the active intellect, see Davidson, *On Intellect*, 79, 124; Jules L. Janssens, "The Notions of *Wāhib*

al-ṣuwar (Giver of Forms) and *Wāhib al-ʿaql* (Bestower of Intelligence) in Ibn Sīnā," in *Intellect et Imagination dans la Philosophie Médiévale*, ed. Maria Cândida Pacheco and José F. Meirinhos (Turnhout: Brepols, 2006), vol. 1, 551–62.

171. Qafiḥ, *Nūr al-ẓalām*, 24 (Hebrew pagination).

172. See Havazelet, *Midrash ha-ḥefets*, 1:62 (Hebrew pagination).

173. His dualistic interpretation of the verses informs Naḥmanides's reading of the passage. See his commentary ad loc.

174. See above, n. 155. This interpretation is cited by Maimonides, in *Mishneh torah*, "Laws of Dispositions," 1:6. Note his use of the reflexive *u-lehiddamot*.

175. For Maimonides's ethics in general, see Herbert A. Davidson, "The Middle Way in Maimonides' Ethics," *Proceedings of the American Academy for Jewish Research* 54 (1987): 31–72; Raymond L. Weiss, *Maimonides' Ethics: The Encounter of Philosophic and Religious Morality* (Chicago: University of Chicago Press, 1991).

176. Chavel, *Rabbenu baḥya*, 1:45-7.

177. For the parallel in *Midrash ha-neʿelam*, see *Zohar Ḥadash* 6d (for an English translation of which, see Wolski, *Zohar* [vol. 10], 30). Note that Baḥya ascribes this interpretation to other sources: *ve-yesh she-pershu*. Chavel, *Rabbenu baḥya*, 1:45 (Hebrew pagination).

RAPHAEL DASCALU is Adjunct Research Associate at Monash University, Melbourne, Australia. His research is focused primarily on medieval Jewish philosophy and biblical exegesis in the Islamic world.

3

COMMENTARIES ON *THE GUIDE OF THE PERPLEXED*

A Brief Literary History

Igor H. de Souza

Theoretical Considerations

It might seem self-evident that one of the primary functions of a commentary is to explain another text.[1] Maimonides himself pointed to the clarification of textual obscurities as a fundamental task of commentary.[2] Yet applying this notion to commentaries written on the *Guide of the Perplexed* raises critical questions. It assumes, first, that the *Guide* is an unclear text for which explanation is either desirable or necessary. Who or what determines that the *Guide* is unclear? Is its explanation deemed necessary by the author, the commentator, or the reader? It assumes that the *Guide* is a text for which explanation is permissible, if the commentary is to be written at all. Must such permission be granted by the author, or may an exegete self-authorize a commentary? Finally, it implies that there is also some sort of deficiency in the reader and hence a *purpose* for the explanation, such as to inform, to persuade, or to promote group cohesion. Nonetheless, what happens when commentary and text work at cross purposes?

In light of such questions, not all of which can be answered here, this chapter suggests that the phenomenon of commentary on the *Guide* can

I wish to thank Joseph Fischel and the editors of this volume for their comments on earlier versions of this chapter and the Department of Jewish Studies at McGill University for a postdoctoral fellowship that supported this research.

problematize the explanatory function of the genre of commentary. By way of introduction, let us consider a matrix with which to consider these issues, a unique literary feature of the *Guide*: in the preface Maimonides forbids his readers to explain or comment on even a single word from the text. As the author of a popular work puts it, "[Maimonides] wished there to be no courses on the *Guide*, nor any commentaries, articles, or books."[3]

To rethink our initial questions through this matrix, Maimonides's prohibition on commentary implies that the author does not find explanation of the text desirable or necessary—quite the contrary. In the case of the *Guide*, the need or desire for commentary is driven exclusively by commentators and/or readers. In this peculiar way, commentaries on the *Guide* foreshadow the much more recent notion of "death of the author," with its emphasis on the roles of critics and readers in creating meaning.[4] Moreover, the prohibition also implies that commentaries on the *Guide* are exclusively self-authorized, which places great power in the commentator while also absolving the author of much responsibility. The genre of commentary on the *Guide* represents an impulse to disseminate that is absent from the *Guide* and is in contradiction with the wishes of the author.

Maimonides's purposes for the prohibition are not entirely clear. He may have wished to prevent accusations of heresy. Alternatively, the prohibition may have been intended to spur commentary through its proscription.[5] In either case, commentary and *Guide* essentially work at cross purposes. The prohibition serves to keep the audience restricted to isolated individuals, who may not connect with one another through the shared text. A commentary, on the other hand, necessarily widens the audience and connects readers with one another, even if only with the commentator.[6] In the ultimate instance, commentaries on the *Guide* facilitate the formation of communities of learning rather than Maimonides's preferred paradigm of individual learning. Any student of the *Guide* in the premodern West would have been expected to parse the text through its commentary tradition. Within this tradition, students encountered a community of interpretation consisting of successive generations of commentators.

I submit that as a result of the tensions symbolized by the prohibition—individual versus communal study and the obligation to conceal versus the impetus to disseminate—commentaries on the *Guide* challenge the notion that commentaries serve to explain an unclear text. Commentaries on the *Guide* at times subsume explanatory aims under larger ideological goals, such as defending Maimonides against hostile critics or fulfilling a propaedeutic pedagogical function. In the face of Maimonides's ban on interpretation, this solution legitimizes commentary by downplaying the explanatory aspect. Yet another response to these tensions is to transform what it means to "explain." For several commentators discussed in this chapter, esoteric explanation—one that conceals as much as it reveals—proved a happy medium between Maimonides's strictures and the purposes of the genre. This creative compromise directly challenges the notion that the primary function of commentary is to explain. Rather, it shows that commentaries can also convey much by not explaining.

The paragraphs to follow shed light on explained and unexplained aspects of commentaries on the *Guide* through a focus on the *discourse* of the tradition—larger textual issues—rather than on the interpretation of specific subjects. As an example of what I mean by discourse, I shall point out that commentators do not typically comment on the entire text. Rather, they choose specific passages on which to comment. A study of such passages, which contemporary scholars designate as lemma (plural, lemmata), can yield valuable insights. Which lemmata are chosen and the reasons that guide a commentator's choices can tell us much about a given commentator's view of Maimonides, of the *Guide*, and of previous commentators.

I begin with a brief history of the tradition, with attention to the ideological goals and the discourse of the commentaries. Next, I examine two literary features of commentaries that subvert the explanatory aspect of the genre: esoteric writing and the technique of rewriting.

Historical Overview

The vast majority of commentaries on the *Guide* are in Hebrew and rely on the Hebrew translation of the *Guide* by Samuel ibn Tibbon (1204, revised 1213). Ibn Tibbon's text, although generally faithful to the Arabic original, is far more difficult to read than Judah al-Ḥarizi's translation (after 1204). Shem Tov ibn Falaquera (thirteenth century) is the only commentator who makes extensive use of the Judeo-Arabic text. His commentary retranslates lemmata into Hebrew and appends a critique of Ibn Tibbon's translation to the commentary as a whole. Finally, there are a small number of commentaries in Arabic; the most notable example is that by Abu 'Abd Allah al-Tabrizi.[7] However, even in Arabic-speaking communities, scholars tended to read and interpret the *Guide* in the translation of Samuel ibn Tibbon.[8]

The legacy of Ibn Tibbon is prominent among commentaries on the *Guide*, and particularly so for the earliest period (thirteenth to fourteenth century).

The difficulty of his translation provides an initial impetus for the technique of rewriting; the commentators also inherit from him the ideal of Maimonides as an esoteric writer, one who addresses distinct audiences through a multi-layered text.[9] While any translation is necessarily also an interpretation, my purpose here is to consider exegetical works built around segments of the text, in which exegetical tensions manifest themselves more openly.

I will now turn to an analysis of the main exegetical trends under two perspectives: chronological and methodological. For my periodization below, I rely on extant primary sources and on scholarly listings of commentaries, along with secondary sources.[10] Our present knowledge of the commentaries still contains many lacunae. My account is tentative, based on commentaries whose authorship has been identified; there still remain a large number of anonymous commentaries, many of which survive in manuscript fragments.

Chronological Distribution: Five Stages of Commentary

I classify the tradition of commentaries on the *Guide* into five major stages. For the purposes of study, each stage can be identified with a distinct geographic/cultural zone.

First stage: Spain, south of France, and Italy, thirteenth–fourteenth centuries. The earliest reception of the *Guide of the Perplexed* was accompanied by much controversy, except in Italy. Some of the earliest commentaries emerge against this background. Certain authorities tended to hold the study of philosophy in high esteem, which was in turn opposed by others. Both the *Guide* and the study of philosophy were bitterly divisive in Spain and France.[11] In this case, the paradigm of commentary as a text that is written on a foundational or canonical text does not seem to apply.[12]

The commentaries by Moses ben Solomon of Salerno (d. 1279), Zeraḥyah ben Isaac ben She'alti'el Ḥen (d. after 1291), and Hillel ben Samuel of Verona (c.1220–c.1295) are among the earliest to be written in Italy. Elsewhere, the major philosophical commentary of the thirteenth century is by Shem Tov ben Joseph ibn Falaquera (probably Spain, c.1225–c.1295), alongside the kabbalistic commentaries by Abraham Abulafia (1240–after 1291) and the glosses by Joseph ben Abraham Giqatilla (1248–c.1305).[13] In the south of France, the most representative commentaries of this period are those of Joseph ibn Kaspi (c.1279–1340) and Moses of Narbonne (1300–1362). Moses of Narbonne's commentary closes this first stage of the tradition.[14] It immediately found a broader readership than any other early commentary on the *Guide*, and so it makes for a convenient end to this early period.

In my view, this period is the most fluid and creative in the history of commentary on the *Guide*. It charted some future trends as interpreters in later stages freely absorbed and critiqued commentators of this period. In the commentaries of the first stage, a number of motifs recur in interpretation of the *Guide*, such as the notion that the text contains "secrets" (Ibn Kaspi) and the view that the *Guide* should be explained against the background of its philosophical sources (Zeraḥyah Ḥen, Ibn Falaquera). With the exception of Ibn Falaquera, commentators in this stage tend to emphasize the close connection between the *Guide* and scripture, sometimes viewing Maimonides's *Guide* as a key to unlock the deeper meaning of the Bible. These first commentaries on the *Guide* are therefore also indispensable for the study of Jewish biblical commentary after Maimonides.

Second stage: Spain, late fourteenth–fifteenth centuries. The most representative commentaries of this stage are those by Efodi (Profiat Duran, c.1350–c.1415), Asher Crescas (possibly from Provence, first half of fifteenth century), and Shem Tov ben Joseph ibn Shem Tov (fl.1461–1489). These commentaries do not presuppose extensive philosophical knowledge on the part of the reader and tend to explain the letter of the text rather than the implications of problematic passages. The commentators borrow from Ibn Falaquera, Ibn Kaspi, and Moses of Narbonne, often without attribution. Also worthy of note at this stage is the earliest known commentary written in Ashkenaz, by Solomon ben Judah ha-Nasi, who hailed from Provence and wrote the commentary for an Ashkenazi patron.[15]

Third stage: Spain, Italy, and Levant, fifteenth–sixteenth centuries. The most representative commentary of this period is that of Isaac Abarbanel (Spain/Italy, 1437–1508). The commentary is erudite, often citing Ibn Kaspi and Moses of Narbonne, but also disputational. Unlike previous commentators on the *Guide*, Abarbanel was a sharp critic of Maimonides and frequently disagreed with him,[16] while another commentator, David ben Judah Messer Leon (c.1470–c.1535) defended Maimonides against critics. Despite these differences, both commentators seek to defend religion as a repository of certain truths not accessible through philosophical study. They hold that philosophical study has value, although it is inferior to the Torah.[17] Thus it emerges that commentary on the *Guide* in this period was put in the service of theological goals. The commentary by Moses ben Avraham Provençal

(Italy, 1503–1575) further illustrates this trend, defending Aristotelianism as indispensable for theology.[18]

Fourth stage: Ashkenaz, sixteenth–seventeenth centuries. Study of science and philosophy in Ashkenaz never developed to the same extent as it did in Sepharad, but two key figures of the sixteenth century provided an opening for a modest flourishing of philosophical study in general and the *Guide* in particular. The Maharal of Prague (R. Judah Loew ben Bezalel, 1512?–1609) acknowledged the authority of Maimonides and cited the *Guide* when it suited his larger purposes. Rama (R. Moses Isserles, Poland, 1520–1572) permitted the study of philosophy, though only what was contained in the *Guide*.[19]

These attitudes coalesce in the thought of R. Mordekhai Jaffe (Prague, c.1535–1612), who studied under Rama and replaced the Maharal as the rabbi of Prague. Jaffe authored a ten-volume code of Jewish law for rabbinical students, one of which was a commentary on the *Guide* entitled *Levush pinnat yiqrat*. By doing so, he effectively placed study of the *Guide* in his rabbinical curriculum. The commentary represented an important stage in the controlled absorption of rationalist philosophy into Eastern European rabbinical culture.[20] Unsurprisingly, the commentary tends to harmonize Maimonides's positions with rabbinical Judaism. Two other commentators of distinction are Joseph ben Isaac Ha-Levi (c.1580–?) and Yom-Tov Lipmann Heller (1579–1654). Ha-Levi used the *Guide* as a textbook to teach philosophy and wrote a commentary on three subjects (divine existence, incorporeality, and unity) entitled *Giv'at ha-Moreh*. Heller, a student of Ha-Levi, wrote a collection of glosses on his teacher's *Giv'at ha-Moreh*, which may be considered a supercommentary on the *Guide*.

Central to our purposes is the fact that both Jaffe and Ha-Levi cite several earlier commentators on the *Guide*. Jaffe relied heavily on Moses of Narbonne, and he also cites Efodi, Shem Tov, and Asher Crescas, which by his time were available in a printed edition of the *Guide* (1553). Ha-Levi was proficient in post-Maimonidean Jewish philosophy, and he too cites the commentaries of Moses of Narbonne, Efodi, Asher Crescas, Shem Tov, and Moses Provençal.

Moses of Narbonne's commentary circulated indirectly in Ashkenaz through the glosses of R. Menaḥem Shalem in the early 1400s.[21] It was cited by another Ashkenazi authority of early 1400s Prague, Yom Tov Lipmann Mühlhausen, who writes in his *Ha-'Eshkol* that he relied on Maimonides and on two commentators on the *Guide*, Moses of Narbonne and (likely)

Solomon ha-Nasi.[22] Commentaries on the *Guide*, in particular that by Moses of Narbonne, constituted an essential bridge between Sepharad and Ashkenaz for the acceptance and dissemination of philosophical study.

Fifth stage: Ashkenaz, eighteenth–nineteenth centuries. The last stage in the tradition of commentary on the *Guide* stands between the premodern and modern worlds. Within Jewish letters, the genre of commentary, characteristic of medieval scholarship, gives way to other scholarly genres such as journal articles and encyclopedia entries, in the context of the academization of Jewish studies in the Wissenschaft des Judentums movement.[23]

This is not to say that modern Jewish scholarship abandoned study of the *Guide*. Rather, it means that contents and functions fulfilled by medieval commentaries transferred to new formats for organizing scholarly discourse.[24] The process was inevitable and had occurred centuries earlier in relation to Aristotelian and other such canonical texts.[25] Nonetheless, the migration of knowledge from one genre into disparate others brought with it a certain loss, a "sort of forgetfulness." In the case of the *Guide*, it set the stage for Leo Strauss's later rereading of Maimonides.[26] I return to this notion below.

The last formal commentary on the *Guide* stands on its own in originality and significance. Entitled *Giv'at ha-Moreh*, it was composed by the neo-Kantian philosopher Solomon Maimon (1753–1800). It relies heavily on Moses of Narbonne's commentary, and both commentaries were printed together. That edition marked the first printing of Moses of Narbonne's commentary more than four centuries after it was written.[27]

Maimon's commentary brings together the medieval and the nascent modern in Jewish philosophy through a rational understanding of religion and exalts the Haskalah (Jewish Enlightenment) in identifying it with the Maimonidean notion of *shlemut* (perfection). It provides a medieval, "traditional" basis to legitimize pursuit of science and philosophy under markedly different social conditions. Moreover, the commentary develops a notion of the Haskalah that is ideologically continuous with medieval precedent rather than as a Jewish form of German *Bildung*.[28]

It is significant that Maimon's *Giv'at ha-Moreh* was modeled after Moses of Narbonne's commentary. As early as Isaac Abarbanel, the radical nature of Moses of Narbonne's interpretation had been singled out for condemnation, since Moses of Narbonne identifies Maimonides with a naturalistic view of religion, that is, religion as instrumental toward the achievement of perfection, an achievement held dependent on the intellect.[29] Through Maimon's commentary, this view found expression in the Haskalah ideal of the "sovereignty of universal reason over religion" and "mirrored the social promise of the Enlightenment [that Jews] might meet with their Christian counterparts as equals within the public sphere of discourse."[30]

Moses of Narbonne's commentary was viewed as radical in terms of its method as well. The early modern scholar Joseph Delmedigo (Crete, b. 1591) states having seen eighteen commentaries on the *Guide*, "both large and small."[31] He likens Moses of Narbonne to the evil son of the Passover Haggadah.[32] In Delmedigo's view Moses of Narbonne grasped the full extent of the *Guide* more than any other commentator but revealed the secrets of the text indiscriminately, exposing them to the eyes of all readers. The sin of Moses of Narbonne, then, is not to hold radical Averroistic positions, but to communicate them openly.[33] Although it is at odds with Maimonidean esotericism, such an ideal of open communication correlates with the Enlightenment ideal of elevating the intellectual level of the masses through universal education. This view may help explain why early Maskilim found much to appreciate in Moses of Narbonne's and Solomon Maimon's commentaries.

I shall close this subsection with a note on the impact of printing. The editio princeps of the Hebrew *Guide* was probably printed in Italy shortly before 1480.[34] The second edition (Venice, 1551) was published with the commentaries of Efodi and Shem Tov, and the third (Sabbioneta, 1553) added Asher Crescas's commentary to those two.[35] No other editions were produced until 1742 (which included the three commentaries). The first printed editions reaffirmed the study of the commentaries together with the *Guide*, which had become the de facto manner of studying the text. For instance, the curriculum proposed by the philosopher-kabbalist Yohanan Alemanno, written in 1470s Italy, recommends study of the *Guide* with the commentaries of Moses of Narbonne, Ibn Falaquera, Efodi, and "Ibn Kaspi's books."[36] Shem Tov, Efodi, and Abarbanel all draw from Ibn Kaspi as well as Moses of Narbonne. Still, prior to the printed editions of the *Guide*, the commentaries of Ibn Falaquera, Ibn Kaspi, and Moses of Narbonne were cited in the course of a dispute between a philosopher and a kabbalist in fifteenth-century Crete.[37] The *Guide* and some commentaries were assured wider dissemination after the advent of printing. But most unprinted commentaries were forgotten: only Moses of Narbonne's commentary continued to be studied and even acquired something of a canonical status within the tradition. While the printing of the *Guide* preserved some commentaries, it also consigned many others to oblivion.

Methodological Distribution

I identify four dominant strains in the commentary tradition, which occasionally overlap: philosophical, kabbalistic, scientific, and pedagogical.

Philosophical commentaries. Several commentators focus on the philosophical layer of the *Guide*, either in conversation with Maimonides's Greco-Arabic sources, or through confrontation with philosophical sources that Maimonides did not employ. Ibn Falaquera's commentary *Moreh ha-Moreh* embodies both of these tendencies. Not only was Ibn Falaquera a reader of the Judeo-Arabic original of the *Guide*, he was also well-versed in the Greco-Arabic canon. As an illustration of the first tendency, Ibn Falaquera reads Maimonides by retranslating and juxtaposing select lemmata with parallels from inter alia Al-Farabi, Ibn Bajja, and Ibn Sina. As for the second tendency, he sets the *Guide* side by side with Ibn Rushd (who was not a source for Maimonides) and brings out their differences concerning major issues.[38] A major effect of this mode of interpretation is to implicitly inscribe the *Guide* into a preexisting philosophical canon, in this case Greco-Arabic.

A second distinct strategy inscribes the *Guide* into the philosophical canon through an examination of language and philosophical-literary style. This form of philosophical interpretation elucidates the text by identifying it with the perceived conventions of philosophical writing, and in particular with Aristotelian writings. Two examples follow from Moses of Salerno and Joseph ibn Kaspi.

Among the seven causes in Maimonides's method of contradictions, the fifth cause is the occurrence of a contradiction between the introductory sketch of a subject and a subsequent detailed explanation. Moses of Salerno illustrates this point using as an example the contradictions between Aristotle's works on logic versus those on natural science. Moses of Salerno likens the Aristotelian use of contradictions to Maimonides's differing accounts of the *ḥayyot* (the "living creatures" of Ezekiel's Account of the Chariot) between the *Book of Knowledge* and the beginning of part 3 of the *Guide*.[39] The implication is clear: the method of writing in the *Guide* accords with the norms of philosophical writing, and part of the commentator's agenda is to point out to the reader how to approach such works.

Before proceeding to the second example of philosophical interpretation, let me note that Moses of Salerno leaves the Maimonidean contradiction unresolved. According to the text of the fifth cause of contradictions, one disjunct (half) of the contradiction is understood to be a broad introductory sketch of the matter, presented as such for pedagogical purposes, and "afterwards, in the appropriate place, that obscure matter is stated in exact terms and explained as it truly is."[40] Moses of Salerno does not tell the reader which passage constitutes the matter "as it truly is," but I shall suggest an interpretation. First, the terms of the contradiction: Moses of Salerno writes that in the *Book of Knowledge*, Maimonides defined the *ḥayyot* as separate forms and identified them as equivalent to the ten rows of angels. Moses of Salerno points out, "They are separate from matter, that is, not corporeal." In the *Guide*, he reports, Maimonides defines the *ḥayyot* as the stars and their spheres, "which are undoubtedly material, even though their matter is not [identical to] ours."[41] The contradiction, then, turns on whether the *ḥayyot* are incorporeal or material. Now for a possible solution: in the *Book of Knowledge*, Maimonides introduces the notion of angels as beings that lack matter in toto; the *ḥayyot* are one category of angels. In the *Guide*, he identifies the *ḥayyot* with angels as well—and therefore incorporeal—but he also notes that each of the *ḥayyot* has a "wheel" associated with it (*'ofanim*); the *'ofanim* correspond to the spheres. Near the end of *Guide* 3:3, Maimonides further notes that the wheels are described by Ezekiel as having bodies but no form; in other words, they are pure matter.[42] There is, then, no contradiction: ultimately, each of the *ḥayyot* is indeed an incorporeal intellect; each is also associated with a certain kind of matter, all while remaining distinct from each other. This refined exposition is taught by introducing the idea in the *Book of Knowledge* that the *ḥayyot* are incorporeal and building on it in the *Guide*.

A second example of philosophical interpretation of the *Guide* is by Joseph ibn Kaspi. One of his exegetical techniques is to explain the text through reference to the norms of philosophical writing, or as he calls it, the "custom of the philosophers" (*minhag ha-filosofim*). In one passage, Ibn Kaspi points out that each chapter of the *Guide* may deviate from its main subject and veer into other matters, but "in all books of science it has been the custom of the philosophers to do the same, namely, the thread of the discussion deviates from the general and primary intention."[43] In terms of literary style, therefore, the *Guide* conforms to the expectations common to philosophical writing. It is not only a matter of language but also of ideology. Numerous statements throughout Ibn Kaspi's commentaries leave no doubt that he considers Maimonides to be a philosopher and the *Guide* a work of philosophy; in fact, the only one that Jews now possess in their own name, since "Christian thieves have come to our gates and attributed our books of science to themselves."[44] In another passage he writes of Maimonides "and those who are like him, namely, the philosophers,"[45] and in his interpretation of the fifth cause of contradictions, Ibn Kaspi writes that "This [contradiction] is not found in the books of the prophets, only in the books of the philosophers, among which is the *Guide*, praise be to God."[46]

There is a more or less continuous tradition of philosophical study of the *Guide* that originates from the earliest stages in Italy and Spain, through Moses of Narbonne, on to late medieval and early modern commentaries, all the way to Solomon Maimon at the dawn of modernity. Partly because of the structure of the genre, study of the *Guide* through commentary can offer a multifaceted perspective on the text—it captures both language and content. In modernity, with the death of commentary, study of the *Guide* becomes more specialized: the linguistic dimension now belongs to a discipline distinct from philosophical arguments. The work of Leo Strauss addresses this gap. However, I would venture that its novel character is but a reminder of how much was lost when commentary ceased to be a living practice.[47]

Kabbalistic commentaries. In the thirteenth century, boundaries between philosophy and Kabbalah were fluid. The key kabbalist commentator on the *Guide* is Abraham Abulafia (1240–after 1291), who taught the *Guide* throughout the Mediterranean.[48] Together with a set of glosses by Joseph ibn Giqatilla (1248–1325), Abulafia's three commentaries comprise the bulk of kabbalistic formal interpretation of the *Guide*. Abulafia internalizes several aspects of the *Guide*: for instance, its "philosophy of nature," along with "neo-Aristotelian metaphysics," and more importantly, Maimonides's psychology. On the basis of the latter, Abulafia builds a system focused on spiritualization of Maimonidean concepts and attainment of the mystical experience.[49] An example is Abulafia's reinterpretation of the notion of "secret" (which is also recurrent in philosophical commentaries) as integral to the process of redemption, both national and personal.[50] Indeed, the first commentary on the *Guide* by Abulafia is entitled *Sefer Ge'ulah* (Book of redemption).

Scientific commentaries. By *scientific commentaries* I refer to those that focus on natural science and physics. Two main trends developed.

The first were commentaries that dealt exclusively with the preface to part 2 of the *Guide*.[51] There Maimonides lists the twenty-five ground principles of Aristotelian physics, "All of which are demonstrated without there being a doubt as to any point concerning them," and to which he adds a twenty-sixth.[52] The preface became known by the shorthand *haqdamot* (premises) in Maimonidean literature. The second development consists of a group of commentaries on *Guide* 1:72.[53]

Commentaries on the *haqdamot* proliferated. Among the earliest commentaries on the *Guide* is a commentary on the *haqdamot* by Abu ʿAbd Allah al-Tabrizi. Little is known regarding the author's life other than that he was a thirteenth-century Persian Muslim scholar. Al-Tabrizi's commentary became an oft-cited source for other commentators on its translation into Hebrew in 1347; an anonymous translation followed.[54] Al-Tabrizi was one of the main sources for Ḥasdai Crescas's *Light of the Lord*; Crescas also cites the commentary by Moses of Narbonne. Other key commentaries on the *haqdamot* are those by Hillel of Verona and Moses Provençal.

Pedagogical commentaries. Certain commentaries reflect the teaching of the *Guide* in a pedagogical environment. In the preface to his commentary, Zeraḥyah Ḥen (d. after 1291) writes that his intended audience is made up of two groups: the first are those who already have some knowledge of the *Guide*, while the second are complete beginners.[55] These two audiences may correspond to Zeraḥyah's introductory and advanced classes on the *Guide*, which he taught at a yeshivah in Rome. It is possible that the commentary was culled from his lecture notes.[56]

The commentaries by Asher Crescas and Mordekhai Jaffe directly advance a utilitarian pedagogical purpose. Crescas writes that he has seen many people pursue study of the *Guide* while lacking in the required preliminary sciences, which he considers a dangerous situation.[57] For this reason, he informs us, he decided to compose a commentary that explains select passages from the *Guide* for the benefit of young students (*rakhei ha-shanim*), and he will deliberately not explain the full depth of the text.[58] Mordekhai Jaffe directs his commentary to a specific student audience: "Even though there are a number of printed commentaries I have supplemented them a bit in accordance with the needs of the inquiring rabbinical student."[59] While he relies on the philosophical commentaries printed with the Sabbioneta edition of the *Guide* and on Moses of Narbonne, the needs and interests of his nonphilosophical audience determine Jaffe's explanations. His interpretation therefore remains at a somewhat introductory level.[60]

It bears repeating that more than one of the four purposes—philosophical, kabbalist, scientific, and pedagogical—can be found in the same commentary. Joseph ibn Kaspi's *Pillars of Silver* (*'Ammudei kesef*), for example, is both philosophical and pedagogical, as is Zeraḥyah Ḥen's commentary. Longer commentaries sometimes include commentary on the "scientific" *haqdamot*. In the same vein, Moses of Salerno's philosophical commentary elaborates pedagogically on the logical background necessary to understand the notion of equivocality in the beginning of the preface to the *Guide*. The commentaries also serve purposes connected with their historical and social contexts, such as polemical and apologetic; and some commentators, such as Jaffe or Abarbanel, emphasize the rabbinical layer of the text over or alongside the philosophical.

Literary Features

The foregoing discussion shows that the tradition of commentary on the *Guide* is highly heterogeneous. It spans several centuries, travels across places and cultures, and advances a variety of purposes and methodologies. Nonetheless, certain literary features can be found in a number of commentaries. I focus below on two techniques, esotericism and rewriting, that hold special literary valence. Both respond to problems inherent in the text, which Tzvetan Todorov terms "textual indices." Such indices serve to mark textual status and to stimulate particular forms of reading. Syntagmatic indices are established on the basis of the relationship between a given segment (lemma) and other segments of the same context, whereas paradigmatic indices originate in the confrontation between the text and the "collective memory" of a society. Textual contradictions and tautologies are examples of syntagmatic indices, while paradigmatic indices are found where the text is grammatically incomprehensible, challenges common knowledge, or breaks with social values.[61]

One prominent textual indice employed within the *Guide* is the presence of textual contradictions, a syntagmatic device that stimulates esoteric reading and writing. Another textual indice is the practice of textual rewriting as a response to grammatical difficulties, which is paradigmatic. While the discussion below mentions these two indices, I will also elaborate on other textual indices that straddle the border between syntagmatic and paradigmatic. In the case of esotericism, the indice is Maimonides's request not to comment on the text. In the case of rewriting, the indice is the selection and rewriting of lemmata for the purpose of transmitting to the reader a certain image of Maimonides.

Esotericism

From the perspective of most commentators, there is an acknowledgment that, at a minimum, passages of the *Guide* may contain hidden meanings, or that some scriptural passages quoted in the *Guide* contain hidden Maimonidean meanings.[62] This does not mean that the commentary will expose these concealed layers. Nonetheless, the premise of the *Guide*'s esotericism renders the practice of commentary on the text into an exercise in exegetical self-awareness and self-restraint.

Let me focus on a tangible aspect of commentary esotericism discussed earlier. I return here to the passage of the *Guide* in which Maimonides asks his readers not to explain the text (the "injunction"). Several commentators claim that a commentary that does not reveal all, or one that focuses on only one aspect of the text, does not breach Maimonides's "fence" around interpretation. I give two examples: Hillel of Verona and Joseph ibn Kaspi.

In his preface, Hillel of Verona gives several reasons why his commentary does not transgress the injunction. He states that he will only focus on the letter of the text (*nusḥah*) and will not interpret Maimonides's intentions behind it (*kavvanah*). Regarding the latter he adds that an "educated individual" (*'ish maskil*) who is familiar with the chapters that follow the *haqdamot* does not need a commentary. Furthermore, Hillel adds, his commentary does not break the injunction because he will comment only on what Maimonides has borrowed from Aristotle, which is restated in the *Guide* "in a particular sequence, and with the addition and omission of some words." This statement builds on the notion of *kavvanah*, Maimonidean intention: it implies that there is a concealed purpose for stating Aristotle's premises in a certain order, for adding some details, and for leaving others out. Last, Hillel of Verona promises to transmit his interpretation through "chapter headings" (*rashei peraqim*), according to his "limited ability" and in an "abbreviated manner."[63]

In light of these statements, we can conclude that Hillel of Verona not only reads the text esoterically—in the sense that it contains a concealed meaning—but that he also writes esoterically. He will restrict the commentary to the surface layer of the text only, concealing deeper notions, and even this layer may be explained only through chapter headings, one of the techniques of esoteric writing that Maimonides employs in the *Guide*. His mention of interpretation in an "abbreviated manner" parallels Maimonides's statement in the *Guide* that the reader should not expect a "complete exposition" of any subject.[64] The esoteric writing of the commentary is explicitly modeled after the esoteric writing of the *Guide*.

A second commentator of the *Guide*, Joseph ibn Kaspi, is well-known for having written both an "exoteric" commentary (*'Ammudei kesef*, Pillars of silver) as well as an "esoteric" commentary (*Maskiyot kesef*, Settings of silver).[65] With respect to the injunction, he gives four reasons why his commentary does not breach it; two are of special interest.[66] The first is Ibn Kaspi's claim that Maimonides himself permitted "a few" of the secrets to be revealed and that Maimonides permits "a few" because there is no defined measurement (*shi'ur mugbal*) of what constitutes "a few." Ibn Kaspi's implication is that Maimonides esoterically permitted commentators to define for themselves what constitutes "a few." A second reason is that Ibn Kaspi claims he will only transmit, translate, or compile (*he'etiq*) the "words of the philosophers" such as Aristotle, who explain these matters in their books.

Ibn Kaspi's first defense for clearing the injunction is that, in his view, Maimonides gives the commentator much discretion in interpretation because there is no objective definition to how much can be revealed. Obviously, a commentator may not reveal everything. While one may reveal "a few," it is still necessary to conceal the remainder. Hence it is necessary to write esoterically. Ibn Kaspi does not spell out the methods of esoteric writing in this passage, but elsewhere he points to the method of employing purposeful contradictions as common to both Maimonides and the philosophers. He describes that method as a "procedure among prophets and wise individuals that allows them to find a concealed place [*maqom ṣanua'*] in which to hide their secrets."[67] It is not surprising, then, that Ibn Kaspi's own works are rife with contradictions.

Ibn Kaspi's second defense for clearing the injunction parallels Hillel of Verona's claim that he will explain only what Maimonides has borrowed from Aristotle. Unlike Hillel, who comments only on the *haqdamot*, Ibn Kaspi does not limit himself to the Aristotelian layer of the *Guide*, despite his claim to do so. This claim, therefore, should not be read literally, but rather as self-authorization to explain certain parts of the *Guide* only. There is a certain common thread between Ibn Kaspi's two defenses of his commentary as explanation that is limited in scope and by source. In both cases, the commentator must determine what constitutes "a few" and what is or is not presumably borrowed from Aristotle: not only how deep to conceal or to reveal but also which passages should be considered at all. Ibn Kaspi thus authorizes himself greater exegetical freedom than Hillel of Verona. Even so, he employs esoteric writing to interpret the *Guide*.

For later commentators, the injunction seems not to pose a cognitive problem and is mentioned infrequently. One possible reason is that earlier commentators had repeatedly breached it. There is a corresponding decrease in esoteric interpretation, although later interpreters still express the idea that the *Guide* is an esoteric work.[68]

Some have argued that Maimonides composed the *Guide* with the foresight that it would breed controversy. According to this line of thinking, he also equipped his supporters with the textual weapons they would need by writing esoterically. This means the text would then be inherently capable of opposite readings, namely, as a radical philosophy as well as a defense of traditional Judaism.[69] If this insight is correct, the eclecticism of the tradition of commentaries is evidence that the esotericism of the *Guide* generated multiple views of Maimonides even within the circle of his supporters. Furthermore, esoteric commentary on the *Guide* becomes a way not to resolve the tension engendered by the esoteric text but rather to reproduce it.

Rewriting

Rewriting important texts was a common medieval practice. This practice applied particularly to philosophical texts. By rewriting I mean reworking a text into a genre distinct from the one in which it was originally composed. Such rewritten genres include inter alia abridgments, encyclopedias, or commentaries. Pragmatic factors that motivate the practice of rewriting include material ones, such as the costs of producing a full manuscript of the source, or the possibility that certain ideas in the source might arouse opposition. Similarly, several introductory texts might be gathered into a textual unit to acquire quick mastery of a large volume of philosophical literature. For advanced students, the difficult parts of a text might be rewritten into a selective commentary or a paraphrase.[70]

The commentaries on the *Guide* also constitute a form of rewriting. The practice manifests itself in one of two ways. First, commentators often chose to comment only on a select set of lemmata rather than the entire text, thereby producing a picture of Maimonides that conforms to the exegete's agenda. Two examples are Ibn Falaquera and Jaffe, whose selection of lemmata imply distinct portrayals of Maimonides. The lemmata in Ibn Falaquera's *Moreh ha-Moreh* deal mostly with psychology, metaphysics, physics, the spheres, and human perfection. Relatively few discuss logic, *ma'aseh merkavah*, or prophecy.[71] Ibn Falaquera's Maimonides, then, is a scientist-metaphysician in the mold of Ibn Rushd. Mordekhai Jaffe's commentary, on the other hand, does not delve into the hidden meanings of the text or its naturalistic allusions.[72] Rather, it presents Maimonides as a conservative thinker whose positions parallel those of rabbinical Judaism. The commentary may be seen as a traditionalist reaction against earlier "radical" commentaries (and thus a form of rewriting of earlier commentators as well).[73] For example, in the discussion on creation, Jaffe takes pains to distance Maimonides from Aristotle and to build a case for Maimonidean creation in time.[74] He does not avoid passages that relate to logic:[75] Jaffe's Maimonides, while traditional, does not shun the sciences entirely, but their role is ancillary. From a formal perspective, in this first form of rewriting the commentator works by selecting passages as they are rather than modifying them.

Second, we encounter a form of rewriting that manipulates the text. Rather than the lemma/interpretation binary, this rewriting blurs the boundaries between the two. In this form, some commentators modify the diction of the *Guide*, in many cases as a response to the syntactical difficulties of the Hebrew version of Samuel ibn Tibbon. They might interpolate their own words into sentences, substitute terms for their synonyms, or rephrase awkward syntactical constructions, while omitting the conventional Hebrew markers that separate text from commentary, for example, "this means . . . ," or "in other words." The final text becomes a hybrid product of Maimonides, Samuel ibn Tibbon, and the commentator's own individual reading.

In my view, the rewritten text of the commentaries subverts the explanatory aspect of the genre. For the first form of rewriting, the judicious selection of lemmata betrays a desire to impose a certain image of Maimonides and the *Guide*; explanation is secondary to and dependent on the choice of lemmata. The explanation of (only) such passages adds further legitimacy to the constructed image. For the second form, rewriting as manipulation of the text mimics translation: it provides an interpreted text rather than an explained text. It smooths out textual difficulties, but not through explanation. As in esoteric writing, rewriting constitutes a multilevel form of writing. Expert readers might gather that the text as given has been rewritten, while casual readers might accept the rewritten text as a verbatim lemma.

Let us now consider an example from Moses of Salerno. It contains two parts. First, a passage of the *Guide* rewritten by the commentator. Moses of Salerno's interpretation then follows this lemma, set off by the marker "Maimonides means by this" [*roṣeh ba-zeh*]. I give first the original passage from the *Guide* so that readers may compare it with the changes made by the commentator.

> *Guide*, preface:
> I do not think that anyone possessing an unimpaired capacity imagines that the words of the Torah referred to here that one contrives, through understanding them, to understand the meaning of the parables, are ordinances concerning the building of tabernacles, the lulav, and the law of four trustees, and all that is similar to them.[76] Rather what this text has in view here is the understanding of obscure matters without any doubt.[77]
>
> *Guide*, preface (Ibn Tibbon):
> ואיני רואה שאחד משלמי הדעות יחשב, כי דברי תורה הרמוז אליהם הנה, אשר הערים בהבנתם משפטי עשיית סכה ולולב ודין ארבעה שומרים וכל הדומה להם; אבל—בהבין עניני המשלים, הם הבנת העמוקות והסתומות, בלא ספק[78]—הכונה היא

Now for Moses of Salerno's commentary. Italics reflect words borrowed from the *Guide*; normal font, the commentator's words:

ואיני רואה שאחד משלימי הדעת יחשוב כי דברי תורה הרמוז אליהם הנה אשר הערים שלמה ע"ה *בהבנתם*,
העמיק[79] *להבין ענייני המשלים* שלהם *הם משפטי עשיַת הסוכה והלולב ודין ארבעה שומרים* כי אילו [צ"ל אלו]
מכח הקבלה נודעו. *אבל הכוונה* הוא הדבר העמוק *בלא ספק.*
רוצה בזה הבנת סודות התורה וסדר משליה שהם מעשה המרכבה ובכללם מעשה בראשית אשר בהם העמיק
ויוצא לאור תעלומותיהן וידע מהן מה שלא ידעו הראשונים שלפניו.[80]

> *I do not think that anyone possessing an unimpaired capacity imagines that the words of the Torah referred to here that* Solomon, may he rest in peace *contrives, through understanding them, to understand* in depth *the meaning of* their *parables, are ordinances concerning the building of tabernacles, the lulab, and the law of four trustees* since these are known by virtue of tradition. *Rather what this text has in view here is* the deep subject *without any doubt.*
>
> He [Maimonides] means by this the understanding of the secrets of the Torah and the sequence of its parables, which are "ma'aseh merkavah" and among them is "ma'aseh bereshit," which he[81] investigated in depth and brings to light their obscurities, and he knew from them that which the ancient [authorities] who preceded him did not know.[82]

Moses of Salerno makes several changes to the text, some of which are syntactical whereas others are substantive. He adds a subject (Solomon); a verb, translated as "in depth" (literally, to understand in depth); and a possessive adverb to clarify that "parables" refers to "words of Torah." He substitutes

Ibn Tibbon's addition "and all that is similar to them" for "since these are known by virtue of tradition." Finally, he substitutes "obscure matters" (*he-ʿamuqot ve-ha-setumot*; "things that are deep and things that are hidden") for "the deep subject" (*ha-davar he-ʿamoq*). The two final substitutions may have been made under the influence of Judah al-Ḥarizi's translation of the *Guide*, with which Moses of Salerno was familiar. In the last sentence of the passage, Al-Ḥarizi's translation has only "the deep" (*he-ʿamoq*; the subject is left out), which Moses of Salerno rewrites as "the deep subject." Finally, the marker "He means by this" implies that what preceded were Maimonides's own words, and what is to follow is the commentary. Thus Moses of Salerno rewrites the text while presenting it as a quotation.[83]

This second process of rewriting, corresponding to textual manipulation, reflects a certain fluidity around the text that is lost as it becomes semicanonical for later generations of commentators. Already in the commentaries by Efodi, Shem Tov, and Asher Crescas, we see a sharper boundary between text and commentary, with more frequent use of expressions that delimit one from the other: "the interpretation is" (*perush*); "another interpretation" (*perush ʾaḥer*); "the intention here is" (*ha-raṣon ba-zeh*). Their use of rewriting is more limited in comparison with the first stage of commentary.[84] The textual fluidity and manipulation of early commentaries does not disappear entirely, but it is replaced with an acceptance of the text as received.

The fact that later commentators do not rewrite the text to the same extent may be due to the labor of early commentators in dispelling doubts in Ibn Tibbon's syntax. Later interpreters could be free to focus on other aspects of the text, such as philosophical or theological implications. This trend is already visible in Ibn Kaspi and Moses of Narbonne, who nevertheless still practice rewriting. By the sixteenth century, syntactical problems had been addressed in earlier commentators, the semicanonical status of the *Guide* had become a reality in many quarters, and the text had been printed—factors that militate against the need to reinterpret through rewriting.

The two techniques outlined here, esoteric writing and rewriting, are initially motivated by intertextual difficulties: Maimonides's injunction, his writing style, and the difficulties of the Hebrew version of Samuel ibn Tibbon. Together they suggest that in the early stage of commentary the *Guide* is not yet canonical. Hence the letter of the text can be disobeyed and the injunction can be breached; the text itself can be modified and rewritten.

The freewheeling attitude toward the text is attenuated in later commentaries, in which the text has become semicanonical, with a corresponding emphasis on the boundary between text and commentary.

Conclusion

Maimonides's injunction proscribing commentary was prominently breached by those among his most conscientious and loyal followers. It may be that the cultural efficacy of the practice of commentary outweighed scruples about following the letter of Maimonides's request. As I outlined earlier, the *Guide* and its commentaries work at opposite purposes: individual versus community, restriction versus dissemination. Commentaries on the *Guide* are indispensable conduits through which "Maimonidean" becomes "Maimonideanist," and through which the *Guide* becomes a central text for a wide range of intellectual communities.[85]

The desire to break with the injunction is therefore comprehensible. But it carries its own risks: it can undermine the authority of the author and facilitate the circulation of flawed interpretations. Hence the genre of commentary on the *Guide* is characterized by inherent tension between following the injunction and breaking it, between concealment and revelation. The tension is most visible in the earliest commentaries: while they lack formal and conceptual models, later commentators could rely on the precedent of the injunction having been already repeatedly breached. Nonetheless, I would maintain that it is only in the modern era that all scruples concerning interpretation and transmission of the *Guide* have been completely abandoned. Most premodern commentaries contain statements on esoteric circumspection concerning interpretation or transmission.[86] Esoteric transmission became a way to minimize the risks brought about by transgression of the injunction.

With transmission, we return full circle to the opening idea: the view that commentaries are meant to explain a text that is presumably unclear. Commentaries on the *Guide* certainly contain much in the way of explanation. But they also subsume explanation to other goals and transform what it means to explain another text. Ultimately, the history of commentary on the *Guide* invites us to think of commentary as more than a vehicle of textual explanation. Rather, it becomes a multidimensional cultural practice encapsulating competing agendas but efficient in the construction of text-centered communities.

Notes

1. Cf. the assertion that "even the most creative and mystical commentator, after all, would presumably maintain that he or she is striving to make the text with which he is concerned more clear to the reader." John Dillon, "Some Thoughts on the Commentary," in *The Commentary Hermeneutically Considered: Four Position Papers*, ed. Edward C. Hobbs (Berkeley, CA: Center for Hermeneutical Studies in Hellenistic and Modern Culture, 1978), 16.

2. Carsten Schliwski, "Moses Ben Maimon, Šarḥ fuṣūl Abuqrāṭ: Der Kommentar des Maimonides zu den Aphorismen des Hippokrates. Kritische Edition des arabischen Textes mit Einführung und Übersetzung" (PhD diss., Cologne University, 2004), 1–3 [Hebrew-Arabic], 165–166 [German]. The necessity for commentary to dispel textual unclarity (*asatheia*) has a long history in late-ancient interpretation of Aristotle and in Galen (Maimonides's source for his commentary). Cf. Jaap Mansfeld, *Prolegomena: Questions to Be Settled before the Study of an Author, or a Text* (Leiden: Brill, 1994), 8, 26, 135.

3. Micah Goodman, *Maimonides and the Book That Changed Judaism: Secrets of the "Guide of the Perplexed"* (Lincoln: University of Nebraska Press, 2015), xix.

4. See "Introduction: Reading Commentaries/Commentaries as Reading," in *Classical Commentary: Histories, Practices, Theory*, ed. Christina Shuttleworth Kraus (Leiden: Brill, 2002), 6–7.

5. The prohibition cannot be traced to any one literary model, whether philosophical prooemia or prefaces to biblical commentaries; this strongly suggests that Maimonides had a specific purpose in mind.

6. As a reflection of this distinction, the *Guide*'s idealized setting is a conversation between two individuals, Maimonides and his student, whereas commentary traditions tend to originate within contexts that bring together students in groups. Cf. Barry Smith, "Textual Deference," *American Philosophical Quarterly* 28 (1991): 6–7; Sten Ebbensen, "Medieval Latin Glosses and Commentaries on Aristotelian Logical Texts of the Twelfth and Thirteenth Centuries," in *Glosses and Commentaries on Aristotelian Logical Texts: The Syriac, Arabic, and Medieval Latin Traditions*, ed. Charles Burnett (London: Warburg Institute, 1993), 130–31.

7. Discussed later in the text. See "Scientific commentaries."

8. Y. Tzvi Langermann, "Study and Commentary on 'The Guide of the Perplexed' in Arabic-Speaking Jewish Communities," in *Tribute to Michael: Studies in Jewish and Muslim Thought Presented to Professor Michael Schwarz*, ed. Sara Klein-Braslavy et al. (Tel-Aviv: Lester and Sally Entin Faculty of Humanities, 2009), 67–90 [Hebrew].

9. Aviezer Ravitzky, *History and Faith: Studies in Jewish Philosophy* (Amsterdam: J. C. Gieben, 1996), 205–303.

10. Moritz Steinschneider, "Die hebräischen Commentare zum 'Führer' des Maimonides, in *Festschrift zum siebzigsten Geburtstage A. Berliner's*, ed. A. Freimann and M. Hildesheimer (Frankfurt: J. Kauffman, 1903), 345–63; Israel J. Dienstag, "The Guide of the Perplexed by Maimonides: A Bibliography of Commentaries and Glosses," in *Gevurot ha-Romaḥ*, ed. Ze'ev Falk (Jerusalem: Mesharim, 1987), 207–37 [Hebrew]. These are seminal studies, but they include genres other than commentary. See also Moritz Steinschneider, *Die hebräischen Übersetzungen des Mittelalters und die Juden als Dolmetscher* (Berlin: Kommissionsverlag des Bibliographischen Bureaus, 1893), 423–26, 433–34.

11. See Moshe Halbertal, *Between Torah and Wisdom: Rabbi Menaḥem ha-Meiri and the Maimonidean Halakhists of Provence* (Jerusalem: Magnes Press, 2000) [Hebrew]; and Bernard Septimus, *Hispano-Jewish Culture in Transition: The Career and Controversies of Ramah* (Cambridge, MA: Harvard University Press, 1982).

12. Jan Assmann, "Introduction," in *Text und Kommentar: Archäologie der literarischen Kommunikation IV*, ed. Jan Assmann and Burkhard Gladigow (Munich: Wilhelm Fink, 1995), 1–33.

13. On Moses of Salerno, see Giuseppe Sermoneta, *Un glossario filosofico ebraico-italiano del XIII secolo* (Rome: Edizioni dell'Ateneo, 1969); on Zeraḥyah, see Aviezer Ravitzky, "The Thought of R. Zerahiah b. Isaac b. Shealtiel Hen & the Maimonidean-Tibbonian Philosophy in the 13th Century" (PhD diss., Hebrew University, 1977) [Hebrew]; on Hillel of Verona, see *Über die Vollendung der Seele*, trans. Yossef Schwartz (Freiburg: Herder, 2009), 9–45; on Ibn Falaquera, see Yair Shiffman, "Shem Tob ibn Falqerah [*sic*] as Interpreter of Maimonides' *Guide of the Perplexed*—Outlines of His Thought," *Maimonidean Studies* 3 (1992–1993), 1–29 [Hebrew section]; on Abulafia and Giqatilla, see Moshe Idel, "Maimonides' *Guide of the Perplexed* and the Kabbalah," *Jewish History* 18 (2004).

14. In light of the broad and continuous dissemination of the commentary, I will return to it within stages two to five that follow.

15. Michael Z. Nehorai, "Rabbi Solomon ben Judah Hanasi and His Commentary on the *Guide of the Perplexed*" (PhD diss., Hebrew University, 1978) [Hebrew]. Hanasi relies on Al-Farabi and Ibn Sina in an original manner unlike either the Sephardic-Provençal or Italian philosophical schools. Nehorai, "Rabbi Solomon," 10–11.

16. There are contrasting views of Abarbanel's attitude toward the *Guide* and the commentaries. Cf. Leo Strauss, "On Abravanel's Philosophical Tendency and Political Teaching," in Green, *Leo Strauss*, 579–613, and Eric Lawee, "'The Good We Accept and the Bad We Do Not': Aspects of Isaac Abarbanel's Stance Towards Maimonides," in *Be'erot Yitzhak: Studies in Memory of Isadore Twersky*, ed. Jay M. Harris (Cambridge, MA: Harvard University Press, 2005), 119–60.

17. Hava Tirosh-Rothschild, *Between Worlds: The Life and Thought of Rabbi David ben Judah Messer Leon* (Albany: State University of New York Press, 1991), 90–98; Eric Lawee, *Isaac Abarbanel's Stance Toward Tradition: Defense, Dissent, and Dialogue* (Albany: State University of New York Press, 2001), 33–34, 55–57, 207–10.

18. Reuven Bonfil, "The Commentary of R. Moses Provençalo on Rambam's Twenty-Five Premises," *Qiryat sefer* 50 (1974/1975): 157 [Hebrew].

19. Leonard Levin, *Seeing with Both Eyes: Ephraim Luntshitz and the Polish-Jewish Renaissance* (Leiden: Brill, 2008), 28–29.

20. Lawrence J. Kaplan, "Rationalism and Rabbinic Culture in Sixteenth-Century Eastern Europe: Rabbi Mordecai Jaffe's 'Levush Pinat Yikrat'" (PhD diss., Harvard University, 1975), 348.

21. Kaplan, "Rationalism," 143.

22. Judah Kaufman, "Rabbi Yom Tov Lipmann Mühlhausen, the Apologete, Cabbalist and Philosophical Writer and His Books *Haeshkol* and *Kawwanath hatefilah*" (PhD diss., Dropsie College, 1919), 127, 145 [Hebrew].

23. On the death of commentary in modernity, see John B. Henderson, *Scripture, Canon, and Commentary: A Comparison of Confucian and Western Exegesis* (Princeton, NJ: Princeton University Press, 1991), 200–24.

24. Stefano Perfetti, "How and When the Medieval Commentary Died Out: The Case of Aristotle's Zoological Writings," in *Il commento filosofico nell'Occidente Latino (secoli XIII–XV)*, ed. Gianfranco Fioravanti et al. (Turnhout: Brepols, 2002), 440.

25. Ibid.

26. *Leo Strauss on Maimonides: The Complete Writings*, ed. Kenneth Hart Green (Chicago: University of Chicago Press, 2013), 44.

27. *Giv'at ha-Moreh* (Berlin, 1791), ed. Shmuel Hugo Bergman and Nathan Rotenstreich (Jerusalem: National Academy of Sciences, 1965, reprint 2000).

28. Abraham Socher, *The Radical Enlightenment of Solomon Maimon: Judaism, Heresy, and Philosophy* (Palo Alto, CA: Stanford University Press, 2006), 83.

29. For Moses of Narbonne the value of the Torah is predominantly ethical and political. *Be'ur le-sefer Moreh Nevukhim*, ed. Jacob Goldenthal (Vienna: K. K. Hof- und Staatsdruckerei, 1852), 2. For an account of Abarbanel's treatment of Moses of Narbonne, see Maurice-Ruben Hayoun, *Moshe Narboni* (Tübingen: J. C. B. Mohr, 1986), 98–108.

30. Socher, *Radical Enlightenment*, 82. Cf. the remarks by Maimon's editor, Isaac Euchel, in ibid., 81.

31. Joseph Delmedigo, "Mikhtav 'aḥuz," in *Melo Chofnajim*, ed. Abraham Geiger (Berlin: L. Fernbach, 1840), 18 [Hebrew], 23–24 [German].

32. *Melo Chofnajim*, ibid.

33. However, Socher proposes that Delmedigo's designation of *rasha'* was "probably meant as a compliment." *Radical Enlightenment*, 81.

34. Steinschneider, *Hebräischen Übersetzungen*, 423.

35. Venice: ed. Moses ben Zekhariah Ha-Kohen of Corfu, printed Alvise Bragadin, 1551. Sabbioneta: Cornelius Adelkind supervised for printer Tobias Foa, 1553.

36. Moshe Idel, *Kabbalah in Italy, 1280–1510: A Survey* (New Haven, CT: Yale University Press, 2011), 342.

37. Aviezer Ravitzky, "The God of the Philosophers versus the God of the Kabbalists: A Controversy in 15th-Century Crete (MS. Vatican Heb. 105 and 254)," in *Studies in Jewish Manuscripts*, ed. Joseph Dan and Klaus Herrman (Tübingen: J. C. B. Mohr, 1999), 139–70.

38. Yair Shiffman, ed., *Moreh ha-Moreh* (Jerusalem: World Union of Jewish Studies), 78–79.

39. For the text of the passage in Moses of Salerno, see my "Philosophical Commentaries on the Preface to the *Guide of the Perplexed*, c.1250–1362" (PhD diss., University of Chicago, 2014), 350–51 [English], 496–97 [Hebrew], and my *Rewriting Maimonides: Early Commentaries on the "Guide of the Perplexed"* (Berlin, Boston: De Gruyter, 2018). Moses of Salerno is contrasting here *Guide* 3:2–4 and *Hilkhot yesodei ha-Torah* 2:3, 7. See *The Guide of the Perplexed*, trans. Shlomo Pines (Chicago: University of Chicago Press, 1963), 417–25 [henceforth *Pines*]; *Sefer ha-Madda'*, ed. Samuel Rabinovitch (Jerusalem: Mossad Harav Kook, 1993), 10, 11.

40. Pines, *The Guide of the Perplexed*, 18.

41. De Souza, "Philosophical Commentaries," 351.

42. *Guide* 3:3, *Pines*, 423. Readers of the *Guide* may remember that 1:76 states that matter is an equivocal term with reference to the sublunary existents and the spheres (Pines, 228).

43. In *'Ammudei kesef*; for the text, see De Souza, "Philosophical Commentaries," 432 [English], 525 [Hebrew]; and *'Ammudei kesef u-maskyiot kesef*, ed. Solomon Werbluner (Frankfurt: Jakob Friedrich Bach, 1848), 5–6. The context of the passage suggests that the problem of determining the "primary intention" of a chapter was a polemical matter among students of the *Guide* in fourteenth-century Provence.

44. In the preface to *'Ammudei kesef*; for the text, see De Souza, "Philosophical Commentaries," 412–13 [English], 520 [Hebrew]; Werbluner, *'Ammudei kesef*, 1. The reference here is to a myth that circulated among Jews, Christians, and Muslims, according to which philosophy arose among the Jews before being cultivated (or stolen) by the Greeks. The myth recurs throughout philosophical commentaries on the *Guide*. For a comprehensive history, see Abraham Melammed, *The Myth of the Jewish Origins of Science and Philosophy* (Jerusalem: Magnes Press, 2010) [Hebrew].

45. *'Ammudei kesef*, in De Souza, "Philosophical Commentaries," 424 [English], 523 [Hebrew]; Werbluner, *'Ammudei kesef*, 4.

46. *Maskiyot kesef*, in De Souza, "Philosophical Commentaries," 446 [English], 533 [Hebrew]; Werbluner, *'Ammudei kesef*, 9.

47. See most recently Alfred Ivry, *Maimonides' "Guide of the Perplexed": A Philosophical Guide* (Chicago: University of Chicago Press, 2016).

48. Idel, "Maimonides' *Guide*," 206.

49. Moshe Idel, "Abulafia's Secrets of the *Guide*: A Linguistic Turn," *Revue de Métaphysique et de Morale* 103 (1998), 501.

50. Idel, "Abulafia's Secrets," 500.

51. Pines, *Guide of the Perplexed*, 235–41.

52. Pines, *Guide of the Perplexed*, 235.

53. On these commentaries, see Gad Freudenthal, "Maimonides' *Guide of the Perplexed* and the Transmission of the Mathematical Tract 'On Two Asymptotic Lines' in the Arabic, Latin, and Hebrew Medieval Traditions," in *Maimonides and the Sciences*, ed. R. S. Cohen and H. Levine (Dordrecht: Kluwer, 2000), 35–56.

54. See text in Maurice Ruben-Hayoun, "Moses Maimonides und Muhammad al-Tabrisi," *Trumah* 5 (1996): 201–45; and Harry A. Wolfson, *Crescas's Critique of Aristotle* (Cambridge, MA: Harvard University Press, 1929), 19–21.

55. See text in De Souza, "Philosophical Commentaries," 390–91 [English], 505–6 [Hebrew]. The source is ms Cambridge Add 1235, ff. 1a–1b.

56. Ravitzky, "Thought of R. Zerahiah," 76.

57. Cf. *Guide* 1:34, *Pines*, 75–76.

58. Cf. Crescas's preface in *The Guide of the Perplexed . . . with the Four Commentaries of Efodi, Shem Tov, Crescas, and Abarbanel* (Warsaw: Y. Goldman, 1872), 1:2b [Hebrew].

59. Kaplan, "Rationalism," 103.

60. Kaplan, "Rationalism," 105.

61. Tzvetan Todorov, *Symbolism and Interpretation* (Ithaca, NY: Cornell University Press, 1982), 30–31.

62. On Maimonides's esoteric exegesis, see James A. Diamond, *Maimonides and the Hermeneutics of Concealment* (Albany: State University of New York Press, 2002).

63. *Sefer Tagmulei ha-Nefesh*, ed. Solomon Halberstam (Lyck: Meqize Nirdamim, 1874), 32b–33a.

64. *Pines, The Guide of the Perplexed*, 6.

65. These labels should be understood along a continuum, as the exoteric commentary also contains esoteric elements. See Adrian Sackson, *Joseph ibn Kaspi: Portrait of a Hebrew Philosopher in Medieval Provence* (Leiden, Boston: Brill, 2017), 109, 125.

66. See *Menorat kesef*, in *'Asarah kelei kesef*, ed. Isaac Last (Pressburg: Adolph Alkalay and Son, 1903), 2:77.

67. *Maskiyot kesef*, in De Souza, "Philosophical Commentaries," 445 [English], 533 [Hebrew]; Werbluner, *'Ammudei kesef*, 8.

68. Cf. the moderate esotericism in Abarbanel's account of the structure of the *Guide*, which connects its chapters with one another: *The Guide of the Perplexed with the Four Commentaries*, 3:73a–74b.

69. Aryeh Motzkin, *Philosophy and the Jewish Tradition: Lectures and Essays*, ed. Yehuda Halper (Leiden: Brill, 2012), 125–26; Tirosh-Rothschild, *Between Worlds*, 95.

70. I owe the insights in this paragraph to Jacqueline Hamesse, "Un exemple de reécriture des textes: les instruments de travail philosophiques médiévaux," in *Ecriture et réécriture des textes philosophiques médiévaux: volume d'hommage offert à Colette Sirat*, ed. Jacqueline Hamesse (Turnhout: Brepols, 2006), 195–213.

71. Shiffman, *Moreh ha-Moreh*, 87.

72. Kaplan, "Rationalism," 347.

73. Kaplan, "Rationalism," 350.

74. Kaplan, "Rationalism," 161.

75. Kaplan, "Rationalism," 112–15.

76. The phrase "and all that is similar to them" is Ibn Tibbon's own addition.

77. Pines, *Guide of the Perplexed*, 11, lines 13–19, modified to reflect the Hebrew.

78. Ed. Yehudah 'Even-Shmu'el (Jerusalem: Mossad Harav Kook, 2000) 10, lines 7–10. Punctuation by editor.

79. In the ms: המעיק.

80. ms Munich Bayerische Staatsbibliothek cod. heb. 370, ff. 5a–5b. Punctuation is my own.

81. It is not clear if the subject of "he" refers to Solomon or to Maimonides—if this ambiguity is by design, it would be an example of esoteric writing.

82. De Souza, "Philosophical Commentaries," 329–30 [English], 490 [Hebrew].

83. It is possible that Moses of Salerno was faithfully reproducing the manuscript copy of the *Guide* that he had at his disposal. However, the phenomenon of rewriting is so widespread among early commentaries that this is unlikely. A future critical edition of the *Guide* would permit a comprehensive comparison.

84. On rewriting in Efodi, see Maud Kozodoy, *The Secret Faith of Maestre Honoratus: Profayt Duran and Jewish Identity in Late Medieval Iberia* (Philadelphia: University of Pennsylvania Press, 2015), 51–52.

85. Cf. *The Cultures of Maimonideanism*, ed. James T. Robinson (Boston: Brill, 2009). On the sociocultural functions of commentary, see Aaron W. Hughes, "Presenting the Past: The Genre of Commentary in Theoretical Perspective," *Method and Theory in the Study of Religion* 15:2 (2003): 148–68.

86. Arthur Melzer characterizes esoteric writing as a "nearly universal practice among Western philosophers prior to the late modern era." *Philosophy between the Lines: The Lost History of Esoteric Writing* (Chicago: University of Chicago Press, 2014), 69.

IGOR H. DE SOUZA is Lecturer in Humanities, Women's, Gender, and Sexuality Studies and Associate Research Scholar in Judaic Studies, Yale University. He is author of *Rewriting Maimonides: Early Commentaries on the Guide of the Perplexed.*

4

PHILOSOPHICAL COMMENTARY AND SUPERCOMMENTARY

The Hebrew Aristotelian Commentaries of the Fourteenth through Sixteenth Centuries

Yehuda Halper

In 1893 Moritz Steinschneider, the great Hebrew bibliographer, mentioned over ninety different Hebrew commentaries on the Corpus Aristotelicum written by over thirty different authors in his enumeration of Hebrew translations of Aristotle's works and Averroes's commentaries on them.[1] Since then, new commentaries have been discovered, unidentified authors have been identified, and misattributions have been corrected.[2] Indeed, it is now possible to characterize the genre of Hebrew Aristotelian commentaries as a phenomenon of the fourteenth through sixteenth centuries that occurred in the northern Mediterranean: Provence, the Iberian Peninsula, the Italian Peninsula, and the Aegean region. Yet few of these commentaries have been critically edited, and most have yet to be studied by modern scholarship. In fact, little is known about many of the Hebrew commentators. In this chapter, I present an overview of what is known about the Hebrew Aristotelian commentators and their commentaries in an effort to outline their general philosophical goals. In some cases it is likely that commentary writing was part of a larger scientific or logic-related project and may not have been seen as an end in itself. These projects locate themselves, to a degree, in the works of Aristotle but often build on those works to form original ideas or to move in a Maimonidean or Averroist direction. We shall end with a detailed look at a single manuscript page containing several commentaries to gain some sense of how these works were read.

While numerous Hebrew works rely significantly on Aristotelian texts, for the purposes of this essay I consider only those works that present a complete, phrase-by-phrase interpretation of a specific Aristotelian text.[3] These commentaries are typically preceded by short introductions and often conclude with brief epilogues but for the most part follow the order and conceptual concerns of the text on which they are commenting. Accordingly, they present a different kind of textual engagement from other genres studied in this volume. While sermons, theological summae, dialogues, poetry, epistles, and encyclopedias may make direct use of a text and even quote extensively from it, they do not require the reader to take up the original text to be understood even in the most basic way, and they do not take up a direct back-and-forth between text and commentary. The commentaries of this genre explicitly identify themselves as commentaries on an Aristotelian text and do not include these comments as digressions or as ways of explaining something else, but rather as a complete text dedicated to explicating another complete text.

In almost every case, however, the Aristotelian text is not actually Aristotle's, since very few of his works appeared in Hebrew during this period.[4] Rather, they are Hebrew translations of Averroes's commentaries on Aristotle's works and Porphyry's *Isagoge*. Hebrew commentaries on the latter—of which there are at least a dozen—were often included in manuscripts containing commentaries on Aristotle's *Categories, De interpretatione*, and other books of the logical *Organon*, even as the Hebrew commentators argued over whether the *Isagoge* is really necessary for studying Aristotelian logic. As a result, the Hebrew Aristotelian commentaries are in fact "supercommentaries" in which there is usually some ambiguity as to which statements are Aristotle's, Porphyry's, or Averroes's. Such ambiguity allowed commentators to present different versions of the "true" Aristotle and attribute what they saw as errors or undesirable conclusions to Averroes or other, later commentators.

It is clear that these commentaries represent a form of intergenerational, intercultural, and interfaith dialogue. The layers of commentary embedded in these manuscripts show Aristotle and Porphyry speaking to Averroes, who along with quotations from Al-Farabi and Al-Ghazali, speaks to medieval Jews, who, especially by the fifteenth century, begin to be greatly influenced by Christian scholastics. Yet at the same time, the interactions are often muddled, as quotations are not preserved correctly, misattributed, or not attributed at all and as the commentators engender a kind of ambiguity as to which author and which commentator holds which idea. The Hebrew commentators are thus some of the greatest tributes to Aristotle in Jewish history, but at the same time, because of their (sometimes implicit) attribution of their own original ideas or the teachings of other thinkers to Aristotle, they result in some of the greatest undermining of Aristotle in Jewish history.

Who Wrote the Commentaries and Why?

Gersonides

Chief among the Hebrew commentators on Aristotle and Porphyry was Gersonides (Levi ben Gershom, 1288–1344), whose access to Aristotelian texts was entirely mediated by Averroes. Over the course of five years, between 1321 and 1325, Gersonides completed Hebrew commentaries on Averroes's *Short Commentaries* on *Physica,*[5] *De Caelo,*[6] *De generatione et corruptione*, *Meteorologica,*[7] *De animalibus,*[8] *De anima,*[9] and *Parva naturalia.*[10] In the same period he also completed commentaries on Averroes's *Middle Commentaries on Porphyry's "Isagoge,"*[11] Aristotle's *Categories*, *De interpretatione*, *Analytica priora*, *Analytica posteriora*, *Topica*, *Sophistica*, *Physica*, and the first book of the *De Caelo.*[12] He also seems to have commented on the pseudo-Aristotelian *De plantis* and at least the first books of Aristotle's *Metaphysics*, though there is no evidence that the latter was ever disseminated in any form.[13] No other Hebrew commentator was as prolific or as comprehensive as Gersonides. Further, many of Gersonides's Aristotelian commentaries are extant in numerous manuscripts (indeed, in some cases dozens of manuscripts survive), and Latin translations of his commentaries on the first three books of the logical *Organon* (*Isagoge*, *Categoriae*, and *De interpretation*) were even printed. No other Hebrew commentator appears to have been as popular as Gersonides. In addition to being the most prolific, most comprehensive, and most popular of the Hebrew Aristotelian commentators, Gersonides is one of the first Hebrew commentators on Aristotle.[14]

Why did Gersonides write Aristotelian commentaries? In his introduction to his commentary on Averroes's *Short Commentary on Aristotle's "Physics,"* he says that his aim is "to explain concisely the epitomes of

Averroes on the physical writings of Aristotle, for even though most of what Averroes says is very clear, there remain some profound things he does not explain."[15] Gersonides presents his commentary as a concise explication and clarification of the text. Gersonides's focus is apparently on the "profound things he does not explain," and his explanations often differ considerably from both Aristotle and Averroes. In his introductions to his commentaries on Averroes's *Middle Commentaries on the "Isagoge"* and *on the "Physics,"* Gersonides is more explicit about actually contradicting Averroes, Porphyry, and Aristotle.[16] His primary allegiance is apparently to the subject matter, rather than to the words of Aristotle, Porophyry or Averroes, even while each subject is defined and laid out by Aristotle, Porphyry, and Averroes. Accordingly, the roots of many of Gersonides's innovations in logic and physics may be found in his commentaries.[17] Another of his goals in writing the commentaries was for the benefit of students.[18] There is no evidence indicating that Gersonides was involved with a school or an academy, but his commentaries may have served as courses on Aristotle for a group of scholars and students who were in correspondence with him.[19]

Still, it is not entirely clear why Gersonides's intensive commenting was limited to 1321 to 1325.[20] We know that in 1317, at the age of twenty-nine, he began work on a treatise on creation that would eventually become part of his magnum opus, *Wars of the Lord*, a work finally completed in 1340. We also know that Gersonides completed a first version of his original contribution to logic, *Ha-heqesh ha-yashar* (The correct syllogism) in 1319 but began an extensive revision of the work in 1323, a revision that took into account newly translated logical works of Averroes into Hebrew and Gersonides's commentaries on them.[21] In other words, we know that at the time he was composing his Aristotelian commentaries, Gersonides was also working on original treatises on logic and creation, which Maimonides had understood as a problem of physics. It is likely, then, that Gersonides's interests in logic and physics led him to study and then comment on those Aristotelian logical and physical works available to him, namely, the short and middle commentaries of Averroes. He may have stopped writing Aristotelian commentaries when he felt he had completed his study of the relevant works, perhaps considering it superfluous to comment on both the short and middle commentaries on the remaining works. If he abandoned his commentary on the *Metaphysics*, we may suppose that he did not see it as analogous to his own interests. Indeed, his approach to theological questions in *Wars* follows his reading of the Bible more closely than Aristotle's *Metaphysics*, and we may suppose that he developed his theological notions in response to his detailed study of the Bible. In the years following his Aristotelian commentary writing (1325–1329), Gersonides wrote both his biblical commentaries and a first edition of books 1–6 of the *Wars*.[22] In short, it seems that Gersonides wrote his Aristotelian commentaries on the logical and physical works when he was writing or preparing to write/rewrite his own logical and physical works and wrote his commentary on the Bible when he was writing his theological works.[23] This conjecture may also explain why Gersonides did not write commentaries on nonlogical and nonphysical works, such as *Ethics* or Averroes's *Commentary on Plato's "Republic."*[24]

That laying the groundwork for his own original work was a primary motivation for his activity as a commentator is also suggested by Gersonides's way of describing Aristotle and Averroes in those commentaries. While Gersonides is often somewhat circumspect in his explicit treatment of Aristotle, he is frequently highly critical of Averroes. Thus, he notes that Averroes's arguments in several places are "worthy of laughter,"[25] "weak," and in some cases "untrue."[26] Yet his objections to Aristotle are frequently to "Aristotle in the words of Averroes,"[27] and sometimes the erroneous arguments in Averroes's *Epitomes* on natural sciences may be corrected with reference to Aristotle, often as explained in Averroes's *Middle Commentaries*.[28] In my view, Gersonides's wording in the commentaries often leaves open the possibility that Aristotle was in fact correct, and that the errors he points out may be attributable to Averroes. Additionally, with some exceptions,[29] Gersonides is more limited in original explanations in his Aristotelian commentaries, and he writes more extensively on his original ideas in his later writings, especially the *Wars of the Lord*.[30] This also gives the impression that his Aristotelian commentaries are a kind of preliminary preparation for his original works.

Gersonides's Circle

There were a number of other Hebrew Aristotelian commentators in southern France, primarily Provence, in the early to mid-fourteenth century who seem to have had a direct connection to Gersonides. Jedaiah ha-Penini (Bedersi) was likely near the same age as Gersonides[31] and refers to the latter respectfully as "the sage."[32] He wrote commentaries on the logical *Organon* (which are no longer extant),[33] *Physica*, and *De Caelo*. Since references to Gersonides appear in Jedaiah's commentaries,[34] we may assume at least some intellectual influence, though it is not clear which, if any, of Gersonides's texts Jedaiah may have read. Another five or six commentary writers may have seen themselves as students of Gersonides: R. Sh. Ha-Levy wrote a commentary on the *Physica*, Solomon of Urgul wrote commentaries on *De generatione* and *Meteorologica*,[35] and we have other commentaries on *De Anima* attributed to Porfash, on *De sensu* attributed to Vital,[36] and anonymous commentaries on the *Organon*[37] and *Physica*.[38] The precise number of these otherwise unknown authors is uncertain. The language of Solomon of Urgul is so similar to that of Porfash and Vital that they may in fact be two people or even one person.[39] Both Ha-Levi and Urgul refer to Gersonides as their teacher, and there is evidence that they exchanged letters and had personal meetings with Gersonides.[40] If Porfash and Vital are not the same as Urgul, they may be assumed to have been in close contact with Urgul (and Ha-Levi as well) because of similarities in language.[41]

Another contemporary of Gersonides, Samuel b. Judah of Marseilles, seems to have written a commentary on at least the first three books of the *Organon*, in which he vehemently attacks Gersonides often ad hominem. Samuel's commentary is not extant but is cited extensively in Judah b. Isaac Cohen's fifteenth-century commentary on the *Organon*.[42] Samuel studied with Abba Mari ben Eligdor, among whose other students, were Qalonimos ben Qalonimos and the author of the anonymous commentary on the *Organon* mentioned above.[43] Like Qalonimos, Samuel is best known for his translations of Averroes's Aristotelian commentaries. Yet Samuel, unlike Gersonides, was apparently influenced by Al-Farabi and a number of scholastic thinkers, including William of Occam. In a sense, Samuel's attitude presages later critiques of Gersonides from commentators familiar with scholastic texts, though his acerbic personal attacks were considered excessive even by Judah Cohen.[44]

Like Gersonides's commentaries, and indeed probably because of their authors' interest in Gersonides, these commentaries concentrate exclusively on logic and natural science. Yet only Samuel ben Judah and the anonymous commentator on the *Organon* make extensive and explicit use of Gersonides's commentaries. Apart from a few references to Gersonides and a few other thinkers, the other commentators reflect primarily on Averroes, Porphyry, and Aristotle. It is not yet clear why these commentaries were written—they may have been intended as teaching manuals but also could have been written as exercises assigned in some manner by Gersonides.[45] What we do know is that a small group of men in the generation of and after

Gersonides wrote commentaries on books on which Gersonides himself wrote commentaries. Without evidence of influence in either direction, we can state that they shared similar interests and saw writing commentaries as a way to pursue that interest. While Jedaiah and Gersonides actively pursued theological, ethical, metaphysical, and perhaps even rhetorical interests[46] in various original works and Bible commentaries, they did not turn to Aristotelian commentary for those pursuits.

Other Fourteenth-Century Commentators

A number of other Hebrew Aristotelian commentaries appeared in the fourteenth century that were apparently not connected with Gersonides or his circle. These include fragments of David ibn Bilia's commentary on Porphyry's *Isagoge*,[47] Moses Narboni's lost commentary on Aristotle's *Physics*,[48] and a commentary on *Isagoge*, *Categories*, and *De Interpretatione* written by "Abigdor."[49] Ibn Bilia's interest in logic seems to have been in defending an interpretive method that could read the Bible and Talmud in accordance with Aristotelian philosophy, perhaps in an Averroist fashion.[50]

Moses Narboni, on the other hand, wrote a large number of commentaries. Though he did write some Biblical commentaries, including one on Lamentations, most of his commentaries are on works not commented on by Gersonides and his circle: for example, on Al-Ghazali's *Maqāṣid al-falāsifah*, on the mystical work *Shi'ur Qomah*, on Ibn Ṭufayl's *Ḥayy ibn Yaqẓan*, on Averroes's treatise on intellectual conjunction, and on Maimonides's *Guide*. His commentaries generally presented philosophical interpretations in accord with what Narboni took to be Averroes's understanding. Whereas Al-Ghazali and even Maimonides present viewpoints that differ from Averroes, Narboni is happy to point out their errors. Although it is not extant,[51] it seems likely that Narboni's commentary on the *Physics* relies heavily on Averroes and presents his interpretation as the correct one.

Abigdor's commentary on *Isagoge*, *Categories*, and *De Interpretatione* is either the work of Abraham Abigdor b. Meshullam of Arles or of an unknown Abigdor. In the latter case, we can say nothing about the work; it may even be a fifteenth-century work. In the former case, it is the work of a prolific translator of scholastic logical works—most importantly Peter's *Tractatus*—and medieval Latin medical works. As a young man, he also wrote *Segullat melakhim* (The royal treasure), the first part of which summarizes Averroes's middle commentaries on logic and the latter two parts of which summarize the physical and metaphysical sections of Al-Ghazali's *Maqāṣid*. Abraham Abigdor's interpretation there depends greatly on Narboni's commentary on the *Maqāṣid*, and, like Narboni, Abigdor is wont to correct Al-Ghazali using Averroes's commentaries.[52] The commentaries on logic, which are critical of Al-Ghazali (as well as Avicenna and even Maimonides), go further in the direction of Averroes, "whose intellect is broader than mine, as I am but a student still learning."[53] Assuming these works are all written by the same person, it is possible that both Abigdor and Narboni were drawn to write commentaries on Aristotle and Averroes through their studies of Al-Ghazali's *Maqāṣid*, in particular through their studies of those parts of the *Maqāṣid* with which they did not agree.[54] Alternatively, they may have simply seen the *Maqāṣid* as a simpler, more accessible introduction to philosophy, which could later be supplemented with the works of Averroes and Aristotle. They may thus have been part of what Steven Harvey has identified as a trend of intense interest in Al-Ghazali's *Maqāṣid* in southern France in the fourteenth century.[55] Though apparently unconnected to Gersonides's circle, which seems to have had no interest in Al-Ghazali,[56] Narboni and Abigdor also commented only on the logical and physical works of Aristotle.

Fifteenth-Century Hebrew Aristotelian Commentaries

The fifteenth century saw a twofold increase in Hebrew Aristotelian commentators, yet these commentaries were clearly distinct from their fourteenth-century predecessors in a number of ways. The most obvious difference was in geography: aside from David ibn Bilia who lived in Portugal, the fourteenth-century commentators were all from southern France (mainly Provence), where the majority of the Aristotelian translation activity took place. In contrast, in the fifteenth century, I know of only one commentary from southern France: Mordecai Nathan's commentary on Averroes's *Short Commentaries on Aristotle's logical "Organon."*[57] The other commentary activity took place in the Italian Peninsula, the Iberian Peninsula, and the Aegean region. The Aragonese and Venetian trade routes connected these regions and allowed for the diffusion of books and ideas among them.

The Italian Peninsula

Two figures stand out among the Italian Hebrew commentators on Aristotle of the fifteenth century: Judah Messer Leon (1425–1498) and Elijah del

Medigo (1458–1493). Both were somehow involved with the university in Padua and both were greatly influenced by scholastic modes. Judah Messer Leon apparently received the title *messer* for his work as a physician for Emperor Frederick III and later received the title *doctor* from the emperor in Padua.[58] Messer Leon seems to have adapted the scholastic style to the Hebrew language. Most of his writings are accordingly expositions or questions following scholastic format: this is so even for his original logical work *Mikhlal yofi*.[59] Messer Leon wrote commentaries on *Isagoge*, *Categories*, *On Interpretation*, *Prior Analytics*, *Posterior Analytics*, *Physics*, *De Anima*, *Metaphysics*, and *Ethics*. The last three are not extant, but the others adopt such features of scholastic commentaries as summarizing theses and questions and answers. Additionally, they engage extensively with Walter Burley, Radulphus Brito, Gaetano of Thiene, Paul of Venice, and numerous other Latin writers in the Paduan style.[60] Messer Leon was also explicitly critical of Gersonides and saw his commentaries as pioneering Hebrew commentaries on Aristotle, despite the existence of those works of Gersonides and his circle.[61]

Unlike Judah Messer Leon, who wrote scholastic-style works in Hebrew, Elijah del Medigo actually wrote Latin works in the scholastic style. His two Hebrew commentaries, on *De substantia orbis* and on Averroes's treatises on intellect and conjunction, are apparently translations of works he originally wrote in Latin.[62] In any case, the stylistic similarities to scholastic writings suggest an effort, similar to that of Messer Leon, to import the Latin university style into Hebrew.

The Iberian Peninsula

Around the middle of the fifteenth century, the Shem Ṭob family produced a number of commentaries on Aristotle and Averroes. While the father of the family, Shem Ṭob ibn Shem Ṭob, was known for his anti-Aristotle, antiphilosophy stance, his sons, Joseph and Isaac, wrote Hebrew Aristotelian philosophical commentaries. Joseph ibn Shem Ṭob wrote commentaries on *Isagoge*, *De anima* (both not extant), and *Ethics*; Isaac wrote a commentary on the *Physics*. Joseph's son, Shem Ṭob b. Joseph ibn Shem Ṭob, also apparently wrote commentaries on the *Physics*, *De generatione*, and *De anima*.[63] These commentaries exhibit the influence of scholastic Christian thought, particularly Thomas Aquinas. Joseph's commentary on the *Ethics* is also highly critical of Gersonides, but neither the critique of Gersonides nor the scholastic influence is the central theme of the commentary. Rather, Joseph tells us in the introduction to the work that study of the *Ethics* can lead to human happiness and to proper appreciation of human life.[64] That is, Joseph apparently saw the study of the *Ethics* and the writing of a commentary on it, especially in light of what he sees as rampant misunderstandings of the work in Hebrew, as an end in itself.[65]

Other Iberian Hebrew Aristotelian commentators were apparently in correspondence with each other and the Shem Ṭob family. Eli Habilio, in particular, is known to have corresponded with the Shem Ṭob family[66] and with Abraham Bibago.[67] Most of Eli Habilio's writings were Latin-Hebrew translations, fifteen of which are extant in manuscripts, as well as various *Quaestiones*.[68] The most significant of these translations was of Antonius Andreas's *Quaestiones super XII Libros Metaphysicorum*, which was a key text of Latin Scotism.[69] In his introduction to that work, he criticizes other Jewish thinkers for over-reliance on Averroes, and explicitly praises a number of other thinkers including Avicenna, Aquinas, Occam, and, chiefly, Duns Scotus. Habilio also wrote a short summarizing commentary on Averroes's *Middle Commentary* on Aristotle's *Metaphysics*, which complemented his translation of Andreas's *Quaestiones* in that it omitted or deemphasized Averroes's statements that contradicted Scotist metaphysical doctrines and adjusted Averroes's words to encourage his readers to seek out Scotist doctrines.[70] Habilio may also have written a commentary on the logical *Organon* as well as a commentary on the physical and metaphysical sections of Al-Ghazali's *Maqāṣid*.[71] Like Judah Messer Leon, Eli Habillo seems to have been interested in enriching Jewish philosophical literature by adopting Latin scholastic literary forms. Moreover, far from criticizing Gersonides, Habillo wrote a commentary on the *Wars of the Lord*, perhaps an epitome, in which he treats the *Wars* as the pinnacle reached after the Aristotelian physics and metaphysics have been scaled.[72] Habillo, though, differs from Gersonides not only in his appreciation of Latin Scholasticism but also in his appreciation of metaphysics.

Abraham Bibago was also an avid reader of scholastic philosophy though his commentaries generally evince only subtle influences of Latin philosophical forms. His *Treatise on the Plurality of Forms* is an exception to this rule, as it is clearly in a scholastic style of *quaestiones*, arguments pro and con, and excursus.[73] However, most of his other works take on other literary forms, for example, sermons, treatises, biblical commentaries, Hebrew Aristotelian commentaries, and his best-known treatise on the intellectual basis of biblical and Talmudic texts, *Derekh emunah* (Way of faith). I have argued extensively elsewhere that Bibago saw his main philosophical activity not in his treatises, particularly *Derekh emunah*, but in his commentary, particularly his commentary on Aristotle's *Metaphysics*.[74] This is apparent in his rhymed introduction to that commentary, in which he likens his interpretation to the messianic salvation of Israel.[75] Moreover, Bibago states repeatedly in both *Derekh emunah* and the metaphysics commentary that man's telos is intellectual and achieved through metaphysical speculation. Faith, Bibago claims (in my view, somewhat disingenuously) in *Derekh emunah* can create an imitation of metaphysical knowledge, but even still, true metaphysical knowledge is gained by studying Aristotelian metaphysics. Bibago wrote other commentaries on *Posterior Analytics*, *Physics*, and *De anima*, of which only the *Posterior Analytics* commentary survives in full.[76] There, Bibago clearly demarcates the study of logic as preliminary to intellectual knowledge, which is apparently acquired through metaphysics.[77] While Bibago may also have viewed his commentaries as teaching tools for his academy at Saragossa,[78] he seems to have considered his Aristotelian commentaries as the highest form of philosophical study.[79]

There were a number of other commentaries in the Spanish school, especially on the *Organon* and *Physics*,[80] the authors of which are still unidentified. Yet we know of one other significant commentator, though nearly nothing is known about his life: Baruch ibn Ya'ish. Ibn Ya'ish was also heavily influenced by Latin writings and translated a number of scholastic works into Hebrew; he probably also translated *De anima*, *Metaphysics*, and *Ethica* into Hebrew on the basis of recent Latin translations, especially those of William of Moerbecke. He wrote commentaries on *De anima*, *Physics*, and possibly *Economica*. A student of his, Samuel b. Solomon A[l]ṭorṭos, wrote a commentary on *Ethics* based on Ibn Ya'ish's lectures.[81] These commentaries demonstrate an interest in Aristotelian philosophy for attaining human happiness. They also display an engagement with Latin writings and an effort to import them into Hebrew.

The Aegean Region

The work of commentary writing around the Aegean in the fifteenth century has not been much studied. Ruth Glasner has shown that Shalom Anavi, Michael Kohen, and several still-unnamed authors wrote commentaries on the first books of Averroes's *Long Commentary on Aristotle's "Physics"* in Constantinople/Istanbul and Candia.[82] Mordecai b. Eliezer Comtino, a denizen of Constantinople/Istanbul, wrote commentaries on Euclid and on some astronomical works and may even have written a now-lost commentary on the *Metaphysics*. In sixteenth-century Salonica, Solomon b. Isaac Halevi wrote a commentary on the *Physics* in Salonica and Moses Almosnino wrote on *Ethics*. Influences on these works are still largely unknown, but it is clear that at least two thinkers shared an interest in writing commentaries on *Ethics* and *Metaphysics* with their Western colleagues.

Trends in Fifteenth-Century Commentaries

We can identify four trends in the fifteenth-century commentaries mentioned here: (1) Geographical distribution of commentators in Italy, Iberia, and the Aegean, rather than in Southern France. (2) Influence of Latin Scholasticism and in some cases the creation of Hebrew writings in scholastic style.[83] While Gersonides and his fourteenth-century contemporaries have certain similarities to Christian scholastics, it is not clear how much these thinkers, whom the fourteenth-century thinkers probably did not read in Latin, affected their readings of Averroes and Aristotle.[84] In contrast, some fifteenth-century Hebrew Aristotelian commentators were directly involved in universities (e.g., at Padua) and considered Latin scientific forms of writing worthy of emulation in Hebrew. (3) Hebrew Aristotelian commentaries of the fifteenth century are especially critical of Gersonides and his commentaries. We saw above that Judah b. Isaac Cohen cited Samuel b. Judah of Marseilles's commentary's attack on Gersonides. We find similar attacks in numerous other commentaries, for example, by Judah Messer Leon, Joseph ibn Shem Ṭob, and Abraham Bibago. Eli Habillo is a notable exception to this trend. (4) Fifteenth-century Hebrew authors wrote commentaries on *Metaphysics*, *Ethics*, and perhaps even the *Economica*. In fourteenth-century France, interest in commentary writing was limited to just the logical and physical works. It seems likely that the newfound interest in *Metaphysics* and *Ethics* in the fifteenth century was part of an effort to examine human intellectual happiness through commentaries on Aristotle's works. This may be in contrast to non-Aristotelian ways of seeking human happiness, for example, through religious writings or works.

The Sixteenth Century and the End of the Commentaries

Evidence of sixteenth-century Hebrew Aristotelian commentators is scant. We have already mentioned Solomon b. Isaac Halevi of Salonica's commentary on the *Physics*, and we could also mention Manoah Sho'ali's commentary on logic. It is likely that the future will reveal a few more sixteenth-century Hebrew commentators. Nevertheless, it seems that Hebrew authors ceased to produce Aristotelian commentaries in the sixteenth century and did not return to producing commentaries on Aristotle until the Zionist era. It is not clear why Hebrew Aristotelian commentaries ceased to be written in the sixteenth century. Latin commentaries continued to be written in France and Italy, especially Padua. Jews increasingly read Latin or the vernacular languages and perhaps did not feel the need to produce works in Hebrew.

Yet sixteenth-century Hebrew readers continued to study the commentaries produced in earlier generations. Indeed, many if not most of the manuscripts we have that contain the Hebrew Aristotelian commentaries were copied in the sixteenth century, suggesting a fairly wide readership. Given the large number of sixteenth-century manuscripts, it is possible that the readership of these commentaries was greater in the sixteenth century than it was in the fifteenth. Without much writing about why these books were being copied, it is difficult to assess why they were read. In what follows, we shall examine one example of a unique sixteenth-century manuscript and make some inferences about its readers.

Example: A Sixteenth-Century Manuscript

The following is a page from a manuscript containing Hebrew commentaries on Porphyry's *Isagoge* found today in the Biblioteca della Comunità Ebraica of Mantua, Italy (Hebrew manuscript, 68). Its script is Italian, probably copied in the sixteenth century.[85] In the center of the page is Averroes's *Middle Commentary on the "Isagoge"* in the thirteenth-century Hebrew translation of Jacob Anatoli. It is flanked on the sides by commentaries by Gersonides (completed 1323) and Judah Messer Leon (completed 1454).[86] Other pages also contain short comments in the margins by an as yet unidentified Joseph.[87] The commentaries of Averroes, Gersonides, and Messer Leon depicted here do not end with the *Isagoge* (though Joseph's does) but continue with complete commentaries on Aristotle's *Categories* and *De Interpretatione*. The page depicted here is thus at the opening of a kind of compendium of commentaries, appearing in Hebrew between the thirteenth and fifteenth centuries, on the first part of Aristotle's logical *Organon*.

A few things are apparent from this image. First, the copyist expects readers to study these commentaries together. The alignment of blocks of

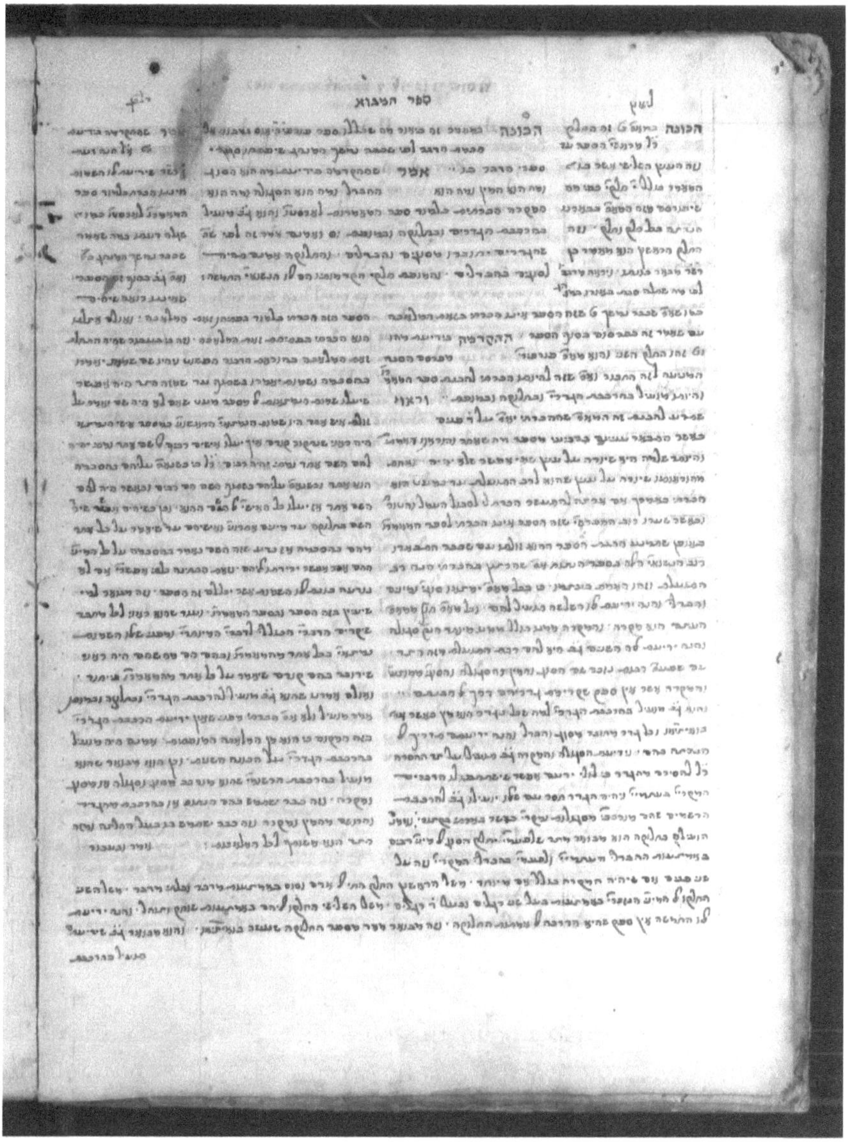

PORPHIRIUS, *Isagoge*. Commentary by AVERROES. Arabic-Hebrew translation titled: *Sefer Mavo*, by YA' AQOV B. ABBA MARI ANATOLI; commentary by LEWI B. GERŠOM, YEHUDAH B. YEHI'EL [Messer Leon] and YOSEF [Yosef ibn Šem Tov?]. Mantova, Biblioteca Comunale Teresiana, Library of the Hebrew Community, Hebrew Ms. Nr. 68, sec. XV–XVI (1/2), f. 3r.

text from the various commentaries on the same page together with some emphasized words at the beginning of sections allow the reader to move with relative ease between corresponding lines of each commentary. That is, the intended readers are expected to engage critically with a number of commentaries, to compare them line by line, and presumably to decide for themselves in cases of disagreement. The graphical similarity to more familiar editions of the Talmud or Midrash with their various commentaries suggests a similar kind of reader: one who wants immediate access to the most important commentaries but in their original text, that is, not corrected or edited to correspond to a more preferred interpretation.[88]

The text commented on is not Porphyry's *Isagoge* here (nor Aristotle's *Categories* or *De interpretatione* later), but Averroes's *Middle Commentary* on each work. Averroes's commentaries are not marked as such by the copyist but appear under the names of the books on which they comment without any mention of their authorship. Jacob Anatoli's introduction to the work, appearing on the first folio of the manuscript, attests to Averroes's authorship, as do the opening lines of Gersonides's and Messer Leon's commentaries. The authorship of the commentary would thus not be misidentified by the critically engaged reader, but the copyist's presentation suggests that the main event here is the *Middle Commentary*, not the original texts, which were not available in Hebrew translation. In the case of *Isagoge*, the separation between commentary and commented-on is even more pronounced, since Porphyry himself describes his work as a "short account" (σύντομος παράδοσις) leading as an "introduction" (εἰσαγωγῇ) to an "elucidation of," or perhaps "commentary on" (διδασκαλία) Aristotle's *Categories*.[89] The above-depicted Hebrew manuscript thus contains multiple layers of commentary, but not the core texts that are the subjects of the commentary.

This leads to a certain amount of ambiguity as to which statement can be attributed to Porphyry, Aristotle, or Averroes. Consider, for example, Gersonides's introductory statement to the entire *Organon*: "Levi ben Gershom said after praise to the Lord: in this book, I saw fit to comment on the short works[90] of Averroes on the books of logic in my own short work (*qiṣuri*). I shall also mention those places where my opinion is different from Aristotle's opinion in this art—according to what Averroes understood of his words. At the same time, in some places I shall investigate things about which Aristotle did not speak according to what Averroes mentioned of his words."[91] Porphyry, somewhat surprisingly, does not appear at all in this statement; he is only mentioned when Gersonides turns to introducing the *Isagoge* specifically. Aristotle is the focus here, but Gersonides acknowledges that Aristotle is virtually inseparable from Averroes and that the former speaks, as it were, in the words of the latter. Even when Gersonides is to broach new topics in the study of logic, his wording suggests some uncertainty as to whether Aristotle did not, in fact, also discuss these topics in some part of the text not recorded by Averroes.[92] Shortly thereafter, when introducing Porphyry's work, Gersonides is even explicitly critical of Averroes: "Averroes' opinion is that knowledge of these terms [discussed in the *Isagoge*] is not necessary for studying the *Categories*—an opinion he revealed when he said, 'it has become customary for the logical corpus to open the *Isagoge*'[93] and when he said at the end of the work that he does not consider the work necessary for beginning this art.[94] However, in our view, it is necessary for beginning this art."[95] Averroes, according to Gersonides, exhibits a fundamental error in his interpretation of the *Isagoge*: he did not think the subject to be necessary. In rectifying this error, Gersonides places himself on the side of Porphyry against Averroes. Gersonides prepares his readers to assume that his own logical contributions, which are interspersed throughout the commentary, are closer to Porphyry's original intention than Averroes's interpretations even, perhaps especially, when Porphyry's own words are not available to a Hebrew audience. That this is no more than a literary feint becomes apparent in Gersonides's numerous criticisms of Porphyry.[96] Still, this literary feint may be a key reason why Gersonides's commentary had a broader readership than his original logical work, *Ha-heqesh ha-yashar*, despite the latter's more significant contribution to the history of logic.[97] Gersonides himself notes in his introductory statement to *Ha-heqesh ha-yashar*, "Many will attribute this [work] to our having brazenness (*'azut meṣaḥ*) and an inadequate understanding of the Philosopher [i.e., of Aristotle]."[98] Gersonides's readers may thus presumably prefer to believe his contributions to be products of a true understanding of the original text than proper innovations. This is not to say that Gersonides's interpretations were in fact close to Aristotle's or Porphyry's original meanings, or even that Gersonides considered them to be, but rather that Gersonides's language in his commentary leaves an opening for his readers to assume, at least at the outset, that his commentary more genuinely reflects Aristotle's or Porphyry's original intentions than Averroes's *Middle Commentaries*.

Judah Messer Leon also presents his commentary as a return to the original meaning, though for Messer Leon that meaning is expressed properly in Averroes's *Middle Commentary*.[99] According to Messer Leon, the true meaning of Porphyry's *Isagoge* has been corrupted by the various commentaries on it in Hebrew. In the words of Messer Leon, "Had those [Hebrew] commentaries been few in quantity but great in quality, I would have held my peace.[100] However, deficiency surrounds them on both sides 'a fence being on this side, and a fence on that side.'[101] The opposite is the case with some of the [other] languages which have filled the houses of the soul with the silver of commentaries, interpretations, and investigations of the demonstrative sciences. Their books have been fruitful, have increased abundantly and have waxed exceedingly mighty.[102] Thus, I could not refrain myself."[103] Messer Leon thus casts his work as a kind of corrective to numerous poor-quality Hebrew commentaries on the *Isagoge*, especially in light of the many good commentaries written in other languages, including Latin. Indeed, his commentary often cites from Boethius, Avicenna, and Al-Ghazali (all of whom he probably read in Latin),[104] and Isaac Husik has shown how Messer Leon draws frequently from Walter Burley's *Expositio super artem veterem*.[105] Messer Leon's blanket criticism of all the previous Hebrew commentaries undoubtedly includes that of Gersonides, whom he repeatedly refers to, not without derision, as "he who is wise in his own eyes" (*he-ḥakham be-ʿeynav*) throughout the commentary.[106] It is likely with Gersonides's "short work"[107] in mind that Messer Leon says: "We do not choose [to use the form of] a short work (*qiṣṣur*) while abandoning what is necessary and beneficial in preparing this treatise [i.e., this commentary]. For that, we suspect, would be complete idiocy. For a 'short work' is attributed to fools. Could we intend to be short with regard to the reach of those treatises that are lacking subjects,[108] which do not have so much of an impression on the object I am following on the grounds that speaking at length about such things is excessive?"[109] Messer Leon then tells us that earlier commentators "have poured out arrogant word[110] and have attributed their intentions to brazenness [*ʿazut meṣaḥ*] and seeking greatness and high stature."[111] The target of these invectives is likely Gersonides, along with other commentators who have written under his influence; Messer Leon decries the long-standing custom of such commentaries, which continuously repeat the same errors. These errors, apparently, are not delving at length into the meanings of the original text and brazenly departing from that text.

Messer Leon, in contrast, will speak at length, in great detail and adhere closely to the original text. He says, "I am following convention in preparing an excellent ordering [of a text]: commenting on each part of the treatise and dividing each part into defined parts so as to make known in each of them the intention of the author regarding the perfect thing contained inside [the work]."[112] However, Messer Leon permits some significant ambiguity regarding who the author is. As part of his preface to his commentary, Messer Leon, like a number of other Hebrew and Latin commentators,[113] discusses four causes of the work in hand. Regarding the efficient cause, he says, "The efficient cause of this book, i.e., the *Isagoge*, was the philosopher, Porphyry, who composed it for one of his students named Chrysaorius, while for the rest of the books [the cause] was Aristotle. However, the treatise is mixed with some of the words of Averroes about these [works] by way of his commentary, as I shall comment upon."[114] Messer Leon, then, strives to adhere to the intention of the author, but the author is not separate from Averroes. However, throughout his commentary he tends to equate Averroes's intention with Aristotle's intention. In doing so, he places himself on the side of Porphyry, Aristotle, and Averroes—"the author"—against the corrupting influence of later commentaries, particularly those of Gersonides. The reader in search of the authentic meaning of the text in Hebrew, Messer Leon implies, ought to read his commentary.

One mystery in which the ambiguity between authors is particularly salient is whether the *Isagoge* is necessary for understanding Aristotle's *Categories*, a question Messer Leon takes up in the folio page depicted earlier. Averroes said explicitly that the *Isagoge* is not necessary, while Porphyry and Gersonides said that it is.[115] Messer Leon resolves the Averroes-Porphyry disparity by appeal to Aristotle:

> "Necessary" is said in four ways, whose meanings have been explained in *Metaphysics* IV.[116] Its true and most perfect meaning is that it indicates something whose not-being would be impossible, but another meaning indicates something which is so useful as to be almost necessary. Such, e.g., is your saying that if I want to become rich, I must necessarily suffer hard work and toil. While most of the commentators considered this book not to be necessary for the *Categories* in the sense that understanding the book would be impossible without it . . . what is intended by necessary here is the most useful.[117]

This solution allows all three of the authors to be right. Porphyry is right that the *Isagoge* is necessary for understanding the *Categories* in the sense that hard work is necessary for becoming rich. Averroes is right that the book is not absolutely necessary—Messer Leon even notes that some people "with naturally subtle intellects," such as Hippocrates and "the one who first came up with logic" can understand logic on their own without any textbooks.[118] Aristotle is right because there are different senses of necessity. Gersonides, by this account, would be wrong, since his criticism of Averroes does not take into account Aristotle's account of the meanings of necessity.

Analysis of this sample text illuminates how commentators can play with what they consider the authentically authored meaning. The tendency of both Gersonides and Messer Leon to present their interpretations as the original intention of the work is emblematic of a general assumption in commentary writing: the master is always right, and the commentator can present to the reader the proper understanding of a master who has been regularly misunderstood by other commentators. Note further that the copyist's decision here to place both Gersonides and Messer Leon on the same page reflects a more open, less judgmental reading of the text. Indeed, the copyist does not determine at all which commentary is right but leaves it open to his readers to inquire freely into all commentaries.

Conclusion

Sylvia Fazzo has argued that from the first century BCE through the seventeenth century CE, "Aristotelianism operated as a commentary tradition."[119] She refers especially to Aristotelian commentaries in antiquity and Latin scholastic writings. Does this statement also apply to medieval Jewish thought? Yes, and no. Medieval and renaissance Hebrew readers certainly approached Aristotle through commentaries, especially Averroes and Al-Farabi, but from the fifteenth century also Thomas Aquinas and numerous other scholastic commentators. On the other hand, Hebrew authors themselves produced relatively few commentaries. Hebrew readers apparently preferred translated commentaries to those originally written in Hebrew.

Moreover, in most cases it is unclear what institutional uses, if any, there may have been for Hebrew Aristotelian commentaries. While we know of various fifteenth-century *yeshibot* that studied Aristotle, we do not know how such study took place or whether the commentaries played a role in that study. Longstanding institutions that studied Aristotle, such as the Platonic Academia in Athens or the Sorbonne in Paris simply have no parallel among medieval Jewry. Accordingly, even if some of the Hebrew Aristotelian commentaries were intended for instruction, they would have been developed with very different curricular concerns. Such Hebrew commentaries may have been employed for correspondence courses of sorts, as we saw with Gersonides and his circle. Other commentaries may have been written in the hope of building courses of the kind taught at Christian universities, such as the writings in the scholastic style of Judah Messer Leon and Elijah del Medigo, both of whom operated in the vicinity of the University of Padua, as we saw. Future scholarship will hopefully shed light on the institutional uses of Hebrew Aristotelian commentaries and the types of courses they were intended to build.

The small number of commentators, probably fewer than fifty, and the significant geographical separations between them suggest that there were also individual, varied reasons for writing Aristotelian commentaries. Our overview has suggested a few of these: some were interested in developing their understanding of Aristotle in order to write other books; some were interested in importing scholastic thought into Hebrew; and others saw commentary writing as a way toward human intellectual happiness.

Notes

1. Moritz Steinschneider, *Die Hebraeischen Übersetzungen des Mittelalters und die Juden als Dolmetscher* (Berlin: Kommissionsverlag des Bibliographischen Bureaus, 1893), interspersed in sections 19–148. An expanded translation of Steinschneider's conspectus of those sections is given in Moritz Steinschneider, *The Hebrew Translations of the Middle Ages and the Jews as Transmitters*, vol. 1, ed., rev., and trans. Charles Manekin, Y. Tzvi Langermann, and Hans Hinrich Biesterfeldt (Dordrecht: Springer, 2013), 232–35. Note that in the conspectus of contents, anonymous commentaries are not always clearly differentiated, and various commentaries on different logical works are listed as simply commentaries on Aristotle's *Organon*. As a result, somewhat fewer commentaries are listed.

2. Steinschneider, for example, considered a number of commentaries on Aristotle's *Physics* to have been written as early as the thirteenth century; this has been convincingly refuted by Ruth Glasner, who argues that those commentaries Steinschneider considered early were in fact products of the fourteenth century. See "Levi Ben Gershom and the Study of Ibn Rushd in the Fourteenth Century," *Jewish Quarterly Review* 86 (1995): 51–90. In some cases, corrections to Steinschneider have themselves turned out to need correction, with conjectures about the dating differing quite widely. Thus, one commentary on the *Physics* was attributed by Steinschneider (*Die Hebraeischen Übersetzungen des Mittelalters und die Juden als Dolmetscher*, section 49) to Isaac Albalag (thirteenth century). Later Harry Wolfson attributed it to Isaac b. Shem Tob (fifteenth century) in "Isaac ibn Shem Tob's Unknown Commentaries on the Physics and His Other Unknown Works," in *Studies in Jewish Bibliography and Related Subjects in Memory of Abraham Solomon Freidus* (New York: Alexander Kohut Memorial Foundation, 1929), 279–90. More recently, Ruth Glasner determined that the manuscripts in question refer to a number of different commentaries on the *Physics* written

by Spanish authors who were apparently in contact with each other in the second half of the fifteenth century. See Ruth Glasner, "Two Notes on the Identification of Some Anonymous Hebrew Commentaries on the *Physics*," *Aleph* 9 (2009): 335–44. For a detailed summary of what is currently known of Hebrew commentaries on Aristotle's *Physica*, see Ruth Glasner, "The Evolution of the Genre of the Philosophical-Scientific Commentary," 182–206, in *Science in Medieval Jewish Cultures*, ed. Gad Freudenthal (Cambridge: Cambridge University Press, 2011).

3. Thus, for example, I do not include here such works as Ṭodros Ṭodrosi's scientific textbook (written in 1334 and preserved in British Library Add., MS 27559, Margoliouth 890 [IMHM 6094]), which includes a commentary on Aristotle's *Physica* in the second part of the work since it is not intended as a complete work. Nor do I include such works as a commentary on Averroes's *Middle Commentary on "Metaphysics Δ,"* chapters 9–10 by someone named Moses included in what was probably his own Hebrew translation of Averroes's *Long Commentary on the "Metaphysics,"* since its inclusion was almost certainly to make up for a significant lacuna in the Arabic text and was accordingly not intended to serve as its own work.

4. For a recent list of scientific and philosophic translations into Hebrew in the Middle Ages, see Mauro Zonta, "Medieval Hebrew Translations of Philosophical and Scientific Texts: A Chronological Table," in Freudenthal, *Science in Medieval Jewish Cultures*, 17–73. The only works of Aristotle translated directly into Hebrew without the mediation of Averroes's commentaries were the *Meteorologica* (Samuel ibn Tibbon translation), *De generatione et corruptione* and *De anima* (both by Zeraḥyah b. Isaac She'altie'l Ḥen), and parts of the *De Animalibus*, which were anonymously translated from Michael Scot's Latin translation of an Arabic translation (see Tamani and Zonta, *Aristoteles Hebraicus*, 42–43).

5. Esti Eisenamann is currently preparing a critical edition of this text.

6. Sasson Horesh is currently preparing a critical edition of this text.

7. An edited text is in Eyal Meiron, "Gersonides' Supercommentary on Averroës' *Epitome of Meteorology* 1–3" (PhD diss., Hebrew University, 2003) [Hebrew].

8. An edited text is in Ahuva Gaziel, "The Biology of Levi ben Gershom [Gersonides]" (PhD diss., Bar-Ilan University, 2008). Note that Averroes's commentary on Aristotle's *De Animalibus* is sometimes considered a middle commentary rather than a short commentary.

9. A section of this work has been edited and translated in Jesse Mashbaum, "Chapters 9–12 of Gersonides' Supercommentary on Averroes' *Epitome of the 'De Anima'*: The Internal Senses" (PhD diss., Brandeis University, 1981). Michael Marcus is currently preparing a complete critical edition of this text.

10. An edition and translation of part of this work is given in Alexander Altmann, "Gersonides' Commentary on Averroes' *Epitome of Parva Naturalia*, II, 3: Annotated Critical Edition," *Proceedings of the American Academy for Jewish Research* 46–7 (1979–1980): 1–31.

11. The beginning of this work is edited in Shalom Rosenberg, "Gersonides' Commentary on the *Ha-Mavo*," *Da'at* 22 (1989): 85–98 [Hebrew].

12. An edited text is in Ofer Elior, "Gersonides' Supercommentary on Averroes' *Middle Commentary on Aristotle's 'De Caelo'*" (MA thesis, Hebrew University, 2004) [Hebrew].

13. Gersonides also wrote commentaries on Euclid and on some Talmudic passages. On Gersonides's commentaries and their dates see Levi Ben Gershom (Gersonides), *The Wars of the Lord*, ed. Ofer Elior and Charles Touati (Tel Aviv: Tel Aviv University Press, 2018), introduction, 33–48; Ruth Glasner, *Gersonides: A Portrait of a Fourteenth-Century*

Philosopher-Scientist (Oxford: Oxford University Press, 2015), 16–17; and Sara Klein-Braslavy, *"Without Any Doubt": Gersonides on Method and Knowledge* (Leiden: Brill, 2009), 181–97. On what might have been included in the commentary on the *Metaphysics*, see Ruth Glasner, "Gersonides' Lost Commentary on the *Metaphysics*," *Medieval Encounters* 4 (1998): 130–57. A list of editions of Gersonides's commentaries is provided in Resianne Fontaine and Steven Harvey, "The Supercommentaries of Gersonides and His Students on Averroes' Epitomes of the *Physica* and the *Meteorologica*," n. 3, in *Gersonides through the Ages*, ed. Ofer Elior, Gad Freudenthal, and David Wirmer (forthcoming).

14. See Ruth Glasner, "Levi ben Gershom and the Study of Ibn Rushd in the Fourteenth Century," *Jewish Quarterly Review* 86 (1995): 51–90. Vatican, Biblioteca Apostolica ebr. 337, contains a manuscript dated 1316 containing a commentary on the *Categories* by Moshe b. Samuel b. Asher. This commentary refers to an even earlier commentary by Joseph b. Isaac Muqatil which is no longer extant. Muqatil's commentary may be the first Hebrew Aristotelian commentary. See Moritz Steinschneider, *The Hebrew Translations of the Middle Ages and the Jews as Transmitters*, vol. 2, ed., rev., and trans. Charles Manekin and Hans Hinrich Biesterfeldt (Dordrecht: Springer, forthcoming). Colette Sirat mentioned to me recently that she has found a manuscript of a commentary on the *De Anima* that may also predate Gersonides.

15. See Mashbaum, "Chapters 9–12," lxv–lxvi, cited in S. Harvey, "Islamic Philosophy and Jewish Philosophy" in *Cambridge Companion to Arabic Philosophy*, ed. Peter Adamson and Richard Taylor (Cambridge: Cambridge University Press, 2005), 362.

16. See S. Harvey, "Islamic Philosophy and Jewish Philosophy," 362, citing Paris BNF héb. 964, f. 4: "In the places where our opinion does not agree with that of Aristotle, we will mention our opinions and refute those of Aristotle." For other examples, see Charles Manekin, "'Composition, Not Commentary': Gersonides' Commentary on the *Isagoge* of Porphyry and its Afterlife," in *Gersonides through the Ages*, ed. Ofer Elior, Gad Freudenthal, and David Wirmer (forthcoming). I thank the author for providing me with an advance copy of this article. We shall discuss Gersonides's introduction to his commentary on Porphyry's *Isagoge* in more detail below.

17. See Glasner, "On the Writings of Gersonides' Philosophical Commentaries," in *Les methods de travail de Gersonide et le maniement du savoir chez les Scolastiques*, ed. Colette Sirat, Sara Klein-Braslavy, and Olga Weijers (Paris: Vrin, 2003), 90–103. See also Glasner, "Gersonides' Theory of Natural Motion," *Early Science and Medicine* 1 (1996): 151–203.

18. In his commentary on the *Middle Commentary on the "Physics,"* Gersonides refers to "the benefit that follows from such a commentary for the students in helping them understand some difficult things." Cited in S. Harvey, "Islamic Philosophy and Jewish Philosophy," 362.

19. See Glasner, "Levi Ben Gershom and the Study of Ibn Rushd in the Fourteenth Century," 61–69. See also Klein-Braslavy, "Gersonides as Commentator on Averroes," 200–201: "Gersonides replaced oral instruction by a written mode, embodied in his supercommentaries."

20. Ruth Glasner, *Gersonides*, 14–18 lists Gersonides's last Aristotelian commentary (on *Parva naturalia*) as dated February 1324. Ofer Elior prefers 1325 as the end of Gersonides's commentary writing years, though it is not entirely clear why. See Levi Ben Gershom (Gersonides), *The Wars of the Lord*, ed. Ofer Elior and Charles Touati, introduction, 37. According to both, there is no evidence that Gersonides continued his Aristotelian commentary writing project after 1325.

21. See Charles Manekin, *The Logic of Gersonides* (Dordrecht: Springer, 1992): 12–52.

22. See Ruth Glasner, *Gersonides*, 14–18.

23. It is quite likely that he continued to rework his physical ideas long after he had abandoned the commentary project.

24. Samuel ben Judah of Marseilles finished translating this work into Hebrew in 1321, thus not giving Gersonides much time to work on it before he abandoned his philosophical commentary project. Further, Gersonides did not comment on *Economics*, *Rhetoric*, *Poetics*, most likely because the *Economics* was not commented on by Averroes and Averroes's commentaries on the *Rhetoric* and *Poetics* were not translated into Hebrew by Ṭodros Ṭodrosi until the early 1330s, a few years after Gersonides had given up writing commentaries.

25. See Manekin, "Preliminary Observations," 93, citing the commentary on the *Prior Analytics*. See also Klein-Braslavy, "*Without Any Doubt*," 210, citing the commentary on the *Meteorology*.

26. Klein-Braslavy, "*Without Any Doubt*," 210–11, citing commentaries to *De caelo* and *De animalibus*.

27. See, e.g., *Commentary on "Isagoge"* cited in section 2 below. See however Paris BNF MS héb. 964, f. 1r, cited in Klein-Braslavy, "*Without Any Doubt*," 192, in which he says he will refute Aristotle's errors explicitly.

28. See Klein-Braslavy, "*Without Any Doubt*," 207.

29. One example is the discussion of choice in the *Commentary on "Parva naturalia"* 2:3. See Altmann, "Gersonides' Commentary," 17–18.

30. See the examples in Klein-Braslavy, "*Without Any Doubt*," 215–18.

31. Glasner, "Levi Ben Gershom and the Study of Ibn Rushd in the Fourteenth Century," 59–61.

32. Ibid., 76.

33. Referred to by Moshe Ḥabib; cf. Steinschneider, *Die Hebraeischen Übersetzungen des Mittelalters und die Juden als Dolmetscher*, 65.

34. See Glasner, "Evolution of the Genre," 189.

35. On Ha-Levy's commentary on the *Physica*, and Solomon of Urgul's commentary on the *Meteorologica*, see Fontaine and Harvey, "Supercommentaries of Gersonides and His Students."

36. These two commentaries are discussed in Glasner, "Levi Ben Gershom and the Study of Ibn Rushd in the Fourteenth Century," 62–63. The texts are found in Paris, BNF héb. 964, ff. 215v–316r and 316b–321r respectively.

37. Philadelphia, University of Pennsylvania Library, MS LJS229, ff. 1r–23r. In this anonymous commentary the author refers to Gersonides as his teacher (*mori*) as well as the "Sage R. Jedaiah ben Abraham Bedersi." See Manekin, "Composition, Not Commentary." According to Manekin, "The commentary was apparently intended to be used in an instructional setting, or perhaps records its use in such a setting. . . . It can be described as part notebook, par summary of doctrine. Occasionally there are 'exercises.' . . . For the most part the author offers explanatory glosses on sections of Averroes' text. . . . For the most part, the anonymous author seems interested in presenting the various doctrines and elucidating the text rather than adjudicating interpretations or engaging in controversy."

38. On this anonymous commentary, which is preserved in two manuscripts (London, British Library Or 1053 Margoliouth 1012/2 and Oxford, Bodleian 2050/4), see Glasner, "Evolution of the Genre," 190. For the connection of this author to Gersonides, Glasner refers to a statement in British Library Or 1053, f. 71r. There, the author refers to a true principle

which he heard from the mouth of his teacher ("העקר האמתי . . . ששמעתי מפי מורי . . .") and then quotes Gersonides (Glasner [in note 64] traces this quote to Paris, France, BNF héb. 965, f. 127r). This suggests that this author was a direct student of Gersonides. Note, however, that he also refers to "Maestre Leon" ("מיאישטרי ליאון") at f. 109v, which Margoliouth takes to prove that he was a student of Judah Messer Leon. See G. Margoliouth, *Catalogue of the Hebrew and Samaritan Manuscripts in the British Museum*, vol. 3 (London: British Museum, 1965), 334. However "Magister Leon" is also used to refer to Gersonides, by, e.g., Judah Cohen; see Manekin, "Composition, Not Commentary." Thus, the author may have been a direct student of Gersonides. Alternatively, it is possible that the author was actually a later fifteenth-century or early sixteenth-century student of Judah Messer Leon, who once heard Messer Leon expounding a doctrine of Gersonides, but did not realize these were Gersonides's words and attributed them to someone else. Or, perhaps, "from the mouth of my teacher" could be a metaphorical reference to something the author read in a book. In short, the matter is deserving of future study.

39. By statistically analyzing their use of language, Ruth Glasner determined that the works of these commentators are extremely close to those of Solomon of Urgul and suggested that either their authors are in fact all one person or else that there were two or three of them who worked together closely. Glasner, "Levi Ben Gershom and the Study of Ibn Rushd in the Fourteenth Century," 66. According to Glasner, this also suggests that the reason the commentaries of the three thinkers appear on one unique manuscript, Paris BNF MS 964 (IMHM F 31361) is that it served as a kind of "notebook" of one of the thinkers. It is also possible the manuscript is just a later attempt to collect somewhat obscure Gersonidean commentaries in one place.

40. See Solomon Urgul's commentary on *Meteorologica*, cited in Glasner, "Levi Ben Gershom and the Study of Ibn Rushd in the Fourteenth Century," 68, in which Urgul refers to Gersonides as "*ha-melammed otanu.*" R. S. Ha-Levi calls Gersonides "*morenu harab*" several times in his commentary on *Physica* (see Glasner, ibid., 63).

41. See note 39.

42. Cf. Mauro Zonta, "Una disputa sugli universali nella logica ebraica del Tracento. Shemuel di Marsiglia contro Gersonides nel 'Supercommento all' Isagoge' di Yehuda b. Ishaq Cohen," *Documenti e studi sulla tradizione filosofica medieval* 11 (2000): 409–58. See also Joseph Shatzmiller, "Étudiants juifs à la faculté de médecine de Montpellier, dernier quart du XIVe siècle," *Jewish History* 6 (1992): 243–45, and Manekin, "Composition, Not Commentary."

43. See Manekin, "Composition, Not Commentary."

44. Ibid.

45. This is suggested by Fontaine and Harvey, "The Supercommentaries of Gersonides and His Students on Averroes' Epitomes of the *Physica* and the *Meteorologica*."

46. At least in the case of Bedersi, who was called *hameliṣ*, "the rhetorician," by Judah Moscato.

47. This is included in a work entitled *Kellalei hahiggayon*, MS Bodl. Mich 342 (Nb. 2168). See Steinschneider, *Die Hebraeischen Übersetzungen des Mittelalters und die Juden als Dolmetscher*, 499.

48. See Ruth Glasner, "Two Notes on the Identification of Some Anonymous Hebrew Commentaries on the *Physics*," 335–44. A commentary on Averroes's *Epitome of Logic*, found in Oxford, Bodl. Ms. Mich. 355 and Oxford, Bodl. Ms. Opp. 575, was thought to be Narboni's but was in fact written by Mordecai Nathan in the second half of the fifteenth century. See

updated Steinschneider (forthcoming; I thank Charles Manekin for sending me an e-mail copy of this entry).

49. MS Munich 63.

50. Cf. Aviram Ravitsky, "Talmudic Methodology and Aristotelian Logic: David ibn Bilia's Commentary on the Thirteen Hermeneutic Principles," *Jewish Quarterly Review* 99 (2009): 184–99.

51. Narboni refers to his commentary on the *Physics* in his commentary on the *Maqāṣid*, MS Cambridge oo.6.30.3 f. 14r.

52. See Steven Harvey and Charles Manekin, "The Curious *Segullat Melakhim* by Abraham Avigdor," in *Écriture et réécriture des textes philosophiques médiévaux*, ed. J. Hamess and O. Weijers (Turnhout: Brepols, 2006): 215–52.

53. MS Munich 63, f. 206v: אב"ר המבאר כי דעתו רחבה מדעתי אמנם כתלמיד מתלמד.

54. Ṭodros Ṭodrosi's scientific textbook, mentioned above in n. 4, also turns to a discussion of Averroes's middle and long commentaries on the *Physics* after a number of excerpts from Avicenna and Al-Ghazali. He also refers to Avicenna and Al-Ghazali repeatedly in his discussion of the *Physics* (See Glasner, "The Evolution of the Genre," 190–91). Ṭodros may thus also be part of this group.

55. See Steven Harvey, "Why Did Fourteenth-Century Jews Turn to Al-Ghazali's Account of Natural Science?" *Jewish Quarterly Review* 91 (2001): 359–76, see 363–64 for the Hebrew translations of the fourteenth century. See also Steven Harvey, "Authors' Introductions as a Gauge for Monitoring Philosophic Influence: The Case of Alghazali," in *Tribute to Michael: Studies in Jewish and Muslim Thought Presented to Professor Michael Schwarz*, ed. Binyamin Abrahamov, et al. (Tel Aviv: Chaim Rosenberg School of Jewish Studies, 2009), 53–66. Most recently, S. Harvey has written, "The Changing Image of Al-Ghazālī in Medieval Jewish Thought," in *Islam and Rationality: The Impact of Al-Ghazālī*, ed. Georges Tamer (Leiden: Brill, 2015), 288–302.

56. Harvey, Why Did Fourteenth-Century Jews Turn to Al-Ghazali's Account of Natural Science?" 364–65.

57. On this work, see Charles Manekin, "When Jews Learned Logic from the Pope: Three Medieval Hebrew Translations of the Tractatus of Peter of Spain," *Science in Context* 10 (1997): 417, 426.

58. On the life and works of Judah Messer Leon, see Yehuda Halper, "Messer Leon, Judah," in *Encyclopedia of Renaissance Philosophy*, ed. Marco Sgrabi (Dordrecht: Springer, 2018); Zonta, *Hebrew Scholasticism*, 209–14; and H. Tirosh-Rothschild, *Between Worlds: The Life and Works of Rabbi David ben Judah Messer Leon* (Albany: State University of New York Press, 1991), 25–33. See also Judah Messer Leon, *The Book of the Honeycomb's Flow, Sepher Nophet Ṣuphim*, ed. and trans. I. Rabinowitz (Ithaca, NY: Cornell University Press, 1983), xvii–l.

59. See Charles Manekin, *Scholastic Logic*, 138, 145–46.

60. See Zonta, *Hebrew Scholasticism*, 213–14.

61. Abraham b. Mordechai Farissol, a student of Messer Leon, wrote a kind of summary of Messer Leon's *Mikhlal Yofi*, a commentary on Maimonides's *Millot Hahigayyon*, and a kind of précis of Aristotle's works on logic that drew heavily on Maimonides's *Millot Hahigayyon*. All of these works are found in Parma, Italy, The Palatina Library, cod. 1957. I shall address this unique collection of commentaries in a future study.

62. See Zonta, "Latin Scholastic Influences on Late Medieval Hebrew Physics," in *Science in Medieval Jewish Cultures*, 215; Giovanni Licata, "Delmedigo, Elijah," in Marco Sgrabi

(ed.), *Encyclopedia of Renaissance Philosophy*, ed. Marco Sgrabi (Dordrecht: Springer, 2018). Michael Engel and Giovanni Licata are currently preparing a Hebrew-Latin dual edition of Elijah del Medigo's Commentary on *De substantia orbis* (Berlin: De Gruyter, expected 2019).

63. See Zonta, *Hebrew Scholasticism*, 18; ibid., *La filosofica antica*, 262. Zonta suggests, however, that these may have been written by students of the Shem Ṭobs. For the commentaries on the *Physics*, see Glasner, "Evolution of the Genre," 198–204.

64. See the edition of the prologue in Chaim M. Neria, "It Cannot Be Valued with the Gold of Ophir (Job 28:16): Rabbi Joseph b. Shem-Ṭob's Commentary on Aristotle's Nicomachean Ethics: Sources and Analysis" (PhD diss., University of Chicago, 2015), 575–76. See also the discussion of the Shem Ṭob family and the various ways other thinkers contrasted the antiphilosophical Shem Ṭob ibn Shem Ṭob with the rest of the family. See especially, Neria's discussion of David, the son of Judah Messer Leon's discussion of this theme, 26–30.

65. Joseph refers to another fifteenth-century commentary on *Ethics*, still anonymous, also probably from Aragon. See Zonta, *Hebrew Scholasticism*, 17.

66. See Jean-Pierre Rothschild, "Questions de philosophie soumises par ʿĒlī Ḥabilio à Šēm Ṭōb, v. 1472," *Archives d'histoire doctrinale et littéraire du Moyen Age* 61 (1994): 105–32.

67. Zonta, *Hebrew Scholasticism*, 167. On the influence of the Saragossa school where Bibago taught, see Colette Sirat and Marc Geoffroy, *L'original arabe du Grand Commentaire d'Averroès au "De Anima" d'Aristote. Prémices de l'édition* (Paris: Vrin, 2005), 79–86.

68. See Zonta, *Hebrew Scholasticism*, 169–75.

69. Mauro Zonta provides an edition of part of the introduction to this text and a summary at Zonta, *Hebrew Scholasticism*, 11*–24* and 175–99, respectively.

70. See Yehuda Halper, "The Only Extant, Complete, and Original Hebrew Commentary on the Entire *Metaphysics* of Aristotle: Eli Habilio and the Influence of Scotism," *Vivarium* 57 (2019): 1–24.

71. See Zonta, *Hebrew Scholasticism*, 170; and Steinschneider, *Die Hebraeischen Übersetzungen des Mittelalters und die Juden als Dolmetscher*, 321.

72. This commentary is contained in MS New York, JTS 2371. See, e.g., f. 1r: המעיין בזה הספר ראוי שיקדם לו העיון בלימודיות ובטבעיות ובאלהיות .

73. Translated in Zonta, *Hebrew Scholasticism*, 45–107.

74. "Abraham Bibago on Intellectual Conjunction and Human Happiness: Faith and Metaphysics according to a 15th Century Jewish Averroist," *Quaestio: Yearbook of the History of Metaphysics* 15 (2015): 309–18; and "Philosophical Allegory in Bibago: Exegetical Duplicity for the Sake of Open Inquiry," *Jewish Quarterly Review* 21 (2014): 261–76.

75. See my "Bibago's Introduction to His *Commentary on Aristotle's 'Metaphysics,'*" *Zutot* 10 (2013): 1–15.

76. Bibago's *Commentary on "Physics"* is not extant. Parts of the *Commentary on "De anima"* may survive as marginal notes. See Colette Sirat and Marc Geoffroy, *L'original arabe du Grand Commentaire d'Averroès au "De Anima" d'Aristote*, 63–68.

77. Bibago's commentary on Aristotle's *Posterior Analytics*, which was completed in Huesca in 1446, is extant in two manuscripts (Vatican, Vatican Library, ebr. 350 and Paris, BNF héb. 959). The introduction and final words are edited in Avraham Nuriel, *Concealed and Revealed in Medieval Jewish Philosophy* (Jerusalem: Magnes Press, 2000), 188–89.

78. See sources cited in note 67 of this chapter. However, little is known about the academy at Saragossa and even less about Bibago's role in it.

79. This is my claim in the sources mentioned in note 78.

80. See Glasner, "Evolution," 196–204.

81. Zonta, *Hebrew Scholasticism*, 109–63. Zonta includes a translation and edition of the commentary on *Ethics* as well as some selections from the commentary on *De anima*.

82. Glasner, "Evolution," 193–95.

83. This is the thesis of Mauro Zonta, *Hebrew Scholasticism in the Fifteenth Century* (Dordrecht: Springer, 2006). According to Zonta, the Hebrew works in the scholastic style "discussed the same questions and used the same methods as contemporary Christian Schoolmen" (1–2). That is, the Aristotelian commentaries of these fifteenth-century authors were Hebrew replications of a currently popular philosophical genre in Latin. Accordingly, Zonta terms them "Hebrew Schoolmen" and their work "Hebrew Scholasticism."

84. For Gersonides, see Sara Klein-Braslavy, *Without Any Doubt*, 18n32. The exceptions to this trend in the fourteenth century, as we saw, are Samuel b. Judah of Marseilles and Abraham Abigdor.

85. See Giuliana Tamani, *Catalogo dei Manoscritti Filosofici, Giuridici e Scientifici nella Biblioteca della Comunità Ebraica di Mantova* (Firenze: Cadmo, 2003), 74–75. The final pages contain the attestation of censors and the year 1618, suggesting that the manuscript must have been completed on or before that year.

86. See Isaac Husik, *Judah Messer Leon's Commentary on the "Vetus Logica"* (Leiden: Brill, 1906), 7.

87. Steinschneider prints the opening text of this commentary in *Die Hebraeischen Übersetzungen des Mittelalters und die Juden als Dolmetscher*, 86–87, n. 297.

88. This is in contrast to the writers of encyclopedic works.

89. A. Busse (ed.), *Porphyrii isagoge et in Aristotelis categorias commentarium* (Commentaria in Aristotelem Graeca 4.1. Berlin: Reimer, 1887), lines 1–8. Jonathan Barnes's English translation avoids the question of the relationship of this work to the commentary tradition or to other commentaries by Porphyry. See Porphyry, introduction, trans. J. Barnes (Oxford: Oxford University Press, 2003), 3. See also the notes on pp. 25–26. For the Hebrew translation of Averroes's adaptation of this claim, see Averroes, *Commentarium Medium In Porphyrii Isagogen EtAristotelis Categorias*, ed. Hebert Davidson (Cambridge, MA: Mediaeval Academy of America and Berkley and Los Angeles: University of California Press, 1969), 4.

90. The Hebrew term I have translated "short work," קצור (see note 7), could be taken to refer to *Epitome* or *Short Commentary*, notwithstanding the fact that Gersonides actually comments on the middle commentaries. Moreover, the form of Gersonides's own commentary is more akin to that of Averroes's long commentaries. My use of "short work" for this term is intended to preserve these ambiguities about what forms of commentary are actually being studied and produced.

91. אמר לוי בן גרשם אחר התהלה לאל, ראיתי בספר הזה לבאר קצורי ן' רשד בספרי ההגיון לארסטו' כפי קצוה. ג"כ אזכור בו במקומות שדעתי זולת דעת ארסטו' בזאת המלאכה לפי מה שהבין ממנו ן' רשד מדבריו. ג"כ במקומות מה אחקור על מה שלא דבר בו ארסטו' ולפי מה שזכר מדבריו ן' רשד. MS Mantua 68, folio 3. This text is slightly different from that printed in Sholom Rosenberg, "Gersonides' Commentary on the *Ha-Mavo*," 90, section אז. Note, however, that some manuscripts of this commentary do not mention Averroes or Aristotle in the first sentence, but they do mention them in the second manuscript. See Charles Manekin, "Composition, Not Commentary."

92. Isaac Husik argues that this passage shows Gersonides's free thinking (*Judah Messer Leon's Commentary*, 9). However, in reaching this conclusion, Husik paraphrases rather than quotes the text and somewhat muddles the role of Averroes in Gersonides's statement. Thus

Husik notes that Gersonides's "object is to indicate the passages where his opinion is different from that of Aristotle," neglecting to mention Gersonides's crucial addition: "according to what Averroes understood of his words."

93. The English wording of this statement is taken from Davidson's translation, p. 6.

94. See Davidson's edition, p. 28 and Davidson's translation p. 27.

95. See text depicted in fig. 1. See also Rosenberg, "Gersonides' Commentary on the *Ha-Mavo*," 90, section אז.

96. See Manekin, "'Composition, Not Commentary': At Least Half of [Gersonides'] Approximately Forty Comments [on *Isagoge*] Are Critical of Porphyry."

97. This is suggested by Rosenberg, "Gersonides' Commentary on the *Ha-Mavo*," 85–86. See also Manekin, "Preliminary Observations," 87 ff.

98. Quoted in Rosenberg, "Gersonides' Commentary on the *Ha-Mavo*," 86. A few lines earlier, Gersonides notes that his understanding of Aristotle is filtered through Averroes. Nevertheless, when he speaks of his brazenness (*ʿazut meṣaḥ*), he mentions going against "the Philosopher."

99. Charles Manekin makes this point generally in "Logic in Medieval Jewish Culture" in *Science in Medieval Jewish Cultures*, 132.

100. Cf. Esther 7:4.

101. Cf. Num. 22:24.

102. Cf. Exod. 1:7 (JPS trans. 1917).

103. Cf. Gen. 45:1. MS Mantua 68, f. 1r: ולו היו הבאורים ההם מעטי הכמות רבי האיכות החרשתי, אבל כי הקיף אותם החסרון משני הצדדים גדר מזה וגדר מזה, והיה הענין בהפך אצל קצת הלשונות אשר מלאו בתי הנפש כסף הבאורים והפירושים והחקירות בחכמות המופתיות ויפרו ספריהם וישרצו ויעצמו במאד מאד, לא יכולתי להתאפק.

104. Steinschneider, *Die Hebraeischen Übersetzungen des Mittelalters und die Juden als Dolmetscher*, 83–84.

105. This is the main thesis of *Judah Messer Leon's Commentary*, but see esp. p. 81. Future studies of Messer Leon's commentary will likely reveal an even deeper engagement with Latin sources.

106. See Husik, *Judah Messer Leon's Commentary*, 93–108.

107. See note 6 in this chapter.

108. I am translating the Hebrew רופס subject in accordance with its use in three Hebrew translations of Maimonides's *Millot Ha-higgayon*, e.g., in chapter 1. See Israel Efros, *Maimonides' Treatise on Logic: The Original Arabic and Three Hebrew Translations* (New York: American Academy for Jewish Research, 1938): p. כד, סח, קג.

109. Mantua 68, f. 1r: ולא נבחר בקצור עם עזיבת ההכרחי והתועלי' בהכנת המאמר. כי זה סכלות גמורה לפי מה שנחשוד. וקצור מיוחס אל הפתאים. האמנם נכוין לקצר בהשלכת המאמרים החסרים מהספורים אשר אין להם רושם כל כך בדרוש אשר אנהג? בו כי האריכות בדברים ההם מותר.

110. Cf. Ps. 94:4.

111. Mantua 68: יְדַבְּרוּ עָתָק וייחסו הענין אל עזות מצח ובקשת הרוממות והתפארת.

112. Mantua 68: הסכמתי לכונן הסדור המעולה לבאר המאמר חלק חלק ולחלק כל חלק לחלקים מוגבלים למען התפרסם בהם כונת המחבר בשלם שבפנים. The word *hiskamti* likely refers to following convention rather than agreement since there is no one in context with whom Messer Leon could be in agreement.

113. See chapter 5 in this volume.

114. אמנם הסבה הפועלית אם מזה הספר, ר"ל המבוא, היה פורפיריאוס הפלוסוף אשר חברו לאחד מתלמידיו נקרא קיסאדורו. ואם מיתר הספרים היה ארסטו' [א]לא שהמאמר מעורב עם קצת דברי בן רשד עליהם על צד הבאור כאשר

אבאר. Mantua 68 has לא rather than אלא, which is not sensible in context. The MSS used by Husik have אלא (see p. 12).

115. See opening line of *Isagoge*. Messer Leon explicitly attributes this position to Porphyry here.

116. See *Metaphysics* Δ, chapter 5. See Zonta's edition.

117. See fig. 1 above.

118. Mantua 68, p. 6: ואפע"פ שמצאנו אנשים דקי השכל בטבעם שהם יגיעו לזה התכלית, רצוני לומר להבחין האמת והשקר מבלי אומנות כי אם מצד הטבע וההרגל כמו הממציא הראשון מההגיון ואיפוקראט שחבר ספרים רבים ברפואה כלם נכוחים וישרים למינן ולא התלמד בזאת המלאכה. מ"מ אי אפשר שיעשה זה דרך האומנות זולתה. גם לא יהיה מן הראוי להמנע מלחקותה בספרים משתמשים בקצתה בטבע למה שמי שיפעל זאת המלאכה בקנין קיים יותר חשוב ממי שיפעלה בהזדמן שהעושה זה באומנות וקנין הוא יודע שהוא מוכיח ושהוא מוליד כפי חקת המלאכה והפועל בהזדמן על צד ההרגל לא ידע דבר מזה. כאשר באר הפלוסוף בראשון מספר ההלצה. ועד הנה הגיע הכוון ממנו בענין לו הסבות, ונבוא אל ביאור המאמר.

119. "Aristotelianism as a Commentary Tradition," in *Philosophy, Science and Exegesis in Greek, Arabic and Latin Commentaries*, ed. Peter Adamson, Han Baltussen, M. W. F. Stone (London: University of London, 2004), 1–19, at 3.

YEHUDA HALPER is Senior Lecturer in the Department of Jewish Philosophy at Bar Ilan University. He is the recipient of the Yigal Alon Fellowship and editor of *Philosophy and the Jewish Tradition: Lectures and Essays by Aryeh Leo Motzkin*.

5

THE AUTHOR'S *HAQDAMAH* AS A LITERARY FORM IN JEWISH THOUGHT

Steven Harvey

Just as it is not proper to enter one's friend's house suddenly without first knocking on the door (cf. BT *Pesaḥim* 112a), so it is not proper to read any book, and in particular this book, without first reading the introduction.

Pinchas Elias Hurwitz, *Sefer ha-Berit*, preface

In the name of the Lord, God of the World[1]

Introduction

Most Jewish philosophically inclined authors of the medieval period, whether by design or by convention, began their works with carefully worded introductions. This custom was not particular to Jewish thinkers but was shared by the medieval Islamic and Christian philosophers as well.[2] Moreover, in an age before flashy covers and, for that matter, even before printing, the author's first few pages were his best chance to entice the potential reader to peruse his book. This was particularly true, but not solely, if the author was not well-known or much respected or if his book's title was not alluring. This is not to suggest that the author's introduction was always intended to persuade the reader to continue. Maimonides's introduction to the *Guide of the Perplexed* comes immediately to mind as one example in which the author actually seems to dissuade the unworthy reader from reading his work. Abraham ibn Da'ud's introduction to *Exalted Faith* is another. As we shall see, different authors had different goals in their introductions. Often we can discern in the introductions the authors' true intentions in composing their books. At times the introductions guide us to understand the books they introduce, and at times they provide the necessary keys for a proper interpretation of their writings.

As the present volume makes clear, Jews conveyed philosophical teachings through a wide variety of genres, including biblical commentaries, commentaries on philosophical and scientific texts, encyclopedias, dialogues, poetry, sermons, translations, paraphrases and summaries of philosophical works, and, of course, independent treatises. One finds *haqdamot* (introductions, prefaces, prologues, prooemia)[3] in all these kinds of philosophical writings, but they appear in certain genres more frequently than in others. Do these various introductions to works that convey philosophical teachings constitute a literary form in themselves? To what extent is their form or structure dictated by convention? Do they often have a common purpose? Are they important for understanding the works they introduce? In this chapter we will address these questions and others through an examination of some of the more interesting introductions of Jewish philosophically-inclined authors of the medieval period. After a few reflections on the Greco-Arabic influence on certain *haqdamah* conventions, we will discuss the introductions themselves in sections on pre-Maimonidean authors, Maimonides, and post-Maimonidean authors of the thirteenth and fourteenth centuries.

The Greco-Islamic Background

There were certain customs or conventions that the medieval author was expected to follow in beginning his book. One such convention, adopted by early Jewish authors writing in an Islamic milieu from the Muslim authors, was to begin their works with a short paragraph of praise to God.[4] Thus Saadia Gaon begins his *Book of Beliefs and Opinions* with the following praise to God: "Blessed be God, the God of Israel, Who is alone deserving of being regarded as the Evident Truth, Who verifies with certainty unto rational beings the existence of their souls, by means of which they assess accurately what they perceive with their senses and apprehend correctly the objects of their knowledge. Uncertainties are thereby removed from them and doubts disappear, so that demonstrations become lucid for them and proofs become clear. May he be lauded, then, above the highest commendation and praise."[5] The actual subject of the book begins in the following paragraph and, in the tradition of the Arab writers, is often introduced with the words *ammā baʿdu* or *ammā ʿalā athari*, which means something like "now after [this customary praise of God]," and indeed Saadia begins his next paragraph in this way. Many of Saadia's other works, such as his commentaries on Psalms, Proverbs, and Job and his *Commentary on Sefer Yeṣirah*, begin in the same fashion.[6] Baḥya ibn Paquda begins his *Duties of the Heart* with similar praise to God, and this convention is likewise found in many other Judeo-Arabic philosophic works, such as those by Solomon ibn Gabirol and Joseph ibn Ṣaddiq, and finds its way into Hebrew philosophic writings with Abraham bar Ḥiyya.[7] Such prescribed or customary praise may not seem of particular interest and often is little more than the pious praise of God, without which the writing of the work would be unthinkable. However, as in the case of Saadia, who unobtrusively weaves themes from his introduction to *Beliefs and Opinions* into his praise, these introductory praises may be far more telling.[8]

Another important custom is found in the early Greek commentators on Aristotle and highlighted by Islamic philosophers, such as Al-Fārābī and Averroes. I have in mind the custom of prefacing one's book with certain bits of information that ought to be known by every reader upon picking up any book. This is the tradition known in the Latin West as the *accessus ad auctores*. Al-Fārābī enumerates and discusses the "matters that the student should know upon opening every book." These are "the aim of the book, its utility, its division, its relation to other subjects, its rank, its title, the name of its author, and the method of instruction that is employed in it."[9] The earliest instance of this custom in Jewish literature appears to be in Isaac ibn Ghiyāth's eleventh-century Judeo-Arabic commentary on Ecclesiastes. Ibn Ghiyāth speaks of the "eight bits of knowledge" that one must grasp upon beginning any book: who the author is, the title of the book and its meaning, the one who wrote it down, the book's rank, whether it is written by divine inspiration, whether there is anything new and hitherto unknown in the book, the foundations on which the book is constructed, and the author's intention.[10] These eight things, it may be noted, are only partly represented in the *accessus* tradition. Full versions of this *accessus* tradition may be found among post-Maimonidean philosophers, likely influenced by Averroes's account of the tradition, such as Samuel ibn Tibbon and Gersonides.[11]

While the *accessus* tradition was adopted by other post-Maimonideans, whether fully or partially, the greatest Islamic influence on the *haqdamot* of the medieval philosophically-inclined Jewish authors were the various rhetorical topoi, which were almost expected in the introductions. Many of these topoi passed from classical Latin works of rhetoric to the Arabic introductions via Syriac authors.[12] Examples of these topoi will be given throughout this chapter.

Pre-Maimonidean Philosophers

Saadia Gaon

Saadia Gaon's *Beliefs and Opinions* is the first of the great medieval Jewish philosophical-theological treatises.[13] His grand introduction to that book and for that matter to the new discipline—that is, new for the Jews of his period—of philosophical speculation is one of the most read and important documents of medieval Jewish thought. Why did Saadia begin his work with an introduction? Saadia's contemporary, Isaac Israeli, for example, rarely prefaced his philosophical works with introductions. Indeed, even Al-Fārābī, despite his great interest in the *accessus* tradition, was wont to begin his independent works without introductions and to get immediately to the point. Not so Saadia. By the time he began his magnum opus, he had already mastered the art of writing introductions, having written numerous lengthy introductions to his various commentaries.[14] What is the purpose of his introduction to *Beliefs and Opinions*?

Saadia's main purpose in his lengthy introduction to *Beliefs and Opinions* is to lure the reader to study the ten treatises of the book that follow. The book has its own purpose, but it cannot be achieved if it is not read. The book's purpose is to save a wayward and confused nation, drowning in a sea of doubts. Saadia states this explicitly at the beginning of the introduction: "I saw in this age of mine many believers whose belief was not pure . . . I saw, furthermore, men who were sunk, as it were in seas of doubt . . . and there was no diver to bring them up from the depths. . . . I thought that it was my duty to help them therewith and my obligation to direct them to the truth."[15] Saadia wishes to guide his fellow Jew away from the doubts and uncertainties that in part had been created by the emergence of numerous secular and religious philosophies and toward the knowledge of truth. Scholars agree that Saadia wrote his book to clarify and prove the principles of Judaism and thereby defend them against contrary teachings, although the exigencies that compelled him to write the work are not so appreciated. Saadia believes that the Jewish nation "is a nation only by virtue of its laws."[16] When he saw that those laws were being set aside and not followed and that the nation was thereby on the threshold of self-annihilation, he realized he needed to defend those laws, encourage their observance, and make them persevere. Saadia's pressing aim in writing *Beliefs and Opinions* is thus the very preservation of the Jewish nation. He was convinced he could use the newly available philosophy and science to prove the existence of a unique, almighty eternal God and to persuade the reader of the principles of Judaism and the truths of Torah on this foundation.[17] His problem was getting his targeted readership, which included the "believers whose belief was not pure," those "sunk in seas of doubt," and even the "deniers of the faith who boasted of their corruption" to peruse his book. His would-be readers had been made skeptical not only by the public teachings of various competing philosophies, religions, and schools of thought but also by the sorry example set by many corrupt leaders of the Jewish establishment. Saadia's strategy was to convince them to return to the teachings of the Torah on the basis of what is accessible to the unassisted human mind, without reliance on divine revelation; he sought to combat philosophy with philosophy. The difficult task of the introduction was to interest would-be readers in his program and almost dare them to read on.

Saadia begins his introduction with a discussion of the causes of uncertainties in our minds, some of which are so powerful that they are taken as truths. Saadia explains that the root of these uncertainties is often poor logic and our tendency to jump to conclusions. He thus states that he will use simple terms and easy language so his book will be easy to follow and so whoever studies it diligently will attain true knowledge. He makes clear to his reader, many of whom are not sure of their beliefs or are nonbelievers, that his emphasis is on reason. Following contemporary Muʿtazila theologians who also held that rational speculation will lead to the knowledge of God and accordingly prefaced their theological works with epistemological introductions, Saadia lists and discusses the sources of certain knowledge.[18] To the three sources of sense perception, intuition, and logic, he adds a fourth: authentic tradition. Throughout the introduction, Saadia wishes to make clear that Judaism does not go counter to reason but harmonizes perfectly with it. Nonetheless, we must be careful how we interpret the data from our knowledge sources, and Saadia provides numerous examples taken from philosophy and science of valid and invalid reasoning and conclusions. Saadia's point to his readers is that if they are careful in their reasoning, they will attain true knowledge.

At this point Saadia turns to his more observant reader and raises the question no doubt on his mind: How can we engage in philosophical speculation when there are those who disapprove, "being of the opinion that speculation leads to unbelief and is conducive to heresy?"[19] Saadia was very much aware that he was doing something radically new in his book that needed the approval of Jewish law. He thus interprets the prohibitions of the sages and explains why philosophical speculation is permitted. But why should believing Jews be interested in such inquiries even if they are permitted? Here Saadia speaks for the first time directly to his reader in the second-person singular: "Know then, may God direct you aright, Oh you who studies this book, that we inquire into and speculate about the matters of our religion with two objectives in mind: to have verified in fact what we have learned from the prophets of God theoretically; [and] . . . to refute him who argues against us in regard to anything pertaining to our religion."[20] Having explained the Jew's need for philosophy, Saadia next considers the opposite question, the philosopher's need for Judaism. After all, if, as he has argued, matters of religious belief may be known through philosophical speculation, why did God bother to teach us things through the prophets that we could have learned by ourselves?[21] Saadia's reply focuses on the length of time needed to attain truth through philosophical reasoning and on the fact that for one reason or another many people might never attain it.

Having explained why the philosophical-theological study that follows should be of interest to every Jew, believer or unbeliever, Saadia then lists the various causes that keep infidels and heretics from engaging in such philosophical speculation, that is, from reading his book. Here, in the closing pages of the introduction, the skeptical, hesitant, and cocksure readers will likely recognize themselves and perhaps be willing to consider the error of their ways. Saadia then gives examples of specific problems, such as unanswered prayers, unpunished evil doers, suffering righteous people, and the mind-boggling notions concerning God and His unity, each of which can cause grave doubts in man. Saadia promises to deal with these and similar issues one by one in the course of his book. He concludes with an enumeration of the ten treatises of his book.[22]

Joseph ibn Ṣaddiq and Abraham ibn Da'ud

Two examples of introductions to medieval Jewish philosophic books, both of which begin with one of the more interesting topoi found in the introductions—one we will call the "question artifice," in which the author states that his book is in response to a question or request by someone—are those in Joseph ibn Ṣaddiq's *Microcosm* and Abraham ibn Da'ud's *Exalted Faith*. Both works were written in Spain in the mid-twelfth century, and both were written in Judeo-Arabic but are extant only in the medieval Hebrew translation. I will consider first Ibn Ṣaddiq's *Microcosm*, which is the earlier work.

The *Microcosm* begins with an introduction of two pages in Horovitz's 1903 edition. As has already been noted, Ibn Ṣaddiq begins with the customary short paragraph of praise to God, the One, the Creator of the world, followed immediately with the *ammā ba'du* (now after). Ibn Ṣaddiq then writes:

> You asked me [O expert student] what the intention of the wise men is in their saying the "permanent good" and the "perfect virtue," for they said that this virtue and this good are not found in this world. They further said that these things ought to be investigated by every intelligent person. Now I have seen this path and it requires much toil, for it is a difficult thing to attain for the few who pursue it and seek it, all the more so in our generation which is an ignorant one, inferior to all the preceding ones, and especially in the knowledge of this matter, which is as nothing to them. The way to accomplish this task requires two fundamental principles: the first is to know the Creator, may He be praised, and the second is to do His will, as the path of truth requires.[23]

Ibn Ṣaddiq writes that he will answer his student's question because of "my love for wisdom and all who seek it." The way to attain this great knowledge requires comprehending the books of the pure philosophers and the divine scholars, and the way to understand them is by training oneself in the quadrivium and logic. All this requires much time, and the beginning student may lose his patience. Ibn Ṣaddiq tells us his intention is thus to explain man's knowledge of himself because as a microcosm, he has some resemblance to everything that is in the world, and so through knowledge of oneself, one can bypass the tedious study of the propaedeutic sciences. Ibn Ṣaddiq concludes his introduction with a division of the book into four treatises and a brief description of each treatise. The introduction makes clear that the terms the student mentioned cannot be simply understood but that the reader will first have to learn philosophy, that is, some logic, physics, theology, and practical science. *Microcosm* thus teaches all these things.

Assuming Ibn Ṣaddiq was asked by a student about these terms, would his goal in writing the *Microcosm*, his only major work, have been simply to answer the student's question or rather to seize the opportunity to present his own philosophical theology? The question artifice awakens the worthy reader's interest and draws him into a well-organized program of study for which he may otherwise have had little patience.

Ibn Da'ud dispenses with the traditional introductory praise of God, and his introduction to the *Exalted Faith* is almost twice as long as Ibn Ṣaddiq's, but it bears much in common with that introduction. It too begins with a question:

> You asked me, may God exalt you, years ago about the problem of necessity and choice, and you mentioned to me the problem you have with each of the two extremes. On the one hand, if God indeed necessitates the sins man commits, how can He punish him for them? How can He prohibit them in His law? And how can He send His prophets to command [against committing] them? On the other hand, if [commandments] are given to man, and he can transgress them if he so wishes or obey them if he wishes, how can there be something over which God has no control?[24]

Ibn Da'ud, presumably still following the questioner, then cites biblical verses to show that scripture itself is not clear on this problem, with many verses to be found in support of each of the views. Ibn Da'ud tells us that he had explained to his questioner that some of the verses need to be interpreted. He had further explained to him that reason argues that there are far less problems with accepting choice than accepting necessity, but he understood that his explanation was not sufficient to convince the questioner or many others among the men of philosophical speculation of this difference. Ibn Da'ud recognizes the deep confusion of many of his fellow Jews over this problem (and others like it) and sees that it results from inadequate study of the principles of Judaism and an insufficient grasp of the agreement that exists between Judaism and true philosophy. He resolves to help his questioner and those like him, that is, those who have begun to study the sciences and are perplexed and disturbed by the seeming lack of agreement between the teachings of the Torah and those of philosophy, but he explains that to do so and to resolve satisfactorily the problem of necessity and choice, he must first give the reader a crash course in physics and metaphysics (outlined in the introduction) and in the basic principles of Judaism. Ibn Da'ud promises to support his scientific teachings with biblical verses and philosophic demonstrations. This latter point is most important in view of his critique of the faulty and misleading logic of popular Neoplatonic thinkers, such as Solomon ibn Gabirol.

Ibn Da'ud thus presents in his introduction the reason and purpose for which he wrote his book, its subject matter, its method of instruction, and its intended readership. Like Ibn Ṣaddiq, he begins with the question artifice, and like him he explains that to answer the question, he must first explain many other matters, which comprise the book's subjects. Scholars have debated whether Ibn Da'ud's real concern in his book was with the problem of free will. While free will is emphasized in the introduction, the fact that it is discussed again in only a few pages toward the book's end could speak for its marginal role in the work. Two recent monographs on the *Exalted Faith* persuasively argue otherwise.[25] The problem of free will *is* the central concern of the book. Yet, even if we accept this conclusion, as I do, it still seems evident that Ibn Da'ud wished to enlighten his worthy reader to the true philosophy, that of Aristotle, which hitherto had not been expounded by any other Jewish thinker. The introduction makes clear that the opening question provided him not only with the occasion and justification for such an account but also the structure and order it would assume.

Judah Ha-Levi

I have suggested the utility of the question artifice for arousing the interest of the reader to the book. Were these questions really asked of the authors, and could a passing question really result in a book? What if the questions had never been asked of Ibn Ṣaddiq and Ibn Da'ud: would their books never have been written? Would they be unknown today as philosophers by students of Jewish philosophy? While we have no certain knowledge about the questions asked of Ibn Ṣaddiq and Ibn Da'ud, we do know something about the question at the beginning of Judah Ha-Levi's *Kuzari*, which was written in Spain in 1140, shortly after the *Microcosm* and shortly before the *Exalted Faith*.

The *Kuzari* begins, without the traditional praise of God, as follows: "I was asked about whatever arguments I had against those who differ with us, such as the philosophers and adherents of [other] religions, as well as the dissenters who differ with the multitude [of Jews]."[26] Ha-Levi tells us that he immediately thought of the report of the arguments that the Jewish sage brought to the king of the Khazars that persuaded him centuries earlier to convert to Judaism. The pagan king had had a recurring dream in which an angel told him that his intentions were pleasing to God but not his actions. This led the king to investigate his own beliefs and eventually convert together with many of his nation to Judaism. Ha-Levi tells us that inasmuch as many of the sage's arguments also convinced him, he decided to answer his questioner by presenting them just as they occurred. The *Kuzari* is thus purportedly an accurate account of the historical discussions between the king of the Khazars and the Jewish sage. Since we are sure today that the account is Ha-Levi's own creation, what about the opening question? Thanks to a letter from the treasures of the Cairo Genizah, we have good reason to believe that Ha-Levi did indeed write the *Kuzari*, or at least an early version of it, in response to a question. Ha-Levi writes in the letter: "As for the Khazarī book, the reason for writing it was a challenge by one of our heretics, living in the land of the Romans, who questioned me concerning certain problems, in reply to which I sent him that book."[27] S. D. Goitein explains that the reference is to a Karaite philosopher from Christian Spain.[28] Tzvi Langermann has argued against Goitein and others that the reference is simply to a heretic, and not specifically a Karaite.[29] Regardless, there really was a question that Ha-Levi felt needed to be addressed. The question arouses the interest of the reader, who no doubt also is curious what arguments the despised religion can bring against the competing philosophies and theologies of the day. The historical background promises an exotic flavor to the defense, and the past success of the arguments along with Ha-Levi's own approval of them assures that the adventure will be not only entertaining but enlightening as well. In addition, with Ha-Levi's own invention of the angel's distinction between intentions and actions, a subtheme is subtly introduced to which the author will return in the course of his book.

* * *

Jewish interest in philosophy, seemingly in slumber for nearly a millennium, awoke with the translation into Arabic of Greek philosophic and scientific texts. Some learned Jews of the time, like contemporary Muslims and Christians, were attracted to the new wisdom and saw how it could be used to strengthen their own religion. Medieval Jewish philosophy became the enterprise of harmonizing the truths of religion with those of reason. But which reason, which school of philosophy, is the true one? How is it to be presented to the Jewish reader, that is, how does the medieval Jew write philosophy? And is it a discipline appropriate and desirable for all Jews to study? Our discussion of representative introductions to well-known works of pre-Maimonidean Jewish thought points to the introduction as an important literary tool for the medieval Jew to address such issues and convey his intent.

Maimonides

As in a study of virtually any area in the history of medieval Jewish philosophy, so in the study of the philosophers' introductions to their works, Maimonides merits a subheading of his own. The way of doing philosophy in the Jewish world changes with Maimonides, and his writings seem to be the inescapable point of departure for later thinkers. I have written an introductory essay on his introductions and will here briefly summarize the relevant conclusions.[30]

Maimonides attributed great importance to the introduction and began all his major works—whether philosophical, legal, or medical—with introductions. Some books have more than one introduction. The *Guide of the Perplexed* has three introductions, one to each of its parts, and an epistle dedicatory that is itself an introduction of sorts. His *Commentary on the Mishnah* also has several introductions—some quite long—and at least one of these introductions itself has an introduction. From these works it emerges that Maimonides was an expert in the art of writing introductions and fully appreciated their power and importance. He knew that the introduction was the appropriate place for providing the premises or principles needed for understanding the book it introduces, and—like Ibn Da'ud—he knew that the introduction could persuade the intended reader to read on, just as it could dissuade the unworthy one not to. Different works had different purposes, were intended for different audiences, and accordingly required different kinds of introductions. Yet each of Maimonides's introductions was carefully crafted, and each accomplished its goal in its own way.

The epistle dedicatory that opens the *Guide of the Perplexed* is not a formal introduction and has few features found in Arabic introductions of the time. It does provide the motivation for the book, although not its purpose; that is, Maimonides felt compelled to write the *Guide* when his student left him, but he does not explain precisely why. It further suggests the intended readership of the book. These issues are addressed with greater clarity in the introduction to part 1.

Maimonides's introduction to part 1, his general introduction to the *Guide*, is one of the outstanding introductions of the medieval period.

It is an ingeniously written piece of art and in a class by itself. It provides most of the information customarily expected in a medieval introduction, in accordance with the *accessus* tradition. This was not lost on fifteenth-century commentator Shem-Ṭov ibn Shem-Ṭov, who listed many of these items found in Maimonides's introduction: "The intention of the book, its end, what its name is [and what it signifies], for whom the book was composed, and the method of instruction employed in it."[31] One could add to this list the utility of the book and its subject matter. What distinguishes the introduction, however, is not its adherence to this tradition, but rather its detailed and carefully formulated account of the treatise's aims and its explicit revelation that the book is an esoteric work—a closed book—with guidelines on how to understand and interpret it. Maimonides states clearly near the beginning of the introduction that a primary purpose of his treatise is to teach us how to read scripture to understand its deeper meanings, but as becomes evident throughout the introduction, the introduction itself provides the worthy with the keys to understanding the deeper meaning of scripture and for that matter any great philosophic book—in particular, the *Guide* itself. Few introductions have ever offered so much.

Post-Maimonidean Philosophers

Among the conventions of pre-Maimonidean Jewish authors discussed above was to begin their works with a short paragraph of praise to God, at times in rhymed prose. This tradition continues, albeit to a lesser extent, among the post-Maimonideans of the thirteenth and fourteenth centuries, for example, in many of the introductions of Shem-Ṭov ibn Falaquera, Joseph ibn Kaspi, and in major works such as Gersonides's *Wars of the Lord*. In many of these opening praises, the reader will discern the rationalist tendencies of the authors: for example, Falaquera praises "the Cause of causes, Who bestows upon man the intelligibles,"[32] and Gersonides appears to allude to his own views on divine providence and the attainment of individual immortality though intellectual perfection.

The question artifice topos continues to be employed among the post-Maimonideans. It is found in one of the first post-Maimonidean philosophic works, Samuel ibn Tibbon's *Ma'amar Yiqqavu ha-Mayim*. Other thirteenth- and fourteenth-century writers who employed this device in their introductions include Nissim of Marseilles in his *Ma'aseh Nissim* and Moses Narboni in his *Ma'amar be-Shelemut ha-Nefesh*. Narboni also employed, in the introduction to his *Commentary on Ḥayy ibn*

Yaqẓān, a similar device: namely, explaining that he is writing the book for those wise students from whom he suddenly has been separated and thus can no longer instruct orally. As for Samuel ibn Tibbon, we will soon see that many of his most important works—according to what Samuel himself writes in his various introductions—were the result of personal entreaties to him. We will return to this shortly, but it will be useful first to distinguish between the literary works of pre-Maimonidean Jewish philosophy and those of the post-Maimonidean Jewish philosophy, as different genres of writing may well call for different kinds of introductions, or at least have different literary conventions.

The most obvious difference between pre- and post-Maimonidean Jewish philosophers is that the former, for the most part, read Arabic and the latter, for the most part, did not and were dependent on Hebrew translations. While Arabic forms and styles of writing introductions were preserved in the translations of Arabic philosophic texts and influenced Hebrew writers in this way, Jews who were not fluent in Arabic or Latin were limited in their knowledge of the conventions in writing introductions to available Hebrew texts.

Another distinction between pre- and post-Maimonidean philosophic works considers the literary genres of these works. Isadore Twersky has observed "the extent to which philosophic material permeate[d] other more conventional literary genres," such as Bible commentary, Talmudic explication, homiletics, legal codification, and poetry, in the post-Maimonidean period.[33] This is certainly true, but I am concerned with the main genres of writing through which philosophy was transmitted. Virtually all the pre-Maimonidean introductions we have mentioned were to the authors' own independent treatises, although some introductions to biblical commentaries were also mentioned. In fact, during the pre-Maimonidean period, there were few Jewish commentaries on philosophic or scientific texts,[34] and until Judah ibn Tibbon, in the second half of the twelfth century, virtually no Hebrew translations of philosophic texts. In contrast, the focus of philosophic writing in the century after Maimonides was directed to the transmission of philosophy in Hebrew. The most sought-after philosophic books, with few notable exceptions, were thus Hebrew translations, Hebrew encyclopedias of science and philosophy, and philosophic biblical commentaries.

Samuel ibn Tibbon

The transition of the language of philosophy for Jews from Arabic to Hebrew that had begun in the twelfth century with Bar Ḥiyya and Ibn Ezra and continued with the translations of Judeo-Arabic classics by Judah ibn Tibbon, reached a turning point immediately after Maimonides's death with Samuel ibn Tibbon. Samuel is most famous for his translation of Maimonides's *Guide* and the appended lexicon of Hebrew philosophic terms used in his translation, but his independent treatise, *Ma'amar Yiqqavu ha-Mayim*, and his philosophic commentary on Ecclesiastes became two of the most popular Hebrew philosophic books of the thirteenth century. Among his translations, that of Aristotle's *Meteorology* was not only the first Aristotelian text to be translated into Hebrew but indeed the first translation into Hebrew of any philosophic text not written by a Jew. Samuel took his introductions seriously. His introduction to his translation of the *Guide* is oft cited, like those of his father, for its enunciation of a methodology of translation. What do we learn from his introductions?

The introduction to the translation of the *Guide* reads in part like an apologia for the work, or more precisely an apologia for his undertaking to translate it. Such apologiae, which conventionally include admission of one's own scholarly limitations, are not at all unusual in introductions to medieval Jewish philosophic texts and can be found already in Saadia's introduction to *Beliefs and Opinions* and Baḥya's introduction to *Duties of the Heart*,[35] but would become commonplace in introductions to medieval Hebrew translations of philosophic texts. In his introduction—after proclaiming that he did not translate the *Guide* because he considered himself especially wise and that he is aware of his shortcomings in the three things a translator of a philosophic texts must know: the language of the book, the language into which the book is to be translated, and the book's meaning—he relates why he undertook to translate the work. The scholars of Provence had a great desire to read the *Guide* and accordingly begged Maimonides to send them a copy. When the copy finally arrived, much to their frustration in the Arabic original, they relentlessly beseeched Samuel ibn Tibbon to translate it, despite his protestations of inadequacy. In the end he could not decline, seeking help from his father's translations and his own personal correspondence with Maimonides. His ultimate justification was "to spread its benefit among our nation, to enlighten them in the belief in God and in His laws, and to direct them to believe the truth and stay far from falsehood." Having said this, he begs the reader to judge him well and correct his mistakes in language, and he gives detailed examples of the kinds of linguistic mistakes he may make and why. His approach to translation was conservative out of fear of changing the meaning Maimonides intended.

His one addition was to number Maimonides's chapters so as to facilitate reference to them.

Six years later when he translated Aristotle's *Meteorology*, he again relates in the introduction that he did so only after repeated beseeching to do so, this time by the "erudite lover of wisdom," Joseph ben Israel, and only after refusing his request to translate the other works on natural science. Once again he explains the specific difficulties of the task: in this case the errors and omissions in the Arabic translation and his "limited intellectual ability." And once again, as in the translation of the *Guide*, he asks God's help to direct him in his translation.

The decision to write *Ma'amar Yiqqavu ha-Mayim* was also in response to someone else's intellectual prodding. The book begins with Samuel ibn Tibbon telling us that one of his "erudite colleagues, who seek *to find words of delight* [Eccles. 12:10]," asked him about the philosophers' response to the physical problem that in this world water does not cover all Earth as one should expect it to in accordance with the theory of the four elements. The citation from Ecclesiastes may also allude to the verse's only citation in Maimonides's *Guide*, in which it refers to the addressee of the book, with the possible implication that Samuel's questioner is no less qualified than Maimonides's addressee. Regardless, Samuel explains that the question posed is a problem only for those who believe in eternity, for believers in creation will answer simply that God changed their nature during creation. Indeed, he continues, according to the beginning of Genesis, before God commanded that the waters be gathered unto one place and the dry land appear, the waters covered all the earth. He tells us that he wrote the book to answer this question and thus called it *Ma'amar Yiqqavu ha-Mayim* because of the importance of Genesis 1:9, "let the waters be gathered," to this question, even though his book treats other related and even more glorious matters. Samuel concludes his short introduction, as is his custom, asking God to keep him from error and also protect his readers from stumbling on his words. May God allow them to judge him favorably, even though his words may seem far from their opinions, for his aim is only the truth.

Samuel ibn Tibbon's lengthy introduction to his *Commentary on Ecclesiastes* is of special interest for its introduction to the Hebrew reader of the *accessus* tradition. The full explication of this tradition is found in his lengthy commentary on Ecclesiastes 1:1.[36] This custom of the commentators may be seen as not so much rhetorical—as many of the devices that we find in the Hebrew traditions—as practical: to provide information that the reader needs to know if he is to understand the book. Samuel's commentary also employs rhetorical devices he has used in his other introductions, such as once again writing at the request of someone, fear of criticism, apology for errors, and request for compassion from the reader, as well as others that he has not yet used but are found in earlier Judeo-Arabic introductions as well as later Hebrew ones, such as the longing for knowledge, survey of existing literature, compulsion to write, and writing for one's own memory.

Thirteenth-Century Translators

The great bulk of the impressive project—impressive in scope and in quality—to translate Arabic texts of Greek philosophy and Islamic philosophy into Hebrew began with Samuel ibn Tibbon and continued for a century and a quarter until Ṭodros Ṭodrosi of Arles in the 1330s. Most of the translations of philosophic texts into Hebrew in the thirteenth century were carried out by Samuel and his relatives: his son Moses ibn Tibbon, his son-in-law, Jacob Anatoli, and his grandson, Jacob ben Makhir. I have discussed these translators and their introductions elsewhere so will limit this section to summarizing the conclusions from my study and a few observations.[37] While Moses wrote introductions to his independent treatises and, like his father, employed the *accessus ad auctores*, which he does in his introduction to his *Commentary on Song of Songs*,[38] he did not begin any of his many translations of Averroes's commentaries (or for that matter, with few exceptions, any of his translations) with introductions. Apparently he felt the task of the translator was to get down to business and translate without any need for introductions. One important exception is his introduction to his 1259 translation of Ibn al-Jazzār's popular medical work *Zād al-musāfir* (*Viaticum peregrinantis*). This scarcely cited introduction provides us with the clearest statement of Moses's method of translation, one acquired from his grandfather and father. Arabic-to-Hebrew translations should be word for word, and eloquence must yield to faithfulness. Like his relatives, Moses states that the three skills needed to translate are knowledge of the two languages involved and knowledge of the subject. And like his relatives and many other translators, he deprecates his own knowledge of languages and science and concludes with a prayer for help and guidance.

Not all thirteenth-century translators wrote introductions to their translations, and of those who did, most did so only for some of their works. But what is most noteworthy about all these introductions is that, unlike most of the introductions to independent philosophic treatises of the period, the goal was not to entice the reader to read the book. In fact, the idea to translate the book was often not the translator's, but that of someone else. The translators also did not feel that they needed to begin their translations with an *accessus ad auctores*, even though some of these same translators—for example, Samuel and Moses ibn Tibbon and Zeraḥyah ben Isaac—began their biblical commentaries with it. Their goal was thus not to introduce or explain the work but simply to translate it. What then was the purpose of their introductions? And why did they employ conventional rhetorical features in them?

The truth is that, for the most part, the translators did not feel introductions were necessary. The main purpose of the introductions of the translators was as an apologia for their undertaking the translation and an explanation of why they did so, particularly when they suspected objections could be raised against the translation of the book: for example, a first translation of a book of Aristotelian logic (Why is this useful? Is it halakhically permissible?), a translation of Aristotelian metaphysics (How can it be understood?), and a work already translated (Why translate it again?). In many introductions, the translators sought to ward off criticism of the translation by confessing their own limited abilities and proclaiming the difficulty of the text, the science it treats, and the shortcomings of Hebrew scientific terminology. In virtually all cases, aid and guidance were sought from God, or at least forgiveness should the translator have done anything wrong. These introductions to the translations help us understand the yearning for science among Jews in thirteenth-century Western Europe and the various forces that motivated the translators to undertake the prodigious task of making available Greek and Arabic science and philosophy to their coreligionists.

Fourteenth-Century Translators

While the thirteenth-century translators saw themselves as pioneers in their work, carefully selected which works to translate, and needed to forge a new Hebrew technical vocabulary, the fourteenth-century translators saw themselves as completing the project, determined which remaining texts were in need of translation, and decided to what extent to adopt the earlier technical vocabulary or to replace these terms with others. What is most interesting about the introductions of the fourteenth-century translators of philosophic and scientific texts into Hebrew, some of them quite long, is that they provide valuable glimpses into the translators' minds that allow us to understand what moved them to translate the works they translated and the importance they attached to these translations.

Consider Qalonymos ben Qalonymos (1287–?), arguably the most active and proficient of the Arabic-to-Hebrew translators of the medieval period. When Qalonymos began his translation activity in southern France in 1306 at the age of nineteen, many of the basic Arabic texts of philosophy and science had already been translated into Hebrew. The first seven years or so of Qalonymos's literary activity were dedicated, apart from a few early medical translations, to expanding what Tony Lévy has called the "mathematical bookshelf of the medieval scholar."[39] Then in 1313 and 1314, while continuing to translate selected Arabic works of geometry, Qalonymos translated Averroes's middle commentaries on Aristotle's *Topics* and on the *Sophistical Refutations* and a few introductory treatises of Al-Fārābī, including the *Enumeration of the Sciences.* This inaugurated perhaps the most important and ambitious translation project of his career: the attempt to complete the Hebrew translation of Averroes's *Corpus commentariorum in Aristotelem.* In 1316 Qalonymos turned to translating systematically the middle commentaries on the scientific books that he believed had not yet been translated. In 1317 he completed his work on the middle commentaries with the translation of the one on the *Metaphysics.* These middle commentaries became popular at once, and it is through them that Jews were able to master Aristotelian science. While Qalonymos's mathematical translations are extant, for the most part, in only one or two manuscripts, those of Averroes's commentaries are extant in dozens of manuscripts and, in the case of the *Middle Commentary on the Physics*, over fifty. These were perhaps the most important Hebrew translations of non-Jewish scientific works in the Middle Ages. We do not know exactly what motivated Qalonymos to prepare them as he did not write any introductions to these translations. Nor can we even be sure of the part he played in the translations of Averroes's long commentaries on *Physics* and *Metaphysics*, as again there are no introductions to these works. Then in 1316, amid his translating of Averroes, he suddenly decided to translate the epistle by the *Ikhwān al-Ṣafā'* on the animals. Indeed, while working on the middle commentaries, he seems to have suspended his translations of works on mathematics and astronomy, and this may have been the only work not by Averroes that he translated during this period. Why did he interrupt his translating of the important

Averroan commentaries for this decidedly non-Aristotelian work? Fortunately, we do have an informative introduction by Qalonymos to this translation that provides answers.

Qalonymos begins his introduction by telling us why he translated the treatise. He makes it abundantly clear that this treatise was not chosen randomly for the sake of translating something, because he was bored, in the mood for translating, or had leisure time. He tells us that he would not undertake a project that had no use. Neither did he translate this treatise for the sake of the filthy rich who like to fill their homes with treasures and beautiful objects, so that they might have one more lovely thing over which to rejoice and gloat. Rather he dedicated himself wholeheartedly to this translation to satisfy the entreaty of "attentive friends" (Song of Sol. 8:13) who desired to "understand the *secrets of wisdom* [Job 11:6]" and who wished for "an explanation of the secrets of the beings" and "yearned to apprehend the mysteries of nature."[40]

Qalonymos's claim that he translated the treatise at the entreaty of friends was almost a commonplace in the introductions of translators. In this case, the friends presumably did not know about the *Ikhwān al-Ṣafā'* but wanted to grasp the secrets of philosophy. Their desire was great, but Qalonymos's translation of Averroes's commentaries on the Aristotelian books of natural science was making it possible for the first time for the Jews of Provence to master the preliminaries needed for learning the secrets. Why did he not suggest to his friends to read the commentaries in their proper order and then turn to Maimonides's *Guide*? And in any case, in what sense did this book provide the elusive secrets? Qalonymos tells us that this treatise was not simply another book of amusing stories and proverbs but rather was intended to teach words of consolation, morals, and profound secrets, scattered throughout its pages, which even scholars could not discern in one reading. The treatise, we are told, is not a demonstrative philosophic work; its methodology, according to Qalonymos, is more narrative and anecdotal than demonstrative. This, he adds, is the style of the epistles of the *Ikhwān al-Safā'*. Qalonymos here tells the reader something about these Islamic savants and suggests that they wrote in anonymity because many of their teachings were not fully in accordance with their religion. But Qalonymos's purpose in translating this treatise was not to hint at theological secrets but rather to convey certain important lessons to his reader.

In Qalonymos's brief account of the *Treatise of the Animals* in his introduction, he makes clear that "the advantage of humans over animals is only with regard to the human intellect when it is *in actu* and its ultimate perfection, and nothing else." Qalonymos adds, "This is a truth with which only an ignoramus or obstinate person would disagree." It was hardly a secret, and Qalonymos's friends could have found it in numerous other writings of the Islamic and Jewish thinkers. Once one prefers one's passions to one's intellect, one strips oneself down to the level of the animals. This was not a profound point, but clearly it was one thing to read it and another thing to grasp it fully. The engaging tale of the animals with its clever dialogue perhaps could awaken his friends and those like them to pursue the true path to human perfection. Qalonymos, in his introduction, describes some of his potential readers as those "who lie upon beds of ivory" (Amos 7:7–8), employing terms that directly reflect the foreboding language of the Bible. He was the prophet who warns his people of their immanent doom if they do not change their ways. He reads to them in private their warning, this treatise, "two, *three, or four columns*" (Jer. 36:23), and hopes they will be wiser than King Jehoiakim.

Why did Qalonymos interrupt his translation of the Averroan commentaries to translate this treatise? In truth, it was not such an interruption. He reveals in the introduction that the translation is often a free translation, that he did not try to translate figures and metaphors that were difficult to translate, and that he completed it within a week. The introduction makes clear that Qalonymos had a practical agenda in translating the treatise that was quite different from that of the Averroes project, for which he felt no introductions were needed.

Another illustration of a rather long introduction to a fourteenth-century philosophic translation is Judah ben Solomon Nathan's introduction to his translation of Al-Ghazālī's *Intentions of the Philosophers*, written around 1330. Judah writes at the request of his uncle, Nathan ben Solomon and his friends, but it is clear from the introduction itself, as we shall see, that this was something to which he attached great importance.[41] Judah's introduction to his translation is typical of many Hebrew introductions to translations of the period: the author tells us he was requested to make the translation and explains that he was hesitant to do so. Judah gives three reasons for his reluctance to translate the work: (1) his own inadequacy—his imperfect knowledge of both Arabic and Hebrew and of the sciences treated in the book, (2) the known difficulty of translation and in particular of books by Al-Ghazālī, and (3) his copy of the work was faulty and contained errors. Nonetheless, he agrees to do so, again for three reasons: (1) his trust in God and the scholars who helped him, (2) the works of those who trod the same path as Al-Ghazālī, and thus through which he could correct the errors in the present book, and (3) the two great benefits that derive from the work, namely, that (i) through it one can learn the sciences and the opinions of the philosophers in as short a time as possible without the need for any other book on the sciences, thus enabling the reader to devote his time to the study of the Talmud, and that (ii) through it the reader may be aroused to avenge our holy Torah against the philosophers . . . and to reply to them through the portals of philosophic speculation. In other words, the *Intentions* provided in a single volume all one needed to know about science and philosophy, and with it one could master these disciplines and know how to reply to the pseudophilosophers who challenge the principles of Judaism. Judah also takes the occasion of the introduction to warn the reader that the *Intentions* is not always completely reliable, for Al-Ghazālī's book contains some non-Aristotelian teachings of Avicenna, "who deviates a little from the path of Aristotle in a few places."[42] Among the rhetorical features one finds in this introduction are those frequently employed in the introductions of Islamic and Jewish philosophers—an emphasis on conciseness, on the work's encyclopedic scope, and on the author's own shortcomings; a reminder that the wisdom of the sages has been lost; mention of the errors of others; and a plea for help from God.

Two other translators who worked around the same time may be mentioned. Samuel ben Judah of Marseilles began translating shortly before Judah. Samuel differs from other translators who have been mentioned in that he wrote appendices instead of introductions. However, his appendices function as typical translators' introductions, with many of the rhetorical features we have seen, such as confessing one's limited abilities, proclaiming the difficulty of the text, mentioning the calamities of the time, and in virtually all cases, seeking aid and guidance from God. Samuel goes beyond most introductions in his detailed account of the reasons for the blunders in his translations, the need for revision, and his own intention to consult with other scholars, including Christian philosophers. We also see through his appendices to his translations of political writings that Samuel saw himself as a pioneer in this. For example he writes in his translation of Averroes's *Commentary on Plato's Republic*: "Until this day, no part of [political] science was translated or came into our possession, neither from the pen of the Philosopher nor from anyone else, except what is to be found in the *Political Regime* of Alfarabi, which many of our nation have. It contains a little of the second part of this science, but nothing of the first part. I am the one who put on strength and was the first to begin to show the preciousness of the splendor of the greatness of this science and to give it existence in our language."[43]

This recognition of the translators of the fourteenth century of works that had already been translated and of the special importance of the books they themselves chose to translate may be seen as well in an introduction of Ṭodros Ṭodrosi of Arles, a close friend of Judah's. He is best known—to the extent he is known—for his translations in 1337 of Averroes's middle commentaries on the *Rhetoric* and the *Poetics*, and of Avicenna's *Salvation* [*al-Najāt*]. His introduction to his translations of Averroes's two middle commentaries is dedicated exclusively, with few rhetorical topoi, to explaining in terms of Aristotle's four causes why he translated them.[44] Actually this sort of explanation is itself a topos found in introductions to medieval Arabic, Hebrew, and Latin philosophical texts. In brief, the final cause was his love of truth and his desire to help his coreligionists distinguish a demonstrative proof from a rhetorical or poetical one. The motive cause was the will to help his coreligionists who were seekers of philosophy to know what they still did not know and to achieve knowledge of the truth, which is the ultimate happiness of human life. The formal cause is his knowledge of the two languages. The material cause is that he had the two books, and, as he explained, to abandon the opportunity to translate the two commentaries of Averroes in his possession, after God had opened his eyes a bit in Arabic, would be "to deal falsely with the truth" (cf. 2 Sam. 18:13). In any event, Ṭodros makes clear that "these two pleasant arts [of rhetoric and poetry], complete the science of logic," and that his goal was "to complete for [our brothers, who cling to philosophical speculation] the translation of the books of the science of logic."[45] When Ṭodros pondered in Arles and its surroundings which important Arabic philosophic texts had still not been translated in the 1330s, the greatest desideratum was likely Averroes's middle commentaries on the *Rhetoric* and the *Poetics*, the only Averroan middle commentaries that had not yet been translated. Ṭodros, as he writes in his introduction, indeed completed the translation of the books of logic, and with them the project of translating Averroes's middle commentaries.

Thirteenth-Century Encyclopedists

In his introduction to *De'ot ha-Filosofim*, the second of the great thirteenth-century Hebrew encyclopedias of science, Shem-Ṭov ibn

Falaquera cites by name perhaps more philosophers than any other thinker of the time in their introductions, bringing fitting quotations from Porphyry, Aristotle, Al-Fārābī, Ibn Bājja, Averroes, and Maimonides. Of particular interest is a comment about Averroes: Averroes was "the last of the commentators, and he incorporated what was best from the [earlier] commentators." For this reason, he explains, his own book need not be original. He will simply gather and translate "the words of Aristotle as explained through Averroes commentaries."[46] This is indeed, more or less, what he does.

After a brief praise to God, the Cause of all being, Falaquera states that it is well-known and agreed on from the Torah and the philosophers that "man's true happiness consists in the apprehension of the Creator according to the capacity of the human intellect" and that this apprehension comes to man through the knowledge of His works. Falaquera brings support for this view from Maimonides (*Guide of the Perplexed* 1, 71). Falaquera next reflects a bit on the progress of science, the need to rely on previous thinkers, and the importance of keeping an open mind and judging teachings on their own merits. Falaquera tells us that he wrote his book to guide the reader who seeks to know God by reason to his goal and ultimate perfection. The main problem is that qualified readers are prevented from engaging in proper scientific inquiry by their physical needs and the hardships of the day, as well as by the large amount of literature, virtually all of which had not been translated into Hebrew, and even in Arabic was often misleading or garbled. Falaquera proposes a single Hebrew book that would sift through all the material and present all one needed to know to attain perfection. "One will not have to weary oneself reading all these books, for all their opinions will be found in this composition." Nonetheless, he tells us that his primary intention is that the book will be a book of remembrance for his old age. Insofar as philosophers agree that the correct opinions of the true philosophers are all contained in Aristotle's works, Falaquera's book will concern itself with these works. He supports this reliance on Aristotle with apt quotes from Al-Fārābī, Maimonides, and Averroes. As we have seen, he will convey Aristotle's philosophy through the words of Averroes. Before concluding his introduction with an outline of the contents and a short philosophic lexicon, he begs the reader not to suspect that he believes anything written in the book that contradicts a word of our faith, for everything in this book is the opinions of the philosopher, and "there is not a thing in this entire composition that I say of my own."[47]

Gersonides

Gersonides, the leading fourteenth-century Jewish philosopher, scientist, and biblical exegete, was familiar with various traditions of introductions to philosophic texts, in particular, the *accessus ad auctores*. He wrote important introductions to his biblical commentaries and shorter ones to his supercommentaries on Aristotle.[48] The introduction to the *Wars of the Lord* is a lengthy one that—at least in part—follows conventional introductions—replete with rhetorical features—of Islamic and Jewish philosophers,[49] and the *accessus* tradition of the commentators. Gersonides writes at the end of the introduction: "We have here explained the purpose and utility of this book, the meaning of its title, its order, the necessary [arrangement] of its parts, and its [rank]. This is what we have intended [in this preface]."[50] Indeed, Gersonides discusses these six subjects of the *accessus* tradition as well as the method of instruction employed in the book, but as Sara Klein-Braslavy notes, they do not serve as the framework around which it is organized. Klein-Braslavy observes that much of the introduction may be read as a response to Maimonides's introduction to the *Guide of the Perplexed*.[51] This is certainly true, but equally striking are the lengthy discussions regarding the proper subjects of philosophic discourse, for example, creation of the world and the possibility of knowledge on this subject and the orderly study of scientific phenomena. Gersonides tells us that his *Wars* is intended for a rather mature reader, learned in the mathematical sciences, the natural sciences, and metaphysics, and that he will presuppose this knowledge of his reader and will engage in mathematical, physical, and metaphysical proofs in seeking to find the truth concerning the extremely difficult topics of his book. More so than in any of the other introductions we have discussed, Gersonides could and did presuppose a worthy reader. Unlike the authors of the previous works, Gersonides was not trying to introduce the reader to a new science but rather to guide a philosophically sophisticated reader to truths concerning certain difficult theological-philosophical issues that are crucial to man's intellectual happiness. Thus his book did not have to begin at the beginning and follow the proper order of pursuit of scientific knowledge, because his reader already possessed this knowledge. He could in his first treatise immediately jump in to the baffling question of the immortality of the soul. This required a new order for his book, and it required a philosophical explanation in the introduction that such knowledge—even though it had eluded his predecessors—was possible. Gersonides's introduction provides a reasoned discussion on the proper order for such philosophic discourse and philosophic argumentation that knowledge of these difficult matters was indeed possible.

Conclusions

Not all philosophical works of the Jewish authors in the medieval period were prefaced with *haqdamot*. However, a great many were, and they comprised a literary form of their own with their own rules and traditions. Yet many of these introductions ignored such formal and/or rhetorical conventions. The *haqdamot* served a great function in introducing the book, convincing the reader to read it (or in rare instances not to read it) and at times providing the key for properly understanding the book. At times, they even served as vehicles for philosophic instruction. Often these introductions made known the motivation of the authors and purposes of the books or simply made known what the author wished to convey to the reader at the outset of his book.

Notes

1. Gen. 21:33.
2. See, e.g., *Les prologues médiévaux*, ed. Jacqueline Hamesse (Turnhout: Brepols, 2001). On the introductions of the Islamic philosophers, see my "The Author's Introduction as a Key to Understanding Trends in Islamic Philosophy," in *Words, Texts and Concepts Cruising the Mediterranean Sea: Studies on the Sources, Contents and Influences of Islamic Civilization and Arabic Philosophy and Science Dedicated to Gerhard Endress on His Sixty-Fifth Birthday*, ed. Rüdiger Arnzen and Jörn Thielmann (Leuven: Peeters, 2004), 15–32.
3. The term is not so important. See Jacques Dalarun, "Épilogue," in Hamesse, *Les prologues médiévaux*, 640–41.
4. Harvey, "Author's Introduction," 15–16.
5. Saadia Gaon, *The Book of Beliefs and Opinions*, trans. Samuel Rosenblatt (New Haven, CT: Yale University Press, 1948), 3.
6. All these works begin with the formula: *Tabāraka allāh ilāh isrā'īl* (Blessed be God, the God of Israel). The second paragraph in *Beliefs and Opinions* begins *ammā 'alā athari*; the second paragraph in the other works begins *ammā ba'du*.
7. For example, Bar Ḥiyya writes at the beginning of *Megillat ha-Megalleh* (ed. Adolf Poznanski [Berlin, 1924], 1), after an opening paragraph of praise to God: "After I have preceded with praise of God, with which one is obliged and commanded to begin." On Bar Ḥiyya's introduction, its structure and intent, see Hannu Töyrylä, *Abraham Bar Hiyya on Time, History, Exile and Redemption: An Analysis of "Megillat ha-Megalleh"* (Leiden: Brill, 2014), 66–77; on its relation to other introductions by Bar Ḥiyya, 66–67.

8. See further, the fascinating article by Baki Tezcan, "The Multiple Faces of the One: The Invocation Section of Ottoman Literary Introductions as a Locus for the Central Argument of the Text," *Middle Eastern Literatures* 12 (2009): 27–41.

9. See, e.g., Al-Fārābī, *Kitāb al-alfāẓ al-musta'mala fī al-manṭiq*, ed. Muhsin Mahdi (Beirut: Dar el-Mashreq, 1968), 94–95. For another clear account of these same eight matters, see Averroes's discussion in Steven Harvey, "The Hebrew Translation of Averroes' Prooemium to his *Long Commentary on Aristotle's Physics*," *Proceedings of the American Academy for Jewish Research* 52 (1985): 55–84. Al-Fārābī and Averroes both refer to the "custom of the commentators" to mention these matters at the beginning of their books.

10. See Isaac ibn Ghiyāth, *Kitāb al-zuhd* (*Sefer ha-Perishut*), ed. and Hebrew trans. by Joseph Kafih in his *Ḥamesh Megillot* (Jerusalem, 1962), 165.

11. On Ibn Tibbon, see James T. Robinson, "Samuel ibn Tibbon's *Commentary on Ecclesiastes* and the Philosopher's Prooemium," in *Studies in Medieval Jewish History and Literature vol.* 3, ed. Isadore Twersky and Jay M. Harris (Cambridge, MA: Harvard University Press, 2000), 83. On Gersonides, see Sara Klein-Braslavy, *"Without Any Doubt": Gersonides on Method and Knowledge* (Leiden: Brill, 2011), 117–50.

12. For a fine account of the Syriac introductions, see Eva Riad, *Studies in the Syriac Preface* (Uppsala: Uppsala University, 1988).

13. An earlier version of this section appeared in Steven Harvey, "Die Einleitung des Autors als Schlüssel zum Verstehen von Strömungen mittelalterlicher jüdischer Philosophie: Von Saadia Gaon bis Ibn Da'ud," *Im Gespräch* 6 (2003): 54–68.

14. See Sarah Stroumsa, "A Literary Genre as an Historical Document: On Saadia's Introduction to His Bible Commentaries," in *"A Word Fitly Spoken": Qur'an and Bible Exegesis, Presented to Haggai Ben-Shammai*, ed. Meir Bar-Asher, et al. (Jerusalem: Ben-Zvi Institute, 2007), 193–204 [Hebrew]. See further Haggai Ben-Shammai, "Saadia's Introduction to Daniel: Prophetic Calculation of the End of Days vs. Astrological and Magical Speculation," *Aleph* 4 (2004): 11–87. Ben-Shammai explains: "In any commentary by Saadia, the introduction occupies an important place. It is where he lays the foundations of the subject that he considers to be the focus of the book in question. In the introduction he also formulates his conclusions" (12). Cf. Henry Malter, *Saadia Gaon: Life and Works* (Philadelphia, PA: Jewish Publication Society, 1921), 146. On the introductions to biblical commentaries, Colette Sirat has written that "Jewish biblical commentaries can be classified into two types, according to the presence or absence of an introduction." This unexpected categorization—although not completely accurate—is ingenious in its simplicity. Of all possible categorizations, why divide the commentaries in this way? Sirat continues: "The commentaries that lack introductions are first the Midrashim, and secondly the commentaries of Rashi (1040–1105) and his successors. . . . Philosophical commentaries, on the other hand, take into account another source of relation to God: reason. . . . All medieval philosophical commentaries have introductions" ("Biblical Commentaries and Christian Influence: The Case of Gersonides," in *Hebrew Scholarship and the Medieval World*, ed. Nicholas de Lange [Cambridge: Cambridge University Press, 2001], 10–212). Sirat briefly outlines the introductions to several early biblical commentaries in her article, such as those of Saadia, Jacob al-Qirqisānī, Ibn Ghiyāth, and Abraham ibn Ezra. As in so many areas, Saadia may well be called the father of the medieval Jewish introduction.

15. Saadia, *Beliefs and Opinions*, introduction, 7.

16. Saadia, *Beliefs and Opinions*, 3: 7, 158.

17. Saadia considered the existence of an immaterial eternal God the "foundation and the axle of the entire book" (*Beliefs and Opinions*, 2, exordium, 94).

18. On the combination of epistemology and theology among Muslim writers and the similarities between them and Saadia, see Franz Rosenthal, *Knowledge Triumphant* (Leiden: Brill, 1970), esp. 208–15. See further, Georges Vajda, "Autour de la théorie de la connaissance chez Saadia," *Revue des études juives* 126 (1967): 135–89, 375–97.

19. Saadia, *Beliefs and Opinions*, introduction, 26.

20. Ibid., 27–28.

21. Ibid., 31–33.

22. Ibid., 33–37.

23. Ibn Ṣaddiq, *Sefer ha-ʿOlam ha-Qaṭan*, ed. S. Horovitz (Breslau, 1903), 1. For a full English translation of this book, see Jacob Haberman, *The Microcosm of Joseph ibn Ṣaddiq* (Madison/Teaneck, NJ: Fairleigh Dickinson University Press, 2003). The introduction is found on 53–55.

24. Ibn Da'ud, *Emunah Ramah*, ed. Simson Weil (Frankfurt am Main, 1852), 1.

25. See T. A. M. Fontaine, *In Defence of Judaism: Abraham ibn Daud* (Assen/Maastricht, Netherlands: Van Gorcum, 1990), 7–8 and 239–52; and Amira Eran, *Me-Emunah Tammah le-Emunah Ramah* (Tel-Aviv: Hakibbutz Hameuchad, 1998), 28–30 and 261–71.

26. Judah Ha-Levi, *The Book of Refutation and Proof on Behalf of the Despised Religion* (*The Kuzari*), trans. Barry S. Kogan and Lawrence V. Berman (New Haven, CT: Yale University Press, forthcoming).

27. S. D. Goitein, *A Mediterranean Society*, vol. 5 (Berkeley: University of California Press, 1988), 465.

28. Ibid., 456.

29. Y. Tzvi Langermann, "Science and the *Kuzari*," *Science in Context* 10 (1997): 501.

30. Steven Harvey, "Maimonides and the Art of Writing Introductions," *Maimonidean Studies* 5 (2008): 85–105.

31. Shem-Ṭov ibn Shem-Ṭov's comments on the *Guide* are printed along with other standard commentaries in the Warsaw 1872 Hebrew edition of the *Guide*. This quotation is found at the end of his comments on the introduction, 11b.

32. Cited from Shem-Ṭov ibn Falaquera, *Reshit Ḥokhmah*, ed. Moritz David (Berlin: M. Poppelauer, 1902), 6.

33. Isadore Twersky, "Aspects of the Social and Cultural History of Provençal Jewry," in *Jewish Society through the Ages*, ed. H. H. Ben-Sasson and S. Ettinger (New York, 1971), 203.

34. One exception is commentaries on *Sefer Yeṣirah*.

35. See, e.g., Saadia, *Beliefs and Opinions*, 8: "I do acknowledge that my learning is far from perfect and admit that my scientific attainments are lacking in excellence, and I am not wiser than my contemporaries . . . [I implore] any scholar who, upon studying the book, sees in it a mistake, that he correct it."

36. The commentary on Eccles. 1:1 has been edited, translated, and discussed in detail in Robinson, "Samuel ibn Tibbon's *Commentary*."

37. See Steven Harvey, "The Introductions of Thirteenth-Century Arabic-to-Hebrew Translators of Philosophic and Scientific Texts," in *Vehicles of Transmission, Translation, and Transformation in Medieval Textual Culture*, ed. Carlos Fraenkel, et al. (Ithaca, NY: Cornell University Press, 2011), 223–34. On the Ibn Tibbon family of translators, see James T. Robinson, "The Ibn Tibbon Family: A Dynasty of Translators in Medieval Provence," in *Be'erot Yitzhak: Studies in Memory of Isadore Twersky*, ed. Jay M. Harris (Cambridge, MA: Harvard University Press, 2005), 193–224, esp. 204–16.

38. See Ottfried Fraisse, *Moses ibn Tibbons Kommentar zum Hohelied und sein poetologisch-philosophisches Programm: Synoptische Edition, Übersetzung und Analyse* (Berlin: de Gruyter, 2004).
39. Tony Lévy, "The Establishment of the Mathematical Bookshelf of the Medieval Hebrew Scholar: Translations and Translators," *Science in Context* 10 (1997): 431–51.
40. Qalonymos ben Qalonymos, *Iggeret Ba'ale Ḥayyim* (Vilna 1874), 2a. The full introduction is on 2a–b.
41. I have discussed Judah's introduction to his translation of Al-Ghazālī's *Intentions of the Philosophers* in my "Authors' Introductions as a Gauge for Monitoring Philosophic Influence: The Case of Alghazali," in *Tribute to Michael: Studies in Jewish Thought Presented to Professor Michael Schwarz*, ed. Sara Klein-Braslavy, et al. (Tel Aviv: Tel Aviv University Press, 2009), 53–66. Cf. the other introductions discussed there. Judah's introduction is printed in Moritz Steinschneider, *Die Handschriften-Verzeichnisse der Koeniglichen Bibliothek zu Berlin* (Berlin, 1878) vol. 1, 130–32.
42. Ibid., 132.
43. Samuel's appendices are translated in Lawrence V. Berman, "Greek into Hebrew: Samuel ben Judah of Marseilles, Fourteenth-Century Philosopher and Translator," in *Jewish Medieval and Renaissance Studies*, ed. Alexander Altmann (Cambridge, MA: Harvard University Press, 1967), 289–320, citation on 310. Al-Fārābī's book was known as *The Book of the Principles of Existing Things* and was translated by Moses ibn Tibbon.
44. *Averrois commentarius in Aristotelis de arte rhetorica libros tres*, ed. J. Goldenthal (Leipzig 1842), 1–4. One example of a rhetorical topos is his alluding to his shortcomings as a translator (4).
45. Ibid., 2 and 4.
46. *De'ot ha-Filosofim*, Parma, Biblioteca Palatina, MS Parm. 3156 (= De Rossi 164), fol. 5r.
47. Ibid., fols. 4r–6r. On Falaquera's introduction, see further Steven Harvey, "Shem-Tov ibn Falaquera's *De'ot ha-Filosofim*: Its Sources and Use of Sources," in *The Medieval Hebrew Encyclopedias of Science and Philosophy*, ed. Steven Harvey (Dordrecht: Kluwer, 2000), 213–18. For introductions by other medieval encyclopedists, see ibid.
48. See Klein-Braslavy, *Gersonides on Method*, 128–79 (biblical commentaries), 184–98 (supercommentaries).
49. For example, opening praise to God, the *ammā ba'du*, brevity, simple—not obscure—language, not composed carelessly, disturbances of the time, division of chapters.
50. Gersonides, *The Wars of the Lord*, trans. Seymour Feldman, vol. 1 (Philadelphia: Jewish Publication Society, 1984), 104. The introduction is on 87–104.
51. Klein-Braslavy, *Gersonides on Method*, 124–28.

STEVEN HARVEY is Professor Emeritus of Medieval Jewish and Islamic Philosophy at Bar-Ilan University. He is President of the Commission for Jewish Philosophy of the Société Internationale pour l'Étude de la Philosophie Médiévale. He has published extensively on the medieval Jewish and Islamic philosophers, with special focus on Averroes's commentaries on Aristotle and on the influence of the Islamic philosophers on Jewish thought. He is author of *Falaquera's Epistle of the Debate: An Introduction to Jewish Philosophy*, and editor of *The Medieval Hebrew Encyclopedias of Science and Philosophy* and *Anthology of the Writings of Avicenna* (in Hebrew).

6

DOES JUDAISM MAKE SENSE?

Early Medieval Kalam as Literature

Gyongyi Hegedus

THIS CHAPTER DESCRIBES THREE MODELS AND THREE DISTINCT voices in which Judaism was articulated in the ninth and tenth centuries. With the appearance of the new triumphant religion of Islam, it became necessary for other Middle Eastern religious traditions to create a rational underpinning for their existence. As a response to this challenge, we know of three treatises composed by Jews during this period: *The Twenty Chapters* (*ʿIšrūn Maqāla*) by Dāwūd ibn Marwān al-Muqammiṣ,[1] *The Book of Beliefs and Opinions* (*Kitāb al-Amānāt wa-l-Iʿtiqādāt*) by Saadya Gaon,[2] and *The Book of Lights and Watchtowers* (*Kitāb al-Anwār wa-l-Marāqib*) by Yaʿqūb al-Qirqisānī.[3]

Although these works are all characterized as masterpieces of Jewish rational theology (kalam), I will show that they are different in structure, that the authors make use of different styles, and that ultimately they offer different answers to the question of what "making sense" means. It should be added, moreover, that while these works provide a Jewish response to the Muslim claim that Islam is the most *sensible* of all religions, these books also appeared in light of an internal Jewish debate, that is, the Rabbanite-Karaite controversy, which centered on the oral tradition, whether Mishnah and Talmud were authentic sources of Jewish law and doctrine.

In what follows I will (1) offer a short presentation of the genre of summa in general and of the structure in order to show how the ordering of material, the formal properties of the texts, reveals an implied methodology;

(2) focus on the deeper structure of these texts by examining the "philosophical" voice of their authors; and (3) touch on how these works understand the notion of "rationality," since all of them would like to prove that Judaism (Rabbanite or Karaite) can be justified by rationality.

Structure: Strict and Sober Order

Summas are medieval summaries and compendia of a certain religious doctrine. They intend to fulfill four conditions: (1) to be coherent and all-inclusive works, touching on all domains of human existence; (2) to make statements that are proved and justified by rational argumentation; (3) to refute all views that contradict the justified "right" opinion; (4) to provide adequate answers to questions and problems that emerge concerning the foundations of the religion in question. The topics generally touched on include the following: the ways to gain valid and reliable knowledge and the way(s) to understand scripture in light of rational knowledge; the origin of the world; its end; last judgment and afterlife; the existence and unity of God; the nature of prophecy and the question of who can claim to be a real prophet; and the origins of religious law. Summas present a coherent and meaningful picture of the world as they claim that humans have the ability and the duty to make sense of the physical world and of scripture.

At the end of his magnum opus, Saadya asks the following question: "Seest thou not, in such matters as things seen and heard and food and drink, much better results are achieved with the help of the concentration of the mind than without it?"[4] This "concentration of the mind" means a universal, rational metalanguage through which the world can be described and understood. It is "philosophical" in nature, scientific and objective and mastered by all adult, sober, and sane humans. As opposed to this language, *faith* is defined as "incomplete knowledge" that, in order to be more vigorous, should be justified by rationality. However, as we will see, this universal language is not the same for all authors, since they had the freedom to employ structures from a large spectrum of models already existing in the Middle East: Aristotelian, Stoic, Neoplatonic, and so forth.

The basic principle of the three analyzed summas is that God created the world and the human mind within it. The most perfect of all creations is human intellect (*'aql*), the basis of similarity between God and humans. However, even if the human intellect can be conceived as an "image" of the Creator, it is deficient in the sense that it is embodied and subject to spatial and temporal limitations. The purpose of these works, to establish a harmony between tradition and intellect, would develop both external and internal dialogues: interreligious debates and an analysis of religious law.

On a more abstract level, summas present a process of translation as they examine the elements that link "mind," "world," and "scripture." The human mind finds itself to be encapsulated into two realities: the sensible/visible world and religious tradition. By reading and making sense of both, the summas present a system that harmonizes faith and knowledge, that justifies and understands scripture in the right way, and that makes sense of the world. According to this view, hermeneutics and natural sciences are organically intertwined. Of course, the foundational principle of the three phenomena is God, the Creator of all. In a sense, mind (*ʿaql*), scripture, and the world are created in three "languages" through which the Creator expresses himself. Summas decode and translate these languages in relation to one another, thereby offering an all-inclusive tool to make sense of the world, to understand scripture, and to lead a virtuous life.

Contemporary scholars often ask questions about the formative, interpretive, and theoretical implications of philosophical genres. According to M. Jordan, "It is not to look for connections between philosophy and something else. It is not to feel the surface of the text as an afterthought. It is, rather, to ask about the shape of the work and what might it mean for the discourse of philosophy 'in' it. Might it be that a work of a certain shape is the only one possible for certain thoughts?"[5] *Shape* in this context means the way ideas are expressed. It is style and genre at the same time. Rationalists always express their thoughts in well-rounded chapters and unequivocal terms. Unlike mystics, they did not want to effect: they intended to explain and unpack. Thus, for our authors shape equals structure, or "form and content are reciprocally responsive to each other."[6]

The general aim of these all-inclusive works is to express through unequivocal technical language that Judaism does not contradict the perception of the senses, that it is in harmony with logic or common sense, that it has laws that are rooted in objective reality (*ḥaqīqa*), and that as a tradition it is justifiable, that is, it makes sense. While reading the three cardinal works of early Jewish kalam, it is clear that their structure and content are homologous. They are composed of clear-cut chapters that build on one another, with the intention of offering a coherent guide to understanding the content of faith and law. In this literary shape, words are not employed for their poetic qualities or power to move the reader. Rather, the terminology is crystal clear and used in such a way as to reinforce the argument.

The mode of expression is almost always impersonal: the "I" never expresses mere personal opinion, but rather a view supported by infallible argumentation. It is typical that a plethora of diverse views and opinions is described, and through rational argumentation one is supported while the others are refuted. The author carefully guides the reader through the labyrinth of different views and subsequently provides the proper view that is supported by logical argumentation. As a first step, I would like to focus on the "articulation" of these works, taking into consideration that the consciously organized sequence of chapters might shed light on the coherence of the form.

Twenty Chapters

The earliest known Jewish theologian in the Middle Ages was Dāwūd ibn Marwān al-Muqammiṣ (early ninth century), a *mutakallim* (that is, a practitioner of kalam).[7] Originally from Raqqa, he lived in Syria and northern Iraq in the first half of the ninth century. For a period of time, he was converted to Christianity by Nānā (Nonnus of Nisibis), and his work was influenced by Christian kalam. In his later years he reconverted to Judaism, although it is not clear whether he followed the Karaite or the Rabbanite faction.[8] He was undoubtedly familiar with the ongoing controversy of his age; however, since in his *Twenty Chapters* his main purpose was to offer to Judaism a solid rational foundation, he was probably unwilling to enter the internal debate.

His magnum opus is the *Twenty Chapters*. In the following section I will provide a brief summary of its contents. The first three treatises of the work focus on establishing the reality (*ḥaqīqa*) of things, of the knowledge concerning them, and of the world. Al-Muqammiṣ employs an empirical approach according to which the objective, tangible reality can be attained by the senses and understood and analyzed by the mind. The first treatise (44–64) is of an epistemological nature. It claims that in order to affirm the real nature of things (*ḥaqāʾiq al-ašyāʾ*), four conditions should be met. These are (1) being (*wujūd*), that is, whether the thing exists or not; (2) quiddity (*māhiyya*), that is, the essence of the thing, such as whether it is a substance or an accident; (3) quality (*kayfiyya*), that is, the definition of the thing; and (4) wherefore (*limmiyya*), namely, the aim of the thing. This Aristotelian frame is used through the whole book to filter out ideas/notions that are unreal or false.[9] In chapter 2 (64–74) the reality of knowledge and truth is justified based on these four conditions. Chapter 3 (74–86) argues that the reality of the world is justified as well. Chapters 4 and 5 focus on proving that the world was created. In chapter 4 (86–92) "accidents" are defined as contingent on substance, with the latter being self-subsistent. Chapter 5 (92–122) deals with creation ex nihilo and proves that both the substances and the accidents of the world are created. At the end of the chapter, the views of those who claim the eternity of the world (*dahriyya*), namely Manichaeans and other dualists, are refuted.[10]

After stating the fact of creation ex nihilo, chapters 6–11 deal with the quiddity and describability of the Creator. Chapter 6 (122–26) defines the quality and the wherefore of the world, stating that it is created. The world's aim and telos is the rational human being and the activity to prove the existence of God. Chapter 7 (126–42) justifies the existence of a Creator based on the createdness of all substances. Chapter 8 (142–84) defines the Creator as one spiritual agent in terms of simplicity and uniqueness in essence and act and argues that the maker of a product is unlike the product. At the end of this chapter, Christians who assert that Jesus was partly human and the notion of Trinity are refuted. Chapter 9 (184–210) touches on the quiddity (wherefore) of God and states that the "how" and the "what" questions cannot be asked concerning the Creator, the only qualities we can claim to know are how God describes himself as "apparent (*ẓāhir*) and hidden (*bāṭin*)," and as the "first (*awwal*) and last (*ākhir*)." At this point the soul and angels are also defined as noncomposite in nature and existing by virtue of themselves. The ideas of the proponents of anthropomorphism (*tajsīm*) are refuted. In chapter 10 (210–24) God is defined as beyond any resemblance (*tašbīh*) and the use of indiscriminate analogies is condemned, since God is above the creatures. In chapter 11 (226–30) the author claims that when God is defined as "our God," it is a mere manner of speech, and it is not said in the "real" sense.

The next part of the book (chapters 12–16) focuses on more practical issues, that is, on how to connect with the Creator and to prove that the prophecy of Moses can be considered guidance to reaching God. Chapter 12 (230–54) explains that God created us benevolently, thereby refuting the views of the determinists (*mujbira*) and explains the four Platonic-Aristotelian virtues of the soul (prudence, fortitude, justice, temperance). Chapter 13 (255–63) defines monotheists as those who accept prophets and argues that prophets obtain extra reward in the afterlife (*dār al-jazāʾ*). Chapter 14 (262–72) deals with the necessary conditions for the veracity of a tradition, and the prophecy of Moses is corroborated based on both common sense and miracles. After explaining the problems resulting from the ultimate unity of God (*tawḥīd*), namely, that it cannot be properly understood or represented by the mind and the confusion that the indescribability of the divine presents, the author delves into the problems of the ways God is connected to humans by justice (*ʿadl*), that is, through law and command and through proportionate compensation in the afterlife. Chapter 15 (272–92) focuses on command and prohibition. Chapter 16 (292–302), concerning reward and punishment, argues for our infinity and that the soul and the body should be punished or rewarded together since they both constitute the human agent.

After several missing chapters (17–19), chapter 20 offers the conclusion, stating that if the account of prophecy in scripture is true, then our antagonists are infidels. Thus, at the end, the description of prophecy in the Bible is invoked, a nonargumentative and revealed witness, supplementing the logically structured "Aristotelian" discourse.

The book of Al-Muqammiṣ is composed of four parts and organized around the four following topics: (1) the world is real, that is, objective, and our senses and speculation bring to us real knowledge; (2) the world was created in time; (3) the Creator is unlike the world: ultimately one and spiritual; (4) through law and command God displays justice in his creation and the prophecy of Moses is justified. This sequence of ideas is typical of rational theologians. The first statement formulates the epistemological foundation of the doctrine of the kalam, the second one states the origin of the world in time, the third deals with the Creator, and the fourth outlines the origins and nature of laws and commandments, reward and punishment. Thus, the text displays a didactical plan of justifying tradition starting with the nature of the mind and knowledge, then asserting creation ex nihilo, from which one can draw conclusions regarding the nature of the Creator, and finally delving into practical questions of how to gain connection with the Creator.

Book of Beliefs and Opinions

Saadya's *Book of Beliefs and Opinions*, composed in 933, can be considered the greatest achievement of Jewish kalam. The Gaon of Baghdad, the most influential Jewish thinker of the tenth century, Saadya succeeded in achieving a double objective. On the one hand, he found a way to articulate Jewish creed using the language and the thought system of the Islamic rationalists (*mutakallimūn*), and on the other he offered a kalamic solution for the demonstration of those articles of faith that are specific to rabbinic Judaism (e.g., the validity of the oral tradition).

The first three treatises of *The Book of Beliefs and Opinions* cover topics parallel to the first three of Al-Muqammiṣ's work, that is: (1) theory of knowledge, (2) creation ex nihilo, and (3) the nature of the Creator. First, the book begins with a relatively long introductory part (1–32) of an epistemological nature, which treats notions related to knowledge, such as that of doubt (*šakk*), truth (*ṣidq*), belief (*īmān*), the sources of knowledge, speculation (*naẓar*), and revelation. The system of epistemology built up in this chapter appears to be based on two principles: (1) that the object and the subject of human knowledge are clearly distinct and (2) that the external and the internal sources of knowledge, that is, the sensible (*maḥsūs*) and the intelligible (*maʿqūl*) realms, correspond to each other, since they reflect the work of the same Creator. Second, after having established these basic principles as ways to achieve knowledge, Saadya addresses the topic of creation ex nihilo in the first treatise of *The Book of Beliefs and Opinions* (33–75). Here he asserts that the origin of the world must be investigated in a speculative manner and offers four proofs demonstrating the creation of the world out of nothing: the world's finitude, its composite nature, the inherence of accidents in it, and its existence in time. Moreover, it is argued that creation ex nihilo implies that there must be an external cause or agent responsible for the creation. At the end of this treatise, Saadya refutes twelve divergent views on the origin of the world that propose theories other than that of creation ex nihilo. Third, the second treatise (76–115) tackles the question of divine unity. On the basis of both the Hebrew Bible and unaided human reason, the treatise attempts to prove that the Creator of the world cannot but be a unique, immaterial agent, impossible to characterize by the ten Aristotelian categories.

Then, in the next three chapters of his book, Saadya turns to questions of how God rules humans by justice (*ʿadl*). In the third treatise concerning command and prohibition (116–49), creation is represented as the expression of God's kindness and bounteousness toward His creatures, a kindness and bounteousness that is manifested by offering them the possibility of attaining perfect happiness through their adherence to the commandments and prohibitions of the Torah. In the fourth treatise, concerning obedience and rebellion, predestination and divine justice (150–68), man is said to be the goal of the work of creation, the most important of all beings. His superiority results from two facts: (1) that he is able to perform good acts as well as evil and (2) that he is endowed with the gift of intelligence, which has been granted to him for the purpose of fulfilling God's commandments. In light of this, man's earthly life, during which he is subjected to pain and suffering, must be complemented by the existence of a hereafter in which divine justice rewards and punishes human beings in accordance with their merits and demerits. The fifth treatise examines the notions of merits and demerits (169–92). God is said to keep a record of man's merits and demerits, and although the bulk of man's retribution for his conduct on earth is reserved for the hereafter, some of it is carried out in this world to serve as a sign of the world to come.

Treatises 6–9 focus on the domains of the "invisible" and the future: the notion of the soul, afterlife, resurrection, and the coming of the Messiah. The sixth treatise (193–217) is composed of two parts, the first one dealing with the essence of the soul and the second part touching on death and on what follows after death. In this treatise the human soul is presented as the noblest and the most exalted substance in the whole of creation, which knows by its essence. The seventh treatise (218–36), concerning the resurrection of the dead in the physical world, focuses on the demonstration of the necessity of the resurrection of the dead at the time of Israel's redemption. It is at this point that Saadya outlines the laws according to which the biblical text needs to be interpreted and proves that the Bible contains explicit references to the doctrine of the bodily resurrection of the dead, references that must not be taken in an allegorical sense. The eighth chapter (237–60) concerns the topic of the redemption and the coming of the Messiah. It enumerates the scriptural passages dealing with the duration of the exile and the prophetic promises made concerning Israel's redemption. The ninth treatise (261–96) concerns the nature of reward and punishment in the world to come.

The tenth treatise (297–324) revises questions related to divine justice: it focuses on the most proper way for man to conduct himself in this world. To begin, Saadya establishes the fact that unity is an attribute appertaining only to the Creator, while everything else in the world is of a composite nature. Thus, human activities must not be dedicated to the attainment of one single goal, like love, collecting wealth, and so forth. Wisdom dictates the regulation of man's impulses and appetites, and it is in the proper blending of pursuits that man's well-being is furthered.

In the characteristic methodology of Saadya, each treatise starts with the establishment of the right view concerning a particular topic, all other views are then refuted, and finally the right view is proven on the basis of scripture. Saadya's opponents, named or anonymous, are numerous. He appears to logically demarcate his position against a wide range of religious and philosophical ideas of his age.

Structural Parallelism

Both works start with an epistemological introduction, then delve into proving creation ex nihilo, and based on the createdness of the world, both attempt to tackle the notion of the Creator. After describing the Creator as unique (*tawḥīd*) and spiritual, both works enter the realm of divine justice (*ʿadl*) and concentrate on how to harmonize human acts with the commands of the Creator. In order to elaborate on these four domains, Saadya adds two more sections: (1) concerning the concepts of the soul, afterlife, and the coming of the Messiah and (2) the ideal human character as a composition of traits.

The Book of Lights and Watchtowers

Yaʿqūb al-Qirqisānī, active in Iraq in the first half of the tenth century, composed a huge handbook of Karaite historiography, in addition to writing heresiographical and legal works. In Karaite Judaism the Bible functions not only as the basic legal norm but also as the primary legal source, alongside reason, consensus, and tradition. Consequently, Karaite halakhic works are exegetical, if not in form, then in content. Legal positions are always grounded in scripture and dissenting views scrutinized as to their exegetical validity.[11] Karaites propose to apply the kalamic methods of analogy (*qiyās*), consensus (*ijmāʿ*), and so forth directly on the text of the Bible and to discredit the Mishnah and the Talmud as legal sources.

As with Saadya, Al-Qirqisānī follows closely the Islamic system of kalam, which, although it incorporates some elements of the Aristotelian system as well as its medieval Neoplatonicized brand, on the whole rejected it. Instead, he focuses on apologetics and polemics. Al-Qirqisānī polemicizes at length against the Rabbanites in general and Saadya in particular, concerning the application of analogical reasoning (*qiyās*) not only to theological questions but also to revealed commandments.[12] Karaites in general, like most Muslim rationalists, insist that a rationally grounded theology is necessary for proper observance of the law; in their view a version of Judaism free from oral law makes more "sense" since it is based exclusively on the unquestionable evidence of scripture and rationality. Thus, both Saadya and Al-Qirqisānī make use of the style of Islamic kalam in defending their different positions.

This chapter focuses only on the first four treatises, since they contain the foundation of Al-Qirqisānī's approach and offer an overview of his general views. The subsequent chapters delve into the details of Jewish law (Sabbath, circumcision, etc.) and contain a practical application of the methods outlined in the first four treatises, so at this point they are less relevant.

The first chapter (3–64)[13] contains the enumeration of Jewish sects and their views, refutes heretics, and puts Judaism in historical context. Al-Qirqisānī quotes Al-Muqammiṣ at length,[14] while defining Christianity as a Jewish sect.[15] In the historical approach of the author of *The Book of Lights and Watchtowers*, Judaism is a dynamic, constantly developing phenomenon with diverse branches and offshoots, and after providing a genealogy of Karaism, it is considered as the version that makes the most sense.

The second chapter (64–179) is mainly epistemological in nature and, like the methodology of Saadya and Al-Muqammiṣ, it enumerates how the knowledge of the real nature of things (*ithbāt al-ḥaqā'iq*) can be generated. This process of knowledge occurs through speculation (*naẓar, baḥth, istidlāl*), consensus (*ijmā'*), and analogy (*qiyās*).[16] Al-Qirqisānī vehemently argues against mere imitation (*taqlīd*) and against Saadya concerning the uncritical acceptance of oral tradition (*naql*).[17] Rabbanites are accused of anthropomorphism (*tajsīm, tašbīh*), and the Talmud and the Mishnah are qualified as nonrevealed texts that are full of "vanities," are characterized as human texts to be replaced by scriptural rational exegesis, namely by analogy (*qiyās*). Human intellect (*'aql*) is the measure (*mi'yār*) and judge (*ḥākim*) of all knowledge;[18] thus in the view of the author, by removing the "oral law" from discussion, Judaism can become a more "sensible" faith. Sensation (*maḥsūs*) and the intuition of the intellect (*ma'qūl*) are considered to be the two sources of knowledge, the former serving as the foundation of the latter. Al-Qirqisānī argues that the natural claim of the intellect, according to which killing is bad, is based on the sensible fact that we are unhappy if people whom we like are killed.[19] As with Saadya,[20] reality (*ḥaqīqa*) for Al-Qirqisānī means reality in the observable, concrete, material sense.[21] Exegesis should be rational as well: the *ẓāhir* (concrete) meaning should serve as the basis of understanding. Nonliteral interpretation can be used only if the scriptural verse contradicts observable reality.[22]

The third part (181–342) of Al-Qirqisānī's work contains the detailed refutation of different sects and views. At first the Christian doctrine of the eternity of the Logos (*qidam al-kalām*) and that of the Trinity are rejected (186–98), then the concept of reward and punishment in the Torah is touched on. As in Saadya's work, Al-Qirqisānī's refutations against Christians work on two levels: on that of epistemology, that is, the opponents misperceive reality since their speculation is incorrect; and that of exegesis, namely, they misread scripture since they do not possess the right exegetical tools. As opposed to Christian law, the laws of the Torah are stated to be generally valid and incumbent on all nations, since the covenant (*ʿahd*) of the Torah is made not only with those who were present but also with all who were not present, that is, with the rest of creation (290). In the same chapter the teachings of Islam are refuted as well since the Torah does not mention Muhammad (294), and since the "miracle of the language of the Qur'an" (*muʿjizāt al-Qurʾān*) does not affect those who do not know Arabic (299). After the rejection of the prophecy of Jesus, based on the lack of miracles, the doctrine of metempsychosis is questioned, then refuted, at first the principle itself, and then the scriptural passages that are quoted by its proponents.

The fourth part of Al-Qirqisānī's magnum opus (343–494) concentrates on the aspects (*wujūh*) and reasons (*asbāb*) of laws. Scripture (*naṣṣ*) is the "raw material," and analogy (*qiyās*) is presented as the way to derive laws from the passages. The main question of the whole work is the following: From what aspects (*wujūh*) can the real nature (*ḥaqāʾiq*) of laws be known? *Ḥaqīqa*, "real nature," here is defined as the exact way to perform legal duties (*farāʾiḍ*): when are they based on the biblical text (*naṣṣ*) in an explicit way (*ẓāhir*) or when are they derived by analogy (*qiyās*) or consensus (*ijmāʿ*) (348).

As a basic method, Al-Qirqisānī draws a parallel between the knowledge of the sensible world (*ḥass/maḥsūs*) and scripture (*naṣṣ/maktūb*). The first needs investigation and speculation (*naẓar* and *istidlāl*), and the second needs interpretation (*tafsīr*) and analogical reasoning (*qiyās*). If the concrete meaning and real sense (*ḥaqīqa*) are not directly available, readers must discover them by the procedures of the intellect (*istikhrāj al-ḥaqāʾiq bi-dalālat al-ʿaql*). In both realms knowledge of the intellect (*maʿqūl*) should be knowledge that is logically necessitated (*iḍṭirār*) (353).

Every duty (*farīḍa*) is stated to have a reason (*ʿilla*) and aim (*ġaraḍ*) (361), that is, the corpus of law is a system that makes sense. As in Saadya's biblical interpretation, in Al-Qirqisānī's interpretation all duties should be understood in the literal sense (*ʿalā ẓāhirihā*), except when the literal understanding does not make sense (*fasād*). Thus, Deuteronomy 14:21, "Do not boil the calf in the milk of the mother," should be taken literally, and the rabbinic explanation prohibiting eating milk with *any* meat is considered an unnecessary allegorical (*bāṭin*) interpretation, since the biblical law can be performed in the literal sense (385–86). "Writing on the tablet of the heart" (Prov. 7:3) or "the circumcision of the heart" (Deut. 10:16), on the other hand, cannot be performed verbatim, and thus the allegorical meaning (*bāṭin*) is preferred. This way, the meaning of the first passage is "thinking of it" (*tafakkur fīhā*) and of the second is "turning ignorance into refined manners" (*ʾizālat al-juhl bi-l-taʾdīb*) (387–88). General advice, like that in Leviticus 19:14,[23] can be understood both in a concrete and in an allegorical sense (387–88). At the end of the methodological introductory parts of his legal code, Al-Qirqisānī states the non-abrogation of Mosaic laws (440–41). Law for him is a dynamic body in which no diminution (*nuqṣān*) is allowed (469). To derive further laws is permitted though, in case there is no direct textual evidence, and if the new law does not go against tradition (*khabar*).

At the final subchapters of part four (470), Al-Qirqisānī defines and illustrates the four methods of kalam: (1) questions (*suʾāl*), (2) answers (*jawāb*), (3) exposition (*muʿāraḍa*), and (4) analysis (*faṣl*). The last part contains a concrete preparation for kalamic debate (*jadal*). The book of Al-Qirqisānī is structured in a different way than that of Saadya and Al-Muqammiṣ. His intention is more exegetical and prescriptive. He does not merely claim that a complete harmony exists between Jewish tradition and the metalanguage of rationality—thus Judaism makes sense and it is justified—but he intends to apply the metalanguage of rationality to find out the exact ways in which the commandments of the revealed books should be fulfilled. The genre of *The Book of Lights and Watchtowers* is a legal code incorporating lengthy heresiographical passages and methodological treatises. However, I would like to claim that its deep structure is exactly the same as that in Saadya and Al-Muqammiṣ. The direction of his argumentation differs, since instead of attempting to discover the "real nature" (*ḥaqīqa*) of human knowledge and of the world, Al-Qirqisānī focuses on the real nature of law and commandments. As stated above, the world as it is perceived, the human capacity of knowledge, and divine revelation are homologous, since they are the works of the same Creator. All three thinkers have in mind to translate these phenomena into each other and to prove that both the world and the word of revelation are the products of divine reason and also available for human reasoning. Al-Qirqisānī's work displays a methodological difference as opposed to the two other works: instead of starting his argument from the description of the mind and proving creation ex nihilo, the exclusive matter of his investigation is the text of the Bible.

The Systematic Presentation of Jewish Belief

Dāwūd's *Twenty Chapters*, Saadya's *Book of Beliefs and Opinions*, and Al-Qirqisānī's *Kitāb al-Anwār* are all well-composed and tightly organized compendia. Their goal is to take the reader from a scattered perplexity of what Judaism consists of to a logically established "safe" or "justified" faith. In so doing, each text seeks to answer questions and concerns and filter out false or misleading beliefs. Thus, the result will be not only a Judaism that is supported by the intellect but also a complete religious map of the Middle East wherein the different views and opposing convictions are refuted one by one. Yet, although the methods used in these three works are somewhat similar, the discourses of the three authors differ in terms of both their styles and aims. It is typical of the kalam style that the methods of research are carefully defined in the introductory part. Those methods appear to differ greatly among the three works.

In the first chapter of *ʿIšrūn Maqāla,* a fourfold Aristotelian system is presented in order to affirm the "real nature" of things (*ḥaqāʾiq al-ašyāʾ*): being (*wujūd*), whether the thing exists or not; quiddity (*māhīya*), the essence of the thing, that is, what it is, whether it is a substance, or an accident; quality (*kayfīya*), the definition of the thing and how it is; and wherefore (*limmiyya*), the final aim of it, or for the sake of what the thing is created. This philosophical frame is used through the book to filter out things/notions that are unreal or false. Al-Muqammiṣ seems to make use of his thorough philosophical education inherited from his "Christian days" as a method to validate the existence of notions, positing philosophy as a framework to test the reality of the concepts.

Saadya's work, on the other hand, follows the method of the Muslim Muʿtazilites:[24] true knowledge is defined as the harmony of sense perception (*maḥsūs*) and the logical intuition of the mind (*maʿqūl*). When there is a discrepancy between these two sources, speculation (*naẓar*) should be applied, as in the case when we see that the moon is changing and we have to investigate the reason for the transformation.

Al-Qirqisānī begins differently with a description of Jewish sects in the introductory part of his work. Judaism for him is not a static faith but constantly evolving and "debated." The most recent Karaite version is presented as the most reasonable branch of religion, free from Mishnaic and Talmudic anthropomorphisms and superstitions. This evolutionary model singles out *The Book of Lights and Watchtowers* as a work that views Judaism as a faith rich in internal divisions.

In the worldview of Islamic theologians, the universe can be divided into two distinct realms: realm of the Creator, an invisible deep structure that can be proven but cannot be described or imagined, and the visible surface structure of creatures in which we can witness order and symmetry, due to the fact that God created them by perfect justice. Both Al-Muqammiṣ and Saadya preserve this distinction of realms as they move between chapters dealing with the unique attributes and activities of the divine (*tawḥīd*) and God's justice (*ʿadl*). The argumentation in both works starts from looking for the temporal origin of the world and proving creation ex nihilo, then logically deriving from this the unity, noncorporeality, eternity, and perfection of God. Divine justice (in sending prophets, designing a law, preparing a well-proportioned reward and punishment) is the consequence of divine perfectness. Language, based on words designating material objects, cannot but deal with the realm of the "visible" created by divine justice; thus, the questions of divine unity, the creative activity of God, and the representation of the divine fall into the category of impossible. This kalamic approach breaks the triumphal march of the fourfold philosophical lens in Al-Muqammiṣ, when he claims that the questions of how (184) and why (228) cannot refer to the Creator. Does it mean then that God does not have a real being? Al-Muqammiṣ would say that God's being is different as it is absolute, and the philosophical categories of Aristotle would fall short of catching it.[25]

This kalamic structure is entirely missing from the chapters of Al-Qirqisānī. His aim to justify a legal code defines his methods. He is much more interested in presenting the right mechanism of how to discover the "proper meaning" (*ḥaqīqa*) of scriptural law. The study of textual interpretation is considerably more important to him than ontology. And although he does not establish a "reading" of the world as consisting of a foundational deep realm of the Creator and of the surface structure of symmetrical visible beings, he makes use of the same system when trying to extract an accurate biblical interpretation. Al-Qirqisānī explicitly draws an analogy between the sensible world (*ḥass*) and the biblical text (*naṣṣ*) (353), in the sense that if the direct/literal meaning of a passage does not make sense, then the intellect should derive it by analogy (*qiyās*). Thus, in the same way as reality has a visible and an invisible (but detectable) aspect, texts also have an apparent (*ẓāhir*) and a hidden (*bāṭin*) meaning.

Thus, Saadya and Al-Qirqisānī would agree that when expressions like "the tablet of the heart" (Prov. 7:3) or the "circumcision of the heart" (Deut. 10:16) are mentioned in scripture, they should be taken in the allegorical sense (in Saadya's usage, *ījāz*; in Al-Qirqisānī, *bāṭin*), that is, writing on the tablet of the heart means "to think of it" (*tafakkur fīhā*), while the "circumcision of the heart" means "replacing ignorance with subtle manners" (*izālat al-jahl bi-l-taʾdīb*) (387–88). However, Al-Qirqisānī's way of interpretation differs from the Rabbanites when he comments on the famous prescription in Deuteronomy 14:21: "Do not boil the calf in the milk of its mother." He claims that it should be understood in the literal sense, since the apparent meaning of the law does not contradict any logical rules and labels the Talmudic restriction of eating any meat with milk as an unnecessary allegorical interpretation (386). In the view of Al-Qirqisānī, allegorical interpretation can be considered as a form of analogy (*qiyās*), and the foundation (*aṣl*) of analogy is defined as "trying to extract the cause from the effect" (*ijrā' al-ʿilla fī-ʿl-maʿlūl*) (358–61). This means that in the Karaite interpretation of *The Book of Lights and Watchtowers*, the real essence (*ḥaqīqa*) of a law is its interpretation, if for some reason the law cannot be performed in the literal sense. And this is in complete harmony with the general rule of kalam, according to which speculation, or analogy (*naẓar*, *istidlāl*, or *qiyās*), is allowed to be used *only* if a certain observation contradicts sense perception (*maḥsūs*) or basic logical rules (*maʿqūl*).[26] When Al-Qirqisānī claims that his interpretation makes "more sense" than that of the Rabbanites, he means that the post-prophetic tradition can and should be replaced by analogy employed directly on the biblical text.

The Multiple Voices of Jewish Kalam

The voice of kalam tends to speak with an impersonal, objective, logical tone. Language is for naming material reality, which also implies its limitations. That which is unwitnessed or immaterial, such as God, soul, creation ex nihilo, and resurrection, cannot be unequivocally expressed, only alluded to. Thus the apparent (*ẓāhir*)/hidden (*bāṭin*) differentiation appears as the result of the limitation of human understanding.

The emotionless, argumentative prose of the summas analyzed in this chapter is not exempt of internal contradictions, however. In a deeper reading, while these thinkers try to give a "sense" to Judaism, we can see a constant negotiation between the two "sense maker" structures: Neoplatonized Aristotelian philosophy and kalam (dialectical theological methods used by Muslim intellectuals). In this struggle between the Greek and the Islamic ways, our authors take highly different positions.

For Al-Muqammiṣ, philosophy—namely, the four Aristotelian conditions mentioned earlier—are used as the litmus test of the true, definable nature of basic notions (knowledge, truth, world, and God). *Virtue* is defined in the Aristotelian way, and the distinction of substance/accident is used through the book. That makes the tone and the style of Al-Muqammiṣ deeply philosophical even if the content and the line of argumentation agrees with the methods of the kalam. Compared to the other two works, scripture is not quoted and prophecy is justified by philosophy and not vice versa.

Saadya walks on the well-paved path of the Muslim mutakallimūn. From time to time he makes use of ideas and concepts originating from philosophy, such as the notions of substance/accident, or the use of the ten Aristotelian categories as a *via negativa* in order to prove the transcendence of God, or the use of philosophical language, likely to differentiate his position from the atomistic view of Islamic mutakallimūn, in describing the subtleness of the notion of the soul.[27] However, philosophy in no form functions as a basic frame of understanding or articulation in Saadya. In the whole *Book of Beliefs and Opinions,* the term "philosophers of old" (*al-falāsifa al-mutaqaddimūn*) occurs only on one occasion in the context of a discussion on miracles: Saadya asserts that the miracle of the manna, in which God miraculously supplied the Israelites with food, had been the most marvelous of all wonders because of its durable nature "for had there been any rational possibility of thinking up a scheme for achieving something of this nature the philosophers of old would have been the first to resort to it" (23). Here, Saadya employs a slightly ironical tone as he describes philosophers as falling short of explaining miracles described in scripture. Saadya's work is a well-structured, all-encompassing handbook of questions and answers touching on Judaism, wherein philosophy is used occasionally as a tool to support kalamic argumentation.[28]

The voice of Al-Qirqisānī echoes that of Saadya. However, he intends to use kalamic methods more radically to argue against the opponents of Judaism and for those supporting the Karaite version; while using analogy (*qiyās*) directly to explain biblical texts, he tries to bracket and avoid the use of oral law. It is somewhat surprising though that in the third chapter (223) of his book he uses an analogy taken from philosophy when he discusses the necessity of biblical interpretation (*tafsīr*):

> In the same way as the books of the philosophers that are not prophetic and whose words are not the word of the Creator . . . needed commentaries that explain and clarify their meaning, like *Alexander of Aphrodisias* and *Porphyrius* and *John the Grammarian* and others who commented on the books of Aristotle, or like *Galen* who commented on *Hippocrates*, whose words were not the words of the Creator (magnified and glorified be He), the more so the deep meanings of the Creator (magnified and exalted be He) and His prophets need commentaries and clarification (*tafsīr wa-šarḥ*), since they are more noble and magnificent (*ašraf wa-ajall*).

In this passage Al-Qirqisānī uses the example of philosophical texts to point out how "scientific" and professional textual interpretation should be performed in order to unpack the meaning of scripture as opposed to Talmudic interpretation that contains anthropomorphisms and unnecessary allegorical interpretations even when the text is unequivocal. Al-Qirqisānī appears to be highly knowledgeable of the philosophical trends and fashions of his day, maybe more than Saadya. In the fourth treatise of *The Book of Lights and Watchtowers* (357–61), he presents a concrete duel between the syllogism (*burhān*) of Aristotelian logic (*manṭiq*) and a faulty *qiyās* of "*mutakallim* style."

With the one-term based analogy (*qiyās*) of the mutakallimūn, one could claim that the Creator should be corporeal, since all agents are corporeal. However, Al-Qirqisānī suggests a different solution: Aristotelian syllogism based on two paradigms (*burhān bi-muqaddimatayni*).

1. Bodies are never free of movement, or rest
2. Movement and rest are created
3. What is never free from created accidents is created

Ergo, bodies are created by a Creator that cannot be corporeal. (If the Creator were corporeal, we would face the problem of infinite regress.)

In this instance Al-Qirqisānī offers an example of how Aristotelian logic might triumph over the *qiyās* of the mutakallimūn. At the very end of the fourth treatise, where this example is mentioned, the author provides advice for people participating in religious debates (*jadal*). The fact that in a Karaite handbook of law an Aristotelian syllogism is presented shows the eclectic structure of the work: Al-Qirqisānī knows precisely how Aristotelian syllogisms function, and he is also cognizant of the shortcomings of kalamic analogy. However, he seems to limit the use of syllogism to exceptional cases, in which one-term based logic falls short. In general, he prefers to apply the methods of kalam, the same ones as Saadya uses, in order to fight him with his own weapon and to adopt the generally used debate style of his day.

Kalam and philosophy can be conceived as two rival languages competing for primacy in Jewish and Islamic medieval thought. Not only do their respective terminologies differ, but also their manner of structuring reality, constructing arguments, and conceiving crucial notions like soul and creation are highly dissimilar. I would like to argue that even though our three authors are highly familiar with both "languages," they choose different ways to synthesize them.

Al-Muqammiṣ, the most "philosophical" of the authors, establishes an original fusion in which philosophically defined notions and significant philosophical content are merged with a kalamic deep structure of argumentation. Philosophy is the lens through which reality is seen and the nature of concepts is defined. The organization of the chapters clearly shows the kalamic distinction of divine uniqueness (*tawḥīd*) and the justice and equilibrium (*ʿadl*) expressed in creation.

Saadya attempts to keep the two "languages" separate. In *The Book of Beliefs and Opinions*, he "talks" pure kalam with occasional episodes borrowed from the repertoire of philosophers (e.g., the description of the notion of the soul as a luminous substance similar to the spheres or the use of the ten Aristotelian categories). His philosophical language is used in other works that are commentaries on more enigmatic texts, such as the *Sēfer Yeẓīra*. When reading visible reality or the text of scripture, the exoteric style of the mutakallimūn is preferred.

Al-Qirqisānī keeps the two languages distinct as well. He takes the pure kalamic approach, while recognizing the validity of philosophy as a parallel domain. In his textual approach based on interpretation, philosophical texts should be commented on in a philosophical style: Aristotle by Alexander of Aphrodisias and medical texts in an appropriate style as well: Hippocrates by Galen. According to him, in the Karaite version of

Judaism, biblical law should be interpreted exclusively in the "language" of kalam, without the methods of philosophers and without considering oral law. Philosophy as a foreign language, however, is acknowledged as a tool for science, but not for Karaite law.

Saadya and Al-Qirqisānī were contemporaries and fierce intellectual enemies. When reading their works and attempting to make sense of them, we can detect an interesting difference. Al-Qirqisānī explicitly refutes the teachings of Islam (the prophecy of Muhammad, the miracle of the Qur'an, etc.) (292–302), whereas Al-Muqammiṣ and Saadya consecrate lengthy passages to refute the dualists (who propose two creating powers behind the world) (48–55), but they do not engage in open debate with Islamic teachings. Of course, Al-Qirqisānī is far from sharing the views of dualists, but is his silence of the same "diplomatic" genre as Saadya's hesitance to refute Islam directly? In the tenth century, Karaism was a movement extremely popular amongst Iranian Jews. Saadya was the official religious leader of Judaism in the eyes of the Islamic Abbasid government, and he had to maintain good relations with the rulers. Al-Qirqisānī was not so bound by political loyalty to the rulers of Baghdad, and perhaps while avoiding launching attacks against the dualists, he displayed some kind of tactfulness vis-à-vis his Zoroastrian neighbors.

The Sense of Tradition

The three works examined in this chapter seek an answer to the question "Is Judaism the closest religion to human nature and understanding?" The responses are three models according to which Jewish tradition can be expressed in rational frameworks. Itt seems likely that the three works created three different subgenres in medieval Jewish rational thought.

Al-Muqammiṣ works to prove that prophecy makes sense, given the fact that appropriate philosophical notions and a kalamic setting offer a structure through which prophecy can be justified. He does not enter into the intricacies of the language of scripture, the grades of prophecy, and its criteria. Rather, he enters the labyrinth of the human mind and understanding. Through a system constructed by an Aristotelian framework and kalamic methods by outlining the necessary conditions for the veracity of a tradition (chapter 14, 264–70), he directs the attention of the reader to the necessity of law (commandment and prohibition) in order to lead a virtuous life and to attain eternal reward. The amalgamated style of Al-Muqammiṣ is clearly detectable even from the order in which these final chapters follow each other: after proving the necessity of prophecy and depicting the prophet as a perfectly virtuous man in philosophical terms (260), he deals with the typically kalamic concerns of command and prohibition and draws a parallel between the pious, law-abiding behavior of the "monotheist" and the virtuous life described by Aristotelians. Then, returning to the style of kalam, he concentrates on the problem of afterlife.

Saadya's main work of theology, *The Book of Beliefs and Opinions*, is ultimately about a transformation through which *amāna*, "faith based on trust," becomes *iʿtiqād* "conviction of the mind supported by logical arguments." A key word for this is *taqrīb* (Hebrew *haqrabah*), "bringing a notion closer to understanding," that is, translating the content of scripture into rational terms. Saadya aims to provide a shield and a sword for the debater for Judaism, and at the same time he establishes the importance of oral tradition as a faint echo of the word of revelation. As opposed to Al-Muqammiṣ, Saadya composed a handbook in pure kalamic style in which Greek thought is a rare guest and figures as a mere illustration.

Al-Qirqisānī's *Book of Lights and Watchtowers* represents a somewhat different genre than the two previously mentioned works. It can be conceived as a huge compendium of "rational *tafsīr*" that translates scripture into a network of legal prescriptions using the method of the Islamic rationalist theologians known as analogy (*qiyās*). He is proud to make Halakah more sensible than Saadya's work by constructing a solid legal structure without the annoying disturbances of the nonprophetic, nontechnical, often anthropomorphic oral tradition. Despite the differences between these three works, we can look at them as attempts to make sense of the divine revelation by translating it into a rational language that is based on the true nature (*ḥaqīqa*) of things.

In the final part of this chapter, I would like to touch on a final question: what is the "metalanguage" of rationality that seems to be universal for human understanding? Do our authors translate revelation into the same metalanguage? I would like to argue that the key notion of this rational metalanguage is *ḥaqīqa*, "the real nature of things, texts, or legal duties." All three authors agree on its being a cornerstone of their thought systems; in fact, they all believe that in issues that look complex and problematic for observation, epistemology, or textual interpretation, an understandable nature can be discovered by thorough investigation (*naẓar, qiyās, istidlāl*). After arriving at this understandable nature at the depth of the problematic issue, the intellect realizes that it is graspable, so the problem disappears because at its root it can be rationalized. Something makes sense or has meaning because it possesses *ḥaqīqa*. The way to this "real nature" can be lengthy, however, and the three philosophers view it differently.

Al-Muqammiṣ offers a fourfold philosophical lens through which the basic concepts in the process of the justification of prophecy make sense. Defining the reality (*ḥaqīqa*) of knowledge, truth, the world, and so on through the four Aristotelian conditions makes them validated, defined, sensible, and solid parts of a coherent worldview. In the *Twenty Chapters*, philosophy as a basic structure of justifying concepts and the kalamic sequence of argumentation as a deeper structure are organically intertwined. This work is far from being a practical handbook providing skillful answers for debaters or questions in order to confuse the opponents. It can rather be conceived as a philosophical meditation, delving into the deep structure of the justification and validity of Mosaic prophetic tradition and its harmony with the intellect.

According to Saadya, *ḥaqīqa* means "true, observable nature";[29] in other words, when the visible, sensible (*maḥsūs*) reality becomes understood by the intellect (*maʿqūl*), the real nature of the thing becomes known. All knowledge touches on the *ḥaqāʾiq*, for example, the intellect realizing that water, vapor, and ice are the three forms in which the same substance appears or when speech sounds have a real, meaningful nature. The final outcome of the investigation is conviction (*iʿtiqād*) when the intellect becomes bound to the real nature of the thing by the bond of rationality created by logical investigation. For Saadya, the most ignorant of all people are those who feign complete ignorance (*mutajāhilūn*). They are "people who, in addition to rejecting the teaching of science [*ʿulūm*], reject also the observation of the senses, asserting that nothing possesses any reality [*ḥaqīqa*] whatever, be it scientific knowledge or sensation" (71). The voice of revelation needs investigation as well when the text is confusing; that is, the content does not agree with the *ḥaqīqa* attainable by the senses or by the intellect. Then one should refer to allegorical interpretation to retrace the real nature of the text, in which it is harmonious with understanding. In Saadya's view the voice of revelation becomes gradually more silent: the revealed words of the Torah are replaced by prophetic inspiration, and after the prophetic period the Talmudic sages might hear the faint echo (*bat qōl*) of the divine words.

Al-Qirqisānī speaks the language of Saadya: kalamic through and through. His views on prophecy are more decisive, as he draws a distinct dividing line between prophecy and nonprophecy, putting the oral tradition into the latter group. His aim is to rewrite Halakah by replacing the Mishnah and the Talmud by rational interpretation. By ignoring the tradition, he claims that each biblical statement of a legal nature should be taken in a literal sense, with the exception of meaning that contradicts reason, or observation, in which case allegorical interpretation can be justified. When speaking about "real nature," Al-Qirqisānī uses the term in the context of legal duties (*ḥaqīqat al-farā'iḍ*). He means by this, the source and foundation from which the law is derived. Thus, it is either the literal understanding of the text (*naṣṣ*) or a derivation by analogy (*qiyās*), or based on common understanding (*ijmā'*) if the first two sources are not available (348). At another instance he enumerates the methods through which knowledge concerning the real nature of things (*ithbāt al-ḥaqā'iq*) can be generated: speculation (*naẓar, baḥth, istidlāl*), consensus (*ijmā'*), and analogy (*qiyās*) (66–68). He claims that each single religious duty has a reason (*'illa*) and an aim (*ġaraḍ*) (361), and thus each duty makes sense for the human mind.

Real nature equals understandability, although each writer uses the concept of "real nature" in different contexts. Unveiling of the *ḥaqīqa* can vary: using the Aristotelian fourfold framework for Al-Muqammiṣ, kalamic investigation for Saadya, and rational *tafsīr* for Al-Qirqisānī. All three books aim to explain Judaism and to give sense to it. Yet the very notion of "sense" differs from one book to the next, largely because each text's intended audience differed. By transformation of faith into knowledge, or by validating prophecy through philosophy, or by building up a legal system based on rational understanding, this harmony between hidden and apparent, sensation and logic, religion and philosophy, visible and invisible meanings is unquestioned. This results in a tranquility of the soul in the thinker and reader that, until Maimonides resets the scene, draws Aristotelian thought into dialogue with scripture.

Notes

1. *Dāwūd ibn Marwān al-Muqammiṣ's Twenty Chapters* (*'Išrūn Maqāla*), ed. and trans. Sarah Stroumsa (Leiden: Brill, 1989).

2. Saadya Gaon, *Kitāb al-Amānāt wa-'l-I'tiqādāt*, ed. and trans. Y. Qafih (Jerusalem, 1970).

3. *Ya'qūb al-Qirqisānī, Kitāb al-Anwār wal-Marāqib* (Code of Karaite Law), ed. L. Nemoy (New York: Alexander Kohut Memorial Foundation, vol. 1, 1939, vol. 2, 1940).

4. *Book of Beliefs and Opinions*, 320 (408).

5. Quoted in J. Lavery, "Philosophical Genres and Literary Forms: A Mildly Polemical Introduction," *Poetics Today* 28:2 (2007): 172.

6. Lavery, "Philosophical Genres and Literary Forms," 181.

7. Haggai Ben-Shammai, "Major Trends in Karaite Philosophy and Polemics in the Tenth and Eleventh Centuries," in *Karaite Judaism, A Guide to its History and Literary Sources*, ed. Meira Pollack (Leiden, Brill, 2003), 340.

8. On the debate concerning the Karaism of Al-Muqammiṣ, see Sarah Stroumsa, *Dāwūd ibn Marwān al-Muqammiṣ's Twenty Chapters*, 17–19.

9. The ultimate basis for this fourfold approach is Aristotle's enumeration of the four types of inquiry in the *Posterior Analytics* 2.1. It influenced the Alexandrian introductions to philosophy, namely that of Olympiodorus and the Neoplatonist commentators of Aristotle (Themistius). In medieval Jewish and Islamic thought, this list of questions is widespread (Isaac Israeli, Ibn Gabirol, Al-Kindi, Al-Tawḥīdī, etc.) in order to prove the "unknowableness" of God. A detailed analysis of this approach can be found in A. Altmann and S. M. Stern, *Isaac Israeli, A Neoplatonic Philosopher of the Early Tenth Century* (Chicago: University of Chicago Press, 2009), 10–23.

10. See J. C. Reeves, *Prolegomena to a History of Islamicate Manicheism* (Sheffield: Equinox, 2011).

11. D. Frank, "Karaite Exegetical and Halakhic Literature in Byzantium and Turkey," in *Karaite Judaism: A Guide to Its History and Literary Sources*, ed. Meira Pollack (Leiden, Brill, 2003), 529.

12. See Ben-Shammai, "Major Trends in Karaite Philosophy and Polemics in the Tenth and Eleventh Centuries," in Pollack, *Karaite Judaism*, 339, 347.

13. Page numbers refer to Nemoy's edition. Yaʿqūb al-Qirqisānī, *Kitāb al-Anwār wal-Marāqib* (Code of Karaite law) ed. Leon Nemoy (New York, Alexander Kohut Memorial Foundation, 1939–1940).

14. Al-Qirqisānī, *Kitāb al-Anwār wal-Marāqib*, 42–47.

15. A relevant text for Islamic criticism on Christianity is ʿAbd al-Jabbār, *Critique of Christian Origins* (*Tathbīt Dalāʾil al-Nubuwwa*), ed. and trans. G. S. Reynolds and K. S. Samir (Provo, UT: Brigham University Press, 2010).

16. Al-Qirqisānī, *Kitāb al-Anwār wal-Marāqib*, 66–68.

17. Al-Qirqisānī, *Kitāb al-Anwār wal-Marāqib*, 123–128.

18. Al-Qirqisānī, *Kitāb al-Anwār wal-Marāqib*, 166.

19. Al-Qirqisānī, *Kitāb al-Anwār wal-Marāqib*, 99–100. Saadya expresses the same view in his *Book of Beliefs and Opinions*, 2.

20. Al-Qirqisānī, *Kitāb al-Anwār wal-Marāqib*, 206.

21. Al-Qirqisānī, *Kitāb al-Anwār wal-Marāqib*, 174.

22. According to Saadya, the Biblical text should be taken in the literal sense (*ʿalā ẓāhirihi*). An allegorical interpretation (*taʾwīl*) is justified only if there is a contradiction between the biblical text and (1) sense perception, (2) the intuition of the intellect, (3) other biblical passages, or (4) tradition (*Book of Beliefs and Opinions*, 190). To state it another way, allegorical interpretation is required when a contradiction arises between the literal meaning of the revealed text and the universal sources of knowledge. To resort to allegorical interpretation in cases in which no such contradiction exists equals unbelief (*lāḥiq bi-ʾl-kāfirīn*).

23. "Do not curse the deaf or put a stumbling block in front of the blind."

24. The first generations of Muslim rationalist theologians lived in the ninth and tenth centuries.

25. This is a statement typical of Aristotelian philosophers. On the absolute existence of God, see Al-Fārābī, *Book of Letters* (*kitāb al- ḥurūf*), ed. Muhsin Mahdi (Beirut: Dar el-Mashreq, 1969), section 242, 219–20.

26. See Saadya, *Book of Beliefs and Opinions*, 13.

27. On the atomism of the mutakallimūn, see Shlomo Pines, *Studies in Islamic Atomism*, trans. M. Schwartz and ed. Y. T. Langermann (Jerusalem: Magnes Press, 1997), 1–40.

28. Saadya's stance concerning philosophy is much more complex. In his commentary on the *Ṣēfer Yeẓīrah*, an enigmatic work used by kabbalists, he defines *philosophy* as becoming wise and as such depicted as similar to the activity of the Creator (*Tafsīr Ṣēfer Yeẓīrah*), p. 4. This work in no way can be considered a summa; it belongs to a different genre of a more Neoplatonic tone.

29. Concerning the importance of sense perception, see Saadya, *Book of Beliefs and Opinions*, 15, also: "Wisdom consists in knowing things as they are in their real, observable character, not as someone would desire or like them to be" (199).

GYONGYI HEGEDUS is Associate Professor in the Department of Philosophy and Religious Studies at Western University (London, Ontario). Her academic interest lies in the history of ideas, medieval thought, Islamic and Jewish kalam (rational theology), and mysticism. She is author of *Saadya Gaon: The Double Path of the Mystic and the Rationalist*.

7

DIALOGUES

Aaron W. Hughes

PHILOSOPHICAL DIALOGUES REVEAL THE INTERSECTION OF THE LITERARY and the philosophical. Since the enterprise of philosophy is inherently dialogical, composed of interlocutors who desire to sharpen their own intellectual positions and to refute those of their opponents, the dialogue becomes a convenient mode of expression. The genre itself would seem to owe its genesis to Plato, who attempted to portray a living and interactive encounter in a written text. The fine balance that Plato struck between philosophy and literature permits the reader entry into an unfolding narrative, thereby allowing him or her to struggle actively with the ideas presented within. Although the dialogue would, in the centuries after Plato, go in and out of vogue, the encounter between antagonistic views, the attempt to convince another of the incorrectness of his or her arguments, and an ultimate resolution offered a convenient vehicle to popularize and disseminate philosophy.[1]

By "philosophical dialogue," I mean nothing more than a series of narrative exchanges between two or more discrete characters whose conversations revolve around a number of philosophical issues. These dialogues usually take place in a particular narrative setting, and the various exchanges permit us to witness the development of not only a set of philosophical arguments but also the protagonists' personalities. Questions that we need to ask include the following: Why might a philosopher have used this genre, as opposed to others, both to create and disseminate their philosophical ideas? What does the genre allow that other genres do not?

How are the literary features of the genre used to construct a philosophical argument?

The Dialogue: Theoretical Issues

Dialogues function as windows through which we are able to examine not only a specific author but also, perhaps more importantly, the broader community of which he was a part. Consequently, the various debates that arise in these dialogues often reflect very real contemporaneous religious, intellectual, and social issues. These issues were often extremely vitriolic, for at stake in the medieval period was Judaism's orientation to other cultures. For instance, what texts should Jews read? Should non-Jewish scientific sources or literary genres play a role in the Jewish educational curriculum? The dialogue now becomes an important lens through which we are able to confront firsthand the dynamics, often nonphilosophical, behind the composition of Jewish philosophy. Having said this, however, it is important not to assume that the reasons behind the composition of each Jewish dialogue were necessarily the same. Sometimes the dialogue could be subversive, as with Judah Halevi's use of the dialogue to offer a Jewish response to Ismaʿili-inflected philosophical ideas, many of which were themselves elaborated in the form of the dialogue. Yet others—for example, those written by Shem Tov ibn Falaquera and Isaac Polleqar—employed the genre as a convenient way to offer thoughtful responses to the Maimonidean Controversies of the thirteenth and fourteenth centuries.

Many medieval Jewish philosophical dialogues are polemical in intent. They involve ideological exchanges between a character who seems to be a stand-in for the author and one or more characters who hold opposing philosophical positions. The protagonist successfully defends his positions and convinces his interlocutors that he alone holds the correct position on any given topic. Once the antagonist accepts the error of his ways, the dialogue moves from polemics to conversation as the protagonist then explains in greater detail a number of his original positions. This leads to the further elucidation of a number of key issues that were only briefly touched on in the initial exchange.

Furthermore, dialogues seek to publicize, popularize, or otherwise disseminate philosophical teachings to as wide a reading audience as possible. They do this primarily by including, in nontechnical fashion, philosophical ideas in a pleasing literary form. Some texts appear to have employed the dialogue form in a fairly wooden fashion, using it for no other reason than to move the conversation along in a rather artificial manner. Other authors, however, create full-blown dialogues that are literary masterpieces in their own right and that are complete with full-blown characters who undergo change in the course of the dialogue. By giving a philosophical treatise various characters, a plot, and a setting, these philosophers were able to create texts that worked on a number of levels. A philosophically inclined reader, for example, would be able to see in such a text a work of philosophy. A more literary-minded reader would be able to see reflected in the same text a work of literature. It is important, however, not to ignore one of these aspects at the expense of the other; for it is ultimately the intersection of philosophy and literature that is not only one of the hallmarks of these dialogues, but the main reason for their popularity.

The Dialogue in Judaism: Origins

Judaism possesses a venerable and ancient tradition of dialogue, at least broadly conceived. Indeed, one could quite easily argue that the history of the Jewish people from antiquity to the present is essentially a series of dialogues and silences between God and Israel. The covenantal relationship, in other words, is one that is based on two sides communicating to one another through and in time. However, this idea of God and Israel engaged in a constant conversation is a concept or a process and not necessarily a literary encounter portrayed in a particular literary genre. The one real exception is the book of Job, wherein we encounter a literal dialogue that revolves around a number of philosophical themes that include theodicy and the suffering of the righteous. Not surprisingly, many Jewish philosophers, beginning with Saadya Gaon (882–942), gravitated to the book of Job and read it as a philosophical dialogue dealing with God's providential relationship to humanity.[2]

The phenomenon of literary disputation also plays a central role in the various sources of rabbinic Judaism. Many of the aggadic stories that appear in the Talmud, for example, provide the rabbinic sages with a means to think about and attempt to resolve the various tensions in their culture.[3] Not unlike philosophical dialogues, in order to understand these stories, we need to situate them within their broader literary, historical, and intellectual contexts.[4] Despite the prevalence for both disputation and literary art, however, the existence of literal dialogues is relatively rare in this literature. One important exception, however, is the series of exchanges between Rabbi Judah the Prince and the enigmatic Antoninus, often believed to be a Roman governor or perhaps even the emperor. In these dialogues, the two characters discuss a number of issues that we might today loosely label as philosophical (e.g., when life begins and the afterlife).[5]

Despite examples such as the book of Job and the dialogic encounters between Rabbi Judah the Prince and Antoninus, there is no evidence that when medieval Jewish philosophers decided to compose their own dialogues they looked to this body of literature. For example, although Jewish philosophers decided to write commentaries, as we have seen, to the book of Job, they rarely, if ever, focused on the dialogic aspect or aspects of this work. They were, in other words, primarily interested in the contents of the book and not its form.

A more likely archetype for the composition of medieval Jewish dialogues would seem to be the work of Plato, the true master of the philosophical dialogue. Yet despite this, it seems highly unlikely that Jewish or Arab philosophers had firsthand knowledge of the Platonic corpus.[6] The majority of Platonic texts reached the medievals by way of Galen's summaries.[7] Islamic and Jewish philosophers had knowledge of the contents but not necessarily the original forms (i.e., dialogues) of the *Sophist*, *Cratylus*, *Euthydemus*, *Statesman*, *Timaeus*, *Laws*,[8] and *Parmenides*, in addition to a paraphrase of the *Republic*.[9] Another important source for knowledge of Plato came from the compilation of his sayings included in *Nawādir al-falāsifa wa-l-ḥukamā'* (Anecdotes of philosophers and sages) by Ḥunayn ibn Isḥāq (809–893). These anecdotes, however, had little or no relation to Plato's actual corpus.[10] Despite the modern importance of the Platonic dialogue to Western thought, it is highly unlikely, if not outright impossible, that the Platonic method of composition would have influenced any Jewish philosopher prior to Judah Abravanel (ca. 1465–after 1521) and the rise of humanism in the Renaissance, which witnessed new editions and translations of Plato's corpus.[11]

On the contrary, it seems likely that some of the earliest dialogues that medieval Jewish philosophers would have encountered emanated not from the Greek-speaking world but from the Arab-speaking one. One of the earliest examples in the Arabo-Islamic world is recorded by Abū Ḥayyān al-Tawḥīdī (ca. 930–1023) as a debate between the grammarian Abū Sa'īd al-Sīrāfī (d. 979) and the philosopher Abū Bishr Mattā b. Yūnus (d. 940).[12] Mattā b. Yūnus, one of the teachers of Al-Farabi, argues in this dialogue that logic is universal science and thus is central to clear thinking; Al-Sīrāfī, who by all accounts wins the debate, counters that logic is not universal, but a Greek linguistic habit and consequently unnecessary for Arab speakers, who have all they need in the rules of Arabic grammar.

It is important to note that one of the earliest Islamic subcultures to employ the dialogue form was the Isma'ilis, a group that had a huge impact on subsequent Islamic and Jewish philosophical speculation.[13] The Isma'ilis seem to have inherited the genre, as they did many other intellectual ideas, from various esoteric groups of late antiquity. In particular, it is worth noting that certain treatises in *Corpus Hermeticum* were written as dialogues, wherein gods reveal esoteric and philosophical truths to humans with requisite preparation and gnosis. The actual chains of transmission of this literature from the late antique period to the early Islamic one, however, are difficult to reconstruct, primarily owing to the fact that it is virtually impossible to know what exactly the earliest Isma'ilis were reading and, equally important, in what literary forms.[14]

Within this context, another important and early dialogue may be found in the debate between the animals and humans in the Isma'ili-influenced *Rasā'il Ikhwān al-Ṣafā'* (Epistles of the Brethren of Purity).[15] This work, in addition to various other proselytizing works composed by Isma'ili missionaries designed to appeal to the philosophically inclined, would have circulated throughout Muslim Spain and North Africa. It would seem that these dialogues—and not biblical, rabbinic, or Platonic precedents—served as the immediate influence on the composition of Jewish philosophical dialogues. Individuals such as Solomon ibn Gabirol, Baḥya ibn Paquda, and Abraham ibn Ezra all seem to have composed their dialogues under the sphere of influence of this Isma'ili philosophical spirituality. Judah Halevi, who composed perhaps the most famous of dialogues in the medieval philosophical tradition, seems likely to have written his *Kuzari* as a way to counter the headway that Isma'ili-infected spirituality was making among Andalusi Jews.

Halevi's *Kuzari*

Judah Halevi (1075–1141) styled himself as a critic of both philosophy and the synthesis of Judeo-Arabic culture. Both of these, according to him, represented an inauthentic Jewish expression. In order to undermine such forms, however, he often resorted to employing the same literary styles as those he sought to critique. Perhaps nowhere is this clearer than in his dialogue *Al-Kuzarī: Kitāb al-radd wa al-dalīl fī'l-dīn al-dhalīl* (The book of refutation and proof in defense of the despised religion),[16] which he seems to have written over the period of about twenty years. The work itself recounts the story of the king of the Khazars, who invites a philosopher, a Muslim, and a Christian to his court in order to ask them questions, with the ultimate aim of converting his kingdom to a new religion. Although he does not invite a Jew to his court, it soon becomes clear from the conversation with the others that he should have. He subsequently does and is so impressed with the Jew's responses that he converts his entire kingdom to Judaism. The dialogue recounts the subsequent conversations between the king and the *ḥaver*, or the spokesperson for Judaism. Although Halevi began the work while still living in Al-Andalus, he completed it in Egypt in 1140, just before he made his way to the land of Israel.[17] This rather lengthy period of composition has led some to conclude that the final version of the *Kuzari* was hastily put together in an "uncrafted and disconnected manner."[18] Yet the very fact that the work is the product of one of the most creative and distinguished of the medieval Hebrew poets should render such a reading problematic.

That Halevi chose to communicate his ideas in the form of a dialogue is surely significant. This genre, as we have seen, was a well-established literary form employed by various Islamicate subcultures to make cases for their exclusive claims to religious authority and gnosis. It was particularly popular among Isma'ili missionaries, many of whom employed dialogues to disseminate their Neoplatonic-inspired brand of Islam. The Isma'ilis were an extremely proselytizing sect within Islam that was predicated on an oath-based system of allegiance to a living Imam, or spiritual leader, who alone was regarded as possessing the proper religious understanding. In addition, Isma'ilis stressed intention (*niyya*) over action (*'amal*) and the esoteric (*bāṭin*) over the exoteric (*zāhir*). The key to maneuvering successfully between these dichotomous positions was an appropriate hermeneutical system (*ta'wīl*). This Isma'ili or Isma'ili-inflected presentation of religious ideas proved particularly popular among many Muslim and Jewish intellectuals who appreciated its presentation of religion using philosophical terminology and categories.[19]

Shlomo Pines has argued that in order to understand the generation of *Kuzari* it is necessary to examine its language, especially the genealogy of certain terms that Halevi employs to make his case for the religious superiority of Judaism.[20] Many of these terms, Pines demonstrates, were not unique to Halevi but actually borrowed from various Islamicate subcultures, most notably the Isma'ilis, and subsequently resignified by Halevi. Rather than compose his treatise in a vacuum, his work must be contextualized within the literary, intellectual, and cultural orbit of eleventh-century Al-Andalus. To ensure as wide an audience as possible for his stinging indictment of Judeo-Arabic synthesis, he would not invent a new genre but employ one that would have been familiar to his contemporaries. The *Kuzari*, thus, presents a pleasing and well-crafted argument that subverts, in its genre no less than its contents, the dominant intellectual and religious paradigms of his day.

Halevi begins the work recounting a dream sequence wherein an angel appears to the non-Jewish king of the Khazars informing him that, while the intention (*niyya*) behind his religious orientation is appropriate, his ritual actions (*a'māl*) are not. These two technical terms form the centerpiece of the beginning of the work, and it is the dissonance between them that informs Halevi's desire to compose the work. Halevi's use of these two technical terms are the opposite of their employment in Isma'ili texts. For the Isma'ilis, the *a'māl* of Islam are the various religious observances and obligations (e.g., prayer, fasting, almsgiving) revealed through the divine law (*sharī'a*) and incumbent on all Muslims. It becomes the goal of the Isma'ili missionary (*dā'ī*) to encourage an initiate to penetrate beyond simple observance of the law to contemplate the spiritual and esoteric truths (*ḥaqā'iq*) that exist beyond such exoteric actions. Not coincidentally, many Isma'ili treatises begin with an elucidation of the difference between intentions and actions.[21]

Juxtaposed against Isma'ili treatises, Halevi begins his treatise with an angel appearing to the king of the Khazars and informing him that it is his actions, *not* his intentions, that are the problem. For Halevi, it is the external acts of religion that, paradoxically, represent the spiritual depths. As a consequence, access to such truth is not confined to the spiritual elite (Isma'ilis or philosophers) but is something that is accessible to the entire Jewish people. Halevi thus frames his work, one of the classics of medieval Jewish thought, using the same genre (a dialogue), the same terminology (actions versus intentions), and a similar narrative structure (a potential disciple asking a potential teacher about their difference) as the Isma'ilis. Unlike them, however, Halevi gives all of these phenomena a completely different interpretation by making true religious experience contingent on the proper, physical performance of ritual, something that has to be accessible to the entire community.

The dialogue, as we have seen, serves as a convenient vehicle to elaborate details of a position, with an individual asking the main protagonist, often a stand-in for the author, questions in such a manner that the latter can elaborate on a particular point. The following encounter between the questioner, the king, and the protagonist, the *ḥaver*, is indicative of this:

THE KING: I have speculated about your authority [*amrakum*] and understand that God desires your survival [*ibqā'kum*], and that He appointed Sabbaths and the holy days [*al-asbāt wa al-a'yād*] among the strongest means of preserving your spark and luster . . . All of these are divine commandments that are incumbent on you [*kullihā awāmir illāhiyya mu'aqqada 'alakum*].

THE ḤAVER: The best [*al-khayr*] among us fulfills the precepts from this divine law [*al-sharī'a al-ilāhiyya*]—circumcision, sabbaths, holy days, and the legal necessities [*lawāzim al-mashrū'*] that come from God. He refrains from the forbidden marriages, using mixtures in plants, clothes, and animals. Keeps the years of release and jubilee, avoids idolatry and the search for knowledge [*talab 'ilm*] without prophecy by means of *urim ve-thummim* or dreams. He does not listen to the soothsayer, astrologer, magician, augur, or necromancer.[22]

The pious and the observant individuals, Halevi speaking through the *ḥaver* makes clear here, should have no need to inquire into the mystical, philosophical, or esoteric properties of the divinely revealed rituals. That they are divine and revealed from heaven should suffice for such an individual. Later on in book three, the *ḥaver* elaborates on this point in response to the Khazar king's questions about the Karaites:

THE KING: I would now like you to tell me about the Karaites and their beliefs, which seem more pious [*al-ta'bbud akthar*] than those of the Rabbanites. I have heard that their arguments are superior and better [*arjaḥ wa-akthar*] when it comes to [understanding] the literal level of the Torah.

THE ḤAVER: Did I not already say that the arbitrariness [*al-taḥakkum*], rational discernment [*al-ta'aqqul*], and conjecture [*al-takharruṣ*] concerning the Law do not lead to the pleasure of God. If this were the case then dualists, materialists, worshippers of spirits, those who withdraw to mountaintops, and those who burn their children all desire to approach God. We have, however, said that one cannot approach God except by His commands [*awāmir Allah*].[23]

The commandments are holy because they come from God, were received by the Israelites on Sinai, and form the core of the divine revelation. They are not holy, the *ḥaver* remarks, because they are subject to esoteric manipulation by a self-styled spiritual elite, whether Isma'ilis, philosophers, or Sufis. This leads to a final major discrepancy between Halevi's dialogue and those composed by the Isma'ilis. Whereas the latter treatises culminate in the conversion of the initiate into the mysteries of the tradition, Halevi's *begins* with the king converting to Judaism. Unlike the Isma'ili initiates, the Khazar king already possessed the proper intention before his conversion to Judaism. What Judaism offers him is the proper physical and bodily outlets to bring his actions into harmony with his intentions. This becomes ever clearer when the king speaks to the representatives of both Islam and Christianity, neither of whom mention the importance of action. Both tell the king what they believe, but it is only the Jew who connects belief to observance as found in the divine law (*al-sharī'a*).

In the final analysis, it should be clear that Halevi's *Kuzari* works not just on the level of ideas, but also on the level of genre. To focus solely on the ideas contained within the work is to overlook the way such ideas are also expressed on the level of both literature and genre. In this regard the ideas and the dialogue mutually reinforce one another.

Other Dialogues in Al-Andalus Prior to Maimonides

Ibn Gabirol (1021–ca. 1058) was one of Al-Andalus's most famous and celebrated Hebrew poets. He was also one of the most original Jewish philosophers prior to Maimonides. His most famous philosophical work is a dialogue entitled *Yanbū' al-hayāh* (translated into Latin in the twelfth century as *Fons Vitae*, both meaning the "fountain of life," hence the Hebrew title of *Meqor Ḥayyim*). *Yanbū' al-hayāh* is one of the most original works of medieval Neoplatonism. Largely devoted to the topic of elucidating the concept of uniformity throughout the cosmos, the work argues that all that exists within the universe is constituted of matter and form. These qualities are manifest throughout the entire universe from the highest limits of the spiritual world to the lowest limits of the physical one. Although all levels of the universe possess this distinction, according to Ibn Gabirol, the farther they are removed from its first source the less spiritual they become. From this structure, we see that Ibn Gabirol's thought is heavily indebted to the intellectualized theology of Neoplatonism, which imagines God as the ultimate reality that infuses all things. In order for the individual to contemplate the universe (and by extension, God) he or she must engage in scientific observation and live an ethical life. This permits the individual to return to his or her source and to reclaim being in the fullest and truest sense of the term.

Because of the novelty and originality of his thought, Ibn Gabirol apparently kept his philosophical speculation free from dogmatic theology. Neither a verse from the Bible nor rabbinic literature is cited in *Yanbūʿ al-hayāh*. Such omissions, despite the originality of his thought, meant that this important philosophical work was largely overlooked by subsequent Jewish philosophers and was instead embraced by Christians and Muslims. In fact, the author of this text was long thought to have been either an Arabo-Muslim thinker or an Augustinian Christian, known by the Latinized name of Avicebron or Avencebrol.[24] Only in the mid-nineteenth century when Salomon Munk "discovered" the text to be written by a Jew did the *Fons Vitae* become, retrospectively, imagined as a work of "Jewish philosophy." Until this time, we had to make do with his religious poetry (such as *Keter Malkhut*) or less original philosophical works (e.g., *On the Improvement of the Moral Qualities*).

Like the great majority of Jewish philosophical dialogues, Ibn Gabirol presents us with a master or teacher who leads his disciple to a proper understanding of the universe through a series of questions and answers. The disciple's questions are often short and to the point, whereas the master's responses provide elaborate responses that enable Ibn Gabirol to articulate his philosophical position. Unlike Halevi, who fully exploits the form of the dialogue, at least in the opening sequence of the *Kuzari*, Ibn Gabirol is not nearly as interested in the genre's literary characteristics. Keeping in mind the dramatic opening section from Halevi's work, we read the following at the beginning of Ibn Gabirol's dialogue:

> Master: Thanks to your natural ability and diligence, you possess the requisite strength to proceed in the study of philosophy. Let us begin with you telling me about matters that are dear to your heart, and then we will eventually arrive to the most important question of all, namely, "Why was man created?" The form of our conversation will be the following: question and answer according to the rules of logical disputation.
>
> Disciple: How can we order our questions and answers according to these rules without talking on and on? Perhaps you should clarify matter before this?

> If you want to follow the rules of logical disputation in all that follows then the work will be long and the toil great.[25]

Without getting into the contents of the work, it should be readily apparent that here we encounter none of the dramatic backdrop that we do in the *Kuzari*. On the contrary, the master informs the disciple that he is ready to begin the study of philosophy and that the rules of their conversation will follow those that govern all logical disputations. In the subsequent exchanges, the disciple asks all the questions, and the master provides all the answers. To cite but one example:

DISCIPLE: Is there an end to human existence?

MASTER: Why shouldn't there be? For everything conforms to the will of the Great One.

DISCIPLE: Please explain this to me.

MASTER: Since the will is the divine strength, it supplies everything and keeps everything apart. It is impossible that something can occur without it.

DISCIPLE: How is this so?[26]

This exchange is typical of the dialogue as a whole. The disciple constantly feeds convenient questions to the master to move the conversation along. Other sections of the dialogue involve lengthy monologues on the part of the master, in which the disciple becomes little more than a passive recipient of his teachings. The role of the dialogue between the two main characters, who are completely undeveloped as personalities, has little to do with the thesis that emerges in the work as a whole, nor is it particularly relevant to its major argument. In fact, so contrived is the dialogue in this treatise that Shem Tov ibn Falaquera (ca. 1225–ca. 1295), who translated the work into Hebrew, seems to have agreed with the assessment of Abraham ibn Da'ud (ca. 1110–ca. 1180) that "perhaps if [*Meqor Ḥayyim's*] contents were refined, [Ibn Gabirol's] words could be included in [a treatise that is] less than one tenth of that treatise."[27] Indeed, when Falaquera translated the work, he chose—despite the fact that he himself, as we shall see shortly, wrote philosophical dialogues—not to retain the dialogue form but simply summarize the main points.

Although it is difficult to prove with certainty that Halevi had the *Meqor Ḥayyim* in mind when he composed his dialogue, he most likely would have known it and its contents. It is perhaps worth noting, however, that a Jew in Al-Andalus composed one of the most important and sustained works of Neoplatonism in the form of a dialogue. It is probably no coincidence that, especially given the highly literary and competitive culture there, that another Jew, Halevi, would present at least the opening of his *Kuzari* using a much more dramatic narrative that employs characters who undergo changes in their personality as the dialogue unfolds. It would seem, then, that Halevi offers his dialogue as an alternative, both philosophical and aesthetic, to something like that composed by Ibn Gabirol.

Another example of a dialogue composed by an Andalusi Jew is Abraham ibn Ezra's *Ḥay ben Meqitz*, which provides an elaborate and poetic description of an unnamed protagonist's ascent through the various levels of the universe, culminating in a dramatic vision. It is, however, also important to note that it is also composed as a dialogue between this protagonist and Ḥay ben Meqitz. Even though Ibn Ezra and Halevi were friends and, according to some accounts, related by marriage, they share radically different conceptions of Judaism and the place of philosophy therein.[28] It seems highly likely, for instance, that Ismaʿili cosmology had a significant role in Ibn Ezra's thought,[29] and, much like Ibn Gabirol, he emphasizes the universal aspects of Judaism at the expense of the particularistic. In the following exchange between the unnamed protagonist and Ḥay ben Meqitz, we encounter the former's initiation into the secrets of the universe:

> He said "Drink the water from its sources
>   The fluids flowing from its well!
> In it your fractures will be healed
>   Your limbs will be dressed
> You will have wings
>   To fly into the heavens."
> I drank from the water of life
>   The water that gives life to souls
> My pain and my affliction left me . . .
>   My sickness was cured.
> He reached out his hands and grabbed me
>   Lifting me from the depths of the spring.[30]

Although he does not employ the Ismaʿili term for initiation (*ʿahd*) here, it seems fairly clear that there is an implication that some kind of initiation has indeed occurred. Only after the baptism in water, for example, can the protagonist continue on his journey of ascent. Again, as we witnessed in the *Kuzari*, such an initiation that takes place external to the halakhic observance of every Jew would be problematic for Halevi. It is against this intellectual and ideological backdrop, once again, that we should situate the literary production of Jewish philosophical texts.

As one final example, let us look briefly at *Kitāb al-hidāya ilā farā'iḍ al-qulūb* (The book of direction to the duties of the heart) by Baḥya ibn Paquda (ca. 1040–ca. 1080). Like Halevi, Baḥya would argue that the ultimate moment for the true believer is suprarational and mystical. Like all of the thinkers discussed so far in this chapter, Baḥya is heavily influenced by Arabo-Islamic speculation, especially that of Sufism or Islamic mysticism.[31] That is, for him, philosophical speculation can only lead the individual so far, at which point reason must surrender to the total submission in the service of God. Parts of this work, but not all, are written in the form of a dialogue. In chapter 3, Baḥya recounts a dialogue between the soul and the intellect concerning the true nature of happiness:

THE SOUL: What is the evil food to which I am accustomed?

THE INTELLECT: It is the blameworthy trait that overcame you from the beginning, and the forces that strength it.

THE SOUL: What are the components of this trait and what are the forces that strengthen it?

THE INTELLECT: Your blameworthy traits are many, but their origins and beginning are two: first, love of the bodily pleasure . . . . these you have acquired from your evil neighbor, the body . . . The second is your love of leadership and honor . . . these cause you to be ungrateful to your Benefactor.[32]

This dialogue between the various faculties within the human is the novelty of Baḥya's dialogue. Here Baḥya gives priority to the intellect, which is able to inform the soul what ails it. The intellect, despite the fact that Baḥya will argue that reason is not the highest function of humans, still plays an important role:

THE SOUL: The finesse and subtlety of this matter is so great that you have made me despair of grasping its meaning, and now you console me. Please reveal to me also the secret of my place in this world and the purpose of my stay on it. Bring me closer to an understanding of divine determination and justice, and briefly as possible, so that I will not be like the man who does not know the right way that leads to his good . . .

THE INTELLECT: The secret is that the Creator formed you out of nothing, among the other spiritual entities created by Him. Intending to raise your position, He elevated you to the level of His chosen favorites who are near to His light, all as a manifestation of His grace and benevolence toward you . . . [God] gave you two chosen viziers . . . The first vizier is the mind, which directs you in the way of God's satisfaction; the second vizier is the instinct that seduces you and leads you to the things that arouse the anger of your Lord and Creator.[33]

Again, we see Baḥya employing a dialogue as a way of discussing philosophical concepts. A conversation between the soul and the intellect over what ails the former is a much more creative way to discuss their relationship than a more technical discursive treatise. It is this, as we shall also see in the example below, that provides the dialogue one of its most important functions in medieval Jewish philosophical literature.

Shem Tov ibn Falaquera's Iggeret ha-vikkuaḥ *and* Sefer ha-mevaqqesh

Increasingly in the thirteenth and fourteenth centuries, the dialogue became intertwined with the Maimonidean Controversies, which witnessed a vitriolic struggle for what Jewish culture, including what should count as its authoritative sources, ought to look like.[34] Dialogues—in addition to other nontraditional forms, such as sermons and philosophically inspired Bible commentaries—played a prominent role in disseminating rationalism to various audiences that neither understood Arabic nor were trained in the technical dimensions of philosophy.

Within this context Shem Tov ibn Falaquera (ca.1225–ca.1295) composed several important philosophical dialogues. Falaquera is generally considered to be one of the great popularizers of Jewish philosophy, someone who not only composed dialogues but also poetry and several encyclopedias. In terms of the dialogue, he exploits the genre's ability to offer multiple antagonistic positions simultaneously and in such a manner that these positions could find ultimate resolution. Here it is important to acknowledge that Falaquera lived during a period of extreme polarization in northern Spain and southern France that revolved around the role of rationalism within Judaism. Falaquera found the genre of the dialogue to be conducive to mediating the acrimonious debates between traditional Judaism and the emerging philosophical discourse by showing their points of intersection and mutual compatibility. Yet it is important to realize that this mediation was primarily textual in the sense that the genre permitted a convenient literary forum to air debates and seek their resolution when, in reality, such resolution was effectively impossible.

In addition to the genre's ability to mediate between opposing views, we also see in Falaquera's dialogues the ability to popularize and disseminate philosophy in a manner that the traditional philosophical treatise could not. Within this context, the generic structure of the dialogue was conducive to instructing those with little formal scientific education about how philosophy could contribute to a better understanding of religion and religious truths. Whenever Falaquera (or others) made the protagonist a philosopher, the various questions that the other characters put to him provided a forum for offering nontechnical descriptions of philosophy, in addition to expounding on the relationship between faith and reason in a nonantagonistic manner.

One of Falaquera's most important dialogues is the *Iggeret ha-vikkuaḥ* (Epistle of the debate),[35] which recounts the debate between a learned pietist (*ḥasid*) and a philosopher (*ḥakham*). The pietist, trained in law but ignorant in matters of philosophy, accuses the philosopher of unbelief. In the course of their debate, however, the philosopher is able to demonstrate to the pietist that there exists a fundamental harmony between the truths of philosophy and religion. Falaquera begins by informing the reader that he has composed the work to demonstrate that the law commands Jews to study philosophy, which, when properly understood, does not contradict the truths of religion. He writes that "The purpose of this epistle, which is written by way of allegory and figure [*ha-mashal ve-ha-melitzah*], is to explain that the study of the true sciences [*ha-ḥokhmot ha-amitiot*] by whomever is worthy of them and whom God in His mercy has favored with an intellect to discover their depths is not prohibited from the point of view of our Law [*torateinu*], and that the truth [*ha-emet*] hidden in them does not contradict a word of our belief [*emunateinu*], as the fools think who are void of truth and disagree with us."[36] The work, then, has a fairly explicit aim, one that is further attested to in the very structure and style that Falaquera chooses to mount his defense. The dialogue, thus, becomes a convenient genre to exploit, and ultimately resolve, the tension between two diametrically opposed positions. It enables him to raise viewpoints and ideologies that are not his own with an eye to reconciling them with those to which he subscribes. *Iggeret ha-vikkuaḥ* is written in clear and simple Hebrew, most of which is composed in a rhyming prose that was popular among contemporaneous Jewish literati, especially among authors of *maqāmāt* (a genre devoted specifically to rhyming prose). Furthermore, Falaquera intersperses biblical and rabbinic phrases throughout the work, undoubtedly to convince further the skeptical reader that the Bible and philosophy are not opposed to one another, at least when properly understood.

Before the actual debate, Falaquera is quick to describe the philosopher as someone who is also a religious person, as someone who studies both law and science, and as someone who learns the true nature of the world from both philosophical and Jewish sources. The pietist and the philosopher, in other words, are not diametrically opposed to one another; rather both share a commitment to religious law and scripture. Where they differ, of course, is in the importance each assigns to philosophy. Keeping in mind the Maimonidean Controversies in the background of this debate, it is important to note that Falaquera does not have the two protagonists attack each other. Rather they engage in civil conversation, and, unlike the real debates that swirled around him, Falaquera's dialogue has a specific and mutually beneficial resolution.

However, just so we do not forget the sociological and intellectual contexts in which he composed the work, Falaquera reminds us what is at stake when he has the pietist threaten the philosopher with a ban (*niddui*), which would effectively excommunicate him, should he not like what the philosopher has to say:

> The philosopher: May God lead you, O pietist, to His truth, may He broaden your intellect, and may the foreskin of our ears and our minds be circumcised. Please be so kind as to tell me what your opinion is about what we said yesterday.
>
> The pietist: May God return you, O philosopher, from the perplexing path of philosophy to the words of the Law and the halakhah. It appears to me that your words are full of sophistry, ugly within though beautiful on the outside. You incline from the path of the Law when you move toward the words of the philosophers. I warn you that if, heaven forbid, your words are heard any more in my presence, I will decree a ban [*niddui*] upon you.[37]

Interestingly, the pietist only utters this threat after he feels that the philosopher has gotten the best of him, owing to the latter's superior logical and rhetorical skills. The role and function of tradition serves as a leitmotif that runs throughout the debate between the pietist and the philosopher.

As was the case for the Maimonidean Controversies, at stake was how one acquires truth:

THE PHILOSOPHER: Now if concerning these things man desires to know their truth and is not satisfied with tradition alone until he knows their cause and their reason, how much more is the case with the things that are the foundation of foundations [*yesodei ha-yesodot*] and the root of roots [*ikkarei ha-ikkarim*], whose reasons man must seek a way to know, and which he must apprehend in truth, not accidentally. This is not necessary for all men, but for the one who is meticulous in his faith and endeavors to ascend to the rank of the perfect man and conceive what he conceives by the intellect [*ha-sekel*], not by way of the imagination. As for the others who do not perceive this degree, tradition without their knowing the reason is sufficient.

THE PIETIST: In your opinion, who showed the philosophers in the first place the paths that lead to truth, and who awakened them since there were not prophets among them?

THE PHILOSOPHER: He who awakes them is God, may He be blessed, in His bestowing upon them the intelligibles among which are the true universal premises . . . God, may He be blessed, gives to him whom he loves a discerning mind to investigate by means of those intelligibles the true reality of the beings. Therefore, the sages may their memory be blessed, arrange that man must ask for them in the beginning of the petition for his needs in prayer.[38]

In this exchange, the philosopher couches his response to the pietist in both philosophical and religious terms. Philosophically, he argues that those who are capable are required by law to use their intellects to investigate the nature of first principles for themselves. However, he also claims that, religiously, this knowledge ultimately derives from God and that one can only seek out knowledge of intelligibles if one is "meticulous in one's faith." Interestingly, and here we see the selective aspect of the genre, the philosopher downplays the tension between faith and reason here by completely leaving out of the discussion the role that the Active Intellect, the last of the ten celestial intellects, plays in the cognitive process. Many critics of philosophy, most notably Halevi, faulted the philosophers for making God only indirectly involved in human cognition by relegating his role in this process in favor of the last of the emanated intellects. At the end of his response, the philosopher goes so far as to claim that the sages of old had philosophy in mind when they composed the fourth benediction of the Amidah.

As we approach the end of the dialogue, the pietist gains a new understanding of the goals and aims of philosophy. In particular, he comes to the realization that philosophy is not tantamount to unbelief and that all philosophers are not, by definition, "Epicureans" (*epikorsim*), that is, unbelievers. Philosophy, when properly defined and its goals correctly understood, is not the enemy of true belief, but the buttress of such belief:

THE PIETIST: What you said is new to me, and if it is as you say, then I have erred in how I regard [the philosophers].

THE PHILOSOPHER: Please be so kind, O pietist, to tell me about this.

THE PIETIST: I regarded them as heretics and Epicureans. I thought that their books were irreligious, that whoever reads them would have no share in the world to come.

THE PHILOSOPHER: You erred greatly! You entertained a suspicion against the worthy. The Epicurean is an extremely impudent man, and he believes that God, may He be blessed and exalted above such a thought, is not present in the world, and that the soul dies after the death of the body. The true philosophers [*ha-filosofim ha-amitiim*]—and these are the ones to which I always refer—bring strong and true proofs for the refutation of [the Epicurean's] belief. They make known with these proofs that there is a God in the world and that the soul remains after the separation from the body.

THE PIETIST: It seems to me that this is close to what is written in our Law: "To love God, [to hearken His voice,] and to cleave to Him [Deut. 30:20].[39]

In addition to *Iggeret ha-vikkuaḥ*, Falaquera also composed *Sefer ha-mevaqqesh* (Book of the seeker),[40] a work that is often referred to not as a dialogue proper but as an "encyclopedia" or even a *maqama*.[41] Although the term itself is anachronistic, scholars of medieval Christianity and Judaism agree that *encyclopedia* can be used accurately to refer to "a well-ordered, easy-to-use, comprehensive account of already existing information."[42] The medieval encyclopedia, not unlike Falaquera's use of the dialogue, represents an attempt to order knowledge with the explicit aim of educating and edifying as large an audience as possible. Unlike his other encyclopedias, however, *Sefer ha-mevaqqesh* is written as a dialogue, and, as a result, the literary aspects of the work need to be considered. Speaking in terms of the larger intellectual context, it was probably no coincidence that the thirteenth century not only witnessed the emergence of Jewish encyclopedias but was also the "age of the encyclopedias" in medieval Christianity.[43]

Within this context, *Sefer ha-mevaqqesh* recounts the story of a young man's search for knowledge. The first part of the book records his conversations with a series of individuals who claim practical knowledge (for example, a merchant, a warrior, a physician, and a poet), and the second part of the work relates the seeker's conversations with those who claim expertise in theoretical knowledge (for example, a mathematician, an astronomer, and a philosopher). The central features, including shortcomings, of each discipline is described through the dialogic exchanges between the seeker and these various individuals, as is the amount of time that should be spent mastering each craft or science. By the end of the work, then, the seeker has accomplished what he had set out to do: he has discovered the various branches of knowledge, the major principles of each branch, and the appropriate length of time that should be devoted to each one.

Unlike the other dialogues examined in this chapter, *Sefer ha-mevaqqesh* does not provide an extended and lengthy conversation between two protagonists. Rather, it gives us a series of vignettes between the seeker and those with whom he believes he can learn. The work itself begins with a description of the seeker about to set out on a quest in search of understanding.[44] What follows is a series of encounters with a variety of individuals who claim to possess knowledge concerning the true nature of human happiness. These individuals are, in the order that the seeker meets them, a rich man, a warrior, a craftsman, a physician, a pious man who teaches ethics, a grammarian, a poet, a religious (and nonphilosophical) Jew, a Jew versed in both religion and philosophy, a mathematician, a geometrician, an optician, an astronomer, a musician, a logician, a physicist, and finally, a philosopher. The seeker spends a set amount of time with each of these individuals, learning and describing for the reader's benefit their crafts and contribution to scientific knowledge. The main exceptions are the rich man and the warrior, both of whom the seeker considers to be vain and arrogant, but who are undoubtedly mentioned here because people generally perceive money and honor to constitute happiness.

The structure of the seeker's encounter with each of these individuals follows a similar pattern. The seeker first challenges the person, who then defends his art or craft, followed by a series of questions by which the seeker tries to understand, and ultimately to point out the weaknesses of, each person's livelihood. Upon departing from each person, the seeker requests additional information, signaled by the phrase "advise me," essentially asking for a summary of the person's art or craft. To illustrate, let us examine the seeker's encounter and subsequent dialogue with the physician. After he follows the physician on his daily routine of house calls, observing him make various diagnoses and cures, the following exchange occurs between them:

THE SEEKER: My soul yearns for your wisdom and "I present my supplication" [Dan 9:20] before you that you may tell me the main principles [*rashei peraqim*] of medicine, its scope [*geder*] and some of the subdivisions [*miqṣat min ha-ḥalaqim*].

THE PHYSICIAN: The scope of this profession is the knowledge of human conditions that make for either health or sickness. It teaches one how to maintain health or, in the case of illness, how to cure the malady.

THE SEEKER: If this is so, is it always edification in preserving health, removing sicknesses and preparing remedies?

THE PHYSICIAN: The physician does, indeed, investigate ways to preserve the patient's health and to cure his sickness, performing all his actions in accordance with the requirements and teachings of his profession, then he hopes that his work will bear fruit.

. . .

THE SEEKER: Does the physician have absolute knowledge in his profession or is his diagnosis conjectural? Can he clearly demonstrate his accuracy, or does this lie beyond him?

THE PHYSICIAN: Know that most medical teachings are based upon logical assessment of the patient's condition, and knowledge in the profession consists of estimate and conjecture. Inasmuch as this profession is conjectural, it is impossible for the physician to be free of error, and he can err, even if he is at the rank of Hippocrates.[45]

The final dialogic exchange in the book is the one with the philosopher. Despite the importance of philosophy in the work—indeed metaphysical truths represent the apex of the seeker's quest—the seeker's conversation with the philosopher is the shortest of any recounted. Yet there may be good reason for this because, as the philosopher says, he cannot reveal the truths of metaphysics to just anyone, only to those who have the requisite intellectual background. Unlike the exchanges with the other figures in the book, the seeker does not attempt to expose the contradictions inherent to the philosopher's craft. Indeed, one of the reasons why the dialogue between them is so brief is because the seeker asks none of the questions that, as in the case of previous encounters, were meant to stump his previous interlocutors by exposing the potential weaknesses of their various crafts and professions. This implies that the arguments of the philosopher, at least when compared to the other crafts and sciences, are ultimately unassailable. One of the few exchanges that does take place between the seeker and the philosopher is the following:

THE SEEKER (IN HIS HEART): This is similar to what Moses, upon whom be peace, says, "The Rock!—His deeds are perfect."

THE SEEKER (TO THE PHILOSOPHER): I request that you answer some of my questions that I have about this science.

THE PHILOSOPHER: I am unable to do so! Philosophers command that we not reveal the secrets of this science. But you can read the books that they composed on this subject, especially the *Metaphysics*, which will explain to you all that you do not know and you will come to understand the truth.[46]

This exchange is interesting for a number of reasons. First, we witness the seeker say one thing in his heart (*bi-libo*) and something different to his interlocutor. Second, what he says "in his heart" is that the philosopher's words correspond to what he already knows from the Torah. As with the *Iggeret ha-vikkuaḥ*, Falaquera again shows the basic and fundamental compatibility between philosophy and religion. Third, and finally, unlike the other dialogic exchanges in which the interlocutor agrees to answer the seeker's question, here the philosopher refuses outright. If the seeker wants to learn the various dimensions of metaphysics, the philosopher informs him, he will have to study them in the work of Aristotle by the same name and as elaborated by the commentaries written about this work. There are, the philosopher intimates, no shortcuts to understanding this science.

Polleqar's *Ezer ha-dat*

Of all the medieval Jewish philosophical dialogues, perhaps none exploits the genre as effectively as *Ezer ha-dat* (Support of the faith) by Isaac Polleqar (fl. mid-fourteenth century in northern Spain).[47] Also written in a rhyming prose, the structure of the work provides a series of dialogues, often with one central dialogue introducing others that further elaborate on the original theme. Moreover, interspersed throughout the work are poetic commentaries and other colorful digressions that maintain the interest of the reader. As with Falaquera's work, we again witness the genre of the dialogue disseminating a rationalist agenda in a popular and easily accessible form for those not necessarily trained in the technical study of philosophy.

We know very little about Polleqar, other than that he was engaged in a number of literary and likely face-to-face exchanges with his former teacher Abner of Burgos (1270–1347). Abner converted to Christianity sometime in the early 1320s and adopted the name Alfonso de Valladolid. Abner looms large in *Ezer ha-dat*, with every chapter of the work responding in some way to his attacks on his former coreligionists. Abner appealed to kabbalah, astrology, determinism, rabbinic aggadot, and criticism of philosophy both to justify his conversion to Christianity and to point out the intransigence of those Jews who did not follow him to his new religion. It is important to note that Abner was a serious thinker who struggled intellectually with the ideas that Jews of his generation inherited from the Maimonidean tradition, ideas that he ultimately found inadequate and which he seems to have associated with Isaac Polleqar. The debate between the two individuals, of which we get a glimpse in *Ezer ha-dat*, is not simply that between Jew and apostate, but also between the Arabo-Islamic philosophical tradition associated with Maimonides and the new scholastic paradigm. Abner and Polleqar were speaking, then, completely different languages on a number of levels.

Although Abner is the main antagonist of the work, he is for all intents and purposes a silent one. In many ways he had to be. For Polleqar to aim a direct critique at a Jewish convert to Christianity, especially a high-profile one who occupied an official position in the church, would have been politically inexpedient. Most Jewish anti-Christian polemics were meant for internal consumption, and if a devastating Jewish critique of Christianity were to fall in the wrong hands, the consequences could be severe. This is especially the case with someone like Abner, who claimed in some of his later writings that Jews should be forcefully encouraged to embrace Christianity. Even though Polleqar does not criticize Abner directly, the primary polemical thrust of his work is to undermine the various ideological principles that Abner used in his justification to apostatize. Polleqar's criticisms, then, are not just leveled against Abner, but against all those who use similar arguments. Implicit in his discussion is that idea that all those who subscribe to kabbalistic, astrological, or uninformed rabbinic principles could end up like Abner of Burgos.

In the second book of *Ezer ha-dat*, Polleqar opens with a description of a visit to Jerusalem recounted by a narrator (*maggid*). One day, walking around its cobblestone streets, he comes across a crowd of men and witnesses a strange sight: "Two men were quarrelling and jesting back and forth, each one trying to outdo the other. One was a venerable old man, his hair a distinguished gray . . . his appearance was glorious and proper, his stature was tall and he was wrapped in a prayer shawl . . . the second was a handsome youth, beautiful to the sight, and all looked admiringly at him. His countenance shined like pearls, his complexion like roses, and his lips were a beautiful red."[48] The personifications of faith and reason are described in terms that are the exact opposite of one another. Whereas the critic of philosophy is elderly, distinguished, and wrapped in a prayer shawl, the philosopher is young, arrogantly relying on his good looks, and unadorned with religious paraphernalia. After expatiating on the greatness of God, the Torah, tradition, and the chosenness of the Jewish people, the old man turns to his junior and accuses him of being influenced by the philosophers:

> **The old man:** The philosophers are grave sinners, who mock our wisdom, speaking a foreign language, that of the Moabites and the Hagarites. Their opinions are strange, their books are irreligious, and their compositions are all derived from foreign sources, namely, Greek wisdom, which is that of the *epikorsim* . . . they attempt to uproot and refute the foundations of true belief [*emunah*].[49]

The young man, however, gives just as good as he receives, in turn accusing the old man of speaking without wisdom (*ḥokhmah*) and intimating that the old man is a fraud, full of malicious intent:

> **The young man:** The [halakhic] dispute between Abbayeh and Raba is but a trifle when compared to the greatness of *ma'aseh merkabah* [i.e., metaphysics]. Perhaps one of the great sages of Israel may have said, "*hokhmah* destroys Torah." Yet others certainly encouraged the study of the theoretical sciences . . . for [science] allows us to judge and understand matters that we do not automatically know . . . without these sciences how are we to differentiate between matters of truth and falsity?[50]

The subsequent debate between the two gets to the heart of the struggle between rationalism and traditionalism in fourteenth-century northern Spain and Provence, a region wherein the vitriol stemming from the Maimonidean Controversies was still in full force. Typical of the intractable debate is the following exchange:

THE OLD MAN: . . . Aristotle, the Greek unbeliever with whom the young man is in a covenant denies the religion of God . . . It is prophecy that allows one to apprehend the hidden matters that the intellect cannot grasp. Torah is all that one needs. It provides an account of the chariot, the secrets of the heavens, the difference between the "upper water" and the "lower water" [i.e., in Gen 1:7], the secret of the *urim* and *thumim* . . . of Metatron, of Gabriel, and the other angels, of the *Sefer Yetsirah*, of *gematria*, of *keter* [the first of the sefirot], and *atarah* [tenth of the sefirot] . . . Now why don't you tell me about your sciences. Where are your miracles and wondrous deeds? What is the profit for us in your sciences? It is no exaggeration to say that there is none except in the customary and habitual occurrences in the world of nature, which we perceive with our eyes and ears every day!

THE YOUNG MAN: The philosophers grasp hidden things, but do so honestly and completely, because the intellect is like a spring and a fountain, in which the unknown becomes evident from what is known. The philosopher is able to do this because he is able to understand the middle term, and bring it to light. He is able to connect the great to the small, and join them so that the answer to every question is derived syllogistically. The philosopher is, thus, able to negotiate around every obstacle. The prophet, however, is able to grasp the essence [*'inyan*] of things, but he does not know how this occurs. If you were to ask him anything about it, he would be unable to respond because he does not know its path. Prophecy dos not occur except in the imaginative faculty. Do not imagine that it occurs in the rational faculty. Because of this a wise man once said, "A *ḥakham* [philosopher] is better than a prophet." This is because a prophet cannot teach another the quiddity of his prophecy.[51]

Here the issue between the disputants revolves around the nature of true knowledge. As the dialogue continues a new character is introduced, a king, to whom the two interlocutors go in order to seek arbitration. After listening to both sides, the king responds by saying that "wisdom cannot exist outside of the Torah, for in it everything is brought to light. A religious person without philosophy in his soul is lost . . . the Torah is a preparation to draw the potential intellect to its actuality, in order to cleave to [the Active Intellect] and unite with it. Whosoever ascends to this level reaches eternity and this is the world to come."[52]

The introduction of the king means that we should not immediately associate the character of the young man with Polleqar. For the latter, as opposed to the former, philosophical and religious truths mutually reinforce one another. Things do not end here, however. Once the narrator returns home, he is confronted by an unnamed antagonist who adopts the position of the old man, although in a manner that invokes the informed criticisms of philosophy offered by the likes of Halevi or the Muslim Al-Ghazali, and a new dialogue subsequently ensues.

Conclusions

Dialogues, as we have seen, serve several important functions in medieval Jewish philosophy. Perhaps most important is the fact that because they are not written as technical treatises, they provide a way to introduce readers, who might not otherwise have exposure to such ideas, to philosophy and rationalism. The dialogue, in other words, provides a convenient vehicle to popularize and thus to disseminate philosophy to a wider reading audience. In addition, and certainly relatedly, the dialogue is a convenient genre in which an author can present multiple positions, but in such a manner that those antagonistic to his own neither compete with nor confuse the reader. Finally, in the proper hands (e.g., Halevi, Falaquera, Polleqar), the genre can be a literary masterpiece that can have appeal far and beyond philosophical circles.

In so doing, the dialogue reveals to us some of the ways in which philosophical ideas, as articulated by the great thinkers such as Maimonides and Gersonides, were received by subsequent generations. In these dialogues we also witness the struggle between philosophy and tradition and the impact that this struggle had on various local communities. We thus begin to see the human face and costs of the philosophical enterprise in Judaism. Nontraditional genres such as dialogues, in the final analysis, help us to understand the various ways in which philosophical ideas were subsequently articulated and popularized to reach and influence a larger reading public.

Notes

1. For a fuller treatment of this topic, see my *The Art of Dialogue in Medieval Jewish Philosophy* (Bloomington: Indiana University Press, 2008), on which this chapter builds.
2. See the important study found in Robert Eisen, *The Book of Job in Medieval Jewish Philosophy* (Oxford: Oxford University Press, 2004).
3. See the comments in Jeffrey L. Rubenstein, *Talmudic Stories: Narrative Art, Composition, and Culture* (Baltimore, MD: Johns Hopkins University Press, 2003), 3.
4. Galit Hasan-Rokem, *The Web of Life: Folklore in Rabbinic Literature* (Tel Aviv: Am Oved, 1996), 78–100 [Hebrew]; Jeffrey L. Rubenstein, *The Culture of the Babylonian Talmud* (Baltimore, MD: Johns Hopkins University Press, 1999); Daniel Boyarin, *Socrates and the Fat Rabbis* (Chicago: University of Chicago Press, 2012), 1–32.

5. E.g., BT Sanhedrin 91a–91b; Avodah Zarah 10a.

6. See the landmark study in Franz Rosenthal, "On the Knowledge of Plato's Philosophy in the Islamic World," *Islamic Culture* 14 (1940): 387–422.

7. Gotthelf Bergsträsser, *Neue Materielien zu Hunain ibn Ishāq's Galen-Bibliographie* (Nendeln, Liechtenstein: Kraus Reprints, 1966 [1932]), 1–24; Dimitri Gutas, "Aspects of Literary Forms and Genre in Arabic Logical Works," in *Glosses and Commentaries on Aristotelian Logical Texts: The Syriac, Arabic, and Medieval Latin Tradition*, ed. Charles Burnett (London: Warburg Institute, 1993), 29–76.

8. Joshua Parens, however, believes that Al-Farabi would have had access to the entire text of the *Laws*, one that "was similar, if not identical, to our own." See his *Metaphysics as Rhetoric: Alfarabi's Summary of Plato's "Laws"* (Albany: State University of New York Press, 1995), xxviii–xxxi.

9. Moritz Steinschneider, *Die arabischen Übersetzung aus dem Griechischen* (Nendeln, Liechtenstein: Kraus Reprints, 1968 [1902]), 54–64.

10. On the pliable use of Socrates in medieval Islam, for example, see Ilai Alon, *Socrates in Medieval Arabic Literature* (Leiden and Jerusalem: Brill and Magnes Press, 1991).

11. See Aaron W. Hughes, *The Art of Dialogue in Jewish Philosophy*, 107–37.

12. Abū Ḥayyān al-Tawḥīdī, *Al-imtāʿ wa-al-mu'ānasa*, vol. 1, ed. Ahmad Amīn and Aḥmad al-Zayn (Cairo: al-Ta'lif, 1939–1944), 108–28. An English translation may be found in D. S. Margoliouth, "The Merits of Logic and Grammar," *Journal of the Royal Asiatic Society* (1905): 111–29. See also, Muhsin Mahdi, "Language and Logic in Classical Islam," in *Logic in Classical Islamic Culture*, ed. G. E. von Grunebaum (Wiesbaden: O. Harassowitz, 1070), 102–13.

13. For the general context, see Alfred L. Ivry, "Neoplatonic Currents in Maimonides," in *Perspectives on Maimonides: Philosophical and Historical Studies*, ed. Joel L. Kraemer (Oxford: Littman Library, 1991), 115–40. For the larger historical and political context, see Josef van Ess, *Chiliastische Erwartungen und die Versuchung der Göttlichkeit der Kalif al-Ḥakīm (386–411 A.H.)* (Heidelberg: Carl Winter Universitätsverlag, 1977).

14. For an attempt to do this, see John T. Walbridge, *The Leaven of the Ancients: Suhrawardī and the Heritage of the Greeks* (Albany: State University of New York Press, 2000).

15. An English translation may be found in *The Case of the Animals versus Man before the King of the Jinn: A Tenth-Century Ecological Fable*, trans. Lenn E. Goodman (Boston, MA: Twayne, 1978). On the relationship between the *Ikhwān* and the Ismaʿilis, see Seyyed Hossein Nasr, *An Introduction to Islamic Cosmological Doctrines*, rev. ed. (Albany: State University of New York Press, 1993), 35–37; Majid Fakhry, *A History of Islamic Philosophy*, 2nd ed. (New York: Columbia University Press, 1983), 164. For a dissenting opinion, see Ian Richard Netton, *Muslim Neoplatonists: An Introduction to the Thought of the Brethren of Purity* (Edinburgh: Edinburgh University Press, 1991), 94–104.

16. The dialogue is still awaiting a definitive translation. In the meantime, see *The Kuzari: An Argument for the Faith of Israel*, trans. Hartwig Hirschfeld (New York: Schocken, 1964). A much better and more accurate translation is found in the French *Le Kuzari: Apologie de la religion méprisée*, trans. Charles Touati (Paris: Verdier, 1994).

17. See the comments in Shlomo Dov Goitein, "The Biography of Rabbi Judah Halevi in Light of the Cairo Genizah," *Proceedings of the American Academy for Jewish Research* 28 (1959): 41–56, at 55–56; also, the translator's introduction in Touati, *Le Kuzari*, viii–ix.

18. This is the opinion of Julius Guttmann, "The Relationship between Religion and Philosophy According to Judah Halevi," in his *Religion and Knowledge: Essays and Lectures*, ed. S. H. Bergman and N. Rostenstreich (Jerusalem: Magnes Press, 1955), 66.

19. It was in Isma'ili circles, for example, that the longer recension of the mystico-philosophical *Theology of Aristotle* seems to have originated. See the comments in Shlomo Pines, "La Longue recension de la Theologie d'Aristote," *Revue des études islamiques* 22 (1954): 7–20. Paul Fenton goes so far as to argue that the work might actually have been the product of Jewish Neoplatonists influenced by Isma'ilism. See his "The Arabic and Hebrew Versions of the *Theology of Aristotle*," in *Pseudo-Aristotle in the Middle Ages: The "Theology" and Other Texts*, ed. Jill Kraye, W. F. Ryan, and C. B. Schmitt (London: Warburg Institute, 1986), 241–64.

20. Shlomo Pines, "Shi'ite Terms and Conceptions in Halevi's *Kuzari*," *Jerusalem Studies in Arabic and Islam* 2 (1980): 165–251. See, more recently, the comments in Diana Lobel, *Between Mysticism and Philosophy: Sufi Language of Religious Experience in Judah Halevi's Kuzari* (Albany: State University of New York Press, 2000), 22–28.

21. For an English translation of such a text, see the tenth-century Abū Ya'qūb al-Sijistānī, *The Wellsprings of Wisdom*, trans. Paul E. Walker (Salt Lake City: University of Utah Press, 1994).

22. *Kuzari* 3:10–11 (Hirschfeld, 142–43).

23. *Kuzari* 3:22–23 (Hirschfeld, 161–62).

24. On Ibn Gabirol's life in general, see Jacques Schlanger, *La Philosophie de Salomon Ibn Gabirol: Étude d'un néoplatonisme* (Leiden: Brill, 1968); see also Sarah Pessin, "Solomon Ibn Gabirol [Avicebron]," *Stanford Encyclopedia of Philosophy*, online at http://plato.stanford.edu/entries/ibn-gabirol/.

25. Shlomo ibn Gabirol, *Sefer Meqor Ḥayyim*, trans. into Hebrew by Jacob Blubstein (Jerusalem: Mossad Harav Kook, 1926), 3.

26. Ibn Gabirol, *Meqor Ḥayyim*, 6.

27. Ibn Da'ud, *The Exalted Faith*, 40.

28. E.g., Tamar Alexander, "Hagiography and Biography: Abraham ibn Ezra as a Character of Hebrew Folktale," in *Abraham ibn Ezra y Su Tiempo*, ed. F. Diaz Esteban (Madrid: Asociación Española de Orientalistas, 1990), 11–16. On their philosophical differences, see the discussion in Zev Harvey, "The First Commandment and the God of Israel: Ibn Ezra and Maimonides versus Halevi and Crescas," *Tarbiz* 57.2 (1988): 2013–16 [Hebrew].

29. See, for example, Y. Tzvi Langermann, "Some Astrological Themes in the Thought of Abraham ibn Ezra," in *Rabbi Abraham ibn Ezra: Studies in the Writings of a Twelfth-Century Jewish Polymath*, ed. Jay Harris and Isadore Twersky (Cambridge. MA: Harvard University Press, 1993), 28–85.

30. Ibn Ezra, *Ḥay ben Meqitz*, 195.

31. See Diana Lobel, *A Sufi-Jewish Dialogue: Philosophy and Mysticism in Bahya ibn Paqūda's "Duties of the Heart"* (Philadelphia: University of Pennsylvania Press, 2007), 21–34.

32. Baḥya ibn Paquda, *The Book of Direction to the Duties of the Heart*, trans. Menahem Mansoor (London: Littman Library of Jewish Civilization, 1973), 181.

33. Baḥya, *The Book of Direction to the Duties of the Heart*, 213–15.

34. The classic study remains Daniel J. Silver, *Maimonidean Criticism and the Maimonidean Controversy, 1180–1240* (Leiden: Brill, 1965). A convenient selection of primary sources maybe found in *After Maimonides: An Anthology of Writings by His Critics, Defenders, and*

Commentators, ed. A. S. Halkin (Jerusalem: Zalman Shazar Center, 1979) [Hebrew]. More recently, see Hava Tirosh-Samuelson, *Happiness in Premodern Judaism: Virtue, Knowledge, Well-Being* (Cincinnati, OH: Hebrew Union College Press, 2003).

35. The full title is *Iggeret ha-Vikuaḥ be-ve'ur ha-haskamah asher ben ha-Torah ve ha-ḥokhmah* (The epistle of the debate, or an explanation of the agreement between the Torah and philosophy). An English translation may be found in *Falaquera's Epistle of the Debate: An Introduction to Jewish Philosophy*, ed. and trans. Steven Harvey (Cambridge, MA: Harvard University Press, 1987).

36. Harvey, *Falaquera's Epistle of the Debate*, 14–15.

37. Harvey, *Falaquera's Epistle of the Debate*, 62.

38. Harvey, *Falaquera's Epistle of the Debate*, 65–66.

39. Harvey, *Falaquera's Epistle of the Debate*, 49–50.

40. An English translation may be found in *The Book of the Seeker by Shem Tov ben Joseph ibn Falaquera*, ed. and trans. M. Herschel Levine (New York: Yeshiva University Press, 1976).

41. For example, Raphael Jospe, *Torah and Sophia: The Life and Thought of Shem Tov ibn Falaquera* (Cincinnati, OH: Hebrew Union College Press, 1988), 46–48; Colette Sirat, *A History of Jewish Philosophy in the Middle Ages* (Cambridge and Paris: Cambridge University Press and Editions de la Maison des Sciences de l'Homme, 1985), 234.

42. Steven Harvey, introduction to *The Medieval Hebrew Encyclopedia of Science and Philosophy*, ed. S. Harvey (Dordrecht: Kluwer, 2000), 9.

43. There is, however, an important difference between Jewish and Christian encyclopedias. The Christian encyclopedia, for example, was primarily intended to give preachers moral instruction; Jewish encyclopedias, as we have just seen, were primarily geared for a socially mobile lay audience. See the comments in Johannes B. Voorbij, "Purpose and Audience: Perspective on the Thirteenth-Century Encyclopedias of Alexander Neckam, Bartholomaeus Angelicus, Thomas of Cantimpré and Vincent of Beauvis," in *The Medieval Hebrew Encyclopedia of Science and Philosophy*, 31–45.

44. This is a fairly typical trope in Islamicate literature, known in Arabic as *ṭalab al-ʿilm*, literally "the search for knowledge."

45. Levine, *Book of the Seeker*, 43–45.

46. Levine, *Book of the Seeker*, 146–47.

47. Isaac Polleqar, *Ezer ha-Dat*, ed. Jacob Levinger (Tel Aviv: Tel Aviv University Press, 1984).

48. Polleqar, *Ezer ha-Dat*, 69.

49. Polleqar, *Ezer ha-Dat*, 70.

50. Polleqar, *Ezer ha-Dat*, 71–72.

51. Polleqar, *Ezer ha-Dat*, 88–89.

52. Polleqar, *Ezer ha-Dat*, 93.

AARON W. HUGHES is the Philip S. Bernstein Professor of Jewish Studies at the University of Rochester. He is the author of many books, including *Rethinking Jewish Philosophy: Beyond Particularism and Universalism*.

8

POETRY

Aaron W. Hughes

THIS CHAPTER EXAMINES THE USE OF POETRY AND poetic expression as a form of philosophical discourse. The genre of poetry, as can be expected, provided philosophers with a way of both popularizing and disseminating their insights to a larger reading audience. However, it is important not to assume that this was the only reason that philosophers wrote in poetic form. Poetry also permitted philosophers—especially so-called Neoplatonic philosophers—to explore, develop, and articulate a set of ontological and epistemological insights that they could not do in more discursive treatises.[1] The result is that poetry functioned as an important philosophical form, and an examination of philosophical poetry helps us begin to dismantle what are now perceived to be natural divisions of medieval Jewish thought (for example, "philosophy," "mysticism," and "literature"). These divisions, largely the product of a nineteenth-century taxonomy, have mostly succeeded in making distinct that which was, for the thinkers under discussion here, a coherent intellectual worldview.[2]

Poetry, however, has long vexed philosophy. The product of the imaginative faculty, it is a literary form that many philosophers tend to categorize as grounded in rhetorical artifice and literary composition rather than reason. A successful poem, for example, is judged on its outer form and not necessarily its content.[3] As a result, many philosophers mistrusted poets on account of the latter's ability to evoke and appeal to the senses at the expense of the intellect. In a philosophical worldview that tended to posit sharp distinctions between body (i.e., matter) and soul (i.e., form), the latter was to be elevated at the expense of the former. Any literary genre perceived to appeal to the senses and the material world in which the soul was temporarily entrapped was believed to take away from the enterprise of philosophy, whose goal was to liberate the soul from the body. This led to the literary, if not historical, antagonism between the philosophers and the poets, perhaps best articulated in book 10 of Plato's *Republic*.[4]

The power of poetry, if left unchecked, threatened philosophy's mission, which was to prepare the soul/intellect for its celestial return following corporeal death. Despite this, or indeed because of this, some thinkers realized that the power of poetry could be harnessed for philosophical purposes. Despite Plato's condemnation of the poets, for example, he himself was certainly a master of literary creativity. The use of metaphor, of allegory, and of metonymy, then, could serve philosophical ends if properly understood and deployed. For this reason, despite the protestations of many, poetry could be used in the service of philosophy. It was just too powerful a form to be ignored.[5]

At the center of this debate is the role and function of the imaginative faculty. Is this faculty, framed as a question, opposed to reason, or can it be employed in its ultimate perfection? These questions became particularly relevant in the rich poetic and philosophical culture of Al-Andalus in the eleventh and twelfth centuries. For the individuals who gave this culture some of its richest expressions, poetry served an important *philosophical* purpose. Since the majority of the great Hebrew poets in Al-Andalus also happened to be important philosophers, we should be cautious of neatly bifurcating their corpora into "philosophy" or "literature." Such a bifurcation needlessly creates artificial rubrics and, in so doing, obfuscates the mutual reinforcement of genres or literary forms. In this way, poetry provides us with an important window into the ways in which medieval thinkers conceptualized both the philosophic and poetic (or, perhaps better, the "philosophico-poetic") enterprise.

Poetry is connected to the larger theme of aesthetics within medieval thought. Within this context, aesthetics refers to a theory of beauty that is primarily interested in delineating the pleasure that arises in the soul of an individual upon viewing an object or upon hearing a poem or harmony.[6] This pleasure, according to medieval Islamic and Jewish philosophers, occurs because physical beauty (often defined in terms of order and harmony) is regarded as participating in a higher order. Such a conception certainly had its origin in Plato's theory of beauty, which made its way into medieval thought through the conduit of Plotinus and other commentators of the late antique period.[7] Yet, as is typical with medieval thought, added to such discourses was a set of issues relevant to monotheistic concerns. What connected the medieval Islamic and Jewish thinkers to their predecessors was the notion that physical beauty (be it oral, aural, or visual) pointed beyond itself.[8] Aesthetics thus takes on an important role in directing the soul of the individual to its true home in the celestial world.

Muthos and *Logos*: Toward a Theory of Poetry in Medieval Philosophy

Although Plato was highly critical of poets and other artists whom, he claims, distort and manipulate for the sake of rhetorical effect, he was a formidable artist who made frequent appeals to mythopoesis. He offers his reason for this in the *Gorgias*: "Listen, then, as they say to a very fine account [*logou*] that you, I suppose, will consider a story [*mythos*], but which I treat as the actual truth [*logon*]. For what I am going to tell you I offer to you as truth."[9] Here Plato hints that what seems like a "myth" to the average person can function as *logos*, the truth, to the person with proper understanding. As a result, the poetic and mythic presentation of the *logos* becomes extremely important to Platonic, and subsequent Neoplatonic, articulations. Mythopoesis, like poetry, bridges the gap between the material and the immaterial in such a way that the ability to access and understand the latter is through the former.

In his definition of artistic beauty, Aristotle focuses more specifically on the various attributes that are responsible for contributing to the quiddity of a beautiful object. In book 8 of the *Metaphysics*, for example, he claims: "The chief forms of beauty are order and symmetry and definiteness, which the mathematical sciences demonstrate in a special degree. And since these are obviously causes of many things, evidently these sciences must treat this sort of cause also in some sense of a cause."[10] Aristotle subsequently argues that beauty is that which gives significance to the form of a natural object.[11] This teleological approach to art and poetry enables Aristotle to connect artistic sentiment to the universal first principles of philosophy. Consequently, Aristotle acknowledges an important interplay between the senses, the emotions, the imagination, and the intellect. This interplay, as he claims in the *Poetics*, proves indispensable to our ability to interact with the world and to form knowledge about it.[12]

Plotinus, the individual who had the biggest impact on medieval philosophical ideas of poetry, argues that sensible beauty awakens the human soul and enables it to recognize its relationship to the immaterial world, which is also its true home. Material beauty, then, functions as a symbol for metaphysical reality. According to Sara Rappe, these symbols function "as crossroads, as junctures that allow the soul to trace its path back to its origins."[13] There exists, in other words, an intimate relationship between the human soul and the divine world. Moreover, this relationship revolves around the symbol and the image. Provided that one does not mistake the image or the symbol for ultimate reality, Plotinus argues that such images double back on themselves. Images and symbols, then, are negative in the sense that they are not the One, yet also positive because they enable the individual to reascend to the One. In this sentiment, we see clearly the paradox of poetry and how it could and would be deployed for philosophical ends.

Subsequent Neoplatonists envisaged a set of analogous correspondences between levels of being and modes of reading. Proclus (ca. 410–484), for example, argues that the surface level of texts (he had in mind the *Iliad* and the *Odyssey*) simultaneously reveals and conceals truths in such a manner that the reader must actively participate in the creation of meaning.[14] The poetic work possesses a similar polysemous structure to the world it mirrors. Just as the universe is composed of material and immaterial parts with the former pointing to and thus participating in the latter, so does poetry—when properly conceived and understood—function in a similar way.

Philosophical understanding of poetry, as should be apparent from this brief survey of ancient and late antique precedents, is predicated on an intimate ontological correspondence between the physicality of this world and the intelligibility of the celestial world. The individual, with his body composed of matter that is defined by corporeal generation and corruption and his soul that has descended from on high, epitomizes this duality on the level of the microcosm. Precisely because of this duality, the only way that one can understand the heavenly world is through the material one. This is why poetry is so important. It points the way. It uses the materiality of language to move beyond language.

Building on these discussions, medieval philosophers all agree that beauty is one of the main attributes of God. When one contemplates a beautiful object, one is drawn to its principles and ideally the subsequent realization that physical objects of beauty derive their essence from a nonmaterial source. Based on medieval epistemology that equates the knower with the known,[15] the individual takes on qualities of nonmaterial beauty that reside in the material object. Because beautiful objects participate in the beauty of the immaterial world, the individual necessarily participates in that world. The result is that one who observes and contemplates beautiful objects and subsequently recognizes beautiful objects for what they are apprehends something of the divine world and, by extension, God.

Poetry and Aesthetics in Medieval Islamic Philosophy

These ideas were subsequently picked up and tuned in a monotheistic key in the Islamic world. Primary for many subsequent discussions are the writings (*rasā'il*) of the Brethren of Purity (*Ikhwān al-Ṣafā'*),[16] a group of individuals from Basra in the late tenth to eleventh century who would have tremendous influence on Jewish Neoplatonic thinkers.[17] They argue that there exists an intimate correspondence between the musical harmony associated with the heavenly spheres and that produced by musical instruments. In a section from their *rasā'il*, entitled "Ḥarakat al-aflāk naghamāt ka-naghamāt al-ʿidān" (The rhythm of the movements of the spheres resembles the rhythms of lutes), they write that "The movement of the spheres and heavenly bodies produces rhythms [*naghamāt*] and melodies [*alḥān*] that are sweet and rejoice the souls of their inhabitants. These rhythms and melodies remind non-composite souls [*al-nufūs al-bāsiṭa*] inhabiting the world of spirits [*ʿālam al-arwāḥ*] that is above the spheres and whose substances are more noble than those of the world of the spheres. This is the world of the souls [*ʿālam al-nufūs*] and the dwelling place whose delight is entirely repose and perfume in the various degrees of paradise as God most high has promised in the Qur'ān."[18]

Although the Brethren will argue that this harmony is based on mathematical principles, they contend that harmony, rhyme, rhythm, and cadence have the composite effect of touching the entire soul of the individual. Listening to music and poetry, then, becomes an important part, and not just a prolegomenon, of intellectual activity and becomes the vehicle that moves the entire individual, not just the intellect, from potentiality to actuality. In a subsequent section, entitled "Aphorisms of the Philosophers on Music" (*nawādir al-falāsifa fī al-mūsīqā*), we read: "When the traces of the beauty [*al-ḥisān*] of sensory things are imprinted on the individual soul [*al-nafs al-juz'iyya*], it conforms to the universal Soul [*al-nafs al-kulliyya*], attunes itself to it, aspires to it, and seeks to join it. Now, when the soul will have left its corporeal residence, it will mount toward the kingdom of heaven and rejoin the intelligible substance."[19] This theme is picked up by Al-Farabi (872–950), who, in his *Views of the Citizens of the Best State* (*Mabādī' ārā' ahl al-madīna al-fāḍila*), defines beauty (*al-jamāl*) as that which "is in its most excellent state of existence and that has attained its ultimate perfection."[20] For him, the beauty of the One surpasses all other types of beauty:

> Since the First is in the most excellent state of existence, its beauty [*al-jamāl*] surpasses the beauty of every other beautiful existent, and the same applies to its splendor [*al-zīna*] and its brilliance [*al-bahā'*]. Further, it has all of these in its substance [*al-jawhar*] and essence [*al-dhāt*] by itself and by thinking its essence. But we have beauty, splendor, and brilliance as a result of accidental qualities, of what our bodies have in them, and because of exterior things, but they are not in our substance. The beautiful [*al-jamīl*] and the beauty [*al-jamāl*] in the First are nothing but one essence, and the same applies to the other things predicated of it.[21]

All types of beauty, with the exception of that of the One, are derivative in the sense that they participate in its beauty. When humans perceive physical or material beauty with their senses, they do so in such a manner that they only perceive a perspective or appearance that is contingent on the arrangement of a particular object or harmony. When we hear a poem, for example, the pleasure we take in it is reminiscent of the pleasure that the One takes in itself. Only the pleasure and self-enjoyment that the One takes from self-contemplation is beyond the ken of our understanding. Nevertheless, the pleasure and enjoyment that we take in the contemplation of beautiful objects and melodies, despite its fleeting and impermanent duration, approximates the self-knowledge of the One insofar as material creatures can approximate the One's immateriality.

Avicenna (980–1037) likewise emphasizes the structure behind beauty and argues that the individual's rational and animal souls are attracted to sensible beauty.[22] However, unlike Al-Farabi, Avicenna contends that physical or sensible beauty appeals to the individual's imaginative faculty, enabling it to align with the rational soul so that the former will resemble the latter.[23] Since the soul is trapped within a body, access to intellectual beauty occurs only through the sensual beauty of concrete particulars: "But whenever [an individual] loves a pleasing form with an intellectual consideration . . . then this is to be considered an approximation to nobility and an increase in goodness. For he covets something whereby he will come nearer to the influence of that which is the first source of influence and the pure object of love, and more similar to the exalted and noble beings . . . For this reason one will never find the wise . . . to be free from having their hearts occupied with a beautiful human form."[24]

Here Avicenna argues that physical beauty is necessary if one is to grasp intellectual beauty. The faculty that bridges both these types of beauty in addition to the animal and the rational souls is the faculty of the imagination.[25] So long as one realizes that the sensible object is not beautiful in and of itself but is based on heavenly beauty in which it participates, one can and should take pleasure in such objects.

It should hopefully be clear by now that medieval Jewish and Islamic philosophers had a distinct theory of aesthetics and that we must situate their poetry within this context. Poetry, according to this reading, is not simply an important philosophical genre or form; it is also intimately connected to the way poets thought about and articulated a distinct system of psychology, ontology, and metaphysics. Although more "strict" Aristotelians (such as Abraham ibn Daud or Maimonides) tended not to write poetry and were, for the most part, quite critical of it, poetry was an important vehicle for those thinkers associated with what is customarily, if not problematically, referred to as "Neoplatonism." In what follows it is important to keep these philosophical reflections on the form of poetry in mind as we try to understand the poem's content. For, ultimately, the form and the content of the philosophical poem cannot be separated from one another.

Andalusian Neoplatonism

Al-Andalus, as is generally well-known, produced a particularly rich, literate, and relatively tolerant society that put pride of place on, among other things, literary grace and poetic expression.[26] Informed intellectually by the Arabic tradition of belles lettres (*adab*) and the various philosophical currents associated with Neoplatonism, Al-Andalus produced one of the most productive and creative chapters in Jewish history. Moses ibn Ezra, in the fifth book of his *Kitāb al-Muḥāḍara wa-l-Mudhākara*, tries to make the case that this was on account of the fact that Andalusi Jews were the direct descendants from those who originated in Jerusalem, where the purest and most graceful Hebrew was spoken.[27] In terms of Hebrew literary production, Al-Andalus witnessed the introduction of Arabic meter into Hebrew poetry by, among others, Dunash ibn Labrat (920–990), a former student of Saadya Gaon and a beneficiary of the Cordovan courtier Ḥasdai ibn Shaprut. Dunash is generally credited with being the first to engage in Hebrew nonliturgical poetry. This period also witnessed the further development of Hebrew grammar by the likes of Judah ben David Hayyuj (ca. 945–ca. 1000).

It was in Al-Andalus, in other words, that Jews began to adapt further the various literary models derived from their contact with Arabic culture.[28] This provided elite Jews with new categories and forms to reframe Judaism. Both philosophy and poetry provided these thinkers with new methods and terms of reference to think about Jewish traditions, narratives, and values.[29] Indeed, many of the thinkers to be discussed in this section seem not to have distinguished between poetry and philosophy as two distinct and mutually exclusive activities. Perhaps it was the Arabic notion of *adab* that permitted them to hold these two activities together in ways that would become more problematic for later thinkers. The notion of what constituted a "proper" philosophical form, in other words, seems to have been largely foreign to these individuals.

The Andalusian poets largely restricted themselves to the semantic field of biblical poetry.[30] In doing this, these poets differed from the linguistic practices of classical piyyut, the tradition of Hebrew liturgical poetry that had developed in late antique Byzantine Palestine, the same environment that had produced many forms of rabbinic literature.[31] Despite the fact that earlier rationalists, most notably Saadya Gaon,[32] had composed piyyutim, its language and style did not find a great deal of favor among the practitioners and theorists of the new poetic forms and styles produced in Al-Andalus. In his commentary to Qoheleth 5:1, for example, the Andalusi Abraham ibn Ezra criticizes the piyyutim of R. Eleazar ha-Qallir as obscure, adulterated with the "language of the Talmud," full of grammatical errors, and too indebted to midrashic and aggadic material.[33] Whereas classical piyyutim was largely free of metrical constraints, Andalusian Hebrew poetry tended to adhere to one of two Arabic models: the monorhymed pattern of the qasida or the alternating rhymes associated with the strophic *muwashshaḥ*.

Despite Abraham ibn Ezra's criticism of the early form and style of the piyyut, he and his contemporaries still engaged in the composition of liturgical Hebrew. Only now they confined their language solely to that of the Bible and adapted religious themes to the more "secular" form of the *muwashshaḥ*. Unlike the earlier tradition of piyyut, the new Andalusi piyyutim were more poetic and, more importantly for the context of this chapter, informed by Neoplatonic themes and motifs.

Within this context, many medieval Jewish philosophers prior to Maimonides were what we might today label as poet-philosophers. Although they certainly wrote "normative" philosophical treatises (e.g., Shlomo ibn Gabirol's *Fons vitae*, Abraham ibn Ezra's *Sefer yesod mora ve-sod ha-Torah*, Judah Halevi, *Kitāb al-Khazarī*), all were equally comfortable giving poetic expression to the ideas expressed in such prose treatises. In both its popular and more technical presentations, Neoplatonism—as witnessed in the previous section—was predicated on a number of themes: the strict ontological separation of form and matter, the doctrine of celestial emanation, and the descent of the human soul from the universal soul into the world of matter, including its subsequent desire to return to its true, celestial home.[34] All of these topics, especially the latter, naturally lent themselves to poetic expression. Much of the poetry produced in Al-Andalus, especially that of the so-called poet-philosophers, dealt with these themes in one way or another.

Perhaps one of the best examples in this regard is the work of Ibn Gabirol (1021–ca. 1057), one of the first Jewish philosophers in Muslim Spain and also a poet of exceptional skill.[35] We discussed his major philosophical work, *Fons Vitae* (Hebrew: *Meqor Hayyim*, Arabic: *Yanbūʿal-hayāh*) in the previous chapter on dialogues; here it suffices to say that his poetry certainly mirrors and builds on many of the themes found in this non-poetic work.[36] While some later medieval Jewish thinkers—most notably, Shem Tov ibn Falaquera, Moses ibn Ezra, Abraham ibn Daud, and Judah Abrabanel—were familiar with *Meqor Hayyim/Yanbūʿ al-hayāh*, it seems that Ibn Gabirol was best known by subsequent generations for his Hebrew poetry, the most famous of which is *Keter malkhut* (variously translated as "kingdom's crown," "the kingly crown," or "the royal crown"). In this latter poem, we encounter poetic variations on numerous themes popular to contemporaneous philosophy. Of God's oneness, for example, he writes,

You are one: the first of every number
  the foundation of all structure.
You are one: the mystery of your oneness
  makes the wise of heart be struck dumb.
They do not know what it is or what You are.

You are one: Your oneness can neither be increased or lessened
  It can neither be reproached nor diminished
You are one: Not something that can be grasped or counted
  Number and change cannot reach You
You can neither be seen nor apprehended.

You are one: my reason cannot put upon you limit or boundary
  Thus I have said I will guard my ways lest my tongue sins
You are one: You are high and exalted
  Beyond abasement and falling
How should the one fall?[37]

In this canto we see Ibn Gabirol equate the oneness and majesty of God using Neoplatonic terminology used to account for the One. Poetry became one of the major vehicles whereby Andalusi thinkers could harmonize the biblical portrait of God with the One of philosophy. These poet-philosophers, as we shall see time and again in the examples that follow, used the poetic idiom—one that was largely confined to the ideals of biblical purism—to show that their potentially radical ideas emerged naturally out of the biblical narrative. If indeed Jewish philosophy is about showing how Judaism and non-Jewish philosophical ideas crosspollinate with one another, poetry becomes an ideal form to show this crosspollination at work. Philosophy, in the deft hands of these poet-philosophers, is not other than the Bible, and the Bible is not other than philosophy. Poetry becomes the way in which philosophy is perceived to emerge naturally from the biblical narrative.

There is probably no better example of this than Abraham ibn Ezra's *Ḥay ben Meqitz*, a work modeled on Avicenna's Arabic *Ḥayy ibn Yaqzān*.[38] The former work ingeniously rewrites or, perhaps better, rearranges the biblical narrative in such a manner that it simultaneously reveals and is made to conform to philosophical truth. Consider, for example, the following description of the boundary between our world (composed of form and matter) and the celestial spheres that the philosopher must cross in order to reach a fuller understanding of the cosmos:

After this boundary there is a consuming fire
  To the heavens it reaches.
Its coals burn
  Its sparks rage.
Its blades are like swords
  Its sparks like stars.
Rains do not extinguish it
  Rivers are unable to flood it.
Rocks are molted by its fire
  Boulders melt from its flame.
I envisioned it
  Staring into its likeness.

My hands were weak
  My knees trembled.
My eyes smoked over from fear
  I fell frightened onto my face.
I was unable to stand
  My whole being was stricken with terror.
He came to see me
  Set me upon my feet
He said, "Do not be afraid
  Do not lose heart
When you walk through fire
  You will not be burned
Though a flame
  It will not harm you."
He passed before me and said
  "Come in, O blessed of the Lord."
He took me swiftly from there
  Moving me into the flame.
I saw the fires touch him
  The sparks surrounding him burned.
The flashes encircled us
  Although surrounded, we were not consumed.[39]

This part of the poem begins with the language of Deuteronomy 4:24, which describes God as "a consuming fire, an impassioned God." From here, Ibn Ezra evokes the language of Song of Songs 8:7 (Rains do not extinguish it/ Rivers are unable to flood it), which, in its original context, describes the insatiable love of the lover for the beloved. From this initial imagery, Ibn Ezra moves to a description of the protagonist's encounter with the fire. In encountering the fire, the individual realizes how everything in this world gives way and succumbs to the majesty of God. Upon comprehending this, he falls down, prostrate with fear—here described using the language of a verse whose original context describes Daniel's encounter with Gabriel (Dan. 8:17). After this initial fear, Hay approaches the unnamed protagonist—unnamed because he is a philosophical everyman—and the language that he uses combines the vocabulary of the call narratives of both Ezekiel and Isaiah: "He set me upon my feet / He said, 'do not be afraid and do not lose heart.'" The first part of this phrase echoes the words uttered to Ezekiel (2:2) after his encounter with the divine chariot; the second part corresponds to

Isaiah's call to go to Ahaz to console him (6:4) and to tell him not to fear, for God was with Judah.

This is significant because in much apocalyptic and *merkabah* literature from the late antique period, the protagonist, upon seeing an angel, falls down in fear and amazement. Ibn Ezra, therefore, had a larger repertoire of autochthonous images to draw on within the Jewish tradition. Although many of these motifs are universal, occurring in contemporaneous philosophical texts, Ibn Ezra firmly grounds them in the specific idiom of Judaism. He uses the language and imagery of the Jewish tradition to add both depth and context to what was originally a non-Jewish narrative. To use the literary critical language of his day, he embellishes well-worn motifs in a new and pleasing way.

Poetry permits Ibn Ezra not only to disseminate philosophical themes in a manner that more technical treatises could not but also to show how such themes are biblical and, by extension, indigenous to Judaism. This, what Ross Brann calls "cultural nationalism," both justified and legitimated the composition of secular work (be it poetry or philosophy) in Al-Andalus.[40] Grammarians, poets, philosophers—often individuals were all three at the same time—envisaged themselves as biblical purists whose work would ensure both the survival and florescence of Israelite antiquity on new soil. What better way to do this than to argue that the form and substance of their adopted culture was ultimately derived from Jewish sources.

Another example of this comes from Ibn Gabirol's *Keter malkhut*, especially those stanzas in which he describes the nature of the relationship between the soul and the body. Interestingly, in this poem he departs from his treatment of this relationship in *Fons Vitae*, a work wherein he describes the soul as existing within a "prison of nature."[41] Ibn Gabirol's portrayal and assessment is not nearly as negative in the poetic work:

> O Lord, who can comprehend your power?
>   You have created for the splendor of your glory
> A pure radiance, hewn from the Rock of rocks
>   Removed from the quarry whence it was dug.
>
> You have given to it the spirit of wisdom
>   And called it soul [*neshamah*].
> The flame of reason you have made its form
>   Like a burning fire you have set it in motion.

You have sent it into the body to serve and protect it
It is like a fire in its midst that does not consume.
It is from the fire of the soul that it has been crafted
It moves from non-existence to existence.
Because the Lord descended upon him in fire.[42]

The poem goes on to celebrate the body as part of God's creation (canto 32). Poetry, then, does not simply translate abstract philosophical themes into a poetic register. It reframes philosophical ideas in such a manner that the poem is not simply derivative or secondary to what are customarily regarded as "normative" philosophical treatises. In the above passage, we witness how the poet describes the soul as hewn from the "Rock of rocks" (*mi-ṣur ha-ṣur nigzerah umi-maqqevet bor nuqqarah*), a verse that is almost identical to Isa. 51:1. The latter verse, though, refers not to the soul's celestial source but to Abraham, the patriarchs, and the matriarchs. As with Ibn Ezra above, Ibn Gabirol here fuses biblical and philosophical motifs, wherein the traditional God of Israel now begins to be identified with the Neoplatonic source of all souls.

Poetic language also enables Ibn Gabirol to maintain a delicate and creative tension between Neoplatonic and biblical cosmologies. Whereas his use of biblical terms and language would suggest to the unsuspecting reader that the God of his poem is one who creates ex nihilo, a closer examination reveals that he envisages the creative process to be one of emanation. However, he also departs significantly from traditional Neoplatonic teaching by making God actively involved in the process of emanation by, for example, making Him the subject of the verbs that imply emanation (for example, those that form around the root *ʿ-s-l*).[43]

Returning to Abraham ibn Ezra's *Ḥay ben Meqitz*, we again witness this constellation of poetic form, biblical language, and philosophical ideas. In the culmination of the work, we read:

There is no God save Him
No Creator except Him.
There is no limit to His knowledge
No bound to His wisdom.
His possessions cannot be enumerated
His contents cannot be known.
From an abundance of greatness
His knowledge is hidden from men.

From the greatness of His appearance
  Seeing Him is prevented,
Just as the sun is hidden by its light
  We cannot know it.
When it rises at dawn
  We barely visualize it.
In this way souls are unable to know Him
  Hearts unable to perceive Him.
He has neither shape nor likeness
  He has no image by which one can compare Him.[44]

Here we see how the form of poetry actually aids in the philosophical enterprise. Just as poetry uses images and motifs that appeal to the imaginative faculty, Ibn Ezra here uses poetic imagery to invoke the immateriality of the divine world. Since the only way in which this world can be imagined is through corporal images, it must also be remembered that these images only point the way. In the proper hands, poetry inculcates in the ideal reader an imageless image, something that cannot be done in more discursive treatises.

We also see these types of images at work in other poets, many of whom are not necessarily or traditionally considered to be philosophers in the strict sense of the term. Moses ibn Ezra (ca. 1055–after 1138), no relation to Abraham, was another one of the great Hebrew poets from Al-Andalus. Poet, belletrist, Torah scholar, aesthetician, and literary critic, Moses ibn Ezra was someone who was interested in the relationship between *majāz* (figurative language) and *ḥaqīqa* (literal language). This relationship, not surprisingly, was intimately connected to theological and philosophical motifs surrounding topics such as anthropomorphism.[45] So even though he is not customarily thought of as a philosopher (at least in the same breath as say Shlomo ibn Gabirol or Abraham ibn Ezra), he nevertheless engaged in quasi-philosophical themes because such themes revolved around literary theory and artistic production. This, in turn, raises another issue surrounding literary form. Although Moses ibn Ezra is not included within the traditional "canon" of medieval Jewish philosophers, his poetry—not to mention his contribution to aesthetics—perhaps ought to make us reconsider his inclusion therein. A reappraisal of our understanding of philosophical forms will subsequently mean that we will have to expand our notion of both medieval Jewish philosophy and medieval Jewish philosophers.

In his "Nafshi ivvitkha ba-layla" (I long for you with my soul in the night), a *seliḥah* or penitential poem, Moses ibn Ezra writes in the opening stanza,

> My soul desires for her place of repose
> Yearns for her Source
> She desires her holy abode
> Searching day and night.[46]

Here we see the common Neoplatonic motif of the soul, trapped in a human body, and its subsequent desire to return to its celestial home, which is described as its source. The title, taken directly from Isaiah 26:9, is now used to designate the rational soul or intellect.[47] The impermanence of this world is, again, starkly juxtaposed with the eternity and permanence of the superlunary world. The search mentioned in the last line of the stanza is something that echoes throughout the poem and implies, as is typical of this literature, that the path toward God, toward the soul's true home, is in contemplation that is often code for the study of philosophy, especially metaphysics. Once again, then, Moses ibn Ezra has picked up on Neoplatonic themes and contributed to their poetic embellishment, even though he is customarily excluded from Jewish philosophy. He is instead referred to as a "medieval Hebrew poet," even though as we see above much of his poetry and literary theory contribute significantly to our understanding of Jewish philosophy in the eleventh century.

Even poets critical of the philosophical enterprise would, perhaps unsurprisingly, couch their criticisms in poetic language. In many ways, they had to because, as witnessed, the Andalusi intellectual scene was one that was defined by literary and semantic parameters associated with the Arab notion of *adab*, or belles lettres. Even to critique a literary form, one had to engage in it if one wanted to find an audience. A perfect example of the poetic criticism of philosophy, especially of philosophy written in poetic form, is the great "anti-philosopher" Judah Halevi (1075–1141). Halevi's magnum opus, the *Kuzari*, was discussed in the chapter on dialogues; here I focus on his use of poetry that has the same intent: a criticism of the Greco-Arabo philosophical enterprise in favor of a return to a more authentic Hebraic expression.[48]

What seemed to bother Halevi the most was that the quantitative meters of Arabic distorted, in his opinion, the purity of biblical diction.[49] His attempts to develop a more authentic meter largely seemed to fail, and by all accounts he resorted back to Arabic meter after he had initially repudiated it upon his departure from Al-Andalus. In terms of philosophy, Halevi is particularly critical of its denial of creation, revelation, and providence. In one of his later poems, he writes:

> Do not let Greek wisdom lure you
> It bears no fruits only flowers.
> Such is its fruit: that the earth was never spread out,
> Nor heaven's tents ever stretched taut;
> That creation had no beginning,
> And the passing of months has no end.
> Hear how the words of its wise are perplexed,
> Built on false groundwork, the whitewashed.
> Your heart will end vacant and emptied,
> Your mouth full of dross and vain breath.[50]

Here Halevi uses the same sort of strophic poetry to undermine that of his more philosophically inclined contemporaries. For him, authentic Jewish life does not reside in speculating about the end of the world but in living a Jewish life in the service of the commandments. Whereas other poets had used poetry to describe the body as a prison and the role of Greek-inflected philosophical speculation as the way to release the soul therefrom, Halevi implies that such a worldview is "full of dross and vain breath" and instead locates such freedom in prayer and ritual. In his "*Shuvi nafshi li-mnuḥayki*" (Return, my soul to your repose), Halevi uses a motif similar to those poet-philosophers discussed above, but now changes the tenor in such a manner that is in keeping with his own understanding:

> I sojourn here, like my ancestors before me
> My years pass like shadows.
> If not now, tell me, when?
> How will you redeem yourself from this prison?
> If you seek He who formed you
> Cleanse yourself from your profanity
> Approach Him, do not be afraid
> Your deeds will bring you near to Him.[51]

Whereas other philosophers stressed study and the philosophical enterprise as the path back to the soul's celestial home, Halevi stresses pious deeds that come from the bodily performance of the commandments. But note how Halevi must still use the themes and motifs even if to dismantle them. As with so much of medieval Judeo-Arabic literature, the poet must improve on a motif in order to lay claim to it.

Aristotelianism and the End of an Era

During the second half of the twelfth century, the philosophical paradigm gradually shifted from the highly literary and eclectic Neoplatonism to the more discursive Aristotelianism. One of the first to introduce Aristotelianism into Jewish philosophy was Abraham ibn Daud (1110–1180), someone who composed his *Emunah Ramah* (Exalted faith) in prose and as a conscious rejoinder to the Neoplatonic-inflected philosophy of Ibn Gabirol. Even though as an elite Cordoban Jew he would have been educated in Arabic belles lettres, Ibn Daud's philosophical system represents a rejection of philosophy composed in poetic form for a more rational articulation of Aristotelian science. In the opening to *Emunah Ramah*, for example, he is highly critical of Ibn Gabirol's style, writing that "perhaps if his content were refined, his words could be included in a book that is less than one tenth of that treatise . . . according to his view imaginary premises in the form of a true syllogism are satisfactory, certainly their content is doubtful."[52]

The towering Maimonides was also extremely critical of poetry, or at least a certain kind of poetry. In *Guide* 1:59, for example, he writes that the utterances of some poets, and here he has in mind the likes of Ibn Gabirol, "contain such rubbish and such perverse imaginings as to make men laugh when they hear them, on account of the nature of these utterances, and to make them weep when they consider that these utterances are applied to God, may He be magnified and glorified."[53] Critical of many of the Andalusian Hebrew poets, Maimonides in the same chapter proclaims that they "predicated attributes of Him and addressed Him in all the terms that they thought permitted and expatiated at such length in this that in their thought they made Him move on account of an affection." In his *Commentary to Avot*, Maimonides finds objectionable the practice of inserting verses from the Torah or the Song of Songs into contemporaneous poetic forms: "Then [such language] departs from the category of the Rejected to the category of the Prohibited and the Cautioned Against, for the Torah prohibited making the worlds of prophecy into forms of song dealing with vices and unseemly matters."[54]

For Ibn Daud and Maimonides, returning to Plato's criticisms of poetry with which this chapter opened, rhetorical and imaginary flourishes potentially get in the way of philosophy. On Ibn Daud's reading, such flourishes lead to faulty reasoning and, for Maimonides, they can lead to misapprehensions of God and the divine world. Yet, like Plato, Maimonides himself was a true master of metaphor and allegory when it suited his philosophical purposes.[55]

Subsequent Spread of the Form

Despite these Maimonidean and other criticisms, the form of poetry as a means of philosophical expression did not disappear. It continued to be used even by philosophers who were no longer interested in Neoplatonism, both in Muslim Spain, Christian Spain, and beyond. As time went on, however, and because Neoplatonism as a philosophical system had largely fallen out of favor, it is difficult to know precisely how these poets used philosophical themes. Was the motif of the body as a prison, for example, used to analyze further a philosophical theme, or, by the thirteenth and fourteenth centuries, had it largely transformed into a literary trope? Rather than become a vehicle for originary philosophical speculation, as it had in the eleventh and twelfth centuries, did later centuries witness it become little more than a recycled form of expression?

The great Nahmanides (1194–1270) composed few poems,[56] but those that he did seem to have been of high quality and they certainly reveal his immersion in Kabbalah and his tenuous relationship to philosophy. In "Before the World Ever Was," we read:

> From the beginning before the world ever was
>   I was held on high with his hidden treasures.
> He brought me forth from nothing and in
>   End I will be withdrawn by the King.
>
> My being flowed from the spheres' foundations
>   Which endowed it with form in evident fashion
> The craftsman's hand weighed its creation
>   So I would be brought to the vaults of the King.[57]

Again we witness the well-used theme of the individual human soul being formed on high and placed in a human body from which it longs to depart. At the time of corporeal death, this soul will be released. Or, in the words of Nahmanides, "The body interred will surely be vanquished/but the soul will ascend through the halls of the King."[58] Although the theme remains, gone are all references to intellectual speculation. Poetry, in the hands of those like Nahmanides, now becomes more relevant to articulating the concerns of mystical (or kabbalistic) speculation, something that in the twelfth and thirteenth centuries increasingly began to define itself against philosophical rationalism.

Poetry, however, was still employed by less mystical and more philosophically inspired thinkers. Yedaya Hapenini (ca. 1270–after 1306) was one such individual. Born in Perpignan (today southern France), he was a biblical commentator heavily influenced by the writings of Averroes, in addition to being a poet and an active participant in the pro-Maimonidean camp during the second phase of the Maimonidean Controversy in 1305.[59] Hapenini's most famous work was *Behinat Olam* (The investigation of the world), a rich belletristic work on ethics that underwent numerous editions and translations over subsequent years. Although *Behinat Olam* employs neither rhyme nor meter, both break out occasionally as in the following example:

> The world is a raging sea
> Whose depth and width are vast,
> And Time is a rickety bridge extending across it.
> Anchored in bonds of absence
> Preceding its existence, it leads one towards eternal bliss
> By the light of the countenance of our King.
> The bridge is wide as the span of man
> Along it there is no railing
> And you live on son of man,
> against your will
> From the day that you were born,
> You've always walked across it.[60]

It is difficult to know if this is tantamount to a work of philosophy. However, we do see in it the articulation of the tense relationship between body and soul, the impermanence of this world, and the hope for future reward. This idea of including poetic sections within more standard philosophical treatises is also found in *Ezer ha-dat*, a philosophical dialogue written in a pleasing rhymed prose, by Isaac Polleqar (first half of fourteenth century). This work was meant as a response to Abner of Burgos/Alfonso de Valladolid, an original Jewish philosopher who had converted to Christianity and who subsequently wrote polemical treatises against his former faith.[61]

In the following poem from *Ezer ha-dat*, we see Polleqar—again writing in the midst of the Maimonidean Controversies—argue that Judaism combines Torah and philosophy:

> If your soul seeks out wisdom with faith,
> And acts in kind, to preserve their bond,
> You'll rejoice, seeing the pleasures
> Of God, the Lord, as faith lives on.
>
> But faith without wisdom means not a thing
> A feast prepared, with no one eating.
> And without the Law, wisdom is worthless:
> Lacking Scripture, its knowledge is thin.
>
> So join the two if you'd pursue
> The strength and power of the purest soul;
> Wisdom, then, will serve all men
> And in its glory, destroy its rebels.[62]

Witness that in these last few poems we are removed from the poetic expression of philosophical ideas witnessed among the early Neoplatonic poet-philosophers. Nevertheless, it is clear that the form still remained in subsequent medieval philosophical speculation.

Conclusions

Poetry, as witnessed in this chapter, served many important purposes in medieval Jewish philosophy. It certainly permitted a broader dissemination of rational ideas. However, equally importantly, it also permitted the fusion of biblical language with philosophical concepts in such a manner that the latter appeared to exist naturally within the former. In this regard poetry succeeded in naturalizing philosophy within Judaism. In the deft hands of Andalusi poets, philosophy simultaneously lead into and out of the rich narrative supplied by the Bible. Finally, in much of the Neoplatonic work examined above, poetry became perhaps the most natural way to express the ineffable nature of the One and to conjure up the nature of the relationship between this world and the celestial world. Within this latter context, poetry became an important vehicle for the expression of philosophical ideas that could not be expressed in more discursive or prose works because the latter lacked the ability to move beyond the written/corporeal world to return to the language-less spiritual world.

By including poetry as a philosophical form, as opposed to something antithetical to philosophy, our understanding of philosophy—its modes of production, the motivations behind it—increases. On this reading, poetry not only supplements philosophy but also becomes a highly creative and imaginative way to express it.

Notes

1. Neoplatonism, to be sure, is an imprecise marker. German scholars originally coined the term *Neuplatonismus* in the nineteenth century to refer pejoratively to those thinkers who came after Plato and were thought to be unoriginal or epigonic because they primarily wrote commentaries, which was perceived to be an unoriginal genre. Although the term is used frequently today, no premodern thinkers would have considered themselves to be "Neoplatonic" philosophers, let alone contributing to a school of "Neoplatonism." Yet despite its imprecision, we still tend to use it. I employ it here with the above caveats.

2. On the history of this categorization, see, for example, David N. Myers, *Re-Inventing the Jewish Past: European Jewish Intellectuals and the Zionist Return to History* (New York: Oxford University Press, 1955), 1–25. Aaron W. Hughes, "'Medieval' and the Politics of Nostalgia: Ideology, Scholarship, and the Creation of the Rational Jew," in *Encountering the Medieval in Modern Jewish Thought*, ed. James A. Diamond and Aaron W. Hughes (Leiden: Brill, 2013), 17–39.

3. As in ancient Greece, poetry in medieval Islamicate culture was considered to be an art or a craft (*ṣināʿa*). Like all other arts or crafts, there existed a canon by which a poem's success was judged. A "good" poem, in other words, had to conform closely to the rules that governed its production. Unlike the modern period, which put overwhelming emphasis on individual creativity and/or artistry, the medieval Hebrew or Arab poet was regarded, first and foremost, as an artisan, someone familiar with the rules and conventions of his field. Poetry, then, was traditional: the poem's success was based primarily on its formal correctness. Poetic beauty resulted when an appropriate form was superadded onto a limited number of poetic themes (*maʿānī*). See the studies in G. E. von Grunebaum, "The Aesthetic Foundations of Arabic Literature," *Comparative Literature* 4 (1952): 323–40; Dan Pagis, *Secular Poetry and Poetic Theory: Moses ibn Ezra and His Contemporaries* (Jerusalem: Bialik Institute, 1970), 51–55 [Hebrew].

4. Plato, *Republic*, in *The Collected Dialogues, including the Letters*, ed. Edith Hamilton and Huntington Cairns (Princeton, NJ: Bollingen, 1989).

5. Gerald F. Else, *Plato and Aristotle on Poetry*, ed. Peter Burian (Chapel Hill: University of North Carolina Press, 1986), 3–5.

6. Witness, for example, Maimonides's comments in *Shemonah Perakim* (Eight chapters) in *Ethical Writings of Maimonides*, ed. and trans. Raymond L. Weiss and Charles E. Butterworth (New York: New York University Press, 1975), esp. 77. Even though Maimonides was highly critical of the poets, he nonetheless writes that pleasing decorations can bring "delight to one's soul for the sake of its health and to drive sickness from it, so that it will be clear and pure to receive the sciences." For the relevant context, see Deborah Black, "Aesthetics in Islamic Philosophy," in *Routledge Encyclopedia of Philosophy*, vol. 1 (London and New York: Routledge,

1998), 75–79; Doris Behrens-Abouseif, *Beauty in Arabic Culture* (Princeton, NJ: Markus Wiener Publishers, 1999), 5–10.

7. E.g., Plato, *Republic* 476, 479; *Symposium* 210b–211e; *Phaedo* 65, 75d, 78d–e; *Phaedrus* 249c–250b.

8. For an important corrective to the notion or assumption that Judaism is or always has been aniconic, see Kalman P. Bland, *The Artless Jew: Medieval and Modern Affirmations and Denials of the Visual* (Princeton, NJ: Princeton University Press, 2000), 15–36. In this regard, see also Ze'ev Levy, "The Status of Aesthetics in Jewish Thought," in *Judaism and Art*, ed. David Cassuto (Bar Ilan: Bar Ilan University Press, 1988), 83–102 [Hebrew].

9. *Gorgias* 523a.

10. *Metaphysics* 1078a35–1078b5. In this regard, see also *Poetics* 1450b34–1451a2.

11. See the discussion in Stephen Halliwell, *The Poetics of Aristotle: Translation and Commentary* (London: Duckworth, 1987), 99.

12. See the comments in Stephen Halliwell, *Aristotle's Poetics* (Chicago: University of Chicago Press, 1986), 97–99.

13. Sara Rappe, *Reading Neoplatonism: Non-discursive Thinking in the Texts of Plotinus, Proclus, and Damascius* (Cambridge: Cambridge University Press, 2000), 12.

14. Rappe, *Reading Neoplatonism*, 75; Robert Lamberton, *Homer the Theologian: Neoplatonist Allegorical Reading and the Growth of the Epic Tradition* (Berkeley, University of California Press, 1986), 186–88.

15. In this regard, the medievals build on the discussion in Aristotle, *De Anima* 3.4 (429a15–429b26). For the various ways in which this plays out in Western thought, see David C. Lindberg, *Theories of Vision from al-Kindi to Kepler* (Chicago: University of Chicago Press, 1976).

16. For requisite historical background, see Ian Netton, *Muslim Neoplatonists: An Introduction to the Thought of the Brethren of Purity* (Edinburgh: Edinburgh University Press, 1991), 1–8; Seyyed Hossein Nasr, *An Introduction to Islamic Cosmological Doctrines*, rev. ed. (Albany: State University of New York Press, 1993), 25–43.

17. See, for example, Paul Fenton, "The Arabic and Hebrew Versions of the Theology of Aristotle," in *Pseudo-Aristotle in the Middle Ages*, ed. J, Kraye, W. Tyan, and C. Schmitt (London: Warburg Institute, 1986), 241–64.

18. *Rasā'il Ikhwān al-Ṣafā'* (Beirut: Dār Sādir, 1957), vol. 1, 183. English translation in Amnon Shiloah, *The Epistle on Music of the Ikhwan al-Safa* (Tel Aviv: Tel Aviv University Press, 1978), 37.

19. *Rasā'il Ikhwān al-Ṣafā'*, vol. 1, 237; Shiloah, *The Epistle on Music*, 69.

20. Al-Farabi, *Al-Fārābī on the Perfect State: Abū Naṣr al-Fārābī's Mabādī' ārā' ahl al-madīna al-fāḍila*, rev. text with intro., trans., and commentary by Richard Walzer (Oxford: Oxford University Press, 1985), 83–85.

21. Al-Farabi, *Mabādī' ārā' ahl al-madīna al-fāḍila*, 84–85.

22. See, for example, Avicenna, *Kitāb al-Najāt*, ed. M. Fakhry (Beirut: n.p., 1986), 281–82; Avicenna, *Risāla fī 'l-'ishq*, in *Traités mystiques d'Abou Ali Hosain b. Abdallah ibn Sina ou d'Avicenne*, IIIième fasc., ed. M. A. F. Mehren (Leiden: Brill, 1894), 14. English translation in Emil Fackenheim, "A Treatise on Love by Ibn Sina," *Mediaeval Studies* 7 (1945): 220.

23. Avicenna, *Risāla fī 'l-'ishq*, 13; Fackenheim, "A Treatise on Love," 219.

24. Avicenna, *Risāla fī 'l-'ishq*, 15; Fackenheim, "A Treatise on Love," 221.

25. See the discussion in Herbert Davidson, *Alfarabi, Avicenna, and Averroes on Intellect: Their Cosmologies, Theories of the Active Intellect, and Theories of the Human Intellect* (New York: Oxford University Press, 1992), 95–102.

26. For some of the political reasons behind this, see David J. Wasserstein, *The Rise and Fall of the Party-Kings, Politics and Society in Islamic Spain, 1002–1086* (Princeton, NJ: Princeton University Press, 1985); ibid., *The Caliphate in the West: An Islamic Political Institution in the Iberian Peninsula* (Oxford: Oxford University Press, 1993). In terms of cultural richness, see the studies found, e.g., in James Monroe, "Hispano-Arabic Poetry during the Age of the Caliphate of Cordoba: Theory and Practice," in *Arabic Poetry: Theory and Development*, ed. G. von Grunebaum (Wiesbaden: Otto Harrassowitz, 1973), 125–54. For relevant background in the Hebrew poetry of Al-Andalus, see Arie Schippers, *Spanish-Hebrew Poetry and the Arabic Literary Tradition: Arabic Themes in Hebrew Andalusian Poetry* (Leiden: Brill, 1994).

27. Moses ibn Ezra, *Kitāb al-Muḥāḍara wa-l-Mudhākara (Sefer ha-ʿiyyunim ve ha-diyyunim)*, ed. and trans. A. S. Halkin (Jerusalem: Mekize Nirdamim, 1975), 28b. For relevant background, see Joseph Dana, *The Poetics of Medieval Hebrew Literature According to Moses ibn Ezra* (Jerusalem: Dvir, 1982), 18–37 [Hebrew].

28. For relevant context, see Rina Drory, *The Emergence of Jewish-Arabic Literary Contacts at the Beginning of the Tenth Century* (Tel Aviv: Tel Aviv University, 1988) [Hebrew]; ibid., *Models and Contacts: Arabic Literature and Its Impact on Medieval Jewish Culture* (Leiden: Brill, 2000).

29. This, of course, is not to say that Jews had not used poetic forms in the past to think about Judaism. Of particular importance is the traditional genre of the piyyut (liturgical poem), which will be discussed below.

30. See the pioneering studies in Raymond Scheindlin, *The Gazelle: Medieval Hebrew Poems on God, Israel, and the Soul* (Philadelphia, PA: Jewish Publication Society of America, 1986); Ross Brann, *The Compunctious Poet: Cultural Ambiguity and Hebrew Poetry in Muslim Spain* (Baltimore, MD: Johns Hopkins University Press, 1991), 23–58.

31. Joseph Yahalom, *Poetry and Society in Jewish Galilee of Late Antiquity* (Tel Aviv: Hakibbutz Hameuchad, 1999), 1–14 [Hebrew]; ibid, *Poetic Language in the Early Piyyut* (Jerusalem: Magnes Press, 1985) [Hebrew]. For a description of the style and forms of piyyutim, consult M. Zulay, *Eretz Israel and Its Poetry: Studies in Piyyutim from the Cairo Genizah*, ed. E. Hazan (Jerusalem: Magnes Press, 1995), 413–527 [Hebrew].

32. M. Zulay, *The Liturgical Poetry of Saadya Gaon and His School* (Jerusalem: Schocken Institute for Jewish Research, 1964) [Hebrew].

33. Z. Malachi, "Abraham ibn Ezra's Criticism of Elazar Hakalir's Poetry," in *Pleasant Words: Chapters from the History of Hebrew Literature* (Lod: Habermann Institute for Literary Research, 1983), 133–56 [Hebrew]; see further, Joseph Yahalom, "The Poetics of Spanish Piyyut in Light of Abraham ibn Ezra's Critique of Pre-Spanish Precedents," in *Abraham ibn Ezra and His Age*, ed. F. Diaz Esteban (Madrid: Asociacíon de Orientalistas, 1990), 387–92; Adena Tanenbaum, *The Contemplative Soul: Hebrew Poetry and Philosophical Theory in Medieval Spain* (Leiden: Brill, 2002), 12–20.

34. I say "popular" and "more technical" because even those poets and belletrists who were not, strictly speaking, philosophers nevertheless recycled many of the categories and tropes of Neoplatonism.

35. Relevant biographical literature may be found in Jacques Schlanger, *La philosophie de Salomon ibn Gabirol: Etude d'un néoplatonisme* (Leiden: Brill, 1968), 1–30. More recently, see Sarah Pessin, "Ibn Gabirol," in the online *Stanford Encyclopedia of Philosophy*.

36. On account of the *Receptionsgeschichte* of *Fons Vitae*, which survived only in Latin translation, it was long assumed that the work was written by the Arab or Christian Avicebron or Avencebrol. It was not until the middle of the nineteenth century that Solomon

Munk discovered a thirteenth-century Hebrew summary by Shem Tov ibn Falaquera that attributed the text to Solomon ibn Gabirol.

37. My translation from the Hebrew text in Solomon ibn Gabirol, "Keter Malkhut," in *Selected Religious Poems of Solomon ibn Gabirol*, ed. Israel Davidson, trans. Israel Zangwill (Philadelphia, PA: Jewish Publication Society of America, 1924), 84.

38. On the relationship between the two texts and the issue of medieval plagiarism, see Aaron W. Hughes, "A Case of Twelfth-Century Plagiarism? Abraham ibn Ezra's *Hay ben Meqitz* and Avicenna's *Hayy ibn Yaqzan*," *Journal of Jewish Studies* 55, no. 2 (2004): 306–31.

39. Translation in Aaron W. Hughes, *The Texture of the Divine: Imagination in Medieval Islamic and Jewish Thought* (Bloomington, Indiana University Press, 2004), 199–200.

40. Brann, *Compunctious Poet*, 37–53.

41. See the comments in Shlomo Pines, "Fragments of the Arabic Original of *Fons Vitae* in Moses ibn Ezra's Work *'Arugat Habossem*" *Tarbiz* 27 (1957–1958): 218–33, at 221–22 [Hebrew].

42. Ibn Gabirol, *Keter malkhut*, canto 29, 103–5.

43. See the comments in Tanenbaum, *Contemplative Soul*, 70–71.

44. In Hughes, *Texture of the Divine*, 206.

45. See Paul Fenton, *Philosophie et exégèse dans "Le Jardin de la métaphore" de Moïse ibn 'Ezra, philosophe et poète du XIIe siècle* (Leiden: Brill, 1995), 258–60.

46. Moses ibn Ezra, *The Collected Liturgical Poetry*, ed. S. Bernstein (Tel Aviv: Massadah, 1957), 68 [Hebrew].

47. See his comments in *Maqālat al-ḥadīqa fī ma'na 'l-majāz wa'l-ḥaqīqa*, Jerusalem, Jewish National and University Library M. 8° 5701, 93.

48. See, e.g., Brann, *The Compunctious Poet*, 84–118; Goodman, "Judah Halevi," *History of Jewish Philosophy*, ed., Daniel H. Frank and Oliver Leaman (London and New York: Routledge, 1997), 188–227, at 196–212.

49. Brann, *The Compunctious Poet*, 90–93.

50. In Hayyim Schirmann, ed., *Hebrew Poetry in Spain and Provence* (Jerusalem: Bialik Institute and Dvir, 1954–1956), vol. 2, 492–94 (lines 27–31) [Hebrew]. English translation in Tanenbaum, *The Contemplative Soul*, 178.

51. In Schirmann, *Hebrew Poetry in Spain and Provence*, vol. 2, 514–15. See the comments in Bernard Septimus, "On the Use of Talmudic Literature in Spanish Hebrew Poetry," *Tarbiz* 53 (1984): 607–14, at 612–13 [Hebrew]. See further the discussion in Tanenbaum, *Contemplative Soul*, 184–94.

52. Abraham ibn Daud, *The Exalted Faith*, trans. Norbert M. Samuelson (Rutherford, NJ: Fairleigh Dickinson University Press, 1986), 40.

53. Maimonides, *Guide of the Perplexed*, translated by Shlomo Pines (Chicago: University of Chicago Press, 1963) 1, 141. This theme is also picked up in his "Book of Commandments." For an English translation of the passage in question, see Isadore Twersky, *A Maimonides Reader* (New York: Behrman, 1972), 427–28.

54. Twersky, *Maimonides Reader*, 393.

55. See, for example, his allegory of the king's palace in the third book of the *Guide*.

56. There are roughly eighteen extant poems attributed to him.

57. Hebrew in *Kitvei Rabbenu Moshe ben Nahman*, ed. C. Chavel (Jerusalem: Mossad Harav Kook, 1963), vol. 1, 392. Translated into English in Peter Cole, *The Dream of the Poem: Hebrew Poetry from Muslim and Christian Spain 950–1492* (Princeton, NJ: Princeton University Press), 234.

58. Ibid.

59. The Maimonidean Controversies were a series of internecine debates over the role and place of philosophy in general and Maimonides's *Guide of the Perplexed* in particular in Judaism. For relevant background and general overview, see Daniel J. Silver, *Maimonidean Criticism and the Maimonidean Controversy 1180–1240* (Leiden: Brill, 1965); and more recently, Hava Tirosh-Samuelson, *Happiness in Premodern Judaism: Virtue, Knowledge, and Well-Being* (Cincinnati, OH: Hebrew Union College Press, 2003), 246–90.

60. Hebrew in *Behinat Olam* (Jerusalem, 1980), poem 142; English translation in Cole, *Dream of the Poem*, 279.

61. See Aaron W. Hughes, *The Art of Dialogue in Jewish Philosophy* (Bloomington: Indiana University Press, 2008), 76–85.

62. Isaac Polleqar, *Ezer ha-dat*, ed. Y. Levinger (Tel Aviv: Tel Aviv University Press, 1984), 93; English translation in Cole, *Dream of the Poem*, 288.

AARON W. HUGHES is the Philip S. Bernstein Professor of Jewish Studies at the University of Rochester. He is the author of many books, including *Rethinking Jewish Philosophy: Beyond Particularism and Universalism.*

9

POETIC SUMMARIES OF SCIENTIFIC AND PHILOSOPHICAL WORKS

Maud Kozodoy

Introduction

In the medieval period, verse was regularly employed to convey scientific and philosophical information. Oral recitation and memorization were central to the Arabic educational institutions of Damascus and Cairo.[1] With the rise of the madrasa in the twelfth century, prose texts came to be versified and original poems to be composed on technical subjects.[2] In the Latin university system, too, versification served pedagogical purposes; poems could serve as brief mnemonic aids or take the form of full-length treatises.[3]

In the Hebrew tradition, by contrast, such verse turns out to be very rare. This rarity may be tied to the lack of enduring institutional contexts, in particular for secular education. Jewish philosophers, as far as we know, tended to study alone or in very small groups.[4] Although memorization was important for the lone scholar, producing a versified philosophical text would have made sense only if a large number of students could take advantage of it. There are, in fact, at most a handful of independent philosophical poems composed by medieval Jews.

Scientific material, for its part, does assume Hebrew poetic form, mainly liturgical; versified versions of the *'avodah* service often include a description of creation and of the heavenly bodies.[5] But to find versification proper of science and philosophy, we must look elsewhere than to piyyut. Paradoxically, it is most fruitful to examine manuscripts of prose texts—which, for reasons to be considered below, on occasion include either a Hebrew poetic prologue or a concluding verse summary. Some of these texts, including the poems treated here, display features that suggest a mnemonic function.

Discussions of mnemonics among medieval Jewish scholars are very rare and late;[6] techniques for memorization first appear in the introduction by Profayt Duran to his 1403 grammatical treatise, *Ma'aseh Efod*.[7] But ease of memorization was a widely and explicitly acknowledged benefit of verse. In what follows I will first consider medieval claims in this regard and then proceed to examine the Hebrew exemplars with an eye to the particular forms and techniques employed by their authors. I will conclude with thoughts about the place of this poetic enterprise within the Jewish culture of, in particular, medieval Iberia.

Here we have a rare opportunity to analyze how some authors went about constructing memory aids and also to reflect on how their poems were experienced. Exploring the consumption of poems outside the *diwan*—in the study hall, in the schoolroom, and in the reading of the manuscript itself—opens windows onto social spaces and the kinds of teaching, learning, and cultural negotiations taking place in them.

One preliminary clarification: what *in this context* constitutes "verse"? Technically speaking, it entails rhyme and meter in the quantitative metrics adopted from Arabic poetic convention; rhymed prose is not verse. But unmetered and unrhymed statements might be considered "poetic" if they were "imitative" or, in other words, used metaphor, simile, and so on to convey truths in a way that affected the imagination:[8] a long-standing debate over the merits of prose versus those of poetry lies in the background here. But that need not concern us; the authors of the poems considered below—by definition—chose to employ the formal elements of meter and rhyme. Whether they also deployed metaphor and simile, biblical allusions, or other rhetorical devices remains to be seen.

Mnemonics and Verse

It has long been recognized that verse is easier to memorize than prose. In his commentary on Ibn Sīnā's medical poem, Ibn Rushd writes: "I have made an effort to comment on the metrical text . . . for this is much better . . . because of its arrangement, which is very appropriate for memorizing and for delighting the soul."[9] Typically the following reasons were given for the superior utility of poetry: "easier reception, charming and lucid brevity, and stronger memory."[10] As Greti Dinkova-Bruun has commented, "The usefulness of metered speech in the process of memorization is a well-known medieval topos."[11]

Recent study of mnemonics in the Latin world has been dominated by the work of Mary Carruthers. She and others, including Jan Ziolkowski, have explicated the *ars memorativa* of the medieval Latin scholastics, based on the monastic techniques of meditation on letters, pictures, and sounds, and later on Ciceronian traditions of locational memory.[12] As in the case of versified late-medieval Latin Bibles, poets relied on "brevity and orderly arrangement" and in some cases also turned to "the use of vivid and striking imagery."[13]

Suzanne Pinckney Stetkevych has written on the shift from early Arabic poetry, composed in the context of an oral culture and shaped by those particular mnemonic requirements, to later Arabic poetry composed in a medieval written culture.[14] She points to the conclusion of Eric Havelock that "virtually all the linguistic features that we classify as 'poetic'—rhyme, meter, assonance, alliteration, antithesis, parallelism, 'poetic diction'—and in particular those figures of speech that we term 'rhetorical devices'—metaphor, simile, metonymy, antithesis—are originally and essentially mnemonic devices that serve to stabilize and preserve the oral 'text.'"[15] These devices remained integral to verse composition even after the move to a written culture.[16]

In the medieval Hebrew tradition, too, verse was considered beneficial for the memory. In the eleventh century, Solomon ibn Gabirol introduces his poem on the rules of Hebrew grammar by remarking: "Since I saw that rhyme is better than anything, even if its way is very constricted, with meter I have metered it; I have made it a poem, rhymed so that it will be a *mazkeret* [reminder]."[17] Moses ibn Ezra likewise notes in his book on rhetoric that, as compared with prose, poetry is easier to remember: "Linguists are divided on the matter of prose and poetry: which of the two is preferable? . . . A few say: prose flies about like sparks, while poetry remains like a carved rock; praise of what is honorable is [kept] forever in rhymes, and the abuse of what is shameful is established forever."[18] In Christian Iberia in the thirteenth century, Shem Tov ibn Falaquera observes in the preface to his own didactic poem on medicine that "matters expressed in rhyme and meter are pleasant to some and easy to remember."[19] In the early-fifteenth-century *Ma'aseh Efod*, Profayt Duran praises the sweetness of song in the context of chanting the Hebrew Bible; Ezra, Duran writes, established the vocalization "so that chanting the scrolls would be easy" and added the cantillation marks "so that there would be sweetness to the reading, so that scripture would stir the desire of men's hearts from the sweetness of the melody of cantillation, and also so that scripture would remain and persist in the faculty of memory—since it is known that song and melody make that which is sung permanent in the faculty of memory, and through these means remembering and recalling become easy."[20] Applying this principle to nonbiblical texts, Duran includes a mnemonic poem summarizing the laws of the calendar in his *Ḥeshev ha-Efod*, because "metrical speech remains longer in the faculty of memory."[21] Finally, Solomon ben Immanuel Dapiera explains that his Hebrew verse translation of an Arabic philosophical poem, to which we shall return, is meant to serve "only as a *mazkeret* [reminder] for students."[22]

The choice to write in verse was not entirely simple; it could, as Ibn Gabirol notes, be "constricting."[23] Another commonplace held that the formal requirements of poetry—rhyme and meter—necessarily curtailed its ability to convey truth. As Dapiera notes: "It is known to all who understand that it is not possible for any sage to speak of science in a metered poem without the meter or the rhyme constraining him to add or remove a little of what was intended."[24] Still, Jewish scholars composed, copied, and consumed poems whose primary purpose was the transmission of true knowledge. This fact suggests that, in these cases, the benefits—the mnemonic benefits—were considered to outweigh the disadvantages.

Prefatory Poems

Prefatory Hebrew poems appear before prose texts written in Hebrew, Arabic, and Aramaic. They were being composed as early as the eleventh century, often drawing on conventional features of the Arabic prose preface. Because prefatory verse has numerous functions quite unrelated to mnemonics, it is important to consider the issue closely.

For example, Moses ibn Ezra wrote an 166-line poem, beginning "Beshem el asher amar," to introduce his Arabic prose philosophical work *Maqālat al-ḥadīqā fī maʿnā al-majāz wa'l-ḥaqīqa*.[25] The prose text is divided into an initial philosophical section and a larger section on biblical metaphor that explores the Hebrew vocabulary for the parts of the human body.[26] The poem seems to have little or no mnemonic role; it serves as a versified introduction to the treatise, displaying structural similarities to the Arabic prose preface. The first words—"Be-shem el asher amar" (In the name of God who spoke")—are a version of the Arabic *basmala*, and the poem's first twenty-five or so lines, as in the standard Arabic *khutbah*, praise God in terms that foreshadow the work's themes. The poem emphasizes the contrast between the many ways that humans define God and his real indescribability, later shifting into an extended depiction of God's creation.[27] A few typical lines:

> And He extends the heavens like a curtain to speak without speech of His glory and His kingship and the living creatures of his pathways;
> Running like a slave, to fulfill the will of its Maker, and to Him to rush in fear and terror;
> He stretched it like a tent, but it was established by the breath of His mouth, and He fixed—without a hand—its clasps and loops.[28]

Written in a high literary style, discursive and studded with biblical allusions, this poem is altogether beautiful. The verse thus also functions as an advertisement for its author's virtuosity, even as it provides a preview of some of the Arabic material to come.[29] None of these roles requires that it be memorized.

Eventually, however, the prefatory poem took on a life of its own in Christian Europe and flourished in the Hebrew manuscripts of the later Middle Ages, ultimately assuming a place in the first Hebrew printed books.[30] Later poems in this mode show a distinct shift from being part of the overall work, a part that just happens to be cast in verse form, to becoming a consciously separate "voice," often engaging the contents of the book itself and/or the presumed interests of the reader. Most briefly present the title and sometimes the author. These title-poems introduce the work to come in flattering terms and in a form that incidentally offers the author a chance to display his literary skill. Ancillary benefits include the fact that the verses visually mark the beginning of the text, as a rubricated incipit does in Latin manuscripts.

A few of these poems seem to indicate, either in their headings or in their form, that they were meant to convey philosophical and/or scientific information in a shape that would be easy to commit to memory. For example, Shem Tov ibn Falaquera, who added prefatory verse to many of his works, has a sixty-one-line verse prologue to *Re'shit ḥokhmah* that explicitly provides an outline of the material to come. The header reads: "The first poem on the parts of philosophy. It is the poem called Philosophy. In it

I have recalled the general principles (*zakharti bah kelalei zeh ha-sefer*) of this book called *Re'shit ḥokhmah*."

Titled by its first line, "Tehilah le-el 'elyon bli ketz tehilato," the poem begins by noting that God has created the world, and man in it, not for the sake of God's own glory but so that man shall praise God. To praise God, man needs to strengthen that part of himself that is divine, namely, the intellect. One can then attain wisdom, or in other words, the sciences, which Falaquera sets out in their usual order: grammar, which makes for correct speech; logic, which "straightens the path of the intellect" and allows one to "distinguish truth from falsehood"; then the mathematical sciences of arithmetic, geometry, music, optics, astrology, and astronomy, and finally physics and metaphysics. Of these, physics receives the largest treatment, in five lines:

> On the science that is concerned with bodies and their natures, and their substance and their accidents and matter and its form.
> And matter without form and the first of all matter; and there is a secret in allegorizing it as "the whiteness of the sapphire stone" [Ex. 24.10; see *Guide* 1.28, 61].
> And how the sphere turns and returns over the earth and the four elements, how their motion is generated.
> And how forms are composed of them and how they return to them and the corruption and generation of what exists.
> And it investigates the cause of created beings: they are matter and form and agent and what its existence is for [i.e., its final cause].

Certainly this poem conveys why a religious reader in particular would wish to continue on to the book; controlling the reading is one of the basic functions of all prefatory poems. But this poem is also meant to present the principles of the prose treatise.

Does it? The prose begins with a discussion of why moral qualities are necessary for the study of science and then—with a digression on the origin and science of language, and on the origin of the sciences in general, that does not seem reflected in the prefatory poem—enumerates those sciences. But the order differs: music, astronomy, and optics get switched around, and mechanics, algebra, politics, law, and dialectics are omitted from the poem altogether. The book does end with a discussion of why philosophy leads to ultimate happiness, an important theme of the poem, but then concludes with a final summary, unrepresented in the poem, of Platonic and Aristotelian philosophy.

Falaquera wrote another long prologue in fifty-two lines for his *Sefer ha-ma'alot*.[31] Called "Aromem el nora' 'alilah she-bara'," it is similarly introduced by him as a poem that "recalls the general principles" of the book to come; this one hews much closer to the contents of the prose text. It presents three groups of men—prophets, scholars, and common folk—ranked according to their intellectual levels in roughly the same proportions as in the book itself. There is but cursory praise of God at the beginning, and a two-line invocation or prayer is situated at the end, but the rest of the poem is devoted to the three types. Six lines are devoted to the prophets:

> And who are the men who approach the living God? I will begin with the holy ones, they are the exalted ones.
> They are called *elohim*, they look to their creator, and bring all hidden things forth into the light.
> And when their intellect is perfected, and they know the secret of the ladder, which their forefather dreamed, and saw in an image,
> Then *shaddai* is revealed to them from above, in a vision of the night, when a deep sleep falls.
> And their souls see new events to come and what will happen to every nation and people.
> And from His spirit God thus pours out to warn Israel, his first-born, away from shame.

The prose text for its part is dry and colorless but offers actual philosophical content: metaphysics, in particular the theory of the agent intellect and its role in prophecy, presented in a series of quotations by philosophers alongside some biblical and rabbinic statements. But the closest the poem comes to addressing this material is the phrase "the intellect is perfected."

Aaron ben Elia of Nicomedia's thirteen lines for his 1346 *'Etz ḥayyim* also sketches out the contents of the work to come, far more briefly, but also more comprehensively. The poem praises the book in its last four lines and includes its title in the last line; it works well as a typical title-poem. But it also summarizes the work to come. Here too there is no one-to-one correspondence between the chapters and the lines of verse. For example, the first four lines of the poem are these:

> Men of intellect and understanding believe in the existence of God and understand His unity.
> And without a body or a faculty borne by any subject, [you should] know the glory of the One who dwells in the [high] places.

And tales of Him are knowledge and not rumor; understand them through faithful miracles.
And they are power and wisdom and life and existence, they are of His essence, without starting and stopping.[32]

The first two lines roughly match the first fifteen chapters of the book, which treat God's existence and incorporeality, and creation. The third line *might* be alluding, although very obliquely, to chapters 16 through 62, on anthropomorphism. Line four points directly to chapters 63 through 77, which are on the unity of God and his inseparable positive attributes: power, knowledge, life, will, and existence. Of the attributes dealt with in the prose treatise, will did not make it into the poem.[33] The poem thus touches only superficially on the content of the book to come, but for mnemonic purposes not much more would have been needed. The main points are listed one after the other in a form that can easily be retained.

Our last example is in an Italian manuscript from the fifteenth or sixteenth century of Moses of Salerno's (southern Italy, d. 1279) commentary on Maimonides's *Guide*. It is a thirty-seven-line poem by one Asher bar Abraham, probably the scribe, who introduces it as "rhymes built upon the twenty-five premises for the existence of God."[34] There follows a summary of the first twenty-five of the philosophical premises that appear at the beginning of book 2 of *Guide*. The first seven (and the last five) lines of the poem assert that proofs for the existence of God based on the existence and nature of the created world, in particular the heavens, are solid and well-founded. The body is made up of the twenty-five premises, one in each line.

For example, the seventh premise in the prose text states that "Everything changeable is divisible. Hence everything movable is divisible and is necessarily a body. But everything that is indivisible is not moveable; hence it will not be a body at all."[35] The verse version is close: "Does not something changeable have part[s] [and] a moving body? Without a body, it has no parts [*u-mishtaneh ha-lo be-ḥeleq guf na' / le-'ein guf ḥalaqim ne'edarim*]" The eighth premise states that "Everything that is moved owing to accident must of necessity come to rest, inasmuch as its motion is not in virtue of its essence. Hence it cannot be moved forever in that accidental motion."[36] This becomes: "And those things that move and wander owing to accident, they will come to rest, with a motion that is not eternal [*ve-ha-na'im ve-ha-nadim be-miqreh / yenuḥun be-tenu'ah bal tedarim*]\"

In these two cases, the premise is crammed into the rhyme and meter with little content lost. But these are two of the shortest premises. In the longer ones, the text is pared of explanations, examples, and proofs. For example, the lengthy seventeenth is condensed to just its first lines: "Everything that is in motion has of necessity a mover; and the mover either may be outside the moved object . . . or the mover may be in the body in motion." It becomes the following: "And every moving thing is moved from within, or externally others cause it to stray [*ve-khol noded meni'o bifenim o' / be-ḥutzah lo yeta'uhu aḥerim*]." For all the premises, there is at least one word in the verse that matches up with a key word in the prose, either in the same form or just using the same root, thereby making obvious the connection between the two.

These poems all offer similar mnemonic benefits. Asher bar Abraham's verses would enable the easy memorization of twenty-five key principles. On the other hand, none of the others presents a strict, line-by-line summary, although they do run through the highlights of the text. Falaquera's "Tehilah le-el 'elyon bli ketz tehilato" seems especially unreliable, skipping over what seem to be important sections in the prose. (Were those sections, one wonders, later additions by Falaquera?)

None of the poems offers any substantive philosophical content. But if, as seems quite possible, they are mnemonic aids for the later discursive prose material, substance would not be their purpose and would merely be redundant. Instead, they seem to offer the reader a structuring tool for mentally organizing the material that is to come. A reader might quickly (and easily) memorize the poem at the outset and then, when reading the prose, use its words to order the material in one's mind for clearer comprehension and easier recall.

Final poems

A few poems were attached to the end of philosophical prose works, where they likely also functioned to help remember the "chapter headings" of the prose text. Consider the Hebrew poem at the end of Baḥya ibn Paquda's eleventh-century Arabic *Duties of the Heart*.[37] Baḥya introduces it in Arabic with these words:

> In order to complete your direction successfully, I found it fit, O my brother, to sum up in ten Hebrew strophes the main points treated in my book. Each one indicates the theme of one chapter, in proper order and sequence. I am ending this book of mine with them in order that they may serve you as a reminder,

which, if you know them by heart, and keep them constantly in your mind and thought, day and night, when at rest or in motion, will help you to think of the contents of this book and will help you remember its principles.[38]

Three lines of the poem:

My son, unite your soul [lit. your unique one] with your Rock, by declaring the unity of the one God, your Creator.
Search and probe, and consider His marvels, and gird yourself with reason and true faith.
Fear God. Observe His statutes and His laws continually. Then your steps will not falter.[39]

These are verses explicitly meant to be memorized, to "serve as a reminder" (a *mazkeret*, in Judah ibn Tibbon's Hebrew translation)[40] of the "principles" in each chapter. Each verse corresponds to one chapter, and the verses are set in proper "order and sequence." In other words, the material is divided into manageable chunks and composed in an ordered series, with the correct order guaranteed by the acrostic of Baḥya's name in the first letters of each line. Moreover, one word in each line links directly back to the chapter's main theme. All of these are well-established mnemonic devices, a point to which we shall return.

A forty-three-line poem sums up the main themes of Meir Aldabi's fourteenth-century philosophical handbook, *Shevilei emunah*. Aldabi introduces the poem, "Be-re'shit kol yesod haven yesodkha," with this brief line, alerting the reader to the book's principles: "And I saw fit to write also these gates and to seal this book with them since it is alluded to (*ramuz*) in them." The poem begins:

At the beginning of every foundation, understand your Foundation. Investigate to find the eternal existence.
In truth, the unique One of the world exists alone. And He is eternal and His eternity is hidden.
And He created existent things and brought forth being by Himself and not through someone or something.
And He has no body or shape or form, and no likeness or quality or quantity.
And His attributes will never change Him and [He displays] no [joy] and no anger or wrath.
And He is one and not of a species or of an enumeration; species does not enter into calculation, nor does "what."
And they—all created things—depend on Him. And the world hangs on nothing.[41]

Without corresponding perfectly to the ten chapters of the book, though it is quite close, the poem picks out Aldabi's most important doctrinal points, running through such topics as God's existence, oneness, and eternity, creation ex nihilo, incorporeality, and providence. It then turns to the names of God, the eternity of the natural order, the miraculous nature of the Torah, the timing of Jewish weeks and holidays, types of exegesis, free will, sacrifices, the soul, the commandments, reward and punishment, Moses, written and oral Torah, levels of revelation, Jerusalem, the destruction of the Temple, redemption, and the resurrection of the dead.

One last example of a concluding poem with an evidently mnemonic function is the one that ends David ibn Shushan's translation/abbreviation of Aristotle's works.[42] Each of the eleven lines alludes more or less directly to one of the Aristotelian books that make up Ibn Shushan's work in terms that are relevant to a general topic in each book. The first two lines, for example, are as follows:

> Listen, lord, give ear; *I heard You with my ears* [Job 42:5] and trust in Your Torah, a hidden creation in Your world.
>
> See, see their praise, the heavens and the earth; their motion and their orbiting in a straight line in their perfection.

The first line uses the root *shin mem ʿayin* three times, a clever allusion to the Hebrew title of Aristotle's *Physics*, while the second weaves in the Hebrew title for *On the Heavens*. This poem, too, is clearly constructed as a mnemonic. It makes no attempt to do anything other than pun on the Hebrew titles of the Aristotelian books in rhythmic, internally rhymed lines. Because of a peculiarity of the meter, which makes each half line begin with the syllables short-long-short-long, several lines simply repeat the first word: see, see (*re'eh, re'eh*), gaze, gaze (*ḥazeh, ḥazeh*), or very, very (*me'od, me'od*).[43]

Perhaps an instructive comparison is to be found in one of the two undated mnemonic poems (not philosophical) published at the end of Falaquera's *Sefer ha-Mevaqqesh*.[44] These are explicitly presented as mnemonic aides, called *simanim*, and are meant to help remember the different individuals interviewed by the seeker of the title in his search for the best path to ultimate felicity. The second of these, for example, is seven independently rhymed couplets that connect each topic to a particular individual, some from the Bible—wealth is Ahav, strength is Samson and Yoav, craft is Bezalel, and so on—and others from the secular world. For medicine, the names to remember are Hippocrates and Galen; for geometry, Euclid; and for astronomy, al-Battani. Once one has memorized the poem and the order of these individuals is fixed in the mind, recalling the contents of the book, in whatever detail necessary, is made far easier.[45]

"Study" Poems

In the poems discussed so far, it is fair to assume that composition of the prose text preceded any verse supplement. The opposite is the case for two lengthy didactic poems on the subject of philosophy, each of which was written as an independent work but then accreted one or more prose commentaries.[46] Didactic verse is not precisely the same thing as mnemonic verse, although didactic verse intended to be memorized should display some of the same features.[47] Thomas Haye has noted that, while mnemonic verse usually offers just isolated bits of knowledge, didactic verse tends to present a systematic and progressive treatment of a particular topic.[48]

The first is *Battei ha-nefesh ve-ha-leḥashim* by Levi ben Abraham of Villefranche-de-Conflent. This 1,846-line poem, completed in 1276, treats some of the same issues that would appear later in the author's prose philosophical work *Livyat ḥen*, though not in the same order or in precisely the same fashion.[49] *Battei ha-nefesh ve-ha-leḥashim* has its own preface, in rhymed prose, and covers the following topics: improvement of the moral qualities, logic, the account of creation, the soul and its faculties, prophecy, the account of the chariot, number and measurement, astronomy and astrology, physics, and metaphysics.[50] Knotty and allusive, the poem draws on the Bible and Talmud and, at least in the section on creation published by Haim Kreisel, offers a thoroughgoing philosophical exegesis of the biblical narrative. It is opaque enough to justify several subsequent commentaries by the author and eventually three others, attempting to explain it.

The second independent philosophical poem really counts as two, as it is extant in both an Arabic and a Hebrew version. Seventy lines long, it was originally written in Arabic by an otherwise unknown Jew, Mūsā ibn Tubi of Seville, and titled *Al-sabʿīnīya* (i.e., a poem in seventy *baits*). As noted earlier, it was translated into Hebrew by Solomon ben Immanuel Dapiera, who called his version *Battei ha-nefesh* (Verses on the soul).[51] The poem opens with the usual argument that—the intellect being the best part of man, and the light of reason purifying man from his base desires—study and learning will lead to ultimate felicity. Seven sciences must be studied: religion, medicine, physics, and metaphysics, but before them logic, astronomy, and geometry. More admonitions about study and a comment about the form of the poem are followed by a philosophical section (lines 46–52) describing what the oneness of God means and that God is the cause and mover of everything. Here are two of its six lines, from the Hebrew:

> Is not that which turns [i.e., the heavens] one? And existence [is] one. Therefore God is one, [the result of] the two premises.
> Who wishes to unify [God] should contemplate [lit. "join"] the subject of one; he denies God who denies His oneness.[52]

From here the poem turns to lists, an ancient mnemonic technique: the two principles of generation and corruption; the three local movements, three worlds, three judges; four elements; five beginnings; six directions, six kinds of motion; seven planets and seven spheres, seven climates and seven metals, the influence of the moon on the seventh day; and so on. This poem, too, is overly compressed and opaque, perhaps even more so than Levi ben Abraham's, and it also acquired a commentary, provided in this case by Dapiera, its Hebrew translator.

These stand-alone philosophical poems are striking in their difficulty.[53] Compression of content makes sense when there is a discursive prose work attached to the verse; if there is none, the verse simply becomes difficult. However, difficulty can be a virtue in certain contexts. For example, Profayt Duran recommends studying texts that, in addition to containing "many general principles together with concision," are "full of rhetorical language and require great investigation and study."[54] We find similar advice in a micro-guide for versification found in two late manuscripts containing Hebrew philosophical and scientific texts. The language of a poem should be *qal ve-tzaḥ* (simple and pure) and pleasurable, we are told, because pleasure enables better understanding. More to the point, the poem's meaning should not be immediately apparent to the reader; one should be obliged to study it carefully, because "many things are contributed by this."[55] As Carruthers reports, the fourteenth-century Giovanni Boccaccio noted that "anything gained through hard work is sweeter than something done without effort; content expressed in plain style delights us but passes casually through our memory."[56] The more difficult the text, then, the more memorable the information extracted from it.

I cannot conclude this section without mentioning in passing the 4,800 lines of *Miqdash me'at*, written in 1415–1416 by Moses ben Isaac da Rieti.[57]

Miqdash me'at is divided into three sections, each representing a different part of the Temple in Jerusalem. The first, five cantos long, is called the "Ulam," or antechamber, and primarily deals with the "external" sciences. The second section of eight cantos, called the "Heikhal," or hall, encompasses Jewish sacred knowledge, while the third section, the "Dvir," the innermost chamber, may have contained esoteric knowledge (it is not extant). Only in the third through fifth cantos of the "Ulam" do we have a sustained presentation of substantive philosophical content: the third canto is an encyclopedic overview of all the sciences, drawn primarily from Al-Farabi's *The Book of the Enumeration of the Sciences* by way of an early fourteenth-century Hebrew translation. The fourth summarizes Porphyry's *Isagoge*, adding some comments by Gersonides. And the fifth restates Aristotle's *Categories* in verse.

Here too, in the introduction, Rieti calls *Miqdash me'at* "a book of the sciences / established by the ancients,"[58] meant for one who has already studied the material:

> The man who has already gotten wisdom
> can use it as an aid to memory [*zikaron*]
> to light his treasury, preserve the shapes therein.
>
> From his own well he first draws wisdom's waters,
> then turns to me to contemplate my verse,
> the parables I've written and their sense.[59]

As we suspected was the case for our previous poems, once a student has done extensive reading, he can turn to verse for reminders. Although space does not permit a full analysis of *Miqdash me'at*, I will note that the form is entirely different from any of the other poems discussed here. *Miqdash me'at* was composed in terza rima, a poetic form employed most famously a century earlier by Dante in his *Divine Comedy*. The lines here are ten syllables long, and the rhyme scheme is aba bcb cdc, and so forth; Arabic quantitative metrics are abandoned altogether.[60]

Mnemonic Techniques

Texts composed as mnemonic aids took on characteristic forms. This was true across languages. For example, in Latin, mnemonic devices can include alliteration, the use of leonine verse (i.e., each line usually contains an internal rhyme), end rhymes with additional internal rhymes, and numbered lists.[61] All of these features appear prominently in our poems, especially the presence of (mostly unnumbered) lists of either the main points, the principles of the book to come, or a series of points of special importance for understanding the prose text.

In general, brevity is an important mnemonic consideration, but only Baḥya's poem, at ten lines, would seem at first glance to qualify. Yet Levi ben Abraham calls his poem, one of the longest, "a short composition including the roots of science and their principles."[62] He has a point if what is important is the brevity of the poetry with respect to the amount of information it conveys. The poems that accompany a prose work are certainly *relatively* brief, extracting general principles and rendering them compactly in verse. As for the two stand-alone versifications of philosophical material, they display a different kind of brevity, being sometimes so compressed and obscure as to necessitate prose explication.

After brevity, another widespread technique involves the subdivision of discursive material into manageable bits, which are then put in order. "What assists memory the most? Division and composition; for order serves memory powerfully,"[63] as one Latin author puts it, and matters are similar in Arabic literary traditions.[64] Following the latter, Maimonides employs *fuṣūl*, short apodictic sayings, for easy memorization. He writes in his introduction to the *Fuṣūl Mūsā* that "works composed in the form of aphorisms are undoubtedly easy to retain."[65]

Most of our poems eschew enjambment. In this respect, they do not differ from most medieval Hebrew poems, but the practice is especially useful here. Baḥya explicitly notes that each separate verse refers to one specific chapter. Asher ben Abraham's poem lists the twenty-five Maimonidean premises in order, one per line.[66] Each line thus functions mnemonically as an aphorism: a brief, self-contained expression of an idea. (Baḥya and Aldabi further facilitate memorization by employing a syntactical pause that corresponds to the caesura between hemistichs, breaking the line up even more.) For these authors, each line is thus both semantically and—through alliteration, assonance, and internal rhyme—acoustically unified. The sounds emphasize each line's independence from the others, as does the internal echo and reecho of sounds within each line.

As for ordering, there is little evidence of a system, such as an alphabetical acrostic—perhaps one constraint too many. Baḥya does employ an acrostic of his name and Musa ibn Tubi relies on serially numbered lists. But the others display no obvious schema. In Meir Aldabi's poem, strikingly, the ends of lines have rhymes or near-rhymes involving not just the ultimate syllable but also the penultimate—for example, "ve-lo mah" and "beli mah," or "kamah" and "ḥamah." These effects serve to link the lines in pairs or, occasionally, triplets. Repetition can sometimes provide structure. In Falaquera's "Tehila le-el nora," we find the word *ḥokhmah* repeated at the inception of every new subject (except grammar): the science of logic, the "sciences" of mathematical fields, the science concerned with bodies, the science concerned with the incorporeal intellect. The word is repeated twice in the first and last lines of the section, as though to mark its beginning and end.

Recall Solomon ibn Gabirol's grammatical poem, divided, as he says, into ten sections, with verses that follow each other like beads on a necklace—or like a bordered garden containing many species of plants, flowers, and trees.

> Therefore I have divided it into ten divisions and I have made for it an edging like a fence.
> Phrase upon phrase and rhyme upon rhyme like pearls upon a necklet.
> It is like a garden bed which appears with every color, and every eye will be aroused.
> Those who walk in it will find varieties of myrtle, camphor, and lily and the boughs of trees.
> I have called it *ʿanaq* as I have given it as a gift to man; also, like a necklace I have placed [it] upon a throat.

One might be permitted to surmise that these two images—of a bordered garden and a necklace—serve a particular mnemonic function in introducing a work on Hebrew grammar. The comparison of a qasida with a necklace was certainly a ubiquitous trope, as was the association of books with gardens. An enclosed garden could serve as an ideal mental structure in which a student might "plant" an ordered series of ideas. A necklace made up of different precious stones could similarly provide a mental chain on which to hang rules of speech. Is Ibn Gabirol here silently supplying the means to facilitate a mastery of Hebrew's grammatical principles?

Stetkevych has written along such lines with respect to the later *badīʿīya* poems, in the process differentiating her approach from Mary Carruthers's notion of "'memorial structures' . . . devised by the memorizer to commit material to memory." To Stetkevych, rather, "*the poetic work itself* serves as a memorial structure, and further, perhaps more precisely, can be understood in terms of the medieval catena, or 'chain'" (emphasis added).[67] Structurally speaking, then, the verse form offers numerous mnemonic benefits, allowing material to be divided up into a series of independent units and presenting this material in clear, straightforward language and, ultimately, ordering the chain of verses into the form of a poem.

So much for brevity, division, and order. What about rhyme and meter?[68] The usual poetic form used in Arabic for didactic and mnemonic poetry was the *muzdawij*, or *qaṣīda muzdawija*, which employed rhyming hemistichs, structurally similar to rhymed couplets.[69] These were popular from the eighth century on—see the early *Urjūza fi-l-ḥudūd* (Poem on the terms) by Al-Fazari (ca. 770–853), of which only a few lines remain[70]—but were considered far inferior to true poetry.[71] In Hebrew poems, however, the monorhymed qasida was preferred.

Not surprisingly, many employ the most common meter, *merubbeh*. The exceptions include Falaquera's "Tehilah le-el 'elyon," composed in the also-popular *arokh*. Falaquera's "Aromem el nora' 'alilah" and the Hebrew translation by Dapiera adopt what's usually called "Dunash's meter." The poem at the end of David ibn Shushan's abbreviation of Aristotle's works is in a version of *marnin* that gives a kind of stuttering effect—the syllables short-long-short-long—at the beginning of each line. And the Arabic poem by Mūsā ibn Tubi is written in a version of the Arabic meter *ramal*, which H. Hirschfeld suggests he took from Hebrew and not Arabic models.[72]

Strikingly, Dunash's meter is associated with a particular rhyme scheme. The line is broken into four parts rather than the more common two, and the first three parts rhyme. Each line thus has three internal rhymes plus the end rhyme that functions as a kind of ground note or continuo: aaax, bbbx, cccx, and so forth. Two of the Hebrew poems, plus Musa ibn Tubi's Arabic poem, use this rhyme scheme. In addition, the *arokh* meter used by another two of our poems likewise breaks the lines into four parts, and the poets can deploy three internal rhymes or half rhymes as often as they wish, which is relatively often.[73] The poem at the end of David ibn Shushan's abbreviation of Aristotle's works is something of an outlier; it is a *muzdawij* poem in which each pair of hemistichs makes a couplet, but each line is further broken into four sections, each with an internal rhyme: thus, four internal rhymes but no linked end rhyme.

It cannot be entirely a coincidence that, despite the admittedly small size of our sample, internal rhymes appear so commonly.[74] Note that the guide for versification mentioned above also directs the versifier that "each verse must be internally rhymed."[75] The technique, like the general use of alliteration, serves to unify each line acoustically, as well as to emphasize the repeating rhythm of meters that break the line into four equal portions.

Rhetorical Devices

So far, we have been considering mechanics; what about aesthetics? Sweetness is consistently singled out as one of the virtues of verse, but here sweetness cannot be said to come from beauty of language. High poetic diction and rhetorical devices have, for the most part, been discarded in favor of treating straightforward content in simple declarative statements.

The case of Moses ibn Ezra's "Be-shem el amar" is particularly instructive as a counterexample; this poem is meant to be a virtuosic performance and is to be considered neither a mnemonic poem nor even a verse summary. For the others, pleasure, if there is any to be had, is evidently to be derived from the rhymes, the extensive alliteration and assonance, and the repetitive, rhythmic meters so many of them use. Notably, these are all *aural* markers, shaping the way the verse is heard by the ear more than how it is absorbed mentally.[76] Carruthers has noted that the term *sweetness* refers to "a definable sensory phenomenon";[77] similarly, as Ross Brann has noted, Judah Halevi in his "Treatise on Hebrew Meters" evaluates the various quantitative meters by the criterion of "what is of lovely tastefulness that transports the natural disposition and *delights the ear*" (emphasis added)[78]—singling out, among others, Dunash's meter and *ha-mitkarev*.[79] The rhythmic patterns of metrical lines would then provide a distinctly sensory pleasure. Dapiera agrees: "I have decided to speak these words in a metered poem so that they will be pleasant to those who hear them and this is because there is nothing more pleasant to the sense of hearing than a metered poem in pure language."[80] How then were these poems and their sweetness experienced? Dapiera refers to "the sense of hearing." Were the poems read or sung aloud or under the breath by those reading them? In the Latin world, as Walter Ong has emphasized, "Manuscripts were commonly read aloud or *sotto voce* even when the reader was alone."[81] If prose was read audibly, presumably the verses were, too. Duran, in *Ma'aseh Efod*, does in fact address the memory-enhancing qualities of chanting aloud. Reading the Hebrew Bible, he writes, should be done first of all "aloud and with perceptible speech. In other words, one should hear what comes out of the mouth."[82] One should also study with "song," Duran writes, referring to biblical cantillation. But consider his discussion of why song is beneficial for study:

> The eighth way, and this is more particular to Scripture, is that you should engage in it with song and melody because, while this is among those things that increase desire and love for engaging in it because of the sweetness of the song that awakens the faculties and strengthens them, it is also among those things that strengthen the faculty of memory. This is because of what happens when the phrase is sung, from the length of time it takes to enunciate the vowels, and from the rests and pauses that enter into it. Along with this, understanding is also perfected, and so is intent concentration on the phrase because of the length of time it takes to sing it. And that is the reason one prays in the synagogue with pleasant voices and sweetness, so that intentness on prayer is perfected.[83]

Conceding that this technique is *more* particular to scripture, Duran seems to suggest that one might chant or sing other texts as well. Might our poetic verses, then, have been chanted melodically aloud by their readers?

Solomon Dapiera's introduction offers some support for this conjecture. Claiming, as was the trope, that the work was written at the request of friends, he asserts that these friends had heard him singing the poem. Might he have been performing it in company on a religious holiday, or were they simply studying together? Either possibility is delightful to imagine. "Therefore, my brothers and friends—who heard me sing this song, as a song, 'in the night when a holy solemnity is kept' [Isa. 30:29]—aroused me to explain it according to my intention [and according to] the intention of the first poet, and I agreed to fulfill their desire."[84] If we take these words at face value, it seems that Dapiera first translated the Arabic poem into Hebrew, presumably for himself, at some point was singing it, and his friends heard and asked for an explanation.

Conclusion

Verse summaries, as we have seen, come in two forms—both, it seems, meant to aid in the recall of more detailed information. The short poems that accrete to a prose text are simple in language and concepts and provide an easy mental structure for the immediate apprehension and later recall of the prose text. Requiring proximity to the material to be recalled, they appear in manuscripts either before or after the relevant text.

The longer, stand-alone poems were probably used as learning aids; the allusiveness of the language requires careful study, making the material itself more memorable. While they might summarize information that can be found in more detail elsewhere, these were transmitted as independent works in the manuscripts. The extant examples of philosophical poems of this type explicitly claim to be intended as a *mazkeret*, a reminder, presumably to be used to recall the contents and material that can be mentally associated with the verses.

The poems examined here constitute a category rarely treated in the wider context of medieval literature, and even more rarely within the narrower field of medieval Hebrew literature. But they offer an unusual perspective on the multifarious roles poetry played in the lives of educated medieval Jews. As we have conjectured, it appears possible that melody of some sort was used to vocalize the poems that appear in philosophical (and other) manuscripts as prologues, as mnemonic aids, as concluding summaries, and even as independent verses to be studied at great length. But what is perhaps most striking is that these poems can often be found inserted in-between prose treatises or scribbled into the margins or flyleaves, suggesting that they had significant meaning not only for their authors but for the later scribes/owners of the manuscripts.

In addition to the many intricately worked compositions such Jews would encounter in their regular prayer routine, poetry served them as a vehicle of knowledge. They would read, and perhaps chant, the poetic prologues that open so many medieval Hebrew prose texts. They might study, and some might teach, verse compositions conveying information and instruction concerning sacred or secular topics, such as the principles of medicine, astronomy, philosophy, or logic. Disentangling questions regarding the composition of poetry from questions about its consumption thus has the potential to illuminate its role from an unfamiliar angle, opening new vistas onto the culture of reading.

Notes

1. Michael Chamberlain, *Knowledge and Social Practice in Medieval Damascus, 1190–1350* (Cambridge: Cambridge University Press, 1994), 146–47; Jonathan Porter Berkey, *The Transmission of Knowledge in Medieval Cairo* (Princeton, NJ: Princeton University Press, 1992), 28. See also Walter J. Ong, "Orality, Literacy, and Medieval Textualization," *New Literary History* 16 (1984): 1–12.

2. Sonja Brentjes, "Teaching the Mathematical Sciences in Islamic Societies Eighth–Seventeenth Centuries" in *Handbook on the History of Mathematics Education*, ed. A. Karp

and G. Schubring (New York: Springer, 2014), 85–107; Geert Jan van Gelder, "Arabic Didactic Verse," in *Centres of Learning: Learning and Location in Pre-Modern Europe and the Near East*, ed. J. W. Drijvers and A. A. MacDonald (Leiden: Brill, 1995), 103–17.

3. Jan M. Ziolkowski, "From Didactic Poetry to Bestselling Textbooks," in *Calliope's Classroom: Studies in Didactic Poetry from Antiquity to the Renaissance*, ed. A. Harder, A. A. MacDonald, and G. J. Reinink (Leuven: Peeters, 2007), 221–40.

4. There are examples of versified halakhic material—poems on the laws of shehitah, piyyutim presenting the laws of Passover, versifications of Talmudic tractates, azharot, poems to remember the order of the books of the Mishnah, and so on; a thorough study of the historical context and mnemonic qualities of these poems has not yet been done.

5. See, for example, Michael D. Swartz and Joseph Yahalom, *Avodah: An Anthology of Ancient Poetry for Yom Kippur* (University Park: Penn State University Press, 2004); also Josefina Rodríguez-Arribas, "Science in Poetic Contexts: Astronomy and Astrology in the Hebrew Poetry of Sepharad," *Miscelánea de Estudios Árabes y Hebraicos* 59 (2010): 167–202 [Hebrew].

6. Explicit treatments of memory often focus on medical aspects. Gerrit Bos, "Jewish Traditions on Strengthening Memory and Leone Modena's Evaluation," *Jewish Studies Quarterly* 2 (1995): 39–58.

7. Also in the fifteenth century, we have a four-page fragment of an *aljamiado*, Art of Memory. James W. Nelson Novoa, "A Sephardic Art of Memory," in *Ars Reminiscendi: Mind and Memory in Renaissance Culture*, ed. D. Beecher and G. Williams (Toronto: Centre for Reformation and Renaissance Studies, 2009), 85–104. See Judah Messer Leon, *Sefer Nofet Tzufim*, book 1, ch. 13: "Memory"; David Margalit, "On Memory: Concerning Lev ha-Arye by Rabbi Judah Aryeh Modena," *Korot* 5 (1975): 759–772; Giuseppe Sermoneta, "Aspetti del pensiero modern nell'Ebraismo Italiano tra Rinascimento e età Baroca," *Italia Judaica Gli Ebrei in Italia tra Rinascimento e Età Barocca*, 17–35 (Rome, 1986); Kalman Bland, "A Jewish Theory of Jewish Visual Culture: Leon Modena's Concept of Image and Their Effect on Locative Memory," *Ars Judaica* 5 (2009): 59–66.

8. See, for example, *Takhyīl: The Imaginary in Classical Arabic Poetics*, ed. M. Hammond & G. J. H. van Gelder (Cambridge: Gibb Memorial Trust, 2008); Deborah Black, *Logic and Aristotle's Rhetoric and Poetics in Medieval Arabic Philosophy* (Leiden: Brill, 1990); Salim Kemal, *The Poetics of Alfarabi and Avicenna* (Leiden: Brill, 1991); Salim Kemal, *The Philosophical Poetics of Alfarabi, Avicenna and Averroës: The Aristotelian Reception* (London: Routledge Curzon, 2003).

9. Averroes, Commentary on *Cantica*, cited in Charles Burnett, "Learned Knowledge of Arabic Poetry, Rhymed Prose, and Didactic Verse from Petrus Alfonsi to Petrarch," in *Poetry and Philosophy in the Middle Ages*, ed. J. Marenbon (Leiden: Brill, 2001), 29–53, 46–47.

10. *Glossa Admirantes* to Alexander de Villa Dei's *Doctrinale*, in Greti Dinkova-Bruun, "The Verse Bible as Aide-mémoire," in *The Making of Memory in the Middle Ages*, ed. Lucie Doležalovà (Leiden: Brill, 2010), 115–31, 115, n. 1.

11. Dinkova-Bruun, "The Verse Bible as Aide-mémoire," 115; Ziolkowski, "From Didactic Poetry to Bestselling Textbooks," 221–44, 229.

12. See Mary Carruthers, *The Book of Memory*, 2nd ed. (Cambridge: Cambridge University Press, 2008); *The Medieval Craft of Memory: An Anthology of Texts and Pictures*, ed. Jan Ziolkowski and Mary Carruthers (Philadelphia: University of Pennsylvania Press, 2002); Mary Carruthers, *The Craft of Thought: Rhetoric, Meditation, and the Making of Images, 400–1200* (Cambridge: Cambridge University Press, 1998).

13. Dinkova-Bruun, "Verse Bible as Aide-mémoire," 124.

14. Suzanne Pinckney Stetkevych, "From Jāhiliyyah to Badīciyyah: Orality, Literacy, and the Transformations of Rhetoric in Arabic Poetry," *Oral Tradition*, 25, no. 1 (2010): 211–30.

15. Stetkevych, "From Jāhiliyyah to Badīciyyah," 212.

16. Stetkevych, "From Jāhiliyyah to Badīciyyah," 214.

17. Angel Saenz-Badillos, "El *'Anaq*, poema lingüístico de Selomoh ibn Gabirol," *Miscelánea de Estudios Árabes y Hebraicos* 29 (1980): 5–28.

18. Moses ibn Ezra, *Kitab al-Muḥāḍara wal-Mudhākara*, ed. and trans. Abraham S. Halkin (Jerusalem: Mekize Nirdamim, 1975), 14b, 27 [Hebrew].

19. Shem Tov ben Joseph Falaquera, *Iggeret Battei Hanhagat ha-Guf ve-ha-Nefesh*, ed. S. Muntner (Jerusalem 1950); Encarnación Varela Moreno, *Shem Tov ibn Falaquera, Versos para la sana conducción del Cuerpo. Versos para la conducción del Alma* (Granada, 1986).

20. Profayt Duran, *Ma'aseh Efod*, ed. J. Friedländer and J. Kohn (Vienna, 1865), 40.

21. Duran, *Ma'aseh Efod* (German section), 43–44.

22. Solomon ben Immanuel Dapiera, *Battei ha-Nefesh*, ed. and trans. (from the Arabic) by H. Hirschfeld (London: Luzac and Co., 1894), 41, 57.

23. Saenz-Badillos, "*El 'Anaq*, poema lingüístico de Selomoh ibn Gabirol," 5–28.

24. Dapiera, *Battei ha-Nefesh*, 26–27.

25. Moshe ibn Ezra, *Shirei Ḥol*, vol. 2, ed. H. Brody (Jerusalem, 1942), 237–245. *Maqālat al-ḥadīqā* also has a prose preface in Arabic with its own *hamdala* and *khutbah*.

26. See also Dan Pagis, *Secular Poetry and Poetic Theory: Moses ibn Ezra and His Contemporaries* (Jerusalem: Mosad Bialik, 1970), 248–52 [Hebrew]; Adena Tanenbaum, *The Contemplative Soul: Hebrew Poetry and Philosophical Theory in Medieval Spain* (Leiden: Brill, 2002), 144n48; and ibid., "Nine Spheres or Ten? A Medieval Gloss on Moses ibn Ezra's 'Be-Shem El Asher Amar,'" *Journal of Jewish Studies* 47 (1996): 294–310.

27. See Tanenbaum, "Nine Spheres or Ten?"

28. Ibn Ezra, *Shirei Hol*, 238, lines 24–32.

29. See Samuel ha-Nagid, *Hilkhata Gavrata*: for the poem, see Samuel ha-Nagid, *Diwan: Ben tehillim*, ed. Dov Jarden (Jerusalem: Hebrew Union College, 1996), 89–95; for extant quotations from the prose, see Samuel ha-Nagid, *Sefer hilkhot ha-nagid*, ed. M. Margaliot (Jerusalem, Keren Yehudah, 1962).

30. See Maud Kozodoy, "Prefatory Poems and the Reception of the *Guide of the Perplexed*," *Jewish Quarterly Review* 103, no. 3 (2016): 257–82.

31. *Sefer ha-Ma'alot*, ed. L. Venetianer (Berlin, 1894).

32. Aaron ben Elia of Nicomedia, *'Etz Ḥayyim: Ahron ben Elia's aus Nikomedien des Karäers System der Religionsphilosophie*, ed. Franz Delitzsch (Leipzig: J. A. Barth, 1841).

33. Aaron ben Elia, *'Etz Ḥayyim*.

34. Cambridge MS add. 672, ff. 139–140, Italy fifteenth to sixteenth centuries. It is written in the same meter and uses the same end rhyme as Levi ben Abraham's poem, discussed below. Its first line is: מעידים על כבוד אלי ברואיו ואותותינו ועדיו היצורים. For the author, see also, NY, Jewish Theological Seminary of America, 80.

35. Guide 2, introduction, second part, 236.

36. Guide 2, introduction, second part, 236.

37. Baḥya ben Joseph ibn Pakuda, *The Book of Direction to the Duties of the Heart*, ed. and trans., M. Mansoor (London: Routledge & Kegan, 1973), 447.

38. Ibn Paquda, *Duties of the Heart*, 445–46.

39. Translated by David Goldstein, in Baḥya ibn Paquda, *The Book of Direction*, 447–48.

40. This term also appears in a number of manuscripts, usually referring to a list, sometimes of books. Jewish National and University Library 8°3739, f. 215v (fourteenth- to fifteenth-century Sephardi hand: a list of *shtarot*, with the names of debtors); Vatican Urbinati ebr. 32, beg. (fourteenth-century Italy: "sections" of books); Munich BS hebr. 510/15h (fifteenth- to sixteenth-century Sephardi hand, books); geniza fragment TS NS 329.94 (fifteenth- to sixteenth-century Mizrahi hand, books); Vatican ebr. 107 (1438–1440, Provencal hand: books); Munich BS hebr. 244, beg. (1438, Sephardi hand: [philosophical] works copied in the "*quntresim*").

41. Meir Aldabi, *Shevile emunah* (Warsaw, 1886–1887). See also Resianne Fontaine, "An Unexpected Source of Meir Aldabi's Shevile Emunah," *Zutot* 4 (2004): 96–100.

42. Oxford Bodleian MS Canonici Or. 7, ff. 210v, fifteenth- to sixteenth-century Sephardi hand. The text is corrupt in places. Each hemistich is copied out separately, in a column, so the fact that some of them were clearly lost in transmission is not evident from a cursory glance.

שמע גביר האזנך [לְ]שֵׁמַע אֹזֶן שְׁמַעְתִּיךָ / והאמן בתורתך חדוש נעלם בעולמך
ראה ראה בהלולם השמים והעולם / תנועתם וגלגולם דרך ישר במכלולם
בנה יסוד והוסד על הויה וההפסד
בלי כלות אחת לצאת זאת היא באה והיא מונאת
חזה חזה בחזיונות רעם רעיון לרעיונות / דמה דמות לדמיונות מופתים אותות ועליונות
ואין לך להנפש עם זן מוליד וגם נפש / הלא בטיט כמו רפש זולת השכל בטוב נפש
עלי דבש בפי יוחש ספר החוש והמוחש / נציר נציר לכל ישך ראשך דמיון והוא נחש
ואין ומה חכם יוש[ה] אם לא הבין ולא נ[ס]ה / לקרוא בשם שמו נש[ה] ספר שינה ויקיצה
מאד מאד בך תשמור דבור זכור וגם שמור / זכור שמור ודע לאמר ריח רוחי כריח מור
מנה מנה בסדורם אורך חיים וקצורם / לכל יצור ואפ הורם מעון [ממ] שפחת רם
פנה זמן בלי שהות ככלית טבע וכאלהות

43. See also versifications of Maimonides's thirteen principles of faith: Alexander Marx, "A List of Poems on the Articles of the Creed," *Jewish Quarterly Review* 9 (1919): 305–36.

44. *Sefer ha-mevaqqesh*, ed. M. Tamah (Hague, 1778), 104.

45. See also diagrams of key points: Vat. BA ebr. 260, f. 81v; Vat. BA ebr. 107, f. 110v; Vat. BA ebr. 353, 56r; Paris BNF 1201, 61r; Paris 1118, f. 2r; Oxford Bodleian Opp. 586, flyleaf.

46. See also medical poems with commentaries: the Hebrew translation of Ibn Sīna's *Urjūza* by Solomon ibn Ayyub, for example.

47. See Ziolkowski, "From Didactic Poetry to Bestselling Textbooks," 221–40.

48. Thomas Haye, *Das lateinische Lehrgedicht im Mittelalter* (Leiden: Brill, 1997), 258.

49. Levi ben Avraham, *Livyat Ḥen*, ed. H. Kreisel (Jerusalem: World Union of Jewish Studies, 2004), 5.

50. Ben Avraham, *Livyat Ḥen*, 4.

51. See Isaiah 3:20. There was evidently some association of the phrase with the genre of didactic poetry. See Joseph ibn Zabara's medical poem, Estori ha-Parhi's ethical poem, and Falaquera's ethical and medical poems; there are ethical poems with other titles, of course: *Musar haskel*, attributed to Hai Gaon; *Qe'arat Kesef* by Joseph Ezovi; *Sheqel ha-Qodesh* by Joseph Kimhi.

52. Dapiera, *Battei ha-Nefesh*, 43.

53. Moses ibn Ezra also provided a lengthy final Hebrew poem, *Eleikhem emunim*, for his Arabic work on rhetoric, introduced in these words: "I have decided to attach a *qasida* to this treatise, a part of whose verses includes all the chapters mentioned in it on the modes of rhetoric, so that you will find it in it [the poem], and you will recognize [them] in it." This

poem gives examples of, or rather models in its own lines, the rhetorical devices that Ibn Ezra describes in the final section of his book. Moses ibn Ezra, *Kitab al-muḥāḍara wal-mudhākara*, ed. and trans. Abraham S. Halkin (Jerusalem: Mekize Nirdamim, 1975), 302–9, 303.

54. Duran, *Ma'aseh Efod*, 18.

55. MS BN Paris héb 1005, f. 28r, also found in Rouen BM Or. 13.

56. Mary Carruthers, *The Experience of Beauty in the Middle Ages* (Oxford: Oxford University Press, 2013), 64.

57. Alessandro Guetta, "Moses da Rieti and His *Miqdash Me'at*," *Prooftexts* 23 (Winter 2003): 4–17.

58. "I whet my intellect and brace myself / to make a book out of the sciences / established by the ancients and arranged / to be their monument [*mishmeret*] after their death." Moses da Rieti, "The Little Temple," trans. Raymond P. Scheindlin, *Prooftexts* 23 (Winter 2003): 25–63, 29.

59. Da Rieti, "Little Temple," 41.

60. Devora Bregman, "A Note on the Style and Prosody of *Miqdash Me'at*," *Prooftexts* 23 (Winter 2003): 18–24.

61. Anna Maria Busse Berger, *Medieval Music and the Art of Memory* (Berkeley: University of California Press, 2005), 100.

62. Israel Davidson, "L'Introduction de Lévi ben Abraham a son encyclopédie poétique," *Revue des études juives* 105 (1940): 80–94.

63. Fortunatianus, Artis rhetoricae libri, 3, 13, in Carruthers and Ziolkowski, *Medieval Craft of Memory*, 295–97.

64. For the Arabic tradition of medical *fusūl*, see Rosa Kuhne Brabant, "Algunos aspectos de la literature didactica entre los médicos árabes," *Actas de las II Jornadas de Cultura Arabe e Islamica (1980)* (Madrid, 1985), 273–80, 274–75; Y. Tzvi Langermann, "Fusūl Mūsā, or On Maimonides' Method of Composition," *Maimonidean Studies* 5 (2000): 325–44.

65. Maimonides, *Medical Aphorisms: Treatises 1–5*, trans. G. Bos (Provo, UT: Brigham Young University Press, 2004), 1, 3–4. Maimonides's aversion to secular poetry is well-known, but he did write prefatory verse to at least three of his own works, including the *Guide*, to which he also added a concluding poem.

66. There are some irregularities: premise 11 gets two lines instead of one, while premise 21 appears to be missing altogether.

67. Stetkevych, "From Jāhiliyyah to Badīciyyah, 224.

68.

Baḥya ibn Paquda

Beni yaḥed yeḥidatkha --˘----˘---˘ /--˘----˘---˘

בני יחד יחידתך לצורך / ביחדך לאל אחד יצרך

Shem Tov ibn Falaquera

Tehilah le-el 'elyon ---˘--˘ /---˘--˘ /---˘--˘ /---˘--˘

ושבח לראש כל ראש / ואדון לכל אדון / ועלה לכל הווה / ונצחו וסבתו

Aromem el nora' /-----˘/-----˘/-----˘/-----˘

ארומם אל נורא / עלילה שברא / ברוחו כל נברא / ושפרה שמימה

David ibn Shushan?

/---˘---˘/---˘-˘-˘/---˘---˘/---˘-˘-˘

שמע גביר האזנך [לְ]שֵׁמַע אֹזֶן שְׁמַעְתִּיךָ / והאמן בתורתך חדוש נעלם בעולמך

Asher bar Abraham

--˘---˘---˘ /--˘---˘---˘

מעידים על כבוד אלי ברואיו ואותותינו ועדיו היצורים

Levi ben Abraham

--˘----˘----˘ /--˘----˘----˘

מיוסד הוא אבל לא באחדים / וחי אך לא כחיי הבשרים

Solomon ben Immanual Dapiera

/-----˘/-----˘/-----˘/-----˘

הלא סובב אחד / והנמצא אחד / ואם כל אל אחד / שתים יולדים

Meir Aldabi

--˘----˘----˘ /--˘----˘----˘

בראשית כל יסוד הבן יסודך / חקור למצוא מציאות הקדומה

Aaron of Nicomedia

--˘----˘----˘ /--˘----˘----˘

מתי שכל ובינה מאמינים / מציאות אל ויחודו מבינים

69. Gustave E. Von Grunebaum, "On the Origin and Early Development of Arabic Muzdawij Poetry," *Journal of Near Eastern Studies* 3 (1944): 9–12; Geert Jan van Gelder, "The Antithesis of Urjūza and Badī'iyya: Two Forms of Arabic Versified Stylistics," in *Calliope's Classroom: Studies in Didactic Poetry from Antiquity to the Renaissance*, ed. A. Harder, A. A. MacDonald, and G. J. Reinink (Leuven: Peeters, 2007), 153–72, 154; see also Van Gelder, "Arabic Didactic Verse."

70. David Pingree, "The Fragments of the Works of Al-Fazari," *Journal of Near Eastern Studies* 29 (1970): 103–23.

71. See Amidu Sanni, *The Arabic Theory of Prosification and Versification: On Ḥall and Naẓm in Arabic Theoretical Discourse* (Beirut: Franz Steiner, 1998).

72. Dapiera, *Battei ha-Nefesh*, 6.

73. See also Moses ibn Ezra's poems, e.g., *Eleikhem emunim* is also written with three internal rhymes per line.

Be-shem el asher amar ----˘-- /----˘-- /----˘-- /----˘--

לראשון בלי ראשית / ואחרון בלי אחרית / ואיך לו יהי תכלית / ואפסו תחלותיו

Eleikhem emunim ---˘-- /---˘-- /---˘-- /---˘--

אליכם אמונים / בחיק הכסילים / מתי רעיונים / כברק לטושים

74. It is not clear to me how many remain to be found in manuscript. See for example Paris BNF héb 977, f. 178v; St. Petersburg IOS RA C22, f. 130r; Parma Pal 2301, at end; Paris BNF héb 1201, f. 60r; Vatican ebr. 343, f. 1r. See also the entry on "Didactic Poetry" in the *Jewish Encyclopedia*. For published studies, see the fourteenth-century versification of Ibn Sīna's *Maqāsid* in Steven Harvey and Charles H. Manekin, "The Curious *Segullat Melakhim* by Abraham Avigdor," in *Écriture et réécriture des textes philosophiques médiévaux*, ed. J. Hamesse and O. Weijers (Turnhout: Brepols, 2006), 215–52; Y. Tzvi Langermann, "Manuscript Moscow Guenzburg 1020: An Important New Yemeni Codex of Jewish Philosophy," *Journal of the American Oriental Society* 115 (1995): 373–87.

75. MS BN Paris héb 1005, f. 28r.

76. Dale Eickelman notes that in the modern period, in the case of memorization of the Quran, a study suggests that "patterns of intonation and rhythm serve as mnemonic markers." Dale Eickelman, "The Art of Memory: Islamic Education and Its Social Reproduction," *Comparative Studies in Society and History* 20 (1978): 485–516, 493n6. And see D. H. Green, "Orality and Reading: The State of Research in Medieval Studies," *Speculum* 65 (1990): 267–80.

77. Mary Carruthers, "Sweetness," *Speculum* 81 (2006): 999–1013, 999.
78. Ross Brann, *The Compunctious Poet: Cultural Ambiguity and Hebrew Poetry in Muslim Spain* (Baltimore, MD: Johns Hopkins University Press, 1991), 104.
79. Brann, *Compunctious Poet*, 104.
80. Dapiera, *Battei ha-Nefesh*, 41, 57.
81. Ong, "Orality, Literacy, and Medieval Textualization," 1, 2.
82. Duran, *Ma'aseh Efod*, 20.
83. Duran, *Ma'aseh Efod*, 20.
84. Dapiera, *Battei ha-Nefesh*, 26–27.

MAUD KOZODOY currently works for the Posen Foundation on the editorial staff of the Posen Library of Jewish Culture and Civilization. Her research interests are medieval Jewish history, the history of science, and, in particular, the interplay between science and literature. She is author of *The Secret Faith of Maestre Honoratus: Profayt Duran and Jewish Identity in Late Medieval Iberia*.

10

THE PHILOSOPHICAL EPISTLE AS A GENRE OF MEDIEVAL JEWISH PHILOSOPHY

Charles H. Manekin

THE PHILOSOPHICAL EPISTLE AS A GENRE GOES BACK to the Greeks, perhaps to Plato.[1] But in considering philosophical epistles among the Jews, our story begins in the Islamicate context, with an occasional look back to Hellenistic writings that were translated into Arabic. For the purposes of this chapter, I will divide philosophical epistles into three categories: the first category, which is the largest, consists of works termed "epistles" by their authors that were not intended, or did not originate, as a work addressed to a specific addressee. I will call these "monographic epistles." The second category consists of letters that touch on philosophical matters but whose context and audience is not restricted to experts in philosophy. The third category contains works that represent actual philosophical correspondence between philosophers. Rather than attempt to make an exhaustive inventory of all works by Jews that could be classified as philosophical epistles, I will select a few specimens. Much remains to be studied, especially in the third category of philosophical correspondence between philosophical experts.

Monographic Epistles

The first category is the largest and in some respects the most philosophically substantive. I am referring to treatises whose titles contain the Hebrew words *iggeret*, *ketav*, *mikhtav*, and so on, which were not intended as actual letters but rather as monographs. Calling such works "epistles" derive from the Arabic literary genre of *risāla*. The term *risāla* (plural: *rasā'il*, *risālāt*) initially denoted the oral transmission of a message but shifted to written text in the eighth century by Sālim Abū 'l-'Alā', secretary of the Umayyad sultan Hishām b. 'Abd al-Malik, who, according to some, translated into Arabic the pseudo-Aristotelian correspondence between Aristotle and his student Alexander; some of this material was later translated into Hebrew. This appeared as bona fide correspondence, albeit invented and pseudepigraphic, so the term *risāla* seems appropriate. But during this period other lengthy *rasā'il* on various topics were written, and in these cases the term *risāla* meant the same as *maqāla*, "treatise," occasionally retaining a more immediate, second-person flavor, with a first-person introduction. In philosophy, from the ninth century onward, both *risāla* and *maqāla* could signify treatises, and length was not always a factor distinguishing them. In fact, Avicenna refers to one of his works both as *risāla* (*Risālat al-quwā al-insāniyya wa-idrākātihā*) and *maqāla* (*al-Maqāla fī 'l-quwā al-insāniyya*).[2]

Some well-known collections of philosophical *rasā'il* are the epistles of the ninth-century philosopher Al-Kindī and the *Epistles of the Brethren of Purity*, which deal with human knowledge arranged according to four groups (mathematics, logic, natural sciences, and metaphysics). These are formulated as letters to an individual addressee called "brother," and it is characteristic of these *rasā'il* that, though monographs, they retain an epistolary flavor. In Al-Andalus, Ibn Bajja and Averroes have collections of their writings with the word *rasā'il* in their titles; in the case of Averroes, the reference is to the so-called Epitomes or Short Treatises on various works of Aristotle. Finally, there are several Judeo-Arabic monographs written in the eleventh and twelfth centuries that are called *risāla*, including the linguistic work by Judah b. Quraysh of Morocco and the grammatical *Risālat at-Tanbīh* by Jonah ibn Janaḥ.

By the time the translation movement brought Arabic and Judeo-Arabic works into Hebrew, especially in the twelfth and thirteenth centuries, the monographic epistle was well-established, and the biblical term *iggeret*, one of the primary terms adopted by the Hebrew translators for *risāla*, was made to capture the same semantic fluidity. I am not sure when the term is first used by the translators for a monographic epistle; the term *ketav* seems to have preceded it, for Al-Farabi's introductory *Risāla fī 'l-'aql* (Epistle on the intellect) was translated into Hebrew, probably in the mid twelfth-century, as *Ketav ha-Da'at*.[3] Both Samuel ibn Tibbon (c. 1165–c.1232) and Judah al-Ḥarizi (1165–1225) use *iggeret* to render *risāla*, and the term is employed in some prominent thirteenth-century Hebrew monographic epistles, such as Shem Tov ibn Falaquera's (c. 1225–1295) *Iggeret ha-vikkuaḥ* (The epistle of the debate) and *Iggeret ha-ḥalom* (The epistle of the dream). Still, as late as 1314, Qalonymos b. Qalonymos (1286–d. after 1328) has to explain the use of the term to his readers; he writes in his introduction of the *Iggeret ba'alei ḥayyim* (The epistle of the animals) that the work is from a great and lengthy composition entitled in Arabic, "The Epistle of Abu al-Safa," "who made little books and called them little epistles, one composition containing fifty-one epistles."[4] This is a reference to the *Epistles of the Brethren of Purity*, and Qalonymos's work is a translation of one of the epistles. It would appear that most of the monographic epistles composed originally in Hebrew are relatively short compositions.

The use of *iggeret* for monographic epistle as well as for an actual epistle addressed to an individual or to a group has been the cause of confusion. So has the failure to distinguish between the *risāla/iggeret* and *maqāla/ma'amar* when an author wrote both sorts of works and intended by them different things. The most popular epistle from the Middle Ages, judging from the number of extant manuscripts, is the *Iggeret teḥiyat ha-metim* (The epistle on resurrection) of Maimonides (1138–1204). Or at least this is how the work is catalogued at the Institute for Microfilmed Hebrew Manuscripts at the National Library of Israel. Yet an examination of the incipits of those manuscripts, as well as of the Judeo-Arabic manuscripts, shows that few of them have the term *iggeret* attached to them. We know that Maimonides himself refers to the work not as a *risāla* but as a *maqāla*, the term he uses to refer inter alia to the *Guide of the Perplexed*.[5] But even if the treatise can be termed *risāla* because of the interchangeability of the terms and even if Maimonides's intention was to have the work disseminated among the learned,[6] there is no reason to believe Maimonides intended it to be a communal letter for the public at large. The work is not addressed to any community, unlike the *Epistle to Yemen*, in which Maimonides urges his interlocutor, Jacob, to send a copy of the epistle "to every community in the cities and the hamlets in order to strengthen the people in their faith."[7] Maimonides mentions in the treatise that he was asked by some Yemenite Jews to explain his views on resurrection and that he responded to their queries. But there is no indication that his answer was intended for the entire community. Similarly, the *Treatise on Resurrection* is by no means a defense of Maimonides's orthodoxy written to "a confused and frightened community."[8] It reads more like a caustic response essay in a scholarly journal by an author who has been misunderstood by other scholars. The "community" to whom the epistle is addressed is the community of students (*ṭulāb*), albeit not necessarily only those trained in philosophy. Yet calling the work "Epistle" and including it within collections of bona fide correspondence and responsa may mislead one to think that the treatise is written for a popular audience, as in the case of the *Epistle to Yemen*. If it is a classical *risāla* at all—and its personal account in the beginning fits into that genre—it should be considered a monographic one.

Epistles, Correspondence, and Such Pertaining to Philosophy

Although the *Treatise on Resurrection* is classified as a monographic epistle, other works of Maimonides should be considered as bona fide epistles. These range from longer works, such as the *Epistle on Astrology* (also known as the *Epistle of the Creation of the World*) that Maimonides sent to the sages of Montpelier,[9] to the personal letters he sent to his student, Joseph b. Judah, and to the Hebrew translator of the *Guide*, Samuel ibn Tibbon, among others. Maimonides is well-known for having introduced philosophical and theological matters within his legal works,[10] and his eminent stature as legal scholar and theologian spurred supporters and detractors alike in dealing with such issues, whether in independent treatises or in epistles.[11] The controversy in the East over Maimonides's views on the resurrection has already been mentioned; with the diffusion of his Hebrew code of law in the West (especially Spain and Provence), a similar controversy broke out with Rabbi Meir ha-Levi Abulafia of Toledo (c. 1165–1244). Maimonides's interpretation of the "world to come" as referring to the survival of the acquired intellect, rather than to a physical world inhabited by resurrected bodies, seemed to some to be a denial, or at least a devaluation, of resurrection. Abulafia sent letters to various rabbinical scholars and academics, some of which he collected; these have been mined by historians of Jewish intellectual history for evidence of the state of the knowledge of philosophy in the Jewish communities of Spain and Provence around the turn of the twelfth century.[12]

Let me take as one example the letter of the Spanish-Jewish savant Sheshet b. Isaac b. Joseph Benveniste (d. c. 1209) in defense of Maimonides.[13] The letter was addressed to Rabbi Jonathan ha-Kohen of Lunel, a prominent rabbinic scholar who had corresponded with Maimonides and whose colleagues had greeted the arrival of Maimonides's *Code of Law* with eagerness.

Abulafia had sent his own letter, critical of Maimonides, to the sages of Lunel, chief of whom was R. Jonathan, and it was this letter to which Sheshet responded. After speaking rather harshly of Abulafia, Sheshet praises Maimonides for denying physical resurrection, since according to Sheshet it is impossible even for God to return the soul to the body. Sheshet's letter shows the impact of Arabic philosophy and allegorical Quranic interpretation on Spanish Jewish scriptural and rabbinic exegesis of the time.[14] He cites approvingly the views of "the philosophers who are called divine" that although the nutritive and appetitive souls die with the body, the rational soul given by God to humans alone is divine, provided that this soul has acquired knowledge in its lifetime. But if this intellect, when impurified by its association with the body, has been overcome by desire and learns nothing, then after separation from the body it yearns only for bodily pleasures, which it can no longer have. Sheshet relates that when he asked Muslim sages about Islam's corporeal descriptions of the afterlife, they told him that these descriptions were intended for Muslims who enjoy food, drink, and love of women, who know nothing of spiritual pleasures. Without these descriptions, such people would have no motivation to obey God and to heed the prophets. The notion that the physical descriptions of resurrection need to be interpreted as allegories is found in Avicenna, as is the notion that the souls of the ignorant yearn for unattainable bodily pleasures after death.[15] Further study of this letter may yield more evidence of Avicennan influence in twelfth-century Spain among the rabbinic and communal aristocracy. By contrast, another response to Abulafia's letter criticizing Maimonides, that of Aaron b. Meshulam of Lunel, does not show any awareness of the spiritualization of the world-to-come found in Spanish Jewish circles.[16]

Two more controversies involving the philosophical interpretations of traditional texts and doctrines broke out in Provence: the first over the study of Maimonides's philosophical writings (1230–1234) and the second over the excessive philosophical allegorization of scripture and the dissemination of such interpretations in public settings (1301–1305).[17] Maimonides refers to the importance of concealing the secrets of the Torah (which he tended to identify with physical and metaphysical doctrines) from those who are not prepared to understand them, and the thirteenth century saw disputes over what those secrets were, which could be revealed, and to whom. Both controversies produced a wealth of epistles that were published in various collections, the most prominent being the *Epistles of Jealousy* for the first controversy and *A Jealousy Offering* for the second.[18] The latter was collected by one of the controversy's protagonists, Abba Mari b. Moses of Lunel. These sources have been examined repeatedly by intellectual historians for evidence of the penetration of philosophy into Spain and so-called Jewish Provence in the thirteenth and early fourteenth centuries and the reactions it provoked.

Jewish philosophers debated their interpretations of Maimonides in correspondence. Thus, Zerahiah b. Shealtiel Ḥen of Barcelona conducted an epistolary controversy with Hillel of Verona in 1290 over the proper interpretation of Maimonides's view that non-Mosaic prophecy, including visions of angels, occurs in dreams. Did such a view mean that Jacob's wrestling with an angel, or the visitation of the angels to Abram and Lot, or the miracle of Balaam's ass speaking, were really prophetic dreams and did not actually occur? And what of the binding of Isaac, in which an angel appeared? These and other questions were raised by Hillel in his letter to Zerahiah, to which Zerahiah composed a short, courteous reply, followed by a lengthy response to all of Hillel's questions. This response apparently did not go over well with Hillel, who responded with an argumentative letter in which he minimized the dream element in these events and interpreted them as actually occurring. This provoked a long and irate response from Zerahiah, who elaborated on his contention that none of these events actually occurred except in the prophetic vision. Of this correspondence we only have Zerahiah's initial courteous reply and his last irate reply.[19] But it is an important record of the division between those interpreters of Maimonides who were deeply influenced by Averroes and those who took a more moderate approach. Of course, some epistles should be noted for their literary style. Especially in his second letter, Zerahiah moves back and forth from lines of rhymed prose, generally full of invective, to simple and direct prose explaining his position.

Another epistolary debate concerning Maimonides's interpretations of the secrets of the Torah, as well as the question of whether they should be revealed, was initiated by the Provençal savant, Joseph ibn Kaspi (1280–1345). Kaspi sent his work, the *Book of the Secret,* and a collection of questions and answers to various parties, including two prominent fourteenth-century philosopher/translators in Salon de Provence, R. Abba Mari b. Eligdor and Moses of Beaucaire, which elicited their replies. We do not possess copies of these materials, but we do have a later version of the *Book of the Secret*, renamed by Kaspi as the *Silver Tower*,[20] and a response that was sent in 1318 to Kaspi by Qalonymos b. Qalonymos at the behest of Abba Mari and Moses of Beaucaire, who were his teachers.[21] Qalonymos was a prolific translator with an impressive range of knowledge. In his response he defends a philosophically moderate interpretation of Maimonides, occasionally disagreeing with his teachers when he felt their response to Kaspi was too generous or weak. Qalonymos responds to Kaspi's interpretations point by point. He writes that even were they correct, it would have been better for Kaspi not to publish them in a book, thereby revealing them to those not worthy. But they are not correct, and Qalonymos appeals to Arabic philosophical authorities to support his case. Though at times overtly cordial (according to the letter, the two had met personally), Qalonymos clearly considers himself superior to Kaspi not only in his interpretation of Maimonides but also in his broader knowledge of philosophy. Kaspi's attempt to explain some of the commandments by referring to contemporary practices and beliefs of Egyptians—he had traveled to Old Cairo in search of authoritative interpreters of Maimonides—is rejected by Qalonymos as anachronistic; who is to say whether today's practices reflect biblical customs? On the contrary, the ascendancy of Islam in the region suggests a reason why the customs are different. (Qalonymos also suggests that Kaspi misunderstood contemporary customs.)[22]

We have already encountered one of the questions considered by Kaspi and Qalonymos: when Maimonides states in the *Guide* that all prophecy aside from that of Moses was in a dream or prophetic vision, exactly how much of the biblical narratives should be understood as prophetic dream? But there are others, some of which exercise scholars today: Was Moses able to manipulate nature through his extraordinary knowledge of it, reaching the level of the separate intellects, or was he able merely to predict the miracles? If Maimonides truly thought that prophecy requires divine volition and is not merely a natural process, why did he cite a scriptural proof text that could be interpreted naturalistically?[23] Qalonymos is also disturbed by Kaspi's boasts that he has uncovered and revealed secrets, which prompts him to list a number of "secrets," that is, difficulties of math, geometry, astronomy, and natural sciences that Kaspi is unable to answer.[24] Qalonymos's response was apparently followed by a second one, of which the opening and closing is preserved in the same manuscript.[25]

Rabbinical responsa that deal with theological matters may be considered a subgenre of philosophical epistles, although these were relatively few. The Spanish rabbi Isaac b. Sheshet Perfet (1326–1408) devotes a responsum to the divine foreknowledge/human choice conundrum. He had criticized

Levi Gersonides (1288–1344) for holding that God knows what ought to befall humans by virtue of their astral fate but that humans have the ability to choose otherwise if they choose according to reason. That prompted the question from Amram b. Marwās Efrati Ibn Marwās to Isaac b. Sheshet: Was not Gersonides's view similar to that of Abraham b. David of Posquières (c. 1125–1198)? R. Abraham had written that God's knowledge is like that of the astrologers, who have knowledge of what humans would do by virtue of their astral fate, except that God, unlike the astrologer, knows the power of their intellects to escape their fate.[26] Isaac replies that there is a great difference between the views. According to Gersonides, God cannot know a rational choice made by humans before they choose; hence, he limits God's knowledge.[27] Moreover, since God learns something new when humans choose according to reason, His knowledge is multiple, which impugns divine unity. Abraham, on the other hand, says that God knows both the power of the constellations and the power of the intellect to overcome their influence, and so he knows which power will overcome the other. Then Isaac offers his own solution: God foreknows what humans will freely choose, that is, both what they will choose and what they could choose otherwise. God's knowledge cannot predetermine the outcome because then he would know that the choice is not free and know it to be free, which is contradictory. He concludes that actual choice does not follow from God's knowledge but rather God's knowledge follows from the actual choice, albeit before the choice is actualized.[28]

Another philosophical epistolary subgenre includes works in religious polemics. Though much of Jewish anti-Christian polemical literature is concerned with exegesis of canonical texts on disputed topics, for example, the messiahship of Jesus, some were devoted to refuting Christian dogma on rational grounds. The conversion of a Jewish savant's colleague to Christianity occasionally resulted in a letter directed to the convert, or from the convert to the Jewish community, or in a series of letters between the parties. These letters may provide a glimpse into the philosophical sources of their authors. For example, the Spanish Jewish savant, Joshua Lorki (d. 1419), in his letter to his teacher Solomon of Burgos (who had converted and become a Christian theologian by the name of Pablo de Santa Maria), concedes that some Christian dogmas, such as the doctrine of the trinity, have traces in the writings of the philosophers. He cites Aristotle's *De Caelo* in the Arabic version without translating it into Hebrew, thus providing another piece of evidence that Spanish Jewish savants were familiar with the

Arabic Aristotle as late as the fifteenth century.[29] The polemical epistles and treatises of the philosopher Abner of Burgos (c. 1270–1347), who converted and took the name of Alfonso de Valladolid, are another important source of the philosophical authorities of the time.[30]

A better-known polemical epistle was written by Lorki's contemporary, the philosopher-scientist Profayt Duran (c. 1350–c. 1415), to his former companion, David Bonet Bonjorn, who had converted to Christianity. *Al tehi ka-avotekha* (Do not be like your father) places rationalist philosophy in the service of anti-Christian polemic and is well-known for its sarcastic tone and rapier wit.[31] While it is no doubt the most famous of his epistles, Duran is the author of two more strictly philosophical epistles—actually, philosophical responsa—to his student, Meir Crescas.[32] In one he responds to a query about the meaning of cryptic remarks by Abraham ibn Ezra regarding the importance accorded the number seven in the Torah. He begins his response by emphasizing the importance of the number seven and by providing explanations that are based mainly on a numerological work by Qalonymos b. Qalonymos. After concluding that seven is the perfect number because it is bereft of all corporeality, he then interprets Ibn Ezra as intimating that when the perfect number (of sacrifices) reaches the Perfect Existence (God), that prepares the mind of the one offering the sacrifice to receive the divine influx.[33] Maud Kozodoy makes the interesting suggestion that Duran does not adopt Qalonymos's view that the number three is the expression of God in the world because of its trinitarian implications. She cites the writing of his contemporary Nicole Oresme, who mentions the Christological interpretation of Aristotle's *De Caelo* as a possible source for Duran.[34] As we just saw, that interpretation was known to Joshua Lorki, and quite likely to other participants in the Jewish-Christian polemic.

Meir's second query deals with the explanation of a saying from the *Book of the Palm Tree*, a work on astral magic, which he interprets in a thoroughly philosophical manner as referring to the path and degrees of human perfection, including prophecy.[35] A third work considered by scholars to be an epistle/response to a query appears to be a student's summary of Duran's treatment of certain philosophical questions about the eternity of the soul's felicity or punishment.[36]

Occasionally, the same scholars who engaged in interreligious polemic conducted a philosophical polemic through epistles. The best-known case of this is found in the correspondence between Abner of Burgos and his erstwhile study partner and student, Isaac Polgar (fl. early fourteenth century). From the interreligious debate, some epistles of the two are extant in Hebrew and in Spanish versions. Additional material found its way into Abner's voluminous dialogue between a master and an errant pupil, *Mostrador de Justicia* (the Hebrew original of which, *Moreh Tzedek*, is no longer extant) and into part 1 of Polgar's *'Ezer ha-dat* (Support of religion).[37] The debate between Abner and Polgar began first in a personal correspondence, albeit one clearly designed to be public, and then in treatises that drew from correspondence. Many, though not all, of these texts have been preserved in Hebrew or Spanish or both.[38]

At the same time as they conducted their Jewish-Christian polemic, Abner and Polgar engaged in a philosophical debate over the proper interpretation of the divine "decree" (*gezerah*), with Abner presenting a strict determinist interpretation and Polgar an Aristotelian indeterminist one. An examination of their arguments reveals them to have been formed entirely within the context of the fourteenth-century Spanish Jewish intellectual, with no Christian predestinarian influence at all. This may be because Abner's determinist views were formed long before his conversion at an advanced age to Christianity, and his "hard determinism" had strong roots in Andalusian Jewish philosophy.[39] As a young man, Abner had defended a theory of celestial determinism in a work entitled *The Secret of Recompense*, no longer extant, but still known years later to Hasdai Crescas (d. 1410) and to Joseph ibn Shem Tov (1400–1460), who composed a rebuttal.[40] There is no evidence that *The Secret of Recompense* initially provoked any reaction, and it was not until years later, after Abner had converted and begun to write anti-Jewish polemical treatises and after he had written another defense of astral determinism called *The Tower of Strength*, that a response came in the form of a philosophical epistle from Polgar entitled *The Refutation of Astrology*. Polgar circulated this epistle with two other epistles attacking Abner's religious and philosophical views. Judging from later sources, these three epistles amounted to a defense of the mainstream philosophical interpretation of Judaism of the period, an interpretation that was heavily indebted to Maimonides and to Averroes. Shortly after receiving *The Refutation of Astrology* and the other letters, Abner responded with a work entitled *A Jealousy Offering* or the *Treatise on Predestination*. By choosing the name *A Jealousy Offering*, Abner may have alluded to the earlier *Jealousy Offering* by Abba Mari of Lunel, which was, in part, an attack on excessive philosophical interpretations of Judaism, and Abner indeed accused Polgar elsewhere of infidelity to the Jewish tradition because of his philosophical interpretations. Polgar responded with a dialogue between a sage and an astrologer in his book *The Support of Religion*, parts of which may have their origin in his epistle *The Refutation of Astrology.* The sage was modeled after him and the astrologer, to a large extent, after Abner.[41]

Abner's conversion and subsequent anti-Jewish literary activity is not mentioned explicitly in either *A Jealousy Offering* or in the dialogue between the sage and the astrologer in *The Support of Religion.* But the conversion is mentioned in the *Treatise on Choice* of Moses Narboni (Moses of Narbonne) (d. after 1362), his answer to Abner's *Epistle on the Decree*, which has sometimes been identified with *A Jealousy Offering.*[42] The identification cannot be ruled out, given that "epistle" can be used either for epistle or treatise. Still, according to Narboni's report of its contents, the *Epistle on the Decree* seems to differ somewhat from the *Jealousy Offering*, which is extant only in the Spanish version, probably made under Abner/Alfonso's supervision. In any event, in the Abner-Polger controversy, we have a public dispute conducted through philosophical epistles that ultimately was recorded in a non-epistolary format.

Philosophical Correspondence

The epistles that we have considered so far deal with issues of religious philosophy and theology. But there were also scientific and "pure" philosophical exchanges between Jewish savants that are contained in letters and treatises that arose from personal contacts. These works have been generally neglected by those more interested in the history of the philosophical interpretations of Judaism than in the history of philosophy written and taught by Jews. Recent years, however, have witnessed the publication of scientific and philosophical works that have added significantly to our knowledge of the Jewish philosophical enterprise. Ruth Glasner edited and analyzed two polemical epistles pertaining to physics by the fourteenth century Provençal poet and philosopher Jedaiah ha-Penini (Bedersi) (born c. 1285).[43] The two works, the *Treatise on Opposite Motions* and the *Book of Confutation* are addressed to an anonymous scholar, whom Glasner was able to identify with Gersonides. She reconstructs the stages of the controversy between the contemporaries from an initial face-to-face encounter, followed by a letter from Gersonides to Jedaiah (no longer extant), then to the latter's response in the *Treatise on Opposite Motions*, and culminating in a final round of Gersonides's criticisms (also no longer extant) and Jedaiah's last word in the *Book of Confutation*. This reconstruction seems plausible, although the evidence for an initial letter by Gersonides is speculative. In any event, the letters provide an important record, albeit one-sided, of an actual scientific controversy by two distinguished Jewish philosophers in fourteenth-century Provence. They are hence of great importance for appreciating the high level of philosophical culture of that period. Whether there was a school of Gersonides, as has been argued by Glasner,[44] we do have evidence of literary connections between contemporaries like Gersonides, Jedaiah ha-Penini, Samuel b. Judah of Marseilles, Abba Mari b. Eligdor, and Qalonymos b. Qalonymos.[45]

Fifteenth-century Spanish Jewish philosophers were also interested in "pure" philosophy, as evidenced by their translations, commentaries, and epistolary exchanges, many of which are still in manuscript. Due to the seminal work of Mauro Zonta and others, we are now familiar not only with the impact of Latin scholasticism on Jewish religious philosophy, but also what Zonta calls "Hebrew Scholasticism," the continuation of Latin scholastic discussions in Hebrew, with little or no input from Jewish culture.[46] Much of Hebrew Scholasticism exists as Hebrew translations of Latin works deemed by the translators to be important for Jewish intellectuals. But some of it is found in correspondence between Jewish intellectuals, with the scholastic component increasing in importance in the decades before the expulsion in 1492. That component is lacking, for example, in Abraham Bibago/Bivach's correspondence with his colleague, Moses Arondi, concerning a passage in Aristotle's *Categories* about motion, namely, whether the term *motion* is said univocally or equivocally and in what circumstances. Bibago was the leading Spanish Jewish philosopher in the second half of the fifteenth century, and several of his writings cite scholastic authorities. Although his correspondence with Arondi does not explicitly mention these authorities, the mode of argumentation is reminiscent of scholastic debate.[47] Another philosophical correspondence between the Spanish Jewish philosophers, Abraham Shalom (d. 1492) and Eli Habillo (late 15th c.), mentions several Latin authorities.[48] Habillo posed two questions to Shalom: whether substance admits of less and more, and whether the generation of a thing from another thing is by nature. These were standard questions in the study of Aristotle, but both Habillo and Shalom base their arguments in part on scholastic thinkers. When Shalom refers to "the sage Marsilius," Habillo claims that the only scholastic work on logic he had read was that of William of Ockham.[49] Here, too, there is moderation, even conservatism, with respect to the philosophical positions taken, but also a real sense of enthusiasm for this activity.

Such enthusiasm for Latin philosophy is perfectly compatible with criticism of the more religiously problematic positions of some of the early Jewish philosophers who drew from the Arabic-Hebrew tradition. For example, the Spanish Jewish poet Solomon Bonafed (end of the fourteenth to the mid-fifteenth century) rails against those of his generation "who promote alien wisdom in order to extirpate the roots of religions."[50] According to Yitzhak Baer, the poet was a "faithful Jew" who "sent a satirical poem to an intellectual who was . . . an adherent of the philosophical school,"[51] which suggests that Bonafed himself was not an adherent. Yet the poet relates in his *Diwan* that he disagreed with a student of Isaac Arondi over the merits of studying scholastic logic. The student had written Solomon that he was studying logic with Arondi, whereupon Solomon answered that he was also studying logic, but in Latin with a Christian sage, whose approach to the subject he praised. This annoyed Arondi's student, who went on to question the worth of Latin logic and to defend the honor of his own teacher.[52] One finds praises of Latin philosophy in translations, treatises, and epistles addressed to an elite fraternity of scholars, but not generally in theological works written for a broader circle of learned people.[53]

The Philosophical Queries of Saul Ha-Kohen Addressed to Don Isaac Abrabanel

In addition to philosophical epistles between colleagues or former colleagues, there is a philosophical responsum from a distinguished scholar to a younger man who posed to him twelve queries. Saul ha-Kohen Ashkenazi of Crete (c. 1470–1523) was thirty-seven years old and living in Constantinople when he sent his queries to an elderly Don Isaac Abrabanel in Venice. Abrabanel had recently moved to Venice after a turbulent career as a scholar, diplomat, and financier in Portugal, Spain, and southern Italy. We know little of Saul ha-Kohen aside from that he composed two treatises (no longer extant) and had studied with philosopher Elia del Medigo in Crete and David ibn Yaḥya in Constantinople. Despite there being a Spanish philosophical center in Constantinople, Saul directed his twelve queries to Abrabanel.[54] The queries concern the textual interpretation of difficult passages in basic works for students of Jewish philosophy. Since the queries and their response provide important testimony for the study of Jewish philosophy in the late fifteenth century, we will look at the work in some detail.

The first three queries have to do with the proper interpretation of passages from the *Guide of the Perplexed.* These queries are given relatively long answers by Abrabanel, who occasionally digresses from Saul's specific questions to provide what he considers the necessary background; in one place he actually chides Saul for not raising a more important issue than the one he raises.[55] Abrabanel writes that although his study of the *Guide* had increased in the years following his exile, "taking from Maimonides the good and leaving the bad,"[56] and although he had explained chapters from the *Guide* in his earlier writings and had written commentaries on selected chapters at the occasional request of his study partners (*ḥaverim*), he had only recently contemplated writing a commentary on the *Guide* as a whole. Abrabanel's reception of Saul's queries, together with one of Saul's books, had led him to believe that a protracted visit from Saul would provide him with a study partner/collaborator who would allow him to complete two other unfinished works and the *Guide* commentary.[57] Since there is no evidence that Abrabanel ever wrote a complete commentary on the *Guide*, his answers to Saul provide important additional material for how he interpreted Maimonides's work.[58]

Some of Saul's questions are rather elementary. For example, he was unable to locate two of Maimonides's references to Aristotle in the *Guide of the Perplexed*; could the master locate them for him? Regarding the first Abrabanel replies that when Maimonides says that something is in Aristotle, one should take him at his word; unfortunately, the only writings of Aristotle at Abrabanel's disposal in Venice are the *Posterior Analytics*, the *Physics*, the third book of the *De Anima*, and the tenth book of the *Metaphysics*.[59] He relates that when he had resided in Naples, his library had been looted during the French occupation and that he had sent the surviving books on to Salonika, where one of his sons lived. Although he does not have an explicit source in Aristotle's works for the first query, he is able to derive the doctrine attributed to Aristotle by Maimonides from several other places. As for the second unknown reference to Aristotle, Abrabanel flatly states that Saul can find it in the *Topics*.[60] Either Abrabanel recalled that from memory, or perhaps he found it in Joseph ibn Shem Tov's commentary on the *Guide*, ad loc.[61]

Two other queries concern the proper explanation of passages in the section on logic of Ghazali's *Intentions of the Philosopher*, a standard work studied by young Jewish intellectuals. After listing the three figures of the categorical syllogism, Ghazali writes cryptically, "The rule for antecedent and consequent in the conditional [syllogism] is that of the subject and the predicate [in the categorical syllogism] with respect to the division of their agreement into these three figures."[62] It seems from this that the three figures of the conditional syllogism relate to the three figures of the categorical syllogism, but Saul is unclear how. If the conditional syllogistic figures reduce to, that is, are derivable from, the categorical syllogistic figures, then why consider them a separate type of syllogism at all? The example cited in the commentary of Moses Narboni is of little help, because it only shows the relationship to the first figure.[63] Saul appeals both to Isaac Abrabanel and to his son Judah to answer his question, since he has no one in his vicinity to help him. Abrabanel replies that what Ghazali intended was that conditional syllogism can reduce to (i.e., be formulated as) a categorical syllogism in any of the standard three figures by reformulating the premises in an equivalent matter. Narboni, says Abrabanel, only cited the first figure because this is the most important one, to which the second and third can be reduced.[64]

Saul's second logical query deals with Ghazali's claim that there is a type of demonstration in which the existence of one effect is inferred from another, where there is a cause common to both of them. This type of demonstration puzzles Saul, who is unable to find it anywhere in Aristotle's book *On Demonstration* (*Posterior Analytics*) and who cannot understand its connection with the types of demonstration proceeding it. Abrabanel explains the type of demonstration, shows the connection, and, after providing his own example, mentions Aristotle's: "This woman gave birth to a child; therefore, she has breast milk and an infant; so if she has breast milk, she has an infant, and vice-versa."[65] He does not mention that Aristotle's example is in *On the Syllogism* (*Prior Analytics* 2.27), which explains why Saul was unable to find it in *On Demonstration*.

Two other queries concern the explanation of cryptic passages in Moses Narboni's commentary on the *Intentions*. In his discussion of divine knowledge and will, Ghazali provides the image of a thumb facing the four fingers and encircling them, which leads Narboni to rhapsodize about the special properties of the Hebrew language, for the word "thumb" (*bohen*) can be understood as "they are in it" (*bo hen*), just as the term for "animal" (*behemah*) can be understood as "*what* is in them" (*bahem mah*). This is interpreted by Narboni to indicate that the spirit of the animal is inseparable from its corporeality and hence does not survive death. Narboni then cites Ecclesiastes' reference to the cherubim, which he interprets allegorically and notes that "cherub" refers to a human being of a tender age,[66] cites scriptural verses about Cain and Abel, and concludes that "Abel represents the correct view." All this confuses Saul, who asks Abrabanel to explain what Narboni is driving at, especially since his conclusion contradicts Narboni's claim in his commentary on the *Guide* that Seth, rather than Abel, represents the correct view.

Abrabanel at first demurs; if Narboni wishes to complicate a difficult passage through unexplained riddles and formulations, why should he bother? But to answer Saul's question, he provides his own interpretation of Narboni's remarks. Narboni, writes Abrabanel, believed in the eternity of the world, and so he understood Adam and his family as a philosophical allegory for different types of humans and different faculties of the soul. Cain (*Kayin*) represents acquisitive individuals, as well as the productive soul; Abel (*Hevel*) represents pragmatic individuals who desire political power, as well as the practical intellect, which is also vanity and wasted breath, certainly in relation to the theoretical intellect. The slaying of Abel by Cain is an allegory for the destruction of the practical intellect, the seat of ethical virtues, by the desire for possessions. Both the productive and the practical intellects do not survive death, although the latter compared with the former can be termed the "correct view"; hence Abel represents the correct view relative to Cain. Only the theoretical intellect is immortal, and Seth, who designates this intellect, is in truth the correct view. Abrabanel concludes with the sardonic remark: "This is the intention of this 'saint' [Narboni] in his verses and contradictions, i.e., to deny the Account of Creation, the origination of the world and its creation, to make figures in his story, and to indicate, as a consequence, that the correct theses are elaborated by the Holy Tongue."[67]

The second passage comes toward the end of Narboni's commentary on Ghazali's disquisition on the rainbow in the *Intentions*. The vapors composing the rainbow are like other vapors, only they differ in their proportion and disposition to receive light. This, Narboni tells us, is like the prophet, whose soul is like other souls, except that it differs in its disposition to receive the light of the intellect:

> The prophet [Ezekiel] when he apprehended the separate [intelligible] said, "the likeness as the appearance of a man," as he said, "the likeness of a throne" because he considered the truth of both to concern the same matter. And

> likewise the Master [Maimonides] explained this with what he brought from *Araboth*. This is like Averroes' statement about those who innovate on the basis of Avicenna, those who say that Aristotle was of this view, who provide an argument that [Averroes] found displeasing. And the Master already said in chapter 72 that demonstration confirms this, and afterwards, an aspect of its opposite. And all the praises made by the Master contain a secret. This is what the praise consists in, and I don't consider it praise. But the glory in my view goes to Averroes, since he possesses perfection.[68]

Saul can't make head or tails of the passage above, and so he asks for guidance from Abrabanel, who responds with a clear, line-by-line explanation of Narboni's "riddles." According to Abrabanel, Narboni follows his explanation of the rainbow with an explanation of the prophet Ezekiel's vision of the heavenly chariot as found in *Guide* 3.1–7, where the likeness of the divine glory is compared to that of a rainbow. Both Maimonides and Narboni interpret the content of Ezekiel's vision as an "investigative question" in which the prophet, like Aristotle, possesses some doubts with respect to celestial science. One such doubt concerns the identity of the mover of the outermost diurnal celestial sphere (*Araboth*). The divine glory ("the appearance of a man") appears closely connected to the outermost sphere ("the likeness of the throne"), but in what manner? According to Averroes, the mover of the sphere is God, the form of the sphere. However, according to Avicenna the mover is the first intellect, caused by God and not to be identified with him.[69] In various places in the *Guide*, Maimonides seems to support the first alternative, but in *Guide* 2.4 he explicitly embraces Avicenna's position, which he characterizes as the view of Aristotle, "as set forth in the work of his followers," and offers a reason for it that, according to Narboni, Averroes found displeasing. As for the reference to *Guide* 1.72, Maimonides writes that on the one hand, God's separateness from the world is demonstrated, whereas on the other, His providence and guidance extends to everything, ending with the praise, "May He whose perfection has dazzled us be glorified!" Artfully using Narboni's commentary to the *Guide*, Abrabanel explains that the "secret" in Maimonides's praise of God, according to Narboni, is that Maimonides does not believe God to be absolutely separate from the world but rather that the first principle is found in everything. But, Narboni continues, the praise of God does not consist in the fact that we are unable to resolve the opposing positions, since they are easily resolved according to Averroes. Indeed, concludes Narboni, the real praise goes to Averroes, who possesses perfection.[70]

After explaining Narboni's enigmatic statements in the *Intentions*, Abrabanel resolves Maimonides's "highly contradictory" view of the mover of the outermost sphere by saying that there is no contradiction: Maimonides accepts the Torah's view that God is the mover of the outermost sphere but not in the Aristotelian/Averroist sense of God being the form of the sphere. His discussion in *Guide* 2.4 concerns the view of Aristotle, as represented by his followers ("according to their reasoning"), that is, Avicenna, and *not* his own view. This is clear from the conclusion of the chapter, in which he announces that he will explain in the following chapters which of these views agree with that of the Torah and which do not.[71]

Saul leaves Ghazali's *Intentions of the Philosophers* and moves on to Averroes's *Epistle on the Possibility of the Conjunction with the Active Intellect*, also with the commentary of Moses Narboni, and asks Abrabanel to explain two passages. Abrabanel replies that he does not possess a copy of the book in Venice. He adds drily that were it a book of legal decisions or tosaphoth (additional commentaries on Talmud), he could borrow it from one of the locals, but "concerning the Intellect, there is here neither conjunction nor possibility," a clever way of dismissing the philosophical level of his fellow Jews in Venice. Nevertheless, Abrabanel tries to explain one passage "like a blind man groping in the darkness" and begs forgiveness from Saul.

As for the other query, which deals with Narboni's interpretation of the concept of "corporeal form," which some philosophers posited in order to endow prime matter with indeterminate tridimensionality, Abrabanel again excuses himself by saying that he does not have Narboni's book in front of him. But he is able to speak to the question of corporeal form based on other writings, and he proceeds to discuss the various interpretations of the concept and provides his own. Saul's question and Abrabanel's answer, which are extremely important for the history of Spanish Jewish philosophy at the turn of the fifteenth century, have recently been studied by Ofer Elior.[72] Like many talented students, Saul appears to have been more familiar with recent discussion of the subject than the elderly Abrabanel; he refers to philosophical correspondence between Eli Habillo and Shem Tov ibn Shem Tov, and a no longer extant treatise by Abraham Bibago that was of the same opinion as the latter.[73] Saul also records the opinion of his teacher, Elia Del Medigo.[74] This prods Abrabanel into reviewing the question and his own earlier views. In his answer, after presenting the prevalent opinions among the classic authorities and posing objections to them, he decides against the existence of a separate form that endows prime matter with indeterminate tridimensionality; rather he argues that the tridimensional nature of matter is an aspect of a thing's substantial form. He then provides the differing opinion of his son, Judah, who, he relates, had recently arrived in Venice.[75] So here is one case in which a query from a young admirer elicits an elderly savant's philosophical reflection and innovation.

Saul's final query concerns whether Aristotle has one or two conceptions of the ultimate happiness of humans. Abrabanel reviews the material from the *Nicomachean Ethics*, the *Metaphysics*, and the *De Anima*. He concludes that he has one conception, which is to apprehend the highest good, for by knowing that good, one will be able to know how to achieve it—and that good is understood by him as intellectual, not practical, although one may need practical virtues in order to develop one's intellectual goals. Just how far humans can achieve intellectual perfection—whether the human intellect can attach themselves to the separate intellect—was not discussed by Aristotle, according to Abrabanel, but by Averroes. Abrabanel goes on to argue that Aristotle provides no reason that intellectual perfection is a sufficient or even a necessary condition for the immortality of the soul. True, Aristotle says that humans become like God through intellectual apprehension, but that refers simply to the act of intellection, not to immortality. Abrabanel concludes that Aristotle, because he did not solve the problem of conjunction, did not prove the immortality of the rational intellect. But we, the believers in the God of Abraham, are vouchsafed immortality through our knowledge and performance of the divine commandments.[76]

Saul ha-Kohen's *Questions* provide us with an unparalleled window into the study of Jewish philosophy, precisely because it was conducted as an epistolary exchange between master and student who lived in different countries. Had the two studied together, we would not have been privy to their conversation. Let us recall that the most famous work of medieval Jewish philosophy, Maimonides's *Guide of the Perplexed*, was written as an epistle/treatise from the author to his student Joseph, after Joseph had left Egypt for Aleppo. Philosophical epistles are important sources for the lives and relationships of those who write and receive them. As a result, philosophical epistles have provided important historical testimony for intellectual historians. But they should not be neglected by historians of philosophy. Saul ha-Kohen's *Questions* has been in print for almost four and a half centuries; many have referred to it, yet few have studied it. And many more philosophical epistles are in manuscript. With interest in the history of "pure" philosophy and science among the Jews on the rise, one expects that these philosophical epistles will receive their proper scholarly attention.

Notes

1. See T. H. Irwin, "Plato: The Intellectual Background," in *The Cambridge Companion to Plato*, ed. Richard Kraut (Cambridge: Cambridge University Press, 1992), 51–89, esp. 78 n. 4.

2. The material in this and the next paragraphs are based on A. Arazi and H. Ben Shammai, "Risāla," *Encyclopedia of Islam, New Edition* (Leiden: Brill, 1995), 8:532–39.

3. See Gad Freudenthal, "*Ketav ha-Da'at* or *Sefer ha-Sekhel we-ha-muskalot*: The Medieval Hebrew Translations of Al-Fārābī's *Risa—lah fī 'l-'aql*. A Study in Text History and in the Evolution of Medieval Hebrew Philosophical Terminology," *Jewish Quarterly Review* 93 (2002): 29–115.

4. See *Iggeret Ba'alei Ḥayyim* (Warsaw, 1879), 2a:
והוא עשה ספרים קטנים וקראם אגרות קטנות והחבור הוא אחד והם חמישים ואחד אגרות

5. See I. Shailat, *Iggerot ha-Rambam* (Jerusalem: Maaliyot, 1987), 415–75, esp. 426, l.9.

6. This is the reason given by Shailat for including the work in his collection of Maimonides's epistles. See *Iggerot ha-Rambam*, 9.

7. In Abraham S. Halkin and David Hartman, *Crisis and Leadership: Epistles of Maimonides* (Philadelphia, PA: Jewish Publication Society of America, 1985), trans. Halkin, 131.

8. Ibid., 247. Cf. Alfred L. Ivry's remark that the *Treatise on Resurrection* and the *Epistle on Astrology* "were also written to affect public attitudes toward issues on which the community held strong views" in *Maimonides' Guide of the Perplexed: A Philosophical Guide* (Chicago: University of Chicago Press, 2016), 21. The *Epistle on Astrology* was addressed to the sages of Montpellier, whom Maimonides believed would continue his philosophical tradition.

9. Shailat, *Iggerot ha-Rambam*, 464–91.

10. He was already preceded in this by several of the Babylonian geonim; see David Sklare, *Samuel Ben Ḥofni Gaon and His Cultural World: Texts and Studies* (Leiden: E. J. Brill, 1996), 64, especially n. 91, which refers to theological discussions in the responsa of the geonim.

11. See Sarah Stroumsa, *Reishit shel pulmus ha-Rambam ba-mizraḥ* (Jerusalem: Ben Tzvi Institute, 1999); and Y. Tzvi Langermann, "The Letter of R. Shmuel ben Eli on Resurrection" *Kovetẓ al Yad* 15 (2000): 41–92 [Hebrew].

12. See Bernard Septimus, *Hispano-Jewish Culture in Transition: The Career and Controversies of Ramah* (Cambridge, MA: Harvard University Press, 1982), 39–60.

13. See Alexander Marx, "Texts by and about Maimonides," *Jewish Quarterly Review* 25 (1934–35): 371–428, esp. 406–28.

14. Sheshet mentions several philosophical sources in Arabic, including the *Book of Doubts*, not identified by Marx, but which appears to be the critique of Galen by Al-Rāzī.

15. See Tariq Jaffer, "Bodies, Souls and Resurrection in Avicenna's *Ar-Risāla al-Aḍḥawīya fī amr al-mā'ād*," in David C. Reisman and Ahmed H. al-Rahim, *Before and After Avicenna: Proceedings of the First Conference of the Avicenna Study Group* (Leiden: Brill, 2003), 163–76.

16. Septimus, *Hispano-Jewish Culture in Transition*, 41.

17. Ibid., 61–74, for the former; for the latter, see Gregg Stern, *Philosophy and Rabbinic Culture: Jewish Interpretation and Controversy in Medieval Languedoc* (Abingdon, Oxon: Routledge, 2009).

18. See *Ḳoveẓ teshuvot ha-Rambam ve-iggerotav*, ed. A. Lichtenberg (Leipzig, 1859) (*Epistles of Jealousy* is the editor's title); and *Minḥat Qenaot*, in *Teshuvot ha-Rashba*, ed. Hayyim Zalman Dimitrovsky (Jerusalem: Mossad Harav Kook, 1990), 225–883.

19. The letters *were* published in "Schreiben des herrn R. Kirchheim an herrn Ignaz Blumenfeld in Wien," *Oẓar Neḥmad* 2 (1857): 117–24 [Hebrew].

20. *Tirat qesef*, in *Mishneh qesef: shenei beurim ʿal ha-Torah*, ed. I. Last (Pressburg: A. Alkqalai 1904), 1–168.

21. See *Kalonymos ben Kalonymos' Sendschreiben an Joseph Kaspi*, ed. P. Perles (Münich: T. Ackermann, 1879).

22. Ibid., 9–10.

23. See Howard Kreisel, *Prophecy: The History of an Idea in Medieval Jewish Philosophy* (Dordrecht: Kluwer Academic Publishers, 2001), 227–28.

24. Perles, *Kalonymos ben Kalonymos' Sendschreiben*, 25–26.

25. Ibid, 27–28.

26. *Hassagot ha-Rabad le-Mishneh Torah: Sefer ha-Madaʿ ve-sefer ha-ahavah*, ed. B. Naor (Jerusalem: B. Naor, 1985), 44–45.

27. Ḥasdai Crescas, Isaac's teacher and colleague, developed the limited-omniscience interpretation of Gersonides's views on God's knowledge. See Charles H. Manekin, "On the Limited-Omniscience Interpretation of Gersonides' Theory of Divine Knowledge," in *Perspectives on Jewish Thought and Mysticism*, ed. A. Ivry, E. Wolfson, and A. Arkush (Reading: Harwood Academic Publishers, 1998), 135–70.

28. *Sheelot u-teshuvot Bar Sheshet*, ed. I Daikhes (Vilna, 1879), no. 118, 24a.

29. *Das apologetische Schreiben des Josua Lorki an den Abtrünnigen Don Salomon Ha-Lewi* (*Paulus De Santa Maria*), ed. L. Landau (Antwerpen: Teitelbaum & Boxenbaum, 1906), 15. The passage in *De Caelo* 1.1 12–15 goes as follows; "And so, having taken these three from nature as (so to speak) laws of it, we make further use of the number three in the worship of the Gods." According to Gerhard Endress, "The *De caelo* quotation is from the standard version of Ibn al-Bitrīq, extant in a number of Arabic mss" (personal communication). It is similar though not identical to the text published in *Fī al-samāʾ wa-l-āthār al-ʿulwiyya*, ed. A. Badawi (Cairo: al-Nahḍa al-Miṣriyya, 1961), 126, which is a partial revision of Ibn al-Bitrīq's edition. The Arabic passage does not appear in the edition of Lorki's letter published by E. Ashkenazi and summarized in Colette Sirat, *A History of Jewish Philosophy in the Middle Ages* (Cambridge: Cambridge University Press, 1985), 348. Lorki subsequently converted to Christianity, took the name Jerome of Santa Fé, and was a protagonist of the Tortosa Disputation in 1413–1414.

30. An examination of Abner's sources is a scholarly desideratum. Some have been investigated by Ryan Szpiech in *From Testimonia to Testimony: Thirteenth-Century Anti-Jewish Polemic and the Mostrador de Justicia of Abner of Burgos/Alfonso of Valladolid* (PhD diss., Yale University, 2009).

31. See Maud Kozodoy, *The Secret Faith of Maestre Honoratus: Profayt Duran and Jewish Identity in Late Medieval Iberia* (Philadelphia: University of Pennsylvania Press, 2015), 115–28.

32. Printed as an appendix to *Maʿaseh Efod*, ed. J. Friedländer and J. Kohn (Vienna, 1865), 181–87.

33. Ibid., 183.

34. Kozodoy, *The Secret Faith of Maestre Honoratus*, 99–100.

35. Friedländer and Kohn, *Ma'aseh Efod*, 185–87. This appears in section 3, but section 2 is not Crescas's query.

36. Kozodoy, *The Secret Faith of Maestre Honoratus*, 64–72. Kozodoy writes on "A third philosophical letter . . . [which] can be found copied elsewhere, is usually collected together with the other two, and is also sometimes said to have been written to Meir Crescas." Yet the beginning reads, "שאלות האדון החוקר יאריך ה' ימיו לטוב לנו" (Questions of the master scholar, may the Lord lengthen his days for our benefit). The lack of any addressee or concluding signature suggests that these are not questions posed to a sage, but rather philosophical questions, that is, investigations.

37. Abner of Burgos/Alfonso de Valladolid, *Mostrador de justicia*, ed. W. Mettmann (Opladen: Westdeutscher Verlag, 1996–1997); Isaac Polgar, *'Ezer ha-dat*, ed. J. Levinger. (Tel-Aviv: Chaim Rosenberg School of Jewish Studies of Tel Aviv University, 1984).

38. The most up-to-date information about Abner can be found in Shalom Sadik, "Abner of Burgos," in *The Stanford Encyclopedia of Philosophy* (Fall 2016 edition), ed. Edward N. Zalta, https://plato.stanford.edu/archives/fall2016/entries/abner-burgos/. For Isaac Polgar, see Rachel Haliva, *Stanford Encyclopedia of Philosophy* (Winter 2017 edition), ed. Edward N. Zalta, https://plato.stanford.edu/archives/winter2016/entries/isaac-polgar/.

39. Yitzhak Baer, *A History of the Jews in Christian Spain* (Philadelphia, PA: Jewish Publication Society of America, 1961), 1:333, who calls Abner's determinism "a curious blend of the Pauline and Augustinian doctrines of predestination, with Moslem fatalism and the lore of astrology." In fact, Abner's determinism blends Avicennan determinism with astrology: see Charles H. Manekin, "Spinoza and the Hard Determinist Tradition in Jewish Philosophy," in *Spinoza and Medieval Jewish Philosophy*, ed. Steven Nadler (Cambridge, Cambridge University Press, 2014), 37–58, esp. 44–50.

40. Ibid., 50.

41. This historical reconstruction of the correspondence is based mainly on Abner's *Ofrenda de zelos*, the Spanish translation of *Minḥat Qenaot*, and part 3 of *'Ezer ha-Dat*. The best edition of the former is in Carlos Sainz de la Maza, "Alfonso de Valladolid: edición y estudio del manuscrito 'Lat. 6423' de la Biblioteca Apostólica Vaticana" (Madrid: Editorial de la Universidad Complutense, 1990). For Polgar, see now Rachel Haliva, "Isaac Polqar—A Jewish Philosopher or a Philosopher and a Jew? A Study of the Relationship between Philosophy and Religion in Isaac Polqar's ''Ezer ha-Dat' [In Support of the Law] and Teshuvat Apikoros [A Response to the Heretic]" (PhD diss., McGill University, 2015).

42. For the text, see Maurice Hayoun, "L'Épître du libre arbitre de Moïse de Narbonne. Édition du texte hébraïque avec traduction française, introduction et notes," *Revue des Études Juives* 141 (1982): 139–67. Translation in Charles H. Manekin, *Medieval Jewish Philosophical Writings* (Cambridge: Cambridge University Press, 2007), 143–52.

43. Ruth Glasner, *Vikuaḥ mada'i filosofi ba-me'ah ha-14: ha-Ma'amar be-hofkhei ha-mahalakh u-Khetav ha-hit'aẓmut* [A fourteenth-century scientific philosophical controversy: Jedaiah Ha-Penini's *Treatise on Opposite Motions* and *Book of Confutation*] (Jerusalem: World Union of Jewish Studies, 1998).

44. Ruth Glasner, "Levi Ben Gershom and the Study of Ibn Rushd in the Fourteenth Century," *Jewish Quarterly Review* 86 (1995): 51–90.

45. On contacts between these savants, see Charles H. Manekin, "Composition, Not Commentary—Gersonides' Commentary on the *Isagoge* of Porphyry and Its Afterlife," in *Gersonides' Afterlife: Studies of the Reception of Levi ben Gershom's Thought in the Medieval*

and Early Modern Hebrew and Latin Cultures, ed. David Wirmer, Ofer Elior, and Gad Freudenthal (Leiden: Brill, forthcoming).

46. Mauro Zonta, *Hebrew Scholasticism in the Fifteenth Century: A History and Source Book* (Dordrecht: Springer, 2006).

47. Mauro Zonta, "The Aragonese Circle of 'Jewish Scholasticism,'" in *Latin-Into-Hebrew: Texts and Studies*, ed. Resianne Fontaine and Gad Freudenthal (Leiden: Brill, 2013), 295–307, esp. 302, in which Zonta suggests that the two employ the Latin method of "disputed question."

48. Zonta, *Hebrew Scholasticism in the Fifteenth Century*, 201–8.

49. Ibid., 207.

50. Cited in Baer, *History*, 2:223.

51. Ibid.

52. See MS Oxford, Bodl. Mich. 155 (formerly 809) [Neubauer 1984], f. 89b, cited in A. Neubauer, *Catalogue of the Hebrew Manuscripts in the Bodleian Library* (Oxford, 1886–1906), 1:674.

53. For some references, see Ram Ben Shalom, "Between Official and Private Dispute: The Case of Christian Spain and Provence in the Late Middle Ages," *Association of Jewish Studies Review* 27 (2003): 23–71, esp. 70. Ben Shalom refers to a "decline" in the study of logic among the Spanish Jews, but there is no evidence for a decline; the evidence simply points to the inadequacy of Arabic-Hebrew tradition of logic in disputations with Christians and the necessity for learning scholastic logic. See Charles H. Manekin, "Scholastic Logic and the Jews," *Bulletin de l'étude de la philosophie médievale* 41 (1999): 123–47.

54. See Y. Hacker, "The Intellectual Activity of the Jews of the Ottoman Empire during the Sixteenth and Seventeenth Centuries," in *Jewish Thought in the Seventeenth Century*, ed. Isadore Twersky and Bernard Septimus (Cambridge, MA: Harvard University Press, 1987), 95–135, esp. 117–19.

55. *She'elot le-ha-ḥakham . . . Sha'ul ha-Kohen . . . sha'al me'et Yizhak Abrabanel* (Venice, 1574), 12a.

56. See Eric Lawee, "'The Good We Accept and the Bad We Do Not': Aspects of Isaac Abarbanel's Stance towards Maimonides," in *Be'erot Yitzhak: Studies in Memory of Isadore Twersky*, ed. Jay M. Harris (Cambridge, MA: Harvard University Press, 2005), 119–60.

57. Ibid., 14d.

58. The manuscripts and the printed edition of Abrabanel's "Commentary on the *Guide of the Perplexed*" contain disconnected explanations on various sections of the *Guide*, with little stylistic coherence. It may be that one or more of the sections represented materials for a commentary, but we have no indication that what we now have is an incomplete commentary. Joseph Solomon Delmedigo claims to have seen all of Abrabanel's commentary, but it is not clear to what he was referring. See David Ben Zazon, "The Commentary of Don Isaac Abrabanel to the *Guide of the Perplexed*," in *Da'at* 76 (2014): 173–89, esp. 178–80. Ben Zazon infers from a scribe's comment "that no more of this matter is found," that it is reasonable to assume that there were other chapters. But this is a standard formula for scribes who sense that something is missing, from which one cannot infer anything else. Cf. the longer discussion in Ben Zazon, *Nevukhim hem: masa' be-ve'uro shel Don Yitsḥaḳ Abravanel be-Moreh ha-nevukhim* (Jerusalem: Ben Zvi Institute, 2015), 1–100, esp. 63–70.

59. According to S. Pines, the reference is to *Metaphysics* 7.6.1071b29–30. Abrabanel did not have a copy of this book of the *Metaphysics* in Venice, nor were there books in philosophy to borrow, as he writes later.

60. Saul's question has to do with Maimonides's reference in *Guide* 2.15, trans. Pines, 292: "You know the text of [Aristotle's] words, which read as follows: 'As for the matters concerning which we have no argument or that are too great in our opinion, it is difficult for us to say: Why is this so? For instance, when we say, Is the world eternal or not.'" Saul writes that he had searched for the reference in Aristotle's metaphysical and physical treatises and that he had asked the savant Moses ibn Habib, who referred him to Themistius's commentary on *De Caelo*, but he found that answer unsatisfactory. In fact, as Pines points out, the reference is to *Topics* 1.11.104b15ff.

61. *Sefer Moreh nevukhim* . . . (Lemberg 1866), 2, 34b. The reference to Shem Tov (albeit incorrectly to "Shem Tov ibn Shem Tov") appears in a marginal gloss of the manuscript underlying the print version of Saul's twelve questions and is brought by the printer.

62. This quotation differs somewhat from the passage as it appears in Gershon B. Chertoff, *The Logical Part of Al-Ghazālī's Maqāsid Al-Falāsifa in an Anonymous Hebrew Translation with the Hebrew Commentary of Moses of Narbonne* (PhD diss., Columbia University, 1952), 56 [Hebrew]:
ומשפט הקודם והנמשך בתנאי המתדבק משפט הנושא והנשוא בחילוק חבורו אל אלה התמונות, וכו'

63. Moses Narboni writes that the conditional syllogism, "'If the sun is rising it is day; behold, it is rising,' reduces to a categorical, i.e., a compound [syllogism]: 'Now the sun is rising; and whenever the sun rises, it is day; hence, it is day.'" This example is missing from the manuscripts underlying Chertoff's edition; I have used Paris BN héb.1079 (IMHM F 15035), 40r.

64. *She'elot le-ha-ḥakham*, 15d.

65. Ibid., 16a.

66. Cf. *Guide* 3:1.

67. *She'elot le-ha-ḥakham*, 17a.

68. Paris BN héb.1079 (IMHM F 15035), 82r.

69. For this dispute see Herbert A. Davidson, *Alfarabi, Avicenna, and Averroes on Intellect: Their Cosmologies, Theories of the Active Intellect, and Theories of Human Intellect* (New York: Oxford University Press, 1992), 223–30.

70. See Moshe Narboni, *Be'ur le-Sefer More nevukhim*, ed. J. Goldenthal (Vienna, 1852), 16b–17a, 27a–b. Cf. Averroës, *The Epistle on the Possibility of Conjunction with the Active Intellect by Ibn Rushd with the Commentary of Moses Narboni*, ed. Kalman J. Bland (New York: Jewish Theological Seminary of America, 1982), 122–26 [Hebrew], 93–95 [English].

71. *She'elot le-ha-ḥakham*, 17d–18a.

72. See Ofer Elior, "Isaac Abravanel's Rejection of Corporeal Form," *Aleph* 12 (2012): 367–402.

73. See Jean-Pierre Rothschild, "Questions de philosophie soumises par Ēli Ḥabilio à Šēm Ṭōb Ibn Šēm Ṭōb, v.1472," *Archives d'histoire doctrinale et littéraire du moyen âge* 61 (1994): 105–32.

74. *She'elot le-ha-ḥakham*, 10a.

75. Ibid., 20a–c.

76. Ibid., 21b.

CHARLES H. MANEKIN is Professor of Philosophy at the University of Maryland. He is editor (with Daniel Davies) of *Interpreting Maimonides*.

11

THE SERMON IN LATE MEDIEVAL JEWISH THOUGHT AS METHOD FOR POPULARIZING PHILOSOPHY

Chaim Meir Neria

Introduction

Haim ibn Musa (c.1380–c.1460), in a letter addressed to his son, complains about preachers' use of "the technique of philosophical investigation" in their sermons: "Their sermons consist of syllogistic arguments and quotations from the philosophers. They mention by name Aristotle, Alexander, Themistius, Plato, Averroes and Ptolemy, while Abbaye and Raba are concealed in their mouths. . . . Happy is the one who shuts his eyes and does not see them, who stops up his ears from hearing their evil words."[1] Ibn Musa's sharp critique of the use of sermons represented a growing opposition to philosophy in fifteenth-century Judaism but represents one end of a continuum along which we find responses to Maimonides's legacy regarding revelation and concealment of philosophical knowledge.

The present chapter will consider the form, style, and content of Jewish sermons as they developed in Spain from the thirteenth to fifteenth centuries as a basis for a more focused examination of their role in the popularization of philosophical knowledge in general, and in Aristotle's *Ethics* in particular. The disdain expressed by Ibn Musa and others for the use of philosophy in sermons, not to mention the support for it among fifteenth-century Spanish Jewry, must be contextualized against inner

Jewish theological development, Jewish-Christian disputations, and the quest for new forms of knowledge during the invention of the printing press.

The Sermon as a Literary Genre

The Jewish sermon has a long history from rabbinic times to the present. Although it has assumed different forms, there is no doubt that the occasion on which the rabbi, the preacher, speaks before his congregation on the Sabbath and other special occasions was and remains a fundamental event of Jewish communal life. Considering the Jewish sermon as a distinct literary genre is not to be taken for granted. Sermons, like speeches, were not conceived as literary works but oral recitations, and, from this perspective, it is difficult to reconstruct the sermon "event." In contrast with Christian practice, in which trained scribes would record sermons as they were being delivered, the Jewish sermon was usually delivered on the Sabbath, which means it could have been written down before or after but not during the event.[2] Furthermore, although preachers would deliver their sermons in whatever language was familiar to their communities at the time, the written sermons that have come down to us are preserved in Hebrew.

In all likelihood, thousands of sermons were delivered orally during the Middle Ages. Few preachers, however, set their sermons down in writing, and of the sermons that were written down, only a small minority have survived. It is reasonable to assume that only sermons with special value beyond the time and place of their delivery were recorded, preserved, and copied. It is clear, then, that the sermon *literature* at our disposal cannot convey the experience of the actual sermon; nor is it representative of the literature as a whole. At the same time, based on the extensive material that has survived in printed volumes or manuscripts, most scholars of sermon literature agree that the authors of these sermons wrote them with an awareness that they were writing a literary work with distinct characteristics, and, therefore, the sermon is undoubtedly worthy of attention as a unique literary form.[3]

From the thirteenth century—when we have our first collections of sermons—to the fifteenth, the formal structure of the sermon was extremely important. In most cases, the preacher would begin with a biblical citation. In the thirteenth century, the opening verse was generally taken from the Writings; beginning in the mid-fourteenth century, the custom took shape of opening with a verse from the Torah, or sometimes with a quotation from aggadic or midrashic literature. In a later stage of the sermon's development, this opening verse or rabbinic saying became known by the technical Hebrew term *nose'* (topic, equivalent to the Latin *thema*).

After the "topic," the opening verse, many preachers would quote a source from the Aggadah or midrash, which became known as the *ma'amar* (framing rabbinic discourse). A third part of the sermon has been given the technical name *perishah*, the "interpretive" or "homiletic" stage. This term refers to the model by which the preacher explains a section of the text verse by verse. The term is parallel to the use of the "homily" among Christian preachers. In the fourteenth and fifteenth centuries, some preachers would raise a series of questions or "doubts," *sefeqot*, during this part of the sermon and then answer them as the sermon developed. Other preachers derived lessons from the central part of the weekly Torah reading (*parashah*) on which the preacher expounded. Over time, additional techniques were added to the sermon, such as permission or apology, brief introductions, and other elements.

An additional development, which deviated from what I call "homiletic sermons" and was closely related to the later development of the "philosophical sermon," were presentations called *derushim*. In this sermon technique the preacher would not explicate a biblical passage but would rather focus on a conceptual problem and discuss it from a religious-philosophical angle. The *derushim* were mostly of a clear didactic and formal nature, raising questions and doubts and resolving them. The structure and development of these sermons were not guided by a need to interpret a biblical passage but by the desire to provide an answer to a theological question raised by the preacher.[4]

The Philosophical Sermon Relative to Other Genres

Marc Saperstein has characterized the Jewish sermon as aiming to connect both with the elite culture of a few highly educated individuals and the Jewish community at large in which the preachers lived. As a historian, he sought in his reading to examine, with the help of the sermons, to what extent philosophy penetrated the popular discourse in Jewish communal life. According to Saperstein, philosophical compositions of various types—treatises, glossaries, commentaries, encyclopedias, summaries, and primers—served as tools for the dissemination of philosophical ideas but were limited in appeal because philosophical writing was difficult to understand and restricted to a small circulation, in part due to their cost. The sermon, in contrast, was directed to the public at large, not just the elite, and thus had to be clear, understandable, and not too complex or intricate. Saperstein suggests that, as a result of this, the presence of direct quotations from and indirect references to philosophical ideas and terms in sermons leads to the conclusion that philosophical thought had become a natural part of contemporary Jewish culture.[5] As we shall see, however, this claim requires much elaboration and qualification.

Rhetoric and the Popularization of Philosophy in Sermons—Research Methodology

The task of tracing the developments in the process of the popularization of philosophy through sermons presents a challenging methodological problem. First, as I have stated, the existing homiletical literature cannot faithfully represent the sermons as they were presented orally, and all we have to rely on today is the existing homiletical literature. In this literature we can distinguish to a certain degree between sermons that try to remain close to the oral presentation and edited sermons in which there is greater distance from the original. In the attempt to conduct a scholarly evaluation of the degree of popularization of philosophy, greater weight must be allotted to the question of whether a particular sermon reflects the original delivery or is a later adaptation. In addition, we must take into account external evidence. As we have seen, Haim ibn Musa, who expresses opposition to integrating philosophical content into sermons, nevertheless provides first-hand testimony of a real phenomenon: preachers were in fact making reference to philosophical literature and using philosophical terminology in their synagogue sermons. We thus conclude that philosophical literature was cited and referenced in sermons in communal context and was not simply the result of later adaptation.

Second, we know, for example, that the sermons were delivered in the vernacular, while the homiletical literature, in contrast, is written in Hebrew, with all philosophical quotations presented in Hebrew translation. Did the preacher, when editing his sermons, add philosophical excerpts in order to lend the sermon a depth and seriousness that he could not transmit orally? When we have a philosophical quotation, assuming that the preacher did relate to it in his sermon, how did he quote it? In Hebrew or in the vernacular? And what sources did he select?

Finally, what is the nature of philosophical quotations in sermons and homiletical literature? Do they have a rhetorical function only? Or are they significant references to philosophical topics and texts? Is it even possible to distinguish between these categories, and how? A reasonable conjecture would be that the deeper and more significant the reference to a philosophical term or idea, the more central a layer it constitutes in the sermon, and the more likely that indeed the original sermon discussed to some extent the same philosophical issue or text. In contrast, the inclusion of a philosophical quotation inserted merely as a rhetorical device arouses suspicion that it is an afterthought, employed as a device to add volume to the sermon's breadth and depth of thought.

Return of Philosophy to Jewish Thought—Provence

The philosophical sermon as we know it began to develop in thirteenth-century Provence among Maimonidean enthusiasts who did not share Maimonides's mistrust of philosophical popularization and his requirement for esotericism.

The first major figure to move in this direction was Jacob Anatoli (c. 1194–1256) Samuel ibn Tibbon's (1165–1232) son-in-law and the first author of a collection of Hebrew sermons. In the preface to his collection of homilies *Malmad ha-talmidim*, he presents as an example the interpretations that he sees as being accepted by the Christians. Anatoli claims that "they attempt to investigate the Bible in depth according to their belief, constantly preaching in public, with the result that their lie is held to be the truth, whereas the Jews are lazy in this regard, with many rabbis content to have the Torah read without delving into its meaning."[6] There is no justification, Anatoli claims, for sharing scientific knowledge only with intellectuals. The objective must be "that we and our offspring be knowers of Your name,"[7] that is, the Jewish aspiration should be that knowledge belongs to everyone, and everyone should take part in it. Esotericism, explains Anatoli, impinges on the ability to understand the Torah, since it leaves the masses in the shadows of ignorance. Moreover, he claims elsewhere, when the correct beliefs are not disseminated among the masses, people become tempted to adopt false beliefs, such as the belief in occult spirits or demons.[8] The dissemination of correct beliefs is not forbidden: and not only is it permitted, but it is imperative.

From a methodological perspective, it was clear to Anatoli that books are elitist in form and are not suited to the purpose of spreading philosophical knowledge among the masses; a new format, therefore, must be created.

The format Anatoli chose was the traditional sermon. The sermon is a tool that by nature is directed at a broad audience of readers or listeners; it aims to spread the elite culture of the educated individuals to the public at large. By composing brief, focused sermons, each of which constitutes a distinct literary unit, Anatoli succeeded in successfully grappling with the philosophical complexity of his subject by turning esoteric knowledge into exoteric opinion. Joseph Dan has already noted that Anatoli, in *Malmad ha-talmidim*, completely crystalized a new genre of "philosophical sermons" whose goal was to make philosophy available to a broad audience of listeners and readers.[9]

And yet it is important to be precise: the "philosophy" disseminated by Anatoli in *Malmad ha-talmidim* is not philosophy in the usual sense, but rather a philosophical-allegorical interpretation of the Bible. In other words, Anatoli does not frequently quote external, non-Jewish philosophical sources but instead relies on radical interpretations of the Bible and rabbinic literature, using it to represent a philosophical meaning of the words of the Torah to the masses.

Anatoli's attempt to spread philosophical wisdom and esoteric knowledge, by applying and teaching a philosophical-allegorical approach to the Bible, was not as successful as he may have hoped, and in fact, by his own report, local communities in southern France prevented him from continuing to expound his ideas in the synagogue. Despite this popular opposition, however, he did inspire a community of avid admirers who rallied around him and who were eager to hear his teachings. For this community of like-minded seekers of wisdom, he arranged his sermons into a book, *Malmad ha-talmidim*.[10] Ultimately the public tension, surrounding Anatoli's allegorical-philosophical sermons on the Torah and related works, started to spread and erupted into a large-scale public debate about the legitimacy of philosophy in Judaism that divided the Jewish population into contending factions. The result was the declaration of a ban on philosophy and philosophical pursuit, imposed by key rabbis including the Rashba (Shlomo ben Adret, d. 1310), dealing a blow to the dissemination of philosophical knowledge in the Jewish communities of Europe and putting the question of philosophical sermons to rest for almost a century.[11]

The Standard Format of the Rabbinic Sermon in Thirteenth- and Fourteenth-Century Spain

In the standard format of the rabbinic sermon in thirteenth- and fourteenth-century Spain, the preacher would generally begin with a verse from the Writings, usually the book of Proverbs. He would suggest different ways of understanding the verse, while focusing on the straightforward meaning of the text and adding ethical advice and words of encouragement. This would reach climax with the postulation of a final way to understand the opening verse so that it could connect with the opening verse of the Torah portion read that week liturgically in the synagogue. Often, the preacher would add a long succession of homilies, rabbinic Aggadot, or halakhic teachings relevant to the day or season at the end; but no philosophy was included.

The Style and Content of the Jewish Sermon in Fifteenth-Century Spain and the Changes in Its Status and Structure

At the end of the fourteenth century and throughout the fifteenth, a significant change occurred in the manner in which sermons were delivered and recorded in the Jewish communities of Europe. In the Spanish diaspora, which will be the focus of the remainder of this chapter, the change was especially apparent and is related in part to the wide circulation and popularization of philosophical ideas.

Changes in the sermon were already discernable at the end of the fourteenth century. For example, sermons of the *derushim* subtype by Nissim b. Reuben of Gerona (Ran, 1310–1373) deviate from the traditional mold. First, they usually open with a saying by the sages or from the Aggadah rather than the Writings. Second, to the extent that they converse with a written text, they relate more to the content of the parashah and thematic units than the interpretation of individual verses. Third, they explore, in a technical way, philosophical and religious issues of universal significance that were not directly related to the Torah portion on whose week they were delivered. These and other reasons, such as their length, have led some scholars to claim that Nissim's sermons are not representative of sermons as a whole.[12] In my view, however, this conclusion is too hasty and based on a misreading of the data—the uniqueness of these sermons indicates not that they are a deviation, but rather that they mark the beginning of a new trend. I believe that the *drushim* of Nissim of Gerona, even if not a representative example of "sermons" that were in fact delivered in the synagogue, reflect the search for a different path and a new literary expression originating in the framework of the public sermon.

The Philosophical Sermon—Precursors and Prototypes

The deviation from the traditional sermon format found, say, in Nissim of Gerona's sermons, is moderate and still constitutes an interpretation of earlier homiletical literature. However, the sermon on the Passover by his student Hasdai Crescas (c. 1340–1410/11), the only sermon preserved in his writings, breaks completely with the earlier stylistic tradition.[13] In Crescas's Passover sermon, the preacher adopts a form from Christian scholastic writings—the "disputed question"—as the rhetorical and literary form for his public sermon delivered on the eve of Passover.

Crescas does not open with a verse, a midrash, or any sort of introduction, but with a question: "Do miracles create rational assent or faith in the human soul, even when willful agreement is lacking, or do they not?" After clarifying the question, he proposes four arguments that negate the role of the will in the surge in faith that follows a miracle. He adopts the second position, according to which miracles and belief in them force themselves upon awareness and will and rejects the other arguments. In the second stage of the sermon, Crescas does return to the traditional *derashah* framework in describing the laws relevant to the occasion, in this case those pertaining to the Passover holiday.

It is important to note that, at the level of content, there is no doubt that Crescas is a Jewish philosopher struggling with the philosophical-allegorical approach of Maimonides. In his struggle against philosophy, Crescas even makes an impressive philosophical effort to undermine the basic physical and metaphysical assumptions of Aristotle, to whom he often refers to simply as "the Greek." At the same time, the style and form through which he fights the war against philosophy are themselves saliently philosophical.

The drastic stylistic change found in Crescas's sermon is startling, but it can be explained as reflecting the effort to express new ideas and to devise for them a suitable literary framework. As a whole, the goal of the popular preacher is to win over his audience. From this perspective, a formal sermon with a rigid structure is not ideal for creating a discourse that seeks to capture the hearts of the listeners. The process by which sermons take on a formal and didactic structure, claims Joseph Dan, discloses a process of the penetration of new and even foreign ideas.[14] Only when the preacher makes an effort to undermine the balance between himself and the audience and to introduce new ideas into the heart of the discourse is he forced to emphasize the Logos of the speech over the pathos and in so doing to amplify the weight of the sermon's formal elements. From this perspective, Crescas's sermon on the Passover is a striking example of a formal and didactic discourse with ideas that, as conservative as they may be, can only be expressed in the language of logic and philosophy.

To what extent, then, does Crescas's sermon on the Passover represent the transition from a homiletical-rabbinic to a homiletical-philosophical style, thereby opening up the possibility for popularizing philosophy within the traditional Jewish community? It is difficult to provide a precise answer, partly because all that we possess is this single sermon. What can be safely stated is that, at the end of the fourteenth century, a change takes place in the style of sermons related to a quest for a new way to express contemporary ideas. It can thus be assumed that from Crescas onwards, sermons will look different. For example, the sermons of Crescas's student Zerahiyah ha-Levi Saladin (d. c. 1455) already belong squarely to the genre of philosophical sermons that developed in fifteenth-century Spain.[15] At the same time, even if a number of sermons can be identified that are solely based on the formal structure and scholastic style of the "disputed question," this specific style did not become dominant in the homiletical literature of fifteenth-century Spain.

The Philosophical Sermons of the Fifteenth Century: Between Conservatism and Innovation

During the fifteenth century, the Sephardic sermon assumed a new and independent well-defined literary form and emerged as a distinct and clear genre aware of its own genesis. The new Sephardic sermon, distinct from its traditional counterpart, barely dealt with matters of halakah or exegesis. Rather, it engaged with theological ideas, rabbinic homilies (midrashim), and polemic with the dominant religion, Christianity. From the audience's perspective, rhetorical, aesthetic, and content-related standards were expected of the preacher. Thus, during this period there was a demand for the instruction of preachers, and the first preaching manuals and rhetorical guidebooks were written in Hebrew, both to aid active preachers and to initiate future preachers into the art.

Naturally, a significant cultural change in a popular genre cannot transpire without reaction. Sephardic Jewry, during this stormy and unpredictable period, was on edge. In political terms, the community was attempting to recuperate from the riots and forced conversions of 1391, to rebuild its public status, to deal with the phenomenon of the new Christians, and to defend itself in public disputations. Moreover, in many areas, the community members were forced to attend public sermons of church officials.[16] Within the community, Jews debated the spiritual roots of the political crisis, questioning whether the Jewish interest in philosophy had weakened the spiritual force of Sephardic Jewry, leading to conversion and the inability to withstand the conversionary attacks from outside.

All of these factors led to a situation in which the sermon took on special significance and became a central organ in the defense of the community, both internally and against the outside world. The community and its spiritual leaders understood that in the struggle against Christian persecution, it was necessary to unite the community and to use the sermons to summon the masses—and not just the elite—to take part in the contemporary struggles and respond to the daily challenges.

In addition to the sermon itself, the competence of the preacher—including his textual abilities, his rhetorical skills, his strategies, and his abilities as a scholar and philosopher—in leading the communal response to external pressure had an effect on the entire community. A popular preacher might strengthen the spirit of someone already possessing strong belief but would find it difficult to formulate a response to philosophical questions and external attacks. A philosophical preacher might deal better with the external attacks, but the price would be a loss of popularity and a weakening of popular belief in tradition. It was this context that gave rise to the debates over the boundaries of the field and the literary sources that the preacher could draw from, particularly in relation to philosophy.

Without a doubt, Haim ibn Musa, who is quoted at the beginning of this chapter, had an authentic disdain for the philosophical sermon, although it is difficult to accept his view as a reflection of the overall public atmosphere. It might be assumed that key portions of the community wished to hear the content offered by the philosophizing preachers, who were not completely divorced from contemporary attitudes among the general populace. As Bernard Septimus so aptly stated,[17] preachers were never completely cut off from market forces. Ibn Musa himself admits that philosophy has utility when used to assist in disputations with the Christians; he even understands that, in his time of political and religious turmoil, ignoring philosophy is impossible. Yet he asks to restrict philosophical investigation to the polemical encounter with Christianity and "not to preach it to the congregation." To the extent that the preacher cannot avoid making reference to philosophy, says Ibn Musa, he must focus on neutral texts "that are not harmful and do not corrupt faith or divert the heart of a single member of the congregation into thinking improper thoughts."[18]

Joseph b. Shem-Tob's '*Ein ha-qore*' and the Rhetorical Art of Preaching

A completely different approach is found in the work *'Ein ha-qore'*, written by Joseph b. Shem-Tob, Ibn Musa's contemporary.[19] *'Ein ha-qore'* is the first book in Hebrew that systematically addresses the genre of the sermon, the status of the preacher, and the rhetorical and aesthetic standards with which he must comply. While Joseph b. Shem-Tob links his instructions to the preacher with the verse, "Cry with full throat, without restraint; Raise your voice like a ram's horn! Declare to My people their transgression, To the House of Jacob their Sin," (Isa. 58:1), his basic premises for evaluating the status of sermon and preacher are predicated on the principles of practical and political philosophy.

Joseph b. Shem-Tob's starting point for the role of the sermon and status of the preacher is the assumption that "man is a political animal." As a proof text, he quotes from Aristotle's *Ethics* together with the verse from Genesis, "It is not good for man to be alone" (Gen. 2:18). The state, as a social entity, needs leadership in the form of kings, rulers, and judges who will direct its leaders to do what is good and just. In this case as well, the sources that he references are Plato's *Republic* together with the biblical injunction "to set a king over yourself" (Deut. 17:15). Joseph b. Shem-Tob goes on to assert that if we require that leaders have the state's best interest in mind, surely the soul requires such a ruler and a guide.

The preacher is the guide, the ruler, the king, the healer of souls who guides the members of the community or the state in the quest to attain eternal life. In contrast to the king, the ruler, or the judge, the preacher does not force the hand of those subordinate to him but encourages their ability to choose good, using "the vivid language and polished rhetoric and best tools of his art in a manner that will make people desire the virtues and choose them freely."[20] As an art, the craft of the sermon is subject to the definitions and conditions that define and are the practice in this art. As a practical art, Joseph b. Shem-Tob claims the sermon must take into consideration its intended audience, its "customers" or the "sick" to whom the preacher is tending.

In Joseph b. Shem-Tob's opinion, there are five types of speech—logical demonstration, sophistry, dialectic, rhetoric, and poetry. The use of logical proof, in the style employed by Crescas, is irrelevant for a sermon for two reasons. The first is that the subject matter of sermons are not arguments that can be refuted or validated using syllogism, but rather matters relating to truths of the Torah. The second reason is that the use of logical proofs in a sermon requires the preacher's mastery of the many components of the complex art of logic, and there are few preachers of this type. In addition, claims Joseph b. Shem-Tob, such a sermon cannot accommodate a varied and popular audience in which the educated sit alongside the masses.

The preacher is also prohibited, according to Joseph b. Shem-Tob, from using the art of sophistry, since the goal of sophistry is to present lies as truth, and if the preacher is a healer of souls, deceiving the public using the tools of sophistry will intensify rather than heal the ailment from which the public suffers. Nor is dialectics suitable for use in sermons, for in dialectical speech the objective is to persuade the audience regarding one's position without relating to the question as to whether it is true.

The art of poetry is disqualified by Joseph b. Shem-Tob because it is removed from the masses and because it has been condemned by the "ancients," that is, Aristotle, who accused Plato of using excessively poetic and obscure language. Thus does the preacher remain with only one choice, namely, rhetoric, whose goal, as defined by Joseph b. Shem-Tob, is to "beautify the [. . .] ideas and to express them through vivid analogies,"[21] and from this perspective it is suitable both for the educated listeners and for the masses, since each type of listener can find in it words that speak to his heart.

Having established this, Joseph b. Shem-Tob sets out to examine and critique the preachers of his generation. First, he critiques the traditional preachers who are content to present and expound on the literal meanings of the midrash and the words of the sages. In his view, these preachers are beneficial neither for the masses nor for the educated elite, as they offer no innovation nor do they challenge or make any meaningful contribution to their listeners. Joseph b. Shem-Tob's underlying message here is that the time of the traditional sermon has passed, and it is no longer able to meet the needs of the community. If the preacher is the community's healer of souls, the traditional preacher using outdated methods is, as it were, using expired medication. Such a preacher lacks a deep understanding of the challenges with which the community is grappling, and he lacks the tools needed to address its crises.

In the second stage of his argument, Joseph b. Shem-Tob critiques the preachers who comprehend correctly that the times are changing—that there is a need for new content, and even for a new style—but fail in transmitting the message. First, he directs his critique at the witty preachers who sometimes use syllogism in a manner that obscures the meaning of their words. Continuing this line of argument, he then critiques those who use sophistical or dialectical claims in a manner that misleads the public. Finally, he attacks those preachers who express themselves in poetic language or inject esoteric content that has a supposed hidden meaning, thereby speaking "over the heads" of the listeners rather than directly to them. The conclusion Joseph b. Shem-Tob reaches is that there is a need for deep but not rigidly structured sermons that employ rhetoric and analogies and avoid language that is either overly poetic or too technical.

Comparing the position of Joseph b. Shem-Tob to that of Ibn Musa, it is clear that the traditional sermon whose demise Ibn Musa laments is perceived as irrelevant by Joseph b. Shem-Tob. Joseph b. Shem-Tob has moved on and, unlike his predecessors, evaluates the status of the preacher and the role of the sermon as rooted entirely in the philosophical-conceptual world and in the role philosophy attributes to rhetoric as a means of persuasion.

The Popularization and Popularity of Aristotle's *Ethics* in Fifteenth-Century Homiletical Literature

Since a complete mapping of the full range of the use of philosophy in sermons is beyond the scope of this chapter, I will confine my focus to two preachers and through them examine the attitudes to and use of Aristotle's *Ethics* in fifteenth-century homiletical literature.

Maimonides, influenced by the Arabic version of the *Nicomachean Ethics* both directly and indirectly, is the first Jewish philosopher to quote from and refer to this work in his writings.[22] Over one hundred years passed from the death of Maimonides until 1321, when the *Nicomachean Ethics* appeared in its first Hebrew translation, entitled *Sefer ha-middot*. The translator was Samuel ben Judah of Marseille (b. 1294),[23] although he did not translate the Aristotelian text itself but rather Averroes's *Middle Commentary* on it.[24]

It was only at the beginning of the fifteenth century that a complete translation of Aristotle's work was made into Hebrew by the chief rabbi of Castile, Don Meir Alguades (d. c. 1410). As a basis for his translation, Alguades relied on Robert Grosseteste's (c. 1170–1253) edition of the Latin text and on Christian scholastic commentaries. His translation was smoother, more eloquent, and clearer than that of Samuel ben Judah. In addition, Alguades, writing in mosaic style, inserted into the text fragments of biblical verses and even gave biblical names to the Aristotelian virtues, giving the reader of the Hebrew text a sense of familiarity rather than alienation toward the Aristotelian text. This "Judaization" of the Aristotelian text gave the Jewish reader a feeling that the text spoke in his language and conversed with his tradition in the deepest manner.[25]

In contrast to the translation of Samuel ben Judah, that of Alguades became tremendously popular, and by the end of the fifteenth century, it was the most frequently cited philosophical source in Jewish homiletical literature. Thus did a remarkable and perhaps unprecedented phenomenon unfold: A book translated in the fifteenth century that, in effect, constituted a fresh or new source of philosophical ideas became more popular than any of the philosophical works that preceded it.

In the case of Sephardic rabbinic thought and sermons of the fifteenth century, the *Ethics* was quoted by Zerahiyah ha-Levi Saladin, Joseph Albo (c. 1380–1444), Moses Arragel (c. 1400–1493), Joseph b. Shem-Tob ibn Shem-Tob (c. 1400–1460), Shem-Tob b. Joseph ibn Shem-Tob (d. c. 1493/1492), Abraham Shalom (d. 1492), Joel ibn Shueib (fl. 1469–1489), Joseph Hayyun (d. 1497), Isaac Abarbanel (c. 1437–1508), and Isaac Arama (c. 1420–1494), along with other anonymous preachers. If in 1442 Joseph b. Shem-Tob complained that Aristotle's *Ethics* was the least known work among the Jews, not much time passed before this claim no longer reflected the reality, inter alia due to the efforts of Joseph b. Shem-Tob himself to accelerate the book's popularization.

The translation of the *Ethics* into a more accessible Hebrew and the efforts to Judaize the text certainly contributed to its popularity, but the popularization of a text cannot be attributed solely to a translation. Additional and even more significant factors must be taken into account. The first is the popularization of the book among the Christian elite. The second is the existence of a conceptual, intellectual, and theological mold that enabled and even advanced the acceptance of Aristotle's *Ethics* in Jewish society. Regarding the first factor—popularization of the book among Christian elites—the two translators of the *Ethics* into Hebrew, Samuel ben Judah and Meir Alguades, expressed their jealousy that the *Ethics* occupied a significant place among the Christians in contrast to the lack of understanding or interest among Jews, including the elite. Samuel ben Judah and

Meir Alguades took part in the task of disseminating the *Ethics* due to their sense that there was a need, even a spiritual necessity, to teach and develop ethical philosophical thinking among the Jewish population.[26] The lack of ethical philosophical literature, together with the popularity of the book itself among the Christian elite, created pressure to disseminate it among the Jewish elite.

At the same time, the second factor, the development of a system of theological thought that could "digest" Aristotle's *Ethics* and was interested in developing a deep dialogue with it, was no less significant. It is clear that in Christian tradition as well, the dialogue with and commentary on the *Ethics* by philosophers such as Albertus Magnus, Thomas Aquinas, and many others contributed to the dissemination of the *Ethics* among the Christian elite, its popularization, and its becoming a canonical text.

It was Maimonides who set down the foundations for a dialogue between Aristotelian ethics and Jewish philosophy. Maimonides adopted Aristotelian concepts such as the "middle way," emphasized the importance of habit in the formation of psychic virtues, and viewed the Torah and its precepts as a practical path for acquiring ethical and intellectual virtues. Although Maimonides's synthesis between Aristotelian ethics and the Jewish Torah was unacceptable to most fifteenth-century Jewish philosophers, thinkers such as Joseph Albo, Zerahiyah ha-Levi Saladin, and especially Joseph b. Shem-Tob proposed alternative formulations of a theological perspective that offered a fruitful basis for dialogue with Aristotle's *Ethics*. Joseph b. Shem-Tob set forth the basic principles of his perspective in a brief book entitled *Kebod Elohim*[27] and subsequently in his long commentary on the *Ethics*, the first ever Hebrew commentary on the work.[28] Using principles proposed by Thomas Aquinas, some of which had been popularized in Hebrew, Joseph b. Shem-Tob sharpened the distinction between religious and ethical action. An ethical act is a secular, human act that a Jew engages in that is no different than what the Greek Aristotle or a Christian neighbor does. For example, a hero, a warrior, or a man of great character with lofty virtues does not carry out his actions in a religious framework. An analysis of his actions must be evaluated in an ethical, human language and as part of a striving for human happiness. On the basis of the human, ethical language—and not necessarily overlapping with it—a religious language can be constructed that strives not for human happiness but rather for divine bliss. Aristotle knows well how to describe the recipe for human success; as for divine bliss, however, only the Torah can provide this.

If we take into account that Joseph b. Shem-Tob is the teacher of Isaac Abarbanel,[29] that his son is Shem-Tob b. Joseph, and that Isaac Arama used Joseph b. Shem-Tob's commentary on the *Ethics*,[30] the direct influence of Joseph b. Shem-Tob on these preachers and on their use of the *Ethics* in their sermons and compositions is clear and profound. In what follows, I will examine the attitude toward philosophy, especially Aristotle's *Ethics*, in the collection of sermons by Zerahiyah ha-Levi Saladin, active at the turn of the fifteenth century. I will then compare it to the attitude toward philosophy reflected in the collection of sermons by Shem-Tob b. Joseph, who wrote at the turn of the sixteenth century.

Popularization of the *Ethics* in the Sermons of Zerahiyah Ha-Levi Saladin

Zerahiyah ha-Levi Saladin was a student of Hasdai Crescas, and a partial collection of his sermons has been published by Ari Ackerman. In addition to his being a scholar of Torah and a prominent rabbinic figure who served as a communal rabbi after Crescas, Zerahiyah undertook the task of translating philosophical literature into Hebrew and was an active member of the poets' association 'Adat Nognim (Minstrels' circle), which was active in Spain during this period.[31] Resembling the lone surviving sermon of Hasdai Crescas, the sermons of Zerahiyah are well constructed and divided into clear parts, usually opening with a brief preliminary description of the structure of the sermon he is about to deliver. The sermon is usually constructed around a single biblical verse, which is the "topic" of the sermon, or in Zerahiyah's words, "the starting point of our topic." One of Zerahiyah's key innovations is the use of logical and philosophical materials. This includes an analysis of a particular verse as a logical axiom, premise, examination of the relationship between subject and object, presentation of "phenomena," and, in general, the use of technical philosophical terminology and Aristotelian logic at every stage of the analysis and discussion.

Given the content, it is difficult to believe that Zerahiyah's sermons were popular. It is unlikely that the general masses could have listened to complex sermons with this kind of structure and terminology. And yet, even if his sermons were not delivered weekly before a large, popular audience, the sermons were apparently authentic, since the written texts are rich with descriptions of the sermon's oral delivery. These include mention of the place in which the sermon was delivered, such as a synagogue, house of mourning, or wedding ceremony.[32]

As for explicit mention of Aristotle, there is one reference to *On the Heavens* and an additional quotation that is likely taken from it,[33] alongside an indirect reference to the topic discussed in that work.[34] There are also allusions to *On the Soul*, a possible reference to the *Metaphysics*,[35] two explicit references to the *Physics*,[36] and other assorted references to the issues discussed there as well. There is one reference to Aristotle's *Posterior Analytics*[37] together with extensive use of Aristotelian logical terminology. There is one reference to Aristotle's *Categories* and yet another on the issues discussed there without mention of the book.[38] And finally, surprisingly, there is a reference to Aristotle's *Politics* via a mention of his critique of Socrates and Plato and their principle supporting shared property and wives.[39]

In contrast to these few mentions, there are many references to the *Ethics*. The first reference to the first book of the *Ethics* is his remark that one cannot say of a man who is still among the living that he has reached complete success and that his life has been good in the absolute sense.[40] An oblique reference to the first book of the *Ethics* is the idea that the greater honor accrues to the person who bestows it, not to the recipient. The preacher's father's interpretation of the verse, "And you shall love the Lord your God" (Deut. 6:5), is that this love is dependent on the previous verse, "the Lord is One," based on Aristotle's idea in the eighth book of the *Ethics* that complete love can only transpire from one individual to another, and if love is divided between a number of people, it is deficient.[41] A mention of the third book of the *Ethics* is in the concept that a person can be praised or condemned only in matters in which he or she has exercised free choice. A further reference to the *Ethics* is his mention that a person who acts in violation of the law or tends toward extremes is not a rightful person.[42] Finally, there is a comprehensive review of the beginning of the *Ethics*, including long excerpts and glosses, but with no explicit mention of the work.[43]

From this general and preliminary comparison, one can see that in contrast to occasional and brief references to various works in Aristotle's corpus, almost all of the mentions and references to the *Ethics* are full, and in some instances clearly defined. Almost all of the references to the *Ethics* are significant to the preacher's claim and not auxiliary rhetorical devices. An outlying exception is the last reference mentioned here, from the sermon on Isaiah 3:10, "Happy is the just man, for he shall fare well," in which the preacher invokes and interprets Aristotle's words as the most essential part—almost one third of the sermon—both quoting them and discussing them at length.

Zerahiyah ha-Levi Saladin's quotations from the *Ethics* are taken from Averroes's *Middle Commentary* as translated by Samuel ben Judah of Marseilles. Zerahiyah does not use Meir Alguades's new translation in his sermons, since when he wrote them, it apparently did not exist. Zerahiyah belonged to the literary group 'Adat Nognim, mentioned above, of which Alguades was also a member. It is likely that the group's familiarity with the *Ethics* and the importance of the book among the Christian Spanish intelligentsia is effectively what led to its translation. In any case, the sermons of Zerahiyah ha-Levi Saladin represent a clear case of the popularization of philosophy in general and of the *Nicomachean Ethics* in particular. The style of his sermons was not completely popular, since they were intended for an educated ear and an intellectual stratum that was capable of understanding them. Even if in some of his sermons he takes a stand against philosophical perspectives, as did his teacher Crescas, he does so as a philosopher.

Popularization of the *Ethics* in the Sermons of Shem-Tob b. Joseph

Like his father, Shem-Tob b. Joseph integrated a broad philosophical education and love of philosophy into his sermons. In an introductory comment woven into the beginning of his book *Sermons on the Torah*, he describes the collection he is writing as written versions of his public sermons. The manuscripts reveal that the collection was completed in 1489 and includes orderly sermons according to the weekly Torah portion, usually one sermon per portion, sometimes more than one. In addition, Shem-Tob included in his collection sermons for weddings, along with sermons on the topic of repentance. The sermons were first published in Salonica in 1525 and twice more in the sixteenth century, though there are discrepancies between the published versions and the manuscripts.

Shem-Tob b. Joseph thought that the influence of the oral sermon was able to—and must—have influence beyond the limited audience to which it was delivered. The condition for this was to record it in writing, since the written sermon has the potential of exerting a religious-ethical influence and reaching an audience that was not present at the oral delivery. Shem-Tob viewed the creation of a written version of the sermon as a necessity due to the miserable historical situation of his people, "who were assaulted by troubles daily." In addition, he considered the written version a model for future preachers. The written sermon would thus continue to have influence on an ever-widening circle of readers and listeners.

As a rule, the sermons of Shem-Tob b. Joseph do not follow a rigid format and are quite varied in nature. Some are more popular, with messages that are relatively easy to grasp, that relate to the life experiences of Spanish Jewry during the period preceding the expulsion; others are profound and intellectual but almost always remain accessible to a popular audience. My overall impression is that Shem-Tob's sermons are not overflowing with philosophical material drawn from external sources, but it is clear that he was intimately familiar with and fluent in philosophical language. In contrast to the philosophical material, he does discuss—sometimes at length—different interpretations of rabbinic Aggadot and biblical texts, many according to Maimonides's *Guide*. For example, in his sermon on the Torah portion Vayetze, he launches into a long exposition of Jacob's "ladder dream," presenting also Maimonides's explanation of it, but without mentioning any non-Jewish philosophical source.

As for Aristotle's *Ethics*, Shem-Tob b. Joseph quotes the work often and as far as can be seen, more than any other philosophical work.[44] Usually, the explicit mentions are mainly rhetorical, a reference to a famous text, a well-known sentence, a familiar principle (such as the "middle way") or an analogy to a particular claim. The exception in this context is Shem-Tob's sermon on Vayiqra. His published collected sermons feature two sermons on this Torah portion. In the first, there is no explicit mention of Aristotle's *Ethics*, but in effect the entire sermon constitutes a summary of broad segments of the first book of the *Ethics*. In the second sermon, Shem-Tob invokes the *Ethics* as proof of the correctness of his position.

The starting point of the first sermon on Vayiqra, on which I will focus, is the verse, "You shall season your every offering of meal with salt" (Lev. 2:13) and the question as to why the Torah instructs that salt be used in the sacrifice. Shem-Tob refers to a midrash that explains that the sacrifice of salt on the sacrifice is a gift and compensation that God grants to the "lower waters," which were separated from the "upper waters" when the world was created.[45] In order to explain this "precious" midrash, Shem-Tob is required to make some preliminary "premises." The first premise is that man has a purpose. The second is that this purpose is unknown, and man must create signs that remind him of this purpose. The third is that, after man knows the purpose, he must attempt to attain it as long as he lives. The fourth is that all of man's deeds must be directed to the attainment of this purpose.

In order to present the first premise, that man has a purpose, Shem-Tob was required to review Aristotle's teleological perspective. He quotes, without stating the source, the statement in Aristotle's *Physics* that "nature does nothing in vain,"[46] citing proofs and analogies from rabbinic literature and from the Bible. Hereafter, Shem-Tob proceeds according to and concisely summarizes parts of the first book of the *Ethics* that explain man's groping for his purpose: happiness and Aristotle's instructions on how to discern the true goal. For example, Shem-Tob presents the Aristotelian principles according to which (1) The ultimate objective is that sought for its own sake and not for another purpose. (2) One who attains the ultimate good is restful and quiet and needs nothing further, but rather is content with his happiness. (3) The human purpose is "for the soul to act according to virtue." Shem-Tob then writes about Aristotle's deliberations as to whether the desired purpose is attained through action, arising from the virtue, or whether it is actually a scholarly pursuit, an intellectual activity that constitutes the essence of the purpose of human action and hope.

As the sermon continues, Shem-Tob then interprets the journey by which "lover" seeks the "beloved" in the Song of Solomon, as the search of the human soul for its purpose and the ultimate good. For example, the experiences of man seeking a purpose—the ultimate good—is expressed in the verse, "Tell me, you whom I love so well; Where do you pasture your sheep? / Where do you rest them at noon?" (Song of Sol. 1:7). The direction given by the lover, "Go follow the tracks of the sheep / And graze your kids / By the tents of the shepherds" (Ibid., v. 8) is perceived by Shem-Tob as an instruction to take counsel with the Jewish scholars and heads of yeshivas regarding this human purpose, as to whether it is action-based or intellectual. The verse "I held him fast, I would not let him go" for Shem-Tob symbolizes that one who attains the ultimate purpose must hold fast to it and rejoice in his happiness, as in the Aristotelian principle (no. 2) presented above.

Concluding his argument, Shem-Tob determines that it has indeed been made clear that man has a purpose, that this purpose is theoretical but that its ultimate goal is practical, in the spirit of the *Guide of the Perplexed*, "to do justice, and to love kindness" (Mic. 6:8) and that the man who recognizes this must labor so that it not slip from his grasp.

To summarize our discussion of Shem-Tob, we see in his writings the popularization of philosophy as a whole and the popularization of the

Ethics particularly, although far more important to him than these is the popularization of Maimonides's ideas in the *Guide*. At the same time, due to Shem-Tob's talent in conveying complex ideas in a popular format, it is difficult, based on the material at hand, to estimate the degree of prior knowledge required from those listening to his sermons and to what extent they absorbed the philosophical knowledge in the sermons, though it appears that sometimes the sermons conveyed real knowledge belonging to philosophical realms, cloaked in terms, expressions, and concepts that were Jewish.

Conclusions

In the fifteenth century, sermons and homiletical literature contain citations of philosophical texts and references to philosophical ideas and terms. For many fifteenth-century preachers, it is impossible to conceive of a discourse, no matter how popular, that would not require philosophical language, values, method, and ideas. It is philosophy that defines the preacher's role, and not the reverse. It is philosophy that provides the necessary terminology and the critical and analytical tools for the preacher, his text, and his audience. Moreover, as exposure to philosophy and philosophical thought redefined homiletical style in fifteenth-century Spain in particular, the need to express new ideas spurred the change in the formal style of preaching that related more directly to essential questions of universal significance. The use of blatantly philosophical sources was, then, merely a manifestation of much broader undercurrents.

And yet, if we accept the position of Joseph b. Shem-Tob expressed in his theoretical book on rhetoric, that the sermon must be analyzed as a rhetorical medium whose foremost objective is persuasion, we must then understand the dissemination of philosophical ideas in the framework of the sermon as a phenomenon that was more incidental than essential. The various genres of philosophical works serve a single goal, namely, the dissemination of philosophy. In contrast, the sermon uses philosophy as a tool for transmitting the homiletical message, that of the preachers. Philosophy is thus subordinate to and functions in the service of homily. The preacher does not teach philosophy in the synagogue. He does not delve into deep philosophical issues per se. At the most, he uses the philosopher as an "authority," as a support for explaining a particular Torah-based position, as a tool for analysis and conceptualization, as an analogy to the claim he is making, and sometimes as an intellectual alternative that he rejects or argues against. For the preacher, introducing philosophy in the synagogue is justified only by harnessing it to the service of Torah.

When the preacher uses philosophy for his own needs, he becomes a purveyor of philosophy. The preacher uses a philosophical text or relates to the philosopher as an authority who supports a Torah position that he seeks to express, and at the same time bolsters the status of the philosopher as an authority. Thus does philosophy "use" the preacher just as the preacher uses it.

This complex interrelation between homily and philosophy did not escape the notice of the preachers of the fifteenth century. In effect, it could be said that their ambivalent relationship with philosophy to a large extent determined the axis along which their intellectual undertaking was positioned. They were unable to feel entirely at peace with philosophy but felt at a loss without it; they used it while simultaneously trying to undermine it; they struggled with it while hanging on to it fiercely.

On reading Isaac Arama's work *Aqedat Yishaq*, a work considered by many the height of homiletical achievement of the generation of the expulsion from Spain, one might find in the frontispiece both admiration for Aristotle in his struggle against the Epicureans and a number of quotations from his books, alongside an emphasis on the Torah's superiority over philosophy and derision of the "philosophers." The choice to characterize Arama as a "philosopher-preacher," a "conservative," or even an "antirationalist" rests entirely with the scholar or the reader and the elements he or she chooses to emphasize.[47]

It seems that despite the gap between the authentic sermon as it was delivered and the written sermon, we have managed to present an array of knowledge on the philosophical sermon and the popularization of philosophy among Jewish laymen in medieval Spain before and after the expulsion and at the dawn of printing. The invention of printed books further strengthened the status of the sermon as a written literary genre through which ideas were transmitted beyond the limited circles of the intellectual elite and the local community.

Notes

1. Translation from M. Saperstein, *Jewish Preaching 1200–1800: An Anthology* (New Haven, CT: Yale University Press, 1989), 384–87.

2. On this comparison, see Saperstein, *Jewish Preaching*, 11, n. 16.

3. See J. Dan, *Sifrut Ha-Musar Ve-Ha-Derush* (Jerusalem: Keter, 1975), 35–36 [Hebrew]; M. Saperstein, *Jewish Preaching*, 5–25; Sh. Regev, *Oral and Written Sermons in the Middle Ages* (Jerusalem: Reuven Mass, 2010), 21–71, 155–200 [Hebrew]; M. Pachter, "Homiletic and Ethical Literature of Safed in the 16th Century" (PhD diss., Hebrew University, 1975), 1–15 [Hebrew].

4. Saperstein, *Jewish Preaching*, 63–79.

5. M. Saperstein, "Sermons as Evidence for the Popularization of Philosophy in Fifteenth-Century Spain," in *Your Voice Like a Ram's Horn: Themes and Texts in Traditional Jewish Preaching* (Cincinnati, OH: Hebrew Union College Press, 1996), 75–88.

6. Jacob Anatoli, *Malmad ha-Talmidim*, ed. L. Silbermann (Lyck: Mekize Nirdamim, 1866), introduction. See also M. Saperstein, "Christians and Christianity in the Sermons of Jacob Anatoli," *Jewish History* 6 (1992): 225–42.

7. Anatoli, *Malmad ha-Talmidim*, introduction.

8. Anatoli, *Malmad ha-Talmidim*, 182b.

9. J. Dan, *Sifrut Ha-Musar Ve-Ha-Derush*, 82.

10. Saperstein, *Jewish Preaching*, 15.

11. See Y. Baer, *A History of the Jews in Christian Spain* (Philadelphia, PA: Jewish Publication Society, 1961), 287–302; M. Saperstein, "The Conflict over the Rashba's Herem on Philosophical Study: A Political Perspective," *Jewish History* 1.2 (1986): 27–38; G. Stern, "What Divided the Moderate Maimonides Scholars of Southern France in 1305?" in *Be'erot Yitzhak: Studies in Memory of Isadore Twersky*, ed. J. Harris (Cambridge, MA: Harvard University Press, 2005), 347–76.

12. Nissim of Gerona, *Derashot Ha-Ran*, ed. L. Feldman (Jerusalem: Mossad Harav Kook, 1967); revised edition with the commentary "Be'erot Moshe" (Jerusalem: Mossad Harav Kook, 2003).

13. Aviezer Ravitzky, *Crescas' Sermon on the Passover and Studies in His Philosophy* (Jerusalem: Israel Academy of Sciences and Humanities, 1988).

14. Joseph Dan, "The Status of Homiletical Literature in Jewish Culture," in *Studies in the History of Popular Culture*, ed. B. Z. Kedar (Jerusalem: Zalman Shazar Center for Jewish History, 1996), 143 [Hebrew].

15. There is no clear information regarding his biography. Ari Ackerman estimates that he died prior to 1445, although from 1414 there is no trace of his activity. Zerahiyah Ha-levi Saladin, *Derashot*, ed. Ari Ackerman (Beer Sheba: Ben-Gurion University, 2012), 11–15.

16. For some early examples, see Jean Régné, *History of the Jews in Aragon* (Jerusalem: Magnes Press, 1978), 41, n. 215; Baer, *History of the Jews*, 167; R. Chazan, "Confrontation in the Synagogue of Narbonne: A Christian Sermon and a Jewish Reply," *Harvard Theological Review* 67 (1974): 437–57.

17. Bernard Septimus, "Yitzhaq Arama and Aristotle's Ethics," in *Jews and Conversos at the Time of the Expulsion*, ed. Yom Tov Assis and Joseph Kaplan (Jerusalem: Zalman Shazar Center, 1999), 7.

18. Saperstein, *Jewish Preaching*, 384–87.

19. Excerpts from the book are in Saperstein, *Jewish Preaching*, 169–79. See also Jean-Pierre Rothschild, "Le 'Eyn ha-qôrê' de Rabbi Joseph B. Shêm Tôb ibn Shêm Tôb: critique de Maïmonide et presence implicite de R. Juda ha-Lévi," in *Torah et science*, ed. Gad Freudenthal, et al. (Paris: Peeters, 2001), 165–211.

20. Saperstein, *Jewish Preaching*, 390.

21. Saperstein, *Jewish Preaching*, 390.

22. Many books and articles have been written about Maimonides's familiarity with the Aristotelian ethical tradition. For background, see Steven Harvey, "The Sources of the Quotations from Aristotle's *Ethics* in the *Guide of the Perplexed* and the *Guide to the Guide*," *Jerusalem Studies in Jewish Thought* 14 (1998): 87–102 [Hebrew]; Herbert Davidson, "Maimonides' Eight Chapters and Alfarabi's Fusul al-Madani," *Proceedings of the American Academy for Jewish Research* 30 (1969): 33–50; Herbert Davidson, "The Middle Way in Maimonides Ethics," *Proceedings of the American Academy for Jewish Research* 54 (1987), 31–72; Raymond L. Weiss, *Maimonides' Ethics: The Encounter of Philosophic and Religious Morality* (Chicago: University of Chicago Press, 1991).

23. L. Berman, "Greek into Hebrew, Samuel Ben Judah of Marseilles, Fourteenth-Century Philosopher and Translator," in *Jewish Medieval and Renaissance Studies*, ed. A. Altman (Cambridge, MA: Harvard University Press, 1967), 289–320.

24. *Averroes' Middle Commentary on Aristotle's Nicomachean Ethics in the Hebrew Version of Samuel Ben Judah*, ed. L. Berman (Jerusalem: Israel Academy of Sciences and Humanities, 1999).

25. For a preliminary edition of Rabbi Don Meir Alguades's Latin-to-Hebrew translation of the *Nicomachean Ethics*, see Chaim M. Neria, "'It Cannot Be Valued with the Gold of Ophir' (Job 28:16): Rabbi Joseph b. Shem-Ṭob's Commentary on Aristotle's *Nicomachean Ethics* Sources and Analysis" (PhD diss., University of Chicago, 2015) appendix 2, 383–566, and references there.

26. See Neria, "It Cannot Be Valued," 411.

27. Joseph b. Shem-Tob, *Kebod Elohim* (*The Glory of God*) (Ferrara: Abraham Usque, 1556).

28. See Neria, "It Cannot Be Valued."

29. In his commentary to the Torah (Exod. 25 and see also 1 Sam. 25), Isaac Abarbanel mentions his studies in the yeshiva of Joseph b. Shem-Tob.

30. Neria, "It Cannot Be Valued," 49–50, 219, 222, and reference there.

31. Haim Shirman, *The History of Hebrew Poetry in Christian Spain and Southern France*, ed. Ezra Fleischer (Jerusalem: Magnes Press, 1997), 594 [Hebrew]; Frank Talmage, "The Francesc de Sant Jordi-Solomon Bonafed Letters," in *Studies in Medieval Jewish History and Literature*, ed. Isadore Twersky (Cambridge, MA: Harvard University Press, 1979), 337–64; Tirza Vardi, "The Group of Poets in Saragossa, Secular Poetry" (PhD diss., Hebrew University, 1996).

32. Ackerman, sermons of Zerahiah Ha-Levi Saladin, introduction.

33. Ibid., 106–7.

34. Ibid., 38.

35. Ibid., 8.

36. Ibid., 41, 42.

37. Ibid., 117.

38. Ibid., 41.

39. Ibid., 112. The book was not translated into Hebrew; therefore, it is reasonable to assume that Zerahiyah saw the book in Latin. Meir Alguades also mentions the book but did not translate it.

40. Ibid., 11.

41. Ibid., 31.

42. Ibid., 164.

43. Ibid., 146–47.

44. I was able to locate mention of the *Ethics* in the following texts: Genesis: Sermon on the Chuppa, "Lekh-Lekha, " "Hayyei Sarah, " "Toldot, " "Vayera, " "Vayehi, " "Shemot, " "Yitro, " "Vayiqra" [two sermons], "Emor, " "Aharei Mot, " "Bahar, " "Behuqotai, " "Tzav, " " Shemini, " "Qedoshim, " "Bahar, " "Qorah, " "Huqqat, " "Balaq, " " Devarim, " "Ki-Tavo, " Sermon on Repentance [several], Yom Kippur Sermon. It is quite likely that there are more mentions that I have not yet identified.

45. For background, see Gen. 1:7 and Rashi's commentary on Lev. 2:13.

46. Averroes, *Epitome of Aristotle's Physics, Hebrew trans. by Moses ibn Tibbon* (1250), (Riva di Trento, 1560), 7a. Cf. *Aristotle in Hebrew: Aristotle's De anima: Translated into Hebrew by Zerahyah b. Isaac b. She'altiel Hen*, ed. G. Bos. (Leiden: E. J. Brill, 1994), 131.

47. See B. Septimus, "Yitzhaq Arama and Aristotle's Ethics," 2–11; M. Pachter, "Homiletic and Ethical Literature of Safed," chapter 4. For a different perspective, see S. Heller-Wilensky, *R. Yitzhak Arama and His Philosophy* (Jerusalem: Bialik Institute, 1956), 68–102, 190 [Hebrew]; Baer, *History of the Jews*, 253.

CHAIM MEIR NERIA is a lecturer at Oranim College of Education, Israel. He wrote his dissertation on Rabbi Joseph b. Shem-Tob's *Commentary on Aristotle's "Nicomachean Ethics."* He is completing a critical edition of Rabbi Don Meir Alguades's Latin-to-Hebrew translation of the *Nicomachean Ethics* in Hebrew.

12

LEXICONS AND LEXICOGRAPHY IN MEDIEVAL JEWISH PHILOSOPHY

James T. Robinson

THE PROCESS OF NAMING THINGS AND DEFINING TERMS has been central in philosophy since its inception. Discussions about language are found throughout the Platonic corpus, especially in *Cratylus*, Socrates's ironic dialogue about etymologies and the relation between words and meanings, terms and ideas. One of the principle aims in the development of logic for Aristotle was the elimination of ambiguity in argumentation through the creation of a precise language of discourse; this is made especially clear in his *Topics* and *Sophistical Refutations*.[1] This concern for precision in language moves from general reflection to proper lexicon in Aristotle's *Metaphysics*, Book Delta, in which he presents a full lexicon of key terms, including *beginning*, *cause*, *element*, *nature*, *necessary*, *one*, *being*, *primary being*, *same*, *opposite*, *before* and *after*, *power*, *quantity*, *quality*, *relations*, *complete*, *limit*, *according to*, *disposition*, *habitude*, *happenings*, *privation*, *to have and to hold*, *to come from something*, *part and whole*, *damaged or mutilated*, *genus*, *false*, and *accidental*.[2]

The lexicographical foundation of philosophy continued and expanded in the Hellenistic and early Islamic periods. Defining terms was a key part of the Hellenistic curriculum, as students began their studies by defining the word *philosophy* itself;[3] and it found full flowering in the commentary tradition, for example, in Themistius's paraphrase of Aristotle's *De caelo*, in which he begins his detailed explanation of Aristotle's work with a lengthy discourse on the various meanings of the word *heavens*.[4] Michael the Interpreter and David the Invincible, late antique Neoplatonists and commentators on Aristotle, both produced lexicographical works focused on the meaning of *philosophy*, the parts of the curriculum, and basic terms related especially to logic, metaphysics, and psychology.[5] These approaches and conventions passed into the Arabic and the Islamic world as well. Al-Kindī continued the Neoplatonic definition tradition with his *Kitāb al-ḥudūd* (Book of definitions), organized conceptually according to the cosmos, from above to below;[6] Al-Fārābī devoted a lengthy treatise to the various meanings of a single word, *'aql*, "intellect";[7] Avicenna produced a brief alphabetical dictionary of philosophical terms;[8] while Averroes and other commentators explained and expanded on Aristotle's lexicon at *Metaphysics*, Book Delta.[9] Even the encyclopedists used linguistic markers to organize knowledge as a whole, as in Ibn Farīghūn's *Jawāmiʿ al-ʿulūm* and Al-Khwārizmī's *Mafātiḥ al-ʿulūm*.[10]

By the tenth century, when a Jewish philosophical literature began to emerge, Jews already had a vast body of lexicography to draw on for inspiration as they worked to create their own unique tradition, which built on the existing Greek and Arabic models and worked innovatively to develop new ones. This process extended, for example, from Isaac Israeli's Neoplatonic "Book of Definitions," to the discussion of a single term in the anonymous *Kitāb maʿānī al-nafs* (Book on the meanings of the soul), to Maimonides's lexicographical discussion in the *Guide of the Perplexed*—which borrowed from and subverted the Aristotelian tradition in order to create a philosophical lexicon for the allegorical interpretation of the Bible—to Samuel ibn Tibbon's very full *Perush ha-Millot ha-Zarot* (Explanation of unusual terms), an alphabetical lexicon that provides coverage of much of the Aristotelian tradition. The later medieval tradition, in both Judeo-Arabic and Hebrew, continued to build on and respond to an ever-expanding corpus of lexicographical writings, both as reference work for the study of philosophy and as a genre of writing philosophy itself.

This chapter will focus on a few prominent examples, written in Judeo-Arabic and Hebrew, which illustrate the diverse approach to lexicography in the medieval Jewish philosophical and theological tradition. The examples will be presented chronologically to give a sense of the overall development of the genre. The goal is not to achieve comprehensiveness but to show variety and richness.

A Neoplatonic Book of Definitions: Isaac Israeli's *Kitāb al-ḥudūd*

As mentioned above, one of the earliest philosophical lexicons produced in the Islamic world was the "Book of Definitions" by Al-Kindī, who was the main figure in a circle of scholars based in Iraq and whose work had decisive influence on Isaac Israeli, among others. Al-Kindī himself—or his school—was responsible for producing a massive corpus of writings covering the entire range of Hellenistic school disciplines, from mathematics to metaphysics.[11] The "Book of Definitions" is, typical of his work more generally, a very short discourse covering a great deal of material in few words. It is organized not alphabetically but thematically, in general moving from above to below and from the more abstract to the more specific. Consisting of some 130 terms defined over just twelve pages (in the most recent English translation),[12] the work begins with the hypostases in the spiritual world and first principles of existence: *first cause*, *intellect*, *nature*, *soul*, *body*, *origination*, *matter*, *form*, *element*; and then continues with terms that correspond more or less with Aristotle's ten categories, including some basic principles of physics: *act*, *action*, *substance*, *choice*, *quantity*, *quality*, *relative*, *motion*, *time*, *place*, *relation*. From the cosmos and first principles, Al-Kindī shifts to the operations of the soul (*imagination*, *sense*, *sensation*, *sensitive faculty*, *sensible*, *deliberation*, *belief*, *compound*, *volition*, *love*, *rhythm*) and epistemology (*necessary*, *possible*, *impossible*, *knowledge*, *truth*, and *falsehood*). The rest of the work is harder to classify, as terms from all areas are combined together with no clear principle of organization, including an extended discussion of the various meanings of the word *philosophy*, defined near the center of the work as a whole. This definition, the longest in the work and one closely related to Israeli's definition of the same term, is cited here in extenso:

> Philosophy: the ancients defined it in a number of ways. (1) From its etymology, which is "love of wisdom," because "philosopher" is composed of philo-, "lover," and -sophia, "wisdom." They also defined it (2) from its action, and said that philosophy is becoming similar to the actions of God, the exalted, to the extent that man is able. [By this] they meant man's becoming perfect in virtue. They also defined it (3) from the point of view of its action, and said "preparation for death." According to them there are two kinds of death: natural death, which is the soul's ceasing to use the body, and second, the killing of desires, which is the death that they intend here. For the killing of

> desires is the path to virtue. Therefore many of the outstanding ancients say pleasure is an evil. This is necessarily so, for there are two uses of the soul, one sensible, the other intellectual. What people call pleasure is what occurs to the senses, because being preoccupied with sensible pleasures means ceasing to use intellect. They also defined it (4) from the point of view of its exalted status, and said: "the art of arts and wisdom of wisdoms." They also defined it (5) by saying, "philosophy is man's knowledge of himself." This statement is noble in the extreme and profound. For example, I say that things are either bodies or not. Things that are bodies are either substances or accidents. Man is body, soul, and accidents. And his soul is a non-bodily substance. Therefore, if someone knows all this [i.e., all the parts of man], then he knows everything. For this reason, wise men call man a microcosm. But as for the definition of philosophy in its very core, it is that philosophy is (6) the knowledge of eternal, universal things, their beings, their essences, and their causes, to the extent of man's ability.[13]

Al-Kindī was based in the East, in Iraq, in the ninth century, but his works transmitted West, so much so that Isaac Israeli, early tenth-century Jewish philosopher and physician based in the Fatimid court in Kairouan, would have had access to them. His own corpus of philosophical writings, expertly translated and explained by Alexander Altmann and Samuel Miklos Stern, show clear resemblance to and affinity with the writings of his Neoplatonic forebear.[14] This applies to the ideas found in his writings, coming out of the Plotinian world but often mediated by Al-Kindī, and in the form of his writings as well, especially in Israeli's "Book of Definitions." Not only does it share a title with Al-Kindī's work of the same name, but also it shows strong similarities in terms of order and content. There are significant differences as well, of course. The brief description of the work given here will emphasize both the similarities and the differences.

The way Israeli's work is organized immediately shows an interest in systematizing in a different way. As Al-Kindī, so Israeli has a clear preference for presenting the cosmos from above to below, including definitions of *wisdom, intellect, soul, sphere,* and *sublunar and celestial body,* followed by terms that relate to the human soul and the processes of the soul, especially as it pertains to epistemological issues, for example, *on the vital spirit, on nature, on reason, absolute knowledge, true knowledge, cognition, opinion, cogitation, memory, recollection, deliberation, retention, discernment, syllogism.* Before getting to the cosmos itself, however, and in sharp contrast to Al-Kindī, Israeli begins with an extended discussion of the four philosophical questions—whether, what, how, and why—followed by a lengthy discourse on the definitions and descriptions of philosophy. The latter, for its similarity to and difference from Al-Kindī's definition of philosophy cited above, is likewise quoted in extenso for comparison.[15]

> When the philosophers understood this and it became clear to them that definition can be composed only from genera and substantial differentiae, and found for "philosophy" no genus from which its definition could be composed, they made a subtle investigation according to their superior deliberation and cogitation and described it by three descriptions: (1) one derived from its name, (2) another from its property, (3) and a third from its traces and actions: (1) The description taken from its name is as follows: Philosophy is the love of wisdom. This is deduced from the name "philosopher:" philosopher is composed of philo- and -sophia, and in Greek philo means "lover" and sophia "wisdom;" thus it is clear that "philosopher" means the lover of wisdom, and if "philosopher" means the lover of wisdom, "philosophy" must mean love of wisdom. (2) The description of philosophy taken from its property is as follows: Philosophy is the assimilation to the works of the Creator, may He be exalted, according to human capacity. By the words "assimilation to the works of the Creator" is meant the understanding of the truth of things, viz., acquiring true knowledge of them and doing what corresponds to the truth; by the words "understanding the truth of things" is meant understanding them from their four natural causes, which are the material, formal, efficient, and final causes.

As can be seen, the first two definitions of Israeli correspond exactly with the first two of Al-Kindī, with brief commentary added and elaboration. Then after a lengthy digression on the meaning of the four causes in both corporeal and spiritual sense, Israeli works his way back to the remaining definitions of philosophy:

> A case of a spiritual final cause is the union of soul and body to the end that the truths of the subject of science may become clear to man; that he may distinguish between good and evil, between what is laudable and what is not; that he may do what corresponds to truth, in justice and rectitude; that he may sanctify, praise, and exalt the Creator, and recognize His dominion; that he may avoid beastly and unclean actions in order thereby to obtain the reward of his Creator, blessed be He, which is the union with the upper soul, and the illumination by the light of intellect and by the beauty and splendor of wisdom. When attaining this rank, he becomes spiritual, and will be joined in union to the light which is created, without mediator, by the power of God, and will become one that exalts and praises the Creator forever and in all eternity. This then will be his paradise and the goodness of his reward, and the bliss of his rest, his perfect rank and unsullied beauty. For this reason Plato said that philosophy is a zeal, a striving, an effort and concern for death. Says Isaac: This is a description of great profundity and elevated meaning. For in saying concern for death the sage meant it to be understood in the sense of the killing of beastly desires and lusts, for in their mortification and avoidance is the highest rank, the supernal splendor and the entry into the realm of truth. And by

> vivifying beastly desires and lusts and by strengthening them, men of intellect are drawn away from that which is due to God in the way of obedience, purity, and attention to prayer at the prescribed hours.

Israeli digresses once again, connecting this Platonic definition of philosophy as a striving for death with a strongly Neoplatonized religious sense of reward and punishment, then ends with his third definition of philosophy: "(3) The description of philosophy from its effect is as follows: Philosophy is man's knowledge of himself. This also is a description of great profundity and elevated intelligence, for the following reason. Man, if he acquires a true knowledge of himself, viz., of his own spirituality and corporeality, comprises the knowledge of everything, viz., of the spiritual and corporeal substance, as in man are joined substance and accident."

Israeli's reordering of the work as a whole, if that is what in fact he did, leads to a remarkably different sort of treatise. In Al-Kindī you have the feel of a cosmological work presented through the key terms of philosophy, at least that is the way it begins. Israeli's work, in contrast, seems a more systematic work of philosophical reflection on terminology and on method more generally. In Israeli's version, beginning with the philosophical questions and an explanation of "definition" and "description" provides the basis for everything that comes after; defining *philosophy* then frames not only the book itself but also the entire world of ideas it describes. It is also more consistent with the Hellenistic Neoplatonic tradition that influenced both Al-Kindī and Israeli, in which defining what philosophy is and what a philosopher does comes at the beginning of the curriculum, a subject one ought to reflect on from the outset and throughout an entire life devoted to a love of wisdom. Finally, while Al-Kindī's six definitions of philosophy are presented in mostly dispassionate prose, Israeli's three definitions (plus one) are presented with a strong moral and metaphysical pathos, linking the definitions of philosophy with religious ideals and Israeli's ever-present aspiration to purify the soul so it can return to its original home in the spiritual realm.

Al-Kindī's work was influential in the East and West. Israeli's work was influential especially in the West, in North Africa, Spain, and Christian Europe. It was cited and paraphrased in Judeo-Arabic works of philosophy and exegesis in Al-Andalus, while the early Hebrew and Latin translations were foundational in the emergence of Hebrew and scholastic philosophy in Christian Europe.[16] As in most writings by Israeli, however, his "Book of Definitions" was important mainly for its innovations; Israeli was, if nothing else, a pioneer. Thus it was soon abandoned for other works which would represent more accurately the ever-changing trends in philosophy and literature.

A Philosophical-Exegetical Reflection on a Single Term: The Anonymous *Kitāb ma'ānī al-nafs*

One of the most interesting, and least studied, works in the history of Jewish thought is the anonymous *Kitāb ma'ānī al-nafs*, "The book on the meanings of the soul." The work was once attributed to Bahya ibn Paquda, the attribution of which is clearly incorrect.[17] Who actually did write it remains a mystery—one recent suggestion is Isaac ibn Ghiyāth, eleventh-century Rabbinic leader, poet, and exegete in Lucena, but this too is unlikely.[18] Whoever the author was, the work itself seems to be from a slightly later moment in the history of Jewish thought, especially since it draws extensively on the Neoplatonic and kalamic resources available in Islamic Spain and also Avicenna. It was likely written during the late eleventh or early twelfth century.

Like Al-Fārābī's "Treatise on Intellect" mentioned above, this anonymous Judeo-Arabic work focuses on the meaning of a single term or notion, *soul,* exploring it in a variety of contexts and from multiple perspectives—philosophical, theological, and exegetical. The book consists of a preface—using standard rhetorical topoi in Arabic literature and presenting a brief outline of the book—and twenty-one chapters, which can be summarized as follows:

Chapter 1 presents a brief survey of different views on the soul, including those held by the naturalists, the materialists, and the metaphysicians, along with Ibn Sina's view and the scriptural view expressed at Ecclesiastes 12:7. Chapter 2 discourses on corporeal versus spiritual substance and introduces the four platonic virtues—courage, wisdom, temperance, and justice—in relation to Ecclesiastes 7:14. Chapter 3 presents a long discussion of creation, using images of darkness and light to describe universal matter and universal form, explaining the esoteric method of presentation and defending scripture as a source of theoretical wisdom while citing Saadia Gaon's commentary on *Sefer yetsirah* and verses from Ezekiel, Ecclesiastes, and other biblical books. Chapter 4 gives a general introduction to the different "souls" and their relation to one another. Chapter 5 discourses on first and final perfection and the body/soul duality, using the image of dead matter versus living soul. Chapter 6 further elaborates on the three souls or faculties (rational, irascible/animal/vital, and concupiscent/vegetable), on the difference between *soul* and *spirit,* and on the term *soul* as a homonym, citing Ibn Sina and Ecclesiastes 3:21 and 12:7 as authorities. Chapter 7 discourses on immortality and the goal of purification—the four humors return to the elements while the soul returns to its original source in the supernal spiritual world.

In chapter 8 the exegetical focus begins to dominate as the author singles out ten biblical terms for the soul (*ner, neshamah, yehidah, hayyah, nefesh, ruah, kavod, almah, shulamit,* and *mehulat ha-mahanayim*), providing relevant prooftexts for each and derivations and giving hints and allusions to the way the allegory of the soul can be read throughout biblical narrative, especially in Song of Songs. Chapter 9 continues this trend, singling out biblical names and verses that can be related to the four platonic virtues, citing examples from the stories of the patriarchs and Moses in particular. Chapter 10 explores the different views on the *neshamah* and when it enters into the fetus according to the book of Job and the Torah, relating to contemporary views about embryology and celestial influence. Chapter 11 focuses on the vegetative or concupiscent soul in particular, drawing again from contemporary scientific views. Chapter 12 then focuses on the animal or spirited or irascible soul, relating again to celestial influence and the question of when the soul enters the body and when and how it starts to act through the body. Chapter 13 works on the standard analogy of body/soul/cosmos. Chapter 14 focuses on the biblical term *neshamah* in relation to the essential names of God and discourses briefly on the giving of the commandments and free will. Chapter 15 relates to the origin of the rational soul and the question of intermediaries, drawing on Saadia's theory of created speech. Chapter 16 moves back to general ideas about principles of existence, introducing the "ten simple spiritual substances": intellect, soul, nature, matter, sphere, planets, fire, air, water, and earth. Chapter 17 describes the descent of the soul and the attendant loss of wisdom, relating to the Platonic doctrine of anamnesis. Chapter 18 presents the upward move, the purification and ascent of the soul as it returns to its spiritual home. Chapter 19 ponders the question, why does the soul descend at all? Chapter 20 relates to the preexistent soul and how it rules the body, and chapter 21, finally, presents a hierarchy of the rational soul according to knowledge and action, reward and punishment.

As can be seen, *Kitāb maʿānī al-nafs* is a highly eclectic work. It is based mainly on Platonic and Neoplatonic ideas about the soul, its origin, and fate, but draws also from kalamic discourse and Ibn Sina's peripatetic writings and frames the entire subject exegetically, relating to biblical terms that, in the author's opinion, refer to psychic and noetic realities. It seems that the exegetical concerns are the primary goal, as the work in effect allows one to decode biblical texts in light of the latest psychological theory. It is through this function that it likely had its most influence, for example, through later biblical commentaries and philosophical-exegetical treatises.

A Lexicographical Introduction to a Single Field: Maimonides's "Treatise on Logic"

A work that fits firmly in the Aristotelian rather than Neoplatonic tradition is Maimonides's "Treatise on Logic," which had extraordinary influence from the thirteenth century to the twentieth. This brief work in fourteen chapters was written in Arabic and translated three times into Hebrew, and the Hebrew versions then served as foundation for a number of commentaries, including those by Mordecai Comtino, Moses Mendelssohn, Isaac Satanov, Leon Roth, and Moses Ventura.[19] It is only in our generation that some skepticism has been expressed about its authorship by Herbert Davidson, though Davidson's view remains the outlier, and the work is still generally accepted as an authentic writing of the master.[20] Regardless of authorship, "Treatise on Logic" remains no less interesting and relevant in any study of lexicography in medieval Jewish thought, a paradigmatic work of introduction focused on terminology.

Each chapter of the "Treatise on Logic" introduces a field or subject within the Aristotelian tradition of logic focusing on the key terms and ends with a list of the various terms in the chapter that have been defined. The best way to illustrate the character of the work is to cite these final statements from each chapter in the very accessible English translation by Israel Efros:[21]

> Chapter 1: "All the terms explained in this chapter are four: predicate, subject, proposition, enunciative sentence."
>
> Chapter 2: "All the terms explained in this chapter are fourteen: affirmative, negative, universal affirmative, particular affirmative, universal negative, particular negative, indesignate, singular, universal negative sign, particular negative sign, universal affirmative sign, particular affirmative sign, quantity of a proposition, quality of a proposition."

Chapter 3: "All the terms explained in this chapter are five: binary sentence, trinary sentence, copulas, word, mode."

Chapter 4: "All the terms explained in this chapter are thirteen: opposition, contrariety, contradiction, opposites, contrary, contradictory, subcontrary, necessary proposition, impossible proposition, proposition of necessity, absolute proposition, possible proposition, actual proposition."

Chapter 5: "All the terms explained in this chapter are four: conversion of a proposition, inversion of a proposition, converted proposition, inverted proposition."

Chapter 6: "All terms explained in this chapter are eleven: syllogism, premise, conclusion, consequent, middle term, first term, major term, last term, minor term, major premise, minor premise."

Chapter 7: "All the terms explained in this chapter are twelve: first figure of the syllogism, second figure, third figure, mood of the syllogistic figure, categorical syllogisms, hypothetical syllogisms, hypothetical conjunctive, hypothetical disjunctive, straight categorical syllogism, apagogic syllogism, inductive syllogism, analogical syllogism."

Chapter 8: "All terms explained in this chapter are seventeen: perception, first ideas, second ideas, conventions, traditions, apodictic proposition, demonstrative syllogism, the art of demonstration, the dialectical syllogism, the art of dialectics, rhetorical syllogism, the art of rhetoric, sophistic syllogism, the art of sophism, poetic syllogism, the art of poetry, enthymeme."

Chapter 9: "All the terms explained in this chapter are ten: matter, agent, form, purpose, proximate causes, remote causes, elements, materia prima, hyle, foundation."

Chapter 10: "All the terms explained in this chapter are seventeen; genus, species, individual, difference, property, accident, permanent accident, separable accident, summum genus, lowest species, subaltern species, component species, summa genera, categories, substance, definition, description."

Chapter 11: "All the terms explained in this chapter are sixteen: per se, per accidens, essential things, accidental things, potentiality, actuality, proximate potentiality, remote potentiality, contraries with an intermediate state, contraries with no intermediate state, habit, privation, correlation, correlative, correlatives, opposites."

Chapter 12: "All the terms explained in this chapter are nine: prior in time, prior in nature, prior in excellence, prior in order, prior in cause, together in time, together in place, together in order, together in nature."

Chapter 13: "All terms explained in this chapter are eighteen: particle, direct noun, oblique noun, indefinite noun, paronyms, the first example, hidden, pronoun, synonyms, distinct, absolute homonym, compound expression of explanation and modification, compound expression of information, univocal, amphibolous, noun used in general and in particular, metaphoric, extended."

> Chapter 14: "All terms explained in this chapter are twenty-five: rational faculty, inner speech, external speech, the art of logic, theoretical arts, productive arts, philosophy, theoretical philosophy, practical philosophy, human philosophy, political philosophy, mathematics, the propaedeutic sciences, physics, theology, metaphysics, habits, moral virtues, moral vices, intellectual virtues, intellectual vices, right, wrong, laws, nomoi."

The work then ends with the same sort of numerical summary: "All the chapters of this treatise are fourteen. All the terms explained in these chapters are one hundred and seventy-five; and these are the most general terms used in logic. Some of them are technical terms used in physics, theology, and political science." There is still much research needed into this short treatise on logic, and not only related to the question of authorship. For example, the exact relationship to the writings of Al-Fārābī and other early Arabic logical treatises still needs to be addressed. For our purposes, however, one fact is clear. It would be hard to find a more effective work of a lexicographical approach to philosophy: a clear, simple, straightforward introduction to the full breadth of logic organized according to its technical terminology.

A Philosophical-Allegorical Lexicon of the Bible: Maimonides's *Guide of the Perplexed*

It was in Aristotle's corpus, as mentioned above, that discussion of language and ambiguity became a central project of philosophy itself, for, as he says in the *Topics*, the only way to achieve precise argument and arrive at the truth is through the elimination of ambiguous and equivocal language.[22] He explains this clearly in *Sophistical Refutations* as well, in which he exposes the various fallacies that result from the use of imprecise language; homonymy is especially problematic, he says, when trying to philosophize toward the truth.[23] The famous lexicon in Book Delta of *Metaphysics*, finally, seems to be Aristotle's way of trying to achieve precisely this: a technical philosophical language, free of homonymy and ambiguity, that can be used to develop his systematic philosophy of everything that follows after physics.

This preoccupation with ambiguity in language and defining terms precisely was carried over into the Aristotelian tradition in the Hellenistic and Muslim periods. The best examples are the ones already singled out above: Themistius's extended discussion of the ambiguous word *heavens* at the beginning of his commentary on *De caelo* and Al-Fārābī's extended reflections on the meaning of a single word, *'aql*. There are many other works in the Aristotelian tradition that begin with the definition of key terminology necessary for thinking on and writing about a certain philosophical subject.

It is precisely this Aristotelian literary tradition and methodology that stands behind the most famous work of medieval Jewish philosophy, Maimonides's *Guide of the Perplexed*. The introduction to part 1 emphasizes the importance of explaining equivocal, ambiguous, and metaphorical terms in scripture, and most of the first part of the work is devoted to lexicography, defining terms related to the main subjects of the book as a whole. Just as Aristotle and Aristotelian philosophers begin with terminology, so Maimonides begins with an explanation of terms. What he does with his terms, however, is the exact opposite of what the Aristotelian tradition aims to achieve. Whereas philosophical works begin with technical terms of philosophy, Maimonides begins with terms from the Hebrew Bible. Whereas Greek and Arabic philosophical works survey the possible meanings of terms in order to eliminate ambiguity, to isolate the one single, precise, technical philosophical meaning against the imprecise, ordinary language meanings of popular discourse, Maimonides surveys the possible meanings of terms in scripture in order to introduce ambiguity, to give all the possible meanings of a term in order to open up alternative understandings, alternative readings, and alternative possibilities, to eliminate the one single, simple literal sense of any key term in scripture. In other words, while the philosophers aim to create a technical lexicon of philosophical language, Maimonides's goal is different: to create a philosophical lexicon of biblical language, to create an opening, in this way, for the figurative reading of the ambiguous text par excellence, the Hebrew Bible.

In total, some thirty-six chapters in part 1 of the *Guide* are devoted to the explication of biblical terms identified as "homonyms," "metaphors," or "ambiguous" terms. Several chapters in part 2 and part 3 focus on terminology as well, especially 2:6–7, 2:30, 3:52, and 3:54. How they work and function, however, is not uniform throughout. In some cases, as at *Guide* 1:6 (the shortest chapter in the book), Maimonides includes little more than a list of possible meanings, cited with biblical proof texts. Other chapters are more complex, providing not only the meanings of a term with proof texts but the beginning of an explanation of a biblical "parable" in which the term plays a prominent role. A good example of this latter form is *Guide* 1:15, which will be used here to illustrate the Maimonidean method as a whole.

As is well-known, one of the paradigmatic "parables" in the *Guide of the Perplexed* is Jacob's dream about the ladder appearing in Genesis 28.[24]

Maimonides singles it out in the preface to part 1 of the *Guide*, identifying it as one type of parable in which every detail has meaning, but he does not explain there what the meanings may be. In *Guide* 1:15 he returns to the parable again, and again in a different way in *Guide* 2:10. Here is how he begins *Guide* 1:15:[25]

> To stand erect [*natsov* or *yatsob*]. Though these two roots are different, their meaning, as you know, is identical in all their various forms. The term is equivocal. Sometimes it has the meaning of rising and being erect. Thus: "and his sister stood erect afar off" (Exod 2:4); "the kings of the earth stood erect" (Ps 2:2); "they came out and stood erect" (Num 16:27). The term has also another meaning: to be stable and permanent. Thus: "thy word stands erect in heaven" (Ps 118:89); this means that it is stable and constant. In all cases where this term occurs with reference to the Creator, it has this meaning. Thus: "and, behold, the Lord stood erect [*nitstsav*] upon it" (Gen 28:13), that is, was stably and constantly upon it—I mean upon the ladder, one end of which is in heaven, while the other end is upon earth. Everyone who ascends does so climbing up this ladder, so that he necessarily apprehends Him who is upon it, as He is stably and permanently at the top of the ladder.

The chapter to this point exemplifies the standard format of a "lexicographical chapter," singling out a term, identifying it as "equivocal," and surveying possible meanings of the term based on scriptural witnesses. It also begins to provide an explanation of the key parable of Jacob's ladder, which points to the fact that the ladder seems to be the cosmos extending from earth to heavens, that God is fixed firmly as first cause at the head of the cosmos and that anyone who ascends, presumably through study of the cosmos, will necessarily apprehend the first cause fixed at the head of the cosmos—a very strong reading indeed. He continues to provide still more decoding of the paradigmatic parable:

> It is clear that what I say here of Him conforms to the parable propounded. For the "angels of God" are the prophets with reference to whom it is clearly said: "and he sent an angel" (Num 20:16); "and an angel of the Lord came up from Gilgal to Bochim" (Judg 2:1). How well put is the phrase "ascending and descending" (Gen 28:12), in which ascent comes before descent. For after the ascent and the attaining of certain rungs of the ladder that may be known comes the descent with whatever decree the prophet has been informed of, with a view of governing and teaching the people of the earth. As we have made clear, it is on this account that this is called "descent."[26]

Here, in just a few sentences, in the context of a survey of the various meanings of an equivocal term in scripture, a clear reading of Jacob's dream emerges. To explain the ambiguous statement that the angels are "ascending and descending" at Genesis 28:12, when it would seem that angels, who originate in the celestial world, should do the opposite—descend first then ascend—Maimonides completes his philosophical reading of the dream with strongly Platonic political orientation. It is prophets rather than angels who ascend and descend; they ascend through attaining certain rungs of the ladder, that is, by mastering the different fields represented by the "ladder of wisdom" toward God, who stands firmly at the metaphysical summit of all learning; and then they descend, after achieving knowledge of the divine purpose, to govern the people on the earth. Within the context of a simple terminological gloss on the Bible, Maimonides transforms a well-known biblical story into a statement about the philosophical way of life, from scientific understanding of the cosmos and God to politics.

Maimonides's lexicographical method in the *Guide*, as shown here in this simple case, was powerful, and while it was considered dangerous by many, it was embraced and expanded by many more, who used Maimonides's lexicon in their own allegorical philosophical readings of scripture and applied the method in the identification and explanation of additional terms and new "parables" that Maimonides had not singled out in the *Guide*.[27] It created the foundation for a strongly exegetical approach to philosophy in traditional Judaism, an approach that would flourish and dominate philosophical debate throughout the later Middle Ages.

Translation, Lexicon, Introduction to Philosophy: Samuel ibn Tibbon's *Perush ha-millot ha-zarot*

In the twelfth and especially the thirteenth and fourteenth centuries, works of Judeo-Arabic and Arabic thought and literature were translated into Hebrew. Dozens of writings in a broad array of fields were rendered into the holy tongue, from grammar and lexicography to wisdom sayings, works of belles lettres, pietistic manuals, legal tracts, theological summas, and the full range of literature coming out of the Aristotelian tradition.[28] Translating Arabic works into Hebrew required the creation of a Hebrew vocabulary and terminology to represent writings that focused on the sciences and other subjects not previously known in Hebrew literature. The translations would often incorporate explanations of foreign terms into the body of the translation itself or in its margins, for example, as brief explanations or simple romance glosses.[29] They also spawned a cognate lexicographical literature, as with the brief glossary of the *Guide* by Judah al-Harizi,[30] the

Hebrew-Romance lexicon of Moses of Salerno,[31] the lexicon of Shem-Tov Falaquera introducing his encyclopedia,[32] and most famously the lexicographical works of Samuel ibn Tibbon.[33] The most foundational work of all in this respect was Ibn Tibbon's *Perush ha-millot ha-zarot*, his "Explanation of unusual terms," which he added to his revised translation of the *Guide* in 1213. It is the fullest of the translation glossaries and serves as both lexicon to one particular book—Ibn Tibbon's translation of the *Guide* into Hebrew—and introduction to philosophy in general.

Ibn Tibbon's explanation begins with a lengthy defense of his translation of the *Guide* and critique of his rival translator, Judah al-Harizi. He gives an extraordinarily clear description of how he himself worked as translator, listing the seven different types of translation terms he created, then sets about undermining Al-Harizi's work, both the translation itself and Al-Harizi's own brief glossary attached to the latter's translation of the *Guide*. Ibn Tibbon's introduction sets up his full lexicon of more than 190 terms[34] that follows, which is organized, for the most part, alphabetically; only the first terms veer from the alphabetical method, as he begins—perhaps influenced by Israeli's approach and the *Isagoge* tradition in Aristotelianism—with discussion of the five predicables, definition and description, and the ten categories.[35] The beginning of the glossary, in other words, presents something like a Hellenistic-style introduction to philosophy, beginning as the Hellenistic tradition did with Porphyry's *Isagoge* and Aristotle's *Categories*. It is rooted in translation, moreover, as it is based almost entirely, and sometimes verbatim, on passages from the most influential Arabic authority in logic, Al-Fārābī (his short treatises on Porphyry's *Isagoge* and Aristotle's *Categories*).[36]

The terms defined by Ibn Tibbon in his explanation vary in length and detail. They cover a broad range of topics, touching on all aspects of the medieval philosophical curriculum, including arithmetic and geometry, astronomy and geography, logic, physics, psychology, metaphysics, political science, and ethics, together with occasional medical terms, foreign names and schools of thought, terms of a theological or religious provenance, and nontechnical terms with no direct relation to the sciences at all, such as *perush* (which Ibn Tibbon explains as meaning not interpretation in the simple sense but extended interpretation, figurative interpretation, that is, translating the Arabic *ta'wīl*). To give a sense of the comprehensive nature of Ibn Tibbon's work, I will provide illustrations from each of these areas.

Mathematics

Ibn Tibbon includes in his glossary many terms related to mathematics, especially in the main three subjects of the classical quadrivium: arithmetic, geometry, and astronomy. For example, he includes brief discourses on *number, perfect number, rational number, point, line, straight, concave, convex, surface, plane, base, circle, center, diameter, circumference, triangle, angle, right angle, quadrangle, diagonal, pentagon, hexagon, dimension, height, length, depth, breadth, sphere, cone, cylinder, contiguity and continuity, discrete, extremity, magnitude, ratio, round, segment, side, solid body, tangent, thickness, transparent, direction, clime, longitude, latitude, pole, celestial pole, terrestrial pole, Arctic and Antarctic, Tropic of Cancer, Tropic of Capricorn, sphere, outer sphere, orbit, circle, equator, ecliptic (sphere of the zodiac), eccentric, deferent, epicycle, inclination, anomaly, obliquity, planet, wandering planets, star, fixed stars, constellation, day, night, diurnal motion* (including a short introduction to Al-Bitruji),[37] *eclipse, solstice, equinox, retrograde, quadrant, the four seasons, year, the horizon*, and the *Almagest*. He also defines the field itself, with a separate entry on the science of mathematics, which reads as follows:

> *Limmudiyyot*, Mathematics: Know that the demonstrative sciences have three divisions: natural science, mathematics, and divine science. We have already explained the first and the last at the letter *het*. As for the second, namely, mathematics, it includes geometry, arithmetic, astronomy—which includes the study of the spheres and planets as well as the judgments of the planets [=astrology]—and the science of melody, which is called "music." The three terms "mathematics," "propadeutic," and "training" are synonyms used for this division of science, since it is like a science that trains, teaches, or serves the other two divisions. I have used these [terms] interchangeably.

The Art of Logic

The medievals were completely taken by logic and the power of logic. Ibn Tibbon was no different in this respect, as discussions of logic are found throughout his writings. Logical terms are well represented in his explanation as well, with entries on the following terms: the five predicables (*genus, species, differentia, property, accident*), *individual, the ten categories, definition* and *description, equivocal, ambiguous*, and *metaphorical terms, synonyms, antonyms*, and *derived terms, true* and *false, possible, impossible*, and *necessary, affirmation* and *negation, conceptualization* and *assent, absolute* and *contingent, postulate, proposition, premise*, and *conclusion, proof* and *argument*, and the various types of syllogism. As with "mathematics," Ibn Tibbon defines the field of logic itself, alluding to the difficulty created by the translation of the Arabic *manṭiq* as *higgayon*. He also presents a full classification of the five types of syllogism following the Hellenistic "context theory."[38] These two entries are given here:

> *Higgayon*, Logic: Some commentators have explained "keep your children from *higgayon*" [TB Berakhot 28b] as referring to the science called "*manṭiq*" in Arabic. The Christians call it "dialectics," [referring to the discipline as a whole] with the name of one of its parts. I have followed the [Talmudic] commentators with respect to this [terminology] and call it "the art of *higgayon*," even though in my opinion it would have been better had they called it "the art of speech" following the [philosophers'] definition of man as "speaking [i.e., rational] animal." Indeed, in my opinion, it ought to be called the "art of reasoning."

And here is his survey of the five types of syllogism:

> *Ma'amar haggadi*, Rhetorical Statement: Know that there are five types of syllogism; Aristotle wrote a book about each. The first is the demonstrative syllogism, in which something is deduced from true premises. He called [his book on this type of syllogism] the "Book on Demonstration" [=*Posterior Analytics*]. The second is the dialectical syllogism, in which something is deduced from generally accepted premises. He called [his book on this type] the "Book on Dispute and Victory" [=*Topics*]. The third type is the rhetorical syllogism, in which the premises are convincing, that is, they convince the vulgar of their truth such that they believe in them. These are inferior to the generally accepted premises; they are certainly inferior to the demonstrative. He called [his book on this type] "Rhetoric." With this type of statement or syllogism, moreover, one preaches to the people in order to exhort them to do something or caution them against doing something, or to fix in their hearts the love of something, so that they approach it, or the hatred of something, so that they distance themselves from it. A statement of this type is called "rhetorical statement," just as a statement of the first type is called "demonstrative statement" and of the second "dialectical statement." The fourth is the poetic syllogism, in which the premises are such that they create an image in the heart of whomever hears them. This image leads such a person to love or hate something, even when he knows there is no truth in those statements. He called [his book on this type] "Poetics." The fifth [type of syllogism] is the sophistical syllogism, of which there are two types: (1) the premises themselves are sophistical, that is, although they appear to be true, when they are examined carefully by a scholar he finds that one or both are false; (2) the premises are true, but their combination does not generate a [true] conclusion, even though it seems to do so. This second type will deceive anyone who fails to examine [the conclusion] carefully or who is not an expert with regard to all of the conditions of syllogisms. The name of the book concerning this fifth type of syllogism is

> the "Book of Sophistry;" it is the book called in Arabic *al-Safsata* and in Romance *Sofistica*. These [five] works were prefaced by Aristotle with his "Book on Syllogism" [=*Prior Analytics*], in which he discusses all of them and makes known [in general] the conditions and properties of the syllogism.

Natural Science

Ibn Tibbon's survey of terms in natural science is also robust and comprehensive, especially when we include meteorology and psychology, which were of special interest to him. Among the terms he includes are the following: *nature, natural, artificial, simple, complex, extension, species of motion, local motion, natural motion, motion or movement through compulsion, time, eternity, the now, atom, atomic, atomic substance, vacuum, adjacent, substrate, natural things/notions, matter, form, natural form, specific form, artificial form, to take on form, first matter, body, corporeality, the four elements, the fifth element/body, generation* and *corruption, lightning, thunder, earthquake, mineral* [*motsa'*], *quarried stone* [*mehtsav*], *quarried ore* [*maqor*], *gem* [*matekhet*], *potential, actual, causation, formal cause, material cause, agent, telos, the nutritive soul* or *faculty, the sensitive soul* or *faculty, the appetitive soul* or *faculty, the imaginative soul* or *faculty, the intellectual soul* or *faculty, the intuitive soul, intellect, potential intellect, acquired emanated intellect, the tenth intellect*, and *the active intellect.* His definition of natural science itself shows how clearly he fits within the Aristotelian tradition coming out of the Hellenistic sources and the works of Al-Fārābī, on the one hand, and Maimonides's reading of rabbinic literature on the other. His entry reads as follows:

> *Hokhmat ha-teva'*, Natural Science: The Master [Maimonides] has indicated that this is what the Sages called the "Work of the Beginning." He meant by this that the secrets of the "Work of the Beginning" represent chapter headings in natural science, namely, the science that investigates all aspects of things that are governed by nature, i.e., all celestial and sublunary bodies and their accidents. The final source of all books in this science are those written by Aristotle, which include the following. 1) "The Discourse on Nature" [i.e., the *Physics*], in which natural things are discussed in general. 2) "On the Heavens and the World" [i.e., *De caelo*], in which the spheres, planets, and stars, along with the four elements and their mixtures, are discussed in general. 3) "On Generation and Corruption," in which the causes of generation and corruption, their attributes and quiddity, are discussed in particular. 4) "The Signs of Heaven" [i.e., *Meteorology*], in which accidents and phenomena that come into existence in the upper part of the atmosphere are discussed; some of these things, when they come into existence, are also found on land or in the sea.

5) "On Minerals and Stones,"[39] in which their quiddity and quality are discussed. 6) "On Plants,"[40] in which the nature of everything that experiences growth is discussed. 7) "On Animals,"[41] in which all accidents that affect both rational and irrational animals is discussed, as well as the utility of their limbs. 8) "On the Soul" [i.e., *De anima*], in which the faculties of the human soul are discussed in general. 9) "On Sense and Sensibilia,"[42] in which the nature of the senses in particular, as well as sleep and being awake, are discussed. As for the chapter headings set forth in the biblical section on Genesis, they cover only a small portion of what is contained in these books: not one in a hundred or even one in two hundred. This follows his [Maimonides's] view regarding the interpretation of that first biblical text and regarding the aim of the Torah in writing it.

Divine Science

There are relatively few terms in the field of metaphysics or divine science in Ibn Tibbon's lexicon. Why this is the case is not clear, though in general Ibn Tibbon, in his own original work—the commentary on Ecclesiastes and *Ma'amar yiqqavu ha-mayyim*—was far more interested in logic and physics than metaphysics. The terms defined include the following: *first philosophy, divine things or notions, being, essence, substance, quiddity, spiritual substances,* and *emanation/overflow,* along with *divine science* itself, which reads as follows: "*Hokhmat ha-elohut,* Divine Science: This is a science which discusses that which has no nature, that is, things that are intelligible and separate from matter, like the Lord, His angels, and other things that derive from the actions of the intellect and from the knowledge of the intellect—they have no action in the sensible world. The root of all books in this science is Aristotle's book entitled *Metaphysics.*"

Politics and Ethics

Political science is also underrepresented in the explanation, which is especially surprising since Ibn Tibbon translated Maimonides's "Eight Chapters" and commentary on Avot in addition to the *Guide*. A few examples of the terms included in these areas: *temperance, natural disposition, habitus,* and *first* and *final perfection,* as well as *political,* which, interestingly, does not relate at all to the field of political philosophy: "*Medini,* Political: An adjective derived from *medinah,* 'city.' One says: 'man is political by nature' [see *Guide* 2:40], which means that he is required to reside in a city or in a place where others of his species collect together into a city. He cannot stay alone in the deserts or in whatever place he might happen to be, like beasts."

Foreign Names and Schools: Religious Terminology

The other two categories listed above, unlike mathematics, logic, physics, metaphysics, and political philosophy, do not fit easily into the Aristotelian tradition that Ibn Tibbon draws from. Some of them, in fact, seem very strange indeed—for what they say and for why they are even needed. Among the foreign terms and names listed are: *Kalām, Muʿtazilite, Asharite, Sabians,* and *Peripatetics,* in which Ibn Tibbon emphasizes the basic meaning of the word: "*Masha'im*, Peripatetics: The name of the philosophical sect that follows Aristotle with respect to all his opinions. Aristotle himself was the first [*rosh*] of the Peripatetics. The meaning of *masha'im* is 'those who walk,' for they used to study while walking outside the city, not while sitting. They did this in order to get exercise while walking in order to preserve their good health."

Somewhat puzzling is the religious terminology listed in Ibn Tibbon's glossary, such as *masses* [*hamon*] and *elite* [*yehidim, segullah*], *principles of religion, divine providence, laws* [*torot*], and *practical laws* [*torot maʿasiyot*]. The latter he defines completely from within the Jewish context, including a biblical proof text; it seems that he preferred to translate Maimonides literally, coining a new term, when an existing term may have been misleading. In any event, it required him to specify what he meant by the artificial term created. Here is what he says: "*Torot maʿasiyot*, Practical Laws: These are the commandments which have some practical component, such as sukkah, lulav, matsah. It is possible they also include negative commandments, when they include the prohibition against doing some action, excluding those laws which have no action, such as the belief that God exists, that He is not many, that He is not originated. It is also possible that the belief that there is no God other than He is of this type. This is the commandment: 'let you not have any other gods than me' [Exod 20:3]."

The influence of Ibn Tibbon's "Explanation of Unusual Terms" cannot be overestimated. It went a long way to saving Ibn Tibbon's translation of the *Guide* itself and establishing it as the primary text of choice—contra Al-Harizi's—among later Jewish philosophers until the twentieth century. It provided a clear guide to understanding his "Arabized" translation terminology, which provided a key not only for the translation of the *Guide* but other translations as well; and in fact Ibn Tibbon's translations as well as his "Explanation" influenced the development of philosophical writing in Hebrew going forward, as later writers, even those who knew no Arabic, employed the "Arabized" and "scientific" terminology created and explained by

Ibn Tibbon. Focusing on the development of the philosophical lexicon itself, Ibn Tibbon's book quickly became the standard reference work. It was read and borrowed from, and it served as a model for later works, for example the Hebrew-Romance lexicon of Moses of Salerno, which followed Ibn Tibbon's *Perush ha-millot ha-zarot* closely, as well as the late medieval *Sefer ha-gedarim* by Menachem Bonafos.[43] Ibn Tibbon's explanation remained standard even into the modern period, despite the scientific lexicographical and philological work done by figures such as Jacob Klatzkin, Israel Efros, Harry Wolfson, Moshe Goshen-Gottstein, and Gad Zarfati.[44] Indeed, even after the work of these foundational figures and continuing into the twenty-first century, Ibn Tibbon's *Perush ha-millot ha-zarot* retains its central importance, relevant even for the latest of the philosophical lexicons: PESHAT—Premodern Philosophic and Scientific Hebrew Terminology, an online project directed by Giuseppe Veltri and hosted by the University of Hamburg.

Notes

1. See, for example, *Topics* 6:1–2, *Sophistical Refutations* 4, 7.
2. See Aristotle, *Metaphysics*, Book Delta, following the translation of Richard Pope (Ann Arbor: University of Michigan Press, 1960), 87–122.
3. See Angela Jaffray, "At the Threshold of Philosophy: Al-Fārābī's Introductory Works on Logic" (PhD diss., Harvard University, 2000), 10–12, with reference to earlier literature.
4. See Themistius, *In Libros Aristotelis De caelo paraphrases hebraice et latine*, ed. S. Landauer, in *Commentaria in Aristotelem graeca V-4* (Berlin, 1902), 1.
5. See G. Furlani, "Il 'libro delle definizioni e divisioni' di Michele L'Interprete," *Memorie della Classe di Scienze, Morali, Storiche e Filogiche* 2:1 (1928), 5–194; Bridget Kendall and Robert Thomson, *Definitions and Divisions of Philosophy by David the Invincible Philosopher* (Scholars Press, 1983).
6. See the text and translation with commentary by Tamar Frank, "Al-Kindī's *Book of Definitions*: Its Place in Arabic Definition Literature" (PhD diss., Yale University, 1975); and the new translation by Peter Adamson and Peter Porman, *The Philosophical Works of Al-Kindī* (Oxford University Press, 2012), 297–311.
7. See Al-Fārābī, *Treatise on Intellect (Risāla fī al-'aql)*, ed. M. Bouyges (Beirut, 1983); partial English translation by A. Hyman, in *Philosophy in the Middle Ages: The Christian, Islamic, and Jewish Traditions* (Indianapolis, IN: Hackett Publishing Company, 1973), 215–21; complete translation in John McGinnis and David Reisman, *Classical Arabic Philosophy: An Anthology of Sources* (Indianapolis, IN: Hackett Publishing, 2007), 68–78.
8. See Kiki Kennedy-Day, *Books of Definition in Islamic Philosophy: The Limits of Words* (London: Routledge, 2003).
9. See especially Yehuda Halper, "Averroes on Metaphysical Terminology: An Analysis and Critical Edition of the Long Commentary on Aristotle's Metaphysics Delta" (PhD diss., Bar-Ilan University, 2010).

10. See Hans Hinrich Biesterefeldt, "Medieval Arabic Encyclopedias of Science and Philosophy," in *The Medieval Hebrew Encyclopedias of Science and Philosophy*, ed. S. Harvey (Dordrecht: Kluwer Academic Publishers, 2000), 84–87.

11. For background, see, in general, Peter Adamson, *Al-Kindi* (Oxford: Oxford University Press, 2006).

12. Adamson and Porman, *Philosophical Works of al-Kindī*, 300–311.

13. Adamson and Porman, *Philosophical Works of al-Kindī*, 304–5.

14. Alexander Altman and Samuel Miklos Stern, *Isaac Israeli: A Neoplatonic Philosopher of the Early Tenth Century* (Chicago: University of Chicago Press, 2009).

15. Based on the translation of Stern in Altman and Stern, *Isaac Israeli*, 23–27. See also Stern's extensive discussion in his commentary ad loc., 27–31.

16. On the translations, see Altmann and Stern, *Isaac Israeli*, 3–9.

17. See Ignaz Goldziher, *Kitāb maʿānī al-nafs, Buch vom Wesen der Seele* (Berlin, 1907).

18. This is suggested by Hagit Mittelmann, "A Commentary on Ecclesiastes in Judeo-Arabic Ascribed to Isaac Ibn Ghiyath" (PhD diss., Hebrew University, 1999) [Hebrew].

19. See Israel Efros, *Maimonides' Treatise on Logic: The Original Arabic and Three Hebrew Translations* (New York: American Academy for Jewish Research, 1938); Yosef Qafih, *Be'ur melekhet ha-higgayon le-Rabbenu Mosheh ben Maimon* (Qiryat Ono, 1996); Jacob Dienstag, "Commentators, Translators, and Editors of Maimonides' Treatise on Logic: A Bio-Bibliographical Survey," *Koroth* 9 (1986): 269–96.

20. See Herbert Davidson, "The Authenticity of Works attributed to Maimonides," in *Me'ah She'arim: Studies in Medieval Jewish Spiritual Life in Memory of Isadore Twersky*, ed. E. Fleischer, G. Blidstein, C. Horowitz, and B. Septimus (Jerusalem: Magnes Press, 2001), 111–33; cf. Ahmad Hasnawi, "Réflexions sur la terminologie logique de Maïmonide et son contexte farabien: le Guide des perplexes et le Traité de logique," in *Maïmonide: Philosophe et Savant (1138–1204)*, ed. T. Lévy and R. Rashed (Leuven: Peeters, 2004), 39–78.

21. Efros, *Maimonides' Treatise on Logic*, 35–41, 47, 49, 51, 54, 57–58, 61, 65.

22. See, e.g., *Topics* 6:1–2.

23. See, e.g., *Sophistical Refutations* 4, 7.

24. For background and bibliography, see James T. Robinson, "On or Above the Ladder? Maimonidean and Anti-Maimonidean Readings of Jacob's Ladder," in *Interpreting Maimonides*, ed. Daniel Davies and Charles Manekin (Cambridge: Cambridge University Press, forthcoming).

25. Cited here according to Pines's translation, *Maimonides, The Guide of the Perplexed* (Chicago: University of Chicago Press, 1963), 40–41.

26. Cited in Pines's translation, *Maimonides, The Guide of the Perplexed*, 41.

27. See, for example, James T. Robinson, "Some Remarks on the Source of Maimonides' Plato in *Guide of the Perplexed* I.17," *Zutot* 3 (2004): 41–49; idem, "Maimonides, Samuel Ibn Tibbon, and the Construction of a Jewish Tradition of Philosophy," in *Maimonides after 800 Years: Essays on Maimonides and His Influence*, ed. Jay M. Harris (Cambridge, MA: Harvard University Press, 2007), 291–306; idem, "We Drink Only from the Master's Water: Maimonides and Maimonideanism in Southern France, 1200–1306," in *Epigonism in Jewish Culture*, ed. Shlomo Berger and Irene Zwiep, *Studia Rosenthaliana* 40 (2007–2008): 27–60; idem, *Samuel Ibn Tibbon's Commentary on Ecclesiastes, The Book of the Soul of Man* (Tübingen: Mohr Siebeck, 2007), 113–20.

28. For introduction to the translation movement with a fairly full bibliography, see James T. Robinson, "Arabic, Latin, and Romance into Hebrew: The Role of Translation in the

Development of European Jewish Culture," in *The Cambridge History of Judaism*, vol. 4, *Jews and Judaism in the Christian World, Seventh through Fifteenth Centuries*, ed. Robert Chazan (Cambridge: Cambridge University Press, forthcoming).

29. See, e.g., Ibn Tibbon's translation of "Eight Chapters," ed. and trans. Joseph Gorfinkle, *The Eight Chapters of Maimonides on Ethics* (New York: Columbia University Press, 1912), 20–21, 24; and, in general, James T. Robinson, "Samuel Ibn Tibbon's *Perush ha-Millot ha-Zarot* and Al-Fārābī's *Eisagoge* and *Categories*," *Aleph* 9 (2009): 70–76.

30. See *Sefer Moreh Nevukhim*, trans. Judah al-Harizi, ed. Lev Schlossberg, annotated by Shimon Scheyer (Vilna, 1929): 7–10.

31. See Giuseppe Sermoneta, *Un glossario filosofico ebraico-italiano del XIII secolo* (Rome, 1969); Jean-Pierre Rothschild, "Remarques sur la tradition manuscrite du glossaire hébreu-italien du commentaire de Moise de Salerne au Guide des égarés (en appendices, note sur les glossaires médicaux hébreux; liste de manuscrits hébreux contenant des glossaires)" in *Lexiques bilingues dans les domaines philosophique et scientifique (Moyen Age—Renaissance)*, ed. Jacqueline Hamesse and Danielle Jacquart (Turnhout: Brepols, 2001), 49–88.

32. See Mauro Zonta, *Un dizionario filosofico ebraico del XIII secolo. L'introduzione al Sefer De'ot ha-filosofim di Shem Tob Ibn Falaquera* (Torino, 1992).

33. See Resianne Fontaine, *Otot ha-Shamayim: Samuel Ibn Tibbon's Hebrew Version of Aristotle's Meteorology* (Leiden: Brill, 1995); J. Finkel, *Maimonides' Treatise on Resurrection (Maqāla fī Tehiyyat ha-Metim): The Original Arabic and Samuel Ibn Tibbon's Hebrew Translation and Glossary* (New York: American Academy for Jewish Research, 1939); and especially his *Perush ha-Millot ha-Zarot*, ed. Yehudah Even-Shemuel, published as an appendix to *Moreh ha-Nevukhim* (Jerusalem: Mossad Harav Kook, 1987).

34. Note that there is considerable variation in the manuscripts, even in the number of terms defined, ranging from 190 to 198 terms.

35. For the *Isagoge* tradition, see Jaffray, "At the Threshold of Philosophy."

36. See Robinson, "Samuel Ibn Tibbon's *Perush ha-Millot ha-Zarot*," 41–76.

37. See James T. Robinson, "The First References in Hebrew to al-Bitrūjī's *On the Principles of Astronomy*," *Aleph* 3 (2003): 145–63.

38. About which see Deborah Black, *Logic and Aristotle's Rhetoric and Poetics in Medieval Arabic Philosophy* (Leiden: E. J. Brill, 1990).

39. Probably referring to book 4 of Meteorology along with pseudo-Aristotelian works, about which see J. Ruska, *Das Steinbuch des Aristoteles, mit literargeschichtlichen Untersuchungen nach der arabischen Handschrift der Bibliothèque nationale* (Heidelberg: Carl Wintke's Universitatsbuchhandlung, 1912).

40. Probably referring to the pseudo-Aristotelian *De plantis*; see *Nicolaus Damascenus De Plantis Five Translations*, ed. and intro. H. J. Drossaart Lulofs and E. L. J. Poortman (Amsterdam, Oxford, New York: North-Holland Publishing, 1989).

41. This work included the three works of the Aristotelian corpus: "History of Animals," "Parts of Animals," and "Generation of Animals."

42. This would have included the books collected in *Parva naturalia*, about which see Rotraud Elisabeth Hansberger, "The Arabic Version of Aristotle's *De divination per somnum*" (MPhil diss., Oxford University, 2002); H. H. Eadem, "The Transmission of Aristotle's *Parva Naturalia* in Arabic" (DPhil diss., Oxford University, 2007). See also Averroes's summary, which was certainly known to Ibn Tibbon. The Arabic original and medieval Hebrew translation, edited by H. Blumberg (Medieval Academy of America, 1954, 1972), are now available online: http://c.ymcdn.com/sites/www.medievalacademy.org/resource/resmgr/maa_books

_online/blumberg_0080_bkmrkdpdf.pdf; http://c.ymcdn.com/sites/www.medievalacademy.org/resource/resmgr/maa_books_online/blumberg_0062_bkmrkdpdf.pdf.

43. See Menachem Bonafos, *Sefer ha-Gedarim* (Berlin, 1798).

44. See especially Israel Efros, *Philosophical Terms in the "Moreh Nebukim"* (New York: Columbia University Press, 1924) and Jacob Klatzkin, *Otsar ha-munahim ha-filosofiyim ve-antologiyah filosofit*, 4 vols. (Berlin, 1928). Harry A. Wolfson's writings are full of explanations of philosophical terminology; see, e.g., the notes to his *Crescas' Critique of Aristotle* (Cambridge, MA: Harvard University Press, 1929), a veritable lexicon of Greek, Latin, Arabic, and Hebrew terms. Moshe Goshen-Gottstein is the founder of the discourse on "Arabized" Hebrew, focused mainly on Ibn Tibbon's language; see his posthumously published dissertation: *Syntax and Vocabulary of Mediaeval Hebrew, As Influenced by Arabic*, revised by Sh. Assif and U. Melammed (Jerusalem: Ben Zvi Institute, 2006) [Hebrew], which includes a bibliography of his relevant articles on translation in Hebrew. See also Gad Zarfati, *Mathematical Terminology in Hebrew Scientific Literature of the Middle Ages* (Jerusalem: Magnes Press, 1968) [Hebrew].

JAMES T. ROBINSON is the Caroline E. Haskell Professor of the History of Judaism, Islamic Studies, and the History of Religions at the University of Chicago Divinity School. He is the author of several books and articles on medieval Jewish philosophy, literature, and biblical exegesis.

13

THEOLOGICAL SUMMAS IN LATE MEDIEVAL JEWISH PHILOSOPHY

Shira Weiss

In the early medieval period, due largely to the influence of Maimonides, Jewish philosophy was perceived to be accessible to the privileged intellectual elite. By the late Middle Ages, there was a sustained effort by philosophers to extend their influence to wider circles of the Jewish community, thereby allowing greater access to philosophical ideas. Three of the most significant works from this later period that have been incorporated into the canon of medieval Jewish philosophy are *Milḥamot ha-Shem* (Wars of the Lord) by Gersonides (1288–1344), *Or ha-Shem* (Light of the Lord) by Hasdai Crescas (1340–1410) and *Sefer ha-ʿiqqarim* (Book of principles) by Joseph Albo (1380–1444). The author of each of these theological summas set out to address the philosophical concerns of his generation and was motivated to correct what he perceived as his predecessors' mistakes or omissions. In response to Maimonides's profound impact, the authors composed comprehensive theological books that either further developed or critiqued Maimonides's Aristotelian-influenced philosophy. These three prominent works encapsulated much of the philosophical debate that consumed philosophers in the late medieval period and offered diverse perspectives and arguments regarding topics that continue to be of interest today.

Medieval philosophical texts were composed in a variety of literary forms. The goal of the summa was to emancipate philosophical or theological subjects from the structure of scripture and discuss the topics comprehensively, often in summary form. Medieval summae are characterized by their overall organizing structure and method of confronting individual problems or questions. Topics are arranged in a systematic style and various arguments for a given position and against it are presented. St. Thomas Aquinas, in his *Summa Theologiae*, the paradigm of medieval theological summae, uses an abbreviated form of the disputed question and presents the objections and authorities in an effort to achieve a rhetorical and a logical effect. Aquinas's work is intended to introduce students of theology to the notion that speculation, not fixed answers, is intrinsic to the philosophical and theological enterprise. He aspires not only to convey information to his readers but also to train them in a certain mode of thinking. In his prologue, Aquinas suggests that a major contribution of his work is its organization of topics and questions, according to the logical order required by the subject.[1] Following Aquinas, the summa became the form for the systematic organization of an entire area of philosophical and theological study, as reflected in the comprehensive discussions that comprise the great works of late medieval Jewish philosophy.

The *Wars of the Lord, Light of the Lord*, and *Book of Principles* reflect qualities of the medieval summa. Gersonides, Crescas, and Albo set out to compose comprehensive philosophical discussions, organized in systematic and logical styles. Embedded within their thorough expositions, they reveal their own arguments, present original ideas, and refute opposing views. Each author aims to ameliorate what he considers to be erroneous beliefs and substantiates his views through well-reasoned arguments. While they present diverse perspectives on a variety of philosophical and theological ideas, Gersonides, Crescas, and Albo attempt to convey to their readers a cohesive philosophical worldview that can fortify their understanding and convictions. Crescas and Albo, in particular, present an explicit delineation of dogma in an effort to offer readers, Jewish and non-Jewish alike, a uniform understanding of the tenets of Judaism.

Milḥamot ha-Shem (Wars of the Lord)

Milḥamot ha-Shem (Wars of the Lord), the philosophical-theological magnum opus of Gersonides (also known as R. Levi b. Gershom and by the acronym Ralbag), presents the author's original and systematic thought in a scholastic, precise, and technical style. The book was written in an accessible Hebrew, as opposed to the Arabic of earlier medieval Jewish philosophy. In his work, Gersonides further develops the Aristotelian philosophy that

Maimonides had incorporated into his *Guide of the Perplexed*. Gersonides's methodology of exposition of different points of view, refutation, and then exposition and demonstration of correct theses was new to Jewish philosophy. However, Gersonides's style not only reflected the influence of Aristotle's method but also the mode of exposition of the Christian scholastics. St. Thomas Aquinas's *Summa Theologiae* presents the same structure: exposition of the question, citation of the difficulties and discussion of them, followed by solutions. Like Aristotle and Aquinas, Gersonides provides a history of the views of others on each topic, enumerates long lists of arguments pro and con, and then puts forth his own opinions supported with both logical argument and biblical citation.

Gersonides's discussion of numerous theories in *Wars of the Lord* is centered on Aristotle's interpretation and was composed at the same time as the commentaries of Averroes. Gersonides presents a comprehensive and critical analysis of the philosophies of Aristotle, Averroes, and Maimonides. Throughout the book, Gersonides presents the views of Averroes and Maimonides, in some instances agreeing with one against the other and on other occasions rejecting both. For Gersonides, Averroes represented the Aristotelian tradition, whereas Maimonides demonstrated loyalty to the Torah and used philosophy to defend it against the criticisms of the Aristotelians. Gersonides maintains that true philosophy is consistent with the teachings of the Torah when properly understood and conceives of true philosophy not as Aristotle's thought, as Averroes argued, nor as incomprehensible to the limits of human reason, as Maimonides claimed. Gersonides refuses to accept that human intellect, the way in which humanity connects with God, is intrinsically imperfect, but rather maintains that with the Torah's guidance one can achieve intellectual perfection through reason.

Similar to Maimonides, Gersonides argues that the Torah is not a political law that constrains the reader to believe falsities. Rather, in the Torah, the reader must interpret the meaning consistent with demonstrated truth. However, unlike in the *Guide of the Perplexed*, in which Maimonides required the reader to search for the meaning that he deliberately concealed in esotericism, Gersonides composes his work in an organized order in which it should be read as he presents the reader with the results of his comprehensive research conducted over a long period of time. He arranges his book in such a way since the knowledge of certain ideas naturally precedes others, with the general preceding the particular.

Wars of the Lord was completed in 1329 after twelve years of writing. The work began as an essay on creation, since Gersonides was dissatisfied with Maimonides's discussion of creation in *Guide of the Perplexed*. However, Gersonides concluded that an exposition of creation needed to be grounded in an analysis of time, motion, and the infinite. He later added discussions of immortality, divination, prophecy, and providence to his philosophical text. The completed work is comprised of six books devoted to the following topics: (1) immortality of the soul, (2) dreams, divination, and prophecy, (3) divine knowledge, (4) providence, (5) the celestial spheres, and (6) creation and miracles. In his introduction to *Wars of the Lord*, Gersonides delineates six questions, each to be examined in a separate book: Is the rational soul immortal? What is the nature of prophecy? Does God know particulars? Does divine providence extend to individuals? What is the nature of astronomical bodies? Is the universe eternal or created?

Gersonides develops an overarching view of God, humanity, and the world that incorporates his ideas on astronomy into his overall system. For Gersonides, the ultimate purpose of astronomy is to understand God, since through the study of orbs and stars, humanity is led to knowledge and appreciation of God.[2] Gersonides's discussion of creation responds to that of Maimonides. In *Guide of the Perplexed*, Maimonides maintains that the topic of creation is beyond rational demonstration and remains loyal to the Torah's literal account of creation ex nihilo. Gersonides, by contrast, devotes his attention in *Wars of the Lord* to proving that the Platonic theory of creation out of an eternal formless matter is rationally demonstrable and argues that the world was created outside of time by a freely willing agent. Whereas Maimonides asserts that no valid inference can be drawn from the nature of the sublunar sphere to that of the superlunary sphere, Gersonides argues that since both spheres contain material elements, knowledge of creation is based on astronomy, which is a human science similar to physics.[3]

In many respects, Gersonides was a more radical thinker than Maimonides, as he deviates from traditional views when he deems philosophical reasoning demands it. Gersonides maintains his conception of the Aristotelian notion of an impersonal God and reconstructs the concepts of providence, prophecy, and miracles accordingly. As Julius Guttmann writes, "Whereas Maimonides had erected a true synthesis of Judaism and Aristotelianism, in Gersonides the Aristotelian element was of decisive importance. . . . Gersonides may be the truest disciple of Aristotle whom medieval Jewish philosophy produced; but because of this, he was essentially alien to those biblical doctrines which in his formulation he seemed to approach."[4]

Like Aristotle, Gersonides argues that providence is general in nature and pertains to a species and only incidentally to particulars of the species. Because of this, God experiences no change in will and therefore does not interact personally in human affairs. Rather, God is in control of the universe in that the motions of the heavenly bodies that implement the laws in the divine mind, which is activated by God's self-intellection act to preserve the species in the sublunar realm in the best possible way.[5] The human species merits the most general providence due to its rank and nobility; however, its members are not protected from harmful chance events. In order to gain protection from such events, one must achieve individual providence by perfecting one's intellect to avoid oncoming danger. Gersonides distinguishes between three types of individual providence: prophecy, providential suffering, and miracles.

Unlike the more traditional notion of God's bestowal of a divine message on the human prophet, Gersonides explains that prophecy occurs when the intellectually perfected individual receives emanations from the Active Intellect that impart information about essences and laws in the divine mind that control the operations of the natural order. Gersonides suggests that the prophet does not receive knowledge of particular future events but rather achieves knowledge of a general form, and he uses his imagination to instantiate such knowledge with particular facts. A prophet can only foresee the future if that future is ordered and predictable, governed by natural causal laws. Thus, the prophet taps into these emanations that are present at all times in order to retrieve information about harmful chance events that have been determined to befall him and then uses such information to circumvent harm and maximize his well-being. The difference between the prophet and the rest of humanity is that he is more attuned to receive universal messages and can apply them to particular circumstances.[6]

If an individual is not worthy of prophecy but still intellectually perfected to merit some form of individual providence, he can receive protection from harmful chance events through providential suffering, which Gersonides associates with the rabbinic concept of "afflictions of love." Rather than the emanations that impart information to the prophet, these emanations instantiate a series of providential laws that cause suffering but that ultimately protect the individual from greater harm. In both types of individual providence, prophecy and providential suffering, God does not participate personally in providential action, but rather humans bring providence on themselves by tapping into ever-present impersonal emanations from God that become operative once intellectual perfection is achieved. Such emanations provide either information or a change of event, both of which benefit the recipient of providence.[7] Gersonides identifies immortality as the highest form of providential reward, which, like Maimonides, he conceives philosophically as the intellect that survives after the body perishes.

Gersonides suggests that miracles function in the same manner as other forms of providence as a result of impersonal laws and do not require a change of divine will or God's personal intervention in the sublunar realm. Miracles operate in a similar way to providential suffering, but instead of a painful obstacle, a series of unusual laws are instantiated that produce miracles for the intellectually perfected. God does not willfully intervene in the natural order, but a series of impersonal laws in the divine mind are activated by the individual's superior intellect. Gersonides "naturalizes" miracles by rejecting both that God can do anything and that God is their direct agent. Instead, he interprets miracles described in the Bible as being brought about through natural phenomenon. Seymour Feldman writes, "Just as the laws of natural, or general, providence governed by the heavenly bodies can be contravened by human choices, so too the law of miracles is conditional. Miracles are lawful and thus natural, but they are also contingent and hence volitional . . . Just as in prophecy, the occurrence of a miracle is 'impersonal.' Whoever is qualified and worthy of receiving it receives it. The recipients of a miracle are those who are worthy of having the providential plan concretized or manifested through them."[8] The Bible's identification of God as the agent of miracles does not necessitate the conclusion that God is the proximate cause of miracles, but rather, God is the origin of all things that are generated.

Gersonides's view of free choice further illustrates his radical position regarding divine omniscience. His affirmation of human free choice may have been in response to Abner of Burgos, though not explicitly stated. Abner advocated absolute determinism, as he argued that human actions flow necessarily from causes, as does the process of nature.[9] Humanity chooses between alternatives, but this choice is not free, for it depends on necessary laws. If human choice were free, God could not know a human decision until the last moment, because it would be unforeseeable and He would thus not be omniscient. Gersonides reconciles divine omniscience while preserving human free choice by redefining the nature of God's knowledge. Emphasizing the teleological nature of astrology, his conception of divine knowledge is predicated on knowledge of the heavenly bodies that are directed toward man's preservation and guidance. Gersonides argues that God's perfect knowledge extends only over that which is knowable, universal, and immutable. For instance, God eternally perceives the general laws of the universe since he knows the structure of the universe and the intelligible order it follows through his unchanging knowledge of his own essence from which the universe proceeds.[10] Human contingents are unknown to God; however, this does not detract from God's omniscience because human choice constantly changes and is not universal or knowable. Rather, God does not know particulars as particulars but as determined by the universal laws of nature, yet human choice influenced by reason can subvert the celestial bodies' general ordering of life. In the previous century, Maimonides maintained God's omniscience and man's freedom by arguing that the nature of God's knowledge and its ability to foreknow man's free acts is incomprehensible to the limits of the human mind. Despite the immutability of God's knowledge, Maimonides does not render objects of God's knowledge necessary. Aristotle argued that God does not know particulars. In an attempt to mediate between the views, Gersonides goes further than Maimonides in his rationalistic attitude by limiting God's knowledge of particulars only insofar as they are ordered. Therefore, God knows that certain states of affairs are contingent but does not know which of the alternatives will be the case. Thus, Gersonides maintains that divine knowledge precludes contingency, since if God knew future contingents before they are actualized, there would be no contingency.[11] In *Wars of the Lord*, Gersonides argues,

> Contingents are defined and ordered in one respect and are contingents in another respect. That being so, it is clear that the respect in which He knows them is the respect in which they are ordered and defined . . . The respect in which he does not know them is the respect in which they are not ordered, which is the respect in which they are contingents. This is because in this respect it is impossible that they should be known. However, from this respect He knows that they are contingents which possibly will not be actualized with regard to the choice which God gave to man in order to perfect what was lacking in the governance of the heavenly bodies. But He does not know which of the two possible alternatives will be actualized from the point of view that they are contingents. The reason for this is that if this were so, there could be no contingency in this world at all . . . The lack of knowledge of which of two possible alternatives qua possible will be actualized, is not a deficiency

> in Him. This is because perfect knowledge of a thing consists in knowing the nature of the thing. Were [the thing] to be conceived to be other than it is, this would be error and not knowledge. This being so, He knows all these things in the most perfect way possible. This is because He knows them with respect to their being ordered in a clear and definite way. In addition He knows those respects in which they are contingent with regard to choice, according to their contingency.[12]

Gersonides here argues that God knows all the infinite possibilities due to his knowledge of scientific and astral determinants of the world but not acts by which humans deviate from their astrological destiny.[13] Since he maintains that it is "a fundamental and pivotal belief of the Torah that there are contingent events in the world,"[14] he holds onto human freedom at the expense of traditional understandings of divine omniscience, a view that was, and continues to be viewed as, controversial and criticized by later philosophers.

Although not explicitly a work of dogma, like those of Crescas and Albo, Gersonides does articulate what he considers to be the most fundamental philosophical and theological topics in Judaism throughout his summa. However, while his biblical commentary was well received, his philosophy was perceived by many to be radical and met opposition, similar to the work of Maimonides. Criticism of his philosophy can be attributed to a number of factors. Social and religious upheaval affected the role of philosophy within the European Jewish community. Facing pogroms, coerced conversions, and forced debates, philosophy or "wisdom of the Greeks" was believed by some to lead to apostasy. Additionally, as the influence of Kabbalah increased and the status of Aristotle in the entire medieval philosophical world began to decline, the Aristotelian conceptual framework that Gersonides espoused was regarded as foreign and dangerous.[15]

However, even opposition reflected the importance of Gersonides's work. The reaction to *Wars of the Lord*, both positive and negative, in his lifetime and posthumously, testifies to its philosophical impact. Many of the most notable Jewish philosophers and theologians during the late medieval and early modern periods refer to Gersonides directly or indirectly and take his philosophy seriously. Hasdai Crescas deals most extensively with *Wars of the Lord*, as he perceives Maimonides and Gersonides to be the chief representatives of Jewish Aristotelianism, a philosophical movement to which he vehemently objects. Thus, the significance and enduring impact of Gersonides may lie not necessarily in solutions to specific philosophical-religious questions, but in the general tenor and thrust of his philosophical program.[16]

Or ha-Shem (Light of the Lord)

Gersonides's radical rationalistic thought, as well as that of Maimonides, was subject to philosophical critique in Hasdai Crescas's *Or ha-Shem* (Light of the Lord). Crescas argues that Maimonides and Gersonides used Aristotle's arguments to undermine Judaism. He maintains that Aristotelian views not only contradict the Jewish tradition but also the rational understanding of the world. Written in Hebrew, Crescas's objection in *Light of the Lord* is not to philosophy per se, but to the dominant scholastic Aristotelian philosophy and its intellectualization of religion.[17] Thus, in a style characterized by precision and free from rhetoric, the author employs philosophical tools to criticize and overturn Aristotelian philosophy through logical analysis and proof. Crescas resents Greek philosophy's domination of Jewish belief and tries to undermine and discredit Aristotelian philosophy in favor of the Torah's Judaism. Crescas's separation of Judaism from Aristotelianism entails a return to the fundamentals of biblical religion. He attempts to replace accepted Aristotelian scientific principles with traditionally religious beliefs and reinvigorate a truer Judaism based on its spiritual and emotional facets instead of its intellectual elements. While Crescas argues that the true meaning of the Torah cannot contradict philosophy, he believes, unlike some of his Jewish philosophical predecessors, that philosophy cannot reveal the entire truth of the Torah, but rather, God's revelation disclosed true beliefs that philosophy cannot discover. Though he generally presents conservative reactions to rationalistic excesses in his work, he also develops untraditional opinions when he feels such positions are warranted.

Light of the Lord's structure is based on a hierarchical arrangement of Jewish dogma and discusses the essential doctrines of Judaism, in the order of their dogmatic importance.[18] In addition to Crescas's opposition to Maimonides's Aristotelianism, he rejects Maimonides's deductive delineation of his thirteen principles of Judaism, which failed to distinguish between more and less fundamental dogmas.[19] The book's division into four parts serves as the framework for Crescas's philosophical discussions. Crescas attributes Maimonides's errors to Aristotelian science and therefore devotes the first volume to a criticism of Aristotelian science in his delineation of the roots or first principles (*shorashim*) of scripture, without which one cannot imagine revelation or divine law, namely, the existence, unity, and incorporeality of God. Crescas objects to Maimonides's argument that the belief in the existence, unity, and incorporeality of God must be based on Aristotelian principles and argues that such beliefs cannot be based on philosophical proofs built on faulty propositions. The second volume, comprised of six parts, explains the bases or cornerstones (*pinnot*) of scripture, without which the existence of the Torah (and in general of all revealed law) is impossible, namely, divine knowledge of individuals, providence, divine power, prophecy, free will, and purposefulness of revelation. The third volume enumerates and explains the eight true doctrines (*de'ot amitiot*) that, while not necessary, render anyone who denies them a heretic, namely, creation, immortality of the soul, reward and punishment, resurrection of the dead, eternity of the Torah, superiority of the prophecy of Moses, ability to prophesy, and messianic redemption. The fourth volume discusses some nonobligatory speculations of scripture (*de'ot u-sevarot*), including future eternity; plurality of worlds; celestial bodies; astral influence; demons; amulets and incantations; reincarnation; future reward of a minor; "heaven" and "hell"; "account of the beginning" and "account of the chariot"; intellect, intelligible, and intellectually cognizing subject; prime mover; and metaphysics.[20]

Light of the Lord was written over a long period of Crescas's life (perhaps as much as fifteen years) and was completed several months before his death. In his introduction, Crescas explains that the book is only the first part of a project, to be called *Ner Elohim* (Candle of God), intended to counter the two major works of Maimonides. The first book is a philosophical work against Maimonides's *Guide of the Perplexed*, while the second was to be a legal book to supplant Maimonides's *Mishneh Torah*, to be called *Ner mitzvah* (The lamp of the divine commandment), in which Crescas would critique Maimonides's legal method and lack of citations of sources from earlier authorities. However, political/religious challenges and communal responsibility prevented him from writing the legal volume. As a leading rabbi of the Aragonian Jewish communities, following the persecutions of 1391 in which his only son was murdered, Crescas sought to reconstruct the decimated Jewish communities. He was therefore unable to accomplish his objective of replacing both the philosophic and halakhic works of Maimonides.

Crescas deviates from Maimonides in his argument that the true perfection of the soul is not rational knowledge but love of God. He suggests that the soul continues immortally after the body perishes, since it is a spiritual substance with a potential for knowledge. Crescas asserts that love of God is not a function of knowledge as Maimonides suggested but is related to the will, the appetitive and imaginative components of the soul, and unrelated to the mind. Crescas instructs humanity to express love of God through obedience to his commands, which he considers the highest spiritual goal for which humans receive spiritual reward after death. While Crescas pays homage to the teachings of Maimonides, he felt that service of God takes precedence over knowledge of him. Crescas argues that the foundation of Maimonides's thought is flawed, since fear and love of God is the path that leads to God, not the knowledge of intelligibles, as Maimonides conceived. Fulfillment of the commandments leads to perfection; knowledge of the commandment is a means to achieving perfection. Crescas criticizes Maimonides for not clarifying the causes of the commandments and their general laws but merely expounding on the number of commandments. *The Lamp of the Divine Commandment* was to have clarified their causes, which are not found in Maimonides's halakhic writings.[21]

Additionally, according to Crescas, Maimonides did not appropriately distinguish between beliefs and commandments. Crescas considers Maimonides's placement of belief in God as the first of the positive commandments to be absurd, because "knowledge of the divine existence is a necessary presupposition: what would be the significance of a commandment if one did not believe in the existence of him who ordained this commandment?"[22] Furthermore, since belief is not the result of will or choice, why should there be punishment for erroneous belief and opinion if the believer is constrained to believe by the arguments over which he has no control? Crescas responds that "reward and punishment are not for the belief itself, but rather for the pleasure one finds in it and the pains one takes to examine it carefully. Even in conduct one is not rewarded or punished for deeds directly but for the intention and desire. Deed without intention is not punished. Intention without deed is; though the two together call for the greatest punishment or reward."[23] This distinction between intention and deed enables Crescas to preserve just retribution in his deterministic scheme.

Crescas deviates from both Gersonides and Maimonides in his attempt to resolve the conflict between divine omniscience and human freedom. He argues that God's omniscience must be maintained even over particulars, since he felt it absurd to suppose that the first universal and absolute cause should be ignorant of its effects, as implied by Gersonides. Crescas finds

Gersonides's theory to be absurd because it attributes to God ignorance of his creatures and impious because it is contrary to the biblical text that records God's knowledge of and interactions with the patriarchs, and Israel. However, if humanity is not free, how can God's reward and punishment be justified? Crescas responds that determinism is not fatalism—humanity is not preordained from eternity to act in a given way, no matter the circumstances. Command, effort, and endeavor are not useless and without effect. However, man's will and conduct are also not causeless and undetermined until the moment of action. Crescas explains that the act of will is contingent in respect to itself but is determined by its cause. If the cause were removed, the act would not be, but given the cause, the effect is necessary.[24] Crescas writes, "The will may indeed be necessitated by causes, yet remain *will*; for considered by itself it can will or not will, although considered from the standpoint of its causes its choice is necessitated. There is a subjective test for distinguishing a voluntary act from an involuntary one: the former, unlike the latter, is not accompanied by feeling of necessity or compulsion."[25] Effort is itself a cause and determines an effect. Commandments and prohibitions are also causes that influence action. "Reward and punishment are not unjust, even though antecedent causes over which man has no control determine his acts, any more than it is unjust that fire burns the one who comes near it, though he did so without intention. Reward and punishment are a necessary consequence of obedience and disobedience."[26] However, Crescas did not want to make this view public, since people would find it as an excuse for the wicked. Since forbidden acts are naturally evil, the punishment of the sinner is not a providential form of punishment but rather the natural consequences of the sinner's act. The goal of the Torah is to guide people to do good. Therefore, the Torah's commands and retribution serve as causes that influence humanity.

Crescas's conception of choice is similar to that of Abner of Burgos. He empties the words *will* and *free will* of their sense, as a human is considered ""willing" when the cause is interiorized and not perceived by him, and "nonwilling" only when an external cause is perceived as forcing him, against his interior assent, into a certain action."[27] Crescas diminishes human liberty in order to safeguard divine knowledge. However, he "attempts to lighten the impact of his deterministic views by asserting that reward and punishment are a consequence of the feelings of pleasure or discomfort which accompanies human actions. One who feels pain at the sin which is committed under compulsion will not be punished."[28] Thus, even though the decision-making process is fundamentally deterministic, the attitudes and feelings behind actions are voluntary. The inner self can either be happy or unhappy with the actions of one's deterministic external person. If one externally sins, while internally one is unhappy, it is not truly a sin because the inner self did not want to sin. Rather, a deterministic process coerced the external person into committing the sin against one's conscience and true will, since the inner will is under human control, while the regular will that decides action is contingent on a deterministic psychological process.[29] Crescas distinguishes between causation and compulsion to explain the justice of reward and punishment. Rewards are merited by one who acts due to causal necessity, but not by one who acts as a result of compulsion. Even if one's acts follow a certain causal route, the act can be considered voluntary in a sense, so long as it was not compelled.[30]

Though Crescas is one of the most original Jewish philosophers in the Middle Ages, his philosophical opinions did not have a lasting impact and were not perpetuated by his students.[31] While *Light of the Lord* presented Crescas's intellectual ingenuity in a comprehensive work, it did not achieve its goal of supplanting Maimonides's magnum opus. Several reasons have been attributed to its lack of influence. Spanish Jewry could not integrate Crescas's new and original mode of thinking due to the devastation of their community as a result of the pogrom of 1391 and the persecutions at the beginning of the fifteenth century and instead reverted back to more traditional thinking. Additionally, Crescas's ideas were complex, and the style and content of his work may have been largely incomprehensible to his general readership. Alternatively, his readers may have rejected his philosophy due to the influence and citation of Christian scholars, such as the apostate Abner of Burgos.[32] Crescas's thought would likely have had longer endurance had he realized his original intention of composing both a legal and philosophical work to counteract the pervasive influence of Maimonides. While *Light of the Lord* did not achieve the status of *Guide of the Perplexed*, Crescas's book reflects philosophic originality that continues to be studied; an English translation was recently published,[33] granting greater access to the complex work.

Sefer ha-ʿiqqarim (Book of Principles)

Sefer ha-ʿiqqarim (Book of principles), composed by Crescas's student, Joseph Albo, reflects the influence of his philosophical predecessors. His work, too, was a book of dogma, but distinct in enumeration and philosophical arguments from that of his teacher. Albo's style is that of a popularizer and homilist, and his philosophical work received greater reception than did his teacher's more philosophically unique *Light of the Lord. The Book of Principles* was widely circulated because of its fluent style, dialectical structure, and interesting expositions (incorporating philosophical interpretations of biblical texts amid descriptions of dogma). The Hebrew language is clear and philosophical arguments are straightforward, making the book accessible to a wide readership. The framework of the book is Albo's principles of faith, which attempt to define the beliefs necessary for a system of divine law. Albo integrates homilies that convey theological lessons within his discussions of dogma, in an effort to defend the authenticity of Judaism and create a uniform set of Jewish doctrine.

Albo served as rabbinic leader and preacher in the community of Daroca in Christian Spain and played a significant role in a particularly turbulent time in Jewish history.[34] He moved to a rabbinic position in Soria in Castille, possibly as a result of the destruction of his community in Daroca (1415), and there completed his major treatise, *The Book of Principles*, in 1425.[35] Scholarly consensus regards Albo as an unoriginal philosopher who merely synthesized the views of his predecessors and contemporaries,[36] sometimes siding with one while at other times with the other.[37] *The Book of Principles* gives the impression of an eclectic compilation in the interest of restoring a moderate conservatism from the radical intellectualism of the previous generations of Jewish philosophers. However, recent scholarship has uncovered original individual philosophical discussions within his work.[38]

Albo was motivated to compile his book in the aftermath of his defense of the Talmud against Christian persecution and coercion in the Tortosa Disputation (1413–1414). He composed *The Book of Principles* as a reaction to the wavering of faith of his coreligionists. He realized from discussions about religious dogma in the disputation that Jews (including his fellow rabbinic defenders of the Talmud) had divergent views concerning Jewish dogma and sought to restore Jewish beliefs by demonstrating that basic teachings of the Jewish religion bore essential characteristics of divine law and was the true religion, while Christianity was spurious. Thus, his work has a two-fold objective: To present a rationalist apologetic for Judaism along with a refutation of Christian doctrines to respond to Christian persecution, as well as to redefine the principles of Judaism in light of internal arguments within Jewish thought. Albo aimed to prove the validity of Judaism to the people of his day in an accessible way. He felt that dogma had not been treated adequately by his predecessors and that there was no agreement among previous writers about the number of the principles or their nature. Maimonides enumerated thirteen principles, David Yom Tov ibn Bilia delineated twenty-six, and Crescas counted six, each without investigating the principles of divine religion. Albo distinguishes between the general principles that pertain to divine legislation common to all religions and principles that are specific to a particular religion.[39] Albo includes all thirteen of Maimonides's dogma, but instead of placing them on the same level of importance, Albo divides them into three categories of descending rank—fundamental principles, derived principles, and true beliefs.

The first volume of *The Book of Principles* deals with the doctrine of the three *'iqqarim*, principles for divine law: existence of God, revelation, and reward and punishment. Upon the urging of his coreligionists, he elaborates on each dogma (and the derivative—*shorashim* [roots] and *'anafim* [true beliefs]) in three subsequent volumes. The derivative principles—beliefs that instill clear and detailed content into the general concept of the principle, derived from the fundamental belief in existence of God—are unity, incorporeality, timelessness, and perfection. The *shorashim* derived from revelation are divine omniscience, prophecy, and authenticity of prophecy. The *shoresh* derived from the principle of reward and punishment is individual providence. The six branches (*'anafim*), beliefs that are true and that every follower of divine law must accept, are creation ex nihilo, superiority of Moses as prophet, immutability, immortality through observance of commandments, resurrection of dead, and the Messiah. Unlike the principles and derivative principles, Albo does not consider denial of the branches to be heresy, but rather a sin that requires atonement.

In an effort to prove the authenticity of Judaism and the refutation of Christianity, Albo distinguishes between true divine law and false religions that claim to be of divine origin. He proposes two criteria: (1) beliefs of true divine law do not contradict any one of the necessary principles of divine law; (2) True divine law demonstrates proof of the credibility of its messenger who transmits the law of divine origin.[40] Albo argues that, despite the risks, religion should be investigated to find what distinguished a divine law from one of human origin. As opposed to Christianity and Islam, Albo deduces that only Judaism fulfills both criteria. Its doctrines are drawn primarily from Maimonides, Crescas, and Albo's contemporary, Simon ben

Zemah Duran (1361–1444), who enumerated the three dogmas that Albo goes on to explicate with greater precision.

As the title reflects, Albo's theory of fundamental principles serves as the focal point and framework of his book. Crescas's influence on Albo is evident in the development of his hierarchy of dogma. However, Albo deviates from his teacher both in his delineation of dogma and in his philosophic conceptions. Consistent with other fifteenth-century Iberian Jewish philosophers, Albo does not maintain the hostile attitude toward rationalism and philosophy that Crescas espoused but presents a more moderate position that defends philosophical speculation in a conservative manner and embraces rational inquiry as a valuable supplement to tradition. Albo's general philosophic approach is perceived to lie between that of the rationalists (most notably Maimonides) and that of philosophers like Crescas, who focus on man's spiritual, rather than intellectual, worship of God. Albo agrees with the rationalists that a human is the noblest form of creation in the sublunar world and that the purpose of his existence is to perfect himself, thus reflecting the influence of Aristotle's thought and that of Maimonides and Gersonides within the Jewish Aristotelian movement. Albo does not, however, conceive of such perfection in terms of theoretical understanding, but rather in terms of finding favor with God. Albo maintains that only the Torah can give humanity full knowledge of the means of obeying God's will and achieving human perfection, representing the Jewish anti-Aristotelian school of thought of Judah Halevi, Naḥmanides, Rashba, Ritba, Nissim ben Reuben Gerondi (RaN), and Hasdai Crescas.

However, Albo's most drastic deviation from the philosophy of Crescas is his conception of human free choice. Albo rejects both Crescas's deterministic teachings that preclude human contingents, as well as Gersonides's radical freedom that limits God's omniscience to universals. Albo criticizes Crescas's theory of contingency:

> What good is there in saying that they are possible considered by themselves, as long as they are determined and necessary from that side that which brings them into existence, namely, the causes? For they cannot come into existence in any other way. They are possible in the theoretical sense that the causes might have been different and then the effect would have been different. But in reality, the effect is necessary when the causes are there and God knows them. It would follow, then, according to this opinion, that there is no thing that may equally be or not be when considered in relation to its causes.[41]

Rather, Albo asserts free choice and reverts back to Maimonides's reconciliatory view that God knows individual contingents, but God's infinite and immutable knowledge, which is part of his essence, does not negate man's free choice, although such divine knowledge is incomprehensible to the human mind.

> Our answer is the same as that of Maimonides' who says [in *Guide of the Perplexed*, 3:20]: that since God's knowledge is essential in Him and not something added to His essence, the investigation of the character of His knowledge is tantamount to an investigation of His essence. But his essence is absolutely unknown; hence, the character of His knowledge is also absolutely unknown. As there is no comparison or similarity between His existence and the existence of other things, so there is no comparison between His knowledge and the knowledge of others . . . The result of all this is that God's knowledge, being infinite, embraces everything that happens in the world without necessitating change in God, and without destroying the category of the contingent. It also embraces the infinite. I have selected this view as the best in this matter.[42]

Despite his Maimonidean influence, Albo does not adopt Maimonides's position that human choice is caused. Later in his work, Albo develops his conception of free choice, which deviates from Maimonides regarding the contingent being indifferent with respect to its causes,[43] since Albo maintains the requirement for the free individual to be able to choose between several possible alternatives. Free choice emerges as a conceptual scheme in many of Albo's homiletical discussions scattered throughout his work on dogma. Albo considers free will to be a necessary condition of the concept of recompense and not in conflict with the existence of an astrological-deterministic system in the universe.

The Book of Principles has become one of the most popular and enduring works of medieval Jewish philosophic theology. It has been published in many editions and languages and has been abridged and commented on in order to accommodate the demand of readers.[44] Albo's work is held in high esteem in both Jewish and Christian theological circles[45] and continues to be analyzed by modern scholars.[46]

Wars of the Lord, *Light of the Lord*, and *The Book of Principles* constitute three of the most comprehensive theological summae within the canon of medieval Jewish philosophy. Each work responds to the thought presented in earlier philosophical texts and seeks to correct erroneous conceptions. The summa genre enables Gersonides, Crescas, and Albo to convey a variety of philosophical arguments in a comprehensive and systematic manner. Readers are able to follow the development of the author's arguments and refutations of opposing views. Each work offers a logical progression of ideas that provides the reader with a cohesive understanding of a broad range of philosophical issues that can be internalized into his worldview and used to strengthen his identity and convictions. During a tumultuous historical period, the attempt to present a uniform system of Jewish dogma was particularly impactful for the Jewish community and was of profound interest among Christians as well. Gersonides, Crescas, and Albo offer diverse (including many original) opinions that contribute meaningfully to the thinking of their coreligionists and also to larger philosophical debates that transcended generations. As Seymour Feldman writes, "All the great philosophers of the past anticipated this dialogue with future generations, just as their own works were often conversations with their predecessors."[47] Thus, the theological and philosophical ideas contested in late medieval theological summae continue to be relevant and significant topics in contemporary philosophical discourse.[48]

Notes

1. Thomas Aquinas, *Summa Theologiae* (Cambridge: Cambridge University Press, 2006).
2. Tamar Rudavsky, "Creation, Time and Infinity in Gersonides," *Journal of the History of Philosophy* 26, no. 1 (1988): 25–44.
3. For Gersonides's discussion of creation, see *Wars of the Lord* 6. English translation by Seymour Feldman, vol. 3 (Philadelphia, PA: Jewish Publication Society, 1999), 217–409.
4. Julius Guttmann, *Philosophies of Judaism: The History of Jewish Philosophy from Biblical Times to Franz Rosenzweig* (New York: Doubleday, 1964), 223–4.
5. Robert Eisen, *Gersonides on Providence, Covenant and the Chosen People* (Albany: State University of New York Press, 1995). For Gersonides's discussion of providence in English, see Feldman, *Wars of the Lord*, 2:155–210.
6. Feldman, *Wars of the Lord*, 2:27–74.
7. J. David Bleich, *Providence and the Philosophy of Gersonides* (New York: Yeshiva University Press, 1973).
8. Seymour Feldman, "Levi Ben Gershom (Gersonides)," in *History of Jewish Philosophy*, ed. D. Frank and O. Leaman (NY: Routledge, 1997), 332.
9. Alexander Altmann, "Free Will and Predestination in Saadia, Bahya and Maimonides," in *Essays in Jewish Intellectual History* (Hanover, NH: University Press of New England, 1981), 35–64; Isaac Baer, *A History of the Jews in Christian Spain*, vol. 1 (Philadelphia, PA: Jewish Publication Society, 1961), 327–54; Colette Sirat, *A History of Jewish Philosophy in the Middle Ages* (Cambridge: Cambridge University Press, 1985), 308–22.
10. Daniel Rynhold, *An Introduction to Medieval Jewish Philosophy* (London: I. B. Tauris, 2009), 169.
11. Sara Klein-Braslavy, "Determinism, Possibility, Choice and Foreknowledge in Ralbag," *Da'at* 22 (1989): 4–53; Tamar Rudavsky, "Divine Omniscience, Contingency and Prophecy in Gersonides," in *Divine Omniscience and Omnipotence in Medieval Philosophy*, ed. T. M. Rudavsky (Dordrecht: D. Reidel, 1984), 161–81; Seymour Feldman, "A Debate

Concerning Determinism in Late Medieval Jewish Philosophy," *Proceedings of the American Academy for Jewish Research* 51 (1984): 15–54; Tamar Rudavsky, "Gersonides," *The Stanford Encyclopedia of Philosophy*, ed. Edward Zalta (2015), https://plato.stanford.edu/archives/win2015/entries/gersonides.

12. *Wars of the Lord*, 3:4, translation from Levi ben Gershom, *Gersonides' The Wars of the Lord, Treatise 3: On God's Knowledge*, trans. Norbert Samuelson (Toronto: Pontifical Institute of Mediaeval Studies, 1977), 232–38.

13. Rynhold, *Introduction to Medieval Jewish Philosophy*, 169.

14. Feldman, *Wars of the Lord*, 2:135.

15. Feldman, *Wars of the Lord*, vol. 1, introduction, 44–45.

16. Ibid., 52.

17. Julius Guttmann, *Philosophies of Judaism*, 226.

18. Crescas challenged Maimonides's delineation of dogma—if he meant fundamental dogmas, there are not as many as thirteen; if Maimonides meant to include "true beliefs," there are more than fifteen. In contrast to Maimonides's 13 principles, Crescas delineated his own set of principles—basic principles to all religions. He argued that belief in the existence of God is not one of the 613 commandments but is the basis for all commandments since commandments imply existence of Commander. Crescas rejects Maimonides's use of Aristotelian proofs for the existence of God but advocates proof out of necessity/contingency since the world is contingent on a designer. See Menachem Kellner, *Dogma in Medieval Jewish Thought from Maimonides to Abravanel* (Oxford: Oxford University Press, 1986).

19. Crescas argued that dogmas should be inductive—beliefs without which Judaism as a religion would collapse. He rejected Maimonides's deductive delineation of dogma—beliefs that have been ordained by the Torah.

20. James T. Robinson, "Hasdai Crescas and Anti-Aristotelianism," in *Cambridge Companion to Medieval Jewish Philosophy*, ed. D. Frank and O. Leaman (New York: Cambridge University Press, 2003), 394. See also Warren Zev Harvey, *Physics and Metaphysics in Ḥasdai Crescas* (Amsterdam: J. C. Gieben, 1988).

21. Sirat, *History of Jewish Philosophy in the Middle Ages*, 358.

22. Ibid., 359.

23. Isaac Husik, *A History of Medieval Jewish Philosophy* (New York: Harper Torchbook, 1966), 398.

24. Ibid., 396–97; Zev Harvey, *Rabbi Hasdai Crescas* (Jerusalem: Zalman Shazar Edition, 2010) [Hebrew].

25. Hasdai Crescas, *Or Adonai* (Light of the Lord). Ferrara, 1544; repr. ed. Shlomo Fisher (Jerusalem, 1990), 2:5:3, translated by Warren Zev Harvey in *Physics and Metaphysics*, 141.

26. Husik, *History of Medieval Jewish Philosophy*, 397.

27. Sirat, *History of Jewish Philosophy in the Middle Ages*, 367.

28. Daniel Lasker, "Chasdai Crescas," in Frank and Leaman, *History of Jewish Philosophy*, 343.

29. Shalom Sadik, "Hasdai Crescas," *The Stanford Encyclopedia of Philosophy*, ed. Edward N. Zalta (2016), https://plato.stanford.edu/archives/win2016/entries/crescas/.

30. Daniel Rynhold, *An Introduction to Medieval Jewish Philosophy* (London: I. B. Tauris, 2009), 175; Seymour Feldman, "A Debate concerning Determinism in Late Medieval Jewish Philosophy," *Proceedings of the American Academy for Jewish Research* 51 (1984): 15–54.

31. Despite the lack of direct influence, Crescas had a profound indirect influence on occidental philosophy and on Spinoza's views of the essence of God and determinism, in particular.

32. Sadik, "Hasdai Crescas."

33. Hasdai Crescas, *Light of the Lord*, trans. Roslyn Weiss (New York: Oxford University Press, 2018)

34. Eliezer Schweid, *Classic Jewish Philosophers: From Saadia through the Renaissance* (Leiden: Brill, 2007), 424.

35. Joseph Albo, *Sefer ha-'Ikkarim* (Book of Principles), ed. and trans. Isaac Husik, 1: 37, 2: 1–2.

36. E.g., Maimonides, Gersonides, Crescas, and Duran.

37. Zev Diesendruck, "Review of Book of Principles," trans. Isaac Husik, *Journal of Philosophy* 28, no. 19 (1931): 526; Isaac Husik, *A History of Medieval Jewish Philosophy* (New York: Harper Torchbook, 1966); Guttmann, *Philosophies of Judaism*, 535–37.

38. Dror Ehrlich, *Haguto shel R. Yosef Albo: Ketivah ezoterit be-shilhi yeme ha-benayim* (Ramat Gan: Bar Ilan University Press, 2009); Zev Harvey, "Albo on Repentance and Coercion," *Jewish Law Annual* 20 (2015); Zev Harvey, "Albo's Discussion of Time," *Jewish Quarterly Review* 70 (1980): 210–38; Zev Harvey, "Albo on the Reasonlessness of True Love," *Iyyun* 49 (2000): 83–86; Shira Weiss, *Joseph Albo on Free Choice: Exegetical Innovation in Medieval Jewish Philosophy* (New York: Oxford University Press, 2017).

39. Albo, introduction to *Book of Principles*, 1:36.

40. Ibid., 1:18.

41. Ibid., 4:1, 7.

42. Ibid., 4:3, 18–23.

43. Josef Stern argues that according to Maimonides, in contrast to Albo, "One can act freely even if he cannot do otherwise as long as he values the act (by his intellect); for by valuing his act, the individual identifies with it, makes it his own, and thus acts autonomously—regardless of necessity . . . Where the individual is in control of the desire, he can freely do what he must do anyway and freely refrain from what is impossible for him to do." See Josef Stern, "Maimonides' Conception of Freedom and the Sense of Shame," in *Freedom and Moral Responsibility: General and Jewish Perspectives*, ed. Charles Manekin and Menachem Kellner (Bethesda: University Press of Maryland, 1997), 263.

44. Seventeen Hebrew editions have been published in addition to translations into Latin, English, German, and Italian. Abridgments: Nibhar Mahrotz, an abridgement of the *'Iqqarim*, by Elijah ben Moses Gershon, Zolkiew, 1772; Tokhahat Haim al Tehilim v'Iyov, taken from Joseph Albo's *'Iqqarim*, Furth, 1805; Twenty-fifth chapter of Treatise Three of *Sefer ha-'Iqqarim*, ed. by Guiseppe Jaré, Liborno, 1876. Commentary: *Ohel Jacob* (The tent of Jacob): Commentary and Explanation of Albo's *Sefer ha-'Iqqarim*, Jacob ben Samuel Bunim Koppelmann, Freiburg, 1584; *Etz Shatul* (A planted tree), Gedaliah ben Solomon Lipschuetz, Venice, 1618.

45. Isaac Arama, Abraham Bibago, and Isaac Abravanel cited Albo's work and contended with his ideas, as well as thinkers in later generations, including Baruch Spinoza and Moses Mendelssohn. Christian theologians influenced by Albo's work include Grotius, Simon, De Voisin, and De Rossi. *The Book of Principles* was perceived as representing a comprehensive Jewish theology, and Albo's arguments were often appropriated by Christian thinkers as they engaged in polemics with Jews and with fellow scholars of other Christian sects. See Sirat, *A History of Jewish Philosophy in the Middle Ages*, 381; J. David Bleich, "Providence in Late Medieval Jewish Philosophy" (PhD diss., New York University, 1974); Sina Rauschenbach, *Josef Albo: Juedische Philosophie Und Christliche Kontroverstheologie In Der Fruehen Neuzeit* (Leiden: Brill, 2002).

46. Dror Ehrlich, *Haguto shel R. Yosef Albo: Ketivah ezoterit be-shilhi yeme ha-benayim* (Ramat Gan: Bar Ilan University, 2009); Shalom Sadik, "Freedom of Choice in the Thought of Rabbi Joseph Albo," *Jewish Studies, an Internet Journal* 11 (2012):1–13 [Hebrew].

47. Seymour Feldman, *Wars of the Lord*, vol. 1, introduction, 51.

48. For example, the debate between foreknowledge and human freedom continues among contemporary philosophers. See Nelson Pike, *God and Timelessness* (New York: Schocken, 1970); Stephen Cahn, *Fate, Logic and Time* (New Haven, CT: Yale University Press, 1967).

SHIRA WEISS is a postdoctoral fellow in the department of Jewish Thought at Ben Gurion University. She is author of *Joseph Albo on Free Choice: Exegetical Innovation in Medieval Jewish Philosophy* as well as articles in *Jewish Quarterly Review, Journal of Religious Ethics*, and *Journal of Jewish Ethics.*

INDEX

Aaron b. Elia of Nicomedia, 244
Aaron b. Meshullam of Lunel, 268
Abarbanel (Abravanel, Abrabanel), Isaac, 55, 56, 83, 85, 86, 91, 301, 303, 276–82
Abrabanel (Abravanel), Judah, 188, 221, 278, 282
Abraham b. David of Posquières, 271
Abba Mari b. Eligdor, 109, 269, 275
Abba Mari b. Moses of Lunel, 269, 273
Abbaye, 207, 288
Abigdor, 110, 111
Abner of Burgos (Alfonso de Valladolid), 206, 231, 272–74, 342, 348, 349
Abraham Abigdor b. Meshullam, 110, 111
Abū al-Barakāt al-Baghdādī, 46
Abū Bishr Mattā b. Yūnus, 188
Abū Ḥayyān al-Tawḥīdī, 188
Abū al-Sa'īd al-Sīrāfī, 188
Abulafia, Abraham, 82, 89
Abulafia, Meir ha-Levi, 267, 268
Ackerman, Ari, 303
'Adanī, David, 50, 59
Aesop, 14
Albertus Magnus, 53, 56, 302
Albo, Joseph, 28, 29, 301, 302, 337, 338, 344, 349, 350–54
Aldabi, Meir, 247, 248, 252
Alemanno, Yoḥanan, 86
Alexander of Aphrodisias, 177, 178, 288
Alexander the Great, 265
Alguades, Don Meir, 300–302, 305
Almosnino, Moses, 115
Altmann, Alexander, 316
Amram b. Marwās Efrati Ibn Marwās, 271
Anatoli, Jacob, 53, 116–118, 148, 292, 293
Anavi, Shalom, 114
Anaxagoras, 56
Andreas, Antonius, 113
Aquinas, Thomas, 56, 112, 113, 122, 302, 338, 339
Arama, Isaac, 301, 303, 309
Aristotle, 3, 21, 23, 29, 56, 135, 141, 153–56, 174, 205, 207, 248, 254, 265, 271, 275, 277, 280–82, 288, 295, 309, 323, 324, 329–32, 339–41, 343–45, 352
  Arabic Aristotle, 272
  Categories, 118, 251, 327
  commentaries on, 104–16, 119, 313–15
  cosmology, 52–53
  esotericism, 92–95
  Isagoge, 121–23
  and literature, 14
  logic, 87, 177, 178
  Metaphysics, 215, 282, 315
  Meteorology, 146, 147
  Nicomachean Ethics, 16, 282, 298–304, 306
  Physics, 307
  Poetics, 154
  Posterior Analytics, 278
  Topics, 150
Arondi, Isaac, 276
Arondi, Moses, 275
Arragel, Moses, 301
Asharite, 332
Asher bar Abraham, 245, 246
Averroes (Ibn Rushd), 3, 16, 48, 53, 104–22, 135, 150–55, 231, 265, 269, 273, 280–82, 288, 314, 339
  and the Christian West, 50
  commentary of, 239, 300, 305
  commentaries on, 87, 148
  and Maimonides, 95
Avicenna (Ibn Sīnā), 3, 87, 111, 120, 153, 154, 239, 269, 280, 281, 319–21
  Ḥayy ibn Yaqzān, 222_
  and the Maimonides Family in Egypt, 47–50
  and Neoplatonism, 53, 265, 314
  psychology of, 218, 219

Baer, Yitzhak, 276
Baḥya ben Asher ibn Ḥalawa, 55, 60
Bar Ḥiyya, Abraham, 135, 145
Baruch ibn Ya'ish, 114
al-Battānī, 249
Ben Sira, 11, 29
Benjamin, Walter, 12
Berakhiah ha-Naqdan, 9–11, 16–20, 27–29
Bibago (Bivach), Abraham, 113–15, 275, 281
Birasaf the Wise, 23, 24
al-Biṭrūjī, 328
Boccaccio, Giovanni, 250
Boethius, 120
Bonafed, Solomon, 276
Bonafos, Menachem, 333
Brann, Ross, 224, 255
Brito, Radulphus, 112
Burley, Walter, 112, 120

Carruthers, Mary, 240, 250, 253, 255
Chrysaorius, 121
Cohen, Hermann, 1, 3
Comtino, Mordecai b. Eliezer, 114, 321
Crescas, Asher, 83, 84, 86, 90, 97
Crescas, Ḥasdai, 54, 90, 273, 295, 296, 299, 303, 305, 337, 338, 244–349, 351–54
Crescas, Meir, 272
Cynics, 22

Dan, Joseph, 293, 295
Dante, 251
Dapiera, Solomon b. Immanuel, 241, 249, 250, 254–56
David Bonet Bonjorn, 272
David the Invincible, 314
Davidson, Herbert, 321
Dāwūd al-Muqammiṣ, 42, 161, 164, 166, 167, 170, 172–74, 176, 178–82
Delmedigo (del Medigo), Elijah (Elia), 112, 123, 276, 281
Delmedigo, Joseph, 86
Democritus, 14, 16
Dinkova-Bruun, Greti, 240
Duns Scotus, 113
Duran, Profayt/Profiat (Efodi), 83, 239–41, 250, 255, 256, 272
Duran, Simon b. Zemah, 351, 352

Efros, Israel, 321, 333
Eleazer ha-Qallir, 220
Elior, Ofer, 281
Empedocles, 56
Epicurean, 202, 309
Euclid, 115, 249

Falaquera, Shem Tov, 28, 29, 81–83, 95, 144, 195, 221, 246, 248, 327
  commentaries of, 86, 87, 94, 155
  dialogues, 186, 198–200, 202, 205, 209
  poetry, 240, 242–44, 253, 254, 261
al-Fārābī (Alfarabi), Abū Naṣr, 3, 47, 87, 105, 109, 122, 136, 155, 188, 265, 314, 323, 327, 330
  Enumeration of the Sciences, 150, 251
  Political Regime, 153
  political thought of, 58, 59
  Treatise on Intellect, 319
  Views of the Citizens of the Best State, 218
al-Fazārī, 254
Fazzo, Sylvia, 122
Feldman, Seymour, 342, 354
Feyerabend, Paul, 18

Gaetano of Thiene, 112
Galen, 56, 177, 178, 188, 249
Gersonides (Levi b. Gershom), 4, 51, 52, 106–13, 116, 118–23, 135, 144, 156, 157, 209, 251, 271, 274, 275, 337–45, 347, 348, 352–54
al-Ghazālī, 105, 111, 113, 120, 152, 153, 209, 277–79, 281
Giqatilla, Joseph b. Abraham, 82, 89
Glasner, Ruth, 114, 274, 275
Goitein, Shlomo Dov, 142
Goshen-Gottstein, Moshe, 333
Grosseteste, Robert, 300
Guttmann, Jakob, 1
Guttmann, Julius, 340

Habilio (Habillo), Eli, 113, 115, 275, 281
Hadot, Pierre, 20, 22
Halevi (Ha-Levi), Judah, 4, 141, 142, 186, 189–97, 201, 209, 221, 227, 228, 255, 352
al-Ḥarizi, Judah, 20, 81, 97, 265, 326, 327, 332
Harvey, Steven, 111
Haskalah, 85, 86
Havelock, Eric, 240

Haye, Thomas, 249
Ḥayyuj, Judah b. David, 220
Ḥayyun, Joseph, 301
Hermes Trismegistus, 56
Hermetic, 48, 189
Hesiod, 14, 16
Hillel of Verona, 82, 90, 92–94, 269
Hippocrates, 121, 177, 178, 204, 249
Hirschfeld, Hartwig, 254
Hishām b. ʿAbd al-Malik, 265
Hobbes, Thomas, 18, 19
Hughes, Aaron W., 3
Hurwitz, Pinchas Elias, 133
Husik, Isaac, 120

Ibn ʿAqnīn, Joseph b. Judah, 46, 47
Ibn Bājja, 87, 155, 265
Ibn Bilia, David, 110, 111, 351
Ibn Daud (Da'ud), Abraham, 46, 133, 138–43, 195, 219, 221, 229, 230
Ibn Ezra, Abraham, 45, 51, 53, 54, 56–58, 145, 189, 196, 220–26, 272
Ibn Ezra, Moses, 44, 219, 221, 226, 227, 240, 241, 255
Ibn Fārighūn, 314
Ibn Gabirol, Solomon (Avicebron, Avencebrol), 4, 44, 135, 140, 189, 193–96, 221, 222, 224–26, 229, 240, 241, 253
Ibn Ghiyāth, Isaac, 44, 45, 51, 135, 319
Ibn Ḥasdai, Abraham, 20, 29
Ibn Janaḥ, Jonah, 265
Ibn al-Jazzār, 148
Ibn Kaspi, Joseph, 27, 52, 82, 83, 86–89, 91–94, 97, 144, 269, 270
Ibn Labrat, Dunash, 219
Ibn Latif, Isaac, 54
Ibn Musa, Ḥaim, 288, 291, 297, 298, 300
Ibn Paquda, Baḥya, 135, 189, 197, 246, 319
Ibn Ṣaddiq, Joseph, 135, 138–141
Ibn Sahula, Isaac, 20–22, 27, 29
Ibn Shaprut, Ḥasdai, 219
Ibn Shem Ṭov, Joseph, 273, 277, 298–303, 308
Ibn Shem Ṭov, Shem Ṭov b. Joseph, 83, 86, 97, 277, 281, 301, 303, 305–308
Ibn Shueib, Joel, 301
Ibn Shushan, David, 248, 254
Ibn Tibbon, Judah, 50, 145, 146, 247
Ibn Tibbon, Moses, 52, 148, 149
Ibn Tibbon, Samuel, 14, 50–52, 81, 95–97, 135, 144–48, 265, 267, 292, 314, 326–33
Ibn Ṭufayl, 110
Ibn Yaḥya, David, 276
Ibn Zabara, Joseph, 20
Ikhwān al-Ṣafā' (Brethren of Purity), 23, 26, 28, 150, 151, 189, 217, 265, 266
Immanuel of Rome, 53
Isaac b. Sheshet Perfet, 270, 271
Isidore of Seville, 56
Ismaili, Ismaʿili, 48–50, 61, 186, 189–91, 193, 196
Israeli, Isaac, 44, 136, 314–18, 327

Jacob b. Makhir, 148
Jedaiah ha-Penini (Yedaya Hapenini), 108–10, 231, 274, 275
Jerome, 56
Jesus, 165, 171, 271
John the Grammarian (Philoponus), 177
Jonathan ha-Kohen of Lunel, 267, 268
Jordan, M., 163
Joseph b. Isaac Ha-Levi, 84
Joseph b. Israel, 147
Judah b. Isaac Cohen, 109, 115
Judah b. Quraysh, 265
Judah b. Solomon Nathan, 152
Judah ha-Kohen of Toledo, 53
Judah Romano, 53

Kabbalah, 2, 54–56, 89, 206, 230, 344
Kalam, 41–44, 61, 161, 163, 164, 166, 167, 169–82, 319, 321, 332
Karaite, 42–44, 57, 142, 161, 162, 164, 169, 170, 174, 175, 177–79, 192
Khazar, 141, 142, 190–93, 221
al-Khwārizmī, 314
al-Kindī, 265, 314–18
Kohen, Michael, 114
Kozodoy, Maud, 272
Klatzkin, Jacob, 333
Klein-Braslavy, Sara, 156
Kreisel, Haim, 249

Langermann, Y. Tzvi, 142
Levi b. Abraham of Villefranche-de-Conflent, 249, 250, 252

Lévy, Tony, 150
Lorki, Joshua, 271, 272

Maharal of Prague (Judah Loew ben Bezalal), 84
Maimon, Solomon, 85, 86, 89
Maimonides, Moses, 3, 4, 13–15, 19, 46-48, 50–53, 59, 107, 110, 156, 182, 193, 255, 273, 277, 288, 300, 302, 330–32, 339, 340
  and allegory, 295
  commentaries on, 47–48, 52, 79–85, 87–98
  criticism of Neoplatonism, 219, 220, 229–30
  epistles, 266–70
  esotericism, of 43
  Guide, 58, 133, 134, 151, 155, 245, 280–82, 306, 308, 349
  Introduction to the *Guide*, 143–47
  lexicographical chapters of the *Guide*, 314, 323–26
  Maimonidean tradition, 206, 209, 292, 337, 342–47, 351–53
  and parables, 26
  Treatise on Logic, 321
Maimonides, Abraham b. Moses, 48, 58, 60
Maimonides, David b. Joshua, 49
Manichean, 165
Manoaḥ Sho'ali, 115
Marsilius, 275
Menaḥem Shalem, 84
Mendelssohn, Moses, 321
Messer Leon, David b. Judah 83
Messer Leon, Judah, 111–13, 115–23
Messiah, 168, 169, 271, 351
Metatron, 208
Michael the Interpreter, 314
Montaigne, Michel de, 22
Mordecai Nathan, 111
Mordekhai Jaffe, 84, 90, 91, 94, 95
Moses b. Avraham Provençal, 83, 84, 90
Moses de León, 55
Moses Isserles (Rama), 84
Moses of Beaucaire, 269
Moses of Narbonne (Narboni), 82–86, 89, 90, 97, 110, 111, 144, 274, 278–81
Moses of Salerno, 82, 87, 88, 91, 96, 97, 245, 327, 333
Muhammad, 171, 179
Munk, Salomon, 194
Mūsā ibn Tubi of Seville, 249, 252, 254
Mu'tazila, Mu'tazilite, 42, 44, 137, 173, 332
Mutakallim, 31–43, 164, 167, 176

Naḥmanides (Moses b. Naḥman), 54, 55, 230, 231, 352
Nathan b. Solomon, 152
Nathaniel b. Isaiah, 49, 59
Nicholas de Lyra, 56
Nissim b. Moses of Marseilles, 52, 144
Nissim b. Reuben of Gerona (Ran), 294, 295, 352

Ong, Walter, 255
Oresme, Nicole, 272
Origen, 48
Orwell, George, 22

Peter of Spain, 110
Philo, 57
Pines, Shlomo, 27, 46, 190, 191
Plato, 3, 13, 16, 56, 108, 153, 185, 188, 214, 215, 229, 230, 264, 288, 298, 299, 304, 313, 317
Pliny, 56
Plotinus, Plotinian, 53–56, 215, 216, 316
Plutarch, 22
Polleqar (Polgar), Isaac, 186, 205, 206, 208, 209, 231, 232, 272–74
Porfash, 109
Porphyry, 56, 105–7, 109, 110, 116, 118–21, 155, 177, 251, 327
Proclus, 216
Ptolemy, Ptolemaic, 43, 52, 56, 288
Pythagoras, 56

Qalonymos (Qalonimos, Qalonymus) b. Qalonymos, 22, 23, 26–29, 109, 150–52, 266, 269, 270, 272, 275
Qimḥi, David, 51, 59
Qimḥi, Joseph, 51
Qimḥi, Moses, 51
al-Qirqisānī, Jacob (Ya'qūb), 43, 44, 161, 169–75, 177–82

Raba, 207, 288
Rabbanite, 42, 43, 57, 161, 162, 164, 169, 170, 175, 192

Rappe, Sara, 216
Rashba (Solomon b. Abraham ibn Adret), 293, 352
Rashi (Solomon b. Isaac of Troyes), 54
Rieti, Moses b. Isaac da, 250, 251
Ritba (Yom Tov b. Abraham al-Ishbili), 352
Roth, Leon, 321

Saadia (Saadya) Gaon, 43, 44, 57, 58, 134–38, 146, 160, 162, 166–82, 187, 219, 220, 319, 320
Sabian, 15, 332
Sālim Abū al-ʿAlā', 265
Sallust, 56
Samuel b. Ḥofni Gaon, 43, 44
Samuel b. Judah (Yehudah) of Marseilles, 16, 109, 115, 153, 275, 305
Samuel b. Solomon A[l]ṭorṭos, 114
Saperstein, Marc, 290, 291
Satanov, Isaac, 321
Saul ha-Kohen Ashkenazi of Crete, 276–82
Seneca, 56
Septimus, Bernard, 297
Sextus Julius Africanus, 56
Sh. Ha-Levy, 109
Shalom, Abraham, 275, 301
Sheshet Benveniste, 267, 268
Socrates, 16, 304, 313
Solomon b. Isaac Halevi of Salonica, 115
Solomon b. Judah ha-Nasi, 83, 85
Solomon of Burgos (Pablo de Santa Maria), 271
Solomon of Urgul, 109
Spinoza, 19, 22
Steinschneider, Moritz, 1, 104
Stern, Samuel Miklos, 316
Stetkevych, Suzanne, 240, 253
Strauss, Leo, 4, 85, 89
Sufi, Sufism, 47–50, 61, 193, 197

al-Tabrīzī, Abū ʿAbd Allah, 81, 90
Tanḥum b. Joseph ha-Yerushalmi, 48
Themistius, 288, 313, 323
Theophrastus, 44
Todorov, Tzvetan, 91
Ṭodros Ṭodrosi, 148, 154
Twersky, Isadore, 145

Valerius Maximus, 56
Ventura, Moses, 321
Virgil, 56
Vital, 109

White, Hayden, 1
William of Occam (Ockham), 109, 113, 275
William of Moerbecke, 114
Wissenschaft des Judentums, 2, 3, 85
Wolfson, Harry Austryn, 333

Yom Ṭov Lipmann Heller, 84
Yom Ṭov Lipmann Mühlhausen, 84

Zarfati, Gad, 333
Zekhariah ha-Rofe, 50, 59
Zeraḥiyah ha-Levi Saladin, 296, 301–3, 305
Zeraḥyah (Zeraḥiah) b. Isaac b. She'alti'el Ḥen, 53, 82, 83, 90, 91, 149, 269
Ziolkowski, Jan, 240
Zonta, Mauro, 275

www.ingramcontent.com/pod-product-compliance
Lightning Source LLC
Chambersburg PA
CBHW021339300426
44114CB00012B/1006
9780253042521